COD
REG(

MW01680170

Title 45
Public Welfare

Parts 200 to 499

Revised as of October 1, 2017

Containing a codification of documents
of general applicability and future effect

As of October 1, 2017

Published by the Office of the Federal Register
National Archives and Records Administration
as a Special Edition of the Federal Register

Table of Contents

Cite this Code: CFR

To cite the regulations in this volume use title, part and section number. Thus, 45 CFR 201.0 *refers to title 45, part 201, section 0.*

Explanation

The Code of Federal Regulations is a codification of the general and permanent rules published in the Federal Register by the Executive departments and agencies of the Federal Government. The Code is divided into 50 titles which represent broad areas subject to Federal regulation. Each title is divided into chapters which usually bear the name of the issuing agency. Each chapter is further subdivided into parts covering specific regulatory areas.

Each volume of the Code is revised at least once each calendar year and issued on a quarterly basis approximately as follows:

Title 1 through Title 16 .... as of January 1
Title 17 through Title 27 .... as of April 1
Title 28 through Title 41 .... as of July 1
Title 42 through Title 50 .... as of October 1

The appropriate revision date is printed on the cover of each volume.

LEGAL STATUS

The contents of the Federal Register are required to be judicially noticed (44 U.S.C. 1507). The Code of Federal Regulations is prima facie evidence of the text of the original documents (44 U.S.C. 1510).

HOW TO USE THE CODE OF FEDERAL REGULATIONS

The Code of Federal Regulations is kept up to date by the individual issues of the Federal Register. These two publications must be used together to determine the latest version of any given rule.

To determine whether a Code volume has been amended since its revision date (in this case, October 1, 2017), consult the "List of CFR Sections Affected (LSA)," which is issued monthly, and the "Cumulative List of Parts Affected," which appears in the Reader Aids section of the daily Federal Register. These two lists will identify the Federal Register page number of the latest amendment of any given rule.

EFFECTIVE AND EXPIRATION DATES

Each volume of the Code contains amendments published in the Federal Register since the last revision of that volume of the Code. Source citations for the regulations are referred to by volume number and page number of the Federal Register and date of publication. Publication dates and effective dates are usually not the same and care must be exercised by the user in determining the actual effective date. In instances where the effective date is beyond the cut-off date for the Code a note has been inserted to reflect the future effective date. In those instances where a regulation published in the Federal Register states a date certain for expiration, an appropriate note will be inserted following the text.

OMB CONTROL NUMBERS

The Paperwork Reduction Act of 1980 (Pub. L. 96–511) requires Federal agencies to display an OMB control number with their information collection request.

Many agencies have begun publishing numerous OMB control numbers as amendments to existing regulations in the CFR. These OMB numbers are placed as close as possible to the applicable recordkeeping or reporting requirements.

PAST PROVISIONS OF THE CODE

Provisions of the Code that are no longer in force and effect as of the revision date stated on the cover of each volume are not carried. Code users may find the text of provisions in effect on any given date in the past by using the appropriate List of CFR Sections Affected (LSA). For the convenience of the reader, a "List of CFR Sections Affected" is published at the end of each CFR volume. For changes to the Code prior to the LSA listings at the end of the volume, consult previous annual editions of the LSA. For changes to the Code prior to 2001, consult the List of CFR Sections Affected compilations, published for 1949-1963, 1964-1972, 1973-1985, and 1986-2000.

"[RESERVED]" TERMINOLOGY

The term "[Reserved]" is used as a place holder within the Code of Federal Regulations. An agency may add regulatory information at a "[Reserved]" location at any time. Occasionally "[Reserved]" is used editorially to indicate that a portion of the CFR was left vacant and not accidentally dropped due to a printing or computer error.

INCORPORATION BY REFERENCE

What is incorporation by reference? Incorporation by reference was established by statute and allows Federal agencies to meet the requirement to publish regulations in the Federal Register by referring to materials already published elsewhere. For an incorporation to be valid, the Director of the Federal Register must approve it. The legal effect of incorporation by reference is that the material is treated as if it were published in full in the Federal Register (5 U.S.C. 552(a)). This material, like any other properly issued regulation, has the force of law.

What is a proper incorporation by reference? The Director of the Federal Register will approve an incorporation by reference only when the requirements of 1 CFR part 51 are met. Some of the elements on which approval is based are:

(a) The incorporation will substantially reduce the volume of material published in the Federal Register.

(b) The matter incorporated is in fact available to the extent necessary to afford fairness and uniformity in the administrative process.

(c) The incorporating document is drafted and submitted for publication in accordance with 1 CFR part 51.

What if the material incorporated by reference cannot be found? If you have any problem locating or obtaining a copy of material listed as an approved incorporation by reference, please contact the agency that issued the regulation containing that incorporation. If, after contacting the agency, you find the material is not available, please notify the Director of the Federal Register, National Archives and Records Administration, 8601 Adelphi Road, College Park, MD 20740-6001, or call 202-741-6010.

CFR INDEXES AND TABULAR GUIDES

A subject index to the Code of Federal Regulations is contained in a separate volume, revised annually as of January 1, entitled CFR INDEX AND FINDING AIDS. This volume contains the Parallel Table of Authorities and Rules. A list of CFR titles, chapters, subchapters, and parts and an alphabetical list of agencies publishing in the CFR are also included in this volume.

An index to the text of "Title 3—The President" is carried within that volume.

The Federal Register Index is issued monthly in cumulative form. This index is based on a consolidation of the "Contents" entries in the daily Federal Register.

A List of CFR Sections Affected (LSA) is published monthly, keyed to the revision dates of the 50 CFR titles.

REPUBLICATION OF MATERIAL

There are no restrictions on the republication of material appearing in the Code of Federal Regulations.

INQUIRIES

For a legal interpretation or explanation of any regulation in this volume, contact the issuing agency. The issuing agency's name appears at the top of odd-numbered pages.

For inquiries concerning CFR reference assistance, call 202–741–6000 or write to the Director, Office of the Federal Register, National Archives and Records Administration, 8601 Adelphi Road, College Park, MD 20740-6001 or e-mail *fedreg.info@nara.gov.*

SALES

The Government Publishing Office (GPO) processes all sales and distribution of the CFR. For payment by credit card, call toll-free, 866-512-1800, or DC area, 202-512-1800, M-F 8 a.m. to 4 p.m. e.s.t. or fax your order to 202-512-2104, 24 hours a day. For payment by check, write to: US Government Publishing Office – New Orders, P.O. Box 979050, St. Louis, MO 63197-9000.

ELECTRONIC SERVICES

The full text of the Code of Federal Regulations, the LSA (List of CFR Sections Affected), The United States Government Manual, the Federal Register, Public Laws, Public Papers of the Presidents of the United States, Compilation of Presidential Documents and the Privacy Act Compilation are available in electronic format via *www.ofr.gov*. For more information, contact the GPO Customer Contact Center, U.S. Government Publishing Office. Phone 202-512-1800, or 866-512-1800 (toll-free). E-mail, *ContactCenter@gpo.gov.*

The Office of the Federal Register also offers a free service on the National Archives and Records Administration's (NARA) World Wide Web site for public law numbers, Federal Register finding aids, and related information. Connect to NARA's web site at *www.archives.gov/federal-register.*

The e-CFR is a regularly updated, unofficial editorial compilation of CFR material and Federal Register amendments, produced by the Office of the Federal Register and the Government Publishing Office. It is available at *www.ecfr.gov.*

OLIVER A. POTTS,
Director,
Office of the Federal Register.
October 1, 2017.

THIS TITLE

Title 45—PUBLIC WELFARE is composed of four volumes. The parts in these volumes are arranged in the following order: Parts 1–199, 200–499, 500–1199, and 1200 to end. Volume one (parts 1–199) contains all current regulations issued under subtitle A—Department of Health and Human Services. Volume two (parts 200–499) contains all current regulations issued under subtitle B—Regulations Relating to Public Welfare, chapter II—Office of Family Assistance (Assistance Programs), Administration for Children and Families, Department of Health and Human Services, chapter III—Office of Child Support Enforcement (Child Support Enforcement Program), Administration for Children and Families, Department of Health and Human Services, and chapter IV—Office of Refugee Resettlement, Administration for Children and Families, Department of Health and Human Services. Volume three (parts 500–1199) contains all current regulations issued under chapter V—Foreign Claims Settlement Commission of the United States, Department of Justice, chapter VI—National Science Foundation, chapter VII—Commission on Civil Rights, chapter VIII—Office of Personnel Management, chapter IX—Denali Commission, chapter X—Office of Community Services, Administration for Children and Families, Department of Health and Human Services, and chapter XI—National Foundation on the Arts and the Humanities. Volume four (part 1200 to end) contains all current regulations issued under chapter XII—Corporation for National and Community Service, chapter XIII—Administration for Children and Families, Department of Health and Human Services, chapter XVI—Legal Services Corporation, chapter XVII—National Commission on Libraries and Information Science, chapter XVIII—Harry S Truman Scholarship Foundation, chapter XXI—Commission of Fine Arts, chapter XXIII—Arctic Research Commission, chapter XXIV—James Madison Memorial Fellowship Foundation, and chapter XXV—Corporation for National and Community Service. The contents of these volumes represent all of the current regulations codified under this title of the CFR as of October 1, 2017.

For this volume, Ann Worley was Chief Editor. The Code of Federal Regulations publication program is under the direction of John Hyrum Martinez, assisted by Stephen J. Frattini.

Title 45—Public Welfare

(This book contains parts 200 to 499)

SUBTITLE B—REGULATIONS RELATING TO PUBLIC WELFARE

Subtitle B—Regulations Relating to Public Welfare

CHAPTER I [RESERVED]

CHAPTER II—OFFICE OF FAMILY ASSISTANCE (ASSISTANCE PROGRAMS), ADMINISTRATION FOR CHILDREN AND FAMILIES, DEPARTMENT OF HEALTH AND HUMAN SERVICES

EDITORIAL NOTE: Nomenclature changes to chapter II appear at 66 FR 39452, July 31, 2001.

PART 200 [RESERVED]

PART 201—GRANTS TO STATES FOR PUBLIC ASSISTANCE PROGRAMS

AUTHORITY: 42 U.S.C. 303, 603, 1203, 1301, 1302, 1316, 1353 and 1383 (note).

SOURCE: 35 FR 12180, July 29, 1970, unless otherwise noted.

§ 201.0 Scope and applicability.

Titles I, X, XIV and XVI (as in effect without regard to section 301 of the Social Security Amendments of 1972) shall continue to apply to Puerto Rico, the Virgin Islands, and Guam. The term *State* as used in such titles means Puerto Rico, the Virgin Islands, and Guam.

[39 FR 8326, Mar. 5, 1974]

§ 201.1 General definitions.

When used in this chapter, unless the context otherwise indicates:

(a) *Act* means the Social Security Act, and titles referred to are titles of that Act;

(b) *Department* means the Department of Health and Human Services;

(c) *Administrator* means the Administrator, Family Support Administration;

(d) *Secretary* means the Secretary of Health and Human Services;

(e) *Administration* means the Family Support Administration;

(f) *Regional Administrator* means the Regional Administrator of the Family Support Administration;

(g) *State* means the several States, the District of Columbia, the Commonwealth of Puerto Rico, the Virgin Islands, Guam, and American Samoa. The term "State" with respect to American Samoa applies to the programs set forth in title IV-A and IV-F of the Act;

(h) *State agency* means the State agency administering or supervising the administration of the State plan or plans under title I, IV-A, IV-F, X, or XVI (AABD) of the Act;

(i) The terms *regional office* and *central office* refer to the regional offices and the central office of the Family Support Administration, respectively.

[35 FR 12180, July 29, 1970, as amended at 39 FR 34543, Sept. 26, 1974; 53 FR 36578, Sept. 21, 1988; 57 FR 30425, July 9, 1992]

Subpart A—Approval of State Plans and Certification of Grants

§ 201.2 General.

The State plan is a comprehensive statement submitted by the State agency describing the nature and scope of its program and giving assurance that it will be administered in conformity with the specific requirements stipulated in the pertinent title of the Act, the regulations in subtitle A and this chapter of this title, and other applicable official issuances of the Department. The State plan contains all information necessary for the Administration to determine whether the plan can be approved, as a basis for Federal financial participation in the State program.

[35 FR 12180, July 29, 1970, as amended at 53 FR 36578, Sept. 21, 1988]

§ 201.3 Approval of State plans and amendments.

The State plan consists of written documents furnished by the State to cover each of its programs under the Act: Old-age assistance (title I); aid and services to needy families with children (part A of title IV); aid to the blind (title X); aid to the permanently and totally disabled (title XIV); or aid to the aged, blind or disabled (title XVI). The State may submit the common material on more than one program as an integrated plan. However, it must identify the provisions pertinent to each title since a separate plan must be approved for each public assistance title. A plan submitted under title XVI encompasses, under a single plan, the programs otherwise covered by three separate plans under titles I, X, and XIV. After approval of the original plan by the Administration, all relevant changes, required by new statutes, rules, regulations, interpretations, and court decisions, are required to be submitted currently so that the Administration may determine whether the plan continues to meet Federal requirements and policies.

(a) *Submittal.* State plans and revisions of the plans are submitted first to the State governor or his designee for review in accordance with § 204.1 of this chapter, and then to the regional office. The States are encouraged to obtain consultation of the regional staff when a plan is in process of preparation or revision.

(b) *Review.* Staff in the regional offices are responsible for review of State plans and amendments. They also initiate discussion with the State agency on clarification of significant aspects of the plan which come to their attention in the course of this review. State plan material on which the regional staff has questions concerning the application of Federal policy is referred with recommendations as required to the central office for technical assistance. Comments and suggestions, including those of consultants in specified areas, may be prepared by the central office for use by the regional staff in negotiations with the State agency.

(c) *Action.* The Regional Administrator, exercised delegated authority to take affirmative action on State plans and amendments thereto on the basis of policy statements or precedents previously approved by the Administrator. The Administrator retains authority for determining that proposed plan material is not approvable, or that a previously approved plan no longer meets the requirements for approval, except that a final determination of disapproval may not be made without prior consultation and discussion by the Administrator with the Secretary. The Regional Administrator, or the Administrator formally notifies the State agency of the actions taken on State plans or revisions.

(d) *Basis for approval.* Determinations as to whether State plans (including plan amendments and administrative practice under the plans) originally meet or continue to meet, the requirements for approval are based on relevant Federal statutes and regulations. Guidelines are furnished to assist in the interpretation of the regulations.

(e) *Prompt approval of State plans.* Pursuant to section 1116 of the Act, the determination as to whether a State plan submitted for approval conforms to the requirements for approval under the Act and regulations issued pursuant thereto shall be made promptly and not later than the 90th day following the date on which the plan submittal is received in the regional office, unless the Regional Administrator, has secured from the State agency a written agreement to extend that period.

(f) *Prompt approval of plan amendments.* Any amendment of an approved State plan may, at the option of the State, be considered as a submission of a new State plan. If the State requests that such amendment be so considered the determination as to its conformity with the requirements for approval shall be made promptly and not later than the 90th day following the date on which such a request is received in the regional office with respect to an amendment that has been received in such office, unless the Regional Administrator, has secured from the State agency a written agreement to extend that period. In absence of request by a State that an amendment of an approved State plan shall be considered as a submission of a new State plan, the procedures under § 201.6 (a) and (b) shall be applicable.

(g) *Effective date.* The effective date of a new plan may not be earlier than the first day of the calendar quarter in which an approvable plan is submitted, and with respect to expenditures for assistance under such plan, may not be earlier than the first day on which the plan is in operation on a statewide basis. The same applies with respect to plan amendments that provide additional assistance or services to persons eligible under the approved plan or that make new groups eligible for assistance or services provided under the approved plan. For other plan amendments the effective date shall be as specified in other sections of this chapter.

[35 FR 12180, July 29, 1970, as amended at 39 FR 34542, Sept. 26, 1974; 42 FR 43977, Sept. 1, 1977; 53 FR 36579, Sept. 21, 1988]

§ 201.4 Administrative review of certain administrative decisions.

Pursuant to section 1116 of the Act, any State dissatisfied with a determination of the Administrator pursuant to § 201.3 (e) or (f) with respect to any plan or amendment may, within 60 days after the date of receipt of notification of such determination, file a petition with the Regional Administrator, asking the Administrator for reconsideration of the issue of whether such plan or amendment conforms to the requirements for approval under the Act and pertinent Federal requirements. Within 30 days after receipt of such a petition, the Administrator shall notify the State of the time and place at which the hearing for the purpose of reconsidering such issue will be held. Such hearing shall be held not less than 30 days nor more than 60 days after the date notice of such hearing is furnished to the State, unless the Administrator and the State agree in writing on another time. For hearing procedures, see part 213 of this chapter. A determination affirming, modifying, or reversing the Administrator's original decision will be made within 60 days of the conclusion of the hearing. Action pursuant to an initial determination by the Administrator described in such § 201.3 (e) or (f) that a plan or amendment is not approvable shall not be stayed pending the reconsideration, but in the event that the Administrator subsequently determines that his original decision was incorrect he shall certify restitution forthwith in a lump sum of any funds incorrectly withheld or otherwise denied.

[35 FR 12180, July 29, 1970, as amended at 42 FR 43977, Sept. 1, 1977; 53 FR 36579, Sept. 21, 1988]

§ 201.5 Grants.

To States with approved plans, grants are made each quarter for expenditures under the plan for assistance, services, training and administration. The determination as to the amount of a grant to be made to a State is based upon documents submitted by the State agency containing information required under the Act and such other pertinent facts, including title IV-A the appropriate Federal share of child support collections made by the State, as may be found necessary.

(a) *Form and manner of submittal.* (1) Time and place: The estimates for public assistance grants for each quarterly period must be forwarded to the regional office 45 days prior to the period of the estimate. They include a certification of State funds available and a justification statement in support of the estimates. A statement of quarterly expenditures and any necessary supporting schedules must be forwarded to the Department of Health and Human Services, Family Support Administration, not later than 30 days after the end of the quarter.

(2) Description of forms: "State Agency Expenditure Projection—Quarterly Projection by Program" represents the State agency's estimate of the total amount and the Federal share of expenditures for assistance, services, training, and administration to be made during the quarter for each of the public assistance programs under the Act. From these estimates the State and Federal shares of the total expenditures are computed. The State's computed share of total estimated expenditures is the amount of State and local funds necessary for the quarter. The Federal share is the basis for the funds to be advanced for the quarter. The

State agency must also certify, on this form or otherwise, the amount of State funds (exclusive of any balance of advances received from the Federal Government) actually on hand and available for expenditure; this certification must be signed by the executive officer of the State agency submitting the estimate or a person officially designated by him, or by a fiscal officer of the State if required by State law or regulation. (A form "Certificate of Availability of State Funds for Assistance and Administration during Quarter" is available for submitting this information, but its use is optional.) If the amount of State funds (or State and local funds if localities participate in the program), shown as available for expenditures is not sufficient to cover the State's proportionate share of the amount estimated to be expended, the certification must contain a statement showing the source from which the amount of the deficiency is expected to be derived and the time when this amount is expected to be made available.

(3) The State agency must also submit a quarterly statement of expenditures for each of the public assistance programs under the Act. This is an accounting statement of the disposition of the Federal funds granted for past periods and provides the basis for making the adjustments necessary when the State's estimate for any prior quarter was greater or less than the amount the State actually expended in that quarter. The statement of expenditures also shows the share of the Federal Government in any recoupment, from whatever source, including for title IV-A the appropriate share of child support collections made by the State, of expenditures claimed in a prior period, and also in expenditures not properly subject to Federal financial participation which are acknowledged by the State agency, including the share of the Federal Government for uncashed and cancelled checks as described at 45 CFR 201.67 and replacement checks as described at 45 CFR 201.70 in this part, or which have been revealed in the course of an audit.

(b) *Review.* The State's estimates are analyzed by the regional office staff and are forwarded with recommendations as required to the central office. The central office reviews the State's estimate, other relevant information, and any adjustments to be made for prior periods, and computes the grant.

(c) *Grant award.* The grant award computation form shows, by program, the amount of the estimate for the ensuing quarter, and the amounts by which the estimate is reduced or increased because of over- or under-estimate for the prior quarter and for other adjustments. This form is transmitted to the State agency to draw the amount of the grant award, as needed, to meet the Federal share of disbursements. The draw is through a commercial bank and the Federal Reserve system against a continuing letter of credit certified to the Secretary of the Treasury in favor of the State payee. A copy of the grant award notice is sent to the State Central Information Reception Agency in accord with section 201 of the Intergovernmental Cooperation Act of 1968.

(d) *Letter of credit payment system.* The letter of credit system for payment of advances of Federal funds was established pursuant to Treasury Department regulations (Circular No. 1075), published in the FEDERAL REGISTER on July 11, 1967 (32 FR 10201). The HEW "Instructions to Recipient Organizations for Use of Letter of Credit" was transmitted to all grantees by memorandum from the Assistant Secretary-Comptroller on January 15, 1968.

(e) *General administrative requirements.* With the following exceptions, the provisions of part 74 of this title, establishing uniform administrative requirements and cost principles, shall apply to all grants made to States under this part:

45 CFR PART 74

Subpart G—Matching and Cost Sharing.

Subpart I—Financial Reporting Requirements.

[35 FR 12180, July 29, 1970, as amended at 38 FR 26320, Sept. 19, 1973; 46 FR 48003, Sept. 30, 1981; 53 FR 24269, June 28, 1988; 53 FR 36579, Sept. 21, 1988]

§ 201.6 Withholding of payment; reduction of Federal financial participation in the costs of social services and training.

(a) *When withheld.* Further payments to a State are withheld in whole or in part if the Administrator, after reasonable notice and opportunity for hearing to the State agency administering or supervising the administration of an approved plan, finds:

(1) That the plan no longer complies with the provisions of section 2, 402, 1002, 1402, or 1602 of the Act; or

(2) That in the administration of the plan there is failure to comply substantially with any such provision.

A question of noncompliance of a State plan may arise from an unapprovable change in the approved State plan, the failure of the State to change its approved plan to conform to a new Federal requirement for approval of State plans, or the failure of the State in practice to comply with a Federal requirement, whether or not its State plan has been amended to conform to such requirement.

(b) *When the rate of Federal financial participation is reduced.* Under title I, X, XIV, or XVI (AABD) of the Act, Federal financial participation in the costs of social services and training approved at the rate of 75 per centum is reduced to 50 per centum if the Administrator, after reasonable notice and opportunity for a hearing to the State agency, finds:

(1) That the plan provision under such title for prescribed services no longer complies with the Federal requirements with respect to such prescribed services; or

(2) That in the administration of the plan there is a failure to comply substantially with such plan provision.

(c) *Information discussions.* Hearings with respect to matters under paragraph (a) or (b) of this section are generally not called, however, until after reasonable effort has been made by the Administration to resolve the questions involved by conference and discussion with State officials. Formal notification of the date and place of hearing does not foreclose further negotiations with State officials.

(d) *Conduct of hearings.* For hearing procedures, see part 213 of this chapter.

(e) *Notification of withholding.* If the Administrator makes a finding of noncompliance with respect to a matter under paragraph (a) of this section, the State agency is notified that further payments will not be made to the State (or, in his discretion, that payments will be limited to categories under or parts of the plan not affected by such failure), until the Administrator is satisfied that there will no longer be any such failure to comply. Until he is so satisfied, no further payments will be made to the State (or will be limited to categories under or parts of the plan not affected by such failure).

(f) *Notification of reduction in the rate of Federal financial participation.* If the Administrator makes a finding of noncompliance with respect to a matter under paragraph (b) of this section, the State agency is notified that further payments will be made to the State at the rate of 50 per centum of the costs of services and training, until the Administrator is satisfied that there will no longer be any failure to comply.

[35 FR 12180, July 29, 1970, as amended at 39 FR 34542, Sept. 26, 1974; 53 FR 36579, Sept. 21, 1988]

§ 201.7 Judicial review.

Any State dissatisfied with a final determination of the Secretary pursuant to § 201.4 or § 201.6(a) may, within 60 days after it has been notified of such determination, file with the U.S. Court of Appeals for the circuit in which such State is located a petition for review of such determination. After a copy of the petition is transmitted by the clerk of the court to the Secretary, the Secretary thereupon shall file in the court the record of proceedings upon which such determination was based as provided in section 2112 of title 28, United States Code. The court is bound by the Secretary's findings of fact, if supported by substantial evidence. The court has jurisdiction to affirm the Secretary's decision, or set it aside in whole or in part, or, for good cause, to remand the case for additional evidence. If the case is remanded, the Secretary may thereupon make new or modified findings of fact, and may modify his previous determination. The Secretary shall certify to the court the transcript and record of the further proceedings. The judgment of the court is subject to review by the Supreme Court of the United States upon certiorari or certification as provided in 28 U.S.C. 1254.

Subpart B—Review and Audits

§ 201.10 Review of State and local administration.

(a) In order to provide a basis for determining that State agencies are adhering to Federal requirements and to the substantive legal and administrative provisions of their approved plans, the Administration conducts a review of State and local public assistance administration. This review includes analysis of procedures and policies of State and local agencies and examination of case records of individual recipients.

(b) Each State agency is required to carry out a continuing quality control program primarily covering determination of eligibility in statistically selected samples of individual cases. The Service conducts a continuing observation of these State systems.

(c) Adherence to other Federal requirements set forth in the pertinent titles of the Act and the regulations in this title is evaluated through review of selected case records and aspects of agency operations.

[35 FR 12180, July 29, 1970, as amended at 53 FR 36579, Sept. 21, 1988]

§ 201.11 Personnel merit system review.

A personnel merit system review is carried out by the Office of State Merit Systems of the Office of the Assistant Secretary for Administration of the Department. The purpose of the review is to evaluate the effectiveness of the State merit system relating to the public assistance programs and to determine whether there is compliance with Federal requirements in the administration of the merit system plan. See part 70 of this title.

§ 201.12 Public assistance audits.

(a) Annually, or at such frequencies as are considered necessary and appropriate, the operations of the State agency are audited by representatives of the Audit Agency of the Department. Such audits are made to determine whether the State agency is being operated in a manner that:

(1) Encourages prudent use of program funds, and

(2) Provides a reasonable degree of assurance that funds are being properly expended, and for the purposes for which appropriated and provided for under the related Act and State plan, including State laws and regulations.

(b) Reports of these audits are released by the Audit Agency simultaneously to program officials of the Department, and to the cognizant State officials. These audit reports relate the opinion of the Audit Agency on the practices reviewed and the allowability of costs audited at the State agency. Final determinations as to actions required on all matters reported are made by cognizant officials of the Department.

§ 201.13 Action on audit and review findings.

(a) If the audit results in no exceptions, the State agency is advised by letter of this result. The general course for the disposition of proposed exceptions resulting from audits involves the submittal of details of these exceptions to the State agency which then has an opportunity to concur in the proposed exceptions or to assemble and submit additional facts for purposes of clearance. Provision is made for the State agency to appeal proposed audit exceptions in which it has not concurred and which have not been deleted on the basis of clearance material. After consideration of a State agency's appeal by the Administrator, the Administration advises the State agency of any expenditures in which the Federal Government may not participate and requests it to include the amount as adjustments in a subsequent statement of expenditures. Expenditures in which it is found the Federal Government may not participate and which are not properly adjusted through the State's claim will be deducted from subsequent grants made to the State agency.

(b) If the Federal or State reviews reveal serious problems with respect to compliance with any Federal requirement, the State agency is required to correct its practice so that there will be no recurrence of the problem in the future.

[35 FR 12180, July 29, 1970, as amended at 53 FR 36579, Sept. 21, 1988]

§201.14 Reconsideration under section 1116(d) of the Act.

(a) *Applicability.* This section applies to any disallowance of any item or class of items for which FFP is claimed under title I, IV, X, XIV, XVI(AABD), or XX of the Act, with respect to which reconsideration was requested prior to March 6, 1978, unless the State by filing a written notice to that effect with the Executive Secretary, Departmental Grant Appeals Board (with proof of service on the head of the constituent agency), within 30 days after mailing of the confirmation of the disallowance by the agency head, elects to have the reconsideration governed by 45 CFR part 16.

(1) Reduction of the Federal share of assistance payments under title IV-A, for failure to certify WIN registrants (section 402(e) of the Act);

(2) Reduction by one per centum of the quarterly amount payable to a State for all expenditures under title IV-A for failure, in certain cases, to carry out the provisions of section 402(a)(15) of the Act which require the offering of and arrangement for the provision of family planning services (section 402(f) of the Act);

(3)–(5) [Reserved]

(6) Any other decision pursuant to sections 3, 403, 422, 455, 1003, 1403, 1603, or 2003, of the Act.

(b) *Notice of disallowance determination.* (1) When the Regional Administrator, determines that a State claim for FFP in expenditures for a particular item or class of items is not allowable, he shall promptly issue a disallowance letter to the State.

(2) This disallowance letter shall include where appropriate:

(i) The date or dates on which the State's claim for FFP was made;

(ii) The time period during which the expenditures in question were made or claimed to have been made;

(iii) The date and amount of any payment or notice of deferral;

(iv) A statement of the amount of FFP claimed, allowed, and disallowed and the manner in which these amounts were calculated;

(v) Findings of fact on which the disallowance determination is based or a reference to other documents previously or contemporaneously furnished to the State (such as a report of a financial review or audit) which contain the findings of fact on which the disallowance determination is based;

(vi) Pertinent citations to the law, regulations, guides and instructions supporting the action taken; and

(vii) Notice of the State's right to request reconsideration of the disallowance under this section and the time within such request must be made.

(c) *Request for reconsideration.* (1) To obtain reconsideration of a disallowance of an item or class of items for FFP, a State shall, within 30 days of the date of the disallowance letter, request reconsideration by the Administrator, with copy to the Regional Administrator, and enclose a copy of the disallowance letter.

(2) The request for reconsideration must be accompanied by a brief statement of the issues in dispute, including an explanation of the State's position with respect to each issue.

(d) *Reconsideration procedures.* (1) The Administrator will promptly acknowledge receipt of a State's request for reconsideration.

(2) Upon receipt of a copy of the request for reconsideration, the Regional Administrator, shall, within 30 days of the request, provide to the Administrator a complete record of all material which he believes to have a bearing on the reconsideration, including any reports of audit or review which were the basis for his decision.

(3) The Administrator shall promptly forward to the State a list of all items currently in the record, including those received from the Regional Administrator, or with respect to the medical assistance program under title XIX, Regional Medicaid Director and make available for examination, inspection and copying any such items not previously received by the State.

(4) Within 60 days from the date of the Administrator's transmittal to the State under paragraph (d)(3) of this

section, the State shall submit in writing to the Administrator any new relevant evidence, documentation, or argument and shall simultaneously submit a copy thereof to the Regional Administrator, or with respect to the medical assistance program under title XIX, Regional Medicaid Director.

(5) The Regional Administrator, or with respect to the medical assistance program under title XIX, Regional Medicaid Director shall, within 60 days of submittal by the State, submit to the Administrator (with a copy to the State) an analysis of the issues relevant to the disallowance including:

(i) A restatement of the findings on which the disallowance was based;

(ii) A response to each issue raised by the State with respect to such findings;

(iii) A response to any other issues raised by the State, providing additional documentation when necessary; and

(iv) Any additional documentation which he deems relevant.

(6) The State may respond to the material submitted by the Regional Administrator, or with respect to the medical assistance program under title XIX, Regional Medicaid Director by submitting to the Administrator within 15 days any supplemental material the State wishes to have entered into the record.

(7) At the time of submitting any additional material pursuant to paragraph (d)(4), the State may obtain, upon request to him, a conference with the Administrator, during which it may discuss with the Administrator its position on the issues. The State may, at its own expense, have such conference transcribed; the transcript shall become part of the administrative record.

(8) In reconsidering the disallowance, the Administrator may request any additional information or documents necessary to his decision.

(9) New relevant evidence received into the record by the Administrator pursuant to paragraph (d)(8) of this section which is not received from, or previously otherwise made available to, the State shall promptly be made available to the State for examination, inspection, and copying and the State will be given appropriate additional time for comment.

(10) All documents, reports, correspondence, and other materials considered by the Administrator in reaching his decision shall constitute the record of the reconsideration proceedings.

(11) After consideration of such record and the laws and regulations pertinent to the issues in question, the Administrator shall issue a written decision, based on the administrative record, which summarizes the facts and cites the regulations or statutes that support the decision. The decision shall constitute final administrative action on the matter and shall be promptly mailed to the head of the State agency.

(12) Either the state or the Regional Administrator, or with respect to the medical assistance program under title XIX, Regional Medicaid Director may request from the Administrator, for good cause, an extension of any of the time limits specified in this section.

(13) No section of this regulation shall be interpreted as waiving the Department's right to assert any provision or exemption in the Freedom of Information Act.

(e) *Implementation of the decision.* If the decision requires an adjustment in the Federal share, either upward or downward, this will be reflected in subsequent grant awards.

(f) For purposes of this section, the Administrator includes the Deputy Administrator, except that whichever official conducts the conference requested pursuant to paragraph (d)(7) of this section will also issue the final administrative decision pursuant to paragraph (d)(11) of this section.

APPENDIX—RECONSIDERATION OF DISALLOWANCES UNDER SECTION 1116 (d) OF THE SOCIAL SECURITY ACT

TRANSFER OF FUNCTIONS

Under the authority of Reorganization Plan No. 1 of 1953, and pursuant to the authorities vested in me as Secretary of Health amd Human Services, I hereby order that, with respect to reconsiderations of disallowances imposed under titles I, IV, VI, X, XIV, XVI (AABD), XIX and XX of the Social Security Act, 42 U.S.C. 301 *et seq.*, 601 *et seq.*, 801 *et seq.*, 1201 *et seq.*, 1351 *et seq.*, 1381 *et seq.* (AABD), 1396 *et seq.* and 1397 *et seq.*, all references to "Administrator" appearing in 45

CFR 201.14 shall be deemed to read "Chairman, Departmental Grant Appeals Board" and all references to "Deputy Administrator" appearing therein shall be deemed to refer to one or more members of the Departmental Grant Appeals Board, designated by the Chairman to decide a reconsideration. States which have previously had or requested a conference pursuant to 45 CFR 201.14(d)(7) will be entitled to a conference with the Chairman of the Departmental Grant Appeals Board acting (as provided above) as successor to the Administrator of the Social and Rehabilitation Service (SRS), or with a member or members of the Board designated by the Chairman to decide the matter, acting as successor to the Deputy Administrator of SRS. The Chairman may, at his option, utilize a Grant Appeals Panel, designated pursuant to 45 CFR 516.4(b), to decide the matter, and may supplement the § 201.14 procedures by utilizing the procedures of 45 CFR part 16 including the authority provided in 45 CFR 16.51 to waive or modify any procedural provision upon a determination that no party will be prejudiced and that the ends of justice will be served.

[40 FR 34592, Aug. 18, 1975; 40 FR 44326, Sept. 26, 1975, as amended at 41 FR 42205, Sept. 27, 1976; 42 FR 43977, Sept. 1, 1977; 42 FR 51583, Sept. 29, 1977; 43 FR 9266, Mar. 6, 1978; 51 FR 9202, Mar. 18, 1986; 53 FR 36579, Sept. 21, 1988]

§ 201.15 Deferral of claims for Federal financial participation.

(a) *Scope.* Except as otherwise provided, this section applies to all claims for Federal financial participation submitted by States pursuant to titles I, IV, X, XIV, XVI (AABD), of the Social Security Act.

(b) *Definitions*—(1) *Deferral Action* means the process of suspending payment with respect to a claim within the scope of paragraph (a) of this section, pending the receipt and analysis of further information relating to the allowability of the claim, under the procedures specified in this section.

(2) *Deferred claim* means a claim within the scope of paragraph (a) of this section upon which a deferral action has been taken.

(c) *Procedures.* (1) A claim or any portion of a claim for reimbursement for expenditures reported on the Quarterly Statement of Expenditures shall be deferred only when the Regional Administrator believes the claim or a specific portion of the claim is of questionable allowability. The deferral action will be taken within 60 days after receipt of a Quarterly Statement of Expenditures prepared in accordance with instructions issued by the Administration.

(2) When deferral action is taken on a claim, the Regional Administrator or the Administrator will within 15 days send written notice to the State identifying the type and amount of the claim and the reason for deferral. In the written notice of the deferral action, the Regional Administrator or the Administrator will request the State to make available for inspection all documents and materials which the Regional office then believes necessary to determine the allowability of the claim.

(3) Within 60 days of receipt of the notice of deferral action described in paragraph (c)(2) of this section the State shall make available to the Regional office, in readily reviewable form, all requested documents and materials, or when necessary, shall identify those documents and items of information which are not available. If the State requires additional time to make the documents and material available, it shall upon request be given an additional 60 days.

(4) The Regional office will normally initiate the review within 30 days of the date that materials become available for review.

(5) If the Regional Administrator finds that the documents and materials are not in readily reviewable form or that supplemental information is required, he will promptly notify the State. The State will have 15 days from the date of notification to complete the action requested. If the Regional Commissioner or the Administrator finds that the documents necessary to determine the allowability of the claim are not made available within the allowed time limits, or that the documents are not made available in readily reviewable form, he shall promptly disallow the claim.

(6) The Regional Administrator or the Administrator will have 90 days after all documentation is available in readily reviewable form to determine the allowability of the deferred claim. If he is unable to complete the review within the time period the claim will be paid subject to a later determination of allowability.

(7) It is the responsibility of the State agency to establish the allowability of a deferred claim.

(8) The Regional Office or the Administrator will notify the State in writing of the decision on the allowability of the deferred claim.

(9) If a deferred claim is disallowed, the Regional Administrator or the Administrator shall advise the State of its right to reconsideration pursuant to § 201.14.

(10) A decision to pay a deferred claim shall not preclude a subsequent disallowance as a result of an audit exception or financial management review. If a subsequent disallowance should occur, the State, upon request shall be granted reconsideration pursuant to § 201.14.

[41 FR 7104, Feb. 17, 1976, as amended at 42 FR 51583, Sept. 29, 1977; 47 FR 7669, Feb. 22, 1982; 53 FR 36579, Sept. 21, 1988]

§ 201.66 Repayment of Federal funds by installments.

(a) *Basic Conditions.* When a State has been reimbursed Federal funds for expenditures claimed under titles I, IV-A, X, XIV, XVI (AABD) which are later determined to be unallowable for Federal financial participation, the State may make repayment of such Federal funds in installments provided:

(1) The amount of the repayment exceeds 2½ percent of the estimated annual State share for the program in which the unallowable expenditure occurred as set forth in paragraph (b) of this section; and

(2) The State has notified the Regional Administrator in writing of its intent to make installment repayments. Such notice must be given prior to the time repayment of the total was otherwise due.

(b) *Criteria governing installment repayments.* (1) The number of quarters over which the repayment of the total unallowable expenditures will be made will be determined by the percentage the total of such repayment is of the estimated State share of the annual expenditures for the specific program against which the recovery is made, as follows:

Total repayment amount as percentage of State share of annual expenditures for the specific program	Number of quarters to make repayment
2.5 pct. or less	1
Greater than 2.5, but not greater than 5	2
Greater than 5, but not greater than 7.5	3
Greater than 7.5, but not greater than 10	4
Greater than 10, but not greater than 15	5
Greater than 15, but not greater than 20	6
Greater than 20 but not greater than 25	7
Greater than 25, but not greater than 30	8
Greater than 30, but not greater than 47.5	9
Greater than 47.5, but not greater than 65	10
Greater than 65, but not greater than 82.5	11
Greater than 82.5, but not greater than 100	12

The quarterly repayment amounts for each of the quarters in the repayment schedule shall not be less than the following percentages of the estimated State share of the annual expenditures for the program against which the recovery is made.

For each of the following quarters	Repayment installment may not be less than these percentages
1 to 4	2.5
5 to 8	5.0
9 to 12	17.5

If the State chooses to repay amounts representing higher percentages during the early quarters, any corresponding reduction in required minimum percentages would be applied first to the last scheduled payment, then to the next to the last payment, and so forth as necessary.

(2) The latest State Agency Statement of Financial Plan for AFDC submitted by the State shall be used to estimate the State's share of annual expenditures for the specific program in which the unallowable expenditures occurred. That estimated share shall be the sum of the State's share of the estimates (as shown on the latest State Agency Statement of Financial Plan for AFDC) for four quarters, beginning with the quarter in which the first installment is to be paid.

(3) In the case of a program terminated by law or by the State, the actual State share—rather than the estimate—shall be used for determining whether the amount of the repayment exceeds 2½% of the annual State share for the program. The annual State

share in these cases will be determined using payments computable for Federal funding as reported for the program by the State on its Quarterly Statement of Expenditures reports submitted for the last four quarters preceding the date on which the program was terminated.

(4) Repayment shall be accomplished through adjustment in the quarterly grants over the period covered by the repayment schedule.

(5) The amount of the repayment for purpose of paragraphs (a) and (b) of this section may not include any amount previously approved for installment repayment.

(6) The repayment schedule may be extended beyond 12 quarterly installments if the total repayment amount exceeds 100% of the estimated State share of annual expenditures. In these circumstances, the criteria in paragraphs (b) (1) and (2) or (3) of this section, as appropriate, shall be followed for repayment of the amount equal to 100% of the annual State share. The remaining amount of the repayment shall be in quarterly amounts not less than those for the 9th through 12th quarters.

(7) The amount of a retroactive claim to be paid a State will be offset against any amounts to be, or already being, repaid by the State in installments, under the same title of the Social Security Act. Under this provision the State may choose to:

(i) Suspend payments until the retroactive claim due the State has, in fact, been offset; or

(ii) Continue payments until the reduced amount of its debt (remaining after the offset), has been paid in full. This second option would result in a shorter payment period. A retroactive claim for the purpose of this regulation is a claim applicable to any period ending 12 months or more prior to the beginning of the quarter in which the payment is to be made by the Administration.

[42 FR 28884, June 6, 1977, as amended at 47 FR 7669, Feb. 22, 1982; 52 FR 273, Jan. 5, 1987; 53 FR 36579, Sept. 21, 1988]

§ 201.67 Treatment of uncashed or cancelled checks.

(a) *Purpose.* This section provides the rules to ensure that States refund the Federal portion of uncashed or cancelled (voided) checks under titles I, IV-A, X, XIV, and XVI (AABD).

(b) *Definitions.* As used in this section—*Check* means a check or warrant that the State or local agency uses to make a payment.

Cancelled (voided) check means a check issued by the State agency or local agency which prior to its being cashed is cancelled (voided) by State or local agency action, thus preventing disbursement of funds.

Uncashed check means a check issued by the State agency or local agency which has not been cashed by the payee.

(c) *Refund of Federal financial participation (FFP) for uncashed checks*—(1) *General provisions.* If a check remains uncashed beyond a period of 180 days from the date it was issued, i.e., the date of the check, it will no longer be regarded as an amount expended because no funds have actually been disbursed. If the State agency has claimed and received FFP for the amount of the uncashed check, it must refund the amount of FFP received.

(2) *Report of refund.* At the end of each calendar quarter, the State agency must identify those checks which remain uncashed beyond a period of 180 days after issuance. The State agency must report on the Quarterly Statement of Expenditures for that quarter all FFP that it received for uncashed checks. Once reported on the Quarterly Statement of Expenditures for a quarter, an uncashed check is not to be reported on a subsequent Quarterly Statement of Expenditures. If an uncashed check is cashed after the refund is made, the State agency may submit a new claim for FFP.

(d) *Refund of FFP for cancelled (voided) checks*—(1) *General provisions.* If the State agency has claimed and received FFP for the amount of a cancelled (voided) check, it must refund the amount of FFP received.

(2) *Report of refund.* At the end of each calendar quarter, the State agency must identify those checks which were cancelled (voided). The State

agency must report on the Quarterly Statement of Expenditures for that quarter all FFP received by the State agency for these checks. Once reported on the Quarterly Statement of Expenditures for a quarter, a cancelled (voided) check is not to be reported on a subsequent Quarterly Statement of Expenditures.

[50 FR 37661, Sept. 17, 1985]

§ 201.70 Treatment of replacement checks.

(a) *Purpose.* This section provides the rules to ensure States do not claim Federal financial participation (FFP) for replacement checks under titles I, VI-A, X, XIV, XVI (AABD) except under the circumstances specified in paragraph (c) of this section.

(b) *Definitions.* As used in this section—

Check means a check or warrant that the State or local agency uses to make a payment.

Replacement check means a check issued by the State or local agency to replace an earlier check.

(c) *Claiming of FFP for replacement checks.* The State agency may not claim FFP for the amount of a replacement check unless:

(1) It makes no claim for FFP for the earlier check;

(2) The earlier check has been cancelled (voided) and FFP refunded, where claimed, pursuant to 45 CFR 201.67(d); or

(3) The earlier check has been cashed and FFP has been refunded.

The State agency shall report the amount of the refund of FFP for the earlier check on the Quarterly Statement of Expenditures for the quarter no later than the quarter in which the replacement check is issued.

[53 FR 24269, June 28, 1988]

PART 204—GENERAL ADMINISTRATION—STATE PLANS AND GRANT APPEALS

Sec.

AUTHORITY: 42 U.S.C. 602(a)(44) and 1302 and sections 1, 5, 6, and 7 of Reorganization Plan No. 1 of 1953, 67 Stat. 631.

§ 204.1 Submittal of State plans for Governor's review.

A State plan under title I, IV-A, IV-B, X, XIV, XVI(AABD) of the Social Security Act, section 101 of the Rehabilitation Act of 1973, or title I of the Mental Retardation Facilities and Community Mental Health Centers Construction Act, must be submitted to the State Governor for his review and comments, and the State plan must provide that the Governor will be given opportunity to review State plan amendments and long-range program planning projections or other periodic reports thereon. This requirement does not apply to periodic statistical or budget and other fiscal reports. Under this requirement, the Office of the Governor will be afforded a specified period in which to review the material. Any comments made will be transmitted to the Family Support Administration with the documents.

(Sec. 1102, 49 Stat. 647 (42 U.S.C. 1302))

[39 FR 34542, Sept. 26, 1974, as amended at 53 FR 36579, Sept. 21, 1988]

§ 204.2 State plans—format.

State plans for Federally-assisted programs for which the Family Support Administration has responsibility must be submitted to the Administration in the format and containing the information prescribed by the Administration, and within time limits set in implementing instructions issued by the Administration. Such time limits will be adequate for proper preparation of plans and submittal in accordance with the requirements for State Governors' review (see § 204.1 of this chapter).

(Sec. 1102, 49 Stat. 647, 42 U.S.C. 1302; sec. 7(b), 68 Stat. 658, 29 U.S.C. 37(b); sec. 139, 84 Stat. 1323, 42 U.S.C. 2677(b))

[38 FR 16872, June 27, 1973, as amended at 53 FR 36579, Sept. 21, 1988]

§ 204.3 Responsibilities of the State.

The State agency shall be responsible for assuring that the benefits and services available under titles IV-A, IV-D, and IV-F are furnished in an integrated manner.

[57 FR 30425, July 9, 1992]

§ 204.4 Grant appeals.

(a) *Scope.* This section applies to certain determinations (as set forth in part 16, appendix A, section C of this title), made with respect to direct, discretionary project grants awarded by the Family Support Administration, and such other grants or grant programs as the Administrator, with the approval of the Secretary, may designate. The statutory authority for current grant programs to which this section applies appears in the appendix to this section. This section is also applicable to determinations with respect to grants which were made under authority which has expired or been repealed since the grants were made, even though such authority does not appear in the appendix.

(b) *Submission.* (1) A grantee who has received notification, as described in § 16.3 (b) and (c) of this title, of a determination described in part 16, appendix A, section C of this title, may request reconsideration by informing the Grants Appeals Officer as identified in the final adverse determination or otherwise designated by the Administrator, Family Support Administration, Washington, DC 20201 of the grantee's intent to contest the determination. The grantee's request for reconsideration must be postmarked no later than 30 days after the postmark date of the written notification of such determination, except when the Grant Appeals Officer grants an extension of time for good cause.

(2) Although the request need not follow any prescribed form, it shall clearly identify the question or questions in dispute and contain a full statement of the grantee's position with respect to such question or questions, and the pertinent facts and reasons in support of such position. The grantee shall attach to his submission a copy of the agency notification specified in § 16.3(b) of this title.

(c) *Action by the Administration on requests for reconsideration.* (1) Upon receipt of such an application the Grant Appeals Officer will inform the grantee that:

(i) His request is under review, and

(ii) If no decision is received within 90 days of the postmark date of the grantee's request for reconsideration, the determination may be appealed to the Departmental Grant Appeals Board.

(2) The Grant Appeals Officer will reconsider the determination appealed from, considering any material submitted by the grantee and any other material necessary.

(3) If the response to the grantee is adverse to the grantee's position, the response will include notification of the grantee's right to appeal to the Departmental Grant Appeals Board.

APPENDIX

This section is issued under sections 1, 5, 6, and 7 of Reorganization Plan No. 1 of 1953, 18 FR 2053, 67 Stat. 631 and is applicable to programs carried out under the following authorities:

(1) Section 222(a) and (b) of the Social Security Amendments of 1972 (Pub. L. 92–603).

(2) Section 426 of the Social Security Act (42 U.S.C. 262).

(3) Section 707 of the Social Security Act (42 U.S.C. 907).

(4) Section 1110 of the Social Security Act (42 U.S.C. 1310).

(5) Section 1115 of the Social Security Act (42 U.S.C. 1315).

(Secs. 1, 5, 6, 7 Reorganization Plan No. 1 of 1953, 67 Stat. 631)

[40 FR 51443, Nov. 5, 1975, as amended at 53 FR 36579, Sept. 21, 1988]

PART 205—GENERAL ADMINISTRATION—PUBLIC ASSISTANCE PROGRAMS

Sec.

AUTHORITY: 42 U.S.C. 602, 603, 606, 607, 1302, 1306(a), and 1320b–7: 42 U.S.C. 1973gg–5.

§ 205.5 Plan amendments.

(a) *State plan requirements.* A State plan under title I, IV-A, X, XIV, or XVI (AABD) of the Social Security Act must provide that the plan will be amended whenever necessary to reflect new or revised Federal statutes or regulations, or material change in any phase of State law, organization, policy or State agency operation.

(b) *Federal financial participation.* Except where otherwise provided, Federal financial participation is available in the additional expenditures resulting from an amended provision of the State plan as of the first day of the calendar quarter in which an approvable amendment is submitted or the date on which the amended provision becomes effective in the State, whichever is later.

[39 FR 34542, Dec. 26, 1974, as amended at 53 FR 36579, Sept. 21, 1988]

§ 205.10 Hearings.

(a) *State plan requirements.* A State plan under title I, IV-A, X, XIV, or XVI(AABD) of the Social Security Act shall provide for a system of hearings under which:

(1) The single State agency responsible for the program shall be responsible for fulfillment of hearing provisions which shall provide for:

(i) A hearing before the State agency, or

(ii) An evidentiary hearing at the local level with a right of appeal to a State agency hearing. Where a State agency adopts a system of evidentiary hearings with an appeal to a State agency hearing, it may, in some political subdivisions, permit local evidentiary hearings, and in others, provide for a single hearing before the State agency. Under this requirement hearings shall meet the due process standards set forth in the U.S. Supreme Court decision in Goldberg v. Kelly, 397 U.S. 254 (1970) and the standards set forth in this section.

(2) Hearing procedures shall be issued and publicized by the State agency. Such procedures shall provide for a face-to-face hearing or, at State option, a hearing by telephone when the applicant or recipient also agrees. Under this provision, the State shall assure that the applicant or recipient is afforded all rights as specified in this section, whether the hearing is face-to-face or by telephone;

(3) Every applicant or recipient shall be informed in writing at the time of application and at the time of any action affecting his claim:

(i) Of his right to a hearing, as provided in paragraph (a)(5) of this section;

(ii) Of the method by which he may obtain a hearing;

(iii) That he may be represented by an authorized representative, such as legal counsel, relative, friend, or other spokesman, or he may represent himself.

(4) In cases of intended action to discontinue, terminate, suspend or reduce assistance or to change the manner or form of payment to a protective, vendor, or two-party payment under § 234.60:

(i) The State or local agency shall give timely and adequate notice, except as provided for in paragraphs (a)(4) (ii), (iii), or (iv) of this section. Under this requirement:

(A) *Timely* means that the notice is mailed at least 10 days before the date of action, that is, the date upon which the action would become effective;

(B) *Adequate* means a written notice that includes a statement of what action the agency intends to take, the reasons for the intended agency action, the specific regulations supporting such action, explanation of the individual's right to request an evidentiary hearing (if provided) and a State agency hearing, the circumstances under which assistance is continued if a hearing is requested, and if the agency action is upheld, that such assistance must be repaid under title IV-A, and must also be repaid under titles I, X, XIV or XVI (AABD) if the State plan provides for recovery of such payments.

(ii) The agency may dispense with timely notice but shall send adequate notice not later than the date of action when:

(A) The agency has factual information confirming the death of a recipient or of the AFDC payee when there is no relative available to serve as new payee;

(B) The agency receives a clear written statement signed by a recipient that he no longer wishes assistance, or that gives information which requires termination or reduction of assistance, and the recipient has indicated, in writing, that he understands that this must be the consequence of supplying such information;

(C) The recipient has been admitted or committed to an institution, and further payments to that individual do not qualify for Federal financial participation under the State plan;

(D) The recipient has been placed in skilled nursing care, intermediate care or long-term hospitalization;

(E) The claimant's whereabouts are unknown and agency mail directed to him has been returned by the post office indicating no known forwarding address. The claimant's check must, however, be made available to him if his whereabouts become known during the payment period covered by a returned check;

(F) A recipient has been accepted for assistance in a new jurisdiction and that fact has been established by the jurisdiction previously providing assistance;

(G) An AFDC child is removed from the home as a result of a judicial determination, or voluntarily placed in foster care by his legal guardian;

(H) For AFDC, the agency takes action because of information the recipient furnished in a monthly report or because the recipient has failed to submit a complete or a timely monthly report without good cause. (See § 233.37);

(I) A special allowance granted for a specific period is terminated and the recipient has been informed in writing at the time of initiation that the allowance shall automatically terminate at the end of the specified period;

(J) The agency has made a presumption of mismanagement as a result of a recipient's nonpayment of rent and provides for post hearings in such circumstances;

(K) An individual's payment is suspended or reduced for failure to meet a payment after performance obligation as set forth at § 233.101(b)(2)(iv) (B) or (C) of this chapter. In addition to the contents set forth in paragraph (a)(4)(i)(B) of this section, the adequate notice must advise the individual of the right to have assistance immediately reinstated retroactive to the date of action at the previous month's level pending the hearing decision if he or she makes a request for a hearing and reinstatement within 10 days after the date of the notice.

(iii) When changes in either State or Federal law require automatic grant adjustments for classes of recipients, timely notice of such grant adjustments shall be given which shall be "adequate" if it includes a statement of the intended action, the reasons for such intended action, a statement of the specific change in law requiring such action and a statement of the circumstances under which a hearing may be obtained and assistance continued.

(iv) When the agency obtains facts indicating that assistance should be discontinued, suspended, terminated, or reduced because of the probable fraud of the recipient, and, where possible, such facts have been verified through collateral sources, notice of such grant adjustment shall be timely if mailed at least five (5) days before action would become effective.

(5) An opportunity for a hearing shall be granted to any applicant who requests a hearing because his or her claim for financial assistance (including a request for supplemental payments under §§ 233.23 and 233.27) is denied, or is not acted upon with reasonable promptness, and to any recipient who is aggrieved by any agency action resulting in suspension, reduction, discontinuance, or termination of assistance, or determination that a protective, vendor, or two-party payment should be made or continued. A hearing need not be granted when either State or Federal law requires automatic grant adjustments for classes of recipients unless the reason for an individual appeal is incorrect grant computation.

(i) A request for a hearing is defined as a clear expression by the claimant (or his authorized representative acting for him), to the effect that he wants the opportunity to present his case to higher authority. The State may require that such request be in written form in order to be effective;

(ii) The freedom to make such a request shall not be limited or interfered with in any way. The agency may assist the claimant to submit and process his request;

(iii) The claimant shall be provided reasonable time, not to exceed 90 days, in which to appeal an agency action;

(iv) Agencies may respond to a series of individual requests for hearing by conducting a single group hearing. Agencies may consolidate only cases in which the sole issue involved is one of State or Federal law or policy or changes in State or Federal law. In all group hearings, the policies governing hearings must be followed. Thus, each individual claimant shall be permitted to present his own case or be represented by his authorized representative;

(v) The agency may deny or dismiss a request for a hearing where it has been withdrawn by the claimant in writing, where the sole issue is one of State or Federal law requiring automatic grant adjustments for classes of recipients, where a decision has been rendered after a WIN hearing before the manpower agency that a participant has, without good cause, refused to accept employment or participate in the WIN program, or has failed to request such a hearing after notice of intended action for such refusal, or where it is abandoned. Abandonment may be deemed to have occurred if the claimant, without good cause therefor, fails to appear by himself or by authorized representative at the hearing scheduled for such claimant.

(6) If the recipient requests a hearing within the timely notice period:

(i) Assistance shall not be suspended, reduced, discontinued or terminated (but is subject to recovery by the agency if its action is sustained), until a decision is rendered after a hearing, unless:

(A) A determination is made at the hearing that the sole issue is one of State or Federal law or policy, or change in State or Federal law and not one of incorrect grant computation;

(B) A change affecting the recipient's grant occurs while the hearing decision is pending and the recipient fails to request a hearing after notice of the change;

(C) The recipient specifically requests that he or she not receive continued assistance pending a hearing decision; or

(D) The agency has made a presumption of mismanagement as a result of a recipient's nonpayment of rent and provides for the opportunity for a hearing after the manner or form of payment has been changed for such cases in accordance with § 234.60 (a)(2) and (a)(11).

(ii) The agency shall promptly inform the claimant in writing if assistance is to be discontinued pending the hearing decision; and

(iii) In any case where the decision of an evidentiary hearing is adverse to the claimant, he shall be informed of and afforded the right to make a written request, within 15 days of the mailing of the notification of such adverse decision, for a State agency hearing and of his right to request a de novo hearing. Unless a de novo hearing is specifically requested by the appellant, the State agency hearing may consist of a review by the State agency hearing officer of the record of the evidentiary hearing to determine whether the decision of the evidentiary hearing officer was supported by substantial evidence in the record. Assistance shall not be continued after an adverse decision to the claimant at the evidentiary hearing.

(7) A State may provide that a hearing request made after the date of action (but during a period not in excess of 10 days following such date) shall result in reinstatement of assistance to be continued until the hearing decision, unless (i) the recipient specifically requests that continued assistance not be paid pending the hearing decision; or (ii) at the hearing it is determined that the sole issue is one of State or Federal law or policy. In any case where action was taken without timely notice, if the recipient requests a hearing within 10 days of the mailing of the notice of the action, and the agency determines that the action resulted from other than the application of State or Federal law or policy or a change in State or Federal law, assistance shall be reinstated and continued until a decision is rendered after the hearing, unless the recipient specifically requests that continued assistance not be paid pending the hearing decision.

(8) The hearing shall be conducted at a reasonable time, date, and place, and adequate preliminary written notice shall be given.

(9) Hearings shall be conducted by an impartial official (officials) or designee of the agency. Under this requirement, the hearing official (officials) or designee shall not have been directly involved in the initial determination of the action in question.

(10) When the hearing involves medical issues such as those concerning a diagnosis, an examining physician's report, or a medical review team's decision, a medical assessment other than that of the person or persons involved in making the original decision shall be obtained at agency expense and made part of the record if the hearing officer considers it necessary.

(11) In respect to title IV-C, when the appeal has been taken on the basis of a disputed WIN registration requirement, exemption determination or finding of failure to appear for an appraisal interview, a representative of the local WIN manpower agency shall, where appropriate, participate in the conduct of the hearing.

(12) The hearing shall include consideration of:

(i) An agency action, or failure to act with reasonable promptness, on a claim for financial assistance, which includes undue delay in reaching a decision on eligibility or in making a payment, refusal to consider a request for or undue delay in making an adjustment in payment, and discontinuance, termination or reduction of such assistance;

(ii) Agency decision regarding:

(A) Eligibility for financial assistance in both initial and subsequent determinations,

(B) Amount of financial assistance or change in payments,

(C) The manner or form of payment, including restricted or protective payments, even though no Federal financial participation is claimed.

(13) The claimant, or his representative, shall have adequate opportunity:

(i) To examine the contents of his case file and all documents and records to be used by the agency at the hearing at a reasonable time before the date of the hearing as well as during the hearing;

(ii) At his option, to present his case himself or with the aid of an authorized representative;

(iii) To bring witnesses;

(iv) To establish all pertinent facts and circumstances;

(v) To advance any arguments without undue interference;

(vi) To question or refute any testimony or evidence, including opportunity to confront and cross-examine adverse witnesses.

(14) Recommendations or decisions of the hearing officer or panel shall be based exclusively on evidence and other material introduced at the hearing. The transcript or recording of testimony and exhibits, or an official report containing the substance of what transpired at the hearing, together with all papers and requests filed in the proceeding, and the recommendation or decision of the hearing officer or

panel shall constitute the exclusive record and shall be available to the claimant at a place accessible to him or his representative at a reasonable time.

(15) Decisions by the hearing authority shall:

(i) In the event of an evidentiary hearing, consist of a memorandum decision summarizing the facts and identifying the regulations supporting the decision;

(ii) In the event of a State agency de novo hearing, specify the reasons for the decision and identify the supporting evidence and regulations.

Under this requirement no persons who participated in the local decision being appealed shall participate in a final administrative decision on such a case.

(16) Prompt, definitive, and final administrative action shall be taken within 90 days from the date of the request for a hearing.

(17) The claimant shall be notified of the decision in writing and, to the extent it is available to him, of his right to appeal to State agency hearing or judicial review.

(18) When the hearing decision is favorable to the claimant, or when the agency decides in favor of the claimant prior to the hearing, the agency shall promptly make corrective payments retroactively to the date the incorrect action was taken.

(19) All State agency hearing decisions shall be accessible to the public (subject to provisions of safeguarding public assistance information).

(b) *Federal financial participation.* Federal financial participation is available for the following items:

(1) Payments of assistance continued pending a hearing decision.

(2) Payments of assistance made to carry out hearing decisions, or to take corrective action after an appeal but prior to hearing, or to extend the benefit of a hearing decision or court order to others in the same situation as those directly affected by the decision or order. Such payments may be retroactive in accordance with applicable Federal policies on corrective payments.

(3) Payments of assistance within the scope of Federally aided public assistance programs made in accordance with a court order.

(4) Administrative costs incurred by the agency for:

(i) Providing transportation for the claimant, his representative and witnesses to and from the place of the hearing;

(ii) Meeting other expenditures incurred by the claimant in connection with the hearing;

(iii) Carrying out the hearing procedures, including expenses of obtaining an additional medical assessment.

[38 FR 22007, Aug. 15, 1973, as amended at 44 FR 17941, Mar. 23, 1979; 45 FR 20480, Mar. 28, 1980; 47 FR 5673, Feb. 5, 1982; 47 FR 47827, Oct. 28, 1982; 51 FR 9202, Mar. 18, 1986; 53 FR 36579, Sept. 21, 1988; 57 FR 30425, July 9, 1992]

§ 205.25 Eligibility of supplemental security income beneficiaries for food stamps or surplus commodities.

(a) In respect to any individual who is receiving supplemental security income benefits under title XVI of the Social Security Act, the State agency shall make the following determinations:

(1) The amount of assistance such individual would have been entitled to receive for any month under the appropriate State plan in effect for December 1973, under title I, X, XIV, or XVI, and for such purpose such individual shall be deemed to be aged, blind, or permanently and totally disabled, as the case may be, under the provisions of such plan.

(2) The bonus value of the food stamps (according to the Food Stamp Schedule effective for July 1973) such individual would have been entitled to receive for such month, assuming the individual were receiving the assistance determined under paragraph (a)(1) of this section.

(3) The amount of benefits such individual is receiving for such month under Title XVI, plus supplementary payments as defined in section 1616(a) of the Social Security Act and payments pursuant to section 212 of Pub. L. 93–66, if any.

(b) If the amount determined in paragraph (a)(1) of this section plus the amount determined in paragraph (a)(2) of this section exceeds the amount determined in paragraph (a)(3) of this section, such individual shall be eligible to participate in the food stamp program established by the Food Stamp Act of 1964 or surplus commodities distribution programs established by the Secretary of Agriculture pursuant to section 416 of the Agricultural Act of 1949, section 32 of Pub. L. 74–320, or any other law, in accordance with regulations and procedures established by the Secretary of Agriculture.

(c) For purposes of paragraph (a)(3) of this section, the State agency shall obtain the amount of the title XVI payment and the amount of any Federally administered State supplementary payment from the Social Security Administration.

(d) The State agency shall redetermine the eligibility of individuals to participate in the food stamp or surplus commodities distribution programs hereunder at such times as the Secretary of Agriculture requires recertification for such stamps or commodities.

[38 FR 34324, Dec. 13, 1973]

§205.30 Methods of administration.

State plan requirements: A State plan for financial assistance under title I, IV-A, X, XIV or XVI (AABD) of the Social Security Act must provide for such methods of administration as are found by the Secretary to be necessary for the proper and efficient operation of the plan.

[45 FR 56684, Aug. 25, 1980]

§205.32 Procedures for issuance of replacement checks.

(a) *State plan requirements.* A State plan under title IV-A of the Social Security Act shall provide that (1) procedures are in effect to ensure that no undue delays occur in issuing a replacement check; and (2) when applicable, prior to the issuance of a replacement check, the State agency must:

(i) Issue a stop payment order on the original AFDC check through appropriate banking procedures; and

(ii) Require recipients to execute a signed statement attesting to the nonreceipt, loss, or theft of the original FDC check. However, if obtaining such a statement from the recipient will cause the issuance of the check to be unduly delayed, the statement may be obtained within a reasonable time after the check is issued.

(b) *State option.* A State plan may provide that as a condition for issuance of a replacement check, a recipient is required to report a lost or stolen AFDC check to the police or other appropriate authorities. Under this provision, the State agency may require that the recipient verify that a report was made to the police or other appropriate authorities and, if so, the agency will establish procedures for such verification.

[51 FR 9203, Mar. 18, 1986]

§205.35 Mechanized claims processing and information retrieval systems; definitions.

Section 205.35 through 205.38 contain State plan requirements for an automated statewide management information system, conditions for FFP and responsibilities of the Administration for Children and Families (ACF). For purposes of §§205.35 through 205.38:

(a) *A mechanized claims processing and information retrieval system,* hereafter referred to as an automated *application processing and information retrieval system* (APIRS), or the *system,* means a system of software and hardware used:

(1) To introduce, control and account for data items in providing public assistance under the Aid to Families with Dependent Children (AFDC) State plan; and

(2) To retrieve and produce utilization and management information about such aid and services as required by the single State agency and Federal government for program administration and audit purposes.

(b) *Planning* means:

(1) The preliminary project activity to determine the requirements necessitating the project, the activities to be undertaken, and the resources required to complete the project;

(2) The preparation of an APD;

(3) The preparation of a detailed project plan describing when and how the computer system will be designed and developed; and

(4) The preparation of a detailed implementation plan describing specific

training, testing, and conversion plans to install the computer system.

(c) The following terms are defined at 45 CFR part 95, subpart F, § 95.605:

Annually updated advance automatic data processing planning document;
Design or *System Design;*
Development;
Initial advance automatic data processing planning document;
Installation;
Operation; and
Software.

[51 FR 45330, Dec. 18, 1986, as amended at 53 FR 36579, Sept. 21, 1988; 55 FR 4379, Feb. 7, 1990; 59 FR 30708, June 15, 1994]

§ 205.36 State plan requirements.

A State plan under title IV-A of the Social Security Act shall, at the option of the State, provide for the establishment and operation, in accordance with an (initial and annually updated) advance automated data processing planning document approved by SSA, of an automated statewide management information system designed effectively and efficiently, to assist management in the administration of an approved AFDC State plan. The submission process to amend the State plan is explained in § 201.3. This system must be designed:

(a) To automatically control and account for—

(1) All the factors in the total eligibility determination process under the plan for aid, including but not limited to:

(i) Identifiable correlation factors (such as social security numbers, names, dates of birth, home addresses, and mailing addresses (including postal ZIP codes), of all applicants and recipients of AFDC and the relative with whom any child who is an applicant or recipient is living).

(A) To assure sufficient compatibility among the systems of different jurisdictions, and

(B) To permit periodic screening to determine whether an individual is or has been receiving benefits from more than one jurisdiction.

(ii) Checking records of applicants and recipients of such aid on a periodic basis with other agencies, both intra and inter-state, for eligibility determination, verification and payment as required by other provisions of the Social Security Act.

(2) The costs, quality, and delivery of funds and services furnished to applicants for and recipients of such aid.

(b) To notify the appropriate State officials of child support, food stamp, social service, and medical assistance programs approved under title XIX whenever a case/recipient for aid and services becomes ineligible or the amount of aid or services is changed.

(c) To electronically refer and exchange information with programs under titles IV-D and IV-F for purposes of assuring that benefits and services are provided in an integrated manner.

(d) To provide for security against unauthorized access to, or use of, the data in the system.

[51 FR 13006, Apr. 17, 1986, as amended at 57 FR 47002, Oct. 14, 1992]

§ 205.37 Responsibilities of the Administration for Children and Families (ACF).

(a) ACF shall not approve the initial and annually updated advance automatic data processing planning document unless the document, when implemented, will carry out the requirements of the law and the objectives of title IV-A (AFDC) Automated Application Processing and Information Retrieval System Guide. The initial advance automatic data processing planning document must include:

(1) A requirements analysis, including consideration of the program mission, functions, organization, services, constraints and current support relating to such system;

(2) A description of the proposed statewide management system, including the description of information flows, input data formats, output reports and uses;

(3) The security and interface requirements to be employed in such statewide management system;

(4) A description of the projected resource requirements including staff and other needs; and the resources available or expected to be available to meet these requirements;

(5) A cost benefit analysis of alternative systems designs, data processing services and equipment in terms of qualitative and quantitative measures.

The alternative systems considered should include the advantages of the proposed system over the alternatives and should indicate the period of time the system will be operated to justify the funds invested. ACF certified systems that are already in place in other States must be included in the alternatives to be considered and evaluated;

(6) A plan for distribution of costs, containing the basis for rates, both direct and indirect, to be in effect under such a statewide management system;

(7) An implementation plan with charts of development events, testing description, proposed acceptance criteria, and backup and fallback procedures to handle possible failure of a system; and

(8) Evidence that the State's system will be compatible with those of the FSA to facilitate the exchange of data between the State and Federal system.

(b) ACF shall on a continuing basis, review, assess, and inspect the planning, design, and operation of, statewide management information systems, with a view to determining whether, and to what extent, these systems meet and continue to meet the requirements under these regulations.

(c) If ACF finds that any statewide management information system referred to in § 205.38 fails to comply substantially with criteria, requirements, and other undertakings prescribed by the approved advance automatic data processing planning document, approval of such document shall be suspended. The State will be given written notice of the suspension. The notice of suspension will state the reason for the suspension, whether the suspended system complies with the criteria for 50 percent FFP under 45 CFR part 95, the actions required for future Federal funding, and the effective date of the suspension. The suspension shall be effective as of the date that the system failed to comply substantially with the approved APD. The suspension shall remain in effect until ACF makes a determination that such system complies with prescribed criteria, requirements, and other undertakings for future Federal funding. Should a State cease development of their approved system, either by voluntary withdrawal or as a result of Federal suspension, all Federal incentive funds invested to date that exceed the normal administrative FFP rate (50 percent) will be subject to recoupment.

(d) ACF shall provide technical assistance to States as is deemed necessary to assist States to plan, design, develop, or install and provide for the security of the management information systems.

(e) Approvals of the systems by ACF under the provisions of this section will be undertaken only as a result of State applications for increased matching. The requirements of 45 CFR part 95, subpart E and subpart F apply.

[51 FR 13006, Apr. 17, 1986, as amended at 53 FR 36579, Sept. 21, 1988; 55 FR 4379, Feb. 7, 1990; 56 FR 1493, Jan. 15, 1991; 59 FR 30709, June 15, 1994]

§ 205.38 Federal financial participation (FFP) for establishing a statewide mechanized system.

(a) Effective July 1, 1981 through March 31, 1994, FFP is available at 90 percent of expenditures incurred for planning, design, development or installation of a statewide automated application processing and information retrieval system which are consistent with an approved ADP. (Beginning April 1, 1994 the match rate available for development of title IV-A automated systems is 50 percent.) The 90 percent FFP includes the purchase or rental of computer equipment and software directly required for and used in the operation of this system.

(b) ACF will approve the system provided the following conditions are met—

(1) ACF determines that the system is likely to provide more efficient, economical, and effective administration of the AFDC program.

(2) The system is compatible with the claims processing and information retrieval systems used in the administration of State plans approved under title XIX, and State programs where there is FFP under title XX.

(3) The system meets the requirements referred to in § 205.36.

(4) The system meets criteria established in the title IV-A (AFDC) Automated Application Processing and Information Retrieval System Guide

issued by ACF and which provides specific standard requirements for major functions, such as automated eligibility determination, grant computation, verification, referral, management control, compability, and data security.

(5) The State agency certifies that—

(i) The State will have all ownership rights in software or modifications thereof and associated documentation designed or developed with 90 percent FFP under this section, except that the Department of Health and Human Services reserves a royalty-free, nonexclusive, and irrevocable license to reproduce, publish, or otherwise use, and to authorize others to use for Federal government purposes, such software, modifications, and documentation;

(ii) Methods and procedures for properly charging the cost of all systems whether acquired from public or private sources shall be in accordance with Federal regulations in part 74 of this title and the applicable ACF title IV-A (AFDC) Automated Application Processing and Information Retrieval System Guide;

(iii) The complete system planned, designed, developed, installed, and hardware acquired, with FFP under these regulations will be used for a period of time which is consistent with the advance planning document as approved, or which ACF determines is sufficient to justify the Federal funds invested;

(iv) Information in the system will be safeguarded in accordance with applicable Federal law; and

(v) Access to the system in all of its aspects, including design, development, and operation, including work performed by any source, and including cost records of contractors and subcontractors, shall be made available to the Federal Government by the State at intervals deemed necessary by ACF to determine whether the conditions for approval are being met and to determine its efficiency, economy and effectiveness.

(c) If ACF suspends approval, as described in § 205.37, of the advance automated data processing planning document and/or system, FFP at the higher matching rate shall not be allowed for any costs incurred, until such time as the conditions for approval are met. Should the State fail to correct the deficiencies which led to the suspension within 90 days of the date of notification of suspension or within a longer period of time agreed to by both the State and ACF, all Federal incentive funds invested to date that exceed the normal administrative FFP rate (50 percent) will be disallowed.

(d) Should a State voluntarily withdraw its approved APD and cease development of the approved system, all Federal incentive funds invested to date that exceed the normal administrative FFP rate (50 percent) will be disallowed.

(e) Once a State is certified as having met the requirements referred to in § 205.36 incentive funding will not be allowable for enhancements or other modifications unless these modifications are authorized by the Administation for Children and Families as a result of Federal legislative or regulatory change.

[51 FR 13007, Apr. 17, 1986, as amended at 53 FR 36579, Sept. 21, 1988; 59 FR 30709, June 15, 1994]

§ 205.44 [Reserved]

§ 205.45 Federal financial participation in relation to State emergency welfare preparedness.

(a) Under title IV-A, Federal financial participation is available at the rate of 50 percent in expenditures for development and planning activities for emergency welfare preparedness. Such activities must relate to emergency welfare situations resulting from natural disasters, civil disorders, and enemy caused disasters, as prescribed in "Guidelines for the Preparation of State Emergency Welfare Services Plan" issued by Social and Rehabilitation Service, DHHS publication No. (SRS) 72–23004. These activities include:

(1) Safekeeping essential documents and records;

(2) Planning and developing emergency operating capability for providing food, lodging, clothing, and welfare registration and inquiry;

(3) Assuring that qualified individuals are responsible for the planning and operation of each welfare function

essential under emergency conditions for care and services for public assistance recipients and potential recipients;

(4) Coordinating with other government and voluntary welfare agencies, and welfare-related business and professional organizations and associations, in developing emergency operating plans and attaining operational readiness;

(5) Preparing and maintaining data on kinds, numbers, and locations of essential welfare resources, including manpower;

(6) Developing ability to assess emergency welfare resources and determining requirements necessary to care for public assistance cases in the event of disaster or attack;

(7) Preparing plans for claiming and distributing the above resources;

(8) Developing mutual aid agreements at State and local levels with neighboring welfare organizations;

(9) Preparing and distributing written emergency operations plans for public assistance agencies and operating units;

(10) Participating in preparedness exercises for the purpose of testing plans and determining the role of public assistance programs in relation to the overall preparedness program; and

(11) Travel incidental to any of the above activities.

(b) Federal financial participation is available at 50 percent under title IV-A for providing training in emergency welfare preparedness for all staff and for volunteers.

(c) In Guam, Puerto Rico, and the Virgin Islands, Federal financial participation is available at the rate of 75 percent in expenditures for emergency welfare preparedness under titles I, X, XIV, XVI (AABD) of the Social Security Act.

(d) The cost of these activities must be allocated to all programs benefited in accordance with part 74, subtitle A of title 45 of the Code of Federal Regulations.

[41 FR 23387, June 10, 1976, as amended at 51 FR 9203, Mar. 18, 1986]

§ 205.50 Safeguarding information for the financial assistance programs.

(a) *State plan requirements.* A State plan for financial assistance under title IV-A of the Social Security Act, must provide that:

(1) Pursuant to State statute which imposes legal sanctions:

(i) The use or disclosure of information concerning applicants and recipients will be limited to purposes directly connected with:

(A) The administration of the plan of the State approved under title IV-A, the plan or program of the State under title IV-B, IV-D, IV-E, or IV-F or under title I, X, XIV, XVI (AABD), XIX, XX, or the Supplemental Security Income (SSI) program established by title XVI. Such purposes include establishing eligibility, determining the amount of assistance, and providing services for applicants and recipients.

(B) Any investigation, prosecution, or criminal or civil proceeding conducted in connection with the administration of any such plans or programs.

(C) The administration of any other Federal or federally assisted program which provides assistance, in cash or in kind, or services, directly to individuals on the basis of need.

(D) The verification to the Employment Security Agency, or other certifying agency that an individual has been an AFDC recipient for at least 90 days or is a WIN or WIN Demonstration participant pursuant to Pub. L. 97–34, the Economic Recovery Tax Act of 1981.

(E) Any audit or similar activity, e.g., review of expenditure reports or financial review, conducted in connection with the administration of any such plan or program by any governmental entity which is authorized by law to conduct such audit or activity.

(F) The administration of a State unemployment compensation program.

(G) The reporting to the appropriate agency or official of information on known or suspected instances of physical or mental injury, sexual abuse or exploitation, or negligent treatment or maltreatment of a child receiving aid under circumstances which indicate that the child's health or welfare is threatened.

(ii) The State agency has authority to implement and enforce the provisions for safeguarding information about applicants and recipients:

(iii) Disclosure of any information that identifies by name or address any applicant or recipient to any Federal, State, or local committee or legislative body other than in connection with any activity under paragraph (a)(1)(i)(E) of this section is prohibited.

(iv) Publication of lists or names of applicants and recipients will be prohibited. *Exception.* In respect to a State plan for financial assistance under title I, IVA, X, XIV, or XVI (AABD) of the Social Security Act, an exception to this restriction may be made by reason of the enactment or enforcement of State legislation, prescribing any conditions under which public access may be had to records of the disbursement of funds or payments under such titles within the State, if such legislation prohibits the use of any list or names obtained through such access to such records for commercial or political purposes.

(v) The State or local agency responsible for the administration of the State plan has authority to disclose the current address of a recipient to a State or local law enforcement officer at his or her request. Such information is disclosed only to law enforcement officers who provide the name and Social Security number of the recipient and satisfactorily demonstrate that:

(A) The recipient is a fugitive felon (as defined by the State);

(B) The location or apprehension of such felon is within the law officer's official duties; and

(C) The request is made in the proper exercise of those duties.

(2) The agency will have clearly defined criteria which govern the types of information that are safeguarded and the conditions under which such information may be released or used. Under this requirement:

(i) Types of information to be safeguarded include but are not limited to:

(A) The names and addresses of applicants and recipients and amounts of assistance provided (unless excepted under paragraph (a)(1)(iv) of this section);

(B) Information related to the social and economic conditions or circumstances of a particular individual including information obtained from any agency pursuant to § 205.55; information obtained from the Internal Revenue Service (IRS) and the Social Security Administration (SSA) must be safeguarded in accordance with procedures set forth by those agencies;

(C) Agency evaluation of information about a particular individual;

(D) Medical data, including diagnosis and past history of disease or disability, concerning a particular individual.

(ii) The release or use of information concerning individuals applying for or receiving financial assistance is restricted to persons or agency representatives who are subject to standards of confidentiality which are comparable to those of the agency administering the financial assistance programs.

(iii) Except in the case of information requested pursuant to §§ 205.55 and 205.56, or in the case of an emergency situation when the individual's prior consent for the release of information cannot be obtained, the family or individual is informed whenever possible of a request for information from an outside source, and permission is obtained to meet the request. In an emergency situation when the individual's consent for the release of information cannot be obtained, the individual will be notified immediately.

(iv) In the event of the issuance of a subpoena for the case record or for any agency representative to testify concerning an applicant or recipient, the court's attention is called, through proper channels to the statutory provisions and the policies or rules and regulations against disclosure of information.

(v) The same policies are applied to requests for information from a governmental authority, the courts, or a law enforcement officer (except as provided for under paragraph (a)(1)(v) with respect to fugitive felons) as from any other outside source.

(3)(i) The agency will publicize provisions governing the confidential nature of information about applicants and recipients, including the legal sanctions imposed for improper disclosure and use, and will make these provisions available to applicants and recipients and to other persons and agencies to whom information is disclosed.

(ii) All information obtained pursuant to the income and eligibility verification requirements at §§ 205.55 and 205.56 will be stored and processed so that no unauthorized personnel can acquire or retrieve the information by any means.

(iii) All persons with access to information obtained pursuant to the income and eligibility verification requirements under §§ 205.55 and 205.56 will be advised of the circumstances under which access is permitted and the sanctions imposed for illegal use or disclosure of the information.

(4) All materials sent or distributed to applicants, recipients, or medical vendors, including material enclosed in envelopes containing checks, will be limited to those which are directly related to the administration of the program and will not have political implications except to the extent required to implement the National Voter Registration Act of 1993 (NVRA), Pub. L. 103–31. Under this requirement:

(i) Specifically excluded from mailing or distribution are materials such as "holiday" greetings, general public announcements, alien registration notices, and partisan voting information.

(ii) Not prohibited from such mailing or distribution are materials in the immediate interest of the health and welfare of applicants and recipients, such as announcements of free medical examinations, availability of surplus food, and consumer protection information;

(iii) Only the names of persons directly connected with the administration of the program are contained in material sent or distributed to applicants, recipients, and vendors, and such persons are identified only in their official capacity with the State or local agency.

(iv) Under NVRA, the agency must distribute voter information and registration materials as specified in NVRA.

(b) *Voluntary voter registration activities.* For States that are exempt from the requirements of NVRA, voter registration may be a voluntary activity so long as the provisions of section 7(a)(5) of NVRA are observed.

(c) *State plan requirements for programs of financial assistance in Puerto Rico, the Virgin Islands, and Guam.* A State plan under title I, X, XIV, or XVI (AABD) of the Social Security Act must meet all the requirements of paragraph (a) of this section, with the exception of paragraphs (a)(1)(i) (D) and (E), of this section, and also provide for disclosure of information concerning applicants and recipients for use by public officials who require such information in connection with their official duties. Under this requirement, such information shall be available only to public officials who certify in writing that:

(1) They are public officials as defined by State or Federal law of general applicability; and

(2) The information to be disclosed and used is required in connection with their official duties.

[45 FR 56684, Aug. 25, 1980, as amended at 47 FR 46506, Oct. 19, 1982; 49 FR 35599, Sept. 10, 1984; 51 FR 7214, Feb. 28, 1986; 51 FR 9203, Mar. 18, 1986; 54 FR 42243, Oct. 13, 1989; 57 FR 30157, July 8, 1992; 58 FR 49220, Sept. 22, 1993; 59 FR 26142, May 19, 1994; 61 FR 58143, Nov. 13, 1996]

§ 205.51 Income and eligibility verification requirements.

(a) A State plan under title I, IV-A, X, XIV or XVI (AABD) of the Social Security Act must provide that there be an Income and Eligibility Verification System in the State. Income and Eligibility Verification System (IEVS) means a system through which the State agency:

(1) Co-ordinates data exchanges with other Federally-assisted benefit programs covered by section 1137(b) of the Act;

(2) Requests and uses income and benefit information as specified in section 1137(a)(2) of the Act and §§ 205.55 and 205.56; and

(3) Adheres to standardized formats and procedures in exchanging information with the other programs and agencies and in providing such information as may be useful to assist Federal, State and local agencies in the administration of the child support program and the Social Security Administration in the administration of the title

II and title XVI (SSI) programs. The State agency (UC) information from the State Wage Information Collection Agency, described in paragraph (b) of this section; from the agency administering the State's unemployment compensation program (UC) under section 3304 of the Internal Revenue Code; from agencies in other States cited in § 205.55(a)(5), as set forth by the Secretary; from SSA, as set forth by the Commissioner of Social Security; and from IRS, as set forth by the Commissioner of Internal Revenue.

(b) A State plan under title I, IV-A, X, XIV or XVI (AABD) of the Social Security Act must provide that, as part of its Income and Eligibility Verification System, there be a State Wage Information Collection Agency in the State. State Wage Information Collection Agency (SWICA) means the State agency receiving quarterly wage reports from employers in the State (which may be the agency administering the State's unemployment compensation program), or an alternative system which has been determined by the Secretary of Labor, in consultation with the Secretary of Agriculture and the Secretary of Health and Human Services, to be as effective and timely in providing employment related income and eligibility information.

(c) Wage information maintained by a SWICA which receives quarterly wage reports from employers but does not use these reports for computation of employment compensation shall:

(1) Contain the social security number, first and last name and middle initial, wages earned for the period of the report, and an identifier of the employer (such as name and address) for each employee;

(2) Include all employers covered by the State's UC law and require such employers to report wage information (as specified above) for each employee within 30 days from the end of each calendar quarter;

(3) Accumulate earnings reported by employers for periods no longer than calendar quarters;

(4) Be machine readable; i.e., maintained in a fashion that permits automated processing; and

(5) Be available to other agencies in the State, to agencies in other States, and to Social Security Administration for establishing or verifying eligibility and benefit amounts under titles II and XVI of the Social Security Act, pursuant to agreements as required in § 205.58.

(d) A State shall obtain prior written approval from the Department, where appropriate, in accordance with 45 CFR 95.611, for any new developmental costs for automatic data processing equipment and services incurred in meeting IEVS requirements.

[51 FR 7214, Feb. 28, 1986]

§ 205.52 Furnishing of social security numbers.

The State plan under title I, IV-A, X, XIV, or CVI (AABD) of the Social Security Act must provide that:

(a) As a condition of eligibility, each applicant for or recipient of aid will be required:

(1) To furnish to the State or local agency a social security account number, hereinafter referred to as the SSN (or numbers, if more than one has been issued); and

(2) If he cannot furnish a SSN (either because such SSN has not been issued or is not known), to apply for such number through procedures adopted by the State or local agency with the Social Security Administration. If such procedures are not in effect, the applicant or recipient shall apply directly for such number, submit verification of such application, and provide the number upon its receipt.

(b) The State or local agency will assist the applicant or recipient in making applications for SSNs and will comply with the procedures and requirements established by the Social Security Administration for application, issuance, and verification of social security account numbers.

(c) The State or local agency will not deny, delay, or discontinue assistance pending the issuance or verfication of such numbers if the applicant or recipient has complied with the requirements of paragraph (a) of this section.

(d) The State or local agency will use such account numbers, in addition to any other means of identification it may determine to employ, in the administration of the plan.

(e) "Applicant" and "recipient" include for the purposes of this section the individuals seeking or receiving assistance and any other individual whose needs are considered in determining the amount of assistance.

(f) The State or local agency shall notify the applicant or recipient that the furnishing of the SSN is a condition of eligibility for assistance required by section 1137 of the Social Security Act and that the SSN will be utilized in the administration of the program.

(g) The State agency will submit all unverified social security numbers to the Social Security Administration (SSA) for verification. The State agency may accept as verified a social security number provided directly to the State agency by SSA or by another Federal or federally-assisted benefit program which has received the number from SSA or has submitted it to SSA for verification.

[51 FR 7217, Feb. 28, 1986]

§ 205.55 Requirements for requesting and furnishing eligibility and income information.

A State plan under title I, IV-A, X, XIV, or XVI (AABD) of the Social Security Act must provide that:

(a) Except as provided in paragraph (b), the State agency will request through the IEVS:

(1) Wage information from the SWICA for all applicants at the first opportunity following receipt of the application and for all recipients on a quarterly basis.

(2) Unemployment compensation information from the agency administering the State's unemployment compensation program under section 3304 of the Internal Revenue Code of 1954 and section 303 of the Act as follows:

(i) For applicants at the first opportunity following receipt of the application and in each of the first three months in which the individual is receiving aid, unless the individual is found to be receiving unemployment compensation, in which case the information will be requested until benefits are exhausted; and

(ii) In each of the first three months following any recipient-reported loss of employment, unless the individual is found to be receiving unemployment compensation, in which case the information will be requested until the benefits are exhausted.

(3) All available information maintained by the Social Security Administration for all applicants at the first opportunity following receipt of the application in the manner set forth by the Commissioner of Social Security. The State agency will also request such information for all recipients as of the effective date of this provision for whom such information has not previously been requested.

(4) Unearned income information from the Internal Revenue Service available under section 6103 (l)(7)(B) of the Internal Revenue Code of 1954, for all applicants at the first opportunity following receipt of the application for all recipients on a yearly basis. The request shall be made at the time and in the manner set forth by the Commissioner of Internal Revenue.

(5) As necessary, any income or other information affecting eligibility available from agencies in the State or other States administering:

(i) An AFDC program (in another State) under title IV-A of the Social Security Act;

(ii) A Medicaid program under title XIX of the Social Security Act;

(iii) An unemployment compensation program (in another State) under section 3304 of the Internal Revenue Code of 1954;

(iv) A Food Stamp program under the Food Stamp Act of 1977, as amended;

(v) Any State program administered under plan approved under title I, X, XIV, or XVI (AABD) of the Social Security Act; and

(vi) A SWICA (in another State).

(b)(1) With respect to individuals who cannot furnish an SSN at application, information specified in paragraph (a) will be requested at the first opportunity provided by each source after the State agency is provided with the SSN.

(2) For the purposes of this section, applicants and recipients shall also include any other individuals whose income or resources are considered in determining the amount of assistance, if the State agency has obtained the SSN of such individuals.

(c) The State agency must furnish, when requested, income, eligibility and benefit information to:

(1) Agencies in the State or other States administering the programs cited in paragraph (a)(5) of this section, in accordance with specific agreements as described in § 205.58;

(2) The agency in the State or other States administering a program under title IV-D of the Social Security Act; and

(3) The Social Security Administration for purposes of establishing or verifying eligibility or benefit amounts under title II and XVI (SSI) of the Social Security Act.

(d) The Secretary may, based upon application from a State, permit a State to obtain and use income and eligibility information from an alternate source or sources in order to meet any requirement of paragraph (a) of this section. The State agency must demonstrate to the Secretary that the alternate source or sources is as timely, complete and useful for verifying eligibility and benefit amounts. The Secretary will consult with the Secretary of Agriculture and the Secretary of Labor prior to approval of a request. The State must continue to meet the requirements of this section unless the Secretary has approved the request.

(e) The State agency must, upon request, reimburse another agency for reasonable costs incurred in furnishing income and eligibility information as prescribed in this section, including new developmental costs associated with furnishing such information, in accordance with specific agreements as described in § 205.58.

[51 FR 7215, Feb. 28, 1986]

§ 205.56 Requirements governing the use of income and eligibility information.

A State plan under title I, IV-A, X, XIV, or XVI (AABD) of the Social Security Act must provide that:

(a) The State agency will use the information obtained under § 205.55, in conjunction with other information, for:

(1) Determining individuals' eligibility for assistance under the State plan and determining the amount of assistance. States wishing to exclude categories of information items from follow-up must submit for the Secretary's approval a follow-up plan describing the categories of information items which it proposes to exclude. For each category, the State must provide a reasonable justification that follow-up is not cost-effective. A formal cost-benefit analysis is not required. A State may exclude information items from the following data sources without written justification if followed up previously from another source: Unemployment compensation information received from the Internal Revenue Service, and earnings information received from the Social Security Administration. Information items in these categories which are not duplicative, but provide new leads, may not be excluded without written justification. A State may submit a follow-up plan or alter its plan at any time by notifying the Secretary and submitting the necessary justification. The Secretary will approve or disapprove categories of information items to be excluded under the plan within 60 days of its submission. Those categories approved by the Secretary will constitute an approved State follow-up plan for IEVS. For those information items not excluded from follow-up,

(i) The State agency shall review and compare the information obtained from each data exchange against information contained in the case record to determine whether it affects the applicant's or the recipient's eligibility or the amount of assistance.

(ii) The State agency shall verify that the information is accurate and applicable to case circumstances either through the applicant or recipient or through a third party, if such verification is determined appropriate based on agency experience or is required under paragraph (b) of this section.

(iii) For applicants, if the information is received during the application period, the State agency shall use such information, to the extent possible, in making the eligibility determination.

(iv) For individuals who are recipients when the information is received or for whom a decision could not be made prior to authorization of benefits, the State agency shall within forty-five (45) days of its receipt, initiate a notice of case action or an entry in the case record that no case action is necessary, except that: Completion of action may be delayed beyond forty-five (45) days on no more than twenty (20) percent of the information items targeted for follow-up, if:

(A) The reason that the action cannot be completed within forty-five (45) days is the nonreceipt of requested third-party verification; and

(B) Action is completed promptly, when third party verification is received or at the next time eligibility is redetermined, whichever is earlier. If action is completed when eligibility is redetermined and third party verification has not been received, the State agency shall make its decision based on information provided by the recipient and any other information in its possession.

(v) The State agency shall use appropriate procedures to monitor the timeliness requirements specified in this subparagraph;

(2) Investigations to determine whether recipients received assistance under the State plan to which they were not entitled; and

(3) Criminal or civil prosecutions based on receipt of assistance under the State plan to which recipients were not entitled.

(b)(1) State agencies shall not take any adverse action to terminate, deny, suspend or reduce benefits to an applicant or recipient, based on information produced by a Federal computer matching program that is subject to the requirements in the Computer Matching and Privacy Protection Act (CMPPA) unless (i) The information has been independently verified in accordance with the independent verification requirements set out in the State agency's written agreement as required by § 205.58 or (ii) The independent verification requirement has been waived by the Department's Data Integrity Board.

(2) The CMPPA defines a matching program as any computerized comparison of (i) Two or more automated systems of records or a system of records with non-Federal records for the purpose of (A) Establishing or verifying the eligibility of, or continuing compliance with statutory and regulatory requirements by, applicants for, recipients or beneficiaries of, participants in, or providers of services with respect to, cash or in-kind assistance or payments under Federal benefit programs, or (B) Recouping payments or delinquent debts under such Federal benefit programs, or (ii) Two or more automated Federal personnel or payroll system of records or a system of Federal personnel or payroll record with non-Federal records.

(c) If the agency intends to reduce, suspend, terminate or deny benefits as a result of the actions taken pursuant to this section, the agency must provide notice and the opportunity for a fair hearing in accordance with § 205.10(a).

[51 FR 7215, Feb. 28, 1986, as amended at 53 FR 52712, Dec. 29, 1988; 57 FR 53859, Nov. 13, 1992]

§ 205.57 Maintenance of a machine readable file; requests for income and eligibility information.

A State plan under title I, IV—A, X, XIV, or XVI (AABD) of the Social Security Act must provide that:

(a) The State agency will maintain a file which is machine readable, i.e., which is maintained in a fashion that permits automated processing, and which contains the first and last name and verified social security number of each person applying for or receiving assistance under the plan.

(b) The State agency will use this file to exchange data with other agencies pursuant to § 205.55.

[51 FR 7216, Feb. 28, 1986]

§ 205.58 Income and eligibility information; specific agreements required between the State agency and the agency supplying the information.

(a) A State plan under title I, IV-A, X, XIV, or XVI (AABD) of the Social

Security Act must provide that, in carrying out the requirements of §§ 205.55 and 205.56, the State agency will enter into specific written agreements as described in paragraph (b) of this section with those agencies providing income and eligibility information. Agreements with Federal agencies are subject to the approval by the appropriate Federal Data Integrity Boards. The agreements will contain the procedure to be used in requesting and providing information.

(b) These agreements will include, but need not be limited to, the following:

(1) Purpose of the request;

(2) Identification of all agency officials, by position with authority to request information;

(3) Methods and timing of the requests for information, including the machine readable format to be used, the period of time needed to furnish the requested information and the basis for establishing this period. Agreements with the SWICA and the agency administering the Unemployment Compensation program in the State must provide that the State agency shall obtain information no less frequently than twice monthly;

(4) The type of information and reporting periods for which information will be provided and the verification methodologies to be used;

(5) Safeguards limiting release or redisclosure as required by Federal or State law or regulation, including the requirements of § 205.50 and as may be required by guidelines issued by the Secretary; and

(6) Reimbursement, if any, for the costs of furnishing the information requested by the State agency, including new developmental costs associated with furnishing such information.

[51 FR 7216, Feb. 28, 1986, as amended at 57 FR 53860, Nov. 13, 1992]

§ 205.60 Reports and maintenance of records.

A State plan under title I, IV—A, X, XIV, or XVI (AABD) of the Social Security Act must provide that:

(a) The State agency will maintain or supervise the maintenance of records necessary for the proper and efficient operation of the plan, including records regarding applications, determination of eligibility, the provision of financial assistance, and the use of any information obtained under § 205.55, with respect to individual applications denied, recipients whose benefits have been terminated, recipients whose benefits have been modified, and the dollar value of these denials, terminations and modifications. Under this requirement, the agency will keep individual records which contain pertinent facts about each applicant and recipient. The records will include information concerning the date of application and the date and basis of its disposition; facts essential to the determination of initial and continuing eligibility (including the individual's social security number, need for, and provision of financial assistance); and the basis for discontinuing assistance.

(b) The agency shall report as the Secretary prescribes for the purpose of determining compliance with the requirements of §§ 205.55 and 205.56 and for evaluating the effectiveness of the Income and Eligibility Verification System.

[51 FR 7216, Feb. 28, 1986]

§ 205.70 Availability of agency program manuals.

State plan requirements. A State plan for financial assistance under title I, IV-A, IV-B, X, XIV, or XVI (AABD) of the Social Security Act must provide that:

(a) Program manuals and other policy issuances which affect the public, including the State agency's rules and regulations governing eligibility, need and amount of assistance, and recipient rights and responsibilities will be maintained in the State office and in each local and district office for examination on regular workdays during regular office hours by individuals, upon request for review, study, or reproduction by the individual.

(b)(1) A current copy of such material will be made available without charge or at a charge related to the cost of reproduction for access by the public through custodians who (i) request the material for this purpose, (ii) are centrally located and publicly accessible to a substantial number of the recipient population they serve, and (iii) agree to accept responsibility for filing all amendments and changes forwarded by the agency.

(2) Under this requirement the material, if requested, must be made available without charge or at a charge related to the cost of reproduction to public or university libraries, the local or district offices of the Bureau of Indian Affairs, and welfare or legal services offices or organizations. The material may also be made available, with or without charge, to other groups and to individuals. Wide availability of agency policy materials is recommended.

(c) Upon request, the agency will reproduce without charge or at a charge related to the cost of reproduction the specific policy materials necessary for an applicant or recipient, or his representative, to determine whether a fair hearing should be requested or to prepare for a fair hearing; and will establish policies for reproducing policy materials without charge, or at a charge related to cost, for any individual who requests such material for other purposes.

[38 FR 26378, Sept. 20, 1973, as amended at 44 FR 17941, Mar. 23, 1979; 45 FR 56685, Aug. 25, 1980]

§ 205.100 Single State agency.

(a)(1) *State plan requirements.* A State plan for financial assistance under title I, IV-A, X, XIV, or XVI (AABD) of the Social Security Act must:

(i) Provide for the establishment or designation of a single State agency with authority to administer or supervise the administration of the plan.

(ii) Include a certification by the attorney general of the State identifying the single State agency and citing the legal authority under which such agency administers, or supervises the administration of, the plan on a statewide basis including the authority to make rules and regulations governing the administration of the plan by such agency or rules and regulations that are binding on the political subdivisions, if the plan is administered by them.

(2) [Reserved]

(b) *Conditions for implementing the requirements of paragraph (a) of this section.* (1) The State agency will not delegate to other than its own officials its authority for exercising administrative discretion in the administration or supervision of the plan including the issuance of policies, rules, and regulations on program matters.

(2) In the event that any rules and regulations or decisions of the single State agency are subject to review, clearance, or other action by other offices or agencies of the State government, the requisite authority of the single State agency will not be impaired.

(3) In the event that any services are performed for the single State agency by other State or local agencies or offices, such agencies and offices must not have authority to review, change, or disapprove any administrative decision of the single State agency, or otherwise substitute their judgment for that of the agency as to the application of policies, rules, and regulations promulgated by the State agency.

[45 FR 56685, Aug. 25, 1980]

§ 205.101 Organization for administration.

(a) A State plan for financial assistance under title I, IV-A, X, XIV, or XVI (AABD) of the Social Security Act shall include a description of the organization and functions of the single State agency and an organizational chart of the agency.

(b) Where applicable, a State plan for financial assistance under title I, IV-A, X, XIV, or XVI (AABD) of the act shall identify the organizational unit within the State agency which is responsible for operation of the plan and shall include a description of its organization and functions and an organizational chart of the unit.

[45 FR 56685, Aug. 25, 1980]

§ 205.120 Statewide operation.

(a) *State plan requirements.* A State plan for financial assistance under title I, IV-A, X, XIV, or XVI (AABD) of the Social Security Act must provide that:

(1) It shall be in operation, through a system of local offices, on a statewide basis in accordance with equitable standards for assistance and administration that are mandatory throughout the State;

(2) If administered by political subdivisions of the State, the plan will be mandatory on such political subdivisions;

(3) The State agency will assure that the plan is continuously in operation in all local offices or agencies through:

(i) Methods for informing staff of State policies, standards, procedures and instructions; and

(ii) Regular planned examination and evaluation of operations in local offices by regularly assigned State staff, including regular visits by such staff; and through reports, controls, or other necessary methods.

(b) [Reserved]

[39 FR 16971, May 10, 1974, as amended at 44 FR 17942, Mar. 23, 1979; 45 FR 56686, Aug. 25, 1980]

§ 205.130 State financial participation.

State plan requirements:

(a) A State plan for financial assistance under title I, IV-A, X, XIV, or XVI (AABD) of the Social Security Act must provide that:

(1) State (as distinguished from local) funds will be used in both assistance and administration; and

(2) State and Federal funds will be apportioned among the political subdivisions of the State on a basis consistent with equitable treatment of individuals in similar circumstances throughout the State.

(b) A State plan under title I, IV-A, X, XIV, or XVI (AABD) of the Act must provide further that State funds will be used to pay a substantial part of the total costs of the assistance programs.

[45 FR 56686, Aug. 25, 1980]

§ 205.150 Cost allocation.

A State plan under title I, IV-A, X, XIV, or XVI (AABD) of the Social Security Act must provide that the State agency will have an approved cost allocation plan on file with the Department in accordance with the requirements contained in subpart E of 45 CFR part 95. Subpart E also sets forth the effect on FFP if the requirements contained in that subpart are not met.

[47 FR 17508, Apr. 23, 1982]

§ 205.160 Equipment—Federal financial participation.

Claims for Federal financial participation in the cost of equipment for the cash assistance programs under titles I, IV-A, X, XIV, XVI [AABD] and for the separate administrative unit established under section 402(a)(19)(G) of the Social Security Act are to be determined in accordance with subpart G or 45 CFR part 95. Requirements concerning the management and disposition of equipment under these titles are also prescribed in subpart G of 45 CFR part 95.

[47 FR 41576, Sept. 21, 1982]

§ 205.170 State standards for office space, equipment, and facilities.

State plan requirements: A State plan for financial assistance under title I, IV-A, X, XIV, or XVI(AABD) of the Social Security Act must provide that:

(a) The State agency will establish and maintain standards for office space, equipment, and facilities that will adequately and effectively meet program and staff needs. Under this requirement, offices must be well marked and clearly identifiable in the community as a public service.

(b) The State agency will assure that the standards are continuously in effect in all State and local offices or agencies, including agency suboffices, and special centers through:

(1) Making information about the standards available to State and local staff and other appropriate persons;

(2) Regular planned evaluation of housing and facilities by regularly assigned staff through visits, reports, controls and other necessary methods;

(3) Methods for enforcement when necessary to secure compliance with State standards.

[36 FR 3862, Feb. 27, 1971, as amended at 45 FR 56686, Aug. 25, 1980]

§ 205.190 Standard-setting authority for institutions.

(a) *State plan requirements.* If a State plan for financial assistance under title I, X, XIV, or XVI(AABD) of the Social Security Act includes aid or assistance to individuals in institutions as defined in § 233.60(b) (1) and (2) of this chapter the plan must:

(1) Provide for the designation of a State authority or authorities which shall be responsible for establishing and maintaining standards for such institutions;

(2) Provide that the State agency will keep on file and make available to FSA, OFA upon request:

(i) A listing of the types or kinds of institutions in which an individual may receive financial assistance;

(ii) A record naming the State authority(ies) responsible for establishing and maintaining standards for such types of institutions;

(iii) The standards to be utilized by such State authority(ies) for approval or licensing of institutions including, to the extent applicable, standards related to the following factors:

(*a*) Health (dietary standards and accident prevention);

(*b*) Humane treatment;

(*c*) Sanitation;

(*d*) Types of construction;

(*e*) Physical facilities, including space and accommodations per person;

(*f*) Fire and safety,

(*g*) Staffing, in number and qualifications, related to the purposes and scope of services of the institution;

(*h*) Resident records;

(*i*) Admission procedures;

(*j*) Administrative and fiscal records;

(*k*) The control by the individual, or his guardian or protective payee, of the individual's personal affairs.

(3) Provide for cooperative arrangements with the standard-setting authority(ies) in the development of standards directed toward assuring adequate quality of care; in upgrading of institutional programs and practice; in actions necessary to close institutions that mistreat or are hazardous to the safety of the patients; and in planning so that institutions may be geographically located in accordance with need.

(b) *Federal financial participation.* (1) Federal financial participation is available in staff and related costs of the State or local agency that are necessary to discharge the responsibilities of the State agency under this section, including such costs for staff:

(i) Participating with other agencies and community groups in activities to set up the authority(ies) and to advise on the formulation of policy for the establishment and maintenance of standards;

(ii) On loan for a time limited period to work with the standard-setting authority(ies) in upgrading institutional care;

(iii) Engaged in the function of coordination in States where there is more than one authority; and

(iv) Engaged in adjusting complaints and making reports and recommendations to the standard-setting authority(ies) on conditions which appear to be in violation of such standards.

(2) Federal financial participation is not available in the costs incurred by the standard-setting authority(ies) in establishing and maintaining standards for institutions.

[36 FR 3862, Feb. 27, 1971, as amended at 45 FR 56686, Aug. 25, 1980; 53 FR 36580, Sept. 21, 1988]

PART 206—APPLICATION, DETERMINATION OF ELIGIBILITY AND FURNISHING ASSISTANCE—PUBLIC ASSISTANCE PROGRAMS

AUTHORITY: Sections 402 and 1102 of the Social Security Act (42 U.S.C. 602 and 1302) and Pub. L. No. 97–248, 96 Stat. 324, and Pub. L. No. 99–603, 100 Stat. 3359.

§206.10 Application, determination of eligibility and furnishing of assistance.

(a) *State plan requirements.* A State plan under title I, IV-A, X, XIV, or XVI(AABD), of that Social Security Act shall provide that:

(1) Each individual wishing to do so shall have the opportunity to apply for assistance under the plan without delay. Under this requirement:

(i) Each individual may apply under whichever of the State plan plans he chooses;

(ii) The agency shall require a written application, signed under a penalty of perjury, on a form prescribed by the State agency, from the applicant himself, or his authorized representative, or, where the applicant is incompetent or incapacitated, someone acting responsibly for him. When an individual is required to be included in an existing assistance unit pursuant to paragraph (a)(1)(vii), such individual will be considered to be included in the application, as of the date he is required to be included in the assistance unit;

(iii) An applicant may be assisted, if he so desires, by an individual(s) of his choice (who need not be a lawyer) in the various aspects of the application process and the redetermination of eligibility and may be accompanied by such individual(s) in contacts with the agency and when so accompanied may also be represented by them.

(iv)–(v) [Reserved]

(vi) Every recipient in a State which provides a supplemental payment under § 233.27 of this chapter shall have an opportunity to request that payment without delay.

(vii) For AFDC only, in order for the family to be eligible, an application with respect to a dependent child must also include, if living in the same household and otherwise eligible for assistance:

(A) Any natural or adoptive parent, or stepparent (in the case of States with laws of general applicability); and

(B) Any blood-related or adoptive brother or sister; *Exception:* needs and income of disqualified alien siblings, pursuant to § 233.50(c), are not considered in determining the eligibility and payment of an otherwise eligible dependent child.

(2)(i) Applicants shall be informed about the eligibility requirements and their rights and obligations under the program. Under this requirement individuals are given information in written form, and orally as appropriate, about coverage, conditions of eligibility, scope of the program, and related services available, and the rights and responsibilities of applicants for and recipients of assistance. Specifically developed bulletins or pamphlets explaining the rules regarding eligibility and appeals in simple, understandable terms are publicized and available in quantity.

(ii) Procedures shall be adopted which are designed to assure that recipients make timely and accurate reports of any change in circumstances which may affect their eligibility or the amount of assistance.

(iii) All applicants for and recipients of assistance shall be notified in writing at the time of application and on redetermination that eligibility and income information will be regularly requested from agencies specified in § 205.55 and will be used to aid in determining their eligibility for assistance.

(3) A decision shall be made promptly on applications, pursuant to reasonable State-established time standards not in excess of:

(i) 45 days for OAA, AFDC, AB, AABD (for aged and blind); and

(ii) 60 days for APTD, AABD (for disabled). Under this requirement, the applicant is informed of the agency's time standard in acting on applications which covers the time from date of application under the State plan to the date that the assistance check, or notification of denial of assistance or change of award is mailed to the applicant or recipient. The State's time standards apply except in unusual circumstances (e.g., where the agency cannot reach a decision because of failure or delay on the part of the applicant or an examining physician, or because of some administrative or other emergency that could not be controlled by the agency), in which instances the case record shows the cause for the delay. The agency's standards of promptness for acting on applications or redetermining eligibility shall not be used as a waiting period before granting aid, or as a basis for denial of an application or for terminating assistance.

(4) Adequate notice shall be sent to applicants and recipients to indicate that assistance has been authorized (including the amount of financial assistance) or that it has been denied or terminated. Under this requirement, adequate notice means a written notice that contains a statement of the action taken, and the reasons for and specific regulations supporting such action, and an explanation of the individual's right to request a hearing.

(5)(i) Financial assistance and medical care and services included in the plan shall be furnished promptly to eligible individuals without any delay attributable to the agency's administrative process, and shall be continued regularly to all eligible individuals until they are found to be ineligible. Under this requirement there must be arrangements to assist applicants and recipients in obtaining medical care and services in emergency situations on a 24-hour basis, 7 days a week.

(ii) Assistance will not be denied, delayed, or discontinued pending receipt of income or other information requested under § 205.55, if other evidence establishes the individual's eligibility for assistance.

(6) Assistance shall begin as specified in the State plan, which:

(i) For financial assistance.

(A) Must be no later than:

(*1*) The date of authorization of payment, or

(*2*) Thirty days in OAA, AFDC, AB, and AABD (as to the aged and blind), and 60 days in APTD and AABD (as to the disabled), from the date of receipt of a signed and completed application form, whichever is earlier: *Provided*, That the individuals then met all the eligibility conditions, and

(B) For purposes of Federal financial participation in OAA, AB, APTD, and AABD, may be as early as the first of the month in which an application has been received and the individual meets all the eligibility conditions; and

(C) In AFDC, for purposes of Federal financial participation, may be as early as the date of application provided that the assistance unit meets all the eligibility conditions; and

(D) In AFDC, States that pay for the month of application must prorate the payment for that month by multiplying the amount payable if payment were made for the entire month including special needs in accordance with § 233.34 by the ratio of the days in the month including and following the date of application (or, at State option, the date of authorization of payment) to the total number of days in such month. The State plan may provide for using a standard 30-day month to determine the prorated amount.

(7) In cases of proposed action to terminate, discontinue, suspend or reduce assistance, the agency shall give timely and adequate notice. Such notice shall comply with the provisions of § 205.10 of this chapter.

(8) Each decision regarding eligibility or ineligibility will be supported by facts in the applicant's or recipient's case record. Under this requirement each application is disposed of by a finding of eligibility or ineligibility unless:

(i) The applicant voluntarily withdraws his application, and there is an entry in the case record that a notice has been sent to confirm the applicant's notification to the agency that he does not desire to pursue his application; or

(ii) There is an entry in the case record that the application has been disposed of because the applicant died or could not be located.

(9) Where an individual has been determined to be eligible, eligibility will be reconsidered or redetermined:

(i) When required on the basis of information the agency has obtained previously about anticipated changes in the individual's situation;

(ii) Promptly, after a report is obtained which indicates changes in the individual's circumstances that may affect the amount of assistance to which he is entitled or may make him ineligible; and

(iii) Periodically, within agency established time standards, but not less frequently than every 12 months in OAA, AB, APTD, and AABD, on eligibility factors subject to change. For recipients of AFDC, all factors of eligibility will be redetermined at least every 6 months except in the case of monthly reporting cases or cases covered by an approved error-prone profiling system as specified in paragraph (a)(9)(iv) of this section. Under the AFDC program, at least one face-to-face redetermination must be conducted in each case once in every 12 months.

(iv) In accordance with paragraph (a)(9)(iii) of this section, under an alternative redetermination plan based on error-prone profiling, which has been approved by the Secretary, and includes:

(A) A description of the statistical methodology used to develop the error-prone profile system upon which the redetermination schedule is based;

(B) The criteria to be used to vary the scope of review and to assign different types of cases; and

(C) A detailed outline of the evaluation system, including provisions for necessary changes in the error-prone output, such as types of cases, types of errors, frequencies of redeterminations and corrective action.

(10) Standards and methods for determination of eligibility shall be consistent with the objectives of the programs, and will respect the rights of individuals under the United States Constitution, the Social Security Act, title VI of the Civil Rights Act of 1964, and all other relevant provisions of Federal and State laws.

(11) [Reserved]

(12) The State agency shall establish and maintain methods by which it shall be kept currently informed about local agencies' adherence to the State plan provisions and to the State agency's procedural requirements for determining eligibility, and it shall take corrective action when necessary.

(b) *Definitions.* For purposes of this section:

(1) *Applicant* is a person who has, directly, or through his authorized representative, or where incompetent or incapacitated, through someone acting responsibly for him, made application for public assistance from the agency administering the program, and whose application has not been terminated.

(2) *Application* is the action by which an individual indicates in writing to the agency administering public assistance (on a form prescribed by the State agency) his desire to receive assistance. The relative with whom a child is living or will live ordinarily makes application for the child for AFDC. An application is distinguished from an inquiry, which is simply a request for information about eligibility requirements for public assistance. Such inquiry may be followed by an application. When an individual is required to be included in an existing assistance unit pursuant to paragraph (a)(1)(vii), such individual will be considered to be included in the application, as of the date he is required to be included in the assistance unit.

(3) *Date of Application* is the date on which the action described in paragraph (b)(2) of this section occurs.

(4) *Redetermination* is a review of factors affecting AFDC eligibility and payment amount; e.g. continued absence, income (including child and spousal support), etc.

(5) *Assistance Unit* is the group of individuals whose income, resources and needs are considered as a unit for purposes of determining eligibility and the amount of payment.

[48 FR 28407, June 21, 1983, as amended at 49 FR 35599, Sept. 10, 1984; 51 FR 7217, Feb. 28, 1986; 51 FR 9203, Mar. 18, 1986; 52 FR 48689, Dec. 24, 1987; 53 FR 30433, Aug. 12, 1988; 57 FR 30157, July 8, 1992]

PART 211—CARE AND TREATMENT OF MENTALLY ILL NATIONALS OF THE UNITED STATES, RETURNED FROM FOREIGN COUNTRIES

Sec.

AUTHORITY: Secs. 1–11, 74 Stat. 308–310; 24 U.S.C. 321–329.

SOURCE: 39 FR 26546, July 19, 1974, unless otherwise noted.

§ 211.1 General definitions.

When used in this part:

(a) *Act* means Pub. L. 86–571, approved July 5, 1960, 74 Stat. 308, entitled "An Act to provide for the hospitalization, at Saint Elizabeths Hospital in the District of Columbia or elsewhere, of certain nationals of the United States adjudged insane or otherwise found mentally ill in foreign countries, and for other purposes";

(b) The term *Secretary* means the Secretary of Health and Human Services;

(c) The term *Department* means the Department of Health and Human Services;

(d) The term *Administrator* means the Administrator, Family Support Administration, Department of Health and Human Services;

(e) The term *eligible person* means an individual with respect to whom the certificates referred to in § 211.3 are furnished to the Administrator in connection with the reception of an individual arriving from a foreign country;

(f) The term *Public Health Service* means the Public Health Service in the Department of Health and Human Services;

(g) The term *agency* means an appropriate State or local public or nonprofit agency with which the Administrator has entered into arrangements for the provision of care, treatment, and assistance pursuant to the Act;

(h) The term *State* includes the District of Columbia, the Commonwealth of Puerto Rico, the Virgin Islands, and Guam;

(i) The term *residence* means residence as determined under the applicable law or regulations of a State or political subdivision for the purpose of determining the eligibility of an individual for hospitalization in a public mental hospital;

(j) The term *legal guardian* means a guardian, appointed by a court, whose powers, duties, and responsibilities include the powers, duties, and responsibilities of guardianship of the person.

[39 FR 26546, July 19, 1974, as amended at 53 FR 36580, Sept. 21, 1988]

§ 211.2 General.

The Administrator shall make suitable arrangements with agencies to the end that any eligible person will be received, upon request of the Secretary of State, at the port of entry or debarkation upon arrival in the United States from a foreign country and be provided, to the extent necessary, with temporary care, treatment, and assistance, pending transfer and release or hospitalization pursuant to the Act. The Administrator shall also make suitable arrangements with appropriate divisions of the Public Health Service, with Saint Elizabeths Hospital in the District of Columbia, with Federal hospitals outside of the Department, or with other public or private hospitals to provide the eligible person with care and treatment in a hospital. The Administrator shall maintain a roster setting forth the name and address of each eligible person currently receiving care and treatment, or assistance, pursuant to the Act.

§ 211.3 Certificates.

The following certificates are necessary to establish that an individual is an eligible person:

(a) *Certificates as to nationality.* A certificate issued by an authorized official of the Department of State, stating that the individual is a national of the United States.

(b) *Certificate as to mental condition.* Either (1) a certificate obtained or transmitted by an authorized official of the Department of State that the individual has been legally adjudged insane in a named foreign country; or (2) a certificate of an appropriate authority or person stating that at the time of such certification the individual was in a named foreign country and was in need of care and treatment in a mental hospital. A statement shall, if possible, be incorporated into or attached to the certificate furnished under this paragraph setting forth all available medical and other pertinent information concerning the individual.

(c) *Appropriate authority or person.* For the purpose of paragraph (b)(2) of this section a medical officer of the Public Health Service or of another agency of the United States, or a medical practitioner legally authorized to provide care or treatment of mentally ill persons in the foreign country, is an "appropriate authority or person," and shall be so identified in his execution of the certificate. If such a medical officer or practitioner is unavailable, an authorized official of the Department of State may serve as an "appropriate authority or person," and shall, in the execution of the certificate, identify himself as serving as such person due to the unavailability of a suitable medical officer or practitioner.

§ 211.4 Notification to legal guardian, spouse, next of kin, or interested persons.

(a) Whenever an eligible person arrives in the United States from a foreign country, or when such person is transferred from one State to another, the Administrator shall, upon such arrival or transfer (or in advance thereof, if possible), provide for notification of his legal guardian, or in the absence of such a guardian, of his spouse or next of kin, or in the absence of any of these, of one or more interested persons, if known.

(b) Whenever an eligible person is admitted to a hospital pursuant to the Act, the Administrator shall provide for immediate notification of his legal guardian, spouse, or next of kin, if known.

§211.5 Action under State law; appointment of guardian.

Whenever an eligible person is incapable of giving his consent to care and treatment in a hospital, either because of his mental condition or because he is a minor, the agency will take appropriate action under State law, including, if necessary, procuring the appointment of a legal guardian, to ensure the proper planning for and provision of such care and treatment.

§211.6 Reception; temporary care, treatment, and assistance.

(a) *Reception.* The agency will meet the eligible person at the port of entry or debarkation, will arrange for appropriate medical examination, and will plan with him, in cooperation with his legal guardian, or, in the absence of such a guardian, with other interested persons, if any, for needed temporary care and treatment.

(b) *Temporary care, treatment, and assistance.* The agency will provide for temporary care, treatment, and assistance, as reasonably required for the health and welfare of the eligible person. Such care, treatment, and assistance may be provided in the form of hospitalization and other medical and remedial care (including services of necessary attendants), food and lodging, money, payments, transportation, or other goods and services. The agency will utilize the Public Health Service General Hospital nearest to the port of entry or debarkation or any other suitable public or private hospital, in providing hospitalization and medical care, including diagnostic service as needed, pending other appropriate arrangements for serving the eligible person.

§211.7 Transfer and release of eligible person.

(a) *Transfer and release to relative.* If at the time of arrival from a foreign country or any time during temporary or continuing care and treatment the Administrator finds that the best interests of the eligible person will be served thereby, and a relative, having been fully informed of his condition, agrees in writing to assume responsibility for his care and treatment, the Administrator shall transfer and release him to such relative. In determining whether his best interest will be served by such transfer and release, due weight shall be given to the relationship of the individuals involved, the financial ability of the relative to provide for such person, and the accessibility to necessary medical facilities.

(b) *Transfer and release to appropriate State authorities, or agency of the United States.* If appropriate arrangements cannot be accomplished under paragraph (a) of this section, and if no other agency of the United States is responsible for the care and treatment of the eligible person, the Administrator shall endeavor to arrange with the appropriate State mental health authorities of the eligible person's State of residence or legal domicile, if any, for the assumption of responsibility for the care and treatment of the eligible person by such authorities and shall, upon the making of such arrangements in writing, transfer and release him to such authorities. If any other agency of the United States is responsible for the care and treatment of the eligible person, the Administrator shall make arrangements for his transfer and release to that agency.

§211.8 Continuing hospitalization.

(a) *Authorization and arrangements.* In the event that appropriate arrangements for an eligible person in need of continuing care and treatment in a hospital cannot be accomplished under §211.7, or until such arrangements can be made, care and treatment shall be provided by the Administrator in Saint Elizabeths Hospital in the District of Columbia, in an appropriate Public

Health Service Hospital, or in such other suitable public or private hospital as the Administrator determines is in the best interests of such person.

(b) *Transfer to other hospital.* At any time during continuing hospitalization, when the Administrator deems it to be in the interest of the eligible person or of the hospital affected, the Administrator shall authorize the transfer of such person from one hospital to another and, where necessary to that end, the Administrator shall authorize the initiation of judicial proceedings for the purpose of obtaining a commitment of such person to the Secretary.

(c) *Place of hospitalization.* In determining the placement or transfer of an eligible person for purposes of hospitalization, due weight shall be given to such factors as the location of the eligible person's legal guardian or family, the character of his illness and the probable duration thereof, and the facilities of the hospital to provide care and treatment for the particular health needs of such person.

§211.9 Examination and reexamination.

Following admission of an eligible person to a hospital for temporary or continuing care and treatment, he shall be examined by qualified members of the medical staff as soon as practicable, but not later than the fifth day after his admission. Each such person shall be reexamined at least once within each six month period beginning with the month following the month in which he was first examined.

§211.10 Termination of hospitalization.

(a) *Discharge or conditional release.* If, following an examination, the head of the hospital finds that the eligible person hospitalized for mental illness (whether or not pursuant to a judicial commitment) is not in need of such hospitalization, he shall be discharged. In the case where hospitalization was pursuant to a judicial commitment, the head of the hospital may, in accordance with laws governing hospitalization for mental illness as may be in force and generally applicable in the State in which the hospital is located, conditionally release him if he finds that this is in his best interests.

(b) *Notification to committing court.* In the case of any person hospitalized under §211.8 who has been judicially committed to the custody of the Secretary, the Secretary will notify the committing court in writing of the discharge or conditional release of such person under this section or of his transfer and release under §211.7.

§211.11 Request for release from hospitalization.

If an eligible person who is hospitalized pursuant to the Act, or his legal guardian, spouse, or adult next of kin, requests his release, such request shall be granted by the Administrator if his best interests will be served thereby, or by the head of the hospital if he is found not to be in need of hospitalization by reason of mental illness. The right of the administrator or the head of the hospital, to refuse such request and to detain him for care and treatment shall be determined in accordance with laws governing the detention, for care and treatment, of persons alleged to be mentally ill as may be in force and applicable generally in the State in which such hospital is located, but in no event shall the patient be detained more than forty-eight hours (excluding any period of time falling on a Sunday or a legal holiday observed by the courts of the State in which such hospital is located) after the receipt of such request unless within such time (a) judicial proceedings for such hospitalization are commenced or (b) a judicial extension of such time is obtained, for a period of not more than five days, for the commencement of such proceedings.

§211.12 Federal payments.

The arrangements made by the Administrator with an agency or hospital for carrying out the purposes of the Act shall provide for payments to such agency or hospital, either in advance or by way of reimbursement, of the costs of reception, temporary care, treatment, and assistance, continuing care and treatment, and transportation, pursuant to the Act, and payments for other expenditures necessarily and reasonably related to providing the same. Such arrangements shall include the methods and procedures for determining the amounts of the advances or reimbursements, and for remittance and adjustment thereof.

§211.13 Financial responsibility of the eligible person; collections, compromise, or waiver of payment.

(a) *For temporary care and treatment.* If an eligible person receiving temporary care, treatment, and assistance, pursuant to the Act, has financial resources available to pay all or part of the costs of such care, the Administrator shall require him to pay for such costs, either in advance or by way of reimbursement, unless in his judgment it would be inequitable or impracticable to require such payment.

(b) *For continuing care and treatment.* Any eligible person receiving continuing care and treatment in a hospital, or his estate, shall be liable to pay or contribute toward the payment of the costs or charges therefor, to the same extent as such person would, if a resident of the District of Columbia, be liable to pay, under the laws of the District of Columbia, for his care and maintenance in a hospital for the mentally ill in that jurisdiction.

(c) *Collections, compromise, or waiver of payment.* The Administrator may, in his discretion, where in his judgment substantial justice will be best served thereby or the probable recovery will not warrant the expense of collection, compromise, or waive the whole or any portion of, any claim for continuing care and treatment, and assistance, and in the process of arriving at such decision, the Administrator may make or cause to be made such investigations as may be necessary to determine the ability of the patient to pay or contribute toward the cost of his continuing care and treatment in a hospital.

§211.14 Disclosure of information.

(a) No disclosure of any information of a personal and private nature with respect to an individual obtained at any time by any person, organization, or institution in the course of discharging the duties of the Secretary under the Act shall be made except insofar:

(1) As the individual or his legal guardian, if any (or, if he is a minor, his parent or legal guardian), shall consent;

(2) As disclosure may be necessary to carry out any functions of the Secretary under the Act;

(3) As disclosure may be directed by the order of a court of competent jurisdiction;

(4) As disclosure may be necessary to carry out any functions of any agency of the United States which are related to the return of the individual from a foreign country, or his entry into the United States; or

(5) As expressly authorized by the Administrator.

(b) An agreement made with an agency or hospital for care, treatment, and assistance pursuant to the Act shall provide that no disclosure will be made of any information of a personal and private nature received by such agency or hospital in the course of discharging the duties under such agreement except as is provided therein, or is otherwise specifically authorized by the Administrator.

(c) Nothing in this section shall preclude disclosure, upon proper inquiry, of information as to the presence of an eligible person in a hospital, or as to his general condition and progress.

§211.15 Nondiscrimination.

(a) No eligible person shall, on the ground of race, color, or national origin, be excluded from participation, be denied any benefits, or otherwise be subjected to discrimination of any nature or form in the provision of any benefits, under the Act.

(b) The prohibition in paragraph (a) of this section precludes discrimination either in the selection of individuals to receive the benefits, in the scope of benefits, or in the manner of providing them. It extends to all facilities and services provided by the Administrator or an agency to an individual, and to the arrangements and the procedures under this part relating thereto, in connection with reception, temporary care, treatment, and assistance, and continuing hospitalization under the Act.

PART 212—ASSISTANCE FOR UNITED STATES CITIZENS RETURNED FROM FOREIGN COUNTRIES

AUTHORITY: Sec. 302, 75 Stat. 142, sec. 1102, 49 Stat. 647; 42 U.S.C. 1313, 1302.

SOURCE: 39 FR 26548, July 19, 1974, unless otherwise noted.

§212.1 General definitions.

When used in this part:

(a) *Act* means section 1113 of the Social Security Act, as amended;

(b) The term *Secretary* means the Secretary of Health and Human Services;

(c) The term *Department* means the Department of Health and Human Services;

(d) The term *Administration* means the Administration for Children and Families, Department of Health and Human Services;

(e) The term *Assistant Secretary* means the Assistant Secretary for Children and Families;

(f) The term *eligible person* means an individual with respect to whom the conditions in §212.3 are met;

(g) The term *State* includes the District of Columbia, the Commonwealth of Puerto Rico, the Virgin Islands, and Guam;

(h) The term *United States* when used in a geographical sense means the States;

(i) The term *agency* means State or local public agency or organization or national or local private agency or organization with which the Assistant Secretary has entered into agreement for the provision of temporary assistance pursuant to the Act;

(j) The term *temporary assistance* means money payments, medical care, temporary billeting, transportation, and other goods and services necessary for the health, or welfare of individuals, including guidance, counseling, and other welfare services.

[39 FR 26548, July 19, 1974, as amended at 53 FR 36580, Sept. 21, 1988; 60 FR 19864, Apr. 21, 1995]

§212.2 General.

The Assistant Secretary shall develop plans and make arrangements for provision of temporary assistance within the United States to any eligible person, after consultation with appropriate offices of the Department of State, the Department of Justice, and the Department of Defense. Temporary assistance shall be provided, to the extent feasible, in accordance with such plans, as modified from time to time by the Assistant Secretary. The Assistant Secretary shall enter into agreements with agencies whose services and facilities are to be utilized for the purpose of providing temporary assistance pursuant to the Act, specifying the conditions governing the provision of such assistance and the manner of payment of the cost of providing therefor.

[39 FR 26548, July 19, 1974, as amended at 60 FR 19864, Apr. 21, 1995]

§212.3 Eligible person.

In order to establish that an individual is an eligible person, it must be found that:

(a) He is a citizen of the United States or a dependent of a citizen of the United States;

(b) A written statement has been transmitted to the Administration by an authorized official of the Department of State containing information which identifies him as having returned, or been brought, from a foreign country to the United States because of the destitution of the citizen of the United States, or the illness of such citizen or any of his dependents, or because of war, threat of war, invasion, or similar crisis. Such statement shall, if possible, incorporate or have attached thereto, all available pertinent information concerning the individual.

In case of war, threat of war, invasion, or similar crisis, a determination by the Department of State that such a condition is the general cause for the return of citizens of the United States and their dependents from a particular foreign country, and evidence that an individual has returned, or, been brought, from such country to the United States shall be considered sufficient identification of the reason for his return to, or entry into the United States; and

(c) He is without resources immediately accessible to meet his needs.

[39 FR 26548, July 19, 1974, as amended at 60 FR 19864, Apr. 21, 1995]

§ 212.4 Reception; initial determination, provisions of temporary assistance.

(a) The Administration, or the agency upon notification by the Administration, will meet individuals identified as provided in § 212.3(b), at the port of entry or debarkation.

(b) The Administration or agency will make findings, setting forth the pertinent facts and conclusions, and an initial determination, according to standards established by the Administration, as to whether an individual is an eligible person.

(c) The Administration or agency will provide temporary assistance within the United States to an eligible person, according to standards of need established by the Administration, upon arrival at the port of entry or debarkation, during transportation to his intermediate and ultimate destinations, and after arrival at such destinations.

(d) Temporary assistance may be furnished only for 90 days from the day of arrival of the eligible person in the United States unless he is handicapped in attaining self-support or self-care for such reasons as age, disability, or lack of vocational preparation. In such cases temporary assistance may be extended upon prior authorization by the Administration for nine additional months.

[39 FR 26548, July 19, 1974, as amended at 40 FR 43218, Sept. 19, 1975; 53 FR 36580, Sept. 21, 1988]

§ 212.5 Periodic review and redetermination; termination of temporary assistance.

(a) The Administration or agency will review the situation of each recipient of temporary assistance at frequent intervals to consider whether or not circumstances have changed that would require a different plan for him.

(b) Upon a finding by the Administration or agency that a recipient of temporary assistance has sufficient resources available to meet his needs, temporary assistance shall be terminated.

[39 FR 26548, July 19, 1974, as amended at 53 FR 36580, Sept. 21, 1988]

§ 212.6 Duty to report.

The eligible person who receives temporary assistance, or the person who is caring for or otherwise acting on behalf of such eligible person, shall report promptly to the Administration or agency any event or circumstance which would cause such assistance to be changed in amount or terminated.

[39 FR 26548, July 19, 1974, as amended at 53 FR 36580, Sept. 21, 1988]

§ 212.7 Repayment to the United States.

(a) An individual who has received temporary assistance shall be required to repay, in accordance with his ability, any or all of the cost of such assistance to the United States, except insofar as it is determined that:

(1) The cost is not readily allocable to such individual;

(2) The probable recovery would be uneconomical or otherwise impractical;

(3) He does not have, and is not expected within a reasonable time to have, income and financial resources sufficient for more than ordinary needs; or

(4) Recovery would be against equity and good conscience.

(b) In determining an individual's resources, any claim which he has against any individual, trust or estate, partnership, corporation, or government shall be considered, and assignment to the United States of such claims shall be taken in appropriate cases.

(c) A determination that an individual is not required to repay the cost of temporary assistance shall be final and binding, unless such determination was procured by fraud or misrepresentation of the individual or some other person, or the individual voluntarily offers to repay.

(d) A determination that an individual is required to repay any or all of the cost of temporary assistance may be reconsidered at any time prior to repayment of the required amount. A further determination shall be made with respect to his liability to repay the balance of such amount on the basis of new evidence as to whether (1) he has, or is expected within a reasonable time to have, income and financial resources sufficient for more than ordinary needs, or (2) recovery would be against equity and good conscience.

§212.8 Federal payments.

(a) The agreement made by the Assistant Secretary with an agency for carrying out the purposes of the Act shall provide for payment to such agency, either in advance or by way of reimbursement, of the cost of temporary assistance provided pursuant to the Act, and payment of the cost of other expenditures necessarily and reasonably related to providing the same. Such agreement shall include the cost of other expenditures necessarily and reasonably related to providing the same. Such agreement shall include the method for determining such costs, as well as the methods and procedures for determining the amounts of advances or reimbursement and for remittance and adjustment thereof.

(b) To receive reimbursements, States, or other agencies, shall request and receive prior approval from the Assistant Secretary for administrative expenses incurred in developing or preparing to implement repatriation plans for groups of eligible persons. Such requests should include a description of the activities to be undertaken, an estimate of the expenses and a rationale for the expenditures. In reviewing requests, the Assistant Secretary will consider the necessity and reasonableness of the costs. Prior approval is not required for administrative expenditures incurred by a State in implementing approved repatriation plans as a result of Federal notification that an evacuation may be necessary.

[39 FR 26548, July 19, 1974, as amended at 60 FR 19864, Apr. 21, 1995]

§212.9 Disclosure of information.

(a) No disclosures of any information of a personal and private nature with respect to an individual obtained at any time by any person, organization, or institution in the course of discharging the duties of the Secretary under the Act shall be made except insofar:

(1) As the individual or his legal guardian, if any (or, if he is a minor, his parent or legal guardian), shall consent;

(2) As disclosure may be necessary to carry out any functions of the Secretary under the Act;

(3) As disclosure may be necessary to carry out any functions of any agency of the United States which are related to the return of the individual from a foreign country, or his entry into the United States; or

(4) As expressly authorized by the Assistant Secretary.

(b) An agreement made with an agency for the provision of temporary assistance pursuant to the Act shall provide that no disclosure will be made of any information of a personal and private nature received by such agency in the course of discharging the duties under such agreement except as is provided therein, or is otherwise specifically authorized by the Assistant Secretary.

[39 FR 26548, July 19, 1974, as amended at 60 FR 19864, Apr. 21, 1995]

§212.10 Nondiscrimination.

(a) No eligible person shall, on the ground of race, color, or national origin be excluded from participation, be denied any benefits, or otherwise be subjected to discrimination of any nature or form in the provision of any benefits under the Act.

(b) The prohibition in paragraph (a) of this section precludes discrimination either in the selection of individuals to receive the benefits, in the scope of benefits, or in the manner of providing them. It extends to all facilities and services provided by the Administration or an agency to an individual, and to the arrangements and the procedures under this part relating thereto, in connection with reception and temporary assistance under the Act.

[39 FR 26548, July 19, 1974, as amended at 60 FR 19864, Apr. 21, 1995]

PART 213—PRACTICE AND PROCEDURE FOR HEARINGS TO STATES ON CONFORMITY OF PUBLIC ASSISTANCE PLANS TO FEDERAL REQUIREMENTS

Subpart A—General

Sec.

Subpart B—Preliminary Matters—Notice and Parties

Subpart C—Hearing Procedures

Subpart D—Posthearing Procedures, Decisions

AUTHORITY: Sec. 1102, 49 Stat. 647; 42 U.S.C. 1302.

SOURCE: 36 FR 1454, Jan. 29, 1971, unless otherwise noted.

Subpart A—General

§ 213.1 Scope of rules.

(a) The rules of procedure in this part govern the practice for hearings afforded by the Department to States pursuant to § 201.4 or § 201.6 (a) or (b) of this chapter, and the practice relating to decisions upon such hearings. These rules may also be applied to hearings afforded by the Department to States in other Federal-State programs for which Federal administrative responsibility has been delegated to the Service.

(b) Nothing in this part is intended to preclude or limit negotiations between the Department and the State, whether before, during, or after the hearing to resolve the issues which are, or otherwise would be, considered at the hearing. Such negotiations and resolution of issues are not part of the hearing, and are not governed by the rules in this part, except as expressly provided herein.

§ 213.2 Records to be public.

All pleadings, correspondence, exhibits, transcripts of testimony, exceptions, briefs, decisions, and other documents filed in the docket in any proceeding may be inspected and copied in the office of the FSA Hearing Clerk. Inquiries may be made at the Central Information Center, Department of Health and Human Services, 330 Independence Avenue SW., Washington, DC 20201.

[36 FR 1454, Jan. 29, 1971, as amended at 53 FR 36580, Sept. 21, 1988]

§ 213.3 Use of gender and number.

As used in this part, words importing the singular number may extend and be applied to several persons or things, and vice versa. Words importing the masculine gender may be applied to females or organizations.

§ 213.4 Suspension of rules.

Upon notice to all parties, the Administrator or the presiding officer, with respect to matters pending before him and within his jurisdiction, may modify or waive any rule in this part upon determination that no party will be unduly prejudiced and the ends of justice will thereby be served.

§ 213.5 Filing and service of papers.

(a) All papers in the proceedings shall be filed with the FSA Hearing Clerk, in an original and two copies. Originals only of exhibits and transcripts of testimony need be filed.

(b) All papers in the proceedings shall be served on all parties by personal delivery or by mail. Service on the party's designated attorney will be deemed service upon the party.

[36 FR 1454, Jan. 29, 1971, as amended at 53 FR 36580, Sept. 21, 1988]

Subpart B—Preliminary Matters—Notice and Parties

§ 213.11 Notice of hearing or opportunity for hearing.

Proceedings are commenced by mailing a notice of hearing or opportunity for hearing from the Administrator to the State. The notice shall state the time and place for the hearing, and the issues which will be considered, and shall be published in the FEDERAL REGISTER.

§ 213.12 Time of hearing.

The hearing shall be scheduled not less than 30 days nor more than 60 days after the date notice of the hearing is furnished to the State.

§ 213.13 Place.

The hearing shall be held in the city in which the regional office of the Department is located or in such other place as is fixed by the Administrator in light of the circumstances of the case, with due regard for the convenience and necessity of the parties or their representatives.

§ 213.14 Issues at hearing.

(a) The Administrator may, prior to a hearing under § 201.6 (a) or (b) of this chapter, notify the State in writing of additional issues which will be considered at the hearing, and such notice shall be published in the FEDERAL REGISTER. If such notice is furnished to the State less than 20 days before the date of the hearing, the State or any other party, at its request, shall be granted a postponement of the hearing to a date 20 days after such notice was furnished, or such later date as may be agreed to by the Administrator.

(b) If, as a result of negotiations between the Department and the State, the submittal of a plan amendment, a change in the State program, or other actions by the State, any issue is resolved in whole or in part, but new or modified issues are presented, as specified by the Administrator, the hearing shall proceed on such new or modified issues.

(c)(1) If at any time, whether prior to, during, or after the hearing, the Administrator finds that the State has come into compliance with Federal requirements on any issue, in whole or in part, he shall remove such issue from the proceedings in whole or in part, as may be appropriate. If all issues are removed, he shall terminate the hearing.

(2) Prior to the removal of any issue from the hearing, in whole or in part, the Administrator shall provide all parties other than the Department and the State (see § 213.15(b)) with the statement of his intention, and the reasons therefor, and a copy of the proposed State plan provision on which the State and he have settled, and the parties shall have opportunity to submit in writing within 15 days, for the Administrator's consideration and for the record, their views as to, or any information bearing upon, the merits of the proposed plan provision and the merits of the Administrator's reasons for removing the issue from the hearing.

(d) The issues considered at the hearing shall be limited to those issues of which the State is notified as provided in § 213.11 and paragraph (a) of this section, and new or modified issues described in paragraph (b) of this section, and shall not include issues or parts of issues removed from the proceedings pursuant to paragraph (c) of this section.

§ 213.15 Request to participate in hearing.

(a) The Department and the State are parties to the hearing without making a specific request to participate.

(b)(1) Other individuals or groups may be recognized as parties, if the issues to be considered at the hearing have caused them injury and their interest is within the zone of interests to be protected by the governing Federal statute.

(2) Any individual or group wishing to participate as a party shall file a petition with the FSA Hearing Clerk within 15 days after notice of the hearing has been published in the FEDERAL REGISTER, and shall serve a copy on each party of record at that time, in accordance with § 213.5(b). Such petition shall concisely state (i) petitioner's interest in the proceeding, (ii) who will appear for petitioner, (iii) the issues on which petitioner wishes to participate, and (iv) whether petitioner intends to present witnesses.

(3) Any party may, within 5 days of receipt of such petition, file comments thereon.

(4) The presiding officer shall promptly determine whether each petitioner has the requisite interest in the proceedings and shall permit or deny participation accordingly. Where petitions to participate as parties are made by individuals or groups with common interests, the presiding officer may request all such petitioners to designate a single representative, or he may recognize one or more of such petitioners to represent all such petitioners. The presiding officer shall give each petitioner written notice of the decision on his petition, and if the petition is denied, he shall briefly state the grounds for denial.

(c)(1) Any interested person or organization wishing to participate as amicus curiae shall file a petition with the FSA Hearing Clerk before the commencement of the hearing. Such petition shall concisely state (i) the petitioner's interest in the hearing, (ii) who will represent the petitioner, and (iii) the issues on which petitioner intends to present argument. The presiding officer may grant the petition if he finds that the petitioner has a legitimate interest in the proceedings, that such participation will not unduly delay the outcome and may contribute materially to the proper disposition of the issues. An amicus curiae is not a party but may participate as provided in this paragraph.

(2) An amicus curiae may present a brief oral statement at the hearing, at the point in the proceedings specified by the presiding officer. He may submit a written statement of position to the presiding officer prior to the beginning of a hearing, and shall serve a copy on each party. He may also submit a brief or written statement at such time as the parties submit briefs, and shall serve a copy on each party.

[36 FR 1454, Jan. 29, 1971, as amended at 53 FR 36580, Sept. 21, 1988]

Subpart C—Hearing Procedures

§ 213.21 Who presides.

(a) The presiding officer at a hearing shall be the Administrator or his designee.

(b) The designation of the presiding officer shall be in writing. A copy of the designation shall be served on all parties.

[39 FR 40850, Nov. 21, 1974]

§ 213.22 Authority of presiding officer.

(a) The presiding officer shall have the duty to conduct a fair hearing, to avoid delay, maintain order, and make a record of the proceedings. He shall have all powers necessary to accomplish these ends, including, but not limited to, the power to:

(1) Change the date, time, and place of the hearing, upon due notice to the parties. This includes the power to continue the hearing in whole or in part. In hearings pursuant to section 1116(a)(2) of the Social Security Act (see § 201.4 of this chapter), changes of time are subject to the requirements of the statute.

(2) Hold conferences to settle or simplify the issues in a proceeding, or to consider other matters that may aid in the expeditious disposition of the proceeding.

(3) Regulate participation of parties and amici curiae and require parties and amici curiae to state their position with respect to the various issues in the proceeding.

(4) Administer oaths and affirmations.

(5) Rule on motions and other procedural items on matters pending before him including issuance of protective

orders or other relief to a party against whom discovery is sought.

(6) Regulate the course of the hearing and conduct of counsel therein.

(7) Examine witnesses.

(8) Receive, rule on, exclude or limit evidence or discovery.

(9) Fix the time for filing motions, petitions, briefs, or other items in matters pending before him.

(10) If the presiding officer is the Administrator, make a final decision.

(11) If the presiding officer is a hearing examiner, certify the entire record including his recommended findings and proposed decision to the Administrator.

(12) Take any action authorized by the rules in this part or in conformance with the provisions of 5 U.S.C. 551 through 559.

(b) The presiding officer does not have authority to compel by subpoena the production of witnesses, papers, or other evidence.

(c) If the presiding officer is a hearing examiner, his authority pertains to the issues of compliance by a State with Federal requirements which are to be considered at the hearing, and does not extend to the question of whether, in case of any noncompliance, Federal payments will not be made in respect to the entire State plan or will be limited to categories under or parts of the State plan affected by such noncompliance.

[40 FR 50272, Oct. 29, 1975]

§213.23 Rights of parties.

All parties may:

(a) Appear by counsel or other authorized representative, in all hearing proceedings.

(b) Participate in any prehearing conference held by the presiding officer.

(c) Agree to stipulations as to facts which will be made a part of the record.

(d) Make opening statements at the hearing.

(e) Present relevant evidence on the issues at the hearing.

(f) Present witnesses who then must be available for cross-examination by all other parties.

(g) Present oral arguments at the hearing.

(h) Submit written briefs, proposed findings of fact, and proposed conclusions of law, after the hearing.

§213.23a Discovery.

The Department and any party named in the notice issued pursuant to §213.11 shall have the right to conduct discovery (including depositions) against opposing parties. Rules 26–37 of the Federal Rules of Civil Procedures shall apply to such proceedings; there will be no fixed rule on priority of discovery. Upon written motion, the Presiding Officer shall promptly rule upon any objection to such discovery action initiated pursuant to this section. The Presiding Officer shall also have the power to grant a protective order or relief to any party against whom discovery is sought and to restrict or control discovery so as to prevent undue delay in the conduct of the hearing. Upon the failure of any party to make discovery, the Presiding Officer may, in his discretion, issue any order and impose any sanction (other than contempt orders) authorized by Rule 37 of the Federal Rules of Civil Procedure.

[40 FR 50272, Oct. 29, 1975]

§213.24 Evidentiary purpose.

The hearing is directed to receiving factual evidence and expert opinion testimony related to the issues in the proceeding. Argument will not be received in evidence; rather it should be presented in statements, memoranda, or briefs, as determined by the presiding officer. Brief opening statements, which shall be limited to statement of the party's position and what he intends to prove, may be made at hearings.

§213.25 Evidence.

(a) *Testimony.* Testimony shall be given orally under oath or affirmation by witnesses at the hearing. Witnesses shall be available at the hearing for cross-examination by all parties.

(b) *Stipulations and exhibits.* Two or more parties may agree to stipulations of fact. Such stipulations, or any exhibit proposed by any party, shall be exchanged at the prehearing conference or otherwise prior to the hearing if the presiding officer so requires.

(c) *Rules of evidence.* Technical rules of evidence shall not apply to hearings conducted pursuant to this part, but rules or principles designed to assure production of the most credible evidence available and to subject testimony to test by cross-examination shall be applied where reasonably necessary by the presiding officer. A witness may be cross-examined on any matter material to the proceeding without regard to the scope of his direct examination. The presiding officer may exclude irrelevant, immaterial, or unduly repetitious evidence. All documents and other evidence offered or taken for the record shall be open to examination by the parties and opportunity shall be given to refute facts and arguments advanced on either side of the issues.

§ 213.26 Exclusion from hearing for misconduct.

Disrespectful, disorderly, or contumacious language or contemptuous conduct, refusal to comply with directions, or continued use of dilatory tactics by any person at the hearing before a presiding officer shall constitute grounds for immediate exclusion of such person from the hearing by the presiding officer.

§ 213.27 Unsponsored written material.

Letters expressing views or urging action and other unsponsored written material regarding matters in issue in a hearing will be placed in the correspondence section of the docket of the proceeding. These data are not deemed part of the evidence or record in the hearing.

§ 213.28 Official transcript.

The Department will designate the official reporter for all hearings. The official transcripts of testimony taken, together with any stipulations, exhibits, briefs, or memoranda of law filed therewith shall be filed with the Department. Transcripts of testimony in hearings may be obtained from the official reporter by the parties and the public at rates not to exceed the maximum rates fixed by the contract between the Department and the reporter. Upon notice to all parties, the presiding officer may authorize corrections to the transcript which involve matters of substance.

§ 213.29 Record for decision.

The transcript of testimony, exhibits, and all papers and requests filed in the proceedings, except the correspondence section of the docket, including rulings and any recommended or initial decision shall constitute the exclusive record for decision.

Subpart D—Posthearing Procedures, Decisions

§ 213.31 Posthearing briefs.

The presiding officer shall fix the time for filing posthearings briefs, which may contain proposed findings of fact and conclusions of law, and, if permitted, reply briefs.

§ 213.32 Decisions following hearing.

(a) If the Administrator is the presiding officer, he shall, when the time for submission of posthearing briefs has expired, issue his decision within 60 days.

(b)(1) If a hearing examiner is the presiding officer, he shall, when the time for submission of posthearing briefs has expired, certify the entire record, including his recommended findings and proposed decision, to the Administrator. The Administrator shall serve a copy of the recommended findings and proposed decision upon all parties, and amici, if any.

(2) Any party may, within 20 days, file with the Administrator exceptions to the recommended findings and proposed decision and a supporting brief or statement.

(3) The Administrator shall thereupon review the recommended decision and, within 60 days of its issuance, issue his own decision.

(c) If the Administrator concludes that a State plan does not comply with Federal requirements, he shall also, in the case of a hearing pursuant to § 201.6(a) of this chapter, specify whether further payments will not be made to the State or whether, in the exercise of his discretion, payments will be limited to categories under or parts of the State plan not affected by such noncompliance. The Administrator may ask the parties for recommendations or briefs or may hold conferences of the parties on this question.

(d) The decision of the Administrator under this section shall be the final decision of the Secretary and shall constitute "final agency action" within the meaning of 5 U.S.C. 704 and a "final determination" within the meaning of section 1116(a)(3) of the Act and § 201.7 of this chapter. The Administrator's decision shall be promptly served on all parties, and amici, if any.

[36 FR 1454, Jan. 29, 1971, as amended at 36 FR 21520, Nov. 10, 1971]

§ 213.33 Effective date of Administrator's decision.

If, in the case of a hearing pursuant to § 201.6(a) of this chapter, the Administrator concludes that a State plan does not comply with Federal requirements, his decision that further payments will not be made to the State, or payments will be limited to categories under or parts of the State plan not affected, shall specify the effective date for the withholding of Federal funds. The effective date shall not be earlier than the date of the Administrator's decision and shall not be later than the first day of the next calendar quarter. The provisions of this section may not be waived pursuant to § 213.4.

PART 225—TRAINING AND USE OF SUBPROFESSIONALS AND VOLUNTEERS

Sec.

AUTHORITY: Sec. 1102, 49 Stat. 647; 42 U.S.C. 1302.

§ 225.1 Definitions.

(a) The classification of subprofessional staff as community service aides refers to persons in a variety of positions in the planning, administration, and delivery of health, social, and rehabilitation services in which the duties of the position are composed of tasks that are an integral part of the agency's service responsibilities to people and that can be performed by persons with less than a college education, by high school graduates, or by persons with little or no formal education.

(b) *Full-time or part-time employment* means that the person is employed by the agency and his position is incorporated into the regular staffing pattern of the agency. He is paid a regular wage or salary in relation to the value of services rendered and time spent on the job.

(c) The term *Volunteer* describes a person who contributes his personal service to the community through the agency's human services program. He is not a replacement or substitute for paid staff but adds new dimensions to agency services, and symbolizes the community's concern for the agency's clientele.

(d) *Partially paid volunteers* means volunteers who are compensated for expenses incurred in the giving of services. Such payment does not reflect the value of the services rendered, or the amount of time given to the agency.

[34 FR 1319, Jan. 28, 1969]

§ 225.2 State plan requirements.

The State plan for financial assistance programs under titles I, X, XIV, or XVI (AABD) of the Social Security Act for Guam, Puerto Rico and the Virgin Islands or for child welfare services under title IV-B of the Act must:

(a) Provide for the training and effective use of subprofessional staff as community service aides through part-time or full-time employment of persons of low income and, where applicable, of recipients and for that purpose will provide for:

(1) Such methods of recruitment and selection as will offer opportunity for full-time or part-time employment of persons of low income and little or no formal education, including employment of young and middle aged adults, older persons, and the physically and mentally disabled, and in the case of a State plan for financial assistance under title I, X, XIV, or XVI (AABD), of recipients: And will provide that such subprofessional positions are subject to merit system requirements, except where special exemption is approved on the basis of a State alternative plan for recruitment and selection among the disadvantaged of persons who have the potential ability for

training and job performance to help assure achievement of program objectives;

(2) An administrative staffing plan to include the range of service personnel of which subprofessional staff are an integral part;

(3) A career service plan permitting persons to enter employment at the subprofessional level and, according to their abilities, through work experience, pre-service and in-service training and educational leave with pay, progress to positions of increasing responsibility and reward;

(4) An organized training program, supervision, and supportive services for subprofessional staff; and

(5) Annual progressive expansion of the plan to assure utilization of increasing numbers of subprofessional staff as community service aides, until an appropriate number and proportion of subprofessional staff to professional staff are achieved to make maximum use of subprofessionals in program operation.

(b) Provide for the use of nonpaid or partially paid volunteers in providing services and in assisting any advisory committees established by the State agency and for that purpose provide for:

(1) A position in which rests responsibility for the development, organization, and administration of the volunteer program, and for coordination of the program with related functions;

(2) Methods of recruitment and selection which will assure participation of volunteers of all income levels in planning capacities and service provision;

(3) A program for organized training and supervision of such volunteers;

(4) Meeting the costs incident to volunteer service and assuring that no individual shall be deprived of the opportunity to serve because of the expenses involved in such service; and

(5) Annual progressive expansion of the numbers of volunteers utilized, until the volunteer program is adequate for the achievement of the agency's service goals.

[34 FR 1320, Jan. 28, 1969, as amended at 41 FR 12015, Mar. 23, 1976; 42 FR 60566, Nov. 28, 1977; 45 FR 56686, Aug. 25, 1980; 51 FR 9204, Mar. 18, 1986]

§ 225.3 Federal financial participation.

Under the State plan for financial assistance programs under titles I, X, XIV, XVI (AABD) or for child welfare services under title IV-B of the Act, Federal financial participation in expenditures for the recruitment, selection, training, and employment and other use of subprofessional staff and volunteers is available at the rates and under related conditions established for training, services, and other administrative costs under the respective titles.

[51 FR 9204, Mar. 18, 1986]

PART 233—COVERAGE AND CONDITIONS OF ELIGIBILITY IN FINANCIAL ASSISTANCE PROGRAMS

Sec.

AUTHORITY: 42 U.S.C. 301, 602, 602 (note), 606, 607, 1202, 1302, 1352, and 1382 (note).

§ 233.10 General provisions regarding coverage and eligibility.

(a) *State plan requirements.* A State plan under title I, IV—A, X, XIV, or XVI, of the Social Security Act must:

(1) Specify the groups of individuals, based on reasonable classifications, that will be included in the program, and all the conditions of eligibility that must be met by the individuals in the groups. The groups selected for inclusion in the plan and the eligibility conditions imposed must not exclude individuals or groups on an arbitrary or unreasonable basis, and must not result in inequitable treatment of individuals or groups in the light of the provisions and purposes of the public assistance titles of the Social Security Act. Under this requirement:

(i) A State shall impose each condition of eligibility required by the Social Security Act; and

(ii) A State may:

(A) Provide more limited public assistance coverage than that provided by the Act only where the Social Security Act or its legislative history authorizes more limited coverage;

(B) Impose conditions upon applicants for and recipients of public assistance which, if not satisfied, result in the denial or termination of public assistance, if such conditions assist the State in the efficient administration of its public assistance programs, or further an independent State welfare policy, and are not inconsistent with the provisions and purposes of the Social Security Act.

(iii) There must be clarity as to what groups are included in the plan, and which are within, and which are outside, the scope of Federal financial participation.

(iv) Eligibility conditions must be applied on a consistent and equitable basis throughout the State.

(v) A plan under title XVI must have the same eligibility conditions and other requirements for the aged, blind, and disabled, except as otherwise specifically required or permitted by the Act.

(vi) Eligibility conditions or agency procedures or methods must not preclude the opportunity for an individual to apply and obtain a determination of eligibility or ineligibility.

(vii) Methods of determining eligibility must be consistent with the objective of assisting all eligible persons to qualify.

(2) Provide that the State agency will establish methods for identifying the expenditures for assistance for any groups included in the plan for whom Federal financial participation in assistance may not be claimed.

(3) In addition, a State plan under title IV-A, X, XIV, or XVI of the Act, must: Provided that no aid or assistance will be provided under the plan to an individual with respect to a period for which he is receiving aid or assistance under a State plan approved under any other of such titles or under title I of the Act.

(b) *Federal financial participation.* (1) The provisions which govern Federal financial participation in assistance payments are set forth in the Social Security Act, throughout this chapter, and in other policy issuances of the Secretary. Where indicated, State plan provisions are prerequisite to Federal financial participation with respect to the applicable group and payments. State plan provisions on need, the amount of assistance, and eligibility determine the limits of Federal financial participation. Federal financial participation is excluded from assistance payments in which the State refuses to participate because of the failure of a local authority to apply such State plan provisions.

(2) The following is a summary statement regarding the groups for whom Federal financial participation is available. (More detailed information is given elsewhere.)

(i) OAA—for needy individuals under the plan who are 65 years of age or older.

(ii) AFDC—for:

(*a*) Needy children under the plan who are:

(*1*) Under the age of 18, or age 18 if a full-time student in a secondary school, or in the equivalent level of vocational or technical training, and reasonably expected to complete the program before reaching age 19;

(*2*) Deprived of parental support or care by reason of the death, continued absence from the home, or physical or mental incapacity of a parent, or unemployment of a principal earner, and

(*3*) Living in the home of a parent or of certain relatives specified in the Act.

(*b*) The parent(s) of a dependent child, a caretaker relative (other than a parent) of a dependent child, and, in certain situations, a parent's spouse.

(iii) AB—for needy individual's under the plan who are blind.

(iv) APTD—for needy individuals under the plan who are 18 years of age or older and permanently and totally disabled.

(v) AABD—for needy individuals under the plan who are aged, blind, or 18 years of age or older and permanently and totally disabled.

(3) Federal financial participation is available in assistance payments made for the entire month in accordance with the State plan if the individual was eligible for a portion of the month, provided that the individual was eligible on the date that the payment was made; except that where it has been determined that the State agency had previously denied assistance to which the individual was entitled, Federal financial participation will be provided in any corrective payment regardless of whether the individual is eligible on the date that the corrective payment is made.

(4) Federal financial participation is available in assistance payments which are continued in accordance with the State plan, for a temporary period during which the effects of an eligibility condition are being overcome, e.g., blindness in AB, disability in APTD, physical or mental incapacity, continued absence of a parent, or unemployment of a principal earner in AFDC.

(5) Where changed circumstances or a hearing decision makes the individual ineligible for any assistance, or eligible for a smaller amount of assistance than was actually paid, Federal financial participation is available in excess payments to such individuals, for not more than one month following the month in which the circumstances changed or the hearing decision was rendered. Federal financial participation is available where assistance is required to be continued unadjusted because a hearing has been requested.

[36 FR 3866, Feb. 27, 1971, as amended at 38 FR 8744, Apr. 6, 1973; 39 FR 26912, July 24, 1974; 40 FR 32958, Aug. 5, 1975; 47 FR 5674, Feb. 5, 1982; 47 FR 47828, Oct. 28, 1982; 51 FR 9204, Mar. 18, 1986; 57 FR 30158, July 8, 1992]

§ 233.20 Need and amount of assistance.

(a) *Requirements for State Plans.* A State Plan for OAA, AFDC, AB, APTD or AABD must, as specified below:

(1) *General.* (i) Provide that the determination of need and amount of assistance for all applicants and recipients will be made on an objective and equitable basis and all types of income will be taken into consideration in the same way except where otherwise specifically authorized by Federal statute and

(ii) Provide that the needs, income, and resources of individuals receiving SSI benefits under title XVI, individuals with respect to whom Federal foster care payments are made, individuals with respect to whom State or local foster care payments are made, individuals with respect to whom Federal adoption assistance payments are made, or individuals with respect to whom State or local adoption assistance payments are made, for the period for which such benefits or payments are received, shall not be included in determining the need and the amount of the assistance payment of an AFDC assistance unit; except that the needs, income, and resources of an individual with respect to whom Federal adoption assistance payments are made, or individuals with respect to whom State or local adoption assistance payments are made are included in determining the need and the amount of the assistance payment for an AFDC assistance unit of which the individual would otherwise be regarded as a member where the amount of the assistance payment that the unit would receive would not be reduced by including the needs, income, and resources of such individual. Under this requirement, "individuals receiving SSI benefits under title XVI" include individuals receiving mandatory or optional State supplementary payments under section 1616(a) of the Social Security Act or under section 212 of Public Law 93–66, and "individuals with respect to whom Federal foster care payments are made" means a child with respect to whom Federal foster care maintenance payments under section 472(b) and defined in section 475(4)(A) of title IV-E of the Social Security Act are made, and a child whose costs in a foster family home or child care institution are covered by the Federal foster care maintenance payments made with respect to his or her minor parent under sections 472(h) and 475(4)(B) of title IV-E. "Individuals with respect to whom Federal adoption assistance payments are made" means a child who receives payments made under an approved title IV-E plan based on an adoption assistance agreement between the State and the adoptive parents of a child with special needs, pursuant to sections 473 and 475(3) of the Social Security Act.

(iii) For AFDC, when an individual who is required to be included in the assistance unit pursuant to § 206.10(a)(1)(vii) is also required to be included in another assistance unit, those assistance units must be consolidated, and treated as one assistance unit for purposes of determining eligibility and the amount of payment.

(iv) For AFDC, when a State learns of an individual who is required to be included in the assistance unit after the date he or she is required to be included in the unit, the State must redetermine the assistance unit's eligibility and payment amount, including the need, income, and resources of the individual. This redetermination must be retroactive to the date that the individual was required to be in the assistance unit either through birth/adoption or by becoming a member of the household. Any resulting overpayment must be recovered or corrective payment made pursuant to § 233.20(a)(13).

(v) In determining need and the amount of payment for AFDC, all income and resources of an individual required to be in the assistance unit, but subject to sanction under § 250.34 or because of an intentional program violation under the optional fraud control program implementing section 416 of the Social Security Act, are considered available to the assistance unit to the same extent that they would be if the person were not subject to a sanction. However, the needs of the sanctioned individual(s) are not considered. In accord with § 250.34(c), if a parent in an AFDC-UP case is sanctioned pursuant to § 233.100(a)(5), the needs of the second parent are not taken into account in determining the family's need for assistance and the amount of the assistance payment unless the second parent is participating in the JOBS program. An individual required to be in an assistance unit pursuant to § 206.10(a)(1)(vii) but who fails to cooperate in meeting a condition of his or her eligibility for assistance is a sanctioned individual whose needs, income, and resources are treated in the manner described above.

(2) *Standards of assistance.* (i) Specify a statewide standard, expressed in money amounts, to be used in determining (*a*) the need of applicants and recipients and (*b*) the amount of the assistance payment.

(ii) In the AFDC plan, provide that by July 1, 1969, the State's standard of assistance for the AFDC program will have been adjusted to reflect fully changes in living costs since such standards were established, and any maximums that the State imposes on the amount of aid paid to families will have been proportionately adjusted. In such adjustment a consolidation of the standard (i.e., combining of items) may not result in a reduction in the content of the standard. In the event the State is not able to meet need in full under the adjusted standard, the State may make ratable reductions in accordance with paragraph (a)(3)(viii) of this section. Nevertheless, if a State maintains a system of dollar maximums these maximums must be proportionately adjusted in relation to the updated standards.

(iii) Provide that the standard will be uniformly applied throughout the State except as provided under § 239.54.

(iv) Include the method used in determining need and the amount of the assistance payment. For AFDC, the method must provide for rounding down to the next lower whole dollar when the result of determining the standard of need or the payment amount is not a whole dollar. Proration under § 206.10(a)(6)(i)(D) to determine the amount of payment for the month of application must occur before rounding to determine the payment amount for that month.

(v) If the State IV-A agency includes special need items in its standard:

(A) Describe those that will be recognized and the circumstances under which they will be included, and

(B) Provide that they will be considered for all applicants and recipients requiring them; except that:

(*1*) Under AFDC, work expenses and child care (or care of incapacitated adults living in the same home and receiving AFDC) resulting from employment or participation in either a CWEP or an employment search program cannot be special needs, and

(*2*) In a State which has a JOBS program under part 250, child care, transportation, work-related expenses, other work-related supportive services, and the costs of education (including tuition, books, and fees) resulting from participation in JOBS (including participation pursuant to §§ 250.46, 250.47, and 250.48) or any other education or training activity cannot be special needs.

(vi) If the State chooses to establish the need of the individual on a basis that recognizes, as essential to his well-being, the presence in the home of other needy individuals, (A) specify the persons whose needs will be included in the individual's need, and (B) provide that the decision as to whether any individual will be recognized as essential to the recipient's well-being shall rest with the recipient.

(vii) [Reserved]

(viii) Provide that the money amount of any need item included in the standard will not be prorated or otherwise reduced solely because of the presence in the household of a non-legally responsible individual; and the agency will not assume any contribution from such individual for the support of the assistance unit except as provided in paragraphs (a)(3)(xiv) and (a)(5) of this section and § 233.51 of this part.

(ix) For AFDC, provide that a State shall consider utility payments made in lieu of any direct rental payment to a landlord or public housing agency to be shelter costs for applicants or recipients living in housing assisted under the U.S. Housing Act of 1937, as amended, and section 236 of the National Housing Act. The amount considered as a shelter payment shall not exceed the total amount the applicant or recipient is expected to contribute for the cost of housing as determined by HUD. *Utility payments* means only those payments made directly to a utility company or supplier which are for gas, electricity, water, heating fuel, sewerage systems, and trash and garbage collection. Utility payments are made "in lieu of any direct rental payment to a landlord or public housing agency" when, and only when, the AFDC family pays its entire required contribution at HUD's direction to one or more utility companies and does not make any direct payment to the landlord or the public housing agency. Housing covered by "the U.S. Housing Act of 1937, as amended, and section 236 of the National Housing Act" means Department of Housing and Urban Development assisted housing which includes Indian and public housing, section 8 new and existing rental housing, and section 236 rental housing.

(3) *Income and resources.* (i)(A) *OAA, AB, APTD, AABD,* Specify the amount and types of real and personal property, including liquid assets, that may be reserved, i.e., retained to meet the

current and future needs while assistance is received on a continuing basis. In addition to the home, personal effects, automobile and income producing property allowed by the agency, the amount of real and personal property, including liquid assets, that can be reserved for each individual recipient shall not be in excess of two thousand dollars. Policies may allow reasonable proportions of income from businesses or farms to be used to increase capital assets, so that income may be increased; and (B) in AFDC—The amount of real and personal property that can be reserved for each assistance unit shall not be in excess of one thousand dollars equity value (or such lesser amount as the State specifies in its State plan) excluding only:

(*1*) The home which is the usual residence of the assistance unit;

(*2*) One automobile, up to $1,500 of equity value or such lower limit as the State may specify in the State plan; (any excess equity value must be applied towards the general resource limit specified in the State plan);

(*3*) One burial plot (as defined in the State plan) for each member of the assistance unit;

(*4*) Bona fide funeral agreements (as defined and within limits specified in the State plan) up to a total of $1,500 in equity value or such lower limit as the State may specify in the State plan for each member of the assistance unit (any excess equity value must be applied towards the general resource limit specified in the State plan). This provision addresses only formal agreements for funeral and burial expenses such as burial contracts, burial trusts or other funeral arrangements (generally with licensed funeral directors) and does not apply to other assets (e.g., passbook bank accounts, simple set-aside of savings, and cash surrender value of life insurance policies);

(*5*) Real property for a period of six consecutive months (or, at the option of the State, nine consecutive months) which the family is making a good faith effort (as defined in the State plan) to sell, subject to the following provisions. The family must sign an agreement to dispose of the property and to repay the amount of aid received during such period that would not have been paid had the property been sold at the beginning of such period, but not to exceed the amount of the net proceeds of the sale. The family has five working days from the date it realizes cash from the sale of the excess real property to repay the overpayment; failure to make repayment within this period results in the cash being considered to be an available resource. If the family becomes ineligible for AFDC for any other reason during the conditional payment period while making a good faith effort to sell the property, or fails to sell the property by the end of the period despite such a good faith effort, then the amount of the overpayment attributable to the real property will not be determined and recovery will not be begun until the property is, in fact, sold. However, if the property was intentionally sold at less than fair market value so that a good faith effort to sell it was not made, or if it is otherwise determined that a good faith effort to sell the property is not being made, the overpayment amount shall be computed using the fair market value determined at the beginning of the period. For applicants, the conditional payment period begins with the first payment month for which all otherwise applicable eligibility conditions are met and payment is authorized. For recipients who acquire property while receiving assistance, the period begins with the payment month in which the recipient receives the property; and

(*6*) At State option, basic maintenance items essential to day-to-day living such as clothes, furniture and other similarly essential items of limited value.

(ii) Provide that in determining need and the amount of the assistance payment, after all policies governing the reserves and allowances and disregard or setting aside of income and resources referred to in this section have been uniformly applied:

(A) In determining need, all remaining income and resources shall be considered in relation to the State's need standard;

(B) In determining financial eligibility and the amount of the assistance payment all remaining income (except unemployment compensation received by an unemployed principal earner) and, except for AFDC, all resources may be considered in relation to either the State's need standard or the State's payment standard. Unemployment compensation received by an unemployed principal earner shall be considered only by subtracting it from the amount of the assistance payment after the payment has been determined under the State's payment method;

(C) States may have policies which provide for allocating an individual's income for his or her own support if the individual is not applying for or receiving assistance; for the support of other individuals living in the same household but not receiving assistance; and for the support of other individuals living in another household. Such other individuals are those who are or could be claimed by the individual as dependents for determining Federal personal income tax liability, or those he or she is legally obligated to support. No income may be allocated to meet the needs of an individual who has been sanctioned under § 224.51, § 232.11(a)(2), § 232.12(d), § 238.22 or § 240.22 or who is required to be included in the assistance unit and has failed to cooperate. The amount allocated for the individual and the other individuals who are living in the home must not exceed the State's need standard amount for a family group of the same composition. The amount allocated for individuals not living in the home must not exceed the amount actually paid.

(D) Income after application of disregards, except as provided in paragraph (a)(3)(xiii) of this section, and resources available for current use shall be considered. To the extent not inconsistent with any other provision of this chapter, income and resources are considered available both when actually available and when the applicant or recipient has a legal interest in a liquidated sum and has the legal ability to make such sum available for support and maintenance.

(E) For AFDC, income tax refunds, but such payments shall be considered as resources; and

(F) When the AFDC assistance unit's income, after applying applicable disregards, exceeds the State need standard for the family because of receipt of nonrecurring earned or unearned lump sum income (including for AFDC, title II and other retroactive monthly benefits, and payments in the nature of a windfall, e.g., inheritances or lottery winnings, personal injury and worker compensation awards, to the extent it is not earmarked and used for the purpose for which it is paid, i.e., monies for back medical bills resulting from accidents or injury, funeral and burial costs, replacement or repair of resources, etc.), the family will be ineligible for aid for the full number of months derived by dividing the sum of the lump sum income and other income by the monthly need standard for a family of that size. Any income remaining from this calculation is income in the first month following the period of ineligibility. The period of ineligibility shall begin with the month of receipt of the nonrecurring income or, at State option, as late as the corresponding payment month. For purposes of applying the lump sum provision, family includes all persons whose needs are taken into account in determining eligibility and the amount of the assistance payment, and includes solely for determining the income and resources of a family an individual who must be in a family pursuant to § 206.10(a)(1)(vii) but who does not meet a condition of his or her eligibility due to a failure to cooperate or is required by law to have his or her needs excluded from an assistance unit's AFDC grant calculation due to the failure to perform some action. A State may shorten the remaining period of ineligibility when: the standard of need increases and the amount the family would have received also changes (e.g., situations involving additions to the family unit during the period of ineligibility of persons who are otherwise eligible for assistance); the lump sum income or a portion thereof becomes unavailable to the family for a reason beyond the control of the family; or the family incurs and pays for medical expenses. If the State chooses to shorten the period of ineligibility, the State plan shall:

(*1*) Identify which of the above situations are included;

(*2*) In the case of situations involving an increase in the need standard and changes in the amount that should have been paid to the family, specify the types of circumstances which will be included;

(*3*) In the case of situations involving the unavailability of the lump sum income, include a definition of unavailability, and specify what reasons will be considered beyond the control of the family; and

(*4*) In the case of situations involving the payment of medical expenses, specify the types of medical expenses the State will allow to be offset against the lump sum income.

For purposes of this paragraph (a)(3): Automobile means a passenger car or other motor vehicle used to provide transportation of persons or goods. (In AFDC, in appropriate geographic areas, one alternate primary mode of transportation may be substituted for the automobile); Equity value means fair market value minus encumbrances (legal debts); Fair market value means the price an item of a particular make, model, size, material or condition will sell for on the open market in the geographic area involved (If a motor vehicle is especially equipped with apparatus for the handicapped, the apparatus shall not increase the value of the vehicle); Liquid assets are those properties in the form of cash or other financial instruments which are convertible to cash and include savings accounts, checking accounts, stocks, bonds, mutual fund shares, promissory notes, mortgages, cash value of insurance policies, and similar properties; Need standard means the money value assigned by the State to the basic and special needs it recognizes as essential for applicants and recipients; Payment standard means the amount from which non-exempt income is subtracted.

(iii) States may prorate income received by individuals employed on a contractual basis over the period of the contract or may prorate intermittent income received quarterly, semiannually, or yearly over the period covered by the income. In OAA, AB, APTD and AABD, they may use the prorated amount to determine need under § 233.23 and the amount of the assistance payment under §§ 233.24 and 233.25. In AFDC, they may use the prorated amount to determine need under § 233.33 and the amount of the assistance payment under §§ 233.34 and 233.35.

(iv) Provide that in determining the availability of income and resources, the following will not be included as income:

(A) Except for AFDC, income equal to expenses reasonably attributable to the earning of income (including earnings from public service employment);

(B) Grants, such as scholarships, obtained and used under conditions that preclude their use for current living costs;

(C) Home produce of an applicant or recipient, utilized by him and his household for their own consumption;

(D) For AFDC, any amounts paid by a State IV-A agency from State-only funds to meet needs of children receiving AFDC, if the payments are made under a statutorily-established State program which has been continuously in effect since before January 1, 1979;

(E) For AFDC, income tax refunds, but such payments shall be considered as resources; and

(F) At State option, small nonrecurring gifts, such as those for Christmas, birthdays and graduations, not to exceed $30 per recipient in any quarter; and

(G) For AFDC, the amount paid to the family by the IV-A agency under § 232.20(d) or, in a State that treats direct support payments as income under § 233.20(a)(3)(v)(B), the first $50 received by the assistance unit which represents a current monthly support obligation or a voluntary support payment. In no case shall the total amount disregarded exceed $50 per month per assistance unit.

(v) Provide that agency policies will assure that:

(A) In determining eligibility for an assistance payment, support payments assigned under § 232.11 of this chapter will be treated in accordance with § 232.20 and § 232.21 of this chapter; and

(B) In determining the amount of an assistance payment, assigned support payments retained in violation of § 232.12(b)(4) of this chapter, will be counted as income to meet need unless the approved IV-A State plan provides that such support payments are subject to IV-D recovery under §§ 302.31(a)(3) and 303.80 of this title or unless such payments are sufficient to render the family ineligible as provided at § 232.20 of this chapter.

(vi)(A) In family groups living together, income of the spouse is considered available for his spouse and income of a parent is considered available for children under 21, except as provided in paragraphs (a)(3)(xiv) and (a)(3)(xviii) of this section for AFDC. If an individual is a spouse or parent who is a recipient of SSI benefits under title XVI, an individual with respect to whom Federal foster care payments are made, an individual with respect to whom State or local foster care payments are made, an individual with respect to whom Federal adoption assistance payments are made, or an individual with respect to whom State or local adoption assistance payments are made, then, for the period for which such benefits or payments are received, his or her income and resources shall not be counted as income and resources available to the AFDC unit except that a child receiving adoption assistance payments will not be excluded if such exclusion would cause the AFDC benefits of the assistance unit of which the child would otherwise be considered a member to be reduced. For purposes of this exception, "a recipient of SSI benefits under title XVI" includes a spouse or parent receiving mandatory or optional State supplementary payments under section 1616(a) of the Social Security Act or under section 212 of Public Law 93–66 and an "individual with respect to whom Federal foster care payments are made" means a child with respect to whom Federal foster care maintenance payments are made under section 472(b) and defined in section 475(4)(A) of the Act, and a child whose costs in a foster family home or child-care institution are covered by the foster care maintenance payments made with respect to his or her minor parent under sections 472(h) and 475(4)(B) of the Act. "Individuals with respect to whom Federal adoption assistance payments are made" means a child who receives payments made under an approved title IV-E plan based on an adoption assistance agreement between the State and the adoptive parents of a child with special needs, pursuant to sections 473 and 475(3) of the Social Security Act.

(B) Income of an alien parent, who is disqualified pursuant to § 233.50(c) is considered available to the otherwise eligible child by applying the stepparent deeming formula at 45 CFR 233.20(a)(3)(xiv).

(vii) If the State agency establishes policy under which assistance from other agencies and organizations will not be deducted in determining the amount of assistance to be paid, provide that no duplication shall exist between such other assistance and that provided by the public assistance agency. In such complementary program relationships, nonduplication shall be assured by provision that such aid will be considered in relation to: (*a*) The different purpose for which the other agency grants aid such as vocational rehabilitation; (*b*) the provision of goods and services that are not included in the statewide standard of the public assistance agency, e.g., a private agency might provide money for special training for a child or for medical care when the public assistance agency does not carry this responsibility; or housing and urban development payments might be provided to cover moving expenses that are not included in the assistance standard; or (*c*) the fact that public assistance funds are insufficient to meet the total amount of money determined to be needed in accordance with the statewide standard. In such instances, grants by other agencies in an amount sufficient to make it possible for the individual to have the amount of money determined to be needed, in accordance with the public assistance agency standard, will not constitute duplication.

(viii) Provide that: (A) Payment will be based on the determination of the amount of assistance needed; (B) if full individual payments are precluded by maximums or insufficient funds, adjustments will be made by methods applied uniformly statewide; (C) in the case of AFDC no payment of aid shall be made to an assistance unit in any month in which the amount of aid prior to any adjustments is determined to be less than $10; and (D) an individual who is denied aid because of the limitation specified in (C) of this section, or because the payment amount is determined to be zero as a result of rounding the payment amount as required by §233.20(a)(2)(iv), shall be deemed a recipient of aid for all other purposes except participation in the Community Work Experience Program.

(ix) Provide that the agency will establish and carry out policies with reference to applicants' and recipients' potential sources of income that can be developed to a state of availability.

(x) Provide that the income and resources of individuals receiving SSI benefits under title XVI, individuals with respect to whom Federal foster care payments are made, individuals with respect to whom State or local foster care payments are made, individuals with respect to whom Federal adoption assistance payments are made, or individuals with respect to whom State or local adoption assistance payments are made, for the period for which such benefits or payments are received, shall not be counted as income and resources of an assistance unit applying for or receiving assistance under title IV-A; except that a child receiving adoption assistance payments will not be excluded if such exclusion would cause the AFDC benefits of the assistance unit of which the child would otherwise be considered a member to be reduced. Under this requirement, "individuals receiving SSI benefits under title XVI" include individuals receiving mandatory or optional State supplementary payments under section 1616(a) of the Social Security Act or under section 212 of Public Law 93–66 and, "individuals with respect to whom Federal foster care payments are made" means a child with respect to whom Federal foster care maintenance payments are made under section 472(b) and defined in section 475(4)(A) of the Act, and a child whose costs in a foster family home or child-care institution are covered by foster care maintenance payments made with respect to his or her minor parent under sections 472(h) and 475(4)(B) of the Act. "Individuals with respect to whom Federal adoption assistance payments are made" means a child who receives payments made under an approved title IV-E plan based on an adoption assistance agreement between the State and the adoptive parents of a child with special needs, pursuant to sections 473 and 475(3) of the Social Security Act.

(xi) In the case of AFDC if the State chooses to count the value of the food stamp coupons as income, provide that the State plan shall:

(A) Identify the amount for food included in its need and payment standards for an assistance unit of the same size and composition. (States which have a flat grant system must estimate the amount based on historical data or some other justifiable procedure.); and

(B) Specify the amount of such food stamp coupons that it will count as income. Under this requirement, the amount of food stamp coupons which a State may count as income may not exceed the amount for food established in its payment standard for an assistance unit of the same size and composition.

(xii) In the case of AFDC if the State chooses to count the value of the governmental rent or housing subsidies as income, provide that the State plan shall:

(A) Identify the amount for shelter included in its need and payment standards for an assistance unit of the same size and composition. (States which have a flat grant system must estimate this amount based on historical data or some other justifiable procedure.); and

(B) Specify the amount of such housing assistance that it will count as income. Under this requirement, the amount of such rent or housing subsidies which a State may count as income may not exceed the amount for shelter established in its payment standard for assistance unit of the same size and composition.

(xiii) Under the AFDC plan, provide that no assistance unit is eligible for aid in any month in which the unit's income (other than the assistance payment) exceeds 185 percent of the State's need standard (including special needs) for a family of the same composition (including special needs), without application of the disregards in paragraph (a)(11)(i) (except to the extent provided for under paragraph (a)(3)(xix)), paragraph (a)(11)(ii) and paragraph (a)(11)(viii) of this section.

(xiv) For AFDC, in States that do not have laws of general applicability holding the stepparent legally responsible to the same extent as the natural or adoptive parent, the State agency shall count as income to the assistance unit the income of the stepparent (i.e., one who is married, under State law, to the child's parent) of an AFDC child who is living in the household with the child after applying the following disregards (exception: if the stepparent is included in the assistance unit, the disregard under paragraph (a)(11) (i) and (ii) of this section apply instead:

(A) The first $90 of the gross earned income of the stepparent;

(B) An additional amount for the support of the stepparent and any other individuals who are living in the home, but whose needs are not taken into account in making the AFDC eligibility determinations except for sanctioned individuals or individuals who are required to be included in the assistance unit but have failed to cooperate and are or could be claimed by the stepparent as dependents for purposes of determining his or her Federal personal income tax liability. This disregarded amount shall equal the State's need standard amount for a family group of the same composition as the stepparent and those other individuals described in the preceding sentence;

(C) Amounts actually paid by the stepparent to individuals not living in the home but who are or could be claimed by him or her as dependents for purposes of determining his or her Federal personal income tax liability; and

(D) Payments by such stepparent of alimony or child support with respect to individuals not living in the household.

(xv) For AFDC, provide for the consideration of the income and resources of an alien's sponsor who is an individual as provided in § 233.51.

(xvi) For AFDC, provide that in considering the availability of income and resources, support and maintenance assistance (including home energy assistance) will be taken into account in accordance with § 233.53.

(xvii) In the case of AFDC, if the State chooses to disregard monthly income of any dependent child when the income is derived from participation in a program under the JTPA, provide that the State plan shall:

(A) Identify from which programs under the JTPA, income will be disregarded;

(B) In the case of earned income, specify what amount will be disregarded, and the length of time the disregard will be applicable (up to six months per calendar year); and

(C) In the case of unearned income, specify what amount will be disregarded, and the length of time per calendar year the disregard will be applicable if any such limit is chosen.

(xviii) For AFDC, in the case of a dependent child whose parent is a minor under the age of 18 (without regard to school attendance), the State shall count as income to the assistance unit the income, after appropriate disregards, of such minor's own parent(s) living in the same household as the minor and dependent child. The disregards to be applied are the same as are applied to the income of a stepparent pursuant to paragraph (a)(3)(xiv) of this section. However, in applying the disregards, each employed parent will receive the benefit of the work expense disregard in paragraph (a)(3)(xiv)(A) of this section.

(xix) In the case of AFDC, if the State chooses to disregard monthly earned income of dependent children who are full-time students in the determination of whether the family's income exceeds the limit under § 233.20(a)(3)(xiii) of this section, provide that the State plan shall specify what amounts will be disregarded and the length of time the disregard will be applicable (up to six months per calendar year) except that earned income derived from participation in a program under the JTPA may only be disregarded under this paragraph, paragraph (a)(3)(xvii) or a combination of both paragraphs for a total of 6 months per calendar year.

(xx) In the case of AFDC, if the State chooses to disregard in the determination of eligibility the monthly earned income of dependent children applying for AFDC who are full-time students, provide that the State plan shall:

(A) Specify the amount that will be disregarded, and

(B) Provide that the disregard shall only apply to the extent that the earned income is also disregarded pursuant to paragraph (a)(3)(xix) of this section.

(xxi) Provide that the principal of a bona fide loan will not be counted as income or resources in the determination of eligibility and the amount of assistance. Interest earned on a loan is counted as unearned income in the month received and as resources thereafter and purchases made with a loan are counted as resources. For purposes of this paragraph, a loan is considered bona fide when it meets objective and reasonable criteria included in the State plan.

(4) *Disregard of income in OAA, AFDC, AB, APTD, OR AABD.* (i) For all programs except AFDC. If the State chooses to disregard income from all sources before applying other provisions for disregarding or setting aside income, specify the amount that is first to be disregarded, but not more than $7.50 per month, of any income of an individual, child or relative claiming assistance. All income must be included such as social security or other benefits, earnings, contributions from relatives, or other income the individual may have.

(ii) Provide that in determining eligibility for public assistance and the amount of the assistance payment, the following will be disregarded as income and resources:

(*a*) In OAA, AB, APTD, and AABD, the value of the coupon allotment under the Food Stamp Act of 1964 in excess of the amount paid for the coupons;

(*b*) The value of the U.S. Department of Agriculture donated foods (surplus commodities);

(*c*) Any payment received under title II of the Uniform Relocation Assistance and Real Property Acquisition Policies Act of 1970;

(*d*) Grants or loans to any undergraduate student for educational purposes made or insured under any programs administered by the Secretary of Education except the programs under the Carl D. Perkins Vocational and Applied Technology Education Act (20 U.S.C. 2301 *et seq.*). Student financial assistance provided under the Carl D. Perkins Vocational and Applied Technology Education Act will be disregarded in accordance with paragraph (a)(4)(ii)(*t*) of this section.

(*e*) Any funds distributed per capita to or held in trust for members of any Indian tribe under Public Law 92–254 or Pub. L. 94–540;

(*f*) Any benefits received under title VII, Nutrition Program for the Elderly, of the Older Americans Act of 1965, as amended;

(*g*) Payments for supporting services or reimbursement of out-of-pocket expenses made to individual volunteers serving as foster grandparents, senior health aides, or senior companions, and to persons serving in the Service Corps of Retired Executives (SCORE) and Active Corps of Executives (ACE) and any other programs under titles II and III, pursuant to section 418 of Pub. L. 93–113;

(*h*) Payments to applicants or recipients participating in the Volunteers in Service to America (VISTA) Program, except that this disregard will not be applied when the Director of ACTION determines that the value of all such payments, adjusted to reflect the number of hours such volunteers are serving, is equivalent to or greater than the minimum wage then in effect under the Fair Labor Standards Act of 1938, or the minimum wage under the laws of the States where the volunteers are serving, whichever is greater. (Section 404(g) of Pub. L. 93–113, as amended by section 9 of Pub. L. 96–143);

(*i*) The value of supplemental food assistance received under the Child Nutrition Act of 1966 as amended, and the special food service program for children under the National School Lunch Act, as amended (Pub. L. 92–433 and Pub. L. 93–150);

(*j*) [Reserved]

(*k*) Pursuant to section 15 of Public Law 100–241, any of the following distributions made to a household, an individual Native, or a descendant of a Native by a Native Corporation established pursuant to the Alaska Native

Claims Settlement Act (ANCSA) (Pub. L. 92–203, as amended):

(*1*) Cash distributions (including cash dividends on stock from a Native Corporation) received by an individual are never counted as income or resources to the extent that such cash does not, in the aggregate, exceed $2,000 in a year. Cash which, in the aggregate, is in excess of $2,000 in a year is not subject to the income and resources disregards in this paragraph (a)(4)(ii)(*k*)(*1*);

(*2*) Stock (including stock issued or distributed by a Native Corporation as a dividend or distribution on stock);

(*3*) A partnership interest;

(*4*) Land or an interest in land (including land or an interest in land received from a Native Corporation as a dividend or distribution on stock); and

(*5*) An interest in a settlement trust.

(*l*) Benefits paid to eligible households under the Low Income Home Energy Assistance Act of 1981 pursuant to section 2605(f) of Pub. L. 97–35;

(*m*) Effective October 17, 1975, pursuant to section 6 of Pub. L. 94–114 (89 Stat. 577, 25 U.S.C. 459e) receipts distributed to members of certain Indian tribes which are referred to in section 5 of Pub. L. 94–114 (89 Stat. 577, 25 U.S.C. 459d).

(*n*) Pursuant to section 7 of Public Law 93–134, as amended by section 4 of Public Law 97–458, Indian judgment funds that are held in trust by the Secretary of the Interior (including interest and investment income accrued while such funds are so held in trust), or distributed per capita to a household or member of an Indian tribe pursuant to a plan prepared by the Secretary of the Interior and not disapproved by a joint resolution of the Congress, and initial purchases made with such funds. This disregard does not apply to proceeds from the sale of initial purchases, subsequent purchases made with funds derived from the sale or conversion of the initial purchases, or to funds or initial purchases which are inherited or transferred.

(*o*) Pursuant to section 2 of Public Law 98–64, all funds held in trust by the Secretary of the Interior for an Indian tribe (including interest and investment income accrued while such funds are so held in trust) and distributed per capita to a household or member of an Indian tribe, and initial purchases made with such funds. This disregard does not apply to proceeds from the sale of initial purchases, subsequent purchases made with funds derived from the sale or conversion of initial purchases, or to funds or initial purchases which are inherited or transferred.

(*p*) Any student financial assistance provided under programs in title IV of the Higher Education Act of 1965, as amended, and under Bureau of Indian Affairs education assistance programs.

(*q*) For AFDC, any payments made as restitution to an individual under title I of Public Law 100–383 (the Civil Liberties Act of 1988) or under title II of Public Law 100–383 (the Aleutian and Pribilof Islands Restitution Act).

(*r*) Any Federal major disaster and emergency assistance provided under the Disaster Relief Act of 1974, as amended by Public Law 100–707 (the Disaster Relief and Emergency Assistance Amendments of 1988) and comparable disaster assistance provided by States, local governments and disaster assistance organizations.

(*s*) Any payments made pursuant to the settlement in the In Re Agent Orange Product liability litigation, M.D.L. No. 381 (E.D.N.Y.).

(*t*) Student financial assistance made available for the attendance costs defined in this paragraph under programs in the Carl D. Perkins Vocational and Applied Technology Education Act (20 U.S.C. 2301 *et seq.*). Attendance costs are: tuition and fees normally assessed a student carrying the same academic workload as determined by the institution, and including costs for rental or purchase of any equipment, materials, or supplies required of all students in the same course of study; and an allowance for books, supplies, transportation, dependent care and miscellaneous personal expenses for a student attending the institution on at least a half-time basis, as determined by the institution.

(*u*) For AFDC, any payments made pursuant to section 6(h)(2) of Public Law 101–426, the Radiation Exposure Compensation Act.

(iii) Provide that income and resources which are disregarded or set aside under this part will not be taken into consideration in determining the need of any other individual for assistance.

(iv) For AFDC, any amounts determined to have been paid by a State from State-only funds to supplement or otherwise increase the amount of aid paid to an assistance unit as computed under § 233.35 for a month in recognition of current or anticipated needs of the assistance unit for that same month shall not be counted as income—to the extent that the total of the State supplemental payment, the AFDC payment and actual income (i.e., the amount of income received during the payment month after subtracting from gross income the $75 work expense disregard (to recognize mandatory payroll deductions, transportation costs, and other work expenses), child care and other applicable disregards) received in that month are not in excess of what the State would have paid for that month to an assistance unit of the same size and composition with no income—in computing the assistance payment under § 233.35 for the corresponding payment month.

(5) *Proration of shelter, utilities, and similar needs in AFDC.* (i) Provide that the State agency may prorate allowances in the need and payment standards for shelter, utilities, and similar needs when the AFDC assistance unit lives together with other individuals as a household; except that, the State shall not prorate with respect to any person receiving SSI to whom the statutory one-third reduction (section 1612(a)(2)(A)(i) of the Act) is applied, or prorate when a bona fide landlord-tenant relationship exists. If the State chooses to prorate under this paragraph, it must prorate both the need standard and payment standard.

(ii) If the State agency elects to prorate allowances for shelter, utilities, and similar needs the State plan must:

(A) Indicate which allowances will be prorated, and describe the procedure which will be used to prorate the allowances;

(B) Provide that the allowances will be prorated on a reasonable basis; and

(C) Specify the circumstances under which proration will occur, including a description of which individuals are considered to be living with an AFDC assistance unit as a household.

(6) *Disregard of earned income; definition.* Provide that for purposes of disregarding earned income the agency policies will include:

(i) A definition of *earned income* in accordance with the provisions of paragraphs (a)(6) (iii) through (ix) of this section; and

(ii) Provision for disregarding earned income for the period during which it is earned, rather than when it is paid, in cases of lump-sum payment for services rendered over a period of more than 1 month.

(iii) The term earned income encompasses income in cash or in kind earned by an individual through the receipt of wages, salary, commissions, or profit from activities in which he is engaged as a self-employed individual or as an employee. For AFDC, *earned income* means gross earned income prior to any deductions for taxes or for any other purposes, except as provided in paragraph (a)(6)(v). Such earned income may be derived from his own employment, such as a business enterprise, or farming; or derived from wages or salary received as an employee. It includes earnings over a period of time for which settlement is made at one given time, as in the instance of sale of farm crops, livestock, or poultry. For OAA, AB, APTD and AABD only, in considering income from farm operation, the option available for reporting under OASDI, namely the *cash receipts and disbursements* method, i.e., a record of actual gross, of expenses, and of net, is an individual determination and is acceptable also for these assistance programs.

(iv) With reference to commissions, wages, or salary, the term *earned income* means the total amount, irrespective of personal expenses, such as income-tax deductions, lunches, and transportation to and from work, and irrespective of expenses of employment which are not personal, such as the cost of tools, materials, special uniforms, or transportation to call on customers.

(v)(A) For OAA, AB, APTD, and AABD, with respect to self-employment, the term *earned income* means the total profit from business enterprise, farming, etc., resulting from a comparison of the gross income received with the *business expenses,* i.e., total cost of the production of the income. Personal expenses, such as income-tax payments, lunches, and transportation to and from work, are not classified as business expenses.

(B) For AFDC, with respect to self-employment the term *earned income* means the total profit from business enterprise, farming, etc., resulting from a comparison of the gross receipts with the *business expenses,* i.e., expenses directly related to producing the goods or services and without which the goods or services could not be produced. However, items such as depreciation, personal business and entertainment expenses, personal transportation, purchase of capital equipment and payments on the principal of loans for capital assets or durable goods are not business expenses.

(vi) The definition shall exclude the following from *earned income:* Returns from capital investment with respect to which the individual is not himself actively engaged, as in a business (for example, under most circumstances, dividends and interest would be excluded from *earned income*); benefits (not in the nature of wages, salary, or profit) accruing as compensation, or reward for service, or as compensation for lack of employment (for example, pensions and benefits, such as United Mine Workers' benefits or veterans' benefits).

(vii) With regard to the degree of activity, earned income is income produced as a result of the performance of services by a recipient; in other words, income which the individual earns by his own efforts, including managerial responsibilities, would be properly classified as earned income, such as management of capital investment in real estate. Conversely, for example, in the instance of capital investment wherein the individual carries no specific responsibility, such as where rental properties are in the hands of rental agencies and the check is forwarded to the recipient, the income would not be classified as earned income.

(viii) Reserves accumulated from earnings are given no different treatment than reserves accumulated from any other sources.

(7) *Disregard of earned income; method.* (i) Provide that for other than AFDC, the following method will be used for disregarding earned income: The applicable amounts of earned income to be disregarded will be deducted from the gross amount of *earned income,* and all work expenses, personal and non-personal, will then be deducted. Only the net amount remaining will be applied in determining need and the amount of the assistance payment.

(ii) In applying the $30 and one-third disregard under paragraph (a)(11)(i)(D) of this section to an applicant for AFDC, there will be a preliminary step to determine whether the assistance unit is eligible without applying the disregard to the individual's earned income, by comparing the applicant's gross earned income (less the disregards in paragraphs (a)(11)(i) (A), (B) and (C)) and all of the assistance unit's other income to the State need standard. This preliminary step does not apply if the individual has received AFDC in one of the four months prior to the month of application.

(8) *Disregard of earned income applicable only to OAA, APTD, or AABD.* If the State chooses to disregard earned income, specify the amount to be disregarded of the first $80 per month of income that is earned by an aged or disabled individual claiming OAA, APTD, or AABD, who is not blind, but not more than $20 per month plus one-half of the next $60 of such earned income.

(9) *Disregard of income and resources applicable only to APTD or AABD.* If the State chooses to disregard income (which may be additional to the income disregarded under paragraph (a)(8) of this section) or resources for a disabled individual to achieve the fulfillment of a plan of self-support, provide that the amounts of additional income and resources will not exceed those found necessary for the period during which the individual is actually undergoing vocational rehabilitation, and specify the period, not in excess of 36 months, for which such amounts are to be disregarded.

(10) *Disregard of income and resources applicable only to AB or AABD.* Provide

that, in determining the need of individuals who are blind, (i) the first $85 per month of earned income of the individual plus one-half of earned income in excess of $85 per month will be disregarded; and (ii) if the individual has a plan for achieving self-support, such additional income and resources as are necessary to fulfill such plan will be disregarded for a period not in excess of 12 months. Such additional income and resources may be disregarded for an additional period not in excess of 24 months (for a total of 36 months), as specified in the State plan.

(11) *Disregard of income and resources applicable only to AFDC.* (i) For purposes of eligibility determination, the State must disregard from the monthly earned income, i.e., earned income as defined in § 233.20(a)(6)(iii), of each individual whose needs are included in the eligibility determination:

(A) Disregard all of the monthly earned income of each child receiving AFDC if the child is a full-time student or is a part-time student who is not a full-time employee. A student is one who is attending a school, college, or university or a course of vocational or technical training designed to fit him or her for gainful employment and includes a participant in the Job Corps program under the Job Training Partnership Act (JTPA).

(B) The first $90.

(C) Where appropriate, an amount equal to $30 plus one-third of the earned income not already disregarded under paragraphs (a)(11)(i), (a)(11)(v) and (a)(11)(vi) of this section of an individual who received assistance in one of the four prior months.

(D) An amount equal to the actual cost for the care of each dependent child or incapacitated adult living in the same home and receiving AFDC, but not to exceed $175 for each dependent child who is at least age two or each incapacitated adult, and not to exceed $200 for each dependent child who is under age two. For individuals not engaged in full-time employment or not employed throughout the month, the $175 and $200 disregard limits may be applied, or the State agency may establish disregard limits less than $175 and $200.

(E) Where appropriate, $30 of the earned income not already disregarded under paragraphs (a)(11) (i), (v), and (vi) of this section, in the case of an individual who reapplies for assistance within the eight-month period that he/she is eligible for the $30 disregard.

(ii) For purposes of benefit calculation for individuals found eligible under paragraph (a)(11)(i) of this section, the following disregards must be made by the State:

(A) Disregard all of the monthly earned income of each child receiving AFDC if the child is a full-time student or is a part-time student who is not a full-time employee. A student is one who is attending a school, college, or university or a course of vocational or technical training designed to fit him or her for gainful employment and includes a participant in the Job Corps program under the Job Training Partnership Act (JTPA).

(B) Disregard from any other individual's earned income the amounts specified in paragraphs (a)(11)(i)(B) and (a)(11)(i)(D) of this section, and $30 plus one-third of the individual's earned income not already disregarded under paragraphs (a)(11)(ii) and (a)(11)(v) of this section. However, the State may not provide the one-third portion of the disregard to an individual after the fourth consecutive month (any month for which the unit loses the $30 plus one-third disregard because of a provision in paragraph (a)(11)(iii) of this section, shall be considered as one of these months) it has been applied to the individual's earned income and may not apply the $30 disregard after the eighth month following the fourth consecutive month (regardless of whether the $30 disregard was actually applied in those months) unless twelve consecutive months have passed during which the individual is not a recipient of AFDC. If income from a recurring source resulted in suspension or termination due to an extra paycheck, the month of ineligibility does not interrupt the accumulation of consecutive months of the $30 plus one-third disregard, nor does it count as one of the consecutive months.

(iii) The applicable earned income disregards in paragraphs (i) (B) and (C) and (ii)(B) of this paragraph do not apply to the earned income of the individual for the month in which one of the following conditions apply to him:

(A) An individual terminated his employment or reduced his earned income without good cause (as specified in the State plan) within the period of 30 days preceding such month;

(B) An individual refused without good cause (as specified in the State plan) within the period of 30 days preceding such month to accept employment in which he is able to engage which is offered through the public employment offices of the State, or is otherwise offered by an employer if the offer of such employer is determined by the State or local agency administering the State plan, after notification by him, to be a bona fide offer of employment;

(C) An individual failed without good cause (as specified in the State plan) to make a timely report (as defined in § 233.37(c)) of that income; or

(D) The individual voluntarily requests assistance to be terminated for the primary purpose of avoiding receiving the $30 and one-third disregard for four consecutive months.

(iv) [Reserved]

(v) The treatment of earned income and expenses under JOBS is as follows:

(A) For earned income from regular employment or on-the-job training, as described at § 250.61, the disregards in paragraphs (a)(11)(i) and (a)(11)(ii)(B) shall apply.

(B) For earned income from a job under the work supplementation component, as described at § 250.62, the disregards in paragraphs (a)(11)(i) and (a)(11)(ii)(B) shall apply unless the State IV-A agency in its State JOBS plan, has elected to provide otherwise under § 250.62(j) and § 250.62(k).

(C) For all activities under JOBS and self-initiated education and training in non-JOBS areas, advance payment or reimbursement to the individual for child care, transportation, work-related expenses, or work-related supportive services is disregarded.

(D) Payment or reimbursement of child care pursuant to part 255 for employed individuals who are not JOBS participants and one-time work-related expenses for individuals who are not JOBS participants pursuant to part 255 are disregarded.

(vi) At State option, disregard all or part of the monthly income of any dependent child applying for or receiving AFDC when the income is derived from a program carried out under the Job Training Partnership Act of 1982, except that in respect to earned income such disregard may not exceed six months per calendar year.

(vii) At State option, disregard all or part of the monthly earned income of any dependent child applying for AFDC, if the child is a full-time student, and that income has been disregarded for purposes of paragraph (a)(3)(xiii) of this section.

(viii) Disregard as income the amount of any earned income tax credit payments received by an applicant or recipient. Disregard as resources, in the month of receipt and the following month, the amount of any earned income tax credit payments received by an applicant or recipient. "Earned income tax credit payments" include: Any advance earned income tax credit payment made to a family by an employer and any earned income tax credit payment made as a refund of Federal income taxes.

(12) *Recoupment of overpayments and correction of underpayments for programs other than AFDC.* Specify uniform Statewide policies for:

(i) Recoupment of overpayments of assistance, including certain overpayments resulting from assistance paid pending hearing decisions.

(A) The State may not recoup any overpayment previously made to a recipient:

(*1*) Unless the recipient has income or resources exclusive of the current assistance payment currently available in the amount by which the agency proposes to reduce payments: except that,

(*2*) Where such overpayments were occassioned or caused by the recipient's willful withholding of information concerning his income, resources or other circumstances which may affect the amount of payment, the State may recoup prior overpayments from current assistance grants irrespective of current income or resources.

(B) Withholding of information which is subject to the provisions of paragraph (a)(12)(i)(A)(*2*) of this section includes the following:

(*1*) Willful misstatements (either oral or written) made by a recipient in response to oral or written questions from the State agency concerning the recipient's income, resources or other circumstances which may affect the amount of payment. Such misstatements may include understatements of amounts of income or resources and omission of an entire category of income or resources;

(*2*) A willful failure by the recipient to report changes in income, resources or other circumstances which may affect the amount of payment, if the State agency has clearly notified the recipient of an obligation to report such changes. The recipient shall be given such notification periodically at times (not less frequently than semiannually) and by methods which the State agency determines will effectively bring such reporting requirements to the recipient's attention:

(*3*) A willfull failure by the recipient (*i*) to report receipt of a payment which the recipient knew represented an erroneous overpayment, or (*ii*) to notify the State agency of receipt of a check which exceeded the prior check by at least the amount which the State agency had previously notified the recipient (pursuant to the provisions of paragraph (a)(12)(i)(A)(*4*) of this section) might represent an overpayment and constitute a sum to which the recipient would not be entitled. In making a determination pursuant to this paragraph (a)(12)(i)(B)(*3*), all relevant circumstances including the amount by which the erroneous payment exceeded the previous payment shall be considered.

(C) Each periodic notification under paragraph (a)(12)(i)(B)(*2*) of this section shall:

(*1*) Include a reminder that it is the recipient's continuing obligation to furnish to the State agency accurate and timely information concerning changes in income, resources, or other circumstances which may affect the amount of payment, within a reasonable specified period after such change. The recipient may also be notified that a failure to so notify the State agency within the designated time period may constitute a willful withholding of such information and permit the State agency to recover any overpayment occasioned or caused by the willful withholding;

(*2*) Specifically and comprehensibly in simple phraseology indicate the type of information to be disclosed by the recipient. Examples shall be furnished of the most frequent types of newly acquired income or resources (e.g., inheritance, wages from a part-time job);

(*3*) Require that, if there is any doubt whether a particular change in circumstances constitutes such reportable information, the recipient contact the State agency or a designated representative thereof within a reasonable specified period of time after such change in circumstances;

(*4*) If the State plan provides for recoupment in the circumstances described in paragraph (a)(12)(i)(B)(*3*)(*ii*) of this section, notify the recipient that if the check received exceeds the prior check by a specified amount (which amount may not be less than that which a reasonable man should have known was erroneous), this increased check may constitute a sum to which the recipient is not entitled. In such instances, the notification may require that the recipient notify the State agency or a designated representative thereof prior to the negotiation of such check, so that corrective action may be taken; the State agency shall respond to such notification within 24 hours. The recipient may also be notified that a failure to so notify the State agency within the designated time period may constitute a willful withholding of such information and permit the State agency to recover such overpayment.

(D) The State agency shall require periodic formal acknowledgement by recipients (on a form utilized for this purpose) that the reporting obligations of this paragraph had been brought to the recipient's attention and that they were understood.

(E) Any recoupment of overpayments made under circumstances other than those specified in paragraph (a)(12)(i)(B) of this section shall be limited to overpayments made during the

12 months preceding the month in which the overpayment was discovered.

(F) Any recoupment of overpayments permitted by paragraph (a)(12)(i)(A)(*2*) of this section may be made from available income and resources (including disregarded, set-aside or reserved items) or from current assistance payment or from both. If recoupments are made from current assistance payments, the State shall, on a case-by-case basis, limit the proportion of such payments that may be deducted in each case, so as not to cause undue hardship to recipients.

(G) The plan may provide for recoupment in all situations specified herein, or only in certain of the circumstances specified herein, and for waiver of the overpayment where the cost of collection would exceed the amount of the overpayment.

(H) Election by the State not to recoup overpayments shall not waive the provisions of §§ 205.40, and 205.41, or any other quality control requirement.

(ii) Prompt correction of underpayments to current recipients, resulting from administrative error where the State plan provides for recoupment of overpayments. Under this requirement:

(*a*) Retroactive corrective payment shall be made only for the 12 months preceding the month in which the underpayment is discovered;

(*b*) For purposes of determining continued eligibility and amount of assistance, such retroactive corrective payments shall not be considered as income or as a resource in the month paid nor in the next following month; and

(*c*) No retroactive payment need be made where the administrative cost would exceed the amount of the payment.

(13) *Recovery of overpayments and correction of underpayments for AFDC.* (i) Specify uniform Statewide policies for recovery of overpayments of assistance, including overpayments resulting from assistance paid pending hearing decisions. Overpayment means a financial assistance payment received by or for an assistance unit for the payment month which exceeds the amount for which that unit was eligible. (The agency may deny assistance for the corresponding payment month rather than recover if the assistance unit was ineligible for the budget month, the State becomes aware of the ineligibility when the monthly report is submitted, the recipient accurately reported the budget month's income and other circumstances, and the assistance unit will be eligible for the following payment month.)

(A) The State must take all reasonable steps necessary to promptly correct any overpayment, except that, as set forth in the plan, a State may waive any overpayment which occurred because receipt of an earned income tax credit payment by a family during the period January 1, 1990, to December 31, 1990, caused ineligibility under the 185 percent gross income limitation in paragraph (a)(3)(xiii) of this section.

(*1*) Any recovery of an overpayment to a current assistance unit, including a current assistance unit or recipient whose overpayment occurred during a prior period of eligibility, must be recovered through repayment (in part or in full) by the individual responsible for the overpayment or recovering the overpayment by reducing the amount of any aid payable to the assistance unit of which he or she is a member, or both.

(*2*) If recovery is made from the grant, such recovery shall result in the assistance unit retaining, for any payment month, from the combined aid, income and liquid resources, (without application of section 402(a)(8) of the Act) not less than 90 percent of the amount payable under the State plan to a family of the same composition with no other income. Where a State chooses to recover at a rate less than the maximum, it must recover promptly.

(B) The State shall recover an overpayment from (*1*) the assistance unit which was overpaid, or (*2*) any assistance unit of which a member of the overpaid assistance unit has subsequently become a member, or (*3*) any individual members of the overpaid assistance unit whether or not currently a recipient. If the State recovers from individuals who are no longer recipients, or from recipients who refuse to repay the overpayment from their income and resources, recovery shall be made by appropriate action under

State law against the income or resources of those individuals.

(C) If through recovery, the amount payable to the assistance unit is reduced to zero, members of the assistance unit are still considered recipients of AFDC.

(D) In cases which have both an underpayment and an overpayment, the State may offset one against the other in correcting the payment.

(E) Prompt recovery of an overpayment: A State must take one of the following three actions by the end of the quarter following the quarter in which the overpayment is first identified:

(1) Recover the overpayment, *(2)* initiate action to locate and/or recover the overpayment from a former recipient, or *(3)* execute a monthly recovery agreement from a current recipient's grant or income/resources.

(ii) Specify uniform Statewide policies for prompt correction of any underpayments to current recipients and those who would be a current recipient if the error causing the underpayment had not occurred. Underpayment means a financial assistance payment received by or for an assistance unit for the payment month which is less than the amount for which the assistance unit was eligible, or failure by the State to issue a financial assistance payment for the payment month to an eligible assistance unit if such payment should have been issued. Under this requirement, for purposes of determining continued eligibility and amount of assistance, such retroactive corrective payments shall not be considered as income, or as a resource in the month paid nor in the next following month.

(iii) Paragraph (a)(13) of this section is effective for incorrect payments which are identified subsequent to September 30, 1981.

(iv) In locating former recipients who have outstanding overpayments the State should use appropriate data sources such as State unemployment insurance files, State Department of Revenue information from tax returns, State automobile registration, Bendex, and other files relating to current or former recipients.

(v) The State must maintain information on the individual and total number and amount of overpayments identified and their disposition for current and former recipients.

(vi) The State may elect not to attempt recovery of an overpayment from an individual no longer receiving aid where the overpayment amount is less than $35. Where the overpayment amount owed by an individual no longer receiving aid is $35 or more, the State can determine when it is no longer cost-effective to continue overpayment recovery efforts, provided it has made reasonable efforts to recover the overpayment from the individual. Reasonable efforts must include notification of the amount of and reason for the overpayment and that repayment is required. States must also maintain information regarding uncollected overpayments as provided under paragraph (a)(13)(v) of this section, to enable the State to recover those overpayments if the individual subsequently becomes a recipient. In cases involving fraud, States must make every effort to recover the overpayment, regardless of the amount.

(14) For Medicaid eligibility only, beginning October 1, 1998, pursuant to section 402(a)(37) of the Act, an assistance unit will be deemed to be receiving AFDC, but only for the purposes of this paragraph, for a period of nine months after the last month the family actually received aid if the loss of AFDC eligibility was solely because a member of the unit was no longer eligible due to the 4 and 12 month time limitations to have the $30 and one-third or the $30 disregard in paragraph (a)(11)(ii)(B) applied to his or her earned income. At State option, an additional period of Medicaid coverage for up to six months may be provided when the assistance unit would be eligible during such additional period to receive AFDC if the $30 and one-third or the $30 disregards were applied to the assistance unit's earned income.

(15) For Medicaid eligibility only, pursuant to section 406(h) of the Act:

(i) Each dependent child and each relative with whom such a child is living (including the eligible spouse of such relative pursuant to section 237.50(b) of this chapter) who becomes ineligible for AFDC wholly or partly because of the initiation of or an increase in the amount of a child or spousal support collection under title IV-D will be deemed to be receiving AFDC, but only for purposes of this paragraph (a)(15), for a period of four consecutive calendar months beginning with the first month of AFDC ineligibility. To be eligible for extended Medicaid coverage pursuant to this paragraph (a)(15), each dependent child and relative must meet the following conditions:

(A) The individual must have become ineligible for AFDC on or after August 16, 1984; and

(B) The individual must have received AFDC in at least three of the six months immediately preceding the month in which the individual becomes ineligible for AFDC; and

(C) The individual must have become ineligible for AFDC wholly or partly as a result of the initiation of or an increase in the amount of a child or spousal support collection under title IV-D.

(ii)(A) Except as provided in paragraph (a)(15)(ii)(B) of this section, individuals who are eligible for extended Medicaid lose this coverage if they move to another State during the 4-month period. However, if they move back to and reestablish residence in the State in which they have extended coverage, they are eligible for any of the months remaining in the 4-month period in which they are residents of the State.

(B) If a State has chosen in its State plan to provide Medicaid to non-residents, the State may continue to provide the 4-month extended benefits to individuals who have moved to another State.

(iii) For purposes of paragraph (i) of this section:

(A) The new collection or increased collection of child or spousal support results in the termination of AFDC eligibility when it actively causes or contributes to the termination. This occurs when:

(*1*) The change in support collection in and of itself is sufficient to cause ineligibility. This rule applies even if the support collection must be added to other, stable income. It also applies even if other independent factors, alone or in combination with each other, might simultaneously cause ineligibility; or

(*2*) The change in support contributes to ineligibility but does not by itself cause ineligibility. Ineligibility must result when the change in support is combined with other changes in income or changes in other circumstances and the other changes in income or circumstances cannot alone or in combination result in termination without the change in support.

(B) In cases of increases in the amounts of both the support collections and earned income, eligibility under this section does not preclude eligibility under paragraph (a)(14) of this section or section 1925 of the Social Security Act (which was added by section 303(a) of the Family Support Act of 1988 (42 U.S.C. 139r–6)). Extended periods result from both an increase in the amount of the support collection and from an increase in earned income must run concurrently.

(b) *Federal financial participation; General.* (1) Federal participation will be available in financial assistance payments made on the basis that (after application of policies governing the allowable reserve, disregard or setting aside of income and resources), all income of the needy individual, together with the assistance payment, do not exceed the State's defined standard of assistance, and available resources of the needy individuals do not exceed the limits under the State plan.

(2) Federal participation is available within the maximums specified in the Federal law, when the payments do not exceed the amount determined to be needed under the statewide standard, and are made in accordance with the State method for determining the amount of the payments, as specified in § 233.31 for AFDC and in §§ 233.24 and 233.25 for OAA, AB, APTD, and AABD.

(3) Federal participation is available in financial assistance payments made on the basis of the need of the individual. This basis may include consideration of needy persons living in the same home with the recipient when such other persons are within the State's policy as essential to his well-being. Persons living in the home who are "essential to the well-being of the recipient," as specified in the State

plan, will govern as the basis for Federal participation (see Guides and Recommendations). When the State includes persons living outside the home or persons not in need, Federal participation is not available for that portion of financial assistance payments attributable to such persons, and the State's claims must, therefore, identify the amounts of any such nonmatchable payments.

(4) For all assistance programs except AFDC, Federal participation is available for supplemental payments in the retrospective budgeting system.

(c) *Federal financial participation in vendor payments for home repairs.* With respect to expenditures made after December 31, 1967, expenditures to a maximum of $500 are subject to Federal financial participation at 50 percent for repairing the home owned by an individual who is receiving aid or assistance (other than Medical Assistance for the Aged) under a State plan for OAA, AFDC, AB, APTD, or AABD if:

(1) Prior to making the expenditures the agency determined that: (i) The home is so defective that continued occupancy is unwarranted; (ii) unless repairs are made the recipient would need to move to rental quarters; and (iii) the rental cost of quarters for the recipient (including the spouse living with him in such home and any other individual whose needs were considered in determining the recipient's need) would exceed (over a period of 2 years) the repair costs needed to make such home habitable together with other costs attributable to continued occupancy of such home.

(2) No expenditures for repair of such home were made previously pursuant to a determination as described in paragraph (c)(1) of this section. This does not preclude more than one payment made at the time repairs are made pursuant to the determination, e.g., separate payments to the roofer, the electrician, and the plumber.

(3) Expenditures for home repairs are authorized in writing by a responsible agency person, records show the eligible person in whose behalf the home repair expenditure was made, and there is sufficient evidence that the home repair was performed.

[34 FR 1394, Jan. 29, 1969]

EDITORIAL NOTE: For FEDERAL REGISTER citations affecting § 233.20, see the List of CFR Sections Affected, which appears in the Finding Aids section of the printed volume and at *www.fdsys.gov*.

EFFECTIVE DATE NOTE: At 47 FR 5678, Feb. 5, 1982, § 233.20(a)(13)(v) was added. This paragraph contains information collection and recordkeeping requirements and will not become effective until approval has been given by the Office of Management and Budget.

§ 233.21 Budgeting methods for OAA, AB, APTD, and AABD.

(a) *Requirements for State plans.* A State plan for OAA, AB, APTD, and AABD shall specify if assistance payments shall be computed using a prospective budgeting system or a retrospective budgeting system. A State electing retrospective budgeting shall specify which options it selects and the State plan shall state that it shall meet the requirements in §§ 233.21 through 233.29. Budgeting methods for AFDC are described in §§ 233.31 through 233.37.

(b) *Definitions.* The following definitions apply to §§ 233.21 through 233.29:

(1) *Prospective budgeting* means that the agency shall compute the amount of assistance for a payment month based on its best estimate of income and circumstances which will exist in that month. This estimate shall be based on the agency's reasonable expectation and knowledge of current, past or future circumstances.

(2) *Retrospective budgeting* means that the agency shall compute the amount of assistance for a payment month based on actual income or circumstances which existed in a previous month, the "budget month".

(3) *Budget month* means the fiscal or calendar month from which the agency shall use income or circumstances of the family to compute the amount of assistance.

(4) *Payment month* means the fiscal or calendar month for which an agency shall pay assistance. Payment is based upon income or circumstances in the budget month. In prospective budgeting, the budget month and the payment month are the same. In retrospective budgeting, the payment month follows the budget month and the payment month shall begin within

32 days after the end of the budget month.

(5) *Make an assistance payment.* In the context of retrospective budgeting, to make an assistance payment means that the check shall be deposited in the U.S. mail, hand delivered to the recipient, or deposited with an intermediary organization, such as a bank.

(6) *Supplemental payment.* In the context of retrospective budgeting, a supplemental payment is a payment which maintains a family during the time it takes for the monthly assistance payment to reflect a change in circumstances or income.

[44 FR 26082, May 4, 1979, as amended at 47 FR 5678, Feb. 5, 1982]

§ 233.22 Determining eligibility under prospective budgeting.

In States which compute the amount of the assistance payment prospectively, the State plan shall provide that the State shall also determine all factors of eligibility prospectively. Thus, the State agency shall establish eligibility based on its best estimate of income and circumstances which will exist in the month for which the assistance payment is made.

[44 FR 26082, May 4, 1979]

§ 233.23 When assistance shall be paid under retrospective budgeting.

(a) A State which uses retrospective budgeting shall specify in its plan that it will make assistance payments within the following time limits to recipients who file a completed report on time, and to those who are not required to file a report. A State shall choose one of two time periods for making assistance payments. The State plan shall provide that payment must be made:

(1) Within 25 days from the close of the budget month; or

(2) Between 25 and 45 days from the close of the budget month.

(b)(1) Where a State makes payments between 25 and 45 days from the close of the budget month, the State plan shall provide that the State will make supplemental payments as provided in § 233.27.

(2) If a State makes payments within 25 days from the close of the budget month, and also makes supplemental payments as provided in § 233.27, the State plan shall so specify.

(c) In States which issue two checks for each payment month, these time periods apply to the first check.

[44 FR 26083, May 4, 1979]

§ 233.24 Retrospective budgeting; determining eligibility and computing the assistance payment in the initial one or two months.

(a) States which make assistance payments within 25 days of the close of the budget month shall determine eligibility and compute the amount of the payment for all recipients prospectively for the initial month of assistance. These States may choose to determine eligibility and compute the payment prospectively for the second month, also.

(b) States which make assistance payments between 25 and 45 days from the close of the budget month shall determine eligibility and compute the amount of the payment prospectively for the initial two months of assistance.

(c) When a person who previously received assistance reapplies during the same month in which a termination became effective, eligibility shall be determined according to paragraph (a) or (b) of this section. However, the amount of the assistance payment for the month of the reapplication shall be computed retrospectively.

[44 FR 26083, May 4, 1979]

§ 233.25 Retrospective budgeting; computing the assistance payment after the initial one or two months.

The State plan shall provide:

(a) After the initial one or two payment months of assistance under § 233.24, the amount of each subsequent month's payment shall be computed retrospectively, i.e., shall be based on earned and unearned income received in the corresponding budget month.

(b) In these subsequent months, other factors of need which affect the amount of the assistance payment may also be based on circumstances in the corresponding budget month, or they may be based on circumstances in the payment month.

(c) For the first month in which retrospective budgeting is used, a State shall not consider income received by the recipient before the date of application. When a person reapplies during the same month in which a termination became effective, the State may consider income received before the date of application.

[44 FR 26083, May 4, 1979]

§ 233.26 Retrospective budgeting; determining eligibility after the initial one or two months.

(a) Under retrospective budgeting, there are three options for determining eligibility. The State plan shall specify that eligibility, following the initial one or two months under § 233.24, shall be determined by one of the following methods:

(1) A State may consider all factors, including income retrospectively, i.e., only from the budget month. For example, if a change in circumstances occurs which affects eligibility, e.g., deprivation ceases, the change may be reported at the end of the budget month and assistance shall be terminated for the corresponding payment month. Thus, even if the agency could have terminated assistance earlier than the corresponding payment month, it shall not do so under retrospective determination of eligibility.

(2) A State may consider all factors, including income, prospectively. For example, if deprivation ceases, and the family becomes ineligible, the agency shall immediately take steps to terminate assistance.

(3) A State may use a combination of the options in paragraphs (a) and (b) of this section by considering factors related to earned and unearned income retrospectively and all other factors prospectively. For example, if a change in income makes the family ineligible, the agency shall wait until the corresponding payment month to terminate assistance. On the other hand, if a change of circumstances other than income makes the family ineligible, the agency shall immediately take steps to terminate assistance.

[44 FR 26083, May 4, 1979; 44 FR 29065, May 18, 1979, as amended at 47 FR 47828, Oct. 28, 1982]

§ 233.27 Supplemental payments under retrospective budgeting.

(a) *General requirements.* A State plan which provides for payments between 25 and 45 days from the close of a budget month, shall provide for supplemental payments to eligible recipients who request them. A State plan which provides for payments within 25 days may provide for supplemental payments:

(1) The supplemental payment shall be paid for the month in which it was requested.

(2) The recipient family is eligible for a supplemental payment if its income for the month is less than 80 percent of the amount the State would pay for a similar family with no income. However, this percentage of the amount the State would pay for a similar family with no income may be set between 80 and 100 percent, as specified in the State plan. The supplemental payment equals the difference between the family's income in the payment month and that percentage.

(3) Supplemental payments shall be issued within 5 working days of request.

(b) *How income is treated.* For purposes of supplemental payments, income includes that month's assistance payment and any income received or expected to be received by the recipient, but does not include work-related expenses.

(1) The amount used for the assistance payment shall be the monthly assistance payment without regard to any recoupments made for prior overpayments or adjustments for prior underpayments.

(2) The agency may include as income cash in hand or available in bank accounts. It may also include as income any cash disregarded in determining need or the amount of the assistance payment, but not cash payments that are disregarded by § 233.20(a)(4)(ii), paragraphs (c) on relocation assistance, (d) on educational grants or loans and (g) on payments for certain services.

[44 FR 26083, May 4, 1979, as amended at 51 FR 9205, Mar. 18, 1986]

§ 233.28 Monthly reporting.

(a) State plans specifying retrospective budgeting shall require that recipients with earned income, other than income from self-employment, report that income to the agency monthly. The State may require recipients with unearned income, no income, or income from self-employment to report monthly. The agency shall provide a form for this purpose, which:

(1) Is written in clear simple language;

(2) Specifies the date by which the agency must receive the form and the consequences of a late or incomplete form, including whether the agency will delay or withhold payment if the form is not returned by the specified date;

(3) Identifies an individual or agency unit the recipient should contact to receive prompt answers to questions about information requested on the form, and provides a telephone number for this purpose;

(4) Includes a statement, to be signed by the recipient, that he or she understands that the information he or she provides may result in changes in assistance, including reduction or termination;

(5) Advises the recipient if supplemental payments are available and the proper procedures for initiating a request; and

(6) Advises the recipient of his or her right to a fair hearing on any decrease or termination of assistance or denial of a supplemental payment.

(b) The agency shall specify the date by which it must receive the monthly report. This date shall be at least 5 days from the end of the budget month and shall also allow the recipient at least 5 days to complete the report.

(c) The agency may consider a monthly report incomplete only if it is unsigned or omits information necessary to determine eligibility or compute the payment amount.

(d) The agency shall provide a stamped, self-addressed envelope for returning the monthly report.

(e) The agency shall make special provisions for persons who are illiterate or have other handicaps so that they cannot complete a monthly report form.

[44 FR 26083, May 4, 1979]

§ 233.29 How monthly reports are treated and what notices are required.

(a) *What happens if a completed monthly report is received on time.* When the agency receives a completed monthly report by the date specified in § 233.28 it shall process the payment. The agency shall notify the recipient of any changes from the prior payment and the basis for its determinations. This notice must meet the requirements of § 205.10(a)(4)(i)(B) of this chapter on adequate notice if the payment is being reduced or assistance is being terminated. This notice must be received by the recipient no later than his or her resulting payment or in lieu of the payment.

(b) *What happens if the completed monthly report is received before the extension deadline.* (1) If the completed monthly report is not received by the date specified in § 233.28, the agency shall send a notice to the recipient. This notice shall inform him or her that the monthly report is overdue or is not complete and that he or she has at least 10 additional days to file. It must inform the recipient that termination may result if that is the agency's policy, if the report is not filed within the extension period. This notice must reach the recipient at least 10 days before the expected payment. However, in States in which the date specified in § 233.28 is within 10 days of the expected payment date, the notice must reach the recipient on or before the expected payment date.

(2) When the report is received within the extension period, the agency may delay payment to the recipient, as follows:

(i) In a State that pays within 25 days of the budget month the payment may be delayed 10 days;

(ii) In a State that pays within 25 to 45 days of the budget month, the payment may not be delayed beyond the 45th day.

(c) *What happens if a monthly report is not received by the end of the extension period.* An agency may terminate assistance if it has not received a report or has received an incomplete report, and the 10 day extension period has expired. If the State decides to terminate assistance, it must send the recipient a notice which meets the requirements of § 205.10(a)(4)(i)(B) on adequate notice.

(d) *How a recipient may delay an adverse action based on a monthly report.* If a recipient's assistance is reduced or terminated based on information in the monthly report, and he or she requests a fair hearing within 10 days, the assistance payment shall be reinstated immediately at the previous month's level pending the hearing decision. The payment shall be made effective from the date assistance was reduced or terminated.

[44 FR 26084, May 4, 1979]

§ 233.31 Budgeting methods for AFDC.

(a) *Requirements for State plans.* A State plan for AFDC shall specify that all factors of eligibility shall be determined prospectively and the amount of the assistance for any month for all assistance units required to file a monthly report for the month designated as the budget month under the State's retrospective budgeting procedures shall be determined using retrospective budgeting as provided in §§ 233.31–233.37 except as provided in § 233.34. The State plan shall specify whether the State uses prospective or retrospective budgeting to determine the amount of the assistance payments for recipients not required to report monthly. Budgeting methods for OAA, AB, APTD, and AABD are described in §§ 233.21–233.29.

(b) *Definitions.* The following definitions apply to §§ 233.31 through 233.37:

(1) *Prospective budgeting* means that the agency shall determine eligibility (and compute the amount of assistance for the first one or two months) based on its best estimate of income and circumstances which will exist in that month. This estimate shall be based on the agency's reasonable expectation and knowledge of current, past or future circumstances.

(2) *Retrospective budgeting* means that the agency shall compute the amount of assistance for a payment month based on actual income or circumstances which existed in a previous month, the "budget month."

(3) *Budget month* means the fiscal or calendar month from which the agency shall use income or circumstances of the family to compute the amount of assistance.

(4) *Payment month* means the fiscal or calendar month for which an agency shall pay assistance. Payment is based upon income or circumstances in the budget month. In prospective budgeting, the budget month and the payment month are the same. In retrospective budgeting, the payment month follows the budget month.

(5) *Recent work history* means the individual received earned income in any one of the two months prior to the budget month.

[47 FR 5678, Feb. 5, 1982, as amended at 49 FR 35602, Sept. 10, 1984; 57 FR 30160, July 8, 1992]

§ 233.32 Payment and budget months (AFDC).

A State shall specify in its plan for AFDC the time period covered by the payment (payment month) and the time period used to determine that payment (budget month) and whether it adopts (a) a one-month or two-month retrospective system; and (b) a one-month or two-month prospective system for the initial payment months. If a State elects to have a two-month retrospective system it must also elect a two-month prospective system.

[47 FR 5678, Feb. 5, 1982]

§ 233.33 Determining eligibility prospectively for all payment months (AFDC).

(a) The State plan for AFDC shall provide that the State shall determine all factors of eligibility prospectively for all payment months. Thus, the State agency shall establish eligibility based on its best estimate of income and circumstances which will exist in the month for which the assistance payment is made.

(b) When a IV-A agency receives an official report of a child support collection it shall consider that information as provided in § 232.20(a) of this chapter. (§ 232.20(a) explains the treatment of child support collections.)

[47 FR 5678, Feb. 5, 1982]

§ 233.34 Computing the assistance payment in the initial one or two months (AFDC).

A State shall compute the amount of the AFDC payment for the initial month of eligibility:

(a) Prospectively (except as in paragraphs (b) and (c) of this section); or

(b) Retrospectively if the applicant received assistance (or would have except for the prohibition on payments of less than $10) for the immediately preceding payment month (except where the State pays the second month after application prospectively); or

(c) Retrospectively if:

(1) Assistance had been suspended as defined in paragraph (d) of this section; and

(2) The initial month follows the month of suspension; and

(3) The family's circumstances for the initial month had not changed significantly from those reported in the corresponding budget month, e.g., loss of job.

(d) A State may suspend, rather than terminate, assistance when:

(1) The agency has knowledge of, or reason to believe that ineligibility would be only for one payment month; and

(2) Ineligibility for that one payment month was caused by income or other circumstances in the corresponding budget month.

(e) If the initial month is computed prospectively as in paragraph (a) of this section, the second month shall be prospective if the State elects a 2-month retrospective budgeting system.

[47 FR 5679, Feb. 5, 1982]

§ 233.35 Computing the assistance payment under retrospective budgeting after the initial one or two months (AFDC).

The State plan for AFDC shall provide:

(a) After the initial one or two payment months of assistance under § 233.34, the amount of each subsequent month's payment shall be computed retrospectively, i.e., shall be based on income and other relevant circumstances in the corresponding budget month except as provided in § 233.20(a)(3)(iii). In any month for which an individual will be determined eligible prospectively and will be added to an existing AFDC assistance unit, the State must meet the individual's needs to the same extent it would if the individual were an applicant for AFDC.

(b) Except as provided in § 233.34(b), for the first and second payment month for which retrospective budgeting is used, the State shall not count income from the budget month already considered for any payment month determined prospectively which is not of a continuous nature.

[47 FR 5679, Feb. 5, 1982]

§ 233.36 Monthly reporting (AFDC).

(a) Except as provided in paragraph (b) of this section, a State plan for AFDC shall require the caretaker relative, or another person designated by the State, to submit, on behalf of each assistance unit whose members have earned income or recent work history, each assistance unit which has income deemed to it from individuals living with the unit who have earned income or a recent work history and, at State option, other assistance units, a completed report form to the agency monthly on:

(1) Budget month income, family composition, and other circumstances relevant to the amount of the assistance payment; and

(2) Any changes in income, resources, or other relevant circumstances affecting continued eligibility which the assistance unit expects to occur in the current month or in future months.

(3) The income of a parent or a legal guardian of a minor parent, a stepparent, or an alien sponsor, as well as the resources of an alien sponsor, where appropriate.

(b) A State may exempt categories of recipients otherwise required to report monthly from reporting each month with prior approval by the Secretary if the State can demonstrate that not requiring these cases to file monthly reports is cost effective. The Secretary will grant waivers under this provision for a period up to one year, at the end of which time the State may request an extension of the waiver. A decision by the Secretary not to approve a request for an exemption is not appealable. The plan shall include criteria for assuring (1) that exempted cases are unlikely to incur changes in circumstances from month to month which would impact their eligibility r amount of assistance and (2) that the administrative cost of requiring those categories to report monthly will be greater than the program savings which would accrue.

(c) States shall also direct recipients to report information as defined in paragraph (a)(2) of this section to the agency as they become aware of expected changes rather than waiting to inform the State on the monthly report.

[47 FR 5679, Feb. 5, 1982, as amended at 49 FR 35602, Sept. 10, 1984; 57 FR 30160, July 8, 1992]

§ 233.37 How monthly reports are treated and what notices are required (AFDC).

(a) *What happens if a completed monthly report is received on time.* When the agency receives a completed monthly report as specified in § 233.36, and if all eligibility conditions are met, it shall process the payment. The agency shall notify the recipient of any changes from the prior payment and the basis for its determinations. This notice must meet the requirements of § 205.10(a)(4)(i)(B) of this chapter on adequate notice if the payment is being reduced or assistance is terminated as a result of information provided in the monthly report. The notice must be mailed to arrive no later than the resulting payment or in lieu of the payment. A recipient has 10 days from the date of the notice to request a hearing in order to receive reinstatement.

(b) *What happens if a completed monthly report is not received by the agency.* An agency may terminate assistance if it has received no report or has received only an incomplete report as defined by the State. In this case, the agency must send the recipient a notice meeting the requirements of § 205.10(a)(4)(i)(B) to arrive not later than the date it would have made payment if the agency had received a completed monthly report on time. If the recipient notifies the agency and files a completed report within 10 days of the date of this notice, the agency must accept the replacement form and make a payment based on the information on the form if the information indicates that the person is still eligible (without the applicable earned income disregards if the State agency determines no good cause exists for failing to file a timely report of earnings). If the recipient is found ineligible or eligible for an amount less than the prior month's payment, the State must promptly notify the recipient of his or her right to a fair hearing and his or her right to have assistance reinstated. A recipient has 10 days from the date of the notice to request a hearing in order to receive reinstatement.

(c) *What happens if a completed monthly report is received but is not timely.* States must specify in their plans a definition of timeliness related to the filing of a monthly report and the number of days an individual has to report changes in earnings which impact eligibility. States must inform recipients what constitutes timeliness and that no disregard of earnings as described in § 233.20(a)(11) (i) and (ii)(B) ($30 and one-third, child care, and work expenses) will be applied to any earnings which are not reported in a timely manner without good cause. The State must provide recipients an opportunity to show good cause for not filing a timely report of earnings. If the State finds good cause, then applicable earned income disregards will be applied in determining payment. If the State does not find good cause, then applicable earned income disregards will not be applied. If the recipient is found ineligible or eligible for an amount less than the prior month's payment, the State must promptly notify the recipient of his or her right to a fair hearing and his or her right to have assistance reinstated. A recipient has 10 days from the date of the notice to request a hearing in order to receive reinstatement.

[47 FR 5679, Feb. 5, 1982]

§ 233.38 Waiver of monthly reporting and retrospective budgeting requirements; AFDC.

(a) States may request waivers of the requirements at §§ 233.31–233.37 to promote compatibility with monthly reporting and budgeting requirements of the Food Stamp Act of 1977 as amended.

(b) The Secretary will not approve requests for waivers unless the information documenting the need for the waiver shows that the waiver would simplify administration of both programs and would not result in a net cost to the Federal government. Approvals for waivers will be for periods up to one year, after which time the State may request an extension of the waiver.

(c) Any decision by the Secretary not to approve a request for a waiver is not appealable.

[49 FR 35602, Sept. 10, 1984]

§ 233.39 Age.

(a) *Condition for plan approval.* A State plan under title I or XVI of the Social Security Act may not impose any age requirement of more than 65 years.

(b) *Federal financial participation.* (1) Federal financial participation is available in financial assistance provided to otherwise eligible persons who were, for any portion of the month for which assistance is paid:

(i) In OAA or AABD with respect to the aged, 65 years of age or over;

(ii) In AFDC, under 18 years of age; or age 18 if a full-time student in a secondary school, or in the equivalent level of vocational or technical training, and reasonably expected to complete the program before reaching age 19.

(iii) In AB or AABD with respect to the blind, any age;

(iv) In APTD or AABD with respect to the disabled, 18 years of age or older.

(2) Federal determination of whether an individual meets the age requirements of the Social Security Act will be made according to the common-law method (under which a specific age is attained the day before the anniversary of birth), unless the State plan specifies that the popular usage method (under which an age is attained on the anniversary of birth), is used.

(3) The State agency may adopt an arbitrary date such as July 1 as the point from which age will be computed in all instances where the month of an individual's birth is not available, but the year can be established.

[36 FR 3866, Feb. 27, 1971. Redesignated and amended at 47 FR 5678, Feb. 5, 1982]

§ 233.40 Residence.

(a) *Condition for plan approval.* A State plan under title I, IV-A, X, XIV, or XVI of the Social Security Act may not impose any residence requirement which excludes any individual who is a resident of the State except as provided in paragraph (b) of this section. For purposes of this section:

(1) A resident of a State is one: (i) Who is living in the State voluntarily with the intention of making his or her home there and not for a temporary purpose. A child is a resident of the State in which he or she is living other than on a temporary basis. Residence may not depend upon the reason for which the individual entered the State, except insofar as it may bear upon whether the individual is there voluntarily or for a temporary purpose; or

(ii) Who, is living in the State, is not receiving assistance from another State, and entered the State with a job commitment or seeking employment in the State (whether or not currently employed). Under this definition, the child is a resident of the State in which the caretaker is a resident.

(2) Residence is retained until abandoned. Temporary absence from the State, with subsequent returns to the State, or intent to return when the purposes of the absence have been accomplished, does not interrupt continuity of residence.

(b) *Exception.* A State plan under title I, X, XIV, or XVI need not include an individual who has been absent from the State for a period in excess of 90 consecutive days (regardless of whether the individual has maintained his or her residence in the State during this period) until he or she has been present in the State for a period of 30 consecutive days (or a shorter period specified by the State) in the case of such individual who has maintained residence in the State during such period of absence or for a period of 90 consecutive days (or a shorter period as specified by the State) in the case of any other such individual. An individual thus excluded under any such plan may not, as a consequence of that exclusion, be excluded from assistance under the State's title XIX plan if otherwise eligible under the title XIX plan (see 42 CFR 436.403).

[45 FR 26962, Apr. 22, 1980]

§ 233.50 Citizenship and alienage.

A State plan under title I (OAA); title IV-A (AFDC); title X (AB); title XIV (APTD); and title XVI (AABD-disabled) of the Social Security Act shall provide that an otherwise eligible individual, dependent child, or a caretaker relative or any other person whose needs are considered in determining the need of the child or relative claiming aid, must be either:

(a) A citizen, or

(b) An alien lawfully admitted for permanent residence or otherwise permanently residing in the United States under color of law, including certain aliens lawfully present in the United States as a result of the application of the following provisions of the Immigration and Nationality Act:

(1) Section 207(c), in effect after March 31, 1980—Aliens Admitted as Refugees.

(2) Section 203(a)(7), in effect prior to April 1, 1980—Individuals who were Granted Status as Conditional Entrant Refugees.

(3) Section 208—Aliens Granted Political Asylum by the Attorney General.

(4) Section 212(d)(5)—Aliens Granted Temporary Parole Status by the Attorney General, or

(c) An alien granted lawful temporary resident status pursuant to section 201, 302, or 303 of the Immigration Reform and Control Act of 1986 (Pub. L. 99–603) who must be either:

(1) A Cuban and Haitian entrant as defined in paragraph (1) or (2)(A) of section 501(e) of Pub. L. 96–422, as in effect on April 1, 1983, or

(2) An adult assistance applicant for OAA, AB, APTD, or AABD, or

(3) An applicant for AFDC who is not a Cuban and Haitian applicant under paragraph (c)(1) of this section who was adjusted to lawful temporary resident status more than five years prior to application.

All other aliens granted lawful temporary or permanent resident status, pursuant to sections 201, 302, or 303 of the Immigration Reform and Control Act of 1986, are disqualified for five years from the date lawful temporary resident status is granted.

[47 FR 5680, Feb. 5, 1982; 47 FR 43383, Oct. 1, 1982, as amended at 52 FR 48689, Dec. 24, 1987; 53 FR 30433, Aug. 12, 1988; 54 FR 10544, Mar. 14, 1989]

§ 233.51 Eligibility of sponsored aliens.

Definition: *Sponsor* is any person who, or any public or private agency or organization that, executed an affidavit(s) of support or similar agreement on behalf of an alien (who is not the child of the sponsor or the sponsor's spouse) as a condition of the alien's entry into the United States. Paragraphs (a) through (d) of this section apply only to aliens who are sponsored by individuals and who filed applications for the first time after September 30, 1981. Paragraphs (e) and (f) apply only to aliens sponsored by public or private agencies or organizations with respect to periods after October 1, 1984. A State plan under title IV-A of the Act shall provide that:

(a) For a period of three years following entry for permanent residence into the United States, a sponsored alien who is not exempt under paragraph (g) of this section, shall provide the State agency with any information and documentation necessary to determine the income and resources of the sponsor and the sponsor's spouse (if applicable and if living with the sponsor) that can be deemed available to the alien, and obtain any cooperation necessary from the sponsor.

(b) The income and resources of a sponsor and the sponsor's spouse shall be deemed to be the unearned income and resources of an alien for three years following the alien's entry into the United States:

(1) Monthly income deemed available to the alien from the sponsor and the sponsor's spouse not receiving AFDC or SSI shall be:

(i) The total monthly unearned and earned income of the sponsor and sponsor's spouse reduced by 20 percent (not to exceed $175) of the total of any amounts received by them in the month as wages or salary or as net earnings from self-employment.

(ii) The amount described in paragraph (b)(1)(i) of this section reduced by:

(A) The cash needs standard under the plan in the alien's State of residence for a family of the same size and composition as the sponsor and those other people living in the same household as the sponsor who are or could be claimed by the sponsor as dependents to determine his or her Federal personal income tax liability but whose needs are not taken into account in making a determination under § 233.20 of this chapter;

(B) Any amounts actually paid by the sponsor or sponsor's spouse to people not living in the household who are or could be claimed by them as dependents to determine their Federal personal income tax liability; and

(C) Actual payments of alimony or child support, with respect to individuals not living in the household.

(2) Monthly resources deemed available to the alien from the sponsor and sponsor's spouse shall be the total amount of their resources determined as if they were applying for AFDC in the alien's State of residence, less $1500.

(c) In any case where a person is the sponsor of two or more aliens, the income and resources of the sponsor and sponsor's spouse, to the extent they would be deemed the income and resources of any one of the aliens under the provisions of this section, shall be divided equally among the sponsored aliens.

(d) Income and resources which are deemed to a sponsored alien shall not be considered in determining the need of other unsponsored members of the alien's family except to the extent the income or resources are actually available.

(e) For a period of three years following entry for permanent residence into the United States, any alien who is not exempt under paragraph (g) of this section and has been sponsored by a public or private agency or organization, shall be ineligible for assistance unless the State agency determines (in accordance with paragraph (f)) that the sponsor no longer exists or has become unable to meet the alien's needs.

(f) The State plan shall set forth the criteria the State agency will use in determining whether an agency or organization no longer exists or is unable to meet the alien's needs and the documentation the agency will require of the alien in making such determination. The sponsored alien shall provide the State agency with any information and documentation necessary for such determination and obtain any cooperation necessary from the sponsor.

(g) The provisions of this section shall not apply to any alien who is:

(1) Admitted as a conditional entrant refugee to the United States as a result of the application, of the provisions of section 203(a)(7) (in effect prior to April 1, 1980) of the Immigration and Nationality Act;

(2) Admitted as a refugee to the United States as a result of the application of the provisions of section 207(c) (in effect after March 31, 1980) of the Immigration and Nationality Act;

(3) Paroled into the United States as a refugee under section 212(d)(5) of the Immigration and Nationality Act;

(4) Granted political asylum by the Attorney General under section 208 of the Immigration and Nationality Act;

(5) A Cuban or Haitian entrant, as defined in section 501(e) of the Refugee Education Assistance Act of 1980 (Pub. L. 96–422); or

(6) The dependent child of the sponsor or sponsor's spouse.

(h) The Secretary shall make information necessary to make a determination under this section and supplied under agreement with the Secretary of State and the Attorney General, available upon request to a concerned State Agency.

[47 FR 5680, Feb. 5, 1982; 47 FR 43383, Oct. 1, 1982; 47 FR 47828, Oct. 28, 1982; 49 FR 35602, Sept. 10, 1984; 57 FR 30160, July 8, 1992]

§ 233.52 Overpayment to aliens.

A State Plan under title IV-A of the Social Security Act, shall provide that:

(a) Any sponsor of an alien and the alien shall be jointly and severally liable for any overpayment of aid under the State plan made to the alien during the three years after the alien's entry into the United States due to the sponsor's failure to provide correct information under the provisions of § 233.51, except as provided in paragraph (b) of this section.

(b) When a sponsor is found to have good cause or to be without fault (as defined in the State plan) for not providing information to the agency, the sponsor will not be held liable for the overpayment and recovery will not be made from this sponsor.

(c) An overpayment for which the alien or the sponsor and the alien are liable (as described in paragraphs (a) and (b) of this section) shall be repaid to the State or recovered in accordance with §233.20(a)(13). If the agency is unable to recover the overpayment through this method, funds to reimburse the agency for the overpayment shall be withheld from future payments to which the alien or the alien and the individual sponsor are entitled under:

(1) Any State administered or supervised program established by the Social Security Act, or

(2) Any federally administered cash benefit program established by the Social Security Act.

[47 FR 5680, Feb. 5, 1982, as amended at 49 FR 35602, Sept. 10, 1984]

§233.53 Support and maintenance assistance (including home energy assistance) in AFDC.

(a) *General.* At State option, certain support and maintenance assistance (including home energy assistance) may be excluded from income and resources.

(b) *Definitions.* The following definitions are limited to the support and maintenance assistance provisions of this section.

Appropriate State agency means the agency designated by the chief executive officer of the State to handle the State's responsibilities with respect to support and maintenance assistance under paragraph (c) of this section.

Based on need means that the assistance is given to or on behalf of an applicant or recipient for the purpose of support and maintenance (including home energy) and meets the criteria established by the State for determining the need for such assistance.

In kind assistance means assistance furnished in any form except direct cash payments to an applicant or recipient or direct payments to an applicant or recipient through other financial instruments which are convertible to cash.

Private, nonprofit organization means a religious, charitable, educational, or other organization such as described in section 501(c) of the Internal Revenue Code of 1954. (Actual tax exempt certification by IRS is not necessary).

Rate-of-return entity means an entity whose revenues are primarily received from the entity's charges to the public for goods or services, and such charges are based on rates regulated by a State or Federal governmental body.

Support and maintenance assistance means any assistance designed to meet the expenses of day to day living. Support and maintenance assistance includes home energy assistance. Home energy assistance means any assistance related to meeting the cost of heating or cooling a home. Home energy assistance includes such items as payments for utility service or bulk fuels; assistance in kind such as portable heaters, fans, blankets, storm doors, or other items which help reduce the costs of heating and cooling such as conservation or weatherization materials and services; etc.

(c) *Requirements for State Plans.* If a State elects to exclude from income and resources support and maintenance assistance, the State plan for AFDC must as specified below:

(1) Provide that an appropriate State agency will certify that support and maintenance assistance is based on need (as defined in paragraph (b) of this section), and that such certification will be accepted for purposes of determining eligibility for and the amount of payments under the AFDC program.

(2) Provide that in joint AFDC/SSI households, support and maintenance assistance furnished to the household which is not excluded under this paragraph will be prorated on a reasonable basis to determine the amount provided to the AFDC assistance unit. The State plan must describe the method that will be used to prorate the assistance in these circumstances.

(3) Provide that the types and amount of support and maintenance assistance that are excluded when received by an AFDC applicant or recipient will also be excluded in determining the income and resources of a parent, stepparent, spouse or alien sponsor whose income is considered available to an AFDC applicant or recipient.

(4) Provide that the State may exclude, from income and resources, support and maintenance assistance (as defined in paragraph (b) of this section) which the appropriate State agency certifies is based on need, if the assistance is furnished by:

(i) A supplier of home heating gas or oil, regardless of whether the assistance is in cash or in kind; or

(ii) A municipal utility providing home energy, regardless of whether the assistance is in cash or in kind; or

(iii) A rate-of-return entity which provides home energy, regardless of whether the assistance is in cash or in kind; or

(iv) A private nonprofit organization, but only if such assistance is in kind.

(5) Provide that, if the State elects to exclude from income and resources any support and maintenance assistance, the State plan must:

(i) Describe the criteria that will be used to determine the need for the assistance;

(ii) Identify the types and amounts of assistance which will be excluded; and

(iii) Provide that any limitations will be made on a reasonable basis.

[51 FR 39533, Oct. 29, 1986, as amended at 56 FR 64204, Dec. 9, 1991]

§ 233.60 Institutional status.

(a) *Federal financial participation.* (1) Federal financial participation under title I, X, XIV, or XVI of the Social Security Act is not available in payments to or in behalf of any individual who is an inmate of a public institution except as a patient in a medical institution.

(2)(i) Federal financial participation under title X or XIV of the Social Security Act is not available in payments to or in behalf of any individual who is a patient in an institution for tuberculosis or mental diseases.

(ii) Federal financial participation under title XVI of the Social Security Act is not available in payments to or in behalf of any individual who has not attained 65 years of age and who is a patient in an institution for tuberculosis or mental diseases.

(3) For purposes of this paragraph:

(i) Federal financial participation is available in payments for the month in which an individual (if otherwise eligible) became an inmate of a public institution, or a patient in an institution for tuberculosis or mental diseases;

(ii) Whether an institution is one for tuberculosis or mental diseases will be determined by whether its overall character is that of a facility established and maintained primarily for the care and treatment of individuals with tuberculosis or mental diseases (whether or not it is licensed);

(iii) An institution for the mentally retarded is not an institution for mental diseases;

(iv) An individual on conditional release or convalescent leave from an institution for mental diseases is not considered to be a patient in such institution.

(b) *Definitions.* For purposes of Federal financial participation under paragraph (a) of this section:

(1) *Institution* means an establishment which furnishes (in single or multiple facilities) food and shelter to four or more persons unrelated to the proprietor, and in addition, provides some treatment or services which meet some need beyond the basic provision of food and shelter.

(2) *In an institution* refers to an individual who is admitted to participate in the living arrangements and to receive treatment or services provided there which are appropriate to his requirements.

(3) *Public institution* means an institution that is the responsibility of a governmental unit or over which a governmental unit exercises administrative control.

(4) *Inmate of a public institution* means a person who is living in a public institution. An individual is not considered an inmate when:

(i) He is in a public educational or vocational training institution, for purposes of securing education or vocational training, or

(ii) He is in a public institution for a temporary emergent period pending other arrangements appropriate to his needs.

(5) *Medical institution* means an institution which:

(i) Is organized to provide medical care, including nursing and convalescent care;

(ii) Has the necessary professional personnel, equipment, and facilities to manage the medical, nursing, and other health needs of patients on a continuing basis in accordance with accepted standards;

(iii) Is authorized under State law to provide medical care;

(iv) Is staffed by professional personnel who have clear and definite responsibility to the institution in the provision of professional medical and nursing services including adequate and continual medical care and supervision by a physician; sufficient registered nurse or licensed practical nurse supervision and services and nurse aid services to meet nursing care needs; and appropriate guidance by a physician(s) on the professional aspects of operating the facility.

(6) *Institution for tuberculosis* means an institution which is primarily engaged in providing diagnosis, treatment, or care of persons with tuberculosis, including medical attention, nursing care, and related services.

(7) *Institution for mental diseases* means an institution which is primarily engaged in providing diagnosis, treatment or care of persons with mental diseases, including medical attention, nursing care, and related services.

(8) *Patient* means an individual who is in need of and receiving professional services directed by a licensed practitioner of the healing arts toward maintenance, improvement, or protection of health, or alleviation of illness, disability, or pain.

[36 FR 3867, Feb. 27, 1971]

§233.70 Blindness.

(a) *State plan requirements.* A State plan under title X or XVI of the Social Security Act must:

(1) Contain a definition of blindness in terms of ophthalmic measurement. The following definition is recommended: An individual is considered blind if he has central visual acuity of 20/200 or less in the better eye with correcting glasses or a field defect in which the peripheral field has contracted to such an extent that the widest diameter of visual field subtends an angular distance of no greater than 20°.

(2) Provide, in any instance in which a determination is to be made whether an individual is blind or continues to be blind as defined under the State plan, that there will be an initial examination or re-examination performed by either a physician skilled in the diseases of the eye or by an optometrist, whichever the individual so selects.

(i) No examination is necessary when both eyes are missing.

(ii) Where an initial eye examination or re-examination is necessary, the physician or optometrist conducting such examination will submit to the State agency a report thereof, on such forms and in such manner, as may be prescribed for such purpose. A determination whether the individual meets the State's definition of blindness under the State plan will be based upon a review of such eye examination report as provided for in paragraph (a)(3) of this section, and other information or additional examination reports as the State deems necessary.

(3) Provide that each initial eye examination report and any subsequent re-examination report will be reviewed by a State reviewing physician skilled in the diseases of the eye (e.g., an ophthalmologist or an eye, ear, nose and throat specialist). Such physician is responsible for making the agency's decision that the applicant or recipient does or does not meet the State's definition of blindness, and for determining if and when reexaminations are necessary in periodic reviews of eligibility, as required in §206.10(a)(9)(iii) of this chapter.

(b) *Federal financial participation*—(1) *Assistance payments.* Federal financial participation is available in assistance provided to or in behalf of any otherwise eligible person who is blind under the State's title X or XVI plan. Blindness may be considered as continuing until a determination by the reviewing physician establishes the fact that the recipient's vision has improved beyond the State's definition of blindness set forth under its State title of X or XVI plan.

(2) *Administrative expenses.* Federal financial participation is available in any expenditures incident to the eye examination necessary to determine whether an individual is blind.

[36 FR 3867, Feb. 27, 1971, as amended at 40 FR 25819, June 19, 1975]

§ 233.80 Disability.

(a) *State plan requirements.* A State plan under title XIV or XVI of the Social Security Act must:

(1) Contain a definition of permanently and totally disabled, showing that:

(i) "Permanently" is related to the duration of the impairment or combination of impairments; and

(ii) "Totally" is related to the degree of disability.

The following definition is recommended:

"Permanently and totally disabled" means that the individual has some permanent physical or mental impairment, disease, or loss, or combination thereof, this substantially precludes him from engaging in useful occupations within his competence, such as holding a job.

Under this definition:

"Permanently" refers to a condition which is not likely to improve or which will continue throughout the lifetime of the individual; it may be a condition which is not likely to respond to any known therapeutic procedures, or a condition which is likely to remain static or to become worse unless certain therapeutic measures are carried out, where treatment is unavailable, inadvisable, or is refused by the individual on a reasonable basis; "permanently" does not rule out the possibility of vocational rehabilitation or even possible recovery in light of future medical advances or changed prognosis; in this sense the term refers to a condition which continues indefinitely, as distinct from one which is temporary or transient;

"Totally" involves considerations in addition to those verified through the medical findings, such as age, training, skills, and work experience, and the probable functioning of the individual in his particular situation in light of his impairment; an individual's disability would usually be tested in relation to ability to engage in remunerative employment; the ability to keep house or to care for others would be the appropriate test for (and only for) individuals, such as housewives, who were engaged in this occupation prior to the disability and do not have a history of gainful employment; eligibility may continue, even after a period of rehabilitation and readjustment, if the individual's work capacity is still very considerably limited (in comparison with that of a normal person) in terms of such factors as the speed with which he can work, the amount he can produce in a given period of time, and the number of hours he is able to work.

(2) Provide for the review of each medical report and social history by technically competent persons—not less than a physician and a social worker qualified by professional training and pertinent experience—acting cooperatively, who are responsible for the agency's decision that the applicant does or does not meet the State's definition of permanent and total disability. Under this requirement:

(i) The medical report must include a substantiated diagnosis, based either on existing medical evidence or upon current medical examination;

(ii) The social history must contain sufficient information to make it possible to relate the medical findings to the activities of the "useful occupation" and to determine whether the individual is totally disabled, and

(iii) The review physician is responsible for setting dates for reexamination; the review team is responsible for reviewing reexamination reports in conjunction with the social data to determine whether disabled recipients whose health condition may improve continue to meet the State's definition of permanent and total disability.

(3) Provide for cooperative arrangements with related programs, such as vocational rehabilitation services.

(b) *Federal financial participation*—(1) *Assistance payments.* Federal financial participation is available in payments to or in behalf of any otherwise eligible individual who is permanently and totally disabled. Permanent and total disability may be considered as continuing until the review team establishes the fact that the recipient's disability is no longer within the State's definition of permanent and total disability.

(2) *Administrative expenses.* Federal financial participation is available in any expenditures incident to the medical examinations necessary to determine whether an individual is permanently and totally disabled.

[36 FR 3867, Feb. 27, 1971]

§ 233.90 Factors specific to AFDC.

(a) *State plan requirements.* A State plan under title IV-A of the Social Security Act shall provide that:

(1) The determination whether a child has been deprived of parental support or care by reason of the death, continued absence from the home, or physical or mental incapacity of a parent, or (if the State plan includes such cases) the unemployment of his or her parent who is the principal earner will be made only in relation to the child's natural or adoptive parent, or in relation to the child's stepparent who is married, under State law, to the child's natural or adoptive parent and is legally obligated to support the child under State law of general applicability which requires stepparents to support stepchildren to the same extent that natural or adoptive parents are required to support their children. Under this requirement, the inclusion in the family, or the presence in the home, of a "substitute parent" or "man-in-the-house" or any individual other than one described in this paragraph is not an acceptable basis for a finding of ineligibility or for assuming the availability of income by the State; and

(2) Where it has reason to believe that a child receiving aid is in an unsuitable environment because of known or suspected instances of physical or mental injury, sexual abuse or exploitation, or negligent treatment or maltreatment of such child, under circumstances which indicate the child's health or welfare is threatened, the State or local agency will:

(i) Bring such condition to the attention of a court, law-enforcement agency, or other appropriate agency in the State, providing whatever data it has with respect to the situation;

(ii) In reporting such conditions, use the same criteria as are used in the State for all other parents and children; and

(iii) Cooperate with the court or other agency in planning and implementing action in the best interest of the child.

(b) *Conditions for plan approval.* (1) A child may not be denied AFDC either initially or subsequently "because of the conditions of the home in which the child resides", or because the home is considered "unsuitable", unless "provision is otherwise made pursuant to a State statute for adequate care and assistance with respect to such child". (Section 404(b) of the Social Security Act.)

(2) An otherwise eligible child who is under the age of 18 years may not be denied AFDC, regardless of whether she attends school (unless she is required to participate in the JOBS program pursuant to § 250.30 and she is assigned to educational activities) or makes satisfactory grades.

(3) A state may elect to include in its AFDC program children age 18 who are full-time students in a secondary school, or in the equivalent level of vocational or technical training, and who may reasonably be expected to complete the program before reaching age 19.

(4)(i) A child may not be denied AFDC either initially or subsequently because a parent or other caretaker relative fails to cooperate with the child support agency in performing any of the activities needed to:

(A) Establish the paternity of a child born out of wedlock; or

(B) Obtain support from a person having a legal duty to support the child.

(ii) Any parent or caretaker relative who fails to so cooperate shall be treated in accordance with § 232.12 of this chapter.

(5) [Reserved]

(6) An otherwise eligible child may not be denied AFDC if a parent is mentally or physically incapacitated as defined in paragraph (c)(1)(iv) of this section.

(c) *Federal financial participation.* (1) Federal financial participation under title IV-A of the Social Security Act in payments with respect to a "dependent child," as defined in section 406(a) of the Act, is available within the following interpretations:

(i) *Needy child deprived by reason of.* The phrase "needy child * * * deprived * * * by reason of" requires that both need and deprivation of parental support or care exist in the individual case. The phrase encompasses the situation of any child who is in need and otherwise eligible, and whose parent—father or mother—either has died, has a physical or mental incapacity, or is continually absent from the home. This interpretation is equally applicable whether the parent was the chief bread winner or devoted himself or herself primarily to the care of the child, and whether or not the parents were married to each other. The determination whether a child has been deprived of parental support or care is made in relation to the child's natural parent or, as appropriate, the adoptive parent or stepparent described in paragraph (a) of this section.

(ii) *Death of a parent.* If either parent of a child is deceased, the child is deprived of parental support or care, and may, if he is in need and otherwise eligible, be included within the scope of the program.

(iii) *Continued absence of the parent from the home.* Continued absence of the parent from the home constitutes the reason for deprivation of parental support or care when the parent is out of the home, the nature of the absence is such as either to interrupt or to terminate the parent's functioning as a provider of maintenance, physical care, or guidance for the child, and the known or indefinite duration of the absence precludes counting on the parent's performance of the function of planning for the present support or care of the child. If these conditions exist, the parent may be absent for any reason, and may have left only recently or some time previously; except that a parent whose absence is occasioned solely by reason of the performance of active duty in the uniformed services of the United States (as defined in section 101(3) of Title 37, United States code) is not considered absent from the home. A parent who is a convicted offender but is permitted to live at home while serving a court-imposed sentence by performing unpaid public work or unpaid community service during the workday is considered absent from the home.

(iv) *"Physical or mental incapacity".* "Physical or mental incapacity" of a parent shall be deemed to exist when one parent has a physical or mental defect, illness, or impairment. The incapacity shall be supported by competent medical testimony and must be of such a debilitating nature as to reduce substantially or eliminate the parent's ability to support or care for the otherwise eligible child and be expected to last for a period of at least 30 days. In making the determination of ability to support, the agency shall take into account the limited employment opportunities of handicapped individuals.

A finding of eligibility for OASDI or SSI benefits, based on disability or blindness is acceptable proof of incapacity for AFDC purposes.

(v) *"Living with [a specified relative] in a place of residence maintained * * * as his * * * own home".* (A) A child may be considered to meet the requirement of living with one of the relatives specified in the Act if his home is with a parent or a person in one of the following groups:

(*1*) Any blood relative, including those of half-blood, and including first cousins, nephews, or nieces, and persons of preceding generations as denoted by prefixes of grand, great, or great-great.

(*2*) Stepfather, stepmother, stepbrother, and stepsister.

(*3*) Person who legally adopt a child or his parent as well as the natural and other legally adopted children of such persons, and other relatives of the adoptive parents in accordance with State law.

(*4*) Spouses of any persons named in the above groups even after the marriage is terminated by death or divorce.

(B) A home is the family setting maintained or in process of being established, as evidenced by assumption and continuation of responsibility for day to day care of the child by the relative with whom the child is living. A home exists so long as the relative exercises responsibility for the care and control of the child, even though either the child or the relative is temporarily absent from the customary family setting. Within this interpretation, the child is considered to be "living with" his relative even though:

(*1*) He is under the jurisdiction of the court (e.g., receiving probation services or protective supervision); or

(*2*) Legal custody is held by an agency that does not have physical possession of the child.

(2) Federal financial participation is available in:

(i) Initial payments made on behalf of a child who goes to live with a relative specified in section 406(a)(1) of the Social Security Act within 30 days of the receipt of the first payment, provided payments are not made for concurrent period for the same child in the home of another relative or as foster care under title IV-E;

(ii) Payments made for the entire month in the course of which a child leaves the home of a specified relative, provided payments are not made for a concurrent period for the same child in the home of another relative or as foster care under title IV-E; and

(iii) Payments made to persons acting for relatives specified in section 406(a)(1) of the Act in emergency situations that deprive the child of the care of the relative through whom he has been receiving aid, for a temporary period necessary to make and carry out plans for the child's continuing care and support.

(iv) At State option, (A) payments with respect to a pregnant woman with no other children receiving assistance, and additionally, at State option, (B) payments for the purpose of meeting special needs occasioned by or resulting from pregnancy both for the pregnant woman with no other children as well as for the pregnant woman receiving AFDC. However, for both paragraphs (c)(2)(iv) (A) and (B) of this section it must be medically verified that the child is expected to be born in the month such payments are made or within the three-month period following such month of payment, and who, if such child had been born and was living with her in the month of payment, would be eligible for aid to families with dependent children. Federal financial participation is not available to meet the needs of the unborn child. (Refer to Medicaid regulations at 42 CFR 435.115 for Medicaid coverage of pregnant women.)

(3) Federal financial participation (at the 50 percent rate) is available in any expenses incurred in establishing eligibility for AFDC, including expenses incident to obtaining necessary information to determine the existence of incapacity of a parent or pregnancy of a mother.

[36 FR 3868, Feb. 27, 1971, as amended at 39 FR 34038, Sept. 23, 1974; 40 FR 27156, June 26, 1975; 44 FR 12424, Mar. 7, 1979; 47 FR 5681, Feb. 5, 1982; 47 FR 41114, Sept. 17, 1982; 48 FR 28409, June 21, 1983; 51 FR 9206, Mar. 18, 1986; 52 FR 28824, Aug. 4, 1987; 54 FR 42243, Oct. 13, 1989; 58 FR 49218, Sept. 22, 1993; 59 FR 26142, May 19, 1994]

§ 233.100 Dependent children of unemployed parents.

(a) Requirements for State Plans. If a State wishes to provide AFDC for children of unemployed parents, the State plan under title IV-A of the Social Security Act must:

(1) Include a definition of an unemployed parent who is the principal earner which shall apply only to families determined to be needy in accordance with the provisions in § 233.20. Such definition must include any such parent who:

(i) Is employed less than 100 hours a month; or

(ii) Exceeds that standard for a particular month, if the work is intermittent and the excess is of a temporary nature as evidenced by the fact that he or she was under the 100-hour standard for the prior 2 months and is expected to be under the standard during the next month; except that at the option of the State, such definition need not include a principal earner who is unemployed because of participation in a labor dispute (other than a strike) or by reason of conduct or circumstances which result or would result in disqualification for unemployment compensation under the State's unemployment compensation law.

(2) Include a definition of a dependent child which shall include any child of an unemployed parent (as defined by the State pursuant to paragraph (a)(1) of this section) who would be, except for the fact that his parent is not dead,

absent from the home, or incapacitated, a dependent child under the State's plan approved under section 402 of the Act.

(3) Provide for payment of aid with respect to any dependent child (as defined by the State pursuant to paragraphs (a)(2) of this section) when the conditions set forth in paragraphs (a)(3) (i), (ii), (iii), and (vii) of this section are met:

(i) His or her parent who is the principal earner has been unemployed for at least 30 days prior to the receipt of such aid.

(ii) Such parent has not without good cause, within such 30-day period prior to the receipt of such aid, refused a bona fide offer of employment or training for employment. Before it is determined that such parent has refused a bona fide offer of employment or training for employment without good cause, the agency must make a determination that such an offer was actually made. (In the case of offers of employment made through the public employment or manpower agencies, the determination as to whether the offer was bona fide, or whether there was good cause to refuse it, will be made by that office or agency.) The parent must be given an opportunity to explain why such offer was not accepted. Questions with respect to the following factors must be resolved:

(*a*) That there was a definite offer of employment at wages meeting any applicable minimum wage requirements and which are customary for such work in the community;

(*b*) Any questions as to the parent's inability to engage in such employment for physical reasons or because he has no way to get to or from the particular job; and

(*c*) Any questions of working conditions, such as risks to health, safety, or lack of worker's compensation protection.

(iii) Such parent (*a*) has six or more quarters of work (as defined in paragraph (a)(3)(iv) of this section), within any 13-calendar-quarter period ending within 1 year prior to the application for such aid, or (*b*) within such 1-year period, received unemployment compensation under an unemployment compensation law of a State or of the United States, or was qualified under the terms of paragraph (a)(3)(v) of this section) for such compensation under the State's unemployment compensation law.

(iv) A "quarter of work" with respect to any individual means a period (of 3 consecutive calendar months ending on March 31, June 30, September 30, or December 31) in which he or she received earned income of not less than $50 (or which is a "quarter of coverage" as defined in section 213(a)(2) of the Act), or in which he or she participated in a community work experience program under section 409 of the Act or the work incentive program established under title IV-C of the Act.

(v) An individual shall be deemed "qualified" for unemployment compensation under the State's unemployment compensation law if he would have been eligible to receive such benefits upon filing application, or he performed work not covered by such law which, if it had been covered, would (together with any covered work he performed) have made him eligible to receive such benefits upon filing application.

(vi)(A) The "parent who is the principal earner" means, in the case of any child, whichever parent, in a home in which both parents of such child are living, earned the greater amount of income in the 24-month period the last month of which immediately precedes the month in which an application is filed for aid under this part on the basis of the unemployment of a parent. If the State cannot secure primary evidence of earnings for this period, the State shall designate the principal earner, using the best evidence available. The earnings of each parent are considered in determining the principal earner regardless of when their relationship began. The principal earner so defined remains the principal earner for each consecutive month for which the family receives such aid on the basis of such application. This requirement applies to both new applicants and current AFDC unemployed parent families who were eligible and receiving aid prior to October 1, 1981.

(B) If both parents earned an identical amount of income (or earned no income) in such 24-month period, the

State shall designate which parent shall be the principal earner.

(vii) The parent who is the principal earner (unless exempt under § 240.14) has met the requirements for participation in an employment search program under part 240 of this chapter.

(4) Provide for entering into cooperative arrangements with the State agency responsible for administering or supervising the administration of vocational education to assure maximum utilization of available public vocational education services and facilities in the State to encourage the retraining of individuals capable of being retrained.

(5) Provide for the denial of such aid to any such dependent child or the relative specified in section 406(a)(1) of the Act with whom such child is living,

(i) If and for so long as such child's parent, unless exempt under § 224.20, is not currently registered for the work incentive program or if exempt under § 224.20(b)(6), is not currently registered with a public employment office in the State, except that in a State with an approved JOBS plan under § 250.20, such child's parent, unless exempt under § 250.30(b), must be currently participating (or available for participation) in a program under part 250, or, if he is exempt under § 250.30(b)(5), must be registered with a public employment office in the State, and

(ii) With respect to any week for which such child's parent qualifies for unemployment compensation under an unemployment compensation law of the State or of the United States but refuses to apply for or accept such unemployment compensation, and

(iii) If the parent who is the principal earner (unless exempt under § 240.14) fails to meet the requirements for participation in a program of employment search established under part 240 of this chapter.

(6) Provide that within 30 days after the receipt of such aid, unemployed principal earners will be certified for participation in the Work Incentive program under part 224 or, if the State IV-A agency has an approved JOBS plan pursuant to § 250.20, will participate or apply for participation in a program under part 250 unless the program is not available in the area where the parent is living.

(b) [Reserved]

(c) *Federal financial participation.* (1) Federal financial participation is available in payments authorized in accordance with the State plan approved under section 402 of the Act as aid to families with dependent children with respect to a child.

(i) Who meets the requirements of section 406(a)(2) of the Act;

(ii) Who is living with any of the relatives specified in section 406(a)(1) of the Act in a place of residence maintained by one or more of such relatives as his (or their) own home;

(iii) Who has been deprived of parental support or care by reason of the fact that his or her parent who is the principal earner is employed less than 100 hours a month; or exceeds that standard for a particular month if his or her work is intermittent and the excess is of a temporary nature as evidenced by the fact that he or she was under the 100-hour standard for 2 prior months and is expected to be under the standard during the next month.

(iv) Whose parent who is the principal earner (*a*) has six or more quarters of work (as defined in paragraph (a)(3)(iv) of this section) within any 13-calendar-quarter period ending within 1 year prior to the application for such aid, (*b*) within such 1-year period, received unemployment compensation under an unemployment compensation law of a State or of the United States, or was qualified (under the terms of paragraph (a)(3)(v) of this section) for such compensation under the State's unemployment compensation law; and

(v) Whose parent who is the principal earner (*a*) is currently registered with the WIN program unless exempt or is registered with the public employment office in the State if exempt from WIN registration under § 224.20(b)(6) or because there is no WIN program in which he can effectively participate; and (*b*) has not refused to apply for or accept unemployment compensation with respect to any week for which such child's parent qualifies for unemployment compensation under an unemployment compensation law of a State or of the United States.

(2) The State may not include in its claim for Federal financial participation payments made as aid under the plan with respect to a child who meets the conditions set forth in paragraph (c)(1) of this section, where such payments were made.

(i) For any part of the 30-day period specified in paragraph (a)(3)(i) of this section;

(ii) For such 30-day period if during that period the parent refused without good cause a bona fide offer of employment or training for employment;

(iii) For any period beginning with the 31st day after receipt of aid, if and for as long as no action is taken during the period to certify the parent for participation in the Work Incentive program under part 224, or if the State IV-A agency has an approved JOBS plan pursuant to § 250.20, no action is taken during the period to undertake appropriate steps directed toward the participation of such parent in a program under part 250; and

(iv) For any part of the sanction period imposed under § 240.22 (for failure to meet the requirements for participation in the employment search program).

(d) For all States (other than Puerto Rico, American Samoa, Guam, and the Virgin Islands) the provisions of this section are suspended through September 30, 1998. For Puerto Rico, American Samoa, Guam, and the Virgin Islands, the provisions of this section are suspended from October 1, 1992, through September 30, 1998.

[34 FR 1146, Jan. 24, 1969, as amended at 36 FR 13604, July 22, 1971; 38 FR 18549, July 12, 1973; 38 FR 26608, Sept. 24, 1973; 46 FR 46769, Sept. 21, 1981; 47 FR 5681, Feb. 5, 1982; 47 FR 41114, Sept. 17, 1982; 47 FR 43383, Oct. 1, 1982; 48 FR 28409, June 21, 1983; 51 FR 9206, Mar. 18, 1986; 54 FR 42244, Oct. 13, 1989; 57 FR 30426, July 9, 1992]

§ 233.101 Dependent children of unemployed parents.

(a) Requirements for State Plans. Effective October 1, 1990 (for Puerto Rico, American Samoa, Guam, and the Virgin Islands, October 1, 1992), a State plan must provide for payment of AFDC for children of unemployed parents. A State plan under title IV-A for payment of such aid must:

(1) Include a definition of an unemployed parent who is the principal earner which shall apply only to families determined to be needy in accordance with the provisions in § 233.20 of this part. Such definition must have a reasonable standard for measuring unemployment and, at a minimum, include any such parent who:

(i) Is employed less than 100 hours a month; or

(ii) Exceeds that standard for a particular month, if the work is intermittent and the excess is of a temporary nature as evidenced by the fact that he or she was under the 100-hour standard for the prior 2 months and is expected to be under the standard during the next month; except that at the option of the State, such definition need not include a principal earner who is unemployed because of participation in a labor dispute (other than a strike) or by reason of conduct or circumstances which result or would result in disqualification for unemployment compensation under the State's unemployment compensation law.

(2) Include a definition of a dependent child which shall include any child of an unemployed parent (as defined by the State pursuant to paragraph (a)(1) of this section) who would be, except for the fact that his parent is not dead, absent from the home, or incapacitated, a dependent child under the State's plan approved under section 402 of the Act.

(3) Provide for payment of aid with respect to any dependent child (as defined by the State pursuant to paragraph (a)(2) of this section) when the conditions set forth in paragraphs (a)(3)(i), (a)(3)(ii), and (a)(3)(iii) of this section are met.

(i) His or her parent who is the principal earner has been unemployed for at least 30 days prior to the receipt of such aid;

(ii) Such parent has not without good cause, within such 30-day period prior to the receipt of such aid, refused a bona fide offer of employment or training for employment. Before it is determined that such parent has refused a bona fide offer of employment or training for employment without good cause, the agency must make a determination that such offer was actually made. (In the case of offers of employment made through the public employment or manpower agencies, the determination as to whether the offer was bona fide, or whether there was good cause to refuse it, shall be made by the title IV-A agency. The IV-A agency may accept the recommendations of such agencies.) The parent must be given an opportunity to explain why such offer was not accepted. Questions with respect to the following factors must be resolved:

(A) That there was a definite offer of employment at wages meeting any applicable minimum wage requirements and which are customary for such work in the community;

(B) Any questions as to the parent's inability to engage in such employment for physical reasons or because he has no way to get to or from the particular job; and

(C) Any questions of working conditions, such as risks to health, safety, or lack of worker's compensation protection.

(iii) Such parent:

(A) Has six or more quarters of work (as defined in paragraph (a)(3)(iv) of this section), within any 13-calendar-quarter period ending within one year prior to the application for such aid, or

(B) Within such 1-year period, received unemployment compensation under an unemployment compensation law of a State or of the United States, or was qualified under the terms of paragraph (a)(3)(v) of this section for such compensation under the State's unemployment compensation law.

(iv) A "quarter of work" with respect to any individual means a period (of 3 consecutive calendar months ending on March 31, June 30, September 30, or December 31):

(A) In which an individual received earned income of not less than $50 (or which is a "quarter of coverage" as defined in section 213(a)(2) of the Social Security Act) or participated in a program under part 250 of this chapter; or

(B) At State option (as specified in the plan), in one or more subdivisions of the State, in which he or she attended, full-time, an elementary school, a secondary school, or a vocational or technical training course that is designed to prepare the individual for gainful employment, or in which the individual participated in an educational or training program established under the Job Training Partnership Act, provided that an individual may qualify for no more than four quarters of work under this paragraph for purposes of the requirement set forth in paragraph (a)(3)(iii)(A) of this section; and

(C) A calendar quarter ending before October 1990 in which an individual participated in CWEP under section 409 of the Social Security Act or the WIN program established under title IV-C of the Social Security Act (as in effect for a State immediately before the effective date of that State's JOBS program).

(v) An individual shall be deemed "qualified" for unemployment compensation under the State's unemployment compensation law if he or she would have been eligible to receive such benefits upon filing an application, or he performed work not covered by such law, which, if it had been covered, would (together with any covered work he performed) have made him eligible to receive such benefits upon filing an application.

(vi)(A) The "parent who is the principal earner" means, in the case of any child, whichever parent, in a home in which both parents of such child are living, earned the greater amount of income in the 24-month period the last month of which immediately precedes the month in which an application is filed for aid under this part on the basis of the unemployment of a parent. If the State cannot secure primary evidence of earnings for this period, the State shall designate the principal earner, using the best evidence available. The earnings of each parent are considered in determining the principal earner regardless of when their relationship began. The principal earner so defined remains the principal earner for each consecutive month for which the family receives such aid on the basis of such application. This requirement applies to both new applicants and current AFDC unemployed parent families who were eligible and receiving aid prior to October 1, 1981.

(B) If both parents earned an identical amount of income (or earned no income) in such 24-month period, the State shall designate which parent shall be the principal earner.

(4) Provide for entering into cooperative arrangements with the State agency responsible for administering or supervising the administration of vocational education to assure maximum utilization of available public vocational education services and facilities in the State to encourage the retraining of individuals capable of being retrained.

(5) Provide that the needs of the child's parent(s) shall not be taken into account in determining the needs and amount of assistance of the child's family:

(i) If and for so long as such child's parent(s), unless exempt under § 250.30(b) of this chapter, is not currently participating (or available for participation) in a program under part 250 of this chapter or, if they are exempt under § 250.30(b)(5) of this chapter (or because a JOBS program has not been established in the subdivision where they reside or they reside in a JOBS subdivision but there is no appropriate JOBS activity in which they can participate), are not registered with a public employment office in the State, and

(ii) With respect to any week for which such child's parent qualifies for unemployment compensation under an unemployment compensation law of the State or of the United States but refuses to apply for or accept such unemployment compensation.

(6) Provide that medical assistance will be furnished under the State's approved plan under title XIX during any month in which an otherwise eligible individual is denied assistance solely by reason of the time limitation provided under paragraph (b)(3) of this section.

(b) *State Plan Options.* A State plan under title IV-A may:

(1) Require the principal earner or both parents to participate in an activity in the JOBS program under part 250 of this chapter, subject to the limitations and conditions of part 250 of this chapter, provided that the participation of each parent in all required activities under the JOBS program does not exceed 40 hours per week, per parent.

(2) Provide cash assistance after the performance of assigned program activities by parents required to participate in an activity in the JOBS program under part 250 of this chapter (as provided in paragraph (b)(1) of this section) so long as the State:

(i) Makes assistance payments at regular intervals at least monthly,

(ii) Prescribes a set of criteria which defines goals or standards for each assigned activity in the JOBS program which must be completed by the participant prior to payment, and

(iii) Prior to, or concurrent with, assignment to an activity, notifies the participant of the prescribed goals or standards and that payment for a period will be withheld unless performance of each assigned activity for that period is completed.

(3) Provide for a State to operate a payment after performance system under which a family is issued an assistance payment after the applicable family member has successfully completed her obligation to participate in JOBS for a specific period. If the applicable family member fails without good cause to satisfy the obligation, the State may:

(i) Impose a sanction in accordance with the JOBS program rules at §§ 250.34, 250.35 and 250.36 of this chapter;

(ii) Reduce the family's assistance payment to which the specific period applies by the amount of the payment attributable to the family member for that period or do not make the payment to the family; or

(iii) Reduce the family's assistance payment to which the specific period applies (or the amount of the payment attributable to the family member for that period) in proportion to the number of required hours that were not completed.

For States that elect to implement paragraphs (b)(3) (ii) or (iii) of this section, the fair hearing requirements set forth at § 205.10(a)(4)(ii)(K) of this chapter apply.

(4) Limit the number of months that a family may receive AFDC-UP under this section when the following conditions are met:

(i) The State did not have on September 26, 1988, an approved AFDC-UP program under section 407 of the Social Security Act.

(ii) The family received such aid (on the basis of the unemployment of the parent who is the principal earner) in at least 6 of the preceding 12 months.

(iii) The State has in effect a program (described in the plan) for providing education, training, and employment services to assist parents in preparing for and obtaining employment throughout the year. Such a program may include education, training and employment activities under the JOBS program which are provided in part 250 of this chapter or under a State-designed program which provides:

(A) Education and instruction for individuals who have not graduated from a secondary school or obtained an equivalent degree,

(B) Training whereby an individual acquires market-oriented skills necessary for self-support, and

(C) Employment services which seek to place individuals in jobs.

(iv) The State must guarantee child care necessary for an individual to participate in an approved, State-designed, non-JOBS program. The regulations at part 255 of this chapter apply to such care.

(v) The State has the option of providing necessary supportive services associated with an individual's participation in a State-designed, non-JOBS program. Federal financial participation is available under sections 403 (k) and (l) of the Social Security Act. The regulations at part 255 of this chapter apply to such supportive services.

(vi) The State must inform an AFDC-UP family at the time of application that AFDC-UP cash assistance will terminate due to a time limitation, that any family with a child who is (or becomes) deprived due to the death, continued absence, or incapacity of a parent may receive cash assistance under the AFDC program during the time limitation for AFDC-UP, and that a program of training, education, and employment services is available to prepare the family to become self-supporting.

(vii) Prior to termination due to a time limitation, the State must notify an AFDC-UP recipient family of the earliest month that it may receive AFDC-UP cash assistance again. This notification may be included in the notice of proposed action which is required pursuant to § 205.10(a)(4) of this chapter. To receive assistance again, the family must make a new application.

(viii) In establishing eligibility upon re-application following months of nonpayment due to the time limitation, an otherwise eligible family that does not receive aid in a month solely by reason of the option to limit assistance under this paragraph shall be deemed, for purposes of determining the period under paragraph (a)(3)(iii)(A) of this section, to be receiving AFDC-UP cash assistance in that month. This provision also applies if, at the time of the family's original application for assistance, eligibility was established based on the provisions of paragraph (a)(3)(iii)(B) of this section, but eligibility could have been established based on the provisions of paragraph (a)(3)(iii)(A) of this section.

(c) *Federal Financial Participation.* (1) Federal financial participation is available for payments authorized in accordance with the State plan approved under section 402 of the Act as aid to families with dependent children with respect to a child:

(i) Who meets the requirements of section 406(a)(2) of the Act;

(ii) Who is living with any of the relatives specified in section 406(a)(1) of the Act in a place of residence maintained by one or more of such relatives as his (or their) own home;

(iii) Who has been deprived of parental support or care by reason of the fact that his or her parent who is the principal earner is employed less than 100 hours a month; or exceeds that standard for a particular month if his or her work is intermittent and the excess is of a temporary nature as evidenced by the fact that he or she was under the 100-hour standard for 2 prior months and is expected to be under the standard during the next month;

(iv) Whose parent who is the principal earner:

(A) Has six or more quarters of work (as defined in paragraph (a)(3)(iv) of this section) within any 13-calendar-quarter period ending within 1 year prior to the application for such aid,

(B) Within such 1-year period, received unemployment compensation under an unemployment compensation law of a State or of the United States, or was qualified (under the terms of paragraph (a)(3)(v) of this section) for such compensation under the State's unemployment compensation law; and

(v) Whose parent who is the principal earner:

(A) Is currently participating in or available to participate in an activity in the JOBS program under part 250 of this chapter, unless exempt, or is registered with the public employment office in the State if exempt from the JOBS program under § 250.30(b)(5) of this chapter; and

(B) Has not refused to apply for or accept unemployment compensation with respect to any week for which such child's parent qualifies for unemployment compensation under an unemployment compensation law of the State or of the United States.

(2) The State may not include in its claim for Federal financial participation payments made as aid under the plan with respect to a child who meets the conditions set forth in paragraph (c)(1) of this section, where such payments were made:

(i) For any part of the 30-day period specified in paragraph (a)(3)(i) of this section;

(ii) For such 30-day period if during that period the parent refused without good cause a bona fide offer of employment or training for employment;

(iii) For any period beginning with the 31st day after the receipt of aid, if and for as long as no action is taken during the period to undertake appropriate steps directed toward the participation of the parent who is the principal earner in a program under part 250 of this chapter;

(iv) To the extent that such payments are made to meet the need of an individual who is subject to a sanction imposed, under part 250 of this chapter (for failure to meet the requirements for participation in the JOBS program).

(3) Federal financial participation is available for child care and supportive services expenditures associated with participation in an approved State-designed program (as provided in paragraph (b)(3)(iii) of this section) under titles IV-A and IV-F of the Act respectively. However, Federal financial participation is not available for any other costs, program or administrative, associated with State-designed programs.

(d) For all States (other than Puerto Rico, American Samoa, Guam, and the Virgin Islands) the provisions of this section are in effect through September 30, 1998. For Puerto Rico, American Samoa, Guam, and the Virgin Islands, the provisions of this section are in effect from October 1, 1992, through September 30, 1998.

[57 FR 30426, July 9, 1992, as amended at 63 FR 42274, Aug. 7, 1998]

§ 233.106 Denial of AFDC benefits to strikers.

(a) *Condition for plan approval.* A State plan under title IV-A of the Social Security Act must:

(1) Provide that participation in a strike shall not constitute good cause to leave, or to refuse to seek or accept, employment.

(2)(i) Provide for the denial of AFDC benefits to any family for any month in which any caretaker relative with whom the child is living is, on the last day of such month, participating in a strike; and

(ii) Provide that no individual's needs shall be included in determining the amount of aid payable for any month to a family under the plan if, on the last day of such month, such individual is participating in a strike.

(b) *Definitions.* (1) The State must define "strike" by using the National Labor Relations Board definition (29 U.S.C. 142(2)) or another definition of the term that is currently in State law.

(2) The State must define the term "participating in a strike."

(3) For purposes of paragraph (a)(2)(i) of this section, "caretaker relative" means any natural or adoptive parent.

[47 FR 5682, Feb. 5, 1982]

§ 233.107 Restriction in payment to households headed by a minor parent.

(a) *State plan requirements.* A State in its title IV-A State plan may provide that a minor parent and the dependent child in his or her care must reside in the household of a parent, legal guardian, or other adult relative, or in an adult-supervised supportive living arrangement in order to receive, AFDC unless:

(1) The minor parent has no living parent or legal guardian whose whereabouts is known;

(2) No living parent or legal guardian of the minor parent allows the minor parent to live in his or her home;

(3) The minor parent lived apart from his or her own parent or legal guardian for a period of at least one year before either the birth of the dependent child or the parent's having made application for AFDC;

(4) The physical or emotional health or safety of the minor parent or dependent child would be jeopardized if they resided in the same residence with the minor parent's parent or legal guardian;

(5) There is otherwise good cause for the minor parent and dependent child to receive assistance while living apart from the minor parent's parent, legal guardian, or other adult relative, or an adult-supervised supportive living arrangement.

(b) *Allegations.* If a minor parent makes allegations supporting the conclusion that paragraph (a)(4) of this section applies, the State agency shall determine whether it is justified.

(c) *Good Cause.* The circumstances justifying a determination of good cause must be set forth in the State plan.

(d) *Protective Payments.* When a minor parent and his or her dependent child are required to live with the minor parent's parent, legal guardian, or other adult relative, or in an adult-supervised supportive living arrangement, then AFDC is paid (where possible) in the form of a protective payment.

(e) *Definitions:* For purposes of this section:

(1) A *minor parent* is an individual who (i) is under the age of 18, (ii) has never been married, and (iii) is either the natural parent of a dependent child living in the same household or eligible for assistance paid under the State plan to a pregnant woman as provided in § 233.90(c)(2)(iv) of this part.

(2) A *household of a parent, legal guardian, or other adult relatives* means the place of residence of (i) a natural or adoptive parent or a stepparent, or (ii) a legal guardian as defined by the State, or (iii) another individual who is age 18 or over and related to the minor parent as specified in § 233.90(c)(1)(v) of this part provided that the residence is maintained as a home for the minor parent and child as provided in § 233.90(c)(1)(v)(B) of this part.

(3) *An adult-supervised supportive living arrangement* means a private family setting or other living arrangement (not including a public institution), which, as determined by the State, is maintained as a family setting, as evidenced by the assumption of responsibility for the care and control of the minor parent and dependent child or the provision of supportive services, such as counseling, guidance, or supervision. For example, foster homes and maternity homes are "adult-supervised supportive living arrangements."

(f) *Notice Requirements.* Minor applicants shall be informed about the eligibility requirements and their rights and obligations consistent with the provisions at § 206.10(a)(2)(i). For example, a State may wish to: (1) Advise the minor of the possible exemptions and specifically ask whether one or more of these exemptions is applicable; and (2) assist the minor in attaining the necessary verifications if one or more of these exemptions is alleged.

[57 FR 30428, July 9, 1992]

§ 233.110 Foster care maintenance and adoption assistance.

(a) *State plan requirements.* A State plan under title IV-A of the Social Security Act must provide that the State has in effect a plan approved under part E, title IV of the Social Security Act, and operates a foster care maintenance and adoption assistance program in conformity with such a plan.

(b) [Reserved]

[51 FR 9206, Mar. 18, 1986]

§ 233.145 Expiration of medical assistance programs under titles I, IV-A, X, XIV and XVI of the Social Security Act.

(a) Under the provisions of section 121(b) of Pub. L. 89–97, enacted July 30,

1965, no payment may be made to any State under title I, IV-A, X, XIV or XVI of the Social Security Act for aid or assistance in the form of medical or any other type of remedial care for any period after December 31, 1969. However, these provisions do not affect the availability of Federal financial participation in the cost of medical or remedial care furnished under title IV-A of the Act (pursuant to sections 403(a)(5) and 406(e)) of the Act, as emergency assistance to needy families with children (see § 233.120 of this part), subject to the provisions of paragraph (c)[1] of this section. Federal financial participation in vendor payments for medical care and services is not otherwise available except under title XIX of the Act.

(b) Under the provisions of section 4(c) of Pub. L. 92–223, enacted December 28, 1971, and the provisions of section 292 of Pub. L. 92–603, enacted October 30, 1972:

(1) In the case of any State which on January 1, 1972, had in effect a State plan approved under title XIX of the Social Security Act, section 1121 of the Act authorizing payments under title I, X, XIV, or XVI of the Act for assistance in the form of institutional services in intermediate care facilities is rescinded; and

(2) In the case of any State which on January 1, 1972, did not have in effect a State plan approved under title XIX of the Act, Federal financial participation is available in assistance in the form of institutional services in intermediate care facilities pursuant to section 1121 of the Act and under the provisions of § 234.130 of this chapter until the first day of the first month after January 1, 1972, that the State has in effect a State plan approved under title XIX.

(c)(1) Under the provisions of section 249D of Pub. L. 92–603, enacted October 30, 1972, Federal matching is not available for any portion of any payment by any State under titles I, IV-A, X, XIV, or XVI of the Social Security Act for or on account of any medical or any other type of remedial care provided by an institution to any individual as an inpatient thereof, in the case of any State which has a plan approved under title XIX of such Act, if such care is (or could be provided, under a State plan approved under title XIX of such Act, by an institution certified under such title XIX. The effective date of this proposed provision will be the date of publication of the final regulation in the FEDERAL REGISTER.

(2) For purposes of this paragraph,

(i) An institution (see § 233.60(b)(1) of this chapter) is considered to provide medical or remedial care if it provides any care or service beyond room and board because of the physical or mental condition (or both) of its inpatients;

(ii) An inpatient is an individual who is living in an institution which provides medical or remedial care and who is receiving care or service beyond room and board because of his physical or mental condition (or both).

(iii) Federal financial participation is not available for any portion of the payment for care of an inpatient. It is immaterial whether such payment is made as a vendor payment or as a money payment or other cash assistance payment. It is also immaterial whether the payment is divided into components, such as separate amounts or payments for room and board, and for care or services beyond room and board, or whether the payment is considered to meet "basic" needs or "special" needs. If, however, a money payment (or protective payment) is made to an individual who is living in an institution, and such payment does not exceed a reasonable rate for room, board and laundry for individuals not living in their own homes, and no additional payment is made for such individual's care in the institution, Federal financial participation is available in the money payment (or protective payment) since the individual may spend the funds at his discretion and obtain room and board at the place of his choice.

(iv) Federal financial participation is available in cash assistance payments to meet the needs of an inpatient for specific medical services, such as dental care or prescription drugs, which generally are not delivered in an institutional setting and in fact are not

[1] See notice published Aug. 29, 1973 (38 FR 23337).

provided by the institution to the inpatient, provided that such services are not available to the individual under the State's approved title XIX plan.

[38 FR 26379, Sept. 20, 1973, as amended at 38 FR 32912, Nov. 29, 1973]

PART 234—FINANCIAL ASSISTANCE TO INDIVIDUALS

Sec.

AUTHORITY: 42 U.S.C. 602, 603, 606, and 1302.

§234.11 Assistance in the form of money payments.

(a) Federal financial participation is available in money payments made under a State plan under title I, IV-A, X, XIV, or XVI of the Social Security Act to eligible families and individuals. Money payments are payments in cash, checks, or warrants immediately redeemable at par, made to the grantee or his legal representative with no restrictions imposed by the agency on the use of funds by the individual.

(b) [Reserved]

[36 FR 22238, Nov. 23, 1971, as amended at 51 FR 9206, Mar. 18, 1986]

§234.60 Protective, vendor and two-party payments for dependent children.

(a) *State plan requirements.* (1) If a State plan for AFDC under title IV-A of the Social Security Act provides for protective, vendor and two-party payments for cases other than failure to participate in the Job Opportunities and Basic Skills Training (JOBS) Program under §250.34(d), or failure by the caretaker relative to meet the eligibility requirements of §232.11, §232.12, or §232.13 of this chapter. It must meet the requirements in paragraphs (a) (2) through (11) of this section. In addition, the plan may provide for protective, vendor, and two-party payments at the request of recipients as provided in paragraph (a)(14) of this section.

(2)(i) Methods will be in effect to identify children whose relatives have demonstrated such an inability to manage funds that payments to the relative have not been or are not currently used in the best interest of the child. This means that the relative has misused funds to such an extent that allowing him or her to manage the AFDC grant is a threat to the health or safety of the child.

(ii) States will establish criteria to determine if mismanagement exists. Under this provision, States may elect to use as one criterion a presumption of mismanagement based on a recipient's nonpayment of rent.

(iii) Under State agency procedures, the recipient shall be notified whenever a creditor requests a protective, vendor, or two-party payment for mismangement on the basis of nonpayment of bills.

(iv) The recipient shall be notified by the agency of a decision not to use a protective, vendor, or two-party payment if such payment has been requested by a creditor.

(v) A statement of the specific reasons that demonstrate the need for making protective, vendor, and two-party payments must be placed in the file of the child involved.

(3) Criteria will be established to identify the circumstances under which protective, vendor, or two-party payments will be made in whole or in part to:

(i) Another individual who is interested in or concerned with the welfare of the child or relative; or

(ii) A person or persons furnishing food, living accommodations or other goods, services, or items to or for the child, relative, or essential person.

(4) Procedures will be established for making protective, vendor, or two-party payments. Under this provision, part of the payment may be made to the family and part may be made to a protective payee or to a vendor, or part may be made in the form of two-party payments, i.e., checks which are drawn jointly to the order of the recipient and the person furnishing goods, services,

or items and negotiable only upon endorsement by both the recipient and the other person.

(5)–(6) [Reserved]

(7) Standards will be established for selection:

(i) Of protective payees, who are interested in or concerned with the recepient's welfare, to act for the recipient in receiving and managing assistance, with the selection of a protective payee being made by the recipient, or with his participation and consent, to the extent possible. If it is in the best interest of the recipient for a staff member of a private agency, of the public welfare department, or of any other appropriate organization to serve as a protective payee, such selection will be made preferably from the staff of an agency or that part of the agency providing protective services for families; and the public welfare department will employ such additional staff as may be necessary to provide protective payees. The selection will not include: The executive head of the agency administering public assistance; the person determining financial eligibility for the family; special investigative or resource staff; or staff handling fiscal processes related to the recipient; or landlords, grocers, or other vendors of goods, services, or items dealing directly with the recipient.

(ii) Of such persons providing goods, services, or items with the selection of such persons being made by the recipient, or with his participation and consent, to the extent possible.

(8) The agency will undertake and continue special efforts to develop greater ability on the part of the relative to manage funds in such manner as to protect the welfare of the family.

(9) Review will be made as frequently as indicated by the individual's circumstances, and at least once every 12 months, of:

(i) The need for protective, vendor, and two-party payments; and

(ii) The way in which a protective payee's responsibilities are carried out.

(10) Provision will be made for termination of protective payments, or payments to a person furnishing goods or services, as follows:

(i) When relatives are considered able to manage funds in the best interest of the child, there will be a return to money payment status.

(ii) When it appears that need for protective, vendor, or two-party payments will continue or is likely to continue beyond 2 years because all efforts have not resulted in sufficiently improved use of assistance in behalf of the child, judicial appointment of a guardian or other legal representative will be sought and such payments will terminate when the appointment has been made.

(11)(i) Opportunity for a fair hearing pursuant to § 205.10 will be given to any individual claiming assistance in relation to the determination:

(A) That a protective, vendor, and two-party payment should be made or continued.

(B) As to the payee selected.

(ii) In cases where the agency has elected the option to presume mismanagement based on a recipient's nonpayment of rent pursuant to paragraph (a)(2)(ii), the agency may also elect the option to provide the opportunity for a fair hearing pursuant to § 205.10 either before or after the manner or form of payment has been changed for these cases.

(12) In cases where an individual is sanctioned for failure to participate in WIN, employment search, CWEP, or JOBS, the State plan must provide that when protective or vendor payments are made pursuant to §§ 224.52(a)(1), 238.22, 240.22(a)(1), 240.22(b)(1) and 250.34(d) of this chapter, only paragraphs (a)(7), (a)(9)(ii), and (a)(11)(i) and (ii) of this section will be applicable. Under these circumstances, when protective payments are made, the entire payment will be made to the protective payee; and when vendor payments are made, at least the greater part of the payment will be through this method. However, if after making all reasonable efforts, the State agency is unable to locate an appropriate individual to whom protective payments can be made, the State may continue to make payments on behalf of the remaining members of the assistance unit to the sanctioned caretaker relative. Provision will be made for termination of protective payments, or payments to a person furnishing goods or

services, with return to money payment status when adults who refused training, employment, or participation in employment search without good cause either accept training, employment, or employment search or agree to do so. In the case of continuing refusal of the relative to participate, payments will be continued for the children in the home in accordance with this paragraph.

(13) For cases in which a caretaker relative fails to meet the eligibility requirements of § 232.11, § 232.12, or § 232.13 of this chapter by failing to assign rights to support or cooperate in determining paternity, securing support, or identifying and providing information to assist the State in pursuing third party liability for medical services, the State plan must provide that only the requirements of paragraphs (a)(7) and (9)(ii) of this section will be applicable. For such cases, the entire amount of the assistance payment will be in the form of protective or vendor payments. These protective or vendor payments will be terminated, with return to money payment status, only upon compliance by the caretaker relative with the eligibility requirements of §§ 232.11, 232.12, and 232.13 of this chapter. However, if after making reasonable efforts, the State agency is unable to locate an appropriate individual to whom protective payments can be made, the State may continue to make payments to the sanctioned caretaker relative on behalf of the remaining members of the assistance unit.

(14) If the plan provides for protective, vendor, or two-party payments:

(i) The State may use any combination of protective, vendor, or two-party payments (at the request of the recipient),

(ii) The request must be in writing from the recipient to whom payment would otherwise be made in an unrestricted manner and must be recorded or retained in the case file, and

(iii) The restriction will be discontinued promptly upon the written request of the recipient who initiated it.

(b) *Federal financial participation.* Federal financial participation is available in payments which otherwise qualify as money payments with respect to an eligible dependent child, but which are made as protective, vendor or two-party payments under this section. Payrolls must identify protective, vendor, or two-party payments either by use of a separate payroll for these cases or by using a special identifying code or symbol on the regular payroll. The payment must be supported by an authorization of award through amendment of an existing authorization document for each case or by preparation of a separate authorization document. In either instance, the authorization document must be a formal agency record signed by a responsible agency official, showing the name of each eligible child and relative, the amount of payment authorized and the name of the protective, vendor or two-party payee.

[37 FR 9025, May 4, 1972, as amended at 37 FR 12202, June 20, 1972; 45 FR 20480, Mar. 28, 1980; 47 FR 5682, Feb. 5, 1982; 49 FR 35603, Sept. 10, 1984; 51 FR 9206, Mar. 18, 1986; 54 FR 42244, Oct. 13, 1989; 56 FR 8932, Mar. 4, 1991; 57 FR 30160, July 8, 1992]

§ 234.70 Protective payments for the aged, blind, or disabled.

(a) *State plan requirements.* If a State plan for OAA, AB, APTD, or AABD under the Social Security Act includes provisions for protective payments, the State plan must provide that:

(1) Methods will be in effect to determine that needy individuals have, by reason of physical or mental condition, such inability to manage funds that making payment to them would be contrary to their welfare; such methods to include medical or psychological evaluations, or other reports of physical or mental conditions including observation of gross conditions such as extensive paralysis, serious mental retardation, continued disorientation, or severe memory loss.

(2) There will be responsibility to assure referral to social services for appropriate action to protect recipients where problems and needs for services and care of the recipients are manifestly beyond the ability of the protective payee to handle. (See paragraph (a)(5) of this section.)

(3) Standards will be established for selection of protective payees who are

interested in or concerned with the individual's welfare, to act for the individual in receiving and managing assistance, with the selection of a protective payee being made by the individual, or with his participation and consent, to the extent possible. If it is in the best interest of the individual for a staff member of a private agency, of the public welfare department, or of any other appropriate organization to serve as a protective payee, such selection will be made preferably from the staff of an agency or that part of the agency providing protective services for families or for the disabled or aged group of which the recipient is a member; and such staff of the public welfare department will be utilized only to the extent that the department has adequate staff for this purpose. The selection will not include: The executive head of the agency administering public assistance; the person determining financial eligibility for the individual; special investigative or resource staff, or staff handling fiscal processes related to the recipient; or landlords, grocers, or other vendors of goods or services dealing directly with the recipient—such as the proprietor, administrator or fiscal agent of a nursing home, or social care, medical or nonmedical institution, except for the superintendent of a public institution for mental diseases or a public institution for the mentally retarded, or the designee of such superintendent, when no other suitable protective payee can be found and there are appropriate staff available to assist the superintendent in carrying out the protective payment function.

(4) Protective payments will be made only in cases in which the assistance payment, with other available income, meets all the needs of the individual, using the State's standards for assistance for the pertinent program, not standards for protective payment cases only.

(5) The agency will undertake and continue special efforts to protect the welfare of such individuals and to improve, to the extent possible, their capacity for self-care and to manage funds.

(6) Reconsideration of the need for protective payments and the way in which a protective payee's responsibilities are carried out will be as frequent as indicated by the individual's circumstances and at least every 6 months.

(7) Provision will be made for appropriate termination of protective payments as follows:

(i) When individuals are considered able to manage funds in their best interest, there will be a return to money payment status.

(ii) When a judicial appointment of a guardian or other legal representative appears to serve the best interest of the individual, such appointment will be sought and the protective payment will terminate when the appointment has been made.

(8) Opportunity for a fair hearing will be given to any individual claiming assistance in relation to the determination that a protective payment should be made or continued, and in relation to the payee selected.

(b) *Federal financial participation.* Federal financial participation is available for payments, which otherwise qualify as money payments with respect to a needy individual, but which are made to a protective payee under paragraph (a)(3) of this section. The payment must be supported by an authorization of award through amendment of an existing authorization document for such case or by preparation of a separate authorization document. In either instance, the authorization document must be a formal agency record signed by a responsible agency official showing the name of each eligible individual, the amount of payment authorized and the name of the protective payee. Payrolls must identify protective payment cases either by use of a separate payroll for these cases or by using a special identifying code or symbol on the regular payroll.

[34 FR 1323, Jan. 28, 1969]

§ 234.75 Rent payments to public housing agencies.

At the option of a State, if its plan approved under title I, X, XIV, or XVI of the Social Security Act so provides, Federal financial participation under such title is available in rent payments made directly to a public housing agency on behalf of a recipient or a group or groups of recipients of OAA, AB, APTD, or AABD. Such Federal financial participation is available in rent payments only to the extent that they do not exceed the amount included for rent under the State's standard of assistance or the amount of rent due under applicable law, whichever is less.

[38 FR 26380, Sept. 20, 1973]

§ 234.120 Federal financial participation.

Federal financial participation is available in assistance payments made under a State plan under title I, IV-A, X, XIV, or XVI of the Social Security Act to any family or individual for periods beginning with the month in which they meet all eligibility conditions under the plan and in which an application has been received by the agency. Such assistance payments include:

(a) Money payments (titles I, IV-A, X, XIV, and XVI, see § 234.11 of this chapter);

(b) Protective and vendor payments for dependent children (title IV-A, see § 234.60 of this chapter);

(c) Protective payments for the aged, blind, or disabled (titles I, X, XIV, and XVI, see § 234.70 of this chapter);

(d) AFDC foster care payments (title IV-A, see § 233.110 of this chapter);

(e) Vendor payments for institutional services in intermediate care facilities (titles I, X, XIV, and XVI), but only in a State that did not, as of January 1, 1972, have an approved plan under title XIX of the act, and only until such State has such a plan in effect (see § 234.130 of this chapter);

(f) Emergency assistance to needy families with children (title IV-A, see § 233.120 of this chapter);

(g) Vendor payments for home repairs (titles I, IV-A, X, XIV, and XVI, see § 233.20(c) of this chapter); and

(h) Rent payments to public housing agencies (titles I, X, XIV, and XVI, see § 234.75 of this chapter).

[38 FR 26380, Sept. 20, 1973]

§ 234.130 Assistance in the form of institutional services in intermediate care facilities.

(a) *Applicability and State plan requirements.* A State which, on January 1, 1972, did not have in effect a State plan approved under title XIX of the Social Security Act may provide assistance under title I, X, XIV, or XVI of the Act in the form of institutional services in intermediate care facilities as authorized under title XI of the Act, until the first day of the first month (occurring after January 1, 1972) that such State does have in effect a State plan approved under title XIX of the Act. In any State which may provide such assistance as authorized under title XI of the Act, a State plan under title I, X, XIV, or XVI of the Act which includes such assistance must:

(1) Provide that such benefits will be provided only to individuals who:

(i) Are entitled (or would, if not receiving institutional services in intermediate care facilities, be entitled) to receive assistance, under the State plan, in the form of money payments; and

(ii) Because of their physical or mental condition (or both) require living accommodations and care which, as a practical matter, can be made available to them only through institutional facilities; and

(iii) Do not have such an illness, disease, injury, or other condition as to require the degree of care and treatment which a hospital or skilled nursing home (as that term is employed in title XIX) is designed to provide.

(2) Provide that, in determining financial eligibility for benefits in the form of institutional services in intermediate care facilities, available income will be applied, first for personal and incidental needs including clothing, and that any remaining income will be applied to the costs of care in the intermediate care facility.

(3) Provide methods of administration that include:

(i) Placing of responsibility, within the State agency, with one or more staff members with sufficient staff time exclusive of other duties to direct and guide the agency's activities with respect to services in intermediate care facilities, including arrangements for consultation and working relationships with the State standard-setting authority and State agencies responsible for mental health and for mental retardation;

(ii) In relation to authorization of benefits, provisions for evaluation by a physician of the individual's physical and mental condition and the kinds and amounts of care he requires; evaluation by the agency worker of the resources available in the home, family and community; and participation by the recipient in determining where he is to receive care, except that in the case of services being provided in a Christian Science Sanatorium, certification by a qualified Christian Science practitioner that the individual meets the requirements specified in paragraphs (a)(1) (ii) and (iii) of this section may be substituted for the evaluation by a physician;

(iii) Provisions for redetermination at least semiannually that the individual is properly a recipient of intermediate care.

(4) Provide for regular, periodic review and reevaluation no less often than annually (by or on behalf of the State agency administering the plan and in addition to the activities described in paragraph (a)(3) of this section) of recipients in intermediate care facilities to determine whether their current physical and mental conditions are such as to indicate continued placement in the intermediate care facility, whether the services actually rendered are adequate and responsive to the conditions and needs identified, and whether a change to other living arrangements, or other institutional facilities (including skilled nursing homes) is indicated. Such reviews must be followed by appropriate action on the part of the State agency administering the plan. They must be conducted by or under the supervision of a physician with participation by a registered professional nurse and other appropriate medical and social service personnel not employed by or having a financial interest in the facility, except that, in the case of recipients who have elected care in a Christian Science sanatorium, review by a physician or other medical personnel is not required.

(5) Provide that all services with respect to social and related problems which the agency makes available to applicants and recipients of assistance under the plan will be equally available to all applicants for and recipients of benefits in the form of institutional services in intermediate care facilities.

(6) Specify the types of facilities, however described, that will qualify under the State plan for participation as intermediate care facilities, and provide for availability to the Department of Health and Human Services, upon request of (i) copies of the State's requirements for licensing of such facilities, (ii) any requirements imposed by the State in addition to licensing and to definition of intermediate care facilities, and (iii) a description of the manner in which such requirements are applied and enforced including copies of agreements or contracts, if any, with the licensing authority for this purpose.

(7) Provide for and describe methods of determining amounts of vendor payments to intermediate care facilities which systematically relate amounts of the payment to the kinds, levels, and quantities of services provided to the recipients by the institutions and to the cost of providing such services.

(b) *Other requirements.* Except when inconsistent with purposes of section 1121 of the Act or contrary to any provision therein, any modification, pursuant thereto, of an approved State plan shall be subject to the same conditions, limitations, rights, and obligations as obtained with respect to such approved State plan. Included specifically among such conditions and limitations are the provisions of titles I, X, XIV, and XVI relating to payments to or care in behalf of any individual who is an inmate of a public institution (except as a patient in a medical institution).

(c) *Federal financial participation.* (1) Federal financial participation is available under section 1121 of the Act in vendor payments for institutional services provided to individuals who are eligible under the respective State plan and who are residents in intermediate care facilities. The rate of participation is the same as for money payments under the respective title or, if the State so elects, at the rate of the Federal medical assistance percentage as defined in section 1905(b) of the Act. Such Federal financial participation ends on the date specified in paragraph (c)(2) of this section, or 12 months after the date when the State first has in effect a State plan approved under title XIX of the Act, whichever is later.

(2) For the period from January 1, 1972, to the date on which a determination is made under the provisions of 42 CFR 449.33 as to a facility's eligibility to receive payments for intermediate care facility services under the medical assistance program, title XIX of the Act, but not later than 12 months following the effective date of these regulations, Federal financial participation in payments for such services under title XIX is governed by the provisions of this section, applied to State plans under title XIX.

(d) *Definition of terms.* For purposes of section 1121 of the Social Security Act, the following definitions apply:

(1) *Institutional services.* The term, *institutional services,* means those items and services provided by or under the auspices of the institution which contribute to the health, comfort, and well-being of the residents thereof; except that the term, *institutional services,* does not include allowances for clothing and incidental expenses for which money payments to recipients are made under the plan, nor does it include medical care, in a form identifiable as such and separable from the routine services of the facility, for which vendor payments may be made under a State plan approved under title XIX.

(2) *Distinct part of an institution.* A *distinct part* of an institution is defined as a part which meets the definition of an intermediate care facility and the following conditions:

(i) *Identifiable unit.* The *distinct part* of the institution is an entire unit such as an entire ward or contiguous wards, wing, floor, or building. It consists of all beds and related facilities in the unit and houses all residents, except as hereafter provided, for whom payment is being made for intermediate care. It is clearly identified and is approved, in writing, by the agency applying the definition of intermediate care facility herein.

(ii) *Staff.* Appropriate personnel are assigned and work regularly in the unit. Immediate supervision of staff is provided in the unit at all time by qualified personnel.

(iii) *Shared facilities and services.* The distinct part may share such central services and facilities as management services, building maintenance and laundry, with other units.

(iv) *Transfers between distinct parts.* In a facility having distinct parts devoted to skilled nursing home care and intermediate care, which facility has been determined by the appropriate State agency to be organized and staffed to provide services according to individual needs throughout the institution, nothing herein shall be construed to require transfer of an individual within the institution when in the opinion of the individual's physician such transfer might be harmful to the physical or mental health of the individual.

(3) *Intermediate care facility.* An intermediate care facility is an institution or a distinct part thereof which:

(i) Is licensed, under State law to provide the residents thereof, on a regular basis, the range or level of care and services as defined in paragraph (d)(4) of this section, which is suitable to the needs of individuals who:

(*a*) Because of their physical or mental limitations or both, require living accommodations and care which, as a practical matter, can be made available to them only through institutional facilities, and

(*b*) Do not have such an illness, disease, injury, or other condition as to require the degree of care and treatment which a hospital or skilled nursing home (as that term is employed in title XIX) is designed to provide:

(ii) Does not provide the degree of care required to be provided by a skilled nursing home furnishing services under a State plan approved under title XIX:

(iii) Meets such standards of safety and sanitation as are applicable to nursing homes under State law; and

(iv) Regularly provides a level of care and service beyond board and room.

The term *intermediate care facility* also includes a Christian Science sanatorium operated, or listed and certified, by the First Church of Christ, Scientist, Boston, Mass.

(4) *Range or level of care and services.* The range or level of care and services suitable to the needs of individuals described in paragraph (d)(3)(i) of this section is to be defined by the State agency. The following items are recommended as a minimum.

(i) *Admission, transfer, and discharge of residents.* The admission, transfer, and discharge of residents of the facility are conducted in accordance with written policies of the institution that include at least the following provisions.

(*a*) Only those persons are accepted into the facility whose needs can be met within the accommodations and services the facility provides;

(*b*) As changes occur in their physical or mental condition, necessitating service or care not regularly provided by the facility, residents are transferred promptly to hospitals, skilled nursing homes, or other appropriate facilities;

(*c*) The resident, his next of kin, and the responsible agency if any, are consulted in advance of the discharge of any resident, and casework services or other means are utilized to assure that adequate arrangements exist for meeting his needs through other resources.

(ii) *Personal care and protective services.* The types and amounts of protection and personal service needed by each resident of the facility are a matter of record and are known to all staff members having personal contact with the resident. At least the following services are provided.

(*a*) There is, at all times, a responsible staff member actively on duty in the facility, and immediately accessible to all residents, to whom residents can report injuries, symptoms of illness, or emergencies, and who is immediately responsible for assuring that appropriate action is taken promptly.

(*b*) Assistance is provided, as needed by individual residents, with routine activities of daily living including such services as help in bathing, dressing, grooming, and management of personal affairs such as shopping.

(*c*) Continuous supervision is provided for residents whose mental condition is such that their personal safety requires such supervision.

(iii) *Social services.* Services to assist residents in dealing with social and related problems are available to all residents through one or more caseworkers on the staff of the facility; and/or, in the case of recipients of assistance, through caseworkers on the staff of the assistance agency; or through other arrangements.

(iv) *Activities.* Activities are regularly available for all residents, including social and recreational activities involving active participation by the residents, entertainment of appropriate frequency and character, and opportunities for participation in community activities as possible and appropriate.

(v) *Food service.* At least three meals a day, constituting a nutritionally adequate diet, are served in one or more dining areas separate from sleeping quarters, and tray service is provided for residents temporarily unable to leave their rooms.

(vi) *Special diets.* If the facility accepts or retains individuals in need of medically prescribed special diets, the menus for such diets are planned by a professionally qualified dietitian, or are reviewed and approved by the attending physician, and the facility provides supervision of the preparation and serving of the meals and their acceptance by the resident.

(vii) *Health services.* Whether provided by the facility or from other sources, at least the following services are available to all residents:

(*a*) Immediate supervision of the facility's health services by a registered professional nurse or a licensed practical nurse employed full-time in the facility and on duty during the day shift except that, where the State recognizes and describes two or more distinct levels of institutions as intermediate care facilities such personnel are not required in any level that serves only individuals who have been determined by their physicians not to be in need of such supervision and whose need for such supervision is reviewed as indicated, and at least quarterly;

(*b*) Continuing supervision by a physician who sees the resident as needed and in no case, less often than quarterly;

(*c*) Under direction by the resident's physician and (where applicable in accordance with (d)(4)(vii)(*a*) of this section), general supervision by the nurse in charge of the facility's health services, guidance, and assistance for each resident in carrying out his personal health program to assure that preventive measures, treatments, and medications prescribed by the physician are properly carried out and recorded;

(*d*) Arrangements for services of a physician in the event of an emergency when the resident's own physician cannot be reached;

(*e*) In the presence of minor illness and for temporary periods, bedside care under direction of the resident's physician including nursing service provided by, or supervised by, a registered professional nurse or a licensed practical nurse;

(*f*) An individual health record for each resident including;

(*1*) The name, address, and telephone number of his physician;

(*2*) A record of the physician's findings and recommendations in the preadmission evaluation of the individual's condition and in subsequent reevaluations and all orders and recommendations of the physician for care of the resident;

(*3*) All symptoms and other indications of illness or injury brought to the attention of the staff by the resident, or from other sources, including the date, time, and action taken regarding each.

(viii) *Living accommodations.* Space and furnishings provide each resident clean, comfortable, and reasonably private living accommodations with no more than four residents occupying a room, with individual storage facilities for clothing and personal articles, and with lounge, recreation and dining areas provided apart from sleeping quarters.

(ix) *Administration and management.* The direction and management of the facility are such as to assure that the services required by the residents are so organized and administered that they are, in fact, available to the residents on a regular basis and that this is accomplished efficiently and with consideration for the objective of providing necessary care within a homelike atmosphere. Staff are employed by the facility sufficient in number and competence, as determined by the appropriate State agency, to meet the requirements of the residents.

[35 FR 8990, June 10, 1970, as amended at 39 FR 2220, Jan. 17, 1974; 39 FR 8918, Mar. 7, 1974]

PART 235—ADMINISTRATION OF FINANCIAL ASSISTANCE PROGRAMS

Sec.

AUTHORITY: 42 U.S.C. 603, 616, and 1302.

§ 235.40 [Reserved]

§ 235.50 State plan requirements for methods of personnel administration.

(a) A State plan for financial assistance programs under title I, IV-A, X, XIV, or XVI (AABD) of the Social Security Act must provide that methods of personnel administration will be established and maintained in public agencies administering or supervising the administration of the program in conformity with the Standards for a Merit System of Personnel Administration, 5 CFR part 900, subpart F, which incorporates the Intergovernmental Personnel Act Merit Principles (Pub. L. 91–648, section 2, 84 Stat. 1909), prescribed by the Office of Personnel Management pursuant to section 208 of the Intergovernmental Personnel Act of 1970 as amended.

[45 FR 25398, Apr. 15, 1980]

§ 235.60 Federal financial participation (FFP) for State and local training.

Sections 235.61 through 235.66 contain (a) State plan requirements for training programs and (b) conditions for Federal financial participation (FFP) for training costs under the State plans. These sections apply to the State plans for the financial assistance programs in all jurisdictions under title I, IV-A, X, XIV, or XVI (AABD) of the Social Security Act.

[45 FR 29833, May 6, 1980]

§ 235.61 Definition of terms.

For purposes of §§ 235.60–235.66:

Act means the Social Security Act, as amended.

A grant to an educational institution means payments to an educational institution for services rendered under a time limited agreement between the State agency and the eligible educational institution which provides for the training of State or local agency employees or persons preparing for employment with the State or local agency.

A training program is the method through which the State agency carries out a plan of educational and training activities to improve the operation of its programs.

(a) *Initial in-service training* means a period of intensive, task-oriented training to prepare new employees to assume job responsibilities.

(b) *Continuing training* means an ongoing program of training planned to enable employees to: (1) Reinforce their basic knowledge and develop the required skills for the performance of specific functions, and (2) acquire additional knowledge and skill to meet changes such as enactment of new legislation, development of new policies, or shifts in program emphasis.

(c) *Full-time training* means training that requires employees to be relieved of all responsibility for performance of current work to participate in a training program.

(d) *Part-time training* means training that allows employees to continue full time in their jobs or requires only partial reduction of work activities to participate in a training program outside of the State or local agency.

(e) *Long-term training* means training for eight consecutive work weeks or longer.

(f) *Short-term training* means training for less than eight consecutive work weeks.

FFP or Federal financial participation means the Federal government's share of expenditures made by a State or local agency under a training program.

Fringe benefits means the employer's share of premiums for industrial compensation, employee's retirement, unemployment compensation, health insurance, and similar expenses.

Persons preparing for employment means individuals who are not yet employed by the State or local agency, but who have received financial assistance from the State agency for training, and have made a legally binding commitment with the State or local agency for future employment under the conditions of these regulations.

Stipend means the basic living allowance paid to a student.

[45 FR 29833, May 6, 1980]

§ 235.62 State plan requirements for training programs.

A State plan under title I, IV-A, X, XIV, or XVI (AABD) of the Act must provide for a training program for agency personnel. The training program must:

(a) Include initial in-service training for newly appointed staff, and continuing agency training opportunities to improve the operation of the program. The training program may also include short-term and long-term training at educational institutions through grants to institutions or by direct financial assistance to students enrolled in institutions who are agency employees or persons preparing for employment with the State or local agency;

(b) Be related to job duties performed or to be performed by the persons trained, and be consistent with the program objectives of the agency; and

(c) Be described in an annual training plan prepared prior to the beginning of the fiscal year. Copies of the training plan shall be made available upon request to the Regional Office of Family

Assistance for review by the Federal staff.

[45 FR 29833, May 6, 1980, as amended at 46 FR 29264, June 1, 1981]

§235.63 Conditions for FFP.

(a) *Who may be trained.* FFP is available only for training provided personnel employed in all classes of positions, volunteers, and persons preparing for employment by the State or local agency administering the program.

(b) *When FFP is available.* FFP is available for personnel employed and persons preparing for employment by the State or local agency provided the following conditions are met, and with the following limitations:

(1) Employees in full-time, long-term training make a commitment to work in the agency for a period of time equal to the period for which financial assistance is granted. A State agency may exempt an employee from fulfilling this commitment only if failure to continue in employment is due to death, disability, employment in a financial assistance program in a public assistance agency in another State, or other emergent circumstances determined by the single State agency head to be valid for exemption;

(2) An employee retains his or her rights and benefits in the agency while on full-time, long-term training leave;

(3) Persons preparing for employment are selected by the State agency and accepted by the school;

(4) Persons preparing for employment are pursuing educational programs approved by the State agency;

(5) Persons preparing for employment are committed to work for State or local agency for a period of time at least equal to the period for which financial assistance is granted if employment is offered within 2 months after training is completed;

(6) The State or local agency offers the individual preparing for employment a job upon completion of training unless precluded by merit system requirements, legislative budget cuts, position freezes, or other circumstances beyond the agency's control; and if unable to offer employment, releases the individual from his or her commitment;

(7) The State agency keeps a record of the employment of persons trained. If the persons are not employed by the State or local agency, the record specifies the reason for non-employment;

(8) The State agency evaluates the training programs; and

(9) Any recoupment of funds by the State from trainees failing to fulfill their commitment under this section shall be treated as a refund and deducted from total training costs for the purpose of determining net costs for FFP.

(c) *Grants to educational institutions.* FFP is available in payments for services rendered under grants to educational institutions provided all of the following conditions are met:

(1) Grants are made for the purpose of developing, expanding, or improving training for personnel employed by the State or local agency or preparing for employment by the State or local agency administering the program. Grants are made for an educational program (curriculum development, classroom instruction, field instruction, or any combination of these) that is directly related to the agency's program. Grants are made for not more than 3 years, but may be renewed, subject to the conditions of this section;

(2) Grants are made to educational institutions and programs that are accredited by the appropriate institutional accrediting body recognized by the U.S. Commissioner of Education. When a specialized program within the institution for which there is a specialized accrediting body is used, that program must be accredited by or have pre-accreditation status from that body. (Part 149 of this title explains the requirements and procedures for obtaining recognition as an accrediting agency or association. Lists of currently recognized accrediting bodies are published in the FEDERAL REGISTER periodically. *See also Nationally Recognized Accrediting Agencies and Associations* published by the Office of Education);

(3) The State agency has written policies establishing conditions and procedures for such grants;

(4) Each grant describes objectives in terms of how the educational program is related to the financial assistance

programs and how it is designed to meet the State or local agency's manpower needs; and

(5) An evaluation of the educational program funded by each grant is made no later than the close of the second year of the grant. The evaluation shall be conducted by representatives from the educational institution and the State agency to determine whether conditions and objectives described in the grant are being met. If the educational program does not meet these conditions and objectives, payment shall be terminated no later than the close of the second year of the grant.

[45 FR 29834, May 6, 1980]

§ 235.64 FFP rates, and activities and costs matchable as training expenditures.

Under title I, IV-A, X, XIV, or XVI(AABD) of the Act, FFP is available at the rate of 50 percent for the following costs:

(a) Salaries, fringe benefits, travel and per diem for:

(1) Staff development personnel (including support staff) assigned full time to training functions and;

(2) Staff development personnel assigned part time to training functions to the extent time is spent performing such functions.

(b) For agency training sessions, FFP is available for:

(1) Salaries, fringe benefits, travel and per diem for employees in initial in-service training of at least one week;

(2) Travel and per diem for employees in agency training sessions away from the employee's work site, or in institutes, seminars or workshops related to the job and sponsored by professional organizations;

(3) Salaries, fringe benefits, travel and per diem for experts outside the agency engaged to develop or conduct special programs; and

(4) Costs of space, postage, teaching supplies, purchase or development of teaching material and equipment, and costs of maintaining and operating the agency library as an essential resource to the agency's training program.

(c) For training and education outside of the agency, FFP is available for:

(1) Salaries, fringe benefits, dependency allowance, travel, tuition, books, and educational supplies for employees in full-time, long-term training programs (with no assigned agency duties);

(2) Salaries, fringe benefits, travel, tuition, books, and educational supplies for employees in full-time, short-term training programs of four or more consecutive work weeks;

(3) Travel, per diem, tuition, books and educational supplies for employees in short-term training programs of less than four consecutive work weeks, or part-time training programs; and

(4) Stipends, travel, tuition, books and educational supplies for persons preparing for employment with the State or local agency.

(d) FFP is available for payments to educational institutions, as described in § 235.63(c) for salaries, fringe benefits, and travel of instructors, clerical assistance, teaching materials and equipment.

[45 FR 29834, May 6, 1980, as amended at 47 FR 5683, Feb. 5, 1982; 59 FR 12861, Mar. 18, 1994]

§ 235.65 Activities and costs not matchable as training expenditures.

FFP is not available for the following expenditures as training costs; however, the expenditures described in this section may be matched as administrative costs, if conditions for such matching are met:

(a) Salaries of supervisors (day-to-day supervision of staff is not a training activity); and

(b) Employment of students on a temporary basis, such as in the summertime.

[45 FR 29835, May 6, 1980]

§ 235.66 Sources of State funds.

(a) *Public funds.* Public funds may be considered as the State's share in claiming Federal reimbursement where the funds:

(1) Are appropriated directly to the State or local agency, or transferred from another public agency (including Indian tribes) to the State or local agency and under its administrative

control, or certified by the contributing public agency as representing expenditures eligible for FFP under §§ 235.60–235.66;

(2) Are not used to match other Federal funds; and

(3) Are not federal funds, or are Federal funds authorized by Federal law to be used to match other Federal funds.

(b) *Private funds.* Funds donated from private sources may be considered as the State's share in claiming Federal reimbursement only where the funds are:

(1) Transferred to the State or local agency and under its administrative control;

(2) Donated without any restriction which would require their use for the training of a particular individual or at particular facilities or institutions; and

(3) Do not revert to the donor's facility or use.

[45 FR 29835, May 6, 1980]

§ 235.70 Prompt notice to child support or Medicaid agency.

(a) A State plan under title IV-A of the Social Security Act must provide for prompt notice to the State or local child support agency designated pursuant to section 454(3) of the Social Security Act and to the State title XIX agency, as appropriate, whenever:

(1) Aid is furnished to a child who has been deserted or abandoned by a parent, to the parent(s) with whom the child lives, or to a pregnant woman under § 233.90(c)(2)(iv), or

(2) Any of the persons in paragraph (a)(1) of this section is deemed to be a recipient of aid under § 233.20(a)(3)(viii)(D).

(b) In this section:

(1) *Aid* means Aid to Families with Dependent Children, or AFDC Foster Care.

(2) *Prompt notice* means written notice including a copy of the AFDC case record, or all relevant information as prescribed by the child support agency. Prompt notice must also include all relevant information as prescribed by the State medicaid agency for the pursuit of liable third parties. The prompt notice shall be provided within two working days of the furnishing of aid or the determination that an individual is a recipient under § 233.20(a)(3)(viii)(D). The title IV-A, IV-D and XIX agencies may agree to provide notice immediately upon the filing of an application for assistance.

(3) *Furnish* means the date on which cash is given to the family, a check or warrant is mailed to the family, a deposit is made in a bank for the family, or other similar circumstances in which an assistance payment is made to the family, or the date on which individuals are determined to be recipients under § 233.20(a)(3)(viii)(D).

(4) *A child who has been deserted or abandoned by a parent* means any child whose eligibility for AFDC is based on continued absence of a parent from the home, and includes a child born out of wedlock without regard to whether the paternity of such child has been established.

[47 FR 5683, Feb. 5, 1982, as amended at 56 FR 8933, Mar. 4, 1991]

§ 235.110 Fraud.

State plan requirements: A State plan under title I, IV-A, X, XIV, or XVI of the Social Security Act must provide:

(a) That the State agency will establish and maintain:

(1) Methods and criteria for identifying situations in which a question of fraud in the program may exist, and

(2) Procedures developed in cooperation with the State's legal authorities for referring to law enforcement officials situations in which there is valid reason to suspect that fraud has been practiced.

The definition of fraud for purposes of this section will be determined in accordance with State law.

(b) For methods of investigation of situations which there is a question of fraud, that do not infringe on the legal rights of persons involved and are consistent with the principles recognized as affording due process of law.

(c) For the designation of official position(s) responsible for referral of situations involving suspected fraud to the proper authorities.

[36 FR 3869, Feb. 27, 1971]

PART 237—FISCAL ADMINISTRATION OF FINANCIAL ASSISTANCE PROGRAMS

AUTHORITY: Section 1102 of the Social Security Act (42 U.S.C. 1302); 49 Stat. 647, as amended.

§ 237.50 Recipient count, Federal financial participation.

Pursuant to the formulas in sections 3, 403, 1003, 1118, 1121, 1403, and 1603 of the Social Security Act, it is necessary to identify expenditures that may be included in claims for Federal financial participation. The quarterly statement of expenditures and recoveries which is required for OAA, AFDC, AB, APTD, and AABD must include, as a part of the basis for computing the amount of Federal participation in such expenditures, the number of eligible recipients each month. However, where the State is making claims under section 1118 of the Act or under optional provisions for Federal sharing specified in such paragraphs no recipient count is involved. Vendor payments for medical care may not be considered if the State has a plan approved under title XIX of the Act. The procedures for determining recipient count are set forth in paragraphs (a), (b) and (c) of this section.

(a) *Adult assistance categories.* For each adult assistance category, under title I, X, XIV, or XVI, of the Act, the recipient count for any month may include:

(1) Eligible recipients who receive money payments or in whose behalf protective payments are made for that month:

Provided, That such payments are not excluded from Federal financial participation under the provisions of § 233.145(c) of this chapter; plus

(2) Other eligible recipients in whose behalf payments are made for institutional services in intermediate care facilities for that month, but only in a State which does not have in effect a plan approved under Title XIX of the Act. (See § 233.145(b)(2) of this chapter.)

(b) *AFDC category.* For the AFDC category under title IV, part A, of the Act:

(1) The recipient count for any month includes:

(i) Eligible recipients in families which receive a money payment, plus

(ii) Eligible recipients in families not otherwise counted on whose behalf protective or nonmedical vendor assistance payments are made for such month in accordance with the vendor payment provisions at § 234.60, provided that such payments are not excluded from Federal financial participation under the provisions of § 233.145(c) of this chapter.

(2) For the purpose of this provision, *recipients* means, if otherwise eligible:

(i) Children;

(ii) In a home with no parent who is the caretaker relative, an otherwise eligible relative of specified degree;

(iii) Parent(s);

(iv) The spouse of such parent, in the case of AFDC eligibility due to incapacity or unemployment;

(3) As used in paragraph (b)(2)(iii) of this section, the term *parent* means the natural or adoptive parent, or the stepparent who is married to the child's natural or adoptive parent and is legally obligated to support the child under a State law of general applicability which requires stepparents to support stepchildren to the same extent that natural or adoptive parents are required to support their children; and the term "spouse" as used in paragraph (b)(2)(iv) of this section means an individual who is the husband or wife of the child's own parent, as defined above, by reason of a legal marriage as defined under State law.

(4) Where there are two or more dependent children living in a place of residence with two other persons and each of such other persons is a relative who has responsibility for the care and control of one or more of the dependent children, there may be two AFDC families (assistance units), if neither family includes a parent or sibling included in the other family pursuant to § 206.10 (a)(1)(vii).

(c) *Essential person.* An *essential person* or other ineligible person who is living with the eligible person may not be counted as a recipient.

[38 FR 32914, Nov. 29, 1973, as amended at 57 FR 30161, July 8, 1992]

PART 260—GENERAL TEMPORARY ASSISTANCE FOR NEEDY FAMILIES (TANF) PROVISIONS

AUTHORITY: 42 U.S.C. 601, 601 note, 603, 604, 606, 607, 608, 609, 610, 611, 619, and 1308.

SOURCE: 64 FR 17878, Apr. 12, 1999, unless otherwise noted.

Subpart A—What Rules Generally Apply to the TANF Program?

§ 260.10 What does this part cover?

This part includes regulatory provisions that generally apply to the Temporary Assistance for Needy Families (TANF) program.

§ 260.20 What is the purpose of the TANF program?

The TANF program has the following four purposes:

(a) Provide assistance to needy families so that children may be cared for in their own homes or in the homes of relatives;

(b) End the dependence of needy parents on government benefits by promoting job preparation, work, and marriage;

(c) Prevent and reduce the incidence of out-of-wedlock pregnancies and establish annual numerical goals for preventing and reducing the incidence of these pregnancies; and

(d) Encourage the formation and maintenance of two-parent families.

§ 260.30 What definitions apply under the TANF regulations?

The following definitions apply under parts 260 through 265 of this chapter:

ACF means the Administration for Children and Families.

Act means Social Security Act, unless otherwise specified.

Adjusted State Family Assistance Grant, or adjusted SFAG, means the SFAG amount, minus any reductions for Tribal Family Assistance Grants paid to Tribal grantees on behalf of Indian families residing in the State and any transfers to the Social Services

Block Grant or the Child Care and Development Block Grant.

Administrative costs has the meaning specified at § 263.0(b) of this chapter.

Adult means an individual who is not a "minor child," as defined elsewhere in this section.

AFDC means Aid to Families with Dependent Children.

Aid to Families with Dependent Children means the welfare program in effect under title IV-A of prior law.

Assistance has the meaning specified at § 260.31.

Basic MOE means the expenditure of State funds that must be made in order to meet the MOE requirement at section 409(a)(7) of the Act.

Cash assistance, when provided to participants in the Welfare-to-Work program (WtW), has the meaning specified at § 260.32.

CCDBG means the Child Care and Development Block Grant Act of 1990, as amended, 42 U.S.C. 9858 *et seq.*

CCDF means the Child Care and Development Fund, or those child care programs and services funded either under section 418(a) of the Act or CCDBG.

Commingled State TANF expenditures means expenditures of State funds that are made within the TANF program and commingled with Federal TANF funds.

Contingency fund means Federal TANF funds available under section 403(b) of the Act, and contingency funds means the Federal monies made available to States under that section. Neither term includes any State funds expended pursuant to section 403(b).

Contingency fund MOE means the MOE expenditures that a State must make in order to meet the MOE requirements at sections 403(b)(6) and 409(a)(10) of the Act and subpart B of part 264 of this chapter and retain contingency funds made available to the State. The only expenditures that qualify for Contingency Fund MOE are State TANF expenditures.

Control group is a term relevant to continuation of a "waiver" and has the meaning specified at § 260.71.

Countable State expenditures has the meaning specified at § 264.0 of this chapter.

Discretionary fund of the CCDF refers to child care funds appropriated under the CCDBG.

EA means Emergency Assistance.

Eligible State means a State that, during the 27-month period ending with the close of the first quarter of the fiscal year, has submitted a TANF plan that we have determined is complete.

Emergency assistance means the program option available to States under sections 403(a)(5) and 406(e) of prior law to provide short-term assistance to needy families with children.

Expenditure means any amount of Federal TANF or State MOE funds that a State expends, spends, pays out, or disburses consistent with the requirements of parts 260 through 265 of this chapter. It may include expenditures on the refundable portions of State or local tax credits, if they are consistent with the provisions at § 260.33. It does not include any amounts that merely represent avoided costs or foregone revenue. Avoided costs include such items as contractor penalty payments for poor performance and purchase price discounts, rebates, and credits that a State receives. Foregone revenue includes State tax provisions—such as waivers, deductions, exemptions, or nonrefundable tax credits—that reduce a State's tax revenue.

Experimental group is a term relevant to continuation of a "waiver" and has the meaning specified at § 260.71.

FAG has the meaning specified at § 264.0(b) of this chapter.

Family Violence Option (or FVO) has the meaning specified at § 260.51.

FAMIS means the automated statewide management information system under sections 402(a)(30), 402(e), and 403 of prior law.

Federal expenditures means expenditures by a State of Federal TANF funds.

Federal TANF funds means all funds provided to the State under section 403 of the Act except WtW funds awarded under section 403(a)(5), including the SFAG, any bonuses, supplemental grants, or contingency funds.

Federally recognized good cause domestic violence waiver has the meaning specified at § 260.51.

Fiscal year means the 12-month period beginning on October 1 of the preceding calendar year and ending on September 30.

FY means fiscal year.

Good cause domestic violence waiver has the meaning specified at § 260.51.

Governor means the Chief Executive Officer of the State. It thus includes the Governor of each of the 50 States and the Territories and the Mayor of the District of Columbia.

IEVS means the Income and Eligibility Verification System operated pursuant to the provisions in section 1137 of the Act.

Inconsistent is a term relevant to continuation of a "waiver" and has the meaning specified at § 260.71.

Indian, Indian Tribe and Tribal Organization have the meaning given such terms by section 4 of the Indian Self-Determination and Education Assistance Act (25 U.S.C. 450b), except that the term "Indian tribe" means, with respect to the State of Alaska, only the Metlakatla Indian Community of the Annette Islands Reserve and the following Alaska Native regional nonprofit corporations:

(1) Arctic Slope Native Association;

(2) Kawerak, Inc.;

(3) Maniilaq Association;

(4) Association of Village Council Presidents;

(5) Tanana Chiefs Council;

(6) Cook Inlet Tribal Council;

(7) Bristol Bay Native Association;

(8) Aleutian and Pribilof Island Association;

(9) Chugachmuit;

(10) Tlingit Haida Central Council;

(11) Kodiak Area Native Association; and

(12) Copper River Native Association.

Individual Development Account, or IDA, has the meaning specified at § 263.20 of this chapter.

Job Opportunities and Basic Skills Training Program means the program under title IV-F of prior law to provide education, training and employment services to welfare recipients.

JOBS means the Job Opportunities and Basic Skills Training Program.

Minor child means an individual who:

(1) Has not attained 18 years of age; or

(2) Has not attained 19 years of age and is a full-time student in a secondary school (or in the equivalent level of vocational or technical training).

MOE means maintenance-of-effort.

Needy State is a term that pertains to the provisions on the Contingency Fund and the penalty for failure to meet participation rates. It means, for a month, a State where:

(1)(i) The average rate of total unemployment (seasonally adjusted) for the most recent 3-month period for which data are published for all States equals or exceeds 6.5 percent; and

(ii) The average rate of total unemployment (seasonally adjusted) for such 3-month period equals or exceeds 110 percent of the average rate for either (or both) of the corresponding 3-month periods in the two preceding calendar years; or

(2) The Secretary of Agriculture has determined that the average number of individuals participating in the Food Stamp program in the State has grown at least 10 percent in the most recent 3-month period for which data are available.

Noncustodial parent means a parent of a minor child who:

(1) Lives in the State; and

(2) Does not live in the same household as the minor child.

Prior law means the provisions of title IV-A and IV-F of the Act in effect as of August 21, 1996. They include provisions related to Aid to Families with Dependent Children (or AFDC), Emergency Assistance (or EA), Job Opportunities and Basic Skills Training (or JOBS), and FAMIS.

PRWORA means the Personal Responsibility and Work Opportunity Reconciliation Act of 1996, or Pub. L. 104–193, 42 U.S.C. 1305 note.

Qualified Aliens has the meaning prescribed under section 431 of PRWORA, as amended, 8 U.S.C. 1641.

Qualified State Expenditures means the total amount of State funds expended during the fiscal year that count for basic MOE purposes. It includes expenditures, under any State program, for any of the following with respect to eligible families:

(1) Cash assistance;

(2) Child care assistance;

(3) Educational activities designed to increase self-sufficiency, job training, and work, excluding any expenditure for public education in the State except expenditures involving the provision of services or assistance of an eligible family that is not generally available to persons who are not members of an eligible family;

(4) Any other use of funds allowable under subpart A of part 263 of this chapter; and

(5) Administrative costs in connection with the matters described in paragraphs (1), (2), (3) and (4) of this definition, but only to the extent that such costs do not exceed 15 percent of the total amount of qualified State expenditures for the fiscal year.

Secretary means Secretary of the Department of Health and Human Services or any other Department official duly authorized to act on the Secretary's behalf.

Segregated State TANF expenditures means expenditures of State funds within the TANF program that are not commingled with Federal TANF funds.

Separate State program, or SSP, means a program operated outside of TANF in which the expenditures of State funds may count for basic MOE purposes.

SFAG means State family assistance grant, as defined in this section.

SFAG payable means the SFAG amount, reduced, as appropriate, for any Tribal Family Assistance Grants made on behalf of Indian families residing in the State and any penalties imposed on a State under this chapter.

Single audit means an audit or supplementary review conducted under the authority of the Single Audit Act at 31 U.S.C. chapter 75.

Social Services Block Grant means the social services program operated under title XX of the Act, pursuant to 42 U.S.C. 1397.

SSBG means the Social Services Block Grant.

State means the 50 States of the United States, the District of Columbia, the Commonwealth of Puerto Rico, the United States Virgin Islands, Guam, and American Samoa, unless otherwise specified.

State agency means the agency that the Governor certifies as the administering and supervising agency for the TANF program, pursuant to section 402(a)(4) of the Act.

State family assistance grant means the amount of the basic block grant allocated to each eligible State under the formula at section 403(a)(1) of the Act.

State MOE expenditures means the expenditure of State funds that may count for purposes of the basic MOE requirements at section 409(a)(7) of the Act and the Contingency Fund MOE requirements at sections 403(b)(4) and 409(a)(10) of the Act.

State TANF expenditures means the expenditure of State funds within the TANF program.

TANF means The Temporary Assistance for Needy Families Program.

TANF program means a State program of family assistance operated by an eligible State under its State TANF plan.

Territories means the Commonwealth of Puerto Rico, the United States Virgin Islands, Guam, and American Samoa.

Title IV-A refers to the title and part of the Act that now includes TANF, but previously included AFDC and EA. For the purpose of the TANF program regulations, this term does not include child care programs authorized and funded under section 418 of the Act, or their predecessors, unless we specify otherwise.

Tribal family assistance grant means a grant paid to a Tribe that has an approved Tribal family assistance plan under section 412(a)(1) of the Act.

Tribal grantee means a Tribe that receives Federal TANF funds to operate a Tribal TANF program under section 412(a) of the Act.

Tribal TANF program means a TANF program developed by an eligible Tribe, Tribal organization, or consortium and approved by us under section 412 of the Act.

Tribe means Indian Tribe or Tribal organization, as defined elsewhere in this section. The definition may include Tribal consortia (i.e., groups of federally recognized Tribes or Alaska Native entities that have banded together in a formal arrangement to develop and administer a Tribal TANF program).

Victim of domestic violence has the meaning specified at § 260.51.

Waiver, when used in subpart C of this part, has the meaning specified at § 260.71.

We (and any other first person plural pronouns) means the Secretary of Health and Human Services or any of the following individuals or organizations acting in an official capacity on the Secretary's behalf: the Assistant Secretary for Children and Families, the Regional Administrators for Children and Families, the Department of Health and Human Services, and the Administration for Children and Families.

Welfare-to-Work means the new program for funding work activities at section 403(a)(5) of the Act.

WtW means Welfare-to-Work.

WtW cash assistance has the meaning specified at § 260.32.

[64 FR 17878, Apr. 12, 1999; 64 FR 40291, July 26, 1999]

§ 260.31 What does the term "assistance" mean?

(a)(1) The term "assistance" includes cash, payments, vouchers, and other forms of benefits designed to meet a family's ongoing basic needs (i.e., for food, clothing, shelter, utilities, household goods, personal care items, and general incidental expenses).

(2) It includes such benefits even when they are:

(i) Provided in the form of payments by a TANF agency, or other agency on its behalf, to individual recipients; and

(ii) Conditioned on participation in work experience or community service (or any other work activity under § 261.30 of this chapter).

(3) Except where excluded under paragraph (b) of this section, it also includes supportive services such as transportation and child care provided to families who are not employed.

(b) It excludes:

(1) Nonrecurrent, short-term benefits that:

(i) Are designed to deal with a specific crisis situation or episode of need;

(ii) Are not intended to meet recurrent or ongoing needs; and

(iii) Will not extend beyond four months.

(2) Work subsidies (i.e., payments to employers or third parties to help cover the costs of employee wages, benefits, supervision, and training);

(3) Supportive services such as child care and transportation provided to families who are employed;

(4) Refundable earned income tax credits;

(5) Contributions to, and distributions from, Individual Development Accounts;

(6) Services such as counseling, case management, peer support, child care information and referral, transitional services, job retention, job advancement, and other employment-related services that do not provide basic income support; and

(7) Transportation benefits provided under a Job Access or Reverse Commute project, pursuant to section 404(k) of the Act, to an individual who is not otherwise receiving assistance.

(c) The definition of the term assistance specified in paragraphs (a) and (b) of this section:

(1) Does not apply to the use of the term assistance at part 263, subpart A, or at part 264, subpart B, of this chapter; and

(2) Does not preclude a State from providing other types of benefits and services in support of the TANF goal at § 260.20(a).

§ 260.32 What does the term "WtW cash assistance" mean?

(a) For the purpose of § 264.1(b)(1)(iii) of this chapter, WtW cash assistance only includes benefits that:

(1) Meet the definition of assistance at § 260.31; and

(2) Are directed at basic needs.

(b) Thus, it includes benefits described in paragraphs (a)(1) and (a)(2) of § 260.31, but excludes benefits described in paragraph (a)(3) of § 260.31.

(c) It only includes benefits identified in paragraphs (a) and (b) of this section when they are provided in the form of cash payments, checks, reimbursements, electronic funds transfers, or any other form that can legally be converted to currency.

§ 260.33 When are expenditures on State or local tax credits allowable expenditures for TANF-related purposes?

(a) To be an allowable expenditure for TANF-related purposes, any tax credit program must be reasonably calculated to accomplish one of the purposes of the TANF program, as specified at § 260.20.

(b)(1) In addition, pursuant to the definition of expenditure at § 260.30, we would only consider the refundable portion of a State or local tax credit to be an allowable expenditure.

(2) Under a State Earned Income Tax Credit (EITC) program, the refundable portion that may count as an expenditure is the amount that exceeds a family's State income tax liability prior to application of the EITC. (The family's tax liability is the amount owed prior to any adjustments for credits or payments.) In other words, we would count only the portion of a State EITC that the State refunds to a family and that is above the amount of EITC used as credit towards the family's State income tax liability.

(3) For other refundable (and allowable) State and local tax credits, such as refundable dependent care credits, the refundable portion that would count as an expenditure is the amount of the credit that exceeds the taxpayer's tax liability prior to the application of the credit. (The taxpayer's liability is the amount owed prior to any adjustments for credits or payments.) In other words, we would count only the portion of the credit that the State refunds to the taxpayer and that is above the amount of the credit applied against the taxpayer's tax bill.

§ 260.34 When do the Charitable Choice provisions of TANF apply?

(a) These Charitable Choice provisions apply whenever a State or local government uses Federal TANF funds or expends State and local funds used to meet maintenance-of-effort (MOE) requirements of the TANF program to directly procure services and benefits from non-governmental organizations, or provides TANF beneficiaries with certificates, vouchers, or other forms of indirect disbursement redeemable from such organizations. For purposes of this section:

(1) *Direct funding or funds provided directly* means that the government or an intermediate organization with the same duties as a governmental entity under this part selects the provider and purchases the needed services straight from the provider (*e.g.*, via a contract or cooperative agreement).

(2) *Indirect funding or funds provided indirectly* means placing the choice of service provider in the hands of the beneficiary, and then paying for the cost of that service through a voucher, certificate, or other similar means of payment.

(b)(1) Religious organizations are eligible, on the same basis as any other organization, to participate in TANF as long as their Federal TANF or State MOE funded services are provided consistent with the Establishment Clause and the Free Exercise Clause of the First Amendment to the United States Constitution.

(2) Neither the Federal government nor a State or local government in its use of Federal TANF or State MOE funds shall, in the selection of service providers, discriminate for or against an organization that applies to provide, or provides TANF services or benefits on the basis of the organization's religious character or affiliation.

(c) No Federal TANF or State MOE funds provided directly to participating organizations may be expended for inherently religious activities, such as worship, religious instruction, or proselytization. If an organization conducts such activities, it must offer them separately, in time or location, from the programs or services for which it receives direct Federal TANF or State MOE funds under this part, and participation must be voluntary for the beneficiaries of those programs or services.

(d) A religious organization that participates in the TANF program will retain its independence from Federal, State, and local governments and may continue to carry out its mission, including the definition, practice and expression of its religious beliefs, provided that it does not expend Federal TANF or State MOE funds that it receives directly to support any inherently religious activities, such as worship, religious instruction, or proselytization. Among other things, faith-based organizations may use space in their facilities to provide TANF-funded services without removing religious art, icons, scriptures, or other symbols.

In addition, a Federal TANF or State MOE funded religious organization retains the authority over its internal governance, and it may retain religious terms in its organization's name, select its board members on a religious basis, and include religious references in its organization's mission statements and other governing documents.

(e) The participation of a religious organization in, or its receipt of funds from, a TANF program does not affect that organization's exemption provided under 42 U.S.C. 2000e–1 regarding employment practices.

(f) A religious organization that receives Federal TANF or State MOE funds shall not, in providing program services or benefits, discriminate against a TANF applicant or recipient on the basis of religion, a religious belief, a refusal to hold a religious belief, or a refusal to actively participate in a religious practice.

(g)(1) If an otherwise eligible TANF applicant or recipient objects to the religious character of a TANF service provider, the recipient is entitled to receive services from an alternative provider to which the individual has no religious objection. In such cases, the State or local agency must refer the individual to an alternative provider of services within a reasonable period of time, as defined by the State or local agency. That alternative provider must be reasonably accessible and have the capacity to provide comparable services to the individual. Such services shall have a value that is not less than the value of the services that the individual would have received from the program participant to which the individual had such objection, as defined by the State or local agency.

(2) The alternative provider need not be a secular organization. It must simply be a provider to which the recipient has no religious objection. States may adopt reasonable definitions of the terms "reasonably accessible," "a reasonable period of time," "comparable," "capacity," and " value that is not less than." We expect States to apply these terms in a fair and consistent manner.

(3) The appropriate State or local governments that administer Federal TANF or State MOE funded programs shall ensure that notice of their right to alternative services is provided to applicants or recipients. The notice must clearly articulate the recipient's right to a referral and to services that reasonably meet the timeliness, capacity, accessibility, and equivalency requirements discussed above.

(h) Religious organizations that receive Federal TANF and State MOE funds are subject to the same regulations as other non-governmental organizations to account, in accordance with generally accepted auditing/accounting principles, for the use of such funds. Religious organizations may keep Federal TANF and State MOE funds they receive for services segregated in a separate account from non-governmental funds. If religious organizations choose to segregate their funds in this manner, only the Federal TANF and State MOE funds are subject to audit by the government under the program.

(i) This section applies whenever a State or local organization uses Federal TANF or State MOE funds to procure services and benefits from non-governmental organizations, or redeems certificates, vouchers, or other forms of disbursement from them whether with Federal funds, or State and local funds claimed to meet the MOE requirements of section 409(a)(7) of the Social Security Act. Subject to the requirements of paragraph (j), when State or local funds are used to meet the TANF MOE requirements, the provisions apply irrespective of whether the State or local funds are commingled with Federal funds, segregated, or expended in separate State programs.

(j) Preemption. Nothing in this section shall be construed to preempt any provision of a State constitution, or State statute that prohibits or restricts the expenditure of segregated or separate State funds in or by religious organizations.

(k) If a non-governmental intermediate organization, acting under a contract or other agreement with a State or local government, is given the authority under the contract or agreement to select non-governmental organizations to provide Federal TANF or MOE funded services, the intermediate organization must ensure that there is compliance with the Charitable Choice statutory provisions and these regulations. The intermediate organization retains all other rights of a non-governmental organization under the Charitable Choice statute and regulations.

(l) Any party which seeks to enforce its right under this section may assert a civil action for injunctive relief exclusively in an appropriate State court against the entity or agency that allegedly commits such violation.

[68 FR 56465, Sept. 30, 2003]

§ 260.35 What other Federal laws apply to TANF?

(a) Under section 408(d) of the Act, the following provisions of law apply to any program or activity funded with Federal TANF funds:

(1) The Age Discrimination Act of 1975;

(2) Section 504 of the Rehabilitation Act of 1973;

(3) The Americans with Disabilities Act of 1990; and

(4) Title VI of the Civil Rights Act of 1964.

(b) The limitation on Federal regulatory and enforcement authority at section 417 of the Act does not limit the effect of other Federal laws, including Federal employment laws (such as the Fair Labor Standards Act (FLSA), the Occupational Safety and Health Act (OSHA) and unemployment insurance (UI)) and nondiscrimination laws. These laws apply to TANF beneficiaries in the same manner as they apply to other workers.

§ 260.40 When are these provisions in effect?

(a) In determining whether a State is subject to a penalty under parts 261 through 265 of this chapter, we will not apply the regulatory provisions in parts 260 through 265 of this chapter retroactively. We will judge State actions that occurred prior to the effective date of these rules and expenditures of funds received prior to the effective date only against a reasonable interpretation of the statutory provisions in title IV-A of the Act.

(b) The effective date of these rules is October 1, 1999.

Subpart B—What Special Provisions Apply to Victims of Domestic Violence?

§ 260.50 What is the purpose of this subpart?

Under section 402(a)(7) of the Act, under its TANF plan, a State may elect to implement a special program to serve victims of domestic violence and to waive program requirements for such individuals. This subpart explains how adoption of these provisions affects the penalty determinations applicable if a State fails to meet its work participation rate or comply with the five-year limit on Federal assistance.

§ 260.51 What definitions apply to this subpart?

Family Violence Option (or FVO) means the provision at section 402(a)(7) of the Act under which a State certifies in its State plan if it has elected the option to implement comprehensive strategies for identifying and serving victims of domestic violence.

Federally recognized good cause domestic violence waiver means a good cause domestic violence waiver that meets the requirements at §§ 260.52(c) and 260.55.

Good cause domestic violence waiver means a waiver of one or more program requirements granted by a State to a victim of domestic violence under the FVO, as described at § 260.52(c).

Victim of domestic violence means an individual who is battered or subject to extreme cruelty under the definition at section 408(a)(7)(C)(iii) of the Act.

§ 260.52 What are the basic provisions of the Family Violence Option (FVO)?

Section 402(a)(7) of the Act provides that States electing the FVO certify that they have established and are enforcing standards and procedures to:

(a) Screen and identify individuals receiving TANF and MOE assistance with a history of domestic violence, while maintaining the confidentiality of such individuals;

(b) Refer such individuals to counseling and supportive services; and

(c) Provide waivers, pursuant to a determination of good cause, of normal program requirements to such individuals for so long as necessary in cases where compliance would make it more difficult for such individuals to escape domestic violence or unfairly penalize those who are or have been victimized by such violence or who are at risk of further domestic violence.

§ 260.54 Do States have flexibility to grant good cause domestic violence waivers?

(a) Yes; States have broad flexibility to grant these waivers to victims of domestic violence. For example, they may determine which program requirements to waive and decide how long each waiver might be necessary.

(b) However, if a State wants us to take the waivers that it grants into account in deciding if it has reasonable cause for failing to meet its work participation rates or comply with the five-year limit on Federal assistance, has achieved compliance or made significant progress towards achieving compliance with such requirements during a corrective compliance period, or qualifies for a reduction in its work penalty under § 261.51 of this chapter, the waivers must be federally recognized good cause domestic violence waivers, within the meaning of §§ 260.52(c) and 260.55, and the State must submit the information specified at § 265.9(b)(5) of this chapter on its strategies and procedures for serving victims of domestic violence and the number of waivers granted.

§ 260.55 What are the additional requirements for Federal recognition of good cause domestic violence waivers?

To be federally recognized, good cause domestic violence waivers must:

(a) Identify the specific program requirements that are being waived;

(b) Be granted appropriately based on need, as determined by an individualized assessment by a person trained in domestic violence and redeterminations no less often than every six months;

(c) Be accompanied by an appropriate services plan that:

(1) Is developed by a person trained in domestic violence;

(2) Reflects the individualized assessment and any revisions indicated by the redetermination; and

(3) To the extent consistent with § 260.52(c), is designed to lead to work.

§ 260.58 What penalty relief is available to a State whose failure to meet the work participation rates is attributable to providing federally recognized good cause domestic violence waivers?

(a)(1) We will determine that a State has reasonable cause if its failure to meet the work participation rates was attributable to federally recognized good cause domestic violence waivers granted to victims of domestic violence.

(2) To receive reasonable cause under the provisions of § 262.5(b) of this chapter, the State must provide evidence that it achieved the applicable rates, except with respect to any individuals who received a federally recognized good cause domestic violence waiver of work participation requirements. In other words, it must demonstrate that it met the applicable rates when such waiver cases are removed from the calculations at §§ 261.22(b) and 261.24(b) of this chapter.

(b)(1) We will reduce a State's penalty based on the degree of noncompliance to the extent that its failure to meet the work participation rates was attributable to federally recognized good cause domestic violence waivers.

(2) To receive a reduction based on degree of noncompliance under the provisions of § 261.51 of this chapter, a State granting federally recognized good cause domestic violence waivers of work participation requirements must demonstrate that it achieved participation rates above the threshold at § 261.51(b)(3) of this chapter, when such waiver cases are removed from the calculations at §§ 261.22(b) and 261.24(b) of this chapter.

(c) We may take federally recognized good cause domestic violence waivers of work requirements into consideration in deciding whether a State has achieved compliance or made significant progress towards achieving compliance in meeting the work participation rates during a corrective compliance period.

(d) To receive the penalty relief specified in paragraphs (a), (b), and (c) of this section, the State must submit the information specified at § 265.9(b)(5) of this chapter.

§ 260.59 What penalty relief is available to a State that failed to comply with the five-year limit on Federal assistance because it provided federally recognized good cause domestic violence waivers?

(a)(1) We will determine that a State has reasonable cause if it failed to comply with the five-year limit on Federal assistance because of federally recognized good cause domestic violence waivers granted to victims of domestic violence.

(2) More specifically, to receive reasonable cause under the provisions at § 264.3(b) of this chapter, a State must demonstrate that:

(i) It granted federally recognized good cause domestic violence waivers to extend time limits based on the need for continued assistance due to current or past domestic violence or the risk of further domestic violence; and

(ii) When individuals and their families are excluded from the calculation, the percentage of families receiving federally funded assistance for more than 60 months did not exceed 20 percent of the total.

(b) We may take federally recognized good cause domestic violence waivers to extend time limits into consideration in deciding whether a State has achieved compliance or made significant progress towards achieving compliance in meeting the five-year limit on Federal assistance during a corrective compliance period.

(c) To receive the penalty relief specified in paragraphs (a) and (b) of this section, the State must submit the information specified at § 265.9(b)(5) of this chapter.

[64 FR 17878, Apr. 12, 1999]

Subpart C—What Special Provisions Apply to States that Were Operating Programs Under Approved Waivers?

§ 260.70 What is the purpose of this subpart?

(a) Under section 415 of the Act, if a State was granted a waiver under section 1115 of the Act and that waiver was in effect on August 22, 1996, the amendments made by PRWORA do not apply for the period of the waiver, to the extent that they are inconsistent with the waiver and the State elects to continue its waiver.

(b) Identification of waiver inconsistencies is relevant for the determination of penalties in three areas:

(1) Under § 261.50 of this chapter for failing to meet the work participation rates at part 261 of this chapter;

(2) Under § 264.2 of this chapter for failing to comply with the five-year limit on Federal assistance at subpart A of part 264 of this chapter; and

(3) Under § 261.54 of this chapter for failing to impose sanctions on individuals who fail to work.

(c) This subpart explains how we will determine waiver inconsistencies and apply them in the penalty determination process for these penalties.

§ 260.71 What definitions apply to this subpart?

(a) *Inconsistent* means that complying with the TANF work participation or sanction requirements at section 407 of the Act or the time-limit requirement at section 408(a)(7) of the Act would necessitate that a State change a policy reflected in an approved waiver.

(b) *Waiver* consists of the work participation or time-limit component of the State's demonstration project under section 1115 of the Act. The component includes the revised AFDC requirements indicated in the State's waiver list, as approved by the Secretary under the authority of section 1115, and the associated AFDC provisions that did not need to be waived.

(c) *Control group* and *experimental group* have the meanings specified in the terms and conditions of the State's demonstration.

§ 260.72 What basic requirements must State demonstration components meet for the purpose of determining if inconsistencies exist with respect to work requirements or time limits?

(a) The policies must be consistent with the requirements of section 415 of the Act and the requirements of this subpart.

(b) The policies must be within the scope of the approved waivers both in terms of geographical coverage and the coverage of the types of cases specified in the waiver approval package.

(c) The State must have applied its waiver policies on a continuous basis from the date that it implemented its TANF program, except that it may have adopted modifications that have the effect of making its policies more consistent with the provisions of PRWORA.

(d) An inconsistency may not apply beyond the earlier of the following dates:

(1) The expiration of waiver authority as determined in accordance with the demonstration terms and conditions; or

(2) For any specific inconsistency, the date upon which the State discontinued the applicable waiver policy.

(e) The State must submit the Governor's certification specified in § 260.75.

(f) In general, the policies in this subpart do not have the effect of delaying the date when a State might be subject to the work or time-limit penalties at §§ 261.50, 261.54, and 264.1 of this chapter or the data collection requirements at part 265 of this chapter.

§ 260.73 How do existing welfare reform waivers affect the participation rates and work rules?

(a) If a State is implementing a work participation component under a waiver, in accordance with this subpart, the provisions of section 407 of the Act will not apply in determining if a penalty should be imposed, to the extent that the provision is inconsistent with the waiver.

(b) For the purpose of determining if the State's demonstration has a work participation component, the waiver list for the demonstration must include one or more specific provisions that directly correspond to the work policies in section 407 of the Act (i.e., change allowable JOBS activities, exemptions from JOBS participation, hours of required JOBS participation, or sanctions for noncompliance with JOBS participation).

(c) Corresponding to the inconsistencies certified by the Governor under § 260.75:

(1) We will calculate the State's work participation rates, by:

(i) Excluding cases exempted from participation under the demonstration component and, if applicable, experimental and control cases not otherwise exempted, in calculating the rate;

(ii) Defining work activities as defined in the demonstration component in determining the numerator; and

(iii) Including cases meeting the required number of hours of participation in work activities in accordance with demonstration component policy, in determining the numerator.

(2) We will determine whether a State is taking appropriate sanctions when an individual refuses to work based on the State's certified waiver policies.

(d) We will use the data submitted by States pursuant to § 265.3 of this chapter to calculate and make public a State's work participation rates under both the TANF requirements and the State's alternative waiver requirements.

§ 260.74 How do existing welfare reform waivers affect the application of the Federal time-limit provisions?

(a)(1) If a State is implementing a time-limit component under a waiver, in accordance with this subpart, the provisions of section 408(a)(7) of the Act will not apply in determining if a penalty should be imposed, to the extent that they are inconsistent with the waiver.

(2) For the purpose of determining if the State's demonstration has a time-limit component, the waiver list for the demonstration must include provisions that directly correspond to the time-limit policies enumerated in section 408(a)(7) of the Act (i.e., address

which individuals or families are subject to, or exempt from, terminations of assistance based solely on the passage of time or who qualifies for extensions to the time limit).

(b)(1) Generally, under an approved waiver, except as provided in paragraph (b)(3) of this section, a State will count, toward the Federal five-year limit, all months for which the head-of-household or spouse of the head-of-household subject to the State time limit receives assistance with Federal TANF funds, just as it would if it did not have an approved waiver.

(2) The State need not count, toward the Federal five-year limit, any months for which a head-of-household or spouse of the head-of-household receives assistance with Federal TANF funds while that individual is exempt from the State's time limit under the State's approved waiver.

(3) Where a State has continued a time limit under waivers that only terminates assistance for adults, the State need not count, toward the Federal five-year limit, any months for which an adult subject to the State time limit receives assistance with Federal TANF funds.

(4) The State may continue to provide assistance with Federal TANF funds for more than 60 months, without a numerical limit, to families provided extensions to the State time limit, under the provisions of the terms and conditions of the approved waiver.

(c) Corresponding to the inconsistencies certified by the Governor under §260.75, we will calculate the State's time-limit exceptions by:

(1) Excluding, from the determination of the number of months of Federal assistance received by a family:

(i) Any month in which the adult(s) were exempt from the State's time limit under the terms of an approved waiver or any months in which the children received assistance under a waiver that only terminated assistance to adults; and

(ii) If applicable, experimental and control group cases not otherwise exempted; and

(2) Applying the State's waiver policies with respect to the availability of extensions to the time limit.

§ 260.75 If a State is claiming a waiver inconsistency for work requirements or time limits, what must the Governor certify?

(a) The Governor of the State must certify in writing to the Secretary that:

(1) The applicable policies have been continually applied in operating the TANF program, as described in §260.72(c);

(2) The inconsistencies claimed by the State are within the scope of the approved waivers, as described in §260.72(b);

(b) The certification must identify the specific inconsistencies that the State chooses to continue with respect to work and time limits.

(1) If the waiver inconsistency claim includes work provisions, the certification must specify the standards that will apply, in lieu of the provisions in subparts B and C of part 261 of this chapter, to determine:

(i) The number of two-parent and all-parent cases that are exempt from participation, if any, for the purpose of determining the denominator of the work participation rate;

(ii) The number of nonexempt two-parent and all-parent cases that are participating in work activities for the purpose of determining the numerator of the work participation rate, including standards applicable to;

(A) Countable work activities; and

(B) Required hours of work for participation for individual participants; and

(iii) The penalty against an individual or family when an individual refuses to work.

(2) If the waiver inconsistency claim includes time-limit provisions, the certification must include the standards that will apply, in lieu of the provisions in §264.1 of this chapter, in determining:

(i) Which families are counted toward the Federal time limit; and

(ii) Whether a family is eligible for an extension of its time limit on federally funded assistance.

(3) If the State is continuing policies for evaluation purposes in accordance with §260.76:

(i) The certification must specify any special work or time-limit standards that apply to the control group and experimental group cases; and

(ii) The State may choose to exclude cases assigned to the experimental and control groups, which are not otherwise exempt, for the purpose of calculating the work participation rate or determining State compliance related to limiting assistance to families including adults who have received 60 months of Federal TANF assistance. In doing so, the State may effectively exclude all experimental group cases and/or control group cases, not otherwise exempt, but may not exclude individual cases on a selective basis.

(c) The certification may include a claim of inconsistency with respect to hours of required participation in work activities only if the State has written evidence that, when implemented, the waiver policies established specific requirements related to hours of work for nonexempt individuals.

(d)(1) The Governor's certification must be provided no later than October 1, 1999.

(2) If a State modifies its waiver policies in a way that has a substantive effect on the determination of its work sanctions, or the calculation of its work participation rates or its time-limit exceptions, it must submit an amended certification no later than the end of the fiscal quarter in which the modifications take effect.

§ 260.76 What special rules apply to States that are continuing evaluations of their waiver demonstrations?

If a State is continuing research that employs an experimental design in order to complete an impact evaluation of a waiver demonstration, the experimental and control groups may continue to be subject to prior AFDC law, except as modified by the waiver.

PART 261—ENSURING THAT RECIPIENTS WORK

Sec.

Subpart A—What Are the Provisions Addressing Individual Responsibility?

Subpart B—What Are the Provisions Addressing State Accountability?

Subpart C—What Are the Work Activities and How Do They Count?

AUTHORITY: 42 U.S.C. 601, 602, 607, and 609; Pub. L. 109–171.

SOURCE: 64 FR 17884, Apr. 12, 1999, unless otherwise noted.

§ 261.1 What does this part cover?

This part includes the regulatory provisions relating to the mandatory work requirements of TANF and State work participation data verification requirements.

[71 FR 37475, June 29, 2006]

§ 261.2 What definitions apply to this part?

(a) The general TANF definitions at §§ 260.30 through 260.33 of this chapter apply to this part.

(b) *Unsubsidized employment* means full-or part-time employment in the public or private sector that is not subsidized by TANF or any other public program.

(c) *Subsidized private sector employment* means employment in the private sector for which the employer receives a subsidy from TANF or other public funds to offset some or all of the wages and costs of employing an individual.

(d) *Subsidized public sector employment* means employment in the public sector for which the employer receives a subsidy from TANF or other public funds to offset some or all of the wages and costs of employing an individual.

(e) *Work experience (including work associated with the refurbishing of publicly assisted housing) if sufficient private sector employment is not available* means a work activity, performed in return for welfare, that provides an individual with an opportunity to acquire the general skills, knowledge, and work habits necessary to obtain employment. The purpose of work experience is to improve the employability of those who cannot find unsubsidized full-time employment. This activity must be supervised by an employer, work site sponsor, or other responsible party on an ongoing basis no less frequently than once in each day in which the individual is scheduled to participate.

(f) *On-the-job training* means training in the public or private sector that is given to a paid employee while he or she is engaged in productive work and that provides knowledge and skills essential to the full and adequate performance of the job.

(g) *Job search and job readiness assistance* means the act of seeking or obtaining employment, preparation to seek or obtain employment, including life skills training, and substance abuse treatment, mental health treatment, or rehabilitation activities. Such treatment or therapy must be determined to be necessary and documented by a qualified medical, substance abuse, or mental health professional. Job search and job readiness assistance activities must be supervised by the TANF agency or other responsible party on an ongoing basis no less frequently than once each day in which the individual is scheduled to participate.

(h) *Community service programs* mean structured programs and embedded activities in which individuals perform work for the direct benefit of the community under the auspices of public or nonprofit organizations. Community service programs must be limited to projects that serve a useful community purpose in fields such as health, social service, environmental protection, education, urban and rural redevelopment, welfare, recreation, public facilities, public safety, and child care. Community service programs are designed to improve the employability of individuals not otherwise able to obtain unsubsidized full-time employment, and must be supervised on an ongoing basis no less frequently than once each day in which the individual is scheduled to participate. A State agency shall take into account, to the extent possible, the prior training, experience, and skills of a recipient in making appropriate community service assignments.

(i) *Vocational educational training (not to exceed 12 months with respect to any individual)* means organized educational programs that are directly related to the preparation of individuals for employment in current or emerging occupations. Vocational educational training must be supervised on an ongoing basis no less frequently than once each day in which the individual is scheduled to participate.

(j) *Job skills training directly related to employment* means training or education for job skills required by an employer to provide an individual with the ability to obtain employment or to advance or adapt to the changing demands of the workplace. Job skills training directly related to employment must be supervised on an ongoing basis no less frequently than once each day in which the individual is scheduled to participate.

(k) *Education directly related to employment, in the case of a recipient who has not received a high school diploma or a certificate of high school equivalency* means education related to a specific occupation, job, or job offer. Education directly related to employment must be supervised on an ongoing basis no less frequently than once each day in which the work-eligible individual is scheduled to participate.

(l) *Satisfactory attendance at secondary school or in a course of study leading to a certificate of general equivalence, in the case of a recipient who has not completed secondary school or received such a certificate* means regular attendance, in accordance with the requirements of the secondary school or course of study, at a secondary school or in a course of study leading to a certificate of general equivalence, in the case of a work-eligible individual who has not completed secondary school or received such a certificate. This activity must be supervised on an ongoing basis no less frequently than once each day in which the individual is scheduled to participate.

(m) *Providing child care services to an individual who is participating in a community service program* means providing child care to enable another TANF or SSP recipient to participate in a community service program. This is an unpaid activity and must be a structured program designed to improve the employability of individuals who participate in this activity. This activity must be supervised on an ongoing basis no less frequently than once each day in which the individual is scheduled to participate.

(n)(1) *Work-eligible individual* means an adult (or minor child head-of-household) receiving assistance under TANF or a separate State program or a non-recipient parent living with a child receiving such assistance unless the parent is:

(i) A minor parent and not the head-of-household;

(ii) A non-citizen who is ineligible to receive assistance due to his or her immigration status; or

(iii) At State option on a case-by-case basis, a recipient of Supplemental Security Income (SSI) benefits or Aid to the Aged, Blind or Disabled in the Territories.

(2) The term also excludes:

(i) A parent providing care for a disabled family member living in the home, provided that there is medical documentation to support the need for the parent to remain in the home to care for the disabled family member;

(ii) At State option on a case-by-case basis, a parent who is a recipient of Social Security Disability Insurance (SSDI) benefits; and

(iii) An individual in a family receiving MOE-funded assistance under an approved Tribal TANF program, unless the State includes the Tribal family in calculating work participation rates, as permitted under § 261.25.

[73 FR 6821, Feb. 5, 2008]

Subpart A—What Are the Provisions Addressing Individual Responsibility?

§ 261.10 What work requirements must an individual meet?

(a)(1) A parent or caretaker receiving assistance must engage in work activities when the State has determined that the individual is ready to engage in work or when he or she has received assistance for a total of 24 months, whichever is earlier, consistent with section 407(e)(2) of the Act.

(2) The State must define what it means to engage in work for this requirement; its definition may include participation in work activities in accordance with section 407 of the Act.

(b) If a parent or caretaker has received assistance for two months, he or she must participate in community service employment, consistent with section 407(e)(2) of the Act, unless the State has exempted the individual from work requirements or he or she is already engaged in work activities as described at § 261.30. The State will determine the minimum hours per week and the tasks the individual must perform as part of the community service employment.

§ 261.11 Which recipients must have an assessment under TANF?

(a) The State must make an initial assessment of the skills, prior work experience, and employability of each recipient who is at least age 18 or who has not completed high school (or equivalent) and is not attending secondary school.

(b) The State may make any required assessments within 30 days (90 days, at State option) of the date an individual becomes eligible for assistance.

§ 261.12 What is an individual responsibility plan?

An individual responsibility plan is a plan developed at State option, in consultation with the individual, on the basis of the assessment made under § 261.11. The plan:

(a) Should set an employment goal and a plan for moving immediately into private-sector employment;

(b) Should describe the obligations of the individual. These could include going to school, maintaining certain grades, keeping school-aged children in school, immunizing children, going to classes, or doing other things that will help the individual become or remain employed in the private sector;

(c) Should be designed to move the individual into whatever private-sector employment he or she is capable of handling as quickly as possible and to increase over time the responsibility and the amount of work the individual handles;

(d) Should describe the services the State will provide the individual to enable the individual to obtain and keep private sector employment, including job counseling services; and

(e) May require the individual to undergo appropriate substance abuse treatment.

§ 261.13 May an individual be penalized for not following an individual responsibility plan?

Yes. If an individual fails without good cause to comply with an individual responsibility plan that he or she has signed, the State may reduce the amount of assistance otherwise payable to the family, by whatever amount it considers appropriate. This penalty is in addition to any other penalties under the State's TANF program.

§ 261.14 What is the penalty if an individual refuses to engage in work?

(a) If an individual refuses to engage in work required under section 407 of the Act, the State must reduce or terminate the amount of assistance payable to the family, subject to any good cause or other exceptions the State may establish. Such a reduction is governed by the provisions of § 261.16.

(b)(1) The State must, at a minimum, reduce the amount of assistance otherwise payable to the family pro rata with respect to any period during the month in which the individual refuses to work.

(2) The State may impose a greater reduction, including terminating assistance.

(c) A State that fails to impose penalties on individuals in accordance with the provisions of section 407(e) of the Act may be subject to the State penalty specified at § 261.54.

§ 261.15 Can a family be penalized if a parent refuses to work because he or she cannot find child care?

(a) No, the State may not reduce or terminate assistance based on an individual's refusal to engage in required work if the individual is a single custodial parent caring for a child under age six who has a demonstrated inability to obtain needed child care, as specified at § 261.56.

(b) A State that fails to comply with the penalty exception at section 407(e)(2) of the Act and the requirements at § 261.56 may be subject to the State penalty specified at § 261.57.

§ 261.16 Does the imposition of a penalty affect an individual's work requirement?

A penalty imposed by a State against the family of an individual by reason of the failure of the individual to comply with a requirement under TANF shall not be construed to be a reduction in any wage paid to the individual.

Subpart B—What Are the Provisions Addressing State Accountability?

SOURCE: 73 FR 6822, Feb. 5, 2008, unless otherwise noted.

§ 261.20 How will we hold a State accountable for achieving the work objectives of TANF?

(a) Each State must meet two separate work participation rates in FY 2006 and thereafter, one—the two-parent rate based on how well it succeeds in helping work-eligible individuals in two-parent families find work activities described at § 261.30, the other—the overall rate based on how well it succeeds in finding those activities for work-eligible individuals in all the families that it serves.

(b) Each State must submit data, as specified at § 265.3 of this chapter, that allows us to measure its success in requiring work-eligible individuals to participate in work activities.

(c) If the data show that a State met both participation rates in a fiscal year, then the percentage of historic State expenditures that it must expend under TANF, pursuant to § 263.1 of this chapter, decreases from 80 percent to 75 percent for that fiscal year. This is also known as the State's TANF "maintenance-of-effort" (MOE) requirement.

(d) If the data show that a State did not meet a minimum work participation rate for a fiscal year, a State could be subject to a financial penalty.

(e) Before we impose a penalty, a State will have the opportunity to claim reasonable cause or enter into a corrective compliance plan, pursuant to §§ 262.5 and 262.6 of this chapter.

§ 261.21 What overall work rate must a State meet?

Each State must achieve a 50 percent minimum overall participation rate in FY 2006 and thereafter, minus any caseload reduction credit to which it is entitled as provided in subpart D of this part.

§ 261.22 How will we determine a State's overall work rate?

(a)(1) The overall participation rate for a fiscal year is the average of the State's overall participation rates for each month in the fiscal year.

(2) The rate applies to families with a work-eligible individual.

(b) We determine a State's overall participation rate for a month as follows:

(1) The number of TANF and SSP–MOE families that include a work-eligible individual who meets the requirements set forth in § 261.31 for the month (i.e., the numerator), divided by,

(2) The number of TANF and SSP–MOE families that include a work-eligible individual, minus the number of such families that are subject to a penalty for refusing to work in that month (i.e., the denominator). However, if a family with a work-eligible individual has been penalized for refusal to participate in work activities for more than three of the last 12 months, we will not exclude it from the participation rate calculation.

(3) At State option, we will include in the participation rate calculation families with a work-eligible individual that have been penalized for refusing to work no more than three of the last 12 months.

(c)(1) A State has the option of not requiring a single custodial parent caring for a child under age one to engage in work.

(2) At State option, we will disregard a family with such a parent from the participation rate calculation for a maximum of 12 months.

(d)(1) If a family receives assistance for only part of a month, we will count it as a month of participation if a work-eligible individual is engaged in work for the minimum average number of hours in each full week that the family receives assistance in that month.

(2) If a State pays benefits retroactively (i.e., for the period between application and approval of benefits), it has the option to consider the family to be receiving assistance during the period of retroactivity.

§ 261.23 What two-parent work rate must a State meet?

Each State must achieve a 90 percent minimum two-parent participation rate in FY 2006 and thereafter, minus any caseload reduction credit to which it is entitled as provided in subpart D of this part.

§ 261.24 How will we determine a State's two-parent work rate?

(a)(1) The two-parent participation rate for a fiscal year is the average of the State's two-parent participation rates for each month in the fiscal year.

(2) The rate applies to two-parent families with two work-eligible individuals. However, if one of the parents is a work-eligible individual with a disability, we will not consider the family to be a two-parent family; i.e., we will not include such a family in either the numerator or denominator of the two-parent rate.

(b) We determine a State's two-parent participation rate for the month as follows:

(1) The number of two-parent TANF and SSP–MOE families in which both parents are work-eligible individuals and together they meet the requirements set forth in § 261.32 for the month (i.e., the numerator), divided by,

(2) The number of two-parent TANF and SSP–MOE families in which both parents are work-eligible individuals during the month, minus the number of such two-parent families that are subject to a penalty for refusing to work in that month (the denominator). However, if a family with a work-eligible individual has been penalized for more than three months of the last 12 months, we will not exclude it from the participation rate calculation.

(3) At State option, we will include in the participation rate calculation families with a work-eligible individual that have been penalized for refusing to

work no more than three of the last 12 months.

(c) For purposes of the calculation in paragraph (b) of this section, a two-parent family includes, at a minimum, all families with two natural or adoptive parents (of the same minor child) who are work-eligible individuals and living in the home, unless both are minors and neither is a head-of-household.

(d)(1) If the family receives assistance for only part of a month, we will count it as a month of participation if a work-eligible individual in the family (or both work-eligible individuals, if they are both required to work) is engaged in work for the minimum average number of hours in each full week that the family receives assistance in that month.

(2) If a State pays benefits retroactively (i.e., for the period between application and approval of benefits), it has the option to consider the family to be receiving assistance during the period of retroactivity.

§ 261.25 Do we count Tribal families in calculating the work participation rate?

At State option, we will include families with a work-eligible individual that are receiving assistance under an approved Tribal family assistance plan or under a Tribal work program in calculating the State's participation rates under §§ 261.22 and 261.24.

Subpart C—What Are the Work Activities and How Do They Count?

§ 261.30 What are the work activities?

The work activities are:

(a) Unsubsidized employment;

(b) Subsidized private-sector employment;

(c) Subsidized public-sector employment;

(d) Work experience if sufficient private-sector employment is not available;

(e) On-the-job training (OJT);

(f) Job search and job readiness assistance;

(g) Community service programs;

(h) Vocational educational training;

(i) Job skills training directly related to employment;

(j) Education directly related to employment, in the case of a recipient who has not received a high school diploma or a certificate of high school equivalency;

(k) Satisfactory attendance at secondary school or in a course of study leading to a certificate of general equivalence, if a recipient has not completed secondary school or received such a certificate; and

(l) Providing child care services to an individual who is participating in a community service program.

§ 261.31 How many hours must a work-eligible individual participate for the family to count in the numerator of the overall rate?

(a) Subject to paragraph (d) of this section, a family with a work-eligible individual counts as engaged in work for a month for the overall rate if:

(1) He or she participates in work activities during the month for at least a minimum average of 30 hours per week; and

(2) At least 20 of the above hours per week come from participation in the activities listed in paragraph (b) of this section.

(b) The following nine activities count toward the first 20 hours of participation: unsubsidized employment; subsidized private-sector employment; subsidized public-sector employment; work experience; on-the-job training; job search and job readiness assistance; community service programs; vocational educational training; and providing child care services to an individual who is participating in a community service program.

(c) Above 20 hours per week, the following three activities may also count as participation: job skills training directly related to employment; education directly related to employment; and satisfactory attendance at secondary school or in a course of study leading to a certificate of general equivalence.

(d)(1) We will deem a work-eligible individual who participates in a work experience or community service program for the maximum number of hours per month that a State may require by dividing the combined monthly TANF or SSP–MOE grant and food stamp allotment by the higher of the Federal or State minimum wage to have participated for an average of 20 hours per week for the month in that activity.

(2) This policy is limited to States that have adopted a Simplified Food Stamp Program option that permits a State to count the value of food stamps in determining the maximum core hours of participation permitted by the FLSA.

(3) In order for Puerto Rico, which does not have a traditional Food Stamp Program, to deem core hours, it must include the value of food assistance benefits provided through the Nutrition Assistance Program in the same manner as a State must include food stamp benefits under subsection (d)(1).

[73 FR 6823, Feb. 5, 2008]

§ 261.32 How many hours must work-eligible individuals participate for the family to count in the numerator of the two-parent rate?

(a) Subject to paragraph (d) of this section, a family with two work-eligible parents counts as engaged in work for the month for the two-parent rate if:

(1) Work-eligible parents in the family are participating in work activities for a combined average of at least 35 hours per week during the month, and

(2) At least 30 of the 35 hours per week come from participation in the activities listed in paragraph (b) of this section.

(b) The following nine activities count for the first 30 hours of participation: unsubsidized employment; subsidized private-sector employment; subsidized public-sector employment; work experience; on-the-job training; job search and job readiness assistance; community service programs; vocational educational training; and providing child care services to an individual who is participating in a community service program.

(c) Above 30 hours per week, the following three activities may also count for participation: job skills training directly related to employment; education directly related to employment; and satisfactory attendance at secondary school or in a course of study leading to a certificate of general equivalence.

(d)(1) We will deem a family with two work-eligible parents in which one or both participates in a work experience or community service program for the maximum number of hours per month that a State may require by dividing the combined monthly TANF or SSP–MOE grant and food stamp allotment by the higher of the Federal or State minimum wage to have participated for an average of 30 hours per week for the month in that activity.

(2) This policy is limited to States that have adopted a Simplified Food Stamp Program option that permits a State to count the value of food stamps in determining the maximum core hours of participation permitted by the FLSA.

(3) In order for Puerto Rico, which does not have a traditional Food Stamp Program, to deem core hours, it must include the value of food assistance benefits provided through the Nutrition Assistance Program in the same manner as a State must include food stamp benefits under paragraph (d)(1) of this section.

(e)(1) Subject to paragraph (f) of this section, if the family receives federally funded child care assistance and an adult in the family does not have a disability or is not caring for a child with a disability, then the work-eligible individuals must be participating in work activities for an average of at least 55 hours per week to count as a two-parent family engaged in work for the month.

(2) At least 50 of the 55 hours per week must come from participation in the activities listed in paragraph (b) of this section.

(3) Above 50 hours per week, the three activities listed in paragraph (c) of this section may also count as participation.

(f)(1) We will deem a family with two work-eligible parents in which one or both participates in a work experience or community service program for the maximum number of hours per month that a State may require by dividing the combined monthly TANF or SSP–MOE grant and food stamp allotment by the higher of the Federal or State minimum wage to have participated for an average of 50 hours per week for the month in that activity.

(2) This policy is limited to States that have adopted a Simplified Food Stamp Program option that permits a State to count the value of food stamps in determining the maximum core hours of participation permitted by the FLSA.

(3) In order for Puerto Rico, which does not have a traditional Food Stamp Program, to deem core hours, it must include the value of food assistance benefits provided through the Nutrition Assistance Program in the same manner as a State must include food stamp benefits under paragraph (d)(1) of this section.

[73 FR 6823, Feb. 5, 2008]

§ 261.33 What are the special requirements concerning educational activities in determining monthly participation rates?

(a) Vocational educational training may only count for a total of 12 months for any individual.

(b)(1) A recipient who is married or a single head-of-household under 20 years old counts as engaged in work in a month if he or she:

(i) Maintains satisfactory attendance at a secondary school or the equivalent during the month; or

(ii) Participates in education directly related to employment for an average of at least 20 hours per week during the month.

(2)(i) For a married recipient, such participation counts as the greater of 20 hours or the actual hours of participation.

(ii) If both parents in the family are under 20 years old, the requirements at § 261.32(d) are met if both meet the conditions of paragraphs (b)(1)(i) or (b)(1)(ii) of this section.

(c) In counting individuals for each participation rate, not more than 30 percent of individuals engaged in work in a month may be included in the numerator because they are:

(1) Participating in vocational educational training; and

(2) In fiscal year 2000 or thereafter, individuals deemed to be engaged in work by participating in educational activities described in paragraph (b) of this section.

§ 261.34 Are there any limitations in counting job search and job readiness assistance toward the participation rates?

Yes. There are four limitations concerning job search and job readiness assistance.

(a) Except as provided in paragraph (b) of this section, an individual's participation in job search and job readiness assistance counts for a maximum of six weeks in the preceding 12-month period.

(b) If the State's total unemployment rate is at least 50 percent greater than the United States' total unemployment rate or if the State meets the definition of a "needy State", specified at § 260.30 of this chapter, then an individual's participation in job search and job readiness assistance counts for a maximum of 12 weeks in that 12-month period.

(c) For purposes of paragraphs (a) and (b) of this section, a week equals 20 hours for a work-eligible individual who is a single custodial parent with a child under six years of age and equals 30 hours for all other work-eligible individuals.

(d) An individual's participation in job search and job readiness assistance does not count for a week that immediately follows four consecutive weeks in which the State reports any hours of such participation in the preceding 12-month period. For purposes of this paragraph a week means seven consecutive days.

(e) Not more than once for any individual in the preceding 12-month period, a State may count three or four days of job search and job readiness assistance during a week as a full week of participation. We calculate a full week of participation based on the average daily hours of participation for three or four days and will prorate participation at that level for the remaining one or two days to determine the total hours for a five-day week. Any prorated hours of participation must be included in the calculation of total hours permitted under the limitation in this section.

[73 FR 6824, Feb. 5, 2008]

§ 261.35 Are there any special work provisions for single custodial parents?

Yes. A single custodial parent or caretaker relative with a child under age six will count as engaged in work if he or she participates for at least an average of 20 hours per week.

§ 261.36 Do welfare reform waivers affect the calculation of a State's participation rates?

A welfare reform waiver could affect the calculation of a State's participation rate, pursuant to subpart C of part 260 and section 415 of the Act.

Subpart D—How Will We Determine Caseload Reduction Credit for Minimum Participation Rates?

SOURCE: 73 FR 6824, Feb. 5, 2008, unless otherwise noted.

§ 261.40 Is there a way for a State to reduce the work participation rates?

(a)(1) If the average monthly number of cases receiving assistance, including assistance under a separate State program (as provided at § 261.42(b)), in a State in the preceding fiscal year was lower than the average monthly number of cases that received assistance, including assistance under a separate State program in that State in FY 2005, the minimum overall participation rate the State must meet for the fiscal year (as provided at § 261.21) decreases by the number of percentage points the prior-year caseload fell in comparison to the FY 2005 caseload.

(2) The minimum two-parent participation rate the State must meet for the fiscal year (as provided at § 261.23) decreases, at State option, by either:

(i) The number of percentage points the prior-year two-parent caseload, including two-parent cases receiving assistance under a separate State program (as provided at § 261.42(b)), fell in comparison to the FY 2005 two-parent caseload, including two-parent cases receiving assistance under a separate State program; or

(ii) The number of percentage points the prior-year overall caseload, including assistance under a separate State program (as provided at § 261.42(b)), fell in comparison to the FY 2005 overall caseload, including cases receiving assistance under a separate State program.

(3) For the credit calculation, we will refer to the fiscal year that precedes the fiscal year to which the credit applies as the "comparison year."

(b)(1) The calculations in paragraph (a) of this section must disregard caseload reductions due to requirements of Federal law and to changes that a State has made in its eligibility criteria in comparison to its criteria in effect in FY 2005.

(2) At State option, the calculation may offset the disregard of caseload reductions in paragraph (b)(1) of this section by changes in eligibility criteria that increase caseloads.

(c)(1) To establish the caseload base for FY 2005 and to determine the comparison-year caseload, we will use the combined TANF and Separate State Program caseload figures reported on the Form ACF–199, TANF Data Report, and Form ACF–209, SSP–MOE Data Report, respectively.

(2) To qualify for a caseload reduction, a State must have reported monthly caseload information, including cases in separate State programs, for FY 2005 and the comparison year for cases receiving assistance as defined at § 261.43.

(d)(1) A State may correct erroneous data or submit accurate data to adjust program data or to include unduplicated cases within the fiscal year.

(2) We will adjust both the FY 2005 baseline and the comparison-year caseload information, as appropriate, based on these State submissions.

(e) We refer to the number of percentage points by which a caseload falls, disregarding the cases described in paragraph (b) of this section, as a caseload reduction credit.

§ 261.41 How will we determine the caseload reduction credit?

(a)(1) We will determine the overall and two-parent caseload reduction credits that apply to each State based on the information and estimates reported to us by the State on eligibility policy changes using application denials, case closures, or other administrative data sources and analyses.

(2) We will accept the information and estimates provided by a State, unless they are implausible based on the criteria listed in paragraph (d) of this section.

(3) We may conduct on-site reviews and inspect administrative records on applications, case closures, or other administrative data sources to validate the accuracy of the State estimates.

(b) In order to receive a caseload reduction credit, a State must submit a Caseload Reduction Report to us containing the following information:

(1) A listing of, and implementation dates for, all State and Federal eligibility changes, as defined at §261.42, made by the State since the beginning of FY 2006;

(2) A numerical estimate of the positive or negative average monthly impact on the comparison-year caseload of each eligibility change (based, as appropriate, on application denials, case closures or other analyses);

(3) An overall estimate of the total net positive or negative impact on the applicable caseload as a result of all such eligibility changes;

(4) An estimate of the State's caseload reduction credit;

(5) A description of the methodology and the supporting data that a State used to calculate its caseload reduction estimates; and

(6) A certification that it has provided the public an appropriate opportunity to comment on the estimates and methodology, considered their comments, and incorporated all net reductions resulting from Federal and State eligibility changes.

(c)(1) A State requesting a caseload reduction credit for the overall participation rate must base its estimates of the impact of eligibility changes on decreases in its comparison-year overall caseload compared to the FY 2005 overall caseload baseline established in accordance with §261.40(d).

(2) A State requesting a caseload reduction credit for its two-parent rate must base its estimates of the impact of eligibility changes on decreases in either:

(i) Its two-parent caseload compared to the FY 2005 base-year two-parent caseload baseline established in accordance with §261.40(d); or

(ii) Its overall caseload compared to the FY 2005 base-year overall caseload baseline established in accordance with §261.40(d).

(d)(1) For each State, we will assess the adequacy of information and estimates using the following criteria: Its methodology; Its estimates of impact compared to other States; the quality of its data; and the completeness and adequacy of its documentation.

(2) If we request additional information to develop or validate estimates, the State may negotiate an appropriate deadline or provide the information within 30 days of the date of our request.

(3) The State must provide sufficient data to document the information submitted under paragraph (b) of this section.

(e) We will not calculate a caseload reduction credit unless the State reports case-record data on individuals and families served by any separate State program, as required under §265.3(d) of this chapter.

(f) A State may only apply to the participation rate a caseload reduction credit that we have calculated. If a State disagrees with the caseload reduction credit, it may appeal the decision as an adverse action in accordance with §262.7 of this chapter.

§261.42 Which reductions count in determining the caseload reduction credit?

(a)(1) A State's caseload reduction credit must not include caseload decreases due to Federal requirements or State changes in eligibility rules since FY 2005 that directly affect a family's eligibility for assistance. These include, but are not limited to, more stringent income and resource limitations, time limits, full family sanctions, and other new requirements that deny families assistance when an individual does not comply with work requirements, cooperate with child support, or fulfill other behavioral requirements.

(2) At State option, a State's caseload reduction credit may include caseload increases due to Federal requirements or State changes in eligibility rules since FY 2005 if used to offset caseload decreases in paragraph (a)(1) of this section.

(3) A State may not receive a caseload reduction credit that exceeds the actual caseload decline between FY 2005 and the comparison year.

(4) A State may count the reductions attributable to enforcement mechanisms or procedural requirements that are used to enforce existing eligibility criteria (e.g., fingerprinting or other verification techniques) to the extent that such mechanisms or requirements identify or deter families otherwise ineligible under existing rules.

(b) A State must include cases receiving assistance in separate State programs as part of its FY 2005 caseload and comparison-year caseload. However, if a State provides documentation that separate State program cases overlap with or duplicate cases in the TANF caseload, we will exclude them from the caseload count.

§ 261.43 What is the definition of a "case receiving assistance" in calculating the caseload reduction credit?

(a) The caseload reduction credit is based on decreases in caseloads receiving TANF- or SSP-MOE-funded assistance (other than those excluded pursuant to § 261.42).

(b)(1) A State that is investing State MOE funds in excess of the required 80 percent or 75 percent basic MOE amount need only include the pro rata share of caseloads receiving assistance that is required to meet basic MOE requirements.

(2) For purposes of paragraph (b)(1) of this section, a State may exclude from the overall caseload reduction credit calculation the number of cases funded with excess MOE. This number is calculated by dividing annual excess MOE expenditures on assistance by the average monthly expenditures on assistance per case for the fiscal year,

(i) Where annual excess MOE expenditures on assistance equal total annual MOE expenditures minus the percentage of historic State expenditures specified in paragraph (v) of this section, multiplied by the percentage that annual expenditures on assistance (both Federal and State) represent of all annual expenditures, and

(ii) Where the average monthly assistance expenditures per case for the fiscal year equal the sum of annual TANF and SSP–MOE assistance expenditures (both Federal and State) divided by the average monthly sum of TANF and SSP–MOE caseloads for the fiscal year.

(iii) If the excess MOE calculation is for a separate two-parent caseload reduction credit, we multiply the number of cases funded with excess MOE by the average monthly percentage of two-parent cases in the State's total (TANF plus SSP–MOE) average monthly caseload.

(iv) All financial data must agree with data reported on the TANF Financial Report (form ACF–196) and all caseload data must agree with data reported on the TANF Data and SSP–MOE Data Reports (forms ACF–199 and ACF–209).

(v) The State must use 80 percent of historic expenditures when calculating excess MOE; however if it has met the work participation requirements for the year, it may use 75 percent of historic expenditures.

§ 261.44 When must a State report the required data on the caseload reduction credit?

A State must report the necessary documentation on caseload reductions for the preceding fiscal year by December 31.

Subpart E—What Penalties Apply to States Related to Work Requirements?

§ 261.50 What happens if a State fails to meet the participation rates?

(a) If we determine that a State did not achieve one of the required minimum work participation rates, we must reduce the SFAG payable to the State.

(b)(1) If there was no penalty for the preceding fiscal year, the base penalty for the current fiscal year is five percent of the adjusted SFAG.

(2) For each consecutive year that the State is subject to a penalty under this part, we will increase the amount of the base penalty by two percentage points over the previous year's penalty. However, the penalty can never exceed 21 percent of the State's adjusted SFAG.

(c) We impose a penalty by reducing the SFAG payable for the fiscal year that immediately follows our final determination that a State is subject to a penalty and our final determination of the penalty amount.

(d) In accordance with the procedures specified at §262.4 of this chapter, a State may dispute our determination that it is subject to a penalty.

§261.51 Under what circumstances will we reduce the amount of the penalty below the maximum?

(a) We will reduce the amount of the penalty based on the degree of the State's noncompliance.

(1) If the State fails only the two-parent participation rate specified at §261.23, reduced by any applicable caseload reduction credit, its maximum penalty will be a percentage of the penalty specified at §261.50. This percentage will equal the percentage of two-parent cases in the State's total caseload.

(2) If the State fails the overall participation rate specified at §261.21, reduced by any applicable caseload reduction credit, or both rates, its maximum penalty will be the penalty specified at §261.50.

(b)(1) In order to receive a reduction of the penalty amounts determined under paragraphs (a)(1) or (a)(2) of this section:

(i) The State must achieve participation rates equal to a threshold level defined as 50 percent of the applicable minimum participation rate at §261.21 or §261.23, minus any caseload reduction credit determined pursuant to subpart D of this part; and

(ii) The adjustment factor for changes in the number of individuals engaged in work, described in paragraph (b)(4) of this section, must be greater than zero.

(2) If the State meets the requirements of paragraph (b)(1) of this section, we will base its reduction on the severity of the failure. For this purpose, we will calculate the severity of the State's failure based on:

(i) The degree to which it missed the target rate;

(ii) An adjustment factor that accounts for changes in the number of individuals who are engaged in work in the State since the prior year; and

(iii) The number of consecutive years in which the State failed to meet the participation rates and the number of rates missed.

(3) We will determine the degree to which the State missed the target rate using the ratio of the following two factors:

(i) The difference between the participation rate achieved by the State and the 50-percent threshold level (adjusted for any caseload reduction credit determined pursuant to subpart D of this part); and

(ii) The difference between the minimum applicable participation rate and the threshold level (both adjusted for any caseload reduction credit determined pursuant to subpart D of this part).

(4) We will calculate the adjustment factor for changes in the number of individuals engaged in work using the following formula:

(i) The average monthly number of individuals engaged in work in the penalty year minus the average monthly number of individuals engaged in work in the prior year, divided by,

(ii) The product of 0.15 and the average monthly number of individuals engaged in work in the prior year.

(5) Subject to paragraph (c) of this section, if the State fails only the two-parent participation rate specified at §261.23, and qualifies for a penalty reduction under paragraph (b)(1) of this section, its penalty reduction will be the product of:

(i) The amount determined in paragraph (a)(1) of this section;

(ii) The ratio described in paragraph (b)(3) of this section computed with respect to two-parent families; and

(iii) The adjustment factor described in paragraph (b)(4) of this section computed with respect to two-parent families.

(6) Subject to paragraph (c) of this section, if the State fails the overall

participation rate specified at § 261.21, or both rates, and qualifies for a penalty reduction under paragraph (b)(1) of this section, its penalty reduction will be the product of:

(i) The amount determined in paragraph (a)(2) of this section;

(ii) The ratio described in paragraph (b)(3) of this section computed with respect to all families; and

(iii) The adjustment factor described in paragraph (b)(4) of this section.

(7) Pursuant to § 260.58 of this chapter, we will adjust the calculations in this section to exclude cases for which a State has granted federally recognized good cause domestic violence waivers.

(c)(1) If the State was not subject to a penalty the prior year, the State will receive:

(i) The full applicable penalty reduction described in paragraph (b)(5) or (b)(6) of this section if it failed only one participation rate; or

(ii) 50 percent of the penalty reduction described in paragraph (b)(6) of this section if it failed both participation rates.

(2) If the penalty year is the second successive year in which the State is subject to a penalty, the State will receive:

(i) 50 percent of the applicable penalty reduction described in paragraph (b)(5) or (b)(6) of this section if it failed only one participation rate; or

(ii) 25 percent of the penalty reduction described in paragraph (b)(6) of this section if it failed both participation rates.

(3) If the penalty year is the third or greater successive year in which the State is subject to a penalty, the State will not receive a penalty reduction described in paragraph (b)(5) or (b)(6) of this section.

(d)(1) We may reduce the penalty if the State failed to achieve a participation rate because:

(i) It meets the definition of a needy State, specified at § 260.30 of this chapter; or,

(ii) Noncompliance is due to extraordinary circumstances such as a natural disaster, regional recession, or substantial caseload increase.

(2) In determining noncompliance under paragraph (d)(1)(ii) of this section, we will consider such objective evidence of extraordinary circumstances as the State chooses to submit.

§ 261.52 Is there a way to waive the State's penalty for failing to achieve either of the participation rates?

(a) We will not impose a penalty under this part if we determine that the State has reasonable cause for its failure.

(b) In addition to the general reasonable cause criteria specified at § 262.5 of this chapter, a State may also submit a request for a reasonable cause exemption from the requirement to meet the minimum participation rate in two specific case situations.

(1) We will determine that a State has reasonable cause if it demonstrates that failure to meet the work participation rates is attributable to its provision of federally recognized good cause domestic violence waivers (i.e., it provides evidence that it achieved the applicable work rates when individuals receiving federally recognized good cause domestic violence waivers of work requirements, in accordance with the provisions at §§ 260.54(b) and 260.55 of this chapter, are removed from the calculations in §§ 261.22(b) and 261.24(b)).

(2) We will determine that a State has reasonable cause if it demonstrates that its failure to meet the work participation rates is attributable to its provision of assistance to refugees in federally approved alternative projects under section 412(e)(7) of the Immigration and Nationality Act (8 U.S.C. 1522(e)(7)).

(c) In accordance with the procedures specified at § 262.4 of this chapter, a State may dispute our determination that it is subject to a penalty.

§ 261.53 May a State correct the problem before incurring a penalty?

(a) Yes. A State may enter into a corrective compliance plan to remedy a problem that caused its failure to meet a participation rate, as specified at § 262.6 of this chapter.

(b) To qualify for a penalty reduction under § 262.6(j)(1) of this chapter, based on significant progress towards correcting a violation, a State must reduce the difference between the participation rate it achieved in the year for which it is subject to a penalty and the rate applicable during the penalty year (adjusted for any caseload reduction credit determined pursuant to subpart D of this part) by at least 50 percent.

§261.54 Is a State subject to any other penalty relating to its work program?

(a) If we determine that, during a fiscal year, a State has violated section 407(e) of the Act, relating to imposing penalties against individuals, we must reduce the SFAG payable to the State.

(b) The penalty amount for a fiscal year will equal between one and five percent of the adjusted SFAG.

(c) We impose a penalty by reducing the SFAG payable for the fiscal year that immediately follows our final determination that a State is subject to a penalty and our final determination of the penalty amount.

§261.55 Under what circumstances will we reduce the amount of the penalty for not properly imposing penalties on individuals?

(a) We will reduce the amount of the penalty based on the degree of the State's noncompliance.

(b) In determining the size of any reduction, we will consider objective evidence of:

(1) Whether the State has established a control mechanism to ensure that the grants of individuals are appropriately reduced for refusing to engage in required work; and

(2) The percentage of cases for which the grants have not been appropriately reduced.

§261.56 What happens if a parent cannot obtain needed child care?

(a)(1) If the individual is a single custodial parent caring for a child under age six, the State may not reduce or terminate assistance based on the parent's refusal to engage in required work if he or she demonstrates an inability to obtain needed child care for one or more of the following reasons:

(i) Appropriate child care within a reasonable distance from the home or work site is unavailable;

(ii) Informal child care by a relative or under other arrangements is unavailable or unsuitable; or

(iii) Appropriate and affordable formal child care arrangements are unavailable.

(2) Refusal to work when an acceptable form of child care is available is not protected from sanctioning.

(b)(1) The State will determine when the individual has demonstrated that he or she cannot find child care, in accordance with criteria established by the State.

(2) These criteria must:

(i) Address the procedures that the State uses to determine if the parent has a demonstrated inability to obtain needed child care;

(ii) Include definitions of the terms "appropriate child care," "reasonable distance," "unsuitability of informal care," and "affordable child care arrangements"; and

(iii) Be submitted to us.

(c) The TANF agency must inform parents about:

(1) The penalty exception to the TANF work requirement, including the criteria and applicable definitions for determining whether an individual has demonstrated an inability to obtain needed child care;

(2) The State's process or procedures (including definitions) for determining a family's inability to obtain needed child care, and any other requirements or procedures, such as fair hearings, associated with this provision; and

(3) The fact that the exception does not extend the time limit for receiving Federal assistance.

[64 FR 17884, Apr. 12, 1999; 64 FR 40291, July 26, 1999]

§261.57 What happens if a State sanctions a single parent of a child under six who cannot get needed child care?

(a) If we determine that a State has not complied with the requirements of §261.56, we will reduce the SFAG payable to the State by no more than five percent for the immediately succeeding fiscal year unless the State demonstrates to our satisfaction that it had reasonable cause or it achieves compliance under a corrective compliance plan pursuant to §§ 262.5 and 262.6 of this chapter.

(b) We will impose the maximum penalty if:

(1) The State does not have a statewide process in place to inform parents about the exception to the work requirement and enable them to demonstrate that they have been unable to obtain child care; or

(2) There is a pattern of substantiated complaints from parents or organizations verifying that a State has reduced or terminated assistance in violation of this requirement.

(c) We may impose a reduced penalty if the State demonstrates that the violations were isolated or that they affected a minimal number of families.

Subpart F—How Do We Ensure the Accuracy of Work Participation Information?

SOURCE: 73 FR 6826, Feb. 5, 2008, unless otherwise noted.

§ 261.60 What hours of participation may a State report for a work-eligible individual?

(a) A State must report the actual hours that an individual participates in an activity, subject to the qualifications in paragraphs (b) and (c) of this section and § 261.61(c). It is not sufficient to report the hours an individual is scheduled to participate in an activity.

(b) For the purposes of calculating the work participation rates for a month, actual hours may include the hours for which an individual was paid, including paid holidays and sick leave. For participation in unpaid work activities, it may include excused absences for hours missed due to a maximum of 10 holidays in the preceding 12-month period and up to 80 hours of additional excused absences in the preceding 12-month period, no more than 16 of which may occur in a month, for each work-eligible individual. Each State must designate the days that it wishes to count as holidays for those in unpaid activities in its Work Verification Plan. It may designate no more than 10 such days. In order to count an excused absence as actual hours of participation, the individual must have been scheduled to participate in a countable work activity for the period of the absence that the State reports as participation. A State must describe its excused absence policies and definitions as part of its Work Verification Plan, specified at § 261.62.

(c) For unsubsidized employment, subsidized employment, and OJT, a State may report projected actual hours of employment participation for up to six months based on current, documented actual hours of work. Any time a State receives information that the client's actual hours of work have changed, or no later than the end of any six-month period, the State must re-verify the client's current actual average hours of work, and may report these projected actual hours of participation for another six-month period.

(d) A State may not count more hours toward the participation rate for a self-employed individual than the number derived by dividing the individual's self-employment income (gross income less business expenses) by the Federal minimum wage. A State may propose an alternative method of determining self-employment hours as part of its Work Verification Plan.

(e) A State may count supervised homework time and up to one hour of unsupervised homework time for each hour of class time. Total homework time counted for participation cannot exceed the hours required or advised by a particular educational program.

§ 261.61 How must a State document a work-eligible individual's hours of participation?

(a) A State must support each individual's hours of participation through documentation in the case file. In accordance with § 261.62, a State must describe in its Work Verification Plan the documentation it uses to verify hours of participation in each activity.

(b) For an employed individual, the documentation may consist of, but is not limited to pay stubs, employer reports, or time and attendance records substantiating hours of participation. A State may presume that an employed individual participated for the total number of hours for which that individual was paid.

(c) The State must document all hours of participation in an activity; however, if a State is reporting projected hours of actual employment in accordance with § 261.60(c), it need only document the hours on which it bases the projection.

(d) For an individual who is self-employed, the documentation must comport with standards set forth in the State's approved Work Verification Plan. Self-reporting by a participant without additional verification is not sufficient documentation.

(e) For an individual who is not employed, the documentation for substantiating hours of participation may consist of, but is not limited to, time sheets, service provider attendance records, or school attendance records. For homework time, the State must also document the homework or study expectations of the educational program.

§ 261.62 What must a State do to verify the accuracy of its work participation information?

(a) To ensure accuracy in the reporting of work activities by work-eligible individuals on the TANF Data Report and, if applicable, the SSP–MOE Data Report, each State must:

(1) Establish and employ procedures for determining whether its work activities may count for participation rate purposes;

(2) Establish and employ procedures for determining how to count and verify reported hours of work;

(3) Establish and employ procedures for identifying who is a work-eligible individual;

(4) Establish and employ internal controls to ensure compliance with the procedures; and

(5) Submit to the Secretary for approval the State's Work Verification Plan in accordance with paragraph (b) of this section.

(b) A State's Work Verification Plan must include the following:

(1) For each countable work activity:

(i) A description demonstrating how the activity meets the relevant definition at § 261.2;

(ii) A description of how the State determines the number of countable hours of participation; and

(iii) A description of the documentation it uses to monitor participation and ensure that the actual hours of participation are reported;

(2) A description of the State's procedures for identifying all work-eligible individuals, as defined at § 261.2;

(3) A description of how the State ensures that, for each work-eligible individual, it:

(i) Accurately inputs data into the State's automated data processing system;

(ii) Properly tracks the hours though the automated data processing system; and

(iii) Accurately reports the hours to the Department;

(4) A description of the procedures for ensuring it does not transmit to the Department a work-eligible individual's hours of participation in an activity that does not meet a Federal definition of a countable work activity; and

(5) A description of the internal controls that the State has implemented to ensure a consistent measurement of the work participation rates, including the quality assurance processes and sampling specifications it uses to monitor adherence to the established work verification procedures by State staff, local staff, and contractors.

(c) We will review a State's Work Verification Plan for completeness and approve it if we believe that it will result in accurate reporting of work participation information.

§ 261.63 When is a State's Work Verification Plan due?

(a) Each State must submit its interim Work Verification Plan for validating work activities reported in the TANF Data Report and, if applicable, the SSP–MOE Data Report no later than September 30, 2006.

(b) If HHS requires changes, a State must submit them within 60 days of receipt of our notice and include all necessary changes as part of a final approved Work Verification Plan no later than September 30, 2007.

(c) If a State modifies its verification procedures for TANF or SSP–MOE work activities or its internal controls for ensuring a consistent measurement of the work participation rate, the State must submit for approval an amended Work Verification Plan by the end of the quarter in which the State modifies the procedures or internal controls.

§ 261.64 How will we determine whether a State's work verification procedures ensure an accurate work participation measurement?

(a) We will determine that a State has met the requirement to establish work verification procedures if it submitted an interim Work Verification Plan by September 30, 2006 and a complete Work Verification Plan that we approved by September 30, 2007.

(b) A "complete" Work Verification Plan means that:

(1) The plan includes all the information required by § 261.62(b); and

(2) The State certifies that the plan includes all the information required by § 261.62(b) and that it accurately reflects the procedures under which the State is operating.

(c) For conduct occurring after October 1, 2007, we will use 45 CFR part 75, subpart F in conjunction with other reviews, audits, and data sources, as appropriate, to assess the accuracy of the data filed by States for use in calculating the work participation rates.

[73 FR 6826, Feb. 5, 2008, as amended at 81 FR 3020, Jan. 20, 2016]

§ 261.65 Under what circumstances will we impose a work verification penalty?

(a) We will take action to impose a penalty under § 262.1(a)(15) of this chapter if:

(1) The requirements under § 261.64(a) and (b) have not been met; or

(2) We determine that the State has not maintained adequate documentation, verification, or internal control procedures to ensure the accuracy of the data used in calculating the work participation rates.

(b) If a State fails to submit an interim or complete Work Verification Plan by the due dates in § 261.64(a), we will reduce the SFAG payable for the immediately succeeding fiscal year by five percent of the adjusted SFAG.

(c) If a State fails to maintain adequate internal controls to ensure a consistent measurement of work participation, we will reduce the adjusted SFAG by the following percentages for a fiscal year:

(1) One percent for the first year;

(2) Two percent for second year;

(3) Three percent for the third year;

(4) Four percent for the fourth year; and,

(5) Five percent for the fifth and subsequent years.

(d) If a State complies with the requirements in this subpart for two consecutive years, then any penalty imposed for subsequent failures will begin anew, as described in paragraph (c) of this section.

(e) If we take action to impose a penalty under § 261.64(b) or (c), we will reduce the SFAG payable for the immediately succeeding fiscal year.

Subpart G—What Nondisplacement Rules Apply in TANF?

§ 261.70 What safeguards are there to ensure that participants in work activities do not displace other workers?

(a) An adult taking part in a work activity outlined in § 261.30 may not fill a vacant employment position if:

(1) Another individual is on layoff from the same or any substantially equivalent job; or

(2) The employer has terminated the employment of any regular employee or caused an involuntary reduction in its work force in order to fill the vacancy with an adult taking part in a work activity.

(b) A State must establish and maintain a grievance procedure to resolve complaints of alleged violations of the displacement rule in this section.

(c) This section does not preempt or supersede State or local laws providing greater protection for employees from displacement.

Subpart H—How Do Welfare Reform Waivers Affect State Penalties?

§ 261.80 How do existing welfare reform waivers affect a State's penalty liability under this part?

A welfare reform waiver could affect a State's penalty liability under this part, subject to subpart C of part 260 of this chapter and section 415 of the Act.

[64 FR 17884, Apr. 12, 1999. Redesignated at 71 FR 37479, June 29, 2006]

PART 262—ACCOUNTABILITY PROVISIONS—GENERAL

AUTHORITY: 31 U.S.C. 7501 *et seq.;* 42 U.S.C. 606, 609, and 610; Sec. 7102, Pub. L. 109–171, 120 Stat. 135; Sec. 4004, Pub. L. 112–96, 126 Stat. 197.

SOURCE: 64 FR 17890, Apr. 12, 1999, unless otherwise noted.

§ 262.0 What definitions apply to this part?

The general TANF definitions at §§ 260.30 through 260.33 of this chapter apply to this part.

§ 262.1 What penalties apply to States?

(a) We will assess fiscal penalties against States under circumstances defined in parts 261 through 265 of this chapter. The penalties are:

(1) A penalty of the amount by which a State misused its TANF funds;

(2) An additional penalty of five percent of the adjusted SFAG if such misuse was intentional;

(3) A penalty of four percent of the adjusted SFAG for each quarter a State fails to submit an accurate, complete and timely required report;

(4) A penalty of up to 21 percent of the adjusted SFAG for failure to satisfy the minimum participation rates;

(5) A penalty of no more than two percent of the adjusted SFAG for failure to participate in IEVS;

(6) A penalty of no more than five percent of the adjusted SFAG for failure to enforce penalties on recipients who are not cooperating with the State Child Support Enforcement (IV-D) agency;

(7) A penalty equal to the outstanding loan amount, plus interest, for failure to repay a Federal loan;

(8) A penalty equal to the amount by which a State fails to meet its basic MOE requirement;

(9) A penalty of five percent of the adjusted SFAG for failure to comply with the five-year limit on Federal assistance;

(10) A penalty equal to the amount of contingency funds that were received but were not remitted for a fiscal year, if the State fails to maintain 100 percent of historic State expenditures in that fiscal year;

(11) A penalty of no more than five percent of the adjusted SFAG for the failure to maintain assistance to an adult single custodial parent who cannot obtain child care for a child under age six;

(12) A penalty of no more than two percent of the adjusted SFAG plus the amount a State has failed to expend of its own funds to replace the reduction to its SFAG due to the assessment of penalties in this section in the immediately succeeding fiscal year;

(13) A penalty equal to the amount of the State's Welfare-to-Work formula grant for failure to meet its basic MOE requirement during a year in which it receives the formula grant;

(14) A penalty of not less than one percent and not more than five percent of the adjusted SFAG for failure to impose penalties properly against individuals who refuse to engage in required work in accordance with section 407 of the Act; and

(15) A penalty of not less than one percent and not more than five percent of the adjusted SFAG for failure to establish or comply with work participation verification procedures.

(16)(i) A penalty of not more than five percent of the adjusted SFAG (in accordance with § 264.61(a) of this chapter), for failure to report annually on the state's implementation and maintenance of policies and practices required in § 264.60 of this chapter.

(ii) A penalty of not more than five percent of the adjusted SFAG (in accordance with § 264.61(b) of this chapter), for FY 2014 and each succeeding fiscal year in which the state does not demonstrate that it has implemented and maintained policies and practices required in § 264.60 of this chapter.

(iii) The penalty under paragraphs (a)(16)(i) and (ii) of this section may be reduced based on the degree of noncompliance of the state.

(iv) Fraudulent activity by any individual receiving TANF assistance in an attempt to circumvent the policies and practices required by § 264.60 of this chapter shall not trigger a state penalty under paragraphs (a)(16)(i) and (ii) of this section.

(b) In the event of multiple penalties for a fiscal year, we will add all applicable penalty percentages together. We will then assess the penalty amount against the adjusted SFAG that would have been payable to the State if we had assessed no penalties. As a final step, we will subtract other (fixed) penalty amounts from the adjusted SFAG.

(c)(1) We will take the penalties specified in paragraphs (a)(1), (a)(2), and (a)(7) of this section by reducing the SFAG payable for the quarter that immediately follows our final decision.

(2) We will take the penalties specified in paragraphs (a)(3) through (6) and (8) through (16) of this section by reducing the SFAG payable for the fiscal year that immediately follows our final decision.

(d) When imposing the penalties in paragraph (a) of this section, the total reduction in an affected State's quarterly SFAG amount must not exceed 25 percent. If this 25-percent limit prevents the recovery of the full penalty amount imposed on a State during a quarter or a fiscal year, as appropriate, we will apply the remaining amount of the penalty to the SFAG payable for the immediately succeeding quarter until we recover the full penalty amount.

(e)(1) In the immediately succeeding fiscal year, a State must expend additional State funds to replace any reduction in the SFAG resulting from penalties.

(2) The State must document compliance with this replacement provision on its TANF Financial Report (or Territorial Financial Report).

[64 FR 17890, Apr. 12, 1999, as amended at 71 FR 37480, June 29, 2006; 81 FR 2104, Jan. 15, 2016]

§ 262.2 When do the TANF penalty provisions apply?

(a) A State will be subject to the penalties specified in § 262.1(a)(1), (2), (7), (8), (9), (10), (11), (12), (13), and (14) for conduct occurring on and after the first day the State operates the TANF program.

(b) A State will be subject to the penalties specified in § 262.1(a)(3), (4), (5), and (6) for conduct occurring on and after July 1, 1997, or the date that is six months after the first day the State operates the TANF program, whichever is later.

(c) For the time period prior to October 1, 1999, we will assess State conduct as specified in § 260.40(b) of this chapter.

(d) The penalty specified in § 262.1(a)(15) takes effect on October 1, 2006, for failure to establish work participation verification procedures and on October 1, 2007, for failure to comply with those procedures.

(e) In accordance with § 264.61(a) and (b) of this chapter, the penalty specified in § 262.1(a)(16) will be imposed for FY 2014 and each succeeding fiscal year.

[64 FR 17890, Apr. 12, 1999, as amended at 71 FR 37480, June 29, 2006; 81 FR 2105, Jan. 15, 2016]

§ 262.3 How will we determine if a State is subject to a penalty?

(a)(1) We will use the single audit under 45 CFR part 75, subpart F, in conjunction with other reviews, audits, and data sources, as appropriate, to determine if a State is subject to a penalty for misusing Federal TANF funds (§ 263.10 of this chapter), intentionally misusing Federal TANF funds (§ 263.12 of this chapter), failing to participate in IEVS (§ 264.10 of this chapter), failing to comply with paternity establishment and child support requirements (§ 264.31 of this chapter), failing to maintain assistance to an adult single custodial parent who cannot obtain child care for a child under 6 (§ 261.57 of this chapter), failing to reduce assistance to a recipient who refuses without good cause to work (§ 261.54 of this chapter), and after October 1, 2007 failing to comply with work participation verification procedures (§ 261.64 of this chapter).

(2) We will also use the single audit as a secondary method of determining if a State is subject to other penalties if an audit detects lack of compliance in other penalty areas.

(b)(1) We will use the TANF Data Report required under part 265 of this chapter to determine if a State failed to meet participation rates (§§ 261.21 and 261.23 of this chapter) or failed to comply with the five-year limit on Federal assistance (§ 264.1 of this chapter).

(2) Data in these reports are subject to our verification in accordance with § 265.7 of this chapter.

(c)(1) We will use the TANF Financial Report (or, as applicable, the Territorial Financial Report) as the primary method for determining if a State has failed to meet the basic MOE requirement (§ 263.8 of this chapter), meet the Contingency Fund MOE requirement (§ 264.76 of this chapter), or replace SFAG reductions with State-only funds (§ 264.50 of this chapter).

(2) Data in these reports are subject to our verification in accordance with § 265.7 of this chapter.

(d) We will determine that a State is subject to the specific penalties for failure to perform if we find information in the reports under paragraphs (b) and (c) of this section to be insufficient to show compliance or if we determine that the State has not adequately documented actions verifying that it has met the participation rates or the time limits.

(e) To determine if a State has met its MOE requirements, we will also use the supplemental information in the annual report required in accordance with § 265.9(c) of this chapter.

(f) States must maintain records in accordance with 45 CFR 75.361 through 75.370.

(g) To determine if a State is subject to a penalty under § 262.1(a)(16), we will use the information provided in annual state reports at § 265.9(b)(10) of this chapter, in accordance with Section 409(a)(16) of the Social Security Act.

[64 FR 17890, Apr. 12, 1999, as amended at 71 FR 37481, June 29, 2006; 81 FR 2105, Jan. 15, 2016; 81 FR 3020, Jan. 20, 2016]

§ 262.4 What happens if we determine that a State is subject to a penalty?

(a) If we determine that a State is subject to a penalty, we will notify the State agency in writing, specifying which penalty we will impose and the reasons for the penalty. This notice will:

(1) Specify the penalty provision at issue, including the penalty amount;

(2) Specify the source of information and the reasons for our decision;

(3) Invite the State to present its arguments if it believes that the information or method that we used were in error or were insufficient or that its actions, in the absence of Federal regulations, were based on a reasonable interpretation of the statute; and

(4) Explain how and when the State may submit a reasonable cause justification under § 262.5 and/or corrective compliance plan under § 262.6.

(b) Within 60 days of when it receives our notification, the State may submit a written response that:

(1) Demonstrates that our determination is incorrect because our information or the method that we used in determining the violation or the amount of the penalty was in error or was insufficient, or that the State acted, in the absence of Federal rules, on a reasonable interpretation of the statute;

(2) Demonstrates that the State had reasonable cause for failing to meet the requirement(s); and/or

(3) Provides a corrective compliance plan, pursuant to § 262.6.

(c) If we find that we determined the penalty erroneously, or that the State has adequately demonstrated that it had reasonable cause for failing to meet one or more requirements, we will not impose the penalty.

(d) Reasonable cause and corrective compliance plans are not available for failing to repay a Federal loan; meet the basic MOE requirement; meet the Contingency Fund MOE requirement; expend additional State funds to replace adjusted SFAG reductions due to the imposition of one or more penalties listed in § 262.1; or maintain 80 percent, or 75 percent, as appropriate, basic MOE during a year in which the State receives a Welfare-to-Work grant.

(e)(1) If we request additional information from a State that we need to determine reasonable cause, the State must ordinarily provide such information within 30 days.

(2) Under unusual circumstances, we may give the State an extension of the time to respond to our request.

(f)(1)(i) We will notify the State in writing of our findings with respect to reasonable cause generally within 60 days of the date when we receive its response to our penalty notice (in accordance with paragraph (b) of this section).

(ii) If the finding is negative and the State has not yet submitted a corrective compliance plan, it may do so in response to this notice in accordance with § 262.6.

(2) We will notify the State of our decision regarding its corrective compliance plan in accordance with the provisions of § 262.6(g).

(g) We will impose a penalty in accord with the provisions in § 262.1(c) after we make our final decision and the appellate process is completed, if applicable. If there is an appellate decision upholding the penalty, we will take the penalty and charge interest back to the date that we formally notified the Governor of the adverse action pursuant to § 262.7(a)(1).

§ 262.5 Under what general circumstances will we determine that a State has reasonable cause?

(a) We will not impose a penalty against a State if we determine that the State had reasonable cause for its failure. The general factors a State may use to claim reasonable cause include:

(1) Natural disasters and other calamities (e.g., hurricanes, earthquakes, fire) whose disruptive impact was so significant as to cause the State's failure;

(2) Formally issued Federal guidance that provided incorrect information resulting in the State's failure; or

(3) Isolated problems of minimal impact that are not indicative of a systemic problem.

(b)(1) We will grant reasonable cause to a State that:

(i) Clearly demonstrates that its failure to submit complete, accurate, and timely data, as required at § 265.8 of this chapter, for one or both of the first two quarters of FY 2000, is attributable, in significant part, to its need to divert critical system resources to Year 2000 compliance activities; and

(ii) Submits complete and accurate data for the first two quarters of FY 2000 by September 30, 2000.

(2) A State may also use the additional factors for claiming reasonable cause for failure to comply with the five-year limit on Federal assistance or the minimum participation rates, as specified at §§ 261.52 and 264.3 and subpart B of part 260 of this chapter.

(c) In determining reasonable cause, we will consider the efforts the State made to meet the requirement, as well as the duration and severity of the circumstances that led to the State's failure to achieve the requirement.

(d)(1) The burden of proof rests with the State to fully explain the circumstances and events that constitute reasonable cause for its failure to meet a requirement.

(2) The State must provide us with sufficient relevant information and documentation to substantiate its claim of reasonable cause.

[64 FR 17890, Apr. 12, 1999; 64 FR 40291, July 26, 1999]

§ 262.6 What happens if a State does not demonstrate reasonable cause?

(a) A State may accept the penalty or enter into a corrective compliance plan that will correct or discontinue the violation in order to avoid the penalty if:

(1) A State does not claim reasonable cause; or

(2) We find that the State does not have reasonable cause.

(b) A State that does not claim reasonable cause will have 60 days from receipt of our notice described in § 262.4(a) to submit its corrective compliance plan.

(c) A State that unsuccessfully claimed reasonable cause will have 60 days from the date that it received our second notice, described in § 262.4(f), to submit its corrective compliance plan.

(d) The corrective compliance plan must include:

(1) A complete analysis of why the State did not meet the requirements;

(2) A detailed description of how the State will correct or discontinue, as appropriate, the violation in a timely manner;

(3) The time period in which the violation will be corrected or discontinued;

(4) The milestones, including interim process and outcome goals, that the State will achieve to assure it comes into compliance within the specified time period; and

(5) A certification by the Governor that the State is committed to correcting or discontinuing the violation, in accordance with the plan.

(e) The corrective compliance plan must correct or discontinue the violation within the following time frames:

(1) For a penalty under § 262.1(a)(4), (a)(9), or (a)(15), by the end of the first fiscal year ending at least six months after our receipt of the corrective compliance plan; and

(2) For the remaining penalties, by a date the State proposes that reflects the minimum period necessary to achieve compliance.

(f) During the 60-day period following our receipt of the State's corrective compliance plan, we may request additional information and consult with the State on modifications to the plan including in the case of a penalty under § 262.1(a)(15), modifications to the State's work verification procedures and Work Verification Plan.

(g) We will accept or reject the State's corrective compliance plan, in writing, within 60 days of our receipt of the plan, although a corrective compliance plan is deemed to be accepted if we take no action during the 60-day period following our receipt of the plan.

(h) If a State does not submit an acceptable corrective compliance plan on time, we will assess the penalty immediately.

(i) We will not impose a penalty against a State with respect to any violation covered by a corrective compliance plan that we accept if the State completely corrects or discontinues, as appropriate, the violation within the period covered by the plan.

(j) Under limited circumstances, we may reduce the penalty if the State fails to completely correct or discontinue the violation pursuant to its corrective compliance plan and in a timely manner. To receive a reduced penalty, the State must demonstrate that it met one or both of the following conditions:

(1) Although it did not achieve full compliance, the State made significant progress towards correcting or discontinuing the violation; or

(2) The State's failure to comply fully was attributable to either a natural disaster or regional recession.

[64 FR 17890, Apr. 12, 1999, as amended at 71 FR 37481, June 29, 2006]

§ 262.7 How can a State appeal our decision to take a penalty?

(a)(1) We will formally notify the Governor and the State agency of an adverse action (i.e., the reduction in the SFAG) within five days after we determine that a State is subject to a penalty under parts 261 through 265 of this chapter.

(2) Such notice will include the factual and legal basis for taking the penalty in sufficient detail for the State to be able to respond in an appeal.

(b)(1) The State may file an appeal of the action, in whole or in part, with the HHS Departmental Appeals Board (the Board) within 60 days after the date it receives notice of the adverse action. The State must submit its brief and supporting documents when it files its appeal.

(2) The State must send a copy of the appeal, and any supplemental filings, to the Office of the General Counsel, Children, Families and Aging Division, Room 411–D, 200 Independence Avenue, SW., Washington, DC 20201.

(c) We will submit our reply brief and supporting documentation within 45 days of the receipt of the State's submission under paragraph (b) of this section.

(d) The State may submit a reply and any supporting documentation within 21 days of its receipt of our reply under paragraph (c) of this section.

(e) The appeal to the Board must follow the provisions of the rules under this section and those at §§16.2, 16.9, 16.10, and 16.13–16.22 of this title, to the extent that they are consistent with this section.

(f) The Board will consider an appeal filed by a State on the basis of the documentation and briefs submitted, along with any additional information the Board may require to support a final decision. Such information may include a hearing if the Board determines that it is necessary. In deciding whether to uphold an adverse action or any portion of such action, the Board will conduct a thorough review of the issues.

(g)(1) A State may obtain judicial review of a final decision by the Board by filing an action within 90 days after the date of such decision. It should file this action with the district court of the United States in the judicial district where the State agency is located or in the United States District Court for the District of Columbia.

(2) The district court will review the final decision of the Board on the record established in the administrative proceeding, in accordance with the standards of review prescribed by 5 U.S.C. 706(2). The court will base its review on the documents and supporting data submitted to the Board.

PART 263—EXPENDITURES OF STATE AND FEDERAL TANF FUNDS

Sec.

Subpart A—What Rules Apply to a State's Maintenance of Effort?

Subpart B—What Rules Apply to the Use of Federal TANF Funds?

Subpart C—What Rules Apply to Individual Development Accounts?

AUTHORITY: 42 U.S.C. 604, 607, 609, and 862a; Pub. L. 109–171.

SOURCE: 64 FR 17893, Apr. 12, 1999, unless otherwise noted.

§263.0 What definitions apply to this part?

(a) Except as noted in §263.2(d), the general TANF definitions at §260.30 through §260.33 of this chapter apply to this part.

(b) The term "administrative costs" means costs necessary for the proper administration of the TANF program or separate State programs.

(1) It excludes direct costs of providing program services.

(i) For example, it excludes costs of providing diversion benefits and services, providing program information to clients, screening and assessments, development of employability plans, work activities, post-employment services, work supports, and case management. It also excludes costs for contracts devoted entirely to such activities.

(ii) It excludes the salaries and benefits costs for staff providing program services and the direct administrative costs associated with providing the services, such as the costs for supplies, equipment, travel, postage, utilities, rental of office space and maintenance of office space.

(2) It includes costs for general administration and coordination of these programs, including contract costs and all indirect (or overhead) costs. Examples of administrative costs include:

(i) Salaries and benefits of staff performing administrative and coordination functions;

(ii) Activities related to eligibility determinations;

(iii) Preparation of program plans, budgets, and schedules;

(iv) Monitoring of programs and projects;

(v) Fraud and abuse units;

(vi) Procurement activities;

(vii) Public relations;

(viii) Services related to accounting, litigation, audits, management of property, payroll, and personnel;

(ix) Costs for the goods and services required for administration of the program such as the costs for supplies, equipment, travel, postage, utilities, and rental of office space and maintenance of office space, provided that such costs are not excluded as a direct administrative cost for providing program services under paragraph (b)(1) of this section;

(x) Travel costs incurred for official business and not excluded as a direct administrative cost for providing program services under paragraph (b)(1) of this section;

(xi) Management information systems not related to the tracking and monitoring of TANF requirements (e.g., for a personnel and payroll system for State staff); and

(xii) Preparing reports and other documents.

Subpart A—What Rules Apply to a State's Maintenance of Effort?

§ 263.1 How much State money must a State expend annually to meet the basic MOE requirement?

(a)(1) The minimum basic MOE for a fiscal year is 80 percent of a State's historic State expenditures.

(2) However, if a State meets the minimum work participation rate requirements in a fiscal year, as required under §§ 261.21 and 261.23 of this chapter, after adjustment for any caseload reduction credit under § 261.41 of this chapter, then the minimum basic MOE for that fiscal year is 75 percent of the State's historic State expenditures.

(3) A State that does not meet the minimum participation rate requirements in a fiscal year, as required under §§ 261.21 and 261.23 of this chapter (after adjustment for any caseload reduction credit under § 261.41 of this chapter), but which is granted full or partial penalty relief for that fiscal year, must still meet the minimum basic MOE specified under paragraph (a)(1) of this section.

(b) The basic MOE level also depends on whether a Tribe or consortium of Tribes residing in a State has received approval to operate its own TANF program. The State's basic MOE level for a fiscal year will be reduced by the same percentage as we reduced the SFAG as the result of any Tribal Family Assistance Grants awarded to Tribal grantees in the State for that year.

§ 263.2 What kinds of State expenditures count toward meeting a State's basic MOE expenditure requirement?

(a) Expenditures of State funds in TANF or separate State programs may count if they are made for the following types of benefits or services:

(1) Cash assistance, including the State's share of the assigned child support collection that is distributed to the family, and disregarded in determining eligibility for, and amount of the TANF assistance payment;

(2) Child care assistance (see § 263.3);

(3) Education activities designed to increase self-sufficiency, job training, and work (see § 263.4);

(4) Any other use of funds allowable under section 404(a)(1) of the Act including:

(i) Nonmedical treatment services for alcohol and drug abuse and some medical treatment services (provided that the State has not commingled its MOE funds with Federal TANF funds to pay for the services), if consistent with the goals at § 260.20 of this chapter; and

(ii) Pro-family healthy marriage and responsible fatherhood activities enumerated in part IV–A of the Act, sections 403(a)(2)(A)(iii) and 403(a)(2)(C)(ii) that are consistent with the goals at § 260.20(c) or (d) of this chapter, but do not constitute "assistance" as defined in § 260.31(a) of this chapter; and

(5)(i) Administrative costs for activities listed in paragraphs (a)(1) through (a)(4) of this section, not to exceed 15 percent of the total amount of countable expenditures for the fiscal year.

(ii) Costs for information technology and computerization needed for tracking or monitoring required by or under part IV–A of the Act do not count towards the limit in paragraph (5)(i) of this section, even if they fall within the definition of "administrative costs."

(A) This exclusion covers the costs for salaries and benefits of staff who develop, maintain, support, or operate the portions of information technology or computer systems used for tracking and monitoring.

(B) It also covers the costs of contracts for the development, maintenance, support, or operation of those portions of information technology or computer systems used for tracking or monitoring.

(b) With the exception of paragraph (a)(4)(ii) of this section, the benefits or services listed under paragraph (a) of this section count only if they have been provided to or on behalf of eligible families. An "eligible family" as defined by the State, must:

(1) Be comprised of citizens or noncitizens who:

(i) Are eligible for TANF assistance;

(ii) Would be eligible for TANF assistance, but for the time limit on the receipt of federally funded assistance; or

(iii) Are lawfully present in the United States and would be eligible for assistance, but for the application of title IV of PRWORA;

(2) Include a child living with a custodial parent or other adult caretaker relative (or consist of a pregnant individual); and

(3) Be financially eligible according to the appropriate income and resource (when applicable) standards established by the State and contained in its TANF plan.

(c) Benefits or services listed under paragraph (a) of this section provided to a family that meets the criteria under paragraphs (b)(1) through (b)(3) of this section, but who became ineligible solely due to the time limitation given under § 264.1 of this chapter, may also count.

(d) Expenditures for the benefits or services listed under paragraph (a) of this section count whether or not the benefit or service meets the definition of assistance under § 260.31 of this chapter. Further, families that meet the criteria in paragraphs (b)(2) and (b)(3) of this section are considered to be eligible for TANF assistance for the purposes of paragraph (b)(1)(i) of this section.

(e) Expenditures for benefits or services listed under paragraph (a) of this section may include allowable costs borne by others in the State (e.g., local government), including cash donations from non-Federal third parties (e.g., a non-profit organization) and the value of third party in-kind contributions if:

(1) The expenditure is verifiable and meets all applicable requirements in 45 CFR 75.2 and 75.306;

(2) There is an agreement between the State and the other party allowing the State to count the expenditure toward its MOE requirement; and,

(3) The State counts a cash donation only when it is actually spent.

(f)(1) The expenditures for benefits or services in State-funded programs listed under paragraph (a) of this section count only if they also meet the requirements of § 263.5.

(2) Expenditures that fall within the prohibitions in § 263.6 do not count.

(g) State funds used to meet the Healthy Marriage Promotion and Responsible Fatherhood Grant match requirement may count to meet the MOE requirement in § 263.1, provided the expenditure also meets all the other MOE requirements in this subpart.

[73 FR 6827, Feb. 5, 2008, as amended at 81 FR 3020, Jan. 20, 2016]

§ 263.3 When do child care expenditures count?

(a) State funds expended to meet the requirements of the CCDF Matching Fund (i.e., as match or MOE amounts) may also count as basic MOE expenditures up to the State's child care MOE amount that must be expended to qualify for CCDF matching funds.

(b) Child care expenditures that have not been used to meet the requirements of the CCDF Matching Fund (i.e., as match or MOE amounts), or any other Federal child care program, may also count as basic MOE expenditures. The limit described in paragraph (a) of this section does not apply.

(c) The child care expenditures described in paragraphs (a) and (b) of this section must be made to, or on behalf of, eligible families, as defined in § 263.2(b).

§ 263.4 When do educational expenditures count?

(a) Expenditures for educational activities or services count if:

(1) They are provided to eligible families (as defined in § 263.2(b)) to increase self-sufficiency, job training, and work; and

(2) They are not generally available to other residents of the State without cost and without regard to their income.

(b) Expenditures on behalf of eligible families for educational services or activities provided through the public education system do not count unless they meet the requirements under paragraph (a) of this section.

§ 263.5 When do expenditures in State-funded programs count?

(a) If a current State or local program also operated in FY 1995, and expenditures in this program would have been previously authorized and allowable under the former AFDC, JOBS, Emergency Assistance, Child Care for AFDC recipients, At-Risk Child Care, or Transitional Child Care programs, then current fiscal year expenditures in this program count in their entirety, provided that the State has met all requirements under § 263.2.

(b) If a current State or local program also operated in FY 1995, and expenditures in this program would not have been previously authorized and allowable under the former AFDC, JOBS, Emergency Assistance, Child Care for AFDC recipients, At-Risk Child Care, or Transitional Child care programs, then countable expenditures are limited to:

(1) The amount by which total current fiscal year expenditures for or on behalf of eligible families, as defined in § 263.2(b), exceed total State expenditures in this program during FY 1995; or, if applicable,

(2) The amount by which total current fiscal year expenditures for pro-family activities under § 263.2(a)(4)(ii) exceed total State expenditures in this program during FY 1995.

[64 FR 17893, Apr. 12, 1999, as amended at 73 FR 6828, Feb. 5, 2008]

§ 263.6 What kinds of expenditures do not count?

The following kinds of expenditures do not count:

(a) Expenditures of funds that originated with the Federal government;

(b) State expenditures under the Medicaid program under title XIX of the Act;

(c) Expenditures that a State makes as a condition of receiving Federal funds under another program that is not in Part IV-A of the Act, except as provided in § 263.3;

(d) Expenditures that a State made in a prior fiscal year;

(e) Expenditures that a State uses to match Federal Welfare-to-Work funds provided under section 403(a)(5) of the Act; and

(f) Expenditures that a State makes in the TANF program to replace the reductions in the SFAG as a result of penalties, pursuant to § 264.50 of this chapter.

[71 FR 37481, June 29, 2006]

§ 263.8 What happens if a State fails to meet the basic MOE requirement?

(a) If any State fails to meet its basic MOE requirement for any fiscal year, then we will reduce dollar-for-dollar the amount of the SFAG payable to the State for the following fiscal year.

(b) If a State fails to meet its basic MOE requirement for any fiscal year, and the State received a WtW formula grant under section 403(a)(5)(A) of the Act for the same fiscal year, we will also reduce the amount of the SFAG payable to the State for the following fiscal year by the amount of the WtW formula grant paid to the State.

§ 263.9 May a State avoid a penalty for failing to meet the basic MOE requirement through reasonable cause or corrective compliance?

No. The reasonable cause and corrective compliance provisions at §§ 262.4, 262.5, and 262.6 of this chapter do not apply to the penalties in § 263.8.

Subpart B—What Rules Apply to the Use of Federal TANF Funds?

§ 263.10 What actions would we take against a State if it uses Federal TANF funds in violation of the Act?

(a) If a State misuses its Federal TANF funds, we will reduce the SFAG payable for the immediately succeeding fiscal year quarter by the amount misused.

(b) If the State fails to demonstrate that the misuse was not intentional, we will further reduce the SFAG payable for the immediately succeeding fiscal year quarter in an amount equal to five percent of the adjusted SFAG.

(c) The reasonable cause and corrective compliance provisions of §§ 262.4 through 262.6 of this chapter apply to the penalties specified in paragraphs (a) and (b) of this section.

§ 263.11 What uses of Federal TANF funds are improper?

(a) States may use Federal TANF funds for expenditures:

(1) That are reasonably calculated to accomplish the purposes of TANF, as specified at § 260.20 of this chapter; or

(2) For which the State was authorized to use IV-A or IV-F funds under prior law, as in effect on September 30, 1995 (or, at the option of the State, August 21, 1996).

(b) We will consider use of funds in violation of paragraph (a) of this section, sections 404 and 408 and other provisions of the Act, section 115(a)(1) of PRWORA, or part 75 of this title to be misuse of funds.

[64 FR 17893, Apr. 12, 1999, as amended at 81 FR 3020, Jan. 20, 2016]

§ 263.12 How will we determine if a State intentionally misused Federal TANF funds?

(a) The State must show, to our satisfaction, that it used these funds for purposes that a reasonable person would consider to be within the purposes of the TANF program (as specified at § 260.20 of this chapter) and consistent with the provisions listed in § 263.11.

(b) We may determine that a State misused funds intentionally if there is supporting documentation, such as Federal guidance or policy instructions, precluding the use of Federal TANF funds for such purpose.

(c) We may also determine that a State intentionally misused funds if the State continues to use the funds in the same or similarly improper manner after receiving notification that we had determined such use to be improper.

§ 263.13 Is there a limit on the amount of Federal TANF funds that a State may spend on administrative costs?

(a)(i) Yes, a State may not spend more than 15 percent of the amount that it receives as its adjusted SFAG, or under other provisions of section 403 of the Act, on "administrative costs," as defined at § 263.0(b).

(ii) Any violation of the limitation in paragraph (a)(i) of this section will constitute a misuse of funds under § 263.11(b).

(b) Expenditures on the information technology and computerization needed for tracking and monitoring required by or under part IV-A of the Act do not count towards the limit specified in paragraph (a) of this section.

(1) This exclusion covers the costs for salaries and benefits of staff who develop, maintain, support or operate the portions of information technology or computer systems used for tracking and monitoring.

(2) It also covers the costs of contracts for development, maintenance. support, or operation of those portions of information technology or computer

systems used for tracking or monitoring.

§263.14 What methodology shall States use to allocate TANF costs?

States shall use a benefiting program cost allocation methodology consistent with the general requirements of subpart E of part 75 of this title to allocate TANF costs.

[73 FR 42721, July 23, 2008, as amended at 81 FR 3020, Jan. 20, 2016]

Subpart C—What Rules Apply to Individual Development Accounts?

§263.20 What definitions apply to Individual Development Accounts (IDAs)?

The following definitions apply with respect to IDAs:

Date of acquisition means the date on which a binding contract to obtain, construct, or reconstruct the new principal residence is entered into.

Eligible educational institution means an institution described in section 481(a)(1) or section 1201(a) of the Higher Education Act of 1965 (20 U.S.C. 1088(a)(1) or 1141(a)), as such sections were in effect on August 21, 1996. Also, an area vocational education school (as defined in subparagraph (C) or (D) of section 521(4) of the Carl D. Perkins Vocational and Applied Technology Education Act (20 U.S.C. 2471(4)) that is in any State (as defined in section 521(33) of such Act), as such sections were in effect on August 21, 1996.

Individual Development Account (IDA) means an account established by, or for, an individual who is eligible for assistance under the TANF program, to allow the individual to accumulate funds for specific purposes. Notwithstanding any other provision of law (other than the Internal Revenue Code of 1986), the funds in an IDA account must be disregarded in determining eligibility for, or the amount of, assistance in any Federal means-tested programs.

Post-secondary educational expenses means a student's tuition and fees required for the enrollment or attendance at an eligible educational institution, and required course fees, books, supplies, and equipment required at an eligible educational institution.

Qualified acquisition costs means the cost of obtaining, constructing, or reconstructing a residence. The term includes any usual or reasonable settlement, financing, or other closing costs.

Qualified business means any business that does not contravene State law or public policy.

Qualified business capitalization expenses means business expenses pursuant to a qualified plan.

Qualified entity means a nonprofit, tax-exempt organization, or a State or local government agency that works cooperatively with a nonprofit, tax-exempt organization.

Qualified expenditures means expenses entailed in a qualified plan, including capital, plant equipment, working capital, and inventory expenses.

Qualified first-time home buyer means a taxpayer (and, if married, the taxpayer's spouse) who has not owned a principal residence during the three-year period ending on the date of acquisition of the new principal residence.

Qualified plan means a business plan that is approved by a financial institution, or by a nonprofit loan fund having demonstrated fiduciary integrity. It includes a description of services or goods to be sold, a marketing plan, and projected financial statements, and it may require the eligible recipient to obtain the assistance of an experienced entrepreneurial advisor.

Qualified principal residence means the place a qualified first-time home buyer will reside in accordance with the meaning of section 1034 of the Internal Revenue Code of 1986 (26 U.S.C. 1034). The qualified acquisition cost of the residence cannot exceed the average purchase price of similar residences in the area.

§263.21 May a State use the TANF grant to fund IDAs?

If the State elects to operate an IDA program, then the States may use Federal TANF funds or WtW funds to fund IDAs for individuals who are eligible for TANF assistance and exercise flexibility within the limits of Federal regulations and the statute.

§ 263.22 Are there any restrictions on IDA funds?

The following restrictions apply to IDA funds:

(a) A recipient may deposit only earned income into an IDA.

(b) A recipient's contributions to an IDA may be matched by, or through, a qualified entity.

(c) A recipient may withdraw funds only for the following reasons:

(1) To cover post-secondary education expenses, if the amount is paid directly to an eligible educational institution;

(2) For the recipient to purchase a first home, if the amount is paid directly to the person to whom the amounts are due and it is a qualified acquisition cost for a qualified principal residence by a qualified first-time home buyer; or

(3) For business capitalization, if the amounts are paid directly to a business capitalization account in a federally insured financial institution and used for a qualified business capitalization expense.

§ 263.23 How does a State prevent a recipient from using the IDA account for unqualified purposes?

To prevent recipients from using the IDA account improperly, States may do the following:

(a) Count withdrawals as earned income in the month of withdrawal (unless already counted as income);

(b) Count withdrawals as resources in determining eligibility; or

(c) Take such other steps as the State has established in its State plan or written State policies to deter inappropriate use.

PART 264—OTHER ACCOUNTABILITY PROVISIONS

Sec.

Subpart A—What Specific Rules Apply for Other Program Penalties?

Subpart B—What are the Requirements for the Contingency Fund?

Subpart C—What Rules Pertain Specifically to the Spending Levels of the Territories?

AUTHORITY: 31 U.S.C. 7501 *et seq.;* 42 U.S.C. 608, 609, 654, 1302, 1308, and 1337.

SOURCE: 64 FR 17896, Apr. 12, 1999, unless otherwise noted.

§264.0 What definitions apply to this part?

(a) The general TANF definitions at §§260.30 through 260.33 of this chapter apply to this part.

(b) The following definitions also apply to this part:

Casino, gambling casino, or gaming establishment means an establishment with a primary purpose of accommodating the wagering of money. It does not include:

(i) A grocery store which sells groceries including staple foods and which also offers, or is located within the same building or complex as, casino, gambling, or gaming activities; or

(ii) Any other establishment that offers casino, gambling, or gaming activities incidental to the principal purpose of the business.

Countable State Expenditures means the amount of qualifying State expenditures, as defined in §264.75, plus the amount of contingency funds expended by the State in the fiscal year.

Electronic benefit transfer transaction means the use of a credit or debit card service, automated teller machine, point-of-sale terminal, or access to an online system for the withdrawal of funds or the processing of a payment for merchandise or a service.

FAG means the Family Assistance Grant granted to a Territory pursuant to section 403(a)(1) of the Act. It is thus the Territorial equivalent of the SFAG, as defined at §260.30 of this chapter.

Food Stamp Trigger means a State's monthly average of individuals participating in the Food Stamp program (as of the last day of the month) for the most recent three-month period that exceeds its monthly average of individuals in the corresponding three-month period in the Food Stamp caseload for FY 1994 or FY 1995, whichever is less, by at least ten percent, assuming that the immigrant provisions of title IV and the Food Stamp provisions under title VII of PRWORA had been in effect in those years.

Liquor store means any retail establishment which sells exclusively or primarily intoxicating liquor. Such term does not include a grocery store which sells both intoxicating liquor and groceries including staple foods (within the meaning of Section 3(r) of the Food and Nutrition Act of 2008 (7 U.S.C. 2012(r))).

Unemployment Trigger means a State's average unemployment rate for the most recent three-month period of at least 6.5 percent and equal to at least 110 percent of the State's unemployment rate for the corresponding three-month period in either of the two preceding calendar years.

[64 FR 17896, Apr. 12, 1999, as amended at 81 FR 2105, Jan. 15, 2016]

Subpart A—What Specific Rules Apply for Other Program Penalties?

§264.1 What restrictions apply to the length of time Federal TANF assistance may be provided?

(a)(1) Subject to the exceptions in this section, no State may use any of its Federal TANF funds to provide assistance (as defined in §260.31 of this chapter) to a family that includes an adult head-of-household or a spouse of the head-of-household who has received Federal assistance for a total of five years (i.e., 60 cumulative months, whether or not consecutive).

(2) The provision in paragraph (a)(1) of this section also applies to a family that includes a pregnant minor head-of-household, minor parent head-of-household, or spouse of such a head-of-household who has received Federal assistance for a total of five years.

(3) Notwithstanding the provisions of paragraphs (a)(1) and (a)(2) of this section, a State may provide assistance under WtW, pursuant to section 403(a)(5) of the Act, to a family that is ineligible for TANF solely because it has reached the five-year time limit.

(b)(1) States must not count toward the five-year limit:

(i) Any month of receipt of assistance by an individual who is not the head-of-household or married to the head-of-household;

(ii) Any month of receipt of assistance by an adult while living in Indian country (as defined in section 1151 of title 18, United States Code) or a Native Alaskan Village where at least 50 percent of the adults were not employed; and

(iii) Any month for which an individual receives only noncash assistance provided under WtW, pursuant to section 403(a)(5) of the Act.

(2) Only months of assistance that are paid for with Federal TANF funds (in whole or in part) count towards the five-year time limit.

(c) States have the option to extend assistance paid for by Federal TANF funds beyond the five-year limit for up to 20 percent of the average monthly number of families receiving assistance during the fiscal year or the immediately preceding fiscal year, whichever the State elects. States are permitted to extend assistance to families only on the basis of:

(1) Hardship, as defined by the State; or

(2) The fact that the family includes someone who has been battered, or subject to extreme cruelty based on the fact that the individual has been subjected to:

(i) Physical acts that resulted in, or threatened to result in, physical injury to the individual;

(ii) Sexual abuse;

(iii) Sexual activity involving a dependent child;

(iv) Being forced as the caretaker relative of a dependent child to engage in nonconsensual sexual acts or activities;

(v) Threats of, or attempts at, physical or sexual abuse;

(vi) Mental abuse; or

(vii) Neglect or deprivation of medical care.

(d) If a State opts to extend assistance to part of its caseload as permitted under paragraph (c) of this section, it would grant such an extension to a specific family once a head-of-household or spouse of a head-of-household in the family has received 60 cumulative months of assistance.

(e) To determine whether a State has failed to comply with the five-year limit on Federal assistance established in paragraph (c) of this section for a fiscal year, we would divide the average monthly number of families with a head-of-household or a spouse of a head-of-household who has received assistance for more than 60 cumulative months by the average monthly number of all families that received assistance during that fiscal year or during the immediately preceding fiscal year.

(f) If the five-year limit is inconsistent with a State's waiver granted under section 1115 of the Act, we will determine State compliance with the Federal time limit in accordance with the provisions of subpart C of part 260.

§ 264.2 What happens if a State does not comply with the five-year limit?

If we determine that a State has not complied with the requirements of § 264.1, we will reduce the SFAG payable to the State for the immediately succeeding fiscal year by five percent of the adjusted SFAG unless the State demonstrates to our satisfaction that it had reasonable cause, or it corrects or discontinues the violation under an approved corrective compliance plan.

§ 264.3 How can a State avoid a penalty for failure to comply with the five-year limit?

(a) We will not impose the penalty if the State demonstrates to our satisfaction that it had reasonable cause for failing to comply with the five-year limit on Federal assistance or it achieves compliance under a corrective compliance plan, pursuant to §§ 262.5 and 262.6 of this chapter.

(b) In addition, we will determine a State has reasonable cause if it demonstrates that it failed to comply with the five-year limit on Federal assistance because of federally recognized good cause domestic violence waivers provided to victims of domestic violence in accordance with provisions of subpart B of part 260.

[64 FR 17896, Apr. 12, 1999; 64 FR 40292, July 26, 1999]

§ 264.10 Must States do computer matching of data records under IEVS to verify recipient information?

(a) Pursuant to section 1137 of the Act and subject to paragraph (a)(2) of that section, States must meet the requirements of IEVS and request the following information from the Internal Revenue Service (IRS), the State Wage Information Collections Agency (SWICA), the Social Security Administration (SSA), and the Immigration and Naturalization Service (INS):

(1) IRS unearned income;

(2) SWICA employer quarterly reports of income and unemployment insurance benefit payments;

(3) IRS earned income maintained by SSA; and

(4) Immigration status information maintained by the INS.

(b) The requirements at §§ 205.51 through 205.60 of this chapter also apply to the TANF IEVS requirement.

[64 FR 17896, Apr. 12, 1999; 64 FR 40292, July 26, 1999]

§ 264.11 How much is the penalty for not participating in IEVS?

If we determine that the State has not complied with the requirements of § 264.10, we will reduce the SFAG payable for the immediately succeeding fiscal year by two percent of the adjusted SFAG unless the State demonstrates to our satisfaction that it had reasonable cause or achieved compliance under a corrective compliance plan pursuant to §§ 262.5 and 262.6 of this chapter.

§ 264.30 What procedures exist to ensure cooperation with the child support enforcement requirements?

(a)(1) The State agency must refer all appropriate individuals in the family of a child, for whom paternity has not been established or for whom a child support order needs to be established, modified or enforced, to the child support enforcement agency (i.e., the IV-D agency).

(2) Referred individuals must cooperate in establishing paternity and in establishing, modifying, or enforcing a support order with respect to the child.

(b) If the IV-D agency determines that an individual is not cooperating, and the individual does not qualify for a good cause or other exception established by the State agency responsible for making good cause determinations in accordance with section 454(29) of the Act or for a good cause domestic violence waiver granted in accordance with § 260.52 of this chapter, then the IV-D agency must notify the IV-A agency promptly.

(c) The IV-A agency must then take appropriate action by:

(1) Deducting from the assistance that would otherwise be provided to the family of the individual an amount equal to not less than 25 percent of the amount of such assistance; or

(2) Denying the family any assistance under the program.

§ 264.31 What happens if a State does not comply with the IV-D sanction requirement?

(a)(1) If we find that, for a fiscal year, the State IV-A agency did not enforce the penalties against recipients required under § 264.30(c), we will reduce the SFAG payable for the next fiscal year by one percent of the adjusted SFAG.

(2) Upon a finding for a second fiscal year, we will reduce the SFAG by two percent of the adjusted SFAG for the following year.

(3) A third or subsequent finding will result in the maximum penalty of five percent.

(b) We will not impose a penalty if:

(1) The State demonstrates to our satisfaction that it had reasonable cause pursuant to § 262.5 of this chapter; or

(2) The State achieves compliance under a corrective compliance plan pursuant to § 262.6 of this chapter.

§ 264.40 What happens if a State does not repay a Federal loan?

(a) If a State fails to repay the amount of principal and interest due at any point under a loan agreement developed pursuant to section 406 of the Act:

(1) The entire outstanding loan balance, plus all accumulated interest, becomes due and payable immediately; and

(2) We will reduce the SFAG payable for the immediately succeeding fiscal

year quarter by the outstanding loan amount plus interest.

(b) Neither the reasonable cause provisions at § 262.5 of this chapter nor the corrective compliance plan provisions at § 262.6 of this chapter apply when a State fails to repay a Federal loan.

§ 264.50 What happens if, in a fiscal year, a State does not expend, with its own funds, an amount equal to the reduction to the adjusted SFAG resulting from a penalty?

(a)(1) When we withhold Federal TANF funds from a State during a fiscal year because of other penalty actions listed at § 262.1 of this chapter, the State must replace these Federal TANF funds with State funds during the subsequent fiscal year.

(2) If the State fails to replace funds during the subsequent year, then we will assess an additional penalty of no more than two percent of the adjusted SFAG during the year that follows the subsequent year.

(b) A State must expend such replacement funds under its TANF program, not under "separate State programs."

(c) We will assess a penalty of no more than two percent of the adjusted SFAG plus the amount equal to the difference between the amount the State was required to expend and the amount it actually expended in the fiscal year.

(1) We will assess the maximum penalty amount if the State made no additional expenditures to compensate for the reductions to its adjusted SFAG resulting from penalties.

(2) We will reduce the percentage portion of the penalty if the State has expended some of the amount required. In such case, we will calculate the applicable percentage portion of the penalty by multiplying the percentage of the required expenditures that the State failed to make in the fiscal year by two percent.

(d) The reasonable cause and corrective compliance plan provisions at §§ 262.5 and 262.6 of this chapter do not apply to this penalty.

§ 264.60 What policies and practices must a state implement to prevent assistance use in electronic benefit transfer transactions in locations prohibited by the Social Security Act?

Pursuant to Section 408(a)(12) of the Act, states are required to implement policies and practices, as necessary, to prevent assistance (defined at § 260.31(a) of this chapter) provided with federal TANF or state TANF MOE funds from being used in any electronic benefit transfer transaction in any: liquor store; casino, gambling casino or gaming establishment; or retail establishment which provides adult-oriented entertainment in which performers disrobe or perform in an unclothed state for entertainment.

[81 FR 2105, Jan. 15, 2016]

§ 264.61 What happens if a state fails to report or demonstrate it has implemented and maintained the policies and practices required in § 264.60?

(a) Pursuant to Section 409(a)(16) of the Act and in accordance with 45 CFR part 262, a penalty of not more than five percent of the adjusted SFAG will be imposed for failure to report by February 22, 2014 and each succeeding fiscal year on the state's implementation of policies and practices required in § 264.60. The penalty will be imposed in the succeeding fiscal year, subject to § 262.4(g) of this chapter.

(b) Pursuant to Section 409(a)(16) of the Act and in accordance with 45 CFR part 262, a penalty of not more than five percent of the adjusted SFAG will be imposed for FY 2014 and each succeeding fiscal year in which the state fails to demonstrate the state's implementation of policies and practices required in § 264.60. The penalty will be imposed in the succeeding fiscal year subject to § 262.4(g) of this chapter.

(c) A penalty applied under paragraphs (a) and (b) of this section may be reduced based on the degree of noncompliance of the state.

(d) Fraudulent activity by any individual in an attempt to circumvent the policies and practices required by § 264.60 shall not trigger a state penalty under paragraphs (a) and (b) of this section.

[81 FR 2105, Jan. 15, 2016]

Subpart B—What Are the Requirements for the Contingency Fund?

§ 264.70 What makes a State eligible to receive a provisional payment of contingency funds?

(a) In order to receive a provisional payment of contingency funds, a State must:

(1) Be a needy State, as defined in § 260.30 of this chapter; and

(2) Submit to ACF a request for contingency funds for an eligible month (i.e., a month in which a State is a needy State).

(b) A determination that a State is a needy State for a month makes that State eligible to receive a provisional payment of contingency funds for two consecutive months.

(c) Only the 50 States and the District of Columbia may receive contingency funds. Territories and Tribal TANF grantees are not eligible.

§ 264.71 What determines the amount of the provisional payment of contingency funds that will be made to a State?

We will make a provisional payment to a State that meets the requirements of § 264.70, within the following limits:

(a) The amount that we will pay to a State in a fiscal year will not exceed an amount equal to 1/12 times 20 percent of that State's SFAG for that fiscal year, multiplied by the number of eligible months for which the State has requested contingency funds;

(b) The total amount that we will pay to all States during a fiscal year will not exceed the amount appropriated for this purpose; and

(c) We will pay contingency funds to States in the order in which we receive requests for such payments.

§ 264.72 What requirements are imposed on a State if it receives contingency funds?

(a)(1) A State must meet a Contingency Fund MOE level of 100 percent of historic State expenditures for FY 1994.

(2) A State must exceed the Contingency Fund MOE level to keep any of the contingency funds that it received. It may be able to retain a portion of the amount of contingency funds that match countable State expenditures, as defined in § 264.0, that are in excess of the State's Contingency Fund MOE level, after the overall adjustment required by section 403(b)(6)(C) of the Act.

(b) A State must complete an annual reconciliation, in accordance with § 264.73, in order to determine how much, if any, of the contingency funds that it received in a fiscal year it may retain.

(c) If required to remit funds under the annual reconciliation, a State must remit all (or a portion) of the funds paid to it for a fiscal year within one year after it has failed to meet either the Food Stamp trigger or the Unemployment trigger, as defined in § 264.0, for three consecutive months.

(d) A State must expend contingency funds in the fiscal year in which they are awarded.

(e) A State may not transfer contingency funds to the Discretionary Fund of the CCDF or the SSBG.

(f) A State must follow the restrictions and prohibitions in effect for Federal TANF funds, including the provisions of § 263.11 of this chapter, in its use of contingency funds.

§ 264.73 What is an annual reconciliation?

(a) The annual reconciliation involves the calculation, for a fiscal year, of:

(1) The amount of a State's qualifying expenditures;

(2) The amount by which a State's countable State expenditures, as defined in § 264.0, exceed the State's required Contingency Fund MOE level; and

(3) The amount of contingency funds that the State may retain or must remit.

(b) If a State exceeded its required Contingency Fund MOE level, it may be able to retain some or all of the contingency funds that it received.

(c) A State determines the amount of contingency funds that it may retain by performing the following calculations:

(1) From the lesser of the following two amounts:

(i) The amount of contingency funds paid to it during the fiscal year; or

(ii) Its countable State expenditures, as defined in § 264.0, minus its required Contingency Fund MOE level, multiplied by:

(A) The State's Federal Medical Assistance Percentage (FMAP) applicable for the fiscal year for which funds were awarded; and

(B) $\frac{1}{12}$ times the number of months during the fiscal year for which the State received contingency funds.

(2) Subtract the State's proportionate remittance (as reported to the State by ACF) for the overall adjustment of the Contingency Fund for that fiscal year required by section 403(b)(6)(C) of the Act.

§ 264.74 How will we determine the Contingency Fund MOE level for the annual reconciliation?

(a)(1) The Contingency Fund MOE level includes the State's share of expenditures for AFDC benefit payments, administration, and FAMIS; EA; and the JOBS program for FY 1994.

(2) We will use the same data sources and date, i.e., April 28, 1995, that we used to determine the basic MOE levels for FY 1994. We will exclude the State's share of expenditures from the former IV-A child care programs (AFDC/JOBS, Transitional and At-Risk child care) in the calculation.

(b) We will reduce a State's Contingency Fund MOE level by the same percentage that we reduce the basic MOE level for any fiscal year in which we reduce the State's annual SFAG allocation to provide funding to Tribal grantees operating a Tribal TANF program.

§ 264.75 For the annual reconciliation, what are qualifying State expenditures?

(a) Qualifying State expenditures are expenditures of State funds made in the State TANF program, with respect to eligible families, for the following:

(1) Cash assistance, including assigned child support collected by the State, distributed to the family, and disregarded in determining eligibility for, and amount of the TANF assistance payment;

(2) Educational activities designed to increase self-sufficiency, job training, and work, excluding any expenditure for public education in the State except expenditures involving the provision of services or assistance to an eligible family that are not generally available to persons who are not members of an eligible family;

(3) Any other services allowable under section 404(a)(1) of the Act and consistent with the goals at § 260.20 of this chapter; and

(4) Administrative costs in connection with the provision of the benefits and services listed in paragraphs (a)(1) through (a)(3) of this section, but only to the extent that such costs are consistent with the 15-percent limitation at § 263.2(a)(5) of this chapter.

(b) Qualifying State expenditures do not include:

(1) Child care expenditures; and

(2) Expenditures made under separate State programs.

§ 264.76 What action will we take if a State fails to remit funds after failing to meet its required Contingency Fund MOE level?

(a) If, for a fiscal year in which it receives contingency funds, a State fails to meet its required Contingency Fund MOE level, we will penalize the State by reducing the SFAG payable for the next fiscal year by the amount of contingency funds not remitted.

(b) A State may appeal this decision, as provided in § 262.7 of this chapter.

(c) The reasonable cause exceptions and corrective compliance regulations at §§ 262.5 and 262.6 of this chapter do not apply to this penalty.

§ 264.77 How will we determine if a State met its Contingency Fund expenditure requirements?

(a) States receiving contingency funds for a fiscal year must complete the quarterly TANF Financial Report. As part of the fourth quarter's report, a State must complete its annual reconciliation.

(b) The TANF Financial Report and State reporting on expenditures are subject to our review.

Subpart C—What Rules Pertain Specifically to the Spending Levels of the Territories?

§ 264.80 If a Territory receives Matching Grant funds, what funds must it expend?

(a) If a Territory receives Matching Grant funds under section 1108(b) of the Act, it must:

(1) Contribute 25 percent of the expenditures funded under the Matching Grant for title IV-A or title IV-E expenditures;

(2) Expend 100 percent of the amount of historic expenditures for FY 1995 for the AFDC program (including administrative costs and FAMIS), the EA program, and the JOBS program; and

(3) Expend 100 percent of the amount of the Family Assistance Grant annual allocation using Federal TANF, title IV-E funds and/or Territory-only funds, without regard to any penalties applied in accordance with section 409 of the Act.

(b) Territories may not use the same Territorial expenditures to satisfy the requirements of paragraphs (a)(1), (a)(2) and (a)(3) of this section.

§ 264.81 What expenditures qualify for Territories to meet the Matching Grant MOE requirement?

To meet the Matching Grant MOE requirements, Territories may count:

(a) Territorial expenditures made in accordance with §§ 263.2, 263.3, 263.4, and 263.6 of this chapter that are commingled with Federal TANF funds or made under a segregated TANF program; and

(b) Territorial expenditures made pursuant to the regulations at 45 CFR parts 1355 and 1356 for the Foster Care and Adoption Assistance programs and section 477 of the Act for the Independent Living program.

§ 264.82 What expenditures qualify for meeting the Matching Grant FAG amount requirement?

To meet the Matching Grant FAG amount requirement, Territories may count:

(a) Expenditures made with Federal TANF funds pursuant to § 263.11 of this chapter;

(b) Expenditures made in accordance with §§ 263.2, 263.3, 263.4, and 263.6 of this chapter that are commingled with Federal TANF funds or made under a segregated TANF program;

(c) Amounts transferred from TANF funds pursuant to section 404(d) of the Act; and

(d) The Federal and Territorial shares of expenditures made pursuant to the regulations at 45 CFR parts 1355 and 1356 for the Foster Care and Adoption Assistance programs and section 477 of the Act for the Independent Living program.

§ 264.83 How will we know if a Territory failed to meet the Matching Grant funding requirements at § 264.80?

We will require the Territories to report the expenditures required by § 264.80(a)(2) and (a)(3) on the quarterly Territorial Financial Report.

§ 264.84 What will we do if a Territory fails to meet the Matching Grant funding requirements at § 264.80?

If a Territory does not meet the requirements at either or both of § 264.80(a)(2) and (a)(3), we will disallow all Matching Grant funds received for the fiscal year.

§ 264.85 What rights of appeal are available to the Territories?

The Territories may appeal our decisions to the Departmental Appeals Board in accordance with our regulations at part 16 of this title if we decide to take disallowances under section 1108(b) of the Act.

PART 265—DATA COLLECTION AND REPORTING REQUIREMENTS

Sec.

AUTHORITY: 42 U.S.C. 603, 605, 607, 609, 611, and 613; Pub. L. 109–171.

SOURCE: 64 FR 17900, Apr. 12, 1999, unless otherwise noted.

§ 265.1 What does this part cover?

(a) This part explains how we will collect the information required by section 411(a) of the Act (data collection and reporting); the information required to implement section 407 of the Act (work participation requirements), as authorized by section 411(a)(1)(A)(xii); the information required to implement section 409 (penalties), section 403 (grants to States), section 405 (administrative provisions), section 411(b) (report to Congress), and section 413 (annual rankings of State TANF programs); and the data necessary to carry out our financial management and oversight responsibilities.

(b) This part describes the information in the quarterly and annual reports that each State must file, as follows:[1]

(1) The case record information (disaggregated and aggregated) on individuals and families in the quarterly TANF Data Report;

(2) The expenditure data in the quarterly TANF Financial Report (or, as applicable, the Territorial Financial Report); and

(3) The definitions and other information on the State's TANF and MOE programs that must be filed annually.

(c) If a State claims MOE expenditures under a separate State program(s), this part describes the case record information (disaggregated and aggregated) on individuals and families in the quarterly SSP–MOE Data Report that each State must file.

(d) This part describes when reports are due, how we will determine if reporting requirements have been met, and how we will apply the statutory penalty for failure to file a timely report. It also specifies electronic filing and sampling requirements.

[64 FR 17900, Apr. 12, 1999, as amended at 71 FR 37482, June 29, 2006]

§ 265.2 What definitions apply to this part?

(a) Except as provided in paragraph (b) of this section, the general TANF definitions at §§ 260.30 through 260.33 and the definitions of a work-eligible individual and the work activities in § 261.2 of this chapter apply to this part.

(b) For data collection and reporting purposes only, family means:

(1) All individuals receiving assistance as part of a family under the State's TANF or separate State program (including noncustodial parents, where required under § 265.5(g)); and

(2) The following additional persons living in the household, if not included under paragraph (b)(1) of this section:

(i) Parent(s) or caretaker relative(s) of any minor child receiving assistance;

(ii) Minor siblings of any child receiving assistance; and

(iii) Any person whose income or resources would be counted in determining the family's eligibility for or amount of assistance.

[71 FR 37482, June 29, 2006]

§ 265.3 What reports must the State file on a quarterly basis?

(a) *Quarterly reports.* (1) Each State must collect on a monthly basis, and file on a quarterly basis, the data specified in the TANF Data Report and the TANF Financial Report (or, as applicable, the Territorial Financial Report).

(2) Each State that claims MOE expenditures for a separate State program(s) must collect on a monthly basis, and file on a quarterly basis, the data specified in the SSP–MOE Data Report.

(b) *TANF Data Report.* The TANF Data Report consists of four sections. Two sections contain disaggregated data elements and two sections contain aggregated data elements.

(1) *Disaggregated Data on Families Receiving TANF Assistance—Section one.* Each State must file disaggregated information on families receiving TANF

[1] The Appendices contain the specific data elements in the quarterly Data Report, the quarterly Financial Report, and the Annual Report on State MOE Programs, as well as the instructions for filing these reports. They also include the form and instructions for the Caseload Reduction Report described at § 261.41(b) of this chapter.

assistance. This section specifies identifying and demographic data such as the individual's Social Security Number and information such as the amount of assistance received, educational level, employment status, work participation activities, citizenship status, and earned and unearned income. The data must be provided for both adults and children.

(2) *Disaggregated Data on Families No Longer Receiving TANF Assistance—Section two.* Each State must file disaggregated information on families no longer receiving TANF assistance. This section specifies the reasons for case closure and data similar to the data required in section one.

(3) *Aggregated Data—Section three.* Each State must file aggregated information on families receiving, applying for, and no longer receiving TANF assistance. This section of the TANF Data Report requires aggregate figures in such areas as: The number of applications received and their disposition; the number of recipient families, adult recipients, and child recipients; the number of births and out-of-wedlock births for families receiving TANF assistance; the number of noncustodial parents participating in work activities; and the number of closed cases.

(4) *Aggregated Caseload Data by Stratum—Section four.* Each State that opts to use a stratified sample to report the quarterly TANF disaggregated data must file the monthly caseload data by stratum for each month in the quarter.

(c) *The TANF Financial Report (or Territorial Financial Report).* (1) Each State must file quarterly expenditure data on the State's use of Federal TANF funds, State TANF expenditures, and State expenditures of MOE funds in separate State programs.

(2) If a State is expending Federal TANF funds received in prior fiscal years, it must file a separate quarterly TANF Financial Report (or, as applicable, Territorial Financial Report) for each fiscal year that provides information on the expenditures of that year's TANF funds.

(3) Territories must report their expenditure and other fiscal data on the Territorial Financial Report, as provided at § 264.85 of this chapter, in lieu of the TANF Financial Report.

(d) *SSP–MOE Data Report.* The SSP–MOE Data Report consists of four sections. Two sections contain disaggregated data elements and two sections contain aggregated data elements.

(1) *Disaggregated Data on Families Receiving SSP–MOE Assistance—Section one.* Each State that claims MOE expenditures for a separate State program(s) must file disaggregated information on families receiving SSP–MOE assistance. This section specifies identifying and demographic data such as the individual's Social Security Number, the amount of assistance received, educational level, employment status, work participation activities, citizenship status, and earned and unearned income. The data must be provided for both adults and children.

(2) *Disaggregated Data on Families No Longer Receiving SSP–MOE Assistance—Section two.* Each State that claims MOE expenditures for a separate State program(s) must file disaggregated information on families no longer receiving SSP–MOE assistance. This section specifies the reasons for case closure and data similar to the data required in section one.

(3) *Aggregated Data—Section three.* Each State that claims MOE expenditures for a separate State program(s) must file aggregated information on families receiving and no longer receiving SSP–MOE assistance. This section of the SSP–MOE Data Report requires aggregate figures in such areas as: The number of recipient families, adult recipients, and child recipients; the total amount of assistance for families receiving SSP–MOE assistance; the number of non-custodial parents participating in work activities; and the number of closed cases.

(4) *Aggregated Caseload Data by Stratum—Section four.* Each State that claims MOE expenditures for a separate State program(s) and that opts to use a stratified sample to report the SSP–MOE quarterly disaggregated data must file the monthly caseload by stratum for each month in the quarter.

(e) *Optional data elements.* A State has the option not to report on some data elements for some individuals in the TANF Data Report and the SSP–MOE

Data Report, as specified in the instructions to these reports.

(f) *Non-custodial parents.* A State must report information on a non-custodial parent (as defined in § 260.30 of this chapter) if the non-custodial parent:

(1) Is receiving assistance as defined in § 260.31 of this chapter;

(2) Is participating in work activities as defined in section 407(d) of the Act; or

(3) Has been designated by the State as a member of a family receiving assistance.

[71 FR 37482, June 29, 2006]

§ 265.4 When are quarterly reports due?

(a) Each State must file the TANF Data Report and the TANF Financial Report (or, as applicable, the Territorial Financial Report) within 45 days following the end of the quarter or be subject to a penalty.

(b) Each State that claims MOE expenditures for a separate State program(s) must file the SSP–MOE Data Report within 45 days following the end of the quarter or be subject to a penalty.

(c) A State that fails to submit the reports within 45 days will be subject to a penalty unless the State files complete and accurate reports before the end of the fiscal quarter that immediately succeeds the quarter for which the reports were required to be submitted.

[71 FR 37483, June 29, 2006]

§ 265.5 May States use sampling?

(a) Each State may report the disaggregated data in the TANF Data Report and the SSP-MOE Data Report on all recipient families or on a sample of families selected through the use of a scientifically acceptable sampling method that we have approved. States may use sampling to generate certain aggregated data elements as identified in the instructions to the reports. States may not use sampling to report expenditure data.

(b) "Scientifically acceptable sampling method" means:

(1) A probability sampling method in which every sampling unit in the population has a known, non-zero chance to be included in the sample; and

(2) Our sample size requirements are met.

(c) In reporting data based on sampling, the State must follow the specifications and procedures in the TANF Sampling Manual.

§ 265.6 Must States file reports electronically?

Each State must file all quarterly reports (i.e., the TANF Data Report, the TANF Financial Report (or, as applicable, the Territorial Financial Report), and the SSP-MOE Data Report) electronically, based on format specifications that we will provide.

§ 265.7 How will we determine if the State is meeting the quarterly reporting requirements?

(a) Each State's quarterly reports (the TANF Data Report, the TANF Financial Report (or Territorial Financial Report), and the SSP-MOE Data Report) must be complete and accurate and filed by the due date.

(b) For a disaggregated data report, "a complete and accurate report" means that:

(1) The reported data accurately reflect information available to the State in case records, financial records, and automated data systems, and include correction of the quarterly data by the end of the fiscal year reporting period;

(2) The data are free from computational errors and are internally consistent (e.g., items that should add to totals do so);

(3) The State reports data for all required elements (i.e., no data are missing);

(4)(i) The State provides data on all families; or

(ii) If the State opts to use sampling, the State reports data on all families selected in a sample that meets the specification and procedures in the TANF Sampling Manual (except for families listed in error); and

(5) Where estimates are necessary (e.g., some types of assistance may require cost estimates), the State uses reasonable methods to develop these estimates.

(c) For an aggregated data report, "a complete and accurate report" means that:

(1) The reported data accurately reflect information available to the State in case records, financial records, and automated data systems;

(2) The data are free from computational errors and are internally consistent (e.g., items that should add to totals do so);

(3) The State reports data on all applicable elements; and

(4) Monthly totals are unduplicated counts for all families (e.g., the number of families and the number of out-of-wedlock births are unduplicated counts).

(d) For the TANF Financial Report (or, as applicable, the Territorial Financial Report), "a complete and accurate report" means that:

(1) The reported data accurately reflect information available to the State in case records, financial records, and automated data systems;

(2) The data are free from computational errors and are internally consistent (e.g., items that should add to totals do so);

(3) The State reports data on all applicable elements; and

(4) All expenditures have been made in accordance with § 75.302(a) of this title.

(e) We will review the data filed in the quarterly reports to determine if they meet these standards. In addition, we will use audits and reviews to verify the accuracy of the data filed by the States.

(f) States must maintain records to adequately support any report, in accordance with §§ 75.361 through 75.370 of this title.

[64 FR 17900, Apr. 12, 1999, as amended at 73 FR 6828, Feb. 5, 2008; 81 FR 3020, Jan. 20, 2016]

§ 265.8 Under what circumstances will we take action to impose a reporting penalty for failure to submit quarterly and annual reports?

(a) We will take action to impose a reporting penalty under § 262.1(a)(3) of this chapter if:

(1) A State fails to file the quarterly TANF Data Report, the quarterly TANF Financial Report (or, as applicable, the Territorial Financial Report), or the quarterly SSP–MOE Data Report (if applicable) within 45 days of the end of the quarter;

(2) The disaggregated data in the TANF Data Report or the SSP–MOE Data Report are not accurate or a report does not include all the data required by section 411(a) of the Act (other than section 411(a)(1)(A)(xii) of the Act) or the nine additional elements necessary to carry out the data collection system requirements, including the social security number;

(3) The aggregated data elements in the TANF Data Report or the SSP–MOE Data Report required by section 411(a) of the Act are not accurate and the report does not include the data elements necessary to carry out the data collection system requirements and to verify and validate the disaggregated data;

(4) The TANF Financial Report (or, as applicable, the Territorial Financial Report) does not contain complete and accurate information on total expenditures and expenditures on administrative costs and transitional services; or

(5) The annual report under § 265.9 does not contain the description of transitional services provided by a State to families no longer receiving assistance due to employment.

(b) If we determine that a State meets one or more of the conditions set forth in paragraph (a) of this section, we will notify the State that we intend to reduce the SFAG payable for the immediately succeeding fiscal year.

(c) We will not impose the penalty at § 262.1(a)(3) of this chapter if the State files the complete and accurate quarterly report or the annual report before the end of the fiscal quarter that immediately succeeds the fiscal quarter for which the reports were required.

(d) If the State does not file all reports as provided under paragraph (a) of this section by the end of the immediately succeeding fiscal quarter, the penalty provisions of §§ 262.4 through 262.6 of this chapter will apply.

(e) Subject to paragraphs (a) through (c) of this section and §§ 262.4 through 262.6 of this chapter, for each quarter for which a State fails to meet the reporting requirements, we will reduce the SFAG payable by an amount equal to four percent of the adjusted SFAG (or a lesser amount if the State achieves substantial compliance under a corrective compliance plan).

[71 FR 37483, June 29, 2006]

§ 265.9 What information must the State file annually?

(a) Each State must file an annual report containing information on the TANF program and the State's MOE program(s) for that year. The report may be filed as:

(1) An addendum to the fourth quarter TANF Data Report; or

(2) A separate annual report.

(b) Each State must provide the following information on the TANF program:

(1) The State's definition of each work activity;

(2) A description of the transitional services provided to families no longer receiving assistance due to employment;

(3) A description of how a State will reduce the amount of assistance payable to a family when an individual refuses to engage in work without good cause pursuant to § 261.14 of this chapter;

(4) The average monthly number of payments for child care services made by the State through the use of disregards, by the following types of child care providers:

(i) Licensed/regulated in-home child care;

(ii) Licensed/regulated family child care;

(iii) Licensed/regulated group home child care;

(iv) Licensed/regulated center-based child care;

(v) Legally operating (i.e., no license category available in State or locality) in-home child care provided by a nonrelative;

(vi) Legally operating (i.e., no license category available in State or locality) in-home child care provided by a relative;

(vii) Legally operating (i.e., no license category available in State or locality) family child care provided by a nonrelative;

(viii) Legally operating (i.e., no license category available in State or locality) family child care provided by a relative;

(ix) Legally operating (i.e., no license category available in State or locality) group child care provided by a nonrelative;

(x) Legally operating (i.e., no license category available in State or locality) group child care provided by a relative; and

(xi) Legally operated (i.e., no license category available in State or locality) center-based child care;

(5) If the State has adopted the Family Violence Option and wants Federal recognition of its good cause domestic violence waivers under subpart B of part 260 of this chapter, a description of the strategies and procedures in place to ensure that victims of domestic violence receive appropriate alternative services and an aggregate figure for the total number of good cause domestic waivers granted;

(6) A description of any nonrecurrent, short-term benefits provided, including:

(i) The eligibility criteria associated with such benefits, including any restrictions on the amount, duration, or frequency of payments;

(ii) Any policies that limit such payments to families that are eligible for TANF assistance or that have the effect of delaying or suspending a family's eligibility for assistance; and

(iii) Any procedures or activities developed under the TANF program to ensure that individuals diverted from assistance receive information about, referrals to, or access to other program benefits (such as Medicaid and food stamps) that might help them make the transition from welfare to work;

(7) A description of the procedures the State has established and is maintaining to resolve displacement complaints, pursuant to section 407(f)(3) of the Act. This description must include the name of the State agency with the lead responsibility for administering this provision and explanations of how the State has notified the public about these procedures and how an individual can register a complaint;

(8) A summary of State programs and activities directed at the third and fourth statutory purposes of TANF (as specified at § 260.20(c) and (d) of this chapter); and

(9) An estimate of the total number of individuals who have participated in subsidized employment under § 261.30(b) or (c) of this chapter.

(10) A comprehensive description of the state's policies and practices to prevent assistance (defined at § 260.31(a) of this chapter) provided with federal TANF or state TANF MOE funds from being used in any electronic benefit transfer transaction in any: liquor store; casino, gambling casino or gaming establishment; or retail establishment which provides adult-oriented entertainment in which performers disrobe or perform in an unclothed state for entertainment. Reports must address:

(i) Procedures for preventing the use of TANF assistance via electronic benefit transfer transactions in any liquor store; any casino, gambling casino, or gaming establishment; and any retail establishment which provides adult-oriented entertainment in which performers disrobe or perform in an unclothed state for entertainment;

(ii) How the state identifies the locations specified in the statute;

(iii) Procedures for ongoing monitoring to ensure policies are being carried out as intended; and

(iv) How the state responds to findings of non-compliance or program ineffectiveness.

(11) The state's TANF Plan must describe how the state will:

(i) Implement policies and procedures as necessary to prevent access to assistance provided under the State program funded under this part through any electronic fund transaction in an automated teller machine or point-of-sale device located in a place described in section 408(a)(12) of the Act, including a plan to ensure that recipients of the assistance have adequate access to their cash assistance; and

(ii) Ensure that recipients of assistance provided under the State program funded under this part have access to using or withdrawing assistance with minimal fees or charges, including an opportunity to access assistance with no fee or charges, and are provided information on applicable fees and surcharges that apply to electronic fund transactions involving the assistance, and that such information is made publicly available.

(c) Each State must provide the following information on the State's program(s) for which the State claims MOE expenditures:

(1) The name of each program and a description of the major activities provided to eligible families under each such program;

(2) Each program's statement of purpose;

(3) If applicable, a description of the work activities in each separate State MOE program in which eligible families are participating;

(4) For each program, both the total annual State expenditures and the total annual State expenditures claimed as MOE;

(5) For each program, the average monthly total number or the total number of eligible families served for which the State claims MOE expenditures as of the end of the fiscal year;

(6) The eligibility criteria for the families served under each program/activity;

(7) A statement whether the program/activity had been previously authorized and allowable as of August 21, 1996, under section 403 of prior law;

(8) The FY 1995 State expenditures for each program/activity not authorized and allowable as of August 21, 1996, under section 403 of prior law (see § 263.5(b) of this chapter); and

(9) A certification that those families for which the State is claiming MOE expenditures met the State's criteria for "eligible families."[7]

(d) If the State has submitted the information required in paragraphs (b) and (c) of this section in the State Plan, it may meet the annual reporting requirements by reference in lieu of re-submission. If the information in the annual report has not changed since the previous annual report, the State may reference this information in lieu of re-submission.

(e) If a State makes a substantive change in certain data elements in paragraphs (b) and (c) of this section, it must file a copy of the change with the

[7] See appendix I for the reporting form for the Annual Report on State Maintenance-of-Effort Programs.

next quarterly data report or as an amendment to its State Plan. The State must also indicate the effective date of the change. This requirement is applicable to the following data elements:

(1) Paragraphs (b)(1), (b)(2), and (b)(3) of this section; and

(2) Paragraphs (c)(1), (c)(2), (c)(3), (c)(6), (c)(7), and (c)(8) of this section.

[64 FR 17900, Apr. 12, 1999, as amended at 81 FR 2105, Jan. 15, 2016]

§ 265.10 When is the annual report due?

The annual report required by § 265.9 is due at the same time as the fourth quarter TANF Data Report.

PART 270—HIGH PERFORMANCE BONUS AWARDS

Sec.

AUTHORITY: 42 U.S.C. 603(a)(4).

SOURCE: 65 FR 52851, Aug. 30, 2000, unless otherwise noted.

§ 270.1 What does this part cover?

This part covers the regulatory provisions relating to the bonus to reward high performing States in the TANF program, as authorized in section 403(a)(4) of the Social Security Act.

§ 270.2 What definitions apply to this part?

The following definitions apply under this part:

Absolute rate means the actual rate of performance achieved in the performance year or the comparison year.

Act means the Social Security Act, as amended.

Bonus year means each of the fiscal years 2002 and 2003 in which TANF bonus funds are awarded, as well as any subsequent fiscal year for which Congress authorizes and appropriates bonus funds.

CCDF means the Child Care and Development Fund.

Comparison year means the fiscal or calendar year preceding the performance year.

Fiscal year means the 12-month period beginning on October 1 of the preceding calendar year and ending on September 30.

Food Stamp Program means the program administered by the United States Department of Agriculture pursuant to the Food Stamp Act of 1977, U.S.C. 2011 *et seq.*

CMS is the Centers for Medicare & Medicaid Services.

Improvement rate means the positive percentage point change between the absolute rate of performance in the performance year and the comparison year, except for the calculation and ranking of States on the increase in success in the work force measure in § 270.5(a)(4).

Medicaid is a State program of medical assistance operated in accordance with a State plan under title XIX of the Act.

MSIS is the Medicaid Statistical Information System.

Performance year means the year in which a State's performance is measured, i.e., the fiscal year or the calendar year immediately preceding the bonus year.

SCHIP is the State Children's Health Insurance Program as described in title XXI of the Act.

Separate State Program (SSP) means a program operated outside of TANF in which the expenditure of State funds may count for TANF maintenance-of-effort (MOE) purposes.

SSP-MOE Data Report is the report containing disaggregated and aggregated data required to be filed on SSP-MOE recipients in separate State programs as specified in § 265.3(d) of this chapter.

State means each of the 50 States of the United States, the District of Columbia, the Commonwealth of Puerto Rico, the United States Virgin Islands, Guam, and American Samoa.

TANF means The Temporary Assistance for Needy Families Program.

We (and any other first person plural pronouns) means the Secretary of Health and Human Services or any of the following individuals or organizations acting in an official capacity on the Secretary's behalf: the Assistant Secretary for Children and Families, the Department of Health and Human Services, and the Administration for Children and Families.

§ 270.3 What is the annual maximum amount we will award and the maximum amount that a State can receive each year?

(a) Except as provided in § 270.9, we will award $200 million in bonus funds annually, subject to Congressional authorization and the availability of the appropriation.

(b) The amount payable to a State in a bonus year may not exceed five percent of a State's family assistance grant.

§ 270.4 On what measures will we base the bonus awards?

(a) *Performance measures: general.* In FY 2002 and beyond, we will base the high performance bonus awards on: four work measures; five measures that support work and self-sufficiency related to participation by low-income working families in the Food Stamp Program, participation of former TANF recipients in the Medicaid and SCHIP programs, and receipt of child care; and one measure on family formation and stability.

(b) *Work measures.* (1) Beginning in FY 2002, we will measure State performance on the following work measures:

(i) Job entry rate;

(ii) Success in the work force rate;

(iii) Increase in the job entry rate; and

(iv) Increase in success in the work force rate.

(2) For any given year, we will score and rank competing States and award bonuses to the ten States with the highest scores in each work measure.

(c) *Measures of participation by low-income working households in the Food Stamp Program*—(1) *Food Stamp absolute measure.* (i) Beginning in FY 2002, we will measure the number of low-income working households with children (*i.e.*, households with children under age 18 which have an income less than 130 percent of poverty and earnings equal to at least half-time, full-year minimum wage) receiving Food Stamps as a percentage of the number of low-income working households with children (as defined in this paragraph) in the State.

(ii) We will rank all States that choose to compete on this measure and will award bonuses to the three States with the highest scores. We will calculate the percentage rate for this measure to two decimal points. If two or more States have the same percentage rate for the measure, we will calculate the rates for these States to as many decimal points as necessary to eliminate the tie.

(2) *Food Stamp improvement measure.* (i) Beginning in FY 2002, we will measure the improvement in the number of low-income working households with children (*i.e.*, households with children under age 18 which have an income less than 130 percent of poverty and earnings equal to at least half-time, full-year Federal minimum wage) receiving Food Stamps as a percentage of the number of low-income working households with children (as defined in this subparagraph) in the State.

(ii) For any given year, we will compare a State's performance on this measure to its performance in the previous year, beginning with a comparison of calendar (CY) 2000 to CY 2001, based on Census Bureau decennial and annual demographic program data.

(iii) We will rank all States that choose to compete on this measure and will award bonuses to the seven States with the greatest percentage point improvement in this measure. We will calculate the percentage rate for this measure to two decimal points. If two or more States have the same percentage rate for this measure, we will calculate the rates for these States to as many decimal points as necessary to eliminate the tie.

(d) Measures of participation by low-income families in the Medicaid/SCHIP Programs. (1) *Medicaid/SCHIP absolute measure.* (i) Beginning in FY 2002, we will measure the number of individuals receiving TANF benefits who are also enrolled in Medicaid or SCHIP, who leave TANF in a fiscal year and are enrolled in Medicaid or SCHIP in the fourth month after leaving TANF assistance, and who are not receiving TANF assistance in the fourth month as a percentage of individuals who left TANF in the fiscal year and are not receiving TANF assistance in the fourth month after leaving.

(ii) We will rank the performance of each State that chooses to compete on this absolute measure and award bonuses to the three States with the highest scores.

(iii) We will calculate the percentage rate for this measure to two decimal points. If two or more States have the same percentage rate for this measure, we will calculate the rates for these States to as many decimal points as necessary to eliminate the tie.

(2) *Medicaid/SCHIP improvement measure.* (i) Beginning in FY 2002, we will measure the improvement in the number of individuals receiving TANF benefits who are also enrolled in Medicaid or SCHIP, who leave TANF in a fiscal year and are enrolled in Medicaid or SCHIP in the fourth month after leaving TANF assistance, and who are not receiving TANF assistance in the fourth month as a percentage of individuals who left TANF in the fiscal year and are not receiving TANF assistance in the fourth month after leaving.

(ii) For any given year, we will compare a State's performance on this improvement measure to its performance in the previous year, beginning with a comparison of FY 2000 to FY 2001, based on a quarterly submission by the State as determined by matching individuals (adults and children) who have left TANF assistance and who are not receiving TANF assistance in the fourth month with Medicaid or SCHIP enrollment data.

(iii) We will rank the performance of all States that choose to compete on this improvement measure and will award bonuses to the seven States with the greatest percentage point improvement in this measure.

(iv) We will calculate the percentage rate for the measure to two decimal points. If two or more States have the same percentage rate for this measure, we will calculate the rates for these States to as many decimal points as necessary to eliminate the tie.

(e) *Child care subsidy measure.* (1) Beginning in FY 2002, we will measure State performance based upon a composite ranking of:

(i) The accessibility of services based on the percentage of children in the State who meet the maximum allowable Federal eligibility requirements for the Child Care and Development Fund (CCDF) who are served by the State during the performance year, and who are included in the data reported on the ACF–800 and ACF–801 for the same fiscal year; and

(ii) The affordability of CCDF services based on a comparison of the reported assessed family co-payment to reported family income and a comparison of the number of eligible children under the State's defined income limits to the number of eligible children under the federal eligibility limits.

(2) Beginning in FY 2003, we will measure State performance based upon a composite ranking of:

(i) The two components described in paragraph (e)(1) of this section; and

(ii) The quality of CCDF services based on a comparison of reimbursement rates during the performance year to the market rates, determined in accordance with 45 CFR 98.43(b)(2), applicable to that year.

(3) For the affordability component in paragraph (e)(1)(ii) of this section, we will compare family income to the assessed State family co-payment as reported on the ACF–801 across four income ranges. These income ranges refer to percentages of the Federal Poverty Guidelines for a family of three persons. The income ranges are as follows:

(i) Income below the poverty level;

(ii) Income at least 100 percent and below 125 percent of poverty;

(iii) Income at least 125 percent and below 150 percent of poverty; and

(iv) Income at least 150 percent and below 175 percent of poverty.

(4)(i) For the affordability component, we will calculate, for each income range, the average of the ratios of family co-payment to family income for each family served; and

(ii) We will calculate a ratio of the number of children eligible under the State's defined income limits compared to the number of children eligible under the Federal eligibility limits in the CCDF, i.e., 85 percent of the State's median income.

(iii) We will rank each State based on each of the four averages calculated in paragraph (e)(4)(i) of this section and the ratio calculated in paragraph (e)(4)(ii) of this section and combine the ranks to obtain the State's score on this component.

(5) For the quality component specified in paragraph (e)(2)(ii) of this section, in FY 2003 and beyond, we will compare the actual rates paid by the State as reported on the ACF–801 (not the published maximum rates) to the market rates applicable to the performance year, i.e., FY 2002. Each State competing on this measure must submit the following data as a part of its market rate survey:

(i) Age-specific rates for children 0–13 years of age reported by the child care centers and family day care homes responding to the State's market rate survey; and

(ii) The provider's county or, if the State uses multi-county regions to measure market rates or set maximum payment rates, the administrative region.

(6) For the quality component, we will compute the percentile of the market represented by the amount paid for each child as reported on the ACF–801 by comparing the actual payment for each child to the array of reported market rates for children of the same age in the relevant county or administrative region. (We will compare payments for children in center-based care to reported center care provider rates. We will compare payments for children in non-center-based care, i.e., family day care and unlicensed child care, to reported family child care provider rates.)

(i) We will take the percentile that results from the per-child comparison of the actual payment to the reported market rates and compute separate State-wide averages for center-based and non-center-based care; and

(ii) We will rank the State according to the two State-wide averages and combine the ranks to obtain the State's score on this component.

(7) For any given year, we will rank the States that choose to compete on the child care measure on each component of the overall measure and award bonuses to the ten States with the highest composite rankings.

(8) We will calculate each component score for this measure to two decimal points. If two or more States have the same score for a component, we will calculate the scores for these States to as many decimal points as necessary to eliminate the tie.

(9)(i) The rank of the measure for the FY 2002 bonus year will be a composite weighted score of the two components at paragraph (e)(1) of this section, with the component at paragraph (e)(1)(i) of this section having a weight of 6 and the component at paragraph (e)(1)(ii) of this section having a weight of 4.

(ii) The rank of the measure for the bonus beginning in FY 2003 will be a composite weighted score of the three components at paragraph (e)(2) of this section, with the component at paragraph (e)(1)(i) of this section having a weight of 5, the component at paragraph (e)(1)(ii) of this section having a weight of 3, and the component at paragraph (e)(2)(ii) of this section having a weight of 2.

(10) We will award bonuses only to the top ten qualifying States that have fully obligated their CCDF Matching Funds for the fiscal year corresponding to the performance year and fully expended their CCDF Matching Funds for the fiscal year preceding the performance year.

(f) *Family formation and stability measure.* (1) Beginning in FY 2002 and beyond, we will measure the increase in the percent of children in each State who reside in married couple families, beginning with a comparison of CY 2000 and CY 2001 data from the Census Bureau. For any given subsequent year we will compare a State's performance on this measure to its performance in the previous year.

(2) We will rank the performance of those States that choose to compete on this measure and will award bonuses to the ten States with the greatest percentage point improvement in this measure.

(3) We will calculate the percentage rate for the measure to two decimal points. If two or more States have the same percentage rate for this measure, we will calculate the rates for these States to as many decimal points as necessary to eliminate the tie.

(g) *Option to compete.* Each State has the option to compete on one, any number of, or none of the measures specified in this section.

[65 FR 52851, Aug. 30, 2000, as amended at 65 FR 75634, Dec. 4, 2000; 66 FR 23859, May 10, 2001]

EFFECTIVE DATE NOTE: At 66 FR 23859, May 10, 2001, in § 270.4(e)(2)(ii) was revised. This paragraph contains information collection and recordkeeping requirements and will not become effective until approval has been given by the Office of Management and Budget.

§ 270.5 What factors will we use to determine a State's score on the work measures?

(a) *Definitions.* The work measures are defined as follows:

(1) The *Job Entry* Rate means the unduplicated number of adult recipients who entered employment for the first time in the performance year (job entries) as a percentage of the total unduplicated number of adult recipients unemployed at some point in the performance year.

(2) The *Success in the Work Force Rate* is composed of two equally weighted sub-measures defined as follows:

(i) The *Job Retention Rate* means the performance year sum of the unduplicated number of employed adult recipients in each quarter one through four who were also employed in the first and second subsequent quarters, as a percentage of the sum of the unduplicated number of employed adult recipients in each quarter. (At some point, the adult might become a former recipient.); and

(ii) The *Earnings Gain Rate* means the performance year sum of the gain in earnings between the initial and second subsequent quarter in each of quarters one through four for adult recipients employed in both these quarters as a percentage of the sum of their initial earnings in each of quarters one through four. (At some point, the adult might become a former recipient.)

(3) The *Increase in the Job Entry Rate* means the positive percentage point difference between the job entry rate for the performance year and the job entry rate for the comparison year; and

(4) The Increase in Success in the Work Force Rate means the positive percentage point difference on at least one sub-measure between the success in the work force rate for the performance year and the success in the work force rate for the comparison year. It is composed of two equally weighted sub-measures defined as follows:

(i) The *Increase in the Job Retention Rate* means the percentage point difference between the job retention rate for the performance year and the job retention rate for the comparison year; and

(ii) The *Increase in the Earning Gain Rate* means the percentage point difference between the earnings gain rate for the performance year and the earnings gain rate for the comparison year.

(b) *Ranking of States.* (1) We will measure State performance in the work measures over the course of an entire fiscal year both for the performance year and the comparison year, if applicable.

(2) We will rank the competing States on the work measures for which they:

(i) Indicate they wish to compete; and

(ii) Submit the data specified in § 270.6 within the time frames specified in § 270.11.

(3) We will rank the States on absolute performance in each of the work measures in paragraphs (a)(1) and (a)(2) of this section. For each of the work measures in paragraphs (a)(3) and (a)(4) of this section, we will rank States based on the percentage point change

in their improvement rate in the performance year compared to the comparison year. The rank of the performance in paragraphs (a)(2) and (a)(4) of this section will be a composite score of the rank of the job retention and the earnings gain measures.

(4) We will calculate the percentage rate for each work measure to two decimal points. If two or more States have the same absolute or improvement rate for a specific work measure, we will calculate the rates for these States to as many decimal points as necessary to eliminate the tie.

§ 270.6 What data and other information must a State report to us?

(a) *Data for work measures.* (1) If a State wishes to compete on any of the work measures specified in § 270.5(a), it must collect quarterly and report semi-annually for the performance year and, if the State chooses to compete on an improvement measure, the comparison year, the identifying information on all adult TANF recipients as specified in program guidance.

(2) Each State must submit the information in this paragraph for both adult TANF recipients and adult SSP-MOE recipients for whom the State would report the data described in paragraph (b) of this section.

(b) *Data on SSP-MOE programs.* In order to compete on any high performance bonus measure, each State must submit the information in Sections One and Three of the SSP-MOE Data Report as specified in § 265.3(d) of this chapter.

(c) *Data for the Medicaid/SCHIP measures.* If a State wishes to compete on the Medicaid/SCHIP measures in § 270.4(d), it must submit the information that we and CMS will specify.

(d) *Data for the child care measure.* If a State wishes to compete on the child care measure in § 270.4(e), it must report the data as required by the CCDF program and additional data on child care market rates that we will specify.

(e) *Intent to compete.* Each State must notify us on which of the measures it will compete in each bonus year.

§ 270.7 What data will we use to measure performance on the work support and other measures?

(a) We will use Census Bureau data to rank States on their performance on the Food Stamp measures in § 270.4(c) and on the measure of family formation and stability in § 270.4(f). We will also use Census Bureau data, along with other information, to rank States on the child care measure in § 270.4(e). We will rank only those States that choose to compete on these measures.

(b) We will rank State performance on the Medicaid/SCHIP measures in § 270.4(d) based on data submitted by those States that choose to compete on these measures, as determined by matching TANF individuals who were enrolled in Medicaid/SCHIP and are no longer receiving TANF assistance with Medicaid/SCHIP enrollment data.

(c) We will rank State performance on the child care measure based on data submitted by those States that choose to compete on this measure. We will use data reported on Forms ACF 800, ACF 801, ACF 696 and other necessary data we will specify.

§ 270.8 How will we allocate the bonus award funds?

(a) In FY 2002 and beyond, we will allocate and award $140 million to the ten States with the highest scores for each work measure as follows, subject to reallocation as specified in § 270.9:

(1) Job Entry Rate—$56 million

(2) Success in the Work Force—$35 million

(3) Increase in Job Entry Rate—$28 million

(4) Increase in Success in the Work Force—$21 million;

(b) In FY 2002 and beyond, we will allocate and award $20 million to the ten States with the highest scores on the Food Stamp measures and $20 million to the ten States with the highest scores on the Medicaid/SCHIP measures, subject to reallocation as specified in § 270.9. For these measures, we will:

(1) Award $6 million to the three States with the highest scores on the Food Stamp absolute measure;

(2) Award $6 million to the three States with the highest scores on the Medicaid/SCHIP absolute measure;

(3) Award $14 million to the seven States with the highest scores on the Food Stamp improvement measure; and

(4) Award $14 million to the seven States with the highest scores on the Medicaid/SCHIP improvement measure.

(c) In FY 2002 and beyond, we will allocate and award $10 million to the ten States with the highest scores on the child care subsidy measure and $10 million to the ten States with the highest scores on the family formation and stability improvement measure.

(d) We will distribute the bonus dollars for each measure based on each State's percentage of the total amount of the State family assistance grants of the States that will receive a bonus.

§ 270.9 How will we redistribute funds if that becomes necessary?

(a) If we cannot distribute the funds as specified in § 270.8, we will reallocate any undistributed funds among the measures listed in § 270.4.

(b) If we still cannot distribute funds within the bonus year, they will remain available for distribution in the next bonus year, to the extent authorized by law.

§ 270.10 How will we annually review the award process?

(a) *Annual determination.* Annually, as needed, we will review the measures, data sources, and funding allocations specified in this part to determine if modifications, adjustments, or technical changes are necessary. We will add new measures or make changes in the funding allocations for the various measures only through regulations.

(b) *Criteria.* We will determine if any modifications, adjustments, or technical changes need to be made based on:

(1) Our experience in awarding high performance bonuses in previous years; and

(2) The availability of national, State-reliable, and objective data.

(c) *Consultation.* We will consult with the National Governors' Association, the American Public Human Services Association, and other interested parties before we make our final decisions on any modification, adjustment, or technical changes for the bonus awards. We will notify States and other interested parties of our decisions through annual program guidance. We will also post this information on the Internet.

§ 270.11 When must the States report the data and other information in order to compete for bonus awards?

(a) *All measures.* Each State must submit a list of the measures on which it is competing by February 28 of each bonus year.

(b) *Work measures.* Each State must collect quarterly and submit semi-annually during the bonus year the data specified in § 270.6(a) as follows:

(1) The data for the first and second quarters of the performance year and, if a State chooses to compete on an improvement measure, the first and second quarters of the comparison year, must be submitted by the dates we will specify in program guidance.

(2) The data for the third and fourth quarters of the performance year and, if a State chooses to compete on an improvement measure, the third and fourth quarters of the comparison year, must be submitted by the dates we will specify in program guidance.

(c) *SSP-MOE reporting.* Each State must collect quarterly its SSP-MOE Data Report as specified in § 270.6(b) and submit it:

(1) At the same time as it submits its quarterly TANF Data Report; or

(2) At the time it seeks to be considered for a high performance bonus as long as it submits the required data for the full period for which this determination will be made.

(d) *Medicaid/SCHIP measures.* Each State must submit the data required to compete on the Medicaid/SCHIP measures by the dates and in a manner that we and CMS will specify.

(e) *Child care subsidy measure.* Each State must submit the data required to compete on the child care measure by the date(s) we will specify.

§ 270.12 Must States file the data electronically?

Each State must submit the data required to compete for the high performance bonus work measures and the

Medicaid/SCHIP measures electronically in a manner that we and CMS will specify.

§ 270.13 What do States need to know about the use of bonus funds?

(a) A State must use bonus award funds to carry out the purposes of the TANF block grant as specified in section 401 (Purpose) and section 404 (Use of Grants) of the Act.

(b) As applicable, these funds are subject to the requirements in and limitations of sections 404 and 408 of the Act and § 263.11 of this chapter.

(c) For Puerto Rico, Guam, the Virgin Islands, and American Samoa, the bonus award funds are not subject to the mandatory ceilings on funding established in section 1108(c)(4) of the Act.

(d) States must report quarterly on the use of the bonus funds.

PART 282 [RESERVED]

PART 283—IMPLEMENTATION OF SECTION 403(A)(2) OF THE SOCIAL SECURITY ACT BONUS TO REWARD DECREASE IN ILLEGITIMACY RATIO

AUTHORITY: 42 U.S.C. 603.

SOURCE: 64 FR 18493, Apr. 14, 1999, unless otherwise noted.

§ 283.1 What does this part cover?

This part explains how States may be considered for the "Bonus to Reward Decrease in Illegitimacy Ratio," as authorized by section 403(a)(2) of the Social Security Act. It describes the data on which we will base the bonus, how we will make the award, and how we will determine the amount of the award.

§ 283.2 What definitions apply to this part?

The following definitions apply to this part:

Abortions means induced pregnancy terminations, including both medically and surgically induced pregnancy terminations. This term does not include spontaneous abortions, i.e., miscarriages.

Act means the Social Security Act.

Bonus refers to the Bonus to Reward Decrease in Illegitimacy Ratio, as set forth in section 403(a)(2) of the Act.

Calculation period refers to the four calendar years used for determining the decrease in the out-of-wedlock birth ratios for a bonus year. (The years included in the calculation period change from year to year.)

Most recent two-year period for which birth data are available means the most recent two calendar years for which the National Center for Health Statistics has released final birth data by State.

Most recent year for which abortion data are available means the year that is two calendar years prior to the current calendar year. (For example, for eligibility determinations made during calendar year 1999, the most recent year for which abortion data are available would be calendar year 1997.)

NCHS means the National Center for Health Statistics, of the Centers for Disease Control and Prevention, U.S. Department of Health and Human Services.

Number of out-of-wedlock births for the State means the final number of births occurring outside of marriage to residents of the State, as reported in NCHS vital statistics data.

Number of total births for the State means the final total number of live births to residents of the State, as reported in NCHS vital statistics data.

Rate of abortions means the number of abortions reported by the State in the most recent year for which abortion data are available divided by the State's total number of resident live births reported in vital statistics for that same year. (This measure is also more traditionally known as the "abortion to live birth ratio.")

Ratio refers to the ratio of live out-of-wedlock births to total live births, as defined in § 283.5(b).

State means the 50 States of the United States, the District of Columbia, the Commonwealth of Puerto Rico, the United States Virgin Islands, Guam, and American Samoa, as provided in section 419(a)(5) of the Act.

Vital statistics data means the data reported by State health departments to NCHS, through the Vital Statistics Cooperative Program (VSCP).

We (and any other first person plural pronouns) means the Secretary of Health and Human Services or any of the following individuals or organizations acting in an official capacity on the Secretary's behalf: the Assistant Secretary for Children and Families, the Regional Administrators for Children and Families, the Department of Health and Human Services, and the Administration for Children and Families.

§ 283.3 What steps will we follow to award the bonus?

(a) For each of the fiscal years 1999 through 2002, we will:

(1) Based on the vital statistics data provided by NCHS as described in § 283.4, calculate the ratios for the most recent two years for which final birth data are available, and for the prior two years, as described in § 283.5;

(2) Calculate the proportionate change between these two ratios, as described in § 283.5.

(3) Identify as potentially eligible a maximum of eight States, i.e., Guam, the Virgin Islands, and American Samoa, and five other States, that have qualifying decreases in their ratios, using the methodology described in § 283.5;

(4) Notify these potentially eligible States that we will consider them for the bonus if they submit data on abortions as stated in § 283.6; and

(5) Identify which of the potentially eligible States that submitted the required data on abortions have experienced decreases in their rates of abortion relative to 1995, as described in § 283.7. These States will receive the bonus.

(b) We will determine the amount of the grant for each eligible State, based on the number of eligible States, and whether Guam, American Samoa, or the Virgin Islands are eligible. No State will receive a bonus award greater than $25 million in any year.

§ 283.4 If a State wants to be considered for bonus eligibility, what birth data must it submit?

(a) To be considered for a bonus, the State must have submitted data on out-of-wedlock births as follows:

(1) The State must have submitted to NCHS the final vital statistics data files for all births occurring in the State. These files must show, among other elements, the total number of live births and the total number of out-of-wedlock live births occurring in the State. These data must conform to the Vital Statistics Cooperative Program contract for all years in the calculation period. This contract specifies, among other things, the guidelines and time-lines for submitting vital statistics data files; and

(2) The State must have submitted these data for the most recent two years for which NCHS reports final data, as well as for the previous two years.

(b) If a State has changed its method of determining marital status for the purposes of these data, the State also must have met the following requirements:

(1) The State has identified all years for which the method of determining marital status is different from that used for the previous year;

(2) For those years identified under paragraph (b)(1) of this section, the State has either:

(i) Replicated as closely as possible a consistent method for determining marital status at the time of birth, and the State has reported to NCHS the resulting alternative number of out-of-wedlock births; or

(ii) If NCHS agrees that such replication is not methodologically feasible, the State may chose to accept an NCHS estimate of what the alternative number would be;

(3) The State has submitted documentation to NCHS on what changes occurred in the determination of marital status for those years and, if appropriate, how it determined the alternative number of out-of-wedlock births for the State; and

(4) For methodological changes that were implemented prior to 1998 and applicable to data collected for the bonus period, the State has submitted the information described in paragraphs (b)(1), (2) and (3) of this section within two months after April 14, 1999. For such changes implemented during or after 1998, the State must submit such information either by the end of calendar year 1999 or according to the same deadline that applies to its vital statistics data for that year, whichever is later.

§ 283.5 How will we use these birth data to determine bonus eligibility?

(a) We will base eligibility determinations on final vital statistics data provided by NCHS showing the number of out-of-wedlock live births and the number of total live births among women living in each State and a factor provided by NCHS to adjust for changes in data reporting for those States that have changed their methodology for collecting data on out-of-wedlock births during the bonus period.

(b) We will use the number of total live births and the number of out-of-wedlock births, adjusted for any changes in data collection or reporting, to calculate the decrease in the ratio of out-of-wedlock to total births for each State as follows:

(1) We will calculate the ratio as the number of out-of-wedlock births for the State during the most recent two-year period for which NCHS has final birth data divided by the number of total births for the State during the same period. We will calculate, to three decimal places, the ratio for each State that submits the necessary data on total and out-of-wedlock births described in § 283.4.

(2) We will calculate the ratio for the previous two-year period using the same methodology.

(3) We will calculate the proportionate change in the ratio as the ratio of out-of-wedlock births to total births for the most recent two-year period minus the ratio of out-of-wedlock births to total births from the prior two-year period, all divided by the ratio of out-of-wedlock births to total births for the prior two-year period. A negative number will indicate a decrease in the ratio and a positive number will indicate an increase in the ratio.

(c) We will identify which States have a decrease in their ratios large enough to make them potentially eligible for the bonus, as follows:

(1) For States other than Guam, American Samoa and the Virgin Islands, we will use this calculated change to rank the States and identify which five States have the largest decrease in their ratios. Only States among the top five will be potentially eligible for the bonus. We will identify fewer than five such States as potentially eligible if fewer than five experience decreases in their ratios. We will not include Guam, American Samoa and the Virgin Islands in this ranking.

(2) If we identify more than five States due to a tie in the decrease, we will recalculate the ratio and the decrease in the ratio to as many decimal places as necessary to eliminate the tie. We will identify no more than five States.

(3) For Guam, American Samoa and the Virgin Islands, we will use the calculated change in the ratio to identify which of these States experienced a decrease that is either at least as large as the smallest qualifying decrease identified in paragraph (c)(1) of this section, or a decrease that ranks within the top five decreases when all States and Territories are ranked together. These identified States will be potentially eligible for the bonus also.

(4) We will notify the potentially eligible States, as identified under paragraphs (a) through (c) of this section that they must submit the information on abortions specified under § 283.6 if they want to be considered for the bonus.

§ 283.6 If a State wants to be considered for bonus eligibility, what data on abortions must it submit?

(a) To be considered further for bonus eligibility, each potentially eligible State, as identified under § 283.5, must submit to ACF data and information on the number of abortions for calendar year 1995 within two months of this notification. This number must measure either of the following:

(1) For calendar year 1995, the total number of abortions performed by all providers within the State; or

(2) For calendar year 1995, the total number of abortions performed by all providers within the State on the total population of State residents only. This is the preferred measure.

(b) States must have obtained these data on abortions for calendar year 1995 within 60 days of publication of the final rule and must include with their submission of 1995 data an official record documenting when they obtained the abortion data.

(c) Within two months of notification by ACF of potential eligibility, the State must submit:

(1) The number of abortions performed for the most recent year for which abortion data are available (as defined in § 283.2 to mean the year that is two calendar years prior to the current calendar year). In measuring the number of abortions, the State must use the same definition, either under paragraph (a)(1) or paragraph (a)(2) of this section, for both 1995 and the most recent year; or

(2) If applicable, the adjusted number and information specified in paragraph (d) of this section.

(d) If the State's data collection or reporting methodology changed between 1995 and the bonus year in such a way as to reflect an increase or decrease in the number of abortions that is different than what actually occurred during the period, the State must:

(1) When submitting the number of abortions for the most recent year under paragraph (c)(2), adjust the number to exclude increases or decreases in the number due to changes in methodology for collecting or reporting the data. For example, this calculation should include adjustments for increases or decreases in response rates for providers in reporting abortion data;

(2) Provide a rationale for the adjustment, i.e., a description of how the data collection or reporting methodology was changed. This could include a description of how legislative, policy or procedural changes affected the collection or reporting of abortion data, or an indication of changes in the response rate of providers in reporting abortion data; and

(3) Provide a certification by the Governor, or his or her designee, that the number of abortions reported to ACF accurately reflects these adjustments for changes in data collection or reporting methodology.

§ 283.7 How will we use these data on abortions to determine bonus eligibility?

(a) For those States that have met all the requirements under §§ 283.1 through 283.6, we will calculate the rate of abortions for calendar year 1995 and for the most recent year for which abortion data are available as defined in § 283.2. These rates will equal the number of abortions reported by the State to ACF for the applicable year, divided by total live births among women living in the State reported by NCHS for the same year. We will calculate the rates to three decimal places.

(b) If ACF determines that the State's rate of abortions for the most recent year for which abortion data are available is less than the rate for 1995, and, if the State has met all the requirements listed elsewhere under this part, the State will receive the bonus.

§ 283.8 What will be the amount of the bonus?

(a) If, for a bonus year, none of the eligible States is Guam, American Samoa or the Virgin Islands, then the amount of the grant shall be:

(1) $20 million per State if there are five eligible States; or

(2) $25 million per State if there are fewer than five eligible States.

(b) If for a bonus year, Guam, the Virgin Islands, or American Samoa is an eligible State, then the amount of the grant shall be:

(1) In the case of such a State, 25 percent of the mandatory ceiling amount as defined in section 1108 of the Act; and

(2) In the case of any other State, $100 million, minus the total amount of any bonuses paid to Guam, the Virgin Islands, and American Samoa, and divided by the number of eligible States other than Guam, American Samoa and the Virgin Islands, not to exceed $25 million per State.

§ 283.9 What do eligible States need to know to access and use the bonus funds?

(a) States must use the bonus funds to carry out the purposes of the Temporary Assistance for Needy Families Block Grant in section 401 and 404 of the Act. This may include statewide programs to prevent and reduce the incidence of out-of-wedlock pregnancies.

(b) As applicable, these funds are subject to the requirements in, and the limitations of, sections 404 and 408 of the Act.

(c) For Puerto Rico, Guam, the Virgin Islands, and American Samoa, the bonus award funds are not subject to the mandatory ceilings on funding established in section 1108(c)(4) of the Act.

PART 284—METHODOLOGY FOR DETERMINING WHETHER AN INCREASE IN A STATE OR TERRITORY'S CHILD POVERTY RATE IS THE RESULT OF THE TANF PROGRAM

Sec.

AUTHORITY: 42 U.S.C. 613(i)

SOURCE: 65 FR 39248, June 23, 2000, unless otherwise noted.

§ 284.10 What does this part cover?

(a) This part describes the methodology for determining the child poverty rates in the States and the Territories, as required by section 413(i) of the Social Security Act, including determining whether the child poverty rate increased by five percent or more as a result of the TANF program(s) in the State or Territory. It also describes the content and duration of the corrective action plan.

(b) The requirements of this part do not apply to any Territory that has never operated a TANF program.

§ 284.11 What definitions apply to this part?

The following definitions apply to this part:

ACF means the Administration for Children and Families.

Act means the Social Security Act, unless otherwise specified.

Census Bureau methodology means the various methods developed by the Census Bureau for estimating the number and percentage of children in poverty in each State. These methods may include national estimates based on the Current Population Survey; the Small Area Income and Poverty Estimates; the annual demographic programs, including the American Community Survey; or any other programs or methods used by the Census Bureau to estimate poverty. "Children in poverty" means children that live in families with incomes below 100 percent of the Census Bureau's poverty threshold.

Child poverty rate means the percentage of all children in a State or Territory which live in families with incomes below 100 percent of the Census Bureau's poverty threshold.

Date of enactment means calendar year 1996.

MOE means maintenance-of-effort. This is a provision in section 409(a)(7) of the Social Security Act that requires States to maintain a certain level of spending based on historical (*i.e.*, FY 1994) expenditure levels.

SAIPE means the Small Area Income and Poverty Estimates, a methodology developed by the Census Bureau to obtain more accurate estimates of poverty and income (including the number and percentage of children in poverty) at the State and county level between decennial censuses.

SSP-MOE means a separate State program operated outside of the TANF program for which the expenditure of State funds may count for MOE purposes.

State means each of the 50 States of the United States and the District of Columbia.

TANF means the Temporary Assistance for Needy Families program under sections 401 through 419 of the Social Security Act, as enacted by the Personal Responsibility and Work Opportunity Reconciliation Act of 1996, sections 101–116 of Pub. L. 104–193 (42 U.S.C. 601–619).

Territories means American Samoa, the Commonwealth of Puerto Rico, Guam, and the United States Virgin Islands.

Tribal TANF program means a TANF program developed by an eligible Tribe, Tribal organization, or consortium of Tribes, and approved by us under section 412 of the Act.

We (and any other first person plural pronouns) means the Secretary of Health and Human Services or any of the following individuals and organizations acting in an official capacity on the Secretary's behalf: The Assistant Secretary for Children and Families, the Regional Administrators for Children and Families, the Department of Health and Human Services, and the Administration for Children and Families.

§ 284.15 Who must submit information to ACF to carry out the requirements of this part?

(a) The Chief Executive Officer of the State, or his or her designee, is responsible for submitting to ACF the information required by this part.

(b) The State should obtain information from and work with the Indian tribe(s) (and Tribal consortia) operating a Tribal TANF program in the State in preparing and submitting the assessment, as specified in § 284.30, and the corrective action plan, as specified in § 284.45.

§ 284.20 What information will we use to determine the child poverty rate in each State?

(a) *General.* We will determine the child poverty rate in each State based on estimates from either the Census Bureau or the State, as described in this section. Each year we will use these data to determine the change in the State's child poverty rate over a two-year period, beginning with calendar years 1996 and 1997.

(b) *Estimates from the Census Bureau.* (1) Annually, we will obtain from the Census Bureau and provide to each State the estimate of the number and percentage of children in poverty in each State. The estimate will be based on the Census Bureau methodology.

(2) In 2000, and annually thereafter, we will determine for each State, at the 90-percent confidence level, the percentage change in the child poverty rate and provide this information to the State. The determination of percentage change in 2000 will cover the change between calendar years 1996 and 1997.

(c) *Estimates from the State.* (1) As an alternative to the Census Bureau estimates provided to the State under paragraph (b) of this section, the State may provide to us data on child poverty in the State derived from an independent source.

(2) If the State provides data on child poverty as described in paragraph (c)(1) of this section, it must:

(i) Provide an estimate of the child poverty rate for the same two calendar years as the Census Bureau estimates provided to the State under paragraph (b)(2) of this section;

(ii) Provide the change in the child poverty rate for the applicable two-calendar-year period at the 90-percent confidence level;

(iii) Use the official definition of poverty as used by the Census Bureau; and

(iv) Describe the methodology used to develop its independent estimates, the sources of data and methodology for collecting the data, any known problems associated with making estimates of this type, the estimate of the standard error, and the power of the sample to detect a five percent change in the child poverty rate.

(3) The State must submit its independent estimates and supporting information within 45 days of the date the State receives the Census Bureau estimates as described in paragraph (b) of this section.

(d) *Determination of the State's child poverty rate.* (1) If we determine that the State's independent estimates of the child poverty rate are more reliable than the Census Bureau estimates, we will accept these estimates.

(2) For all other States, we will determine the State's child poverty rate based on the Census Bureau's estimates.

§ 284.21 What will we do if the State's child poverty rate increased five percent or more over the two-year period?

(a) If we determine, based on § 284.20, that the State's child poverty rate did not increase by five percent or more over the applicable two-year period at the 90-percent confidence interval, we will:

(1) Conclude that the State has satisfied the statutory requirements of section 413(i) of the Act; and

(2) Notify the State that no further information from or action by the State is required for the applicable two-calendar-year period.

(b) If we determine, based on § 284.20, that the State's child poverty rate increased by five percent or more over the applicable two-year period at the 90-percent confidence level, we will notify the State that it has 90 days from the date of its receipt of our notification to submit an assessment of the impact of the TANF program(s) in the State, as specified in § 284.30.

§ 284.30 What information must the State include in its assessment of the impact of the TANF program(s) in the State on the increase in child poverty?

(a) The State's assessment must:

(1) Cover the same two-calendar-year period as the Census Bureau estimates provided to the State in § 284.20(b)(2);

(2) Directly address the issue of whether the State's child poverty rate increased as a result of the TANF program(s) in the State and include the State's analysis, explanation, and conclusions in relation to this issue; and

(3) Include the information on which the assessment was based.

(b) The State's assessment may be supported by any materials the State believes to be pertinent to its analysis, explanation, and conclusions. The following are examples of such materials:

(1) The number of families receiving TANF cash assistance payments under the State TANF program and, if applicable, the Tribal TANF program(s);

(2) The total amount of State and Tribal spending on TANF cash assistance payments;

(3) The number and/or percentage of eligible families with children in the State who are participating in the Food Stamp Program or other State supportive and assistance programs;

(4) The proportion of students certified for free or reduced-price school lunches;

(5) TANF income eligibility rules that show that client participation was not limited or cash benefits did not decrease;

(6) Examples of efforts that the State and the Indian tribe(s), as appropriate, have taken using TANF and other funds to support families entering the work force;

(7) The percentage of eligible individuals in the State receiving TANF assistance;

(8) Information on TANF program participation such as the number of applications disapproved or denied, or cases sanctioned;

(9) The number of TANF cases closed as a result of time-limit restrictions or non-compliance with work requirements;

(10) The amount of total cash assistance expenditures that can be claimed for SSP-MOE purposes;

(11) Information based on Unemployment Insurance wage record data showing, for example, increases in the number of TANF participants entering jobs, retaining jobs, and increasing their earnings;

(12) The number of families receiving work subsidies, *i.e.*, payments to employers or third parties to help cover the costs of employee wages, benefits, supervision, and training;

(13) Information that a State met the definition of "needy State" under section 403(b)(6) of the Act for an extended period of time within the applicable two-calendar-year period;

(14) Examples of past efforts that the State and the Indian tribe(s), as appropriate, have taken to mitigate or address child poverty;

(15) Any other data on the TANF program(s) in the State that would support the State's conclusions; and

(16) Information on other circumstances in the State that may have contributed to the increase in child poverty such as changes in economic or social conditions, *e.g.*, an increase in the State's unemployment rate.

§ 284.35 What action will we take in response to the State's assessment and other information?

(a) We will review the State's assessment along with other available information. If we determine that the increase in the child poverty rate of five percent or more is not the result of the TANF program(s) in the State, we will notify the State that no further information from, or action by, the State is required for the applicable two-calendar-year period.

(b) Based on our review of the State's assessment and other information, if we determine that the increase in the State's child poverty rate of five percent or more is the result of the TANF program(s) in the State, we will notify the State that it must submit a corrective action plan as specified in §§ 284.40 and 284.45.

§ 284.40 When is a corrective action plan due?

Each State must submit a corrective action plan to ACF within 90 days of the date the State receives notice of our determination that, as a result of the TANF program(s) in the State, its child poverty rate increased by five percent or more for the applicable two-calendar-year period.

§ 284.45 What are the contents and duration of the corrective action plan?

(a) The State must include in the corrective action plan:

(1) An outline of the manner in which the State or Territory will reduce its child poverty rate;

(2) A description of the actions it will take under the plan; and

(3) Any actions to be taken under the plan by the Indian tribe(s) (or Tribal consortia) operating a TANF program in the State.

(b) The State must implement the corrective action plan until it determines and notifies us that its child poverty rate, as determined in § 284.20, is less than the lowest child poverty rate on the basis of which the State was required to submit the corrective action plan. The "lowest child poverty rate" means the five percent threshold above the first year in the two-year comparison period.

§ 284.50 What information will we use to determine the child poverty rate in each Territory?

(a) Our intent is that, to the extent that reliable data are available and the procedures are appropriate, the Territories must meet the requirements in §§ 284.11 through 284.45 as specified for the 50 States and the District of Columbia.

(b) When reliable Census Bureau data are available for the Territories, we will:

(1) Notify the Territories through guidance of our intent to use these data in the implementation of this part; and

(2) Begin the process by providing to each Territory the number and percent of children in poverty in each jurisdiction, as specified in § 284.20(b).

PART 285 [RESERVED]

PART 286—TRIBAL TANF PROVISIONS

Subpart A—General Tribal TANF Provisions

Subpart B—Tribal TANF Funding

Subpart C—Tribal TANF Plan Content and Processing

Subpart D—Accountability and Penalties

Subpart E—Data Collection and Reporting Requirements

AUTHORITY: 42 U.S.C. 601, 604, and 612; Public Law 111–5.

SOURCE: 65 FR 8530, Feb. 18, 2000, unless otherwise noted.

Subpart A—General Tribal TANF Provisions

§ 286.1 What does this part cover?

Section 412 of the Social Security Act allows Indian tribes to apply to operate a Tribal Family Assistance program. This part implements section 412. It specifies:

(a) who can apply to operate a Tribal Family Assistance program;

(b) the requirements for the submission and contents of a Tribal Family Assistance Plan;

(c) the determination of the amount of a Tribal Family Assistance Grant; and

(d) other program requirements and procedures.

§ 286.5 What definitions apply to this part?

The following definitions apply under this part:

ACF means the Administration for Children and Families.

Act means the Social Security Act, unless otherwise specified.

Administrative cost means costs necessary for the proper administration of the TANF program.

(1) It excludes the direct costs of providing program services.

(i) For example, it excludes costs of providing diversion benefits and services, providing program information to clients, screening and assessments, development of employability plans, work activities, post-employment services, work supports, information on and referral to Medicaid, Child Health Insurance Program (CHIP), Food Stamp and Native Employment Works (NEW) programs and case management.

(ii) It excludes the salaries and benefit costs for staff providing program services and the direct administrative costs associated with providing the services, such as the costs for supplies, equipment, travel, postage, utilities, rental of office space and maintenance of office space, and

(iii) It excludes information technology and computerization needed for tracking and monitoring.

(2) It includes the costs for general administration and coordination of this program, including contract costs for these functions and indirect (or overhead) costs. Some examples of administrative costs include, but are not limited to:

(i) Salaries and benefits and all other direct costs not associated with providing program services to individuals, including staff performing administrative and coordination functions;

(ii) Preparation of program plans, budgets, and schedules;

(iii) Monitoring of programs and projects;

(iv) Fraud and abuse units;

(v) Procurement activities;

(vi) Public relations;

(vii) Services related to accounting, litigation, audits, management of property, payroll, and personnel;

(viii) Costs for the goods and services required for administration of the program such as the costs for supplies, equipment, travel, postage, utilities, and rental of office space and maintenance of office space, provided that such costs are not excluded as a direct administrative cost for providing program services under paragraph (1) of this definition;

(ix) Travel costs incurred for official business and not excluded as a direct administrative cost for providing program services under paragraph (1) of this definition;

(x) Management information systems not related to the tracking and monitoring of TANF requirements (*e.g.*, for a personnel and payroll system for Tribal staff); and

(xi) Preparing reports and other documents related to program requirements.

Adult means an individual who is not a "minor child," as defined below.

Alaska Tribal TANF entity means the twelve Alaska Native regional non-profit corporations in the State of Alaska and the Metlakatla Indian Community of the Annette Islands Reserve.

Assistant Secretary means the Assistant Secretary for Children and Families, Department of Health and Human Services.

Cash assistance, when provided to participants in the Welfare-to-Work program, has the meaning specified at § 286.130.

Comparability means similarity between State and Tribal TANF programs in the State of Alaska. Comparability, when defined related to services provided, does not necessarily mean identical or equal services.

Consortium means a group of Tribes working together for the same identified purpose and receiving combined TANF funding for that purpose.

The Department means the Department of Health and Human Services.

Duplicative Assistance means the receipt of services/ assistance from two or more TANF programs for the same purpose.

Eligible families means all families eligible for TANF funded assistance under the Tribal TANF program funded under section 412(a), including:

(1) All U.S. citizens who meet the Tribe's criteria for Tribal TANF assistance;

(2) All qualified aliens, who meet the Tribe's criteria for Tribal TANF assistance, who entered the U.S. before August 22, 1996;

(3) All qualified aliens, who meet the Tribe's criteria for Tribal TANF assistance, who entered the U.S. on or after August 22, 1996, who have been in the U.S. for at least 5 years beginning on the date of entry into the U.S. with a qualified alien status, are eligible beginning 5 years after the date of entry into the U.S. There are exceptions to this 5-year bar for qualified aliens who enter on or after August 22, 1996, and the Tribal TANF program must cover these excepted individuals:

(a) An alien who is admitted to the U.S. as a refugee under section 207 of the Immigration and Nationality Act;

(b) An alien who is granted asylum under section 208 of such Act;

(c) An alien whose deportation is being withheld under section 243(h) of such Act; and

(d) An alien who is lawfully residing in any State and is a veteran with an honorable discharge, is on active duty in the Armed Forces of the U.S., or is the spouse or unmarried dependent child of such an individual;

(4) All permanent resident aliens who are members of an Indian tribe, as defined in section 4(e) of the Indian Self-Determination and Education Assistance Act;

(5) All permanent resident aliens who have 40 qualifying quarters of coverage as defined by Title II of the Act.

Eligible Indian tribe means any Tribe or intertribal consortium that meets the definition of Indian tribe in this section and is eligible to submit a Tribal TANF plan to ACF.

Family Violence Option (or FVO) means the provision at section 402(a)(7) of the Act made available to Tribes under which a Tribe may certify in its Tribal TANF plan that it has elected the option to implement comprehensive strategies for identifying and serving victims of domestic violence.

Fiscal year means the 12-month period beginning on October 1 of the preceding calendar year and ending on September 30.

FY means fiscal year.

Good cause domestic violence waiver means a waiver of one or more program requirements granted by a Tribe to a victim of domestic violence under the FVO, as described in § 286.140(a)(3).

Grant period means the period of time that is specified in the Tribal TANF grant award document.

Indian, Indian tribe and Tribal Organization have the same meaning given such terms by section 4 of the Indian Self-Determination and Education Assistance Act (25 U.S.C. 450b), except that the term "Indian tribe" means, with respect to the State of Alaska, only the Metlakatla Indian Community of the Annette Islands Reserve and the following Alaska Native regional non-profit corporations:

(1) Arctic Slope Native Association;

(2) Kawerak, Inc.;

(3) Maniilaq Association;

(4) Association of Village Council Presidents;

(5) Tanana Chiefs Council;

(6) Cook Inlet Tribal Council;

(7) Bristol Bay Native Association;

(8) Aleutian and Pribilof Island Association;

(9) Chugachmuit;

(10) Tlingit Hàida Central Council;

(11) Kodiak Area Native Association; and

(12) Copper River Native Association.

Indian country has the meaning given the term in 18 U.S.C. 1151.

Minor child means an individual who:

(1) Has not attained 18 years of age; or

(2) Has not attained 19 years of age and is a full-time student in a secondary school (or in the equivalent level of vocational or technical training).

Minor Head-of-Household means an individual under age 18, or 19 and a full-time student in a secondary school, who is the custodial parent of a minor child.

PRWORA means the Personal Responsibility and Work Opportunity Reconciliation Act of 1996.

Qualified Aliens has the same meaning given the term in 8 U.S.C. 1641 except that it also includes members of an Indian tribe, as defined in section 4(e) of the Indian Self-Determination and Education Assistance Act, who are lawfully admitted under 8 U.S.C. 1359.

Retrocession means the process by which a Tribe voluntarily terminates and cedes back (or returns) a Tribal TANF program to the State which previously served the population covered by the Tribal TANF plan. Retrocession includes the voluntary relinquishment of the authority to obligate previously awarded grant funds before that authority would otherwise expire.

Secretary means the Secretary of the Department of Health and Human Services.

Scientifically acceptable sampling method means a probability sampling method in which every sampling unit has a known, non-zero chance to be included in the sample and the sample size requirements are met.

SFAG or State Family Assistance Grant means the amount of the block grant funded under section 403(a) of the Act for each eligible State.

SFAP or State Family Assistance Plan is the plan for implementation of a State TANF program under PRWORA.

State means, except as otherwise specifically provided, the 50 States of the United States, the District of Columbia, the Commonwealth of Puerto Rico, the United States Virgin Islands, Guam, and American Samoa.

TANF means the Temporary Assistance for Needy Families Program, which is authorized under title IV-A of the Social Security Act.

TANF funds mean funds authorized under section 412(a) of the Act.

TFAG or Tribal Family Assistance Grant means the amount of the block grant funded under section 412(a) of the Act for each eligible Tribe.

TFAP or Tribal Family Assistance Plan means the plan for implementation of the Tribal TANF program under section 412(b) of the Act.

Title IV-A refers to the title of the Social Security Act that now includes TANF, but previously included AFDC and EA. For the purpose of the TANF program regulations, this term does not include child care programs authorized and funded under section 418 of the Act, or their predecessors, unless we specify otherwise.

Title IV-F refers to the title of the Social Security Act that was eliminated with the creation of TANF and previously included the Job Opportunities and Basic Skills Training Program (JOBS).

Tribal TANF expenditures means expenditures of TANF funds, within the Tribal TANF program.

Tribal TANF program means a Tribal program subject to the requirements of section 412 of the Act that is funded by

TANF funds on behalf of eligible families.

Victim of domestic violence means an individual who is battered or subject to extreme cruelty under the definition at section 408(a)(7)(C)(iii) of the Act.

We (and any other first person plural pronouns) refers to The Secretary of Health and Human Services, or any of the following individuals or organizations acting in an official capacity on the Secretary's behalf: the Assistant Secretary for Children and Families, the Regional Administrators for Children and Families, the Department of Health and Human Services, and the Administration for Children and Families.

Welfare-related services means all activities, assistance, and services funded under Tribal TANF provided to an eligible family. See definition of "Assistance" in §286.10.

Welfare-to-Work means the program for funding work activities at section 412(a)(2)(C) of the Act.

WtW means Welfare-to-Work.

WtW cash assistance, when provided to participants in the Welfare-to-Work program, has the meaning specified at §286.130.

§286.10 What does the term "assistance" mean?

(a) The term "assistance" includes cash, payments, vouchers, and other forms of benefits designed to meet a family's ongoing basic needs (*i.e.*, for food, clothing, shelter, utilities, household goods, personal care items, and general incidental expenses).

(1) It includes such benefits even when they are:

(i) Provided in the form of payments by a TANF agency, or other agency on its behalf, to individual recipients; and

(ii) Conditioned on participation in work experience or community service or any other work activity.

(2) Except where excluded under paragraph (b) of this section, it also includes supportive services such as transportation and child care provided to families who are not employed.

(b) It excludes:

(1) Nonrecurring, short-term benefits that:

(i) Are designed to deal with a specific crisis situation or episode of need;

(ii) Are not intended to meet recurrent or ongoing needs; and

(iii) Will not extend beyond four months.

(2) Work subsidies (*i.e.*, payments to employers or third parties to help cover the costs of employee wages, benefits, supervision, and training);

(3) Supportive services such as child care and transportation provided to families who are employed;

(4) Refundable earned income tax credits;

(5) Contributions to, and distributions from, Individual Development Accounts;

(6) Services such as counseling, case management, peer support, child care information and referral, information on and referral to Medicaid, Child Health Insurance Program (CHIP), Food Stamp and Native Employment Works (NEW) programs, transitional services, job retention, job advancement, and other employment-related services that do not provide basic income support; and

(7) Transportation benefits provided under a Job Access or Reverse Commute project, pursuant to section 404(k) of the Act, to an individual who is not otherwise receiving assistance.

(c) The definition of the term assistance specified in paragraphs (a) and (b) of this section does not preclude a Tribe from providing other types of benefits and services consistent with the purposes of the TANF program.

§286.15 Who is eligible to operate a Tribal TANF program?

(a) An Indian tribe that meets the definition of Indian tribe given in §286.5 is eligible to apply to operate a Tribal Family Assistance Program.

(b) In addition, an intertribal consortium of eligible Indian tribes may develop and submit a single TFAP.

Subpart B—Tribal TANF Funding

§286.20 How is the amount of a Tribal Family Assistance Grant (TFAG) determined?

(a) We will request and use data submitted by a State to determine the amount of a TFAG. The State data that we will request and use are the total Federal payments attributable to

State expenditures, including administrative costs (which includes systems costs) for fiscal year 1994 under the former Aid to Families With Dependent Children, Emergency Assistance and Job Opportunities and Basic Skills Training programs, for all Indian families residing in the geographic service area or areas identified in the Tribe's letter of intent or Tribal Family Assistance Plan.

(1) A Tribe must indicate its definition of "Indian family" in its Tribal Family Assistance Plan. Each Tribe may define "Indian family" according to its own criteria.

(2) When we request the necessary data from the State, the State will have 30 days from the date of the request to submit the data.

(i) If we do not receive the data requested from the State at the end of the 30-day period, we will so notify the Tribe.

(ii) In cases where data is not received from the State, the Tribe will have 45 days from the date of the notification in which to submit relevant information. Relevant information may include, but is not limited to, Census Bureau data, data from the Bureau of Indian Affairs, data from other Federal programs, and Tribal records. In such a case, we will use the data submitted by the Tribe to assist us in determining the amount of the TFAG. Where there are inconsistencies in the data, follow-up discussions with the Tribe and the State will ensue.

(b) We will share the data submitted by the State under paragraph (a)(2)(i) of this section with the Tribe. The Tribe must submit to the Secretary a notice as to the Tribe's agreement or disagreement with such data no later than 45 days after the date of our notice transmitting the data from the State. During this 45-day period we will help resolve any questions the Tribe may have about the State-submitted data.

(c) We will notify each Tribe that has submitted a TFAP of the amount of the TFAG. At this time, we will also notify the State of the amount of the reduction in its SFAG.

(d) We will prorate TFAGs that are initially effective on a date other than October 1 of any given Federal fiscal year, based on the number of days remaining in the Federal fiscal year.

§ 286.25 How will we resolve disagreements over the State-submitted data used to determine the amount of a Tribal Family Assistance Grant?

(a) If a Tribe disagrees with the data submitted by a State, the Tribe may submit additional relevant information to the Secretary. Relevant information may include, but is not limited to, Census Bureau data, data from the Bureau of Indian Affairs, data from other Federal programs, and Tribal records.

(1) The Tribe must submit any relevant information within 45 days from the date it notifies the Secretary of its disagreement with State submitted data under § 286.20(b).

(2) We will review the additional relevant information submitted by the Tribe, together with the State-submitted data, in order to make a determination as to the amount of the TFAG. We will determine the amount of the TFAG at the earliest possible date after consideration of all relevant data.

§ 286.30 What is the process for retrocession of a Tribal Family Assistance Grant?

(a) A Tribe that wishes to terminate its TFAG prior to the end of its three-year plan must—

(1) Notify the Secretary and the State in writing of the reason(s) for termination no later than 120 days prior to the effective date of the termination, or

(2) Notify the Secretary in writing of the reason(s) for termination no later than 30 days prior to the effective date of the termination, where such effective data is mutually agreed upon by the Tribe and the affected State(s).

(b) The effective date of the termination must coincide with the last day of a calendar month.

(c) For a Tribe that retrocedes, the provisions of 45 CFR part 75 will apply with regard to closeout of the grant. All unobligated funds will be returned by the Tribe to the Federal government.

(d) The SFAG will be increased by the amount of the TFAG available for the subsequent quarterly installment.

(e) A Tribe's application to implement a TANF program subsequent to its retrocession will be treated as any other application to operate a TANF program, except that we may take into account when considering approval—

(1) Whether the circumstances that the Tribe identified for termination of its TANF program remain applicable and the extent to which—

(i) The Tribe has control over such circumstances, and

(ii) Such circumstances are reasonably related to program funding accountability, and

(2) Whether any outstanding funds and penalty amounts are repaid.

(f) A Tribe which retrocedes a Tribal TANF program is responsible for:

(1) Complying with the data collection and reporting requirements and all other program requirements for the period before the retrocession is effective;

(2) Any applicable penalties (see subpart D) for actions occurring prior to retrocession; the provisions of 45 CFR part 75;

(3) compliance with other Federal statutes and regulations applicable to the TANF program; and

(4) any penalties resulting from audits covering the period before the effective date of retrocession.

[65 FR 8530, Feb. 18, 2000, as amended at 81 FR 3020, Jan. 20, 2016]

§ 286.35 What are proper uses of Tribal Family Assistance Grant funds?

(a) Tribes may use TFAGs for expenditures that:

(1) Are reasonably calculated to accomplish the purposes of TANF, including, but not limited to, the provision to low income households with assistance in meeting home heating and cooling costs; assistance in economic development and job creation activities, the provision of supportive services to assist needy families to prepare for, obtain, and retain employment; the provision of supportive services to prevent of out-of-wedlock pregnancies, and assistance in keeping families together, or

(2) Were an authorized use of funds under the State plans for Parts A or F of title IV of the Social Security Act, as such parts were in effect on September 30, 1995.

(b) [Reserved]

§ 286.40 May a Tribe use the Tribal Family Assistance Grant to fund IDAs ?

(a) If the Tribe elects to operate an IDA program, it may use Federal TANF funds or WtW funds to fund IDAs for individuals who are eligible for TANF assistance and may exercise flexibility within the limits of Federal regulations and the statute.

(b) The following restrictions apply to IDA funds:

(1) A recipient may deposit only earned income into an IDA.

(2) A recipient's contributions to an IDA may be matched by, or through, a qualified entity.

(3) A recipient may withdraw funds only for the following reasons:

(i) To cover post-secondary education expenses, if the amount is paid directly to an eligible educational institution;

(ii) For the recipient to purchase a first home, if the amount is paid directly to the person to whom the amounts are due and it is a qualified acquisition cost for a qualified principal residence by a qualified first-time buyer; or

(iii) For business capitalization, if the amounts are paid directly to a business capitalization account in a federally insured financial institution and used for a qualified business capitalization expense.

(c) To prevent recipients from withdrawing funds held in an IDA improperly, Tribes may do the following:

(1) Count withdrawals as earned income in the month of withdrawal, unless already counted as income,

(2) Count withdrawals as resources in determining eligibility, or

(3) Take such other steps as the Tribe has established in its Tribal plan or written Tribal policies to deter inappropriate use.

§ 286.45 What uses of Tribal Family Assistance Grant funds are improper?

(a) A Tribe may not use Tribal Family Assistance Grant funds to provide assistance to:

(1) Families or individuals that do not otherwise meet the eligibility criteria contained in the Tribal Family Assistance Plan (TFAP); or

(2) For more than the number of months as specified in a Tribe's TFAP (unless covered by a hardship exemption); or

(3) Individuals who are not citizens of the United States or qualified aliens or who do not otherwise meet the definition of "eligible families" at § 286.5.

(b) Tribal Family Assistance Grant funds may not be used to contribute to or to subsidize non-TANF programs.

(c) A Tribe may not use Tribal Family Assistance Grant funds for services or activities prohibited by 45 CFR part 75, subpart E.

(d) All provisions in 45 CFR part 75 are applicable to the Tribal TANF program.

(e) Tribal TANF funds may not be used for the construction or purchase of facilities or buildings.

(f) Tribes must use program income generated by the Tribal Family Assistance grant for the purposes of the TANF program and for allowable TANF services, activities and assistance.

[65 FR 8530, Feb. 18, 2000, as amended at 81 FR 3020, Jan. 20, 2016]

§ 286.50 Is there a limit on the percentage of a Tribal Family Assistance Grant that can be used for administrative costs?

(a) ACF will negotiate a limitation on administrative costs with each Tribal TANF applicant individually for the first year of a program's operation based on the applicant's proposed administrative cost allocation. No Tribal TANF grantee may expend more than 35 percent of its Tribal Family Assistance Grant for administrative costs during the first year.

(b) ACF will negotiate a limitation on administrative costs with each Tribal TANF applicant individually for the second year of a program's operation based on the applicant's proposed administrative cost allocation. No Tribal TANF grantee may expend more than 30 percent of its TFAG for administrative costs during the second year.

(c) ACF will negotiate a limitation on administrative costs with each Tribal TANF applicant individually for the third and all subsequent years of a program's operation based on the applicant's proposed administrative cost allocation. As negotiated, a Tribal TANF grantee may not expend more than 25 percent of its TFAG for administrative costs during any subsequent grant period.

(1) For the purposes of determining administrative costs, Tribes with approved plans who have been operating Tribal TANF programs prior to the effective date of this regulation will be able to negotiate a reasonable adjustment in their approved administrative cost rate, not to exceed the limitations in the Final Rule delineated above.

(2) [Reserved]

(d) ACF will negotiate limitations on administrative costs based on, but not limited to, a Tribe's TANF funding level, economic conditions, and the resources available to the Tribe, the relationship of the Tribe's administrative cost allocation proposal to the overall purposes of TANF, and a demonstration of the Tribe's administrative capability.

§ 286.55 What types of costs are subject to the administrative cost limit on Tribal Family Assistance Grant funds?

(a) Activities that fall within the definition of "administrative costs" at § 286.5 are subject to the limit determined under § 286.50.

(b) Information technology and computerization for tracking, data entry and monitoring, including personnel and other costs associated with the automation activities needed for Tribal TANF monitoring, data entry and tracking purposes, are excluded from the administrative cost cap, even if they fall within the definition of "administrative costs."

(c) Designing, administering, monitoring, and controlling a sample are not inherent parts of information technology and computerization and, thus, costs associated with these tasks must be considered administrative costs.

(d) Indirect Costs negotiated by BIA, the Department's Division of Cost Allocation, or another federal agency must be considered to be part of the total administrative costs.

§ 286.60 Must Tribes obligate all Tribal Family Assistance Grant funds by the end of the fiscal year in which they are awarded?

No. A Tribe may reserve amounts awarded to it, without fiscal year limitation, to provide assistance, benefits, and services in accordance with the requirements under § 286.35 or § 286.40, if applicable.

[74 FR 25163, May 27, 2009]

Subpart C—Tribal TANF Plan Content and Processing

§ 286.65 How can a Tribe apply to administer a Tribal Temporary Assistance For Needy Families (TANF) Program?

(a) Any eligible Indian tribe, Alaska Native organization, or intertribal consortium that wishes to administer a Tribal TANF program must submit a three-year TFAP to the Secretary of the Department of Health and Human Services. The original must be submitted to the appropriate ACF Regional Office with a copy to the ACF Central Office.

(b) A Tribe currently operating a Tribal TANF program must submit to the appropriate ACF Regional Office, with a copy to the ACF Central Office, no later than 120 days prior to the end of the three-year grant period, either—

(1) A letter of intent, with a copy to the affected State or States, which specifies they do not intend to continue operating the program beyond the end of the three-year grant period; or

(2) A letter of intent, with a copy to the affected State or States, which specifies they intend to continue program operations with no changes to the geographic service area or service population; or

(3) A new three-year plan which indicates a change in either the geographic service area or service population.

(c) For Tribes choosing option (b)(2) above, a new three-year plan must be submitted to the appropriate ACF Regional Office, with a copy to the ACF Central Office, no later than 60 days before the end of the current three-year grant period.

§ 286.70 Who submits a Tribal Family Assistance Plan?

(a) A TFAP must be submitted by the chief executive officer of the Indian tribe and be accompanied by a Tribal resolution supporting the TFAP.

(b) A TFAP from a consortium must be forwarded under the signature of the chief executive officer of the consortium and be accompanied by Tribal resolutions from all participating Tribes that demonstrate each individual Tribe's support of the consortium, the delegation of decision-making authority to the consortium's governing board, and the Tribe's recognition that matters involving operation of the Tribal TANF consortium are the express responsibility of the consortium's governing board.

(c) When one of the participating Tribes in a consortium wishes to withdraw from the consortium, the Tribe needs to both notify the consortium and the Secretary of this fact.

(1) This notification must be made at least 120 days prior to the effective date of the withdrawal.

(2) The time frame in paragraph (c)(i) of this section is applicable only if the Tribe's withdrawal will cause a change to the service area or population of the consortium.

(d) When one of the participating Tribes in a consortium wishes to withdraw from the consortium in order to operate its own Tribal TANF program, the Tribe needs to submit a Tribal TANF plan that follows the requirements at § 286.75 and § 286.165.

§ 286.75 What must be included in the Tribal Family Assistance Plan?

(a) The TFAP must outline the Tribe's approach to providing welfare-related services for the three-year period covered by the plan, including:

(1) Information on the general eligibility criteria the Tribe has established, which includes a definition of "needy family," including income and resource limits and the Tribe's definition of "Tribal member family" or "Indian family."

(2) A description of the assistance, services, and activities to be offered, and the means by which they will be offered. The description of the services,

assistance, and activities to be provided includes whether the Tribe will provide cash assistance, and what other assistance, services, and activities will be provided.

(3) If the Tribe will not provide the same services, assistance, and activities in all parts of the service area, the TFAP must indicate any variations.

(4) If the Tribe opts to provide different services to specific populations, including teen parents and individuals who are transitioning off TANF assistance, the TFAP must indicate whether any of these services will be provided and, if so, what services will be provided.

(5) The Tribe's goals for its TANF program and the means of measuring progress towards those goals;

(6) Assurance that a 45-day public comment period on the Tribal TANF plan concluded prior to the submission of the TFAP.

(7) Assurance that the Tribe has developed a dispute resolution process to be used when individuals or families want to challenge the Tribe's decision to deny, reduce, suspend, sanction or terminate assistance.

(8) Tribes may require cooperation with child support enforcement agencies as a condition of eligibility for TANF assistance. Good cause and other exceptions to cooperation shall be defined by the Tribal TANF program.

(b) The TFAP must identify which Tribal agency is designated by the Tribe as the lead agency for the overall administration of the Tribal TANF program along with a description of the administrative structure for supervision of the TANF program.

(c) The TFAP must indicate whether the services, assistance and activities will be provided by the Tribe itself or through grants, contracts or compacts with inter-Tribal consortia, States, or other entities.

(d) The TFAP must identify the population to be served by the Tribal TANF program.

(1) The TFAP must identify whether it will serve Tribal member families only, or whether it will serve all Indian families residing in the Tribal TANF service area.

(2) If the Tribe wishes to serve any non-Indian families (and thus include non-Indians in its service population), an agreement with the State TANF agency must be included in the TFAP. This agreement must provide that, where non-Indians are to be served by Tribal TANF, these families are subject to Tribal TANF program rules.

(e) The TFAP must include a description of the geographic area to be served by the Tribal TANF program, including a specific description of any "near reservation" areas, as defined at 45 CFR 20.1(r), or any areas beyond "near reservation" to be included in the Tribal TANF service area.

(1) In areas beyond those defined as "near reservation", the TFAP must demonstrate the Tribe's administrative capacity to serve such areas and the State(s)', and if applicable, other Tribe(s)' concurrence with the proposed defined boundaries.

(2) A Tribe cannot extend its service area boundaries beyond the boundaries of the State(s) in which the reservation and BIA near-reservation designations are located.

(3) For Tribes in Oklahoma, if the Tribe defines its service area as other than its "tribal jurisdiction statistical area" (TJSA), the Tribe must include an agreement with the other Tribe(s) reflecting agreement to the service area. TJSAs are areas delineated by the Census Bureau for each federally-recognized Tribe in Oklahoma without a reservation.

(f) The TFAP must provide that a family receiving assistance under the plan may not receive duplicative assistance from other State or Tribal TANF programs and must include a description of the means by which the Tribe will ensure duplication does not occur.

(g) The TFAP must identify the employment opportunities in and near the service area and the manner in which the Tribe will cooperate and participate in enhancing such opportunities for recipients of assistance under the plan, consistent with any applicable State standards. This should include:

(1) A description of the employment opportunities available, in both the public and private sector, within and near the Tribal service area; and

(2) A description of how the Tribe will work with public and private sector employers to enhance the opportunities available for Tribal TANF recipients.

(h) The TFAP must provide an assurance that the Tribe applies the fiscal accountability provisions of section 5(f)(1) of the Indian Self-Determination and Education Assistance Act (25 U.S.C. 450c(f)(1)), relating to the submission of a single-agency audit report required by chapter 75 of title 31, United States Code.

§ 286.80 What information on minimum work participation requirements must a Tribe include in its Tribal Family Assistance Plan?

(a) To assess a Tribe's level of success in meeting its TANF work objectives, a Tribe that submits a TFAP must negotiate with the Secretary minimum work participation requirements that will apply to families that receive Tribal TANF assistance that includes an adult or minor head of household receiving such assistance.

(b) A Tribe that submits a TFAP must include in the plan the Tribe's proposal for minimum work participation requirements, which includes the following:

(1) For each fiscal year covered by the plan, the Tribe's proposed participation rate(s) for all families, for all families and two-parent families, or for one-parent families and two-parent families;

(2) For each fiscal year covered by the plan, the Tribe's proposed minimum number of hours per week that adults and minor heads of household will be required to participate in work activities;

(i) If the Tribe elects to include reasonable transportation time to and from the site of work activities in determining the hours of work participation, it must so indicate in its TFAP along with a definition of "reasonable" for purposes of this subsection, along with:

(A) An explanation of how the economic conditions and/or resources available to the Tribe justify inclusion of transportation time in determining work participation hours; and

(B) An explanation of how counting reasonable transportation time is consistent with the purposes of TANF;

(3) The work activities that count towards these work requirements;

(4) Any exemptions, limitations and special rules being established in relation to work requirements; and

(5) The Tribe must provide rationale for the above, explaining how the proposed work requirements relate to and are justified based on the Tribe's needs and conditions.

(i) The rationale must address how the proposed work requirements are consistent with the purposes of TANF and with the economic conditions and resources of the Tribe.

(ii) Examples of the information that could be included to illustrate the Tribe's proposal include, but are not limited to: poverty, unemployment, jobless and job surplus rates; education levels of adults in the service area; availability of and/or accessibility to resources (educational facilities, transportation) to help families become employable and find employment; and employment opportunities on and near the service area.

§ 286.85 How will we calculate the work participation rates?

(a) Work participation rate(s) will be the percentage of families with an adult or minor head-of-household receiving TANF assistance from the Tribe who are participating in a work activity approved in the TFAP for at least the minimum number of hours approved in the TFAP.

(b) The participation rate for a fiscal year is the average of the Tribe's participation rate for each month in the fiscal year.

(c) A Tribe's participation rate for a month is expressed as the following ratio:

(1) The number of families receiving TANF assistance that include an adult or a minor head-of-household who is participating in activities for the month (numerator), divided by

(2) The number of families that include an adult or a minor head-of-household receiving TANF assistance during the month excluding:

(i) Families that were penalized for non-compliance with the work requirements in that month as long as they have not been sanctioned for more than three months (whether or not consecutively) out of the last 12 months; and

(ii) Families with children under age one, if the Tribe chooses to exempt these families from participation requirements.

(d) If a family receives assistance for only part of a month or begins participating in activities during the month, the Tribe may count it as a month of participation if an adult or minor head-of-household in the family is participating for the minimum average number of hours in each full week that the family receives assistance or participates in that month.

(e) Two-parent families in which one of the parents is disabled are considered one-parent families for the purpose of calculating a Tribe's participation rate.

§ 286.90 How many hours per week must an adult or minor head-of-household participate in work-related activities to count in the numerator of the work participation rate?

During the month, an adult or minor head-of-household must participate in work activities for at least the minimum average number of hours per week specified in the Tribe's approved Tribal Family Assistance Plan.

§ 286.95 What, if any, are the special rules concerning counting work for two-parent families?

Parents in a two-parent family may share the number of hours required to be considered as engaged in work.

§ 286.100 What activities count towards the work participation rate?

(a) Activities that count toward a Tribe's participation rate may include, but are not limited to, the following:

(1) Unsubsidized employment;

(2) Subsidized private sector employment;

(3) Subsidized public sector employment;

(4) Work experience;

(5) On-the-job training (OJT);

(6) Job search and job readiness assistance; (see § 286.105)

(7) Community service programs;

(8) Vocational educational training; (see § 286.105)

(9) Job skills training directly related to employment;

(10) Education directly related to employment, in the case of a recipient who has not received a high school diploma or a certificate of high school equivalency;

(11) Satisfactory attendance at secondary school or in a course of study leading to a certificate of general equivalence, if a recipient has not completed secondary school or received such a certificate;

(12) Providing child care services to an individual who is participating in a community service program; and

(13) Other activities that will help families achieve self-sufficiency.

(b) [Reserved]

§ 286.105 What limitations concerning vocational education, job search and job readiness assistance exist with respect to the work participation rate?

(a) Tribes are not required to limit vocational education for any one individual to a period of 12 months.

(b) There are two limitations concerning job search and job readiness:

(1) Job search and job readiness assistance only count for 6 weeks in any fiscal year.

(2) If the Tribe's unemployment rate in the Tribal TANF service area is at least 50 percent greater than the United States' total unemployment rate for that fiscal year, then an individual's participation in job search or job readiness assistance counts for up to 12 weeks in that fiscal year.

(c) If job search or job readiness is an ancillary part of another activity, then there is no limitation on counting the time spent in job search/job readiness.

§ 286.110 What safeguards are there to ensure that participants in Tribal TANF work activities do not displace other workers?

(a) An adult or minor head-of-household taking part in a work activity outlined in § 286.100 cannot fill a vacant employment position if:

(1) Any other individual is on layoff from the same or any substantially equivalent job; or

(2) The employer has terminated the employment of any regular employee or otherwise caused an involuntary reduction in its work force in order to fill the vacancy with the TANF participant.

(b) A Tribe must establish and maintain a grievance procedure to resolve complaints of alleged violations of this displacement rule.

(c) This regulation does not preempt or supersede Tribal laws providing greater protection for employees from displacement.

§286.115 What information on time limits for the receipt of assistance must a Tribe include in its Tribal Family Assistance Plan?

(a) The TFAP must include the Tribe's proposal for:

(1) Time limits for the receipt of Tribal TANF assistance;

(2) Any exceptions to these time limits; and

(3) The percentage of the caseload to be exempted from the time limit due to hardship or if the family includes an individual who has been battered or subjected to extreme cruelty.

(b) The Tribe must also include the rationale for its proposal in the plan. The rationale must address how the proposed time limits are consistent with the purposes of TANF and with the economic conditions and resources of the Tribe.

(1) Examples of the information that could be included to illustrate the Tribe's proposal include, but are not limited to: Poverty, unemployment, jobless and job surplus rates; education levels of adults in the service area; availability of and/or accessibility to resources (educational facilities, transportation) to help families become employable and find employment; and employment opportunities on and near the service area.

(c) We may require that the Tribe submit additional information about the rationale before we approve the proposed time limits.

(d) Tribes must not count towards the time limit:

(1) Any month of receipt of assistance to a family that does not include an adult head-of-household;

(2) A family that does not include a pregnant minor head-of-household, minor parent head-of-household, or spouse of such a head-of-household; and

(3) Any month of receipt of assistance by an adult during which the adult lived in Indian country or in an Alaskan Native Village in which at least 50 percent of the adults were not employed.

(e) A Tribe must not use any of its TFAG to provide assistance (as defined in §286.10) to a family that includes an adult or minor head-of-household who has received assistance beyond the number of months (whether or not consecutive) that is negotiated with the Tribe.

§286.120 Can Tribes make exceptions to the established time limit for families?

(a) Tribes have the option to exempt families from the established time limits for:

(1) Hardship, as defined by the Tribe, or

(2) The family includes someone who has been battered or has been subject to extreme cruelty.

(b) If a Tribe elects the hardship option, the Tribe must specify in its TFAP the maximum percent of its average monthly caseload of families on assistance that will be exempt from the established time limit under paragraph (a) of this section.

(c) If the Tribe proposes to exempt more than 20 percent of the caseload under paragraph (a) of this section, the Tribe must include a rationale in the plan.

§286.125 Does the receipt of TANF benefits under a State or other Tribal TANF program count towards a Tribe's TANF time limit?

Yes, the Tribe must count prior months of TANF assistance funded with TANF block grant funds, except for any month that was exempt or disregarded by statute, regulation, or under any experimental, pilot, or demonstration project approved under section 1115 of the Act.

§ 286.130 Does the receipt of Welfare-to-Work (WtW) cash assistance count towards a Tribe's TANF time limit?

(a) For purposes of an individual's time limit for receipt of TANF assistance as well as the penalty provision at § 286.195(a)(1), WtW cash assistance counts towards a Tribe's TANF time limit only if:

(1) Such assistance satisfies the definition at § 286.10; and

(2) Is directed at ongoing basic needs.

(b) Only cash assistance provided in the form of cash payments, checks, reimbursements, electronic funds transfers, or any other form that can legally be converted to currency is subject to paragraph (a) of this section.

§ 286.135 What information on penalties against individuals must be included in a Tribal Family Assistance Plan?

(a) The TFAP must include the Tribe's proposal for penalties against individuals who refuse to engage in work activities. The Tribe's proposal must address the following:

(1) Will the Tribe impose a pro rata reduction, or more at Tribal option, or will it terminate assistance to a family?

(2) After consideration of the provision specified at § 286.150, what will be the proposed Tribal policies related to a single custodial parent, with a child under the age of 6, who refuses to engage in work activities because of a demonstrated inability to obtain needed child care?

(3) What good cause exceptions, if any, does the Tribe propose that will allow individuals to avoid penalties for failure to engage in work?

(4) What other rules governing penalties does the Tribe propose?

(5) What, if any, will be the Tribe's policies related to victims of domestic violence consistent with § 286.140?

(b) The Tribe's rationale for its proposal must also be included in the TFAP.

(1) The rationale must address how the proposed penalties against individuals are consistent with the purposes of TANF, consistent with the economic conditions and resources of the Tribe, and how they relate to the requirements of section 407(e) of the Act.

(2) Examples of the information that could be included to illustrate the Tribe's proposal include, but are not limited to; poverty, unemployment, jobless and job surplus rates; education levels of adults in the service area; availability of and/or accessibility to resources (educational facilities, transportation) to help families become employable and find employment; and employment opportunities on and near the service area.

(c) We may require a Tribe to submit additional information about the rationale before we approve the proposed penalties against individuals.

§ 286.140 What special provisions apply to victims of domestic violence?

(a) Tribes electing the Family Violence Option (FVO) must certify that they have established and are enforcing standards and procedures to:

(1) Screen and identify individuals receiving TANF assistance with a history of domestic violence, while maintaining the confidentiality of such individuals;

(2) Refer such individuals to counseling and supportive services; and

(3) Provide waivers, pursuant to a determination of good cause, of TANF program requirements to such individuals for so long as necessary in cases where compliance would make it more difficult for such individuals to escape domestic violence or unfairly penalize those who are or have been victimized by such violence or who are at risk of further domestic violence.

(b) Tribes have broad flexibility to grant waivers of TANF program requirements, but such waivers must:

(1) Identify the specific program requirement being waived;

(2) Be granted based on need as determined by an individualized assessment by a person trained in domestic violence and redeterminations no less than every six months;

(3) Be accompanied by an appropriate services plan that:

(i) Is developed in coordination with a person trained in domestic violence;

(ii) Reflects the individualized assessment and any revisions indicated by any redetermination; and

(iii) To the extent consistent with paragraph (a)(3) of this section, is designed to lead to work.

(c) If a Tribe wants us to take waivers that it grants under this section into account in deciding if it has reasonable cause for failing to meet its work participation rates or comply with the established time limit on TANF assistance, has achieved compliance or made significant progress towards achieving compliance with such requirements during a corrective compliance period, the waivers must comply with paragraph (b) of this section.

(d) We will determine that a Tribe has reasonable cause for failing to meet its work participation rates or to comply with established time limits on assistance if—

(1) Such failures were attributable to good cause domestic violence waivers granted to victims of domestic violence;

(2) In the case of work participation rates, the Tribe provides evidence that it achieved the applicable rates except with respect to any individuals who received a domestic violence waiver of work participation requirements. In other words, the Tribe must demonstrate that it met the applicable rates when such waiver cases are removed from the calculation of work participation rate;

(3) In the case of established time limits on assistance, the Tribe provides evidence that it granted good cause domestic violence waivers to extend time limits based on the need for continued assistance due to current or past domestic violence or the risk of further domestic violence, and individuals and their families receiving assistance beyond the established time limit under such waivers do not exceed 20 percent of the total number of families receiving assistance.

(e) We may take good cause domestic violence waivers of work participation or waivers which extend the established time limits for assistance into consideration in deciding whether a Tribe has achieved compliance or made significant progress toward achieving compliance during a corrective compliance period.

(f) Tribes electing the FVO must submit the information specified at § 286.275(b)(7).

§ 286.145 What is the penalty if an individual refuses to engage in work activities?

If an individual refuses to engage in work activities in accordance with the minimum work participation requirements specified in the approved TFAP, the Tribe must apply to the individual the penalties against individuals that were established in the approved TFAP.

§ 286.150 Can a family, with a child under age 6, be penalized because a parent refuses to work because (s)he cannot find child care?

(a) If the individual is a single custodial parent caring for a child under age six, the Tribe may not reduce or terminate assistance based on the parent's refusal to engage in required work if he or she demonstrates an inability to obtain needed child care for one or more of the following reasons:

(1) Appropriate child care within a reasonable distance from the home or work site is unavailable;

(2) Informal child care by a relative or under other arrangements is unavailable or unsuitable; or

(3) Appropriate and affordable formal child care arrangements are unavailable.

(b) Refusal to work when an acceptable form of child care is available is not protected from sanctioning.

(c) The Tribe will determine when the individual has demonstrated that he or she cannot find child care, in accordance with criteria established by the Tribe. These criteria must:

(1) Address the procedures that the Tribe uses to determine if the parent has a demonstrated inability to obtain needed child care;

(2) Include definitions of the terms "appropriate child care," "reasonable distance," "unsuitability of informal care," and "affordable child care arrangements"; and

(3) Be submitted to us.

(d) The Tribal TANF agency must inform parents about:

(1) The penalty exception to the Tribal TANF work requirement, including the criteria and applicable definitions for determining whether an individual has demonstrated an inability to obtain needed child care;

(2) The Tribe's procedures (including definitions) for determining a family's inability to obtain needed child care, and any other requirements or procedures, such as fair hearings, associated with this provision; and

(3) The fact that the exception does not extend the time limit for receiving Federal assistance.

§ 286.155 May a Tribe condition eligibility for Tribal TANF assistance on assignment of child support to the Tribe?

(a) Tribes have the option to condition eligibility for Tribal TANF assistance on assignment of child support to the Tribe consistent with paragraph (b) of this section.

(b) For Tribes choosing to condition eligibility for Tribal TANF assistance on assignment of child support to the Tribe, the TFAP must address the following—

(1) Procedures for ensuring that assigned child support collections in excess of the amount of Tribal TANF assistance received by the family will not be retained by the Tribe; and

(2) How any amounts generated under an assignment and retained by the Tribe will be used to further the Tribe's TANF program, consistent with § 286.45(f).

[65 FR 8530, Feb. 18, 2000, as amended at 69 FR 16672, Mar. 30, 2004]

§ 286.160 What are the applicable time frames and procedures for submitting a Tribal Family Assistance Plan?

(a) A Tribe must submit a Tribal TANF letter of intent and/or a TFAP to the Secretary according to the following time frames:

Implementation date:	Letter of intent due to ACF and the State:	Formal plan due to ACF:	ACF notification to the State due:
January 1, February 1 or March 1.	July 1 of previous year	September 1 of previous year	October 1 of previous year.
April 1, May 1 or June 1	October 1 of previous year	December 1 of previous year	January 1 of same year.
July 1, August 1 or September 1.	January 1 of same year	March 1 of same year	April 1 of same year.
October 1, November 1 or December 1.	April 1 of same year	June 1 of same year	July 1 of same year.

(b) A Tribe that has requested and received data from the State and has resolved any issues concerning the data more than six months before its proposed implementation date is not required to submit a letter of intent.

(c) The effective date of the TFAP must be the first day of any month.

(d) The original TFAP must be sent to the appropriate ACF Regional Administrator, with a copy sent to the Division of Tribal Services, Office of Community Services, Administration for Children and Families.

(e) A Tribe that submits a TFAP or an amendment to an existing plan that cannot be approved by the Secretary will be given the opportunity to make revisions in order to make the TFAP, or an amendment, approvable.

(f) Tribes operating a consolidated Public Law 102–477 program must submit a TFAP plan to the Secretary for review and approval prior to the consolidation of the TANF program into the Public Law 102–477 plan.

§ 286.165 How is a Tribal Family Assistance Plan amended?

(a) An amendment to a TFAP is necessary if the Tribe makes any substantial changes to the plan, including those which impact an individual's eligibility for Tribal TANF services or participation requirements, or any other program design changes which alter the nature of the program.

(b) A Tribe must submit a plan amendment(s) to the Secretary no later than 30 days prior to the proposed implementation date. Proposed implementation dates shall be the first day of any month.

(c) We will promptly review and either approve or disapprove the plan amendment(s).

(d) Approved plan amendments are effective no sooner than 30 days after date of submission.

(e) A Tribe whose plan amendment is disapproved may petition for an administrative review of such disapproval under § 286.170 and may appeal our final written decision to the Departmental Appeals Board no later than 30 days from the date of the disapproval. This appeal to the Board should follow the provisions of the rules under this subpart and those at 45 CFR part 16, where applicable.

§ 286.170 How may a Tribe petition for administrative review of disapproval of a TFAP or amendment?

(a) If, after a Tribe has been provided the opportunity to make revisions to its TFAP or amendment, the Secretary determines that the TFAP or amendment cannot be approved, a written Notice of Disapproval will be sent to the Tribe. The Notice of Disapproval will indicate the specific grounds for disapproval.

(b) A Tribe may request reconsideration of a disapproval determination by filing a written Request for Reconsideration to the Secretary within 60 days of receipt of the Notice of Disapproval. If reconsideration is not requested, the disapproval is final and the procedures under paragraph (f) of this section must be followed.

(1) The Request for Reconsideration must include—

(i) All documentation that the Tribe believes is relevant and supportive of its TFAP or amendment; and

(ii) A written response to each ground for disapproval identified in the Notice of Disapproval indicating why the Tribe believes that its TFAP or amendment conforms to the statutory and regulatory requirements for approval.

(c) Within 30 days after receipt of a Request for Reconsideration, the Secretary or designee will notify the Tribe of the date and time a hearing for the purpose of reconsideration of the Notice of Disapproval will be held. Such a hearing may be conducted by telephone conference call.

(d) A hearing conducted under § 286.170(c) must be held not less than 30 days nor more than 60 days after the date of the notice of such hearing is furnished to the Tribe, unless the Tribe agrees in writing to an extension.

(e) The Secretary or designee will make a written determination affirming, modifying, or reversing disapproval of the TFAP or amendment within 60 days after the conclusion of the hearing.

(f) If a TFAP or amendment is disapproved, the Tribe may appeal this final written decision to the Departmental Appeals Board (the Board) within 30 days after such party receives notice of determination. The party's appeal to the Board should follow the provisions of the rules under this section and those at 45 CFR part 16, where applicable.

§ 286.175 What special provisions apply in Alaska?

A Tribe in the State of Alaska that receives a TFAG must use the grant to operate a program in accordance with program requirements comparable to the requirements applicable to the State of Alaska's Temporary Assistance for Needy Families program. Comparability of programs must be established on the basis of program criteria developed by the Secretary in consultation with the State of Alaska and the Tribes in Alaska. The State of Alaska has authority to waive the program comparability requirement based on a request by an Indian tribe in the State.

§ 286.180 What is the process for developing the comparability criteria that are required in Alaska?

We will work with the Tribes in Alaska and the State of Alaska to develop an appropriate process for the development and amendment of the comparability criteria.

§ 286.185 What happens when a dispute arises between the State of Alaska and the Tribal TANF eligible entities in the State related to the comparability criteria?

(a) If a dispute arises between the State of Alaska and the Tribes in the State on any part of the comparability criteria, we will be responsible for making a final determination and notifying the State of Alaska and the Tribes in the State of the decision.

(b) Any of the parties involved may appeal our decision, in whole or in part, to the HHS Departmental Appeals Board (the Board) within 60 days after such party receives notice of determination. The party's appeal to the Board should follow the provisions of the rules under this section and those at 45 CFR part 16, where applicable.

§ 286.190 If the Secretary, the State of Alaska, or any of the Tribal TANF eligible entities in the State of Alaska want to amend the comparability criteria, what is the process for doing so?

(a) At such time that any of the above parties wish to amend the comparability document, the requesting party should submit a request to us, with a copy to the other parties, explaining the requested change(s) and supplying background information in support of the change(s).

(b) After review of the request, we will make a determination on whether or not to accept the proposed change(s).

(c) If any party wishes to appeal the decision regarding the adoption of the proposed amendment, they may appeal using the appeals process pursuant to § 286.165.

Subpart D—Accountability and Penalties

§ 286.195 What penalties will apply to Tribes?

(a) Tribes will be subject to fiscal penalties and requirements as follows:

(1) If we determine that a Tribe misused its Tribal Family Assistance Grant funds, including providing assistance beyond the Tribe's negotiated time limit under § 286.115, we will reduce the TFAG for the following fiscal year by the amount so used;

(2) If we determine that a Tribe intentionally misused its TFAG for an unallowable purpose, the TFAG for the following fiscal year will be reduced by an additional five percent;

(3) If we determine that a Tribe failed to meet the minimum work participation rate(s) established for the Tribe, the TFAG for the following fiscal year will be reduced. The amount of the reduction will depend on whether the Tribe was under a penalty for this reason in the preceding year. If not, the penalty reduction will be a maximum of five percent. If a penalty was imposed on the Tribe in the preceding year, the penalty reduction will be increased by an additional 2 percent, up to a maximum of 21 percent. In determining the penalty amount, we will take into consideration the severity of the failure and whether the reasons for the failure were increases in the unemployment rate in the TFAG service area and changes in TFAG caseload size during the fiscal year in question; and

(4) If a Tribe fails to repay a Federal loan provided under section 406 of the Act, we will reduce the TFAG for the following fiscal year by an amount equal to the outstanding loan amount plus interest.

(b) In calculating the amount of the penalty, we will add together all applicable penalty percentages, and the total is applied to the amount of the TFAG that would have been payable if no penalties were assessed against the Tribe. As a final step, we will subtract other (non-percentage) penalty amounts.

(c) When imposing the penalties in paragraph (a) of this section, we will not reduce an affected Tribe's grant by more than 25 percent. If the 25 percent limit prevents the recovery of the full penalty imposed on a Tribe during a fiscal year, we will apply the remaining amount of the penalty to the TFAG payable for the immediately succeeding fiscal year.

(1) If we reduce the TFAG payable to a Tribe for a fiscal year because of penalties that have been imposed, the Tribe must expend additional Tribal funds to replace any such reduction. The Tribe must document compliance with this provision on its TANF expenditure report.

(2) We will impose a penalty of not more than 2 percent of the amount of the TFAG on a Tribe that fails to expend additional Tribal funds to replace amounts deducted from the TFAG due to penalties. We will apply this penalty

to the TFAG payable for the next succeeding fiscal year, and this penalty cannot be excused (see §286.235).

(d) If a Tribe retrocedes the program, the Tribe will be liable for any penalties incurred for the period the program was in operation.

§286.200 How will we determine if Tribal Family Assistance Grant funds were misused or intentionally misused?

(a) We will use the single audit or Federal review or audit to determine if a Tribe should be penalized for misusing Tribal Family Assistance Grant funds under §286.195(a)(1) or intentionally misusing Tribal Family Assistance Grant funds under §286.195(a)(2).

(b) If a Tribe uses the TFAG in violation of the provisions of the Act, the provisions of 45 CFR part 75, or any Federal statutes and regulations applicable to the TANF program, we will consider the funds to have been misused.

(c) The Tribe must show, to our satisfaction, that it used the funds for purposes that a reasonable person would consider to be within the purposes of the TANF program (as specified at §286.35) and the provisions listed in §286.45.

(d) We will consider the TFAG to have been intentionally misused under the following conditions:

(1) There is supporting documentation, such as Federal guidance or policy instructions, indicating that TANF funds could not be used for that purpose; or

(2) After notification that we have determined such use to be improper, the Tribe continues to use the funds in the same or similarly improper manner.

(e) If the single audit determines that a Tribe misused Federal funds in applying the negotiated time limit provisions under §286.115, the amount of the penalty for misuse will be limited to five percent of the TFAG amount.

(1) This penalty shall be in addition to the reduction specified under §286.195(a)(1).

(2) [Reserved]

[65 FR 8530, Feb. 18, 2000, as amended at 81 FR 3020, Jan. 20, 2016]

§286.205 How will we determine if a Tribe fails to meet the minimum work participation rate(s)?

(a) We will use the Tribal TANF Data Reports required under §286.255 to determine if we will assess the penalty under §286.195(a)(3) for failure to meet the minimum participation rate(s) established for the Tribe.

(b) Each Tribal TANF Grantee's quarterly reports (the TANF Data Report and the Tribal TANF Financial Report) must be complete and accurate and filed by the due date. The accuracy of the reports are subject to validation by us.

(1) For a disaggregated data report, "a complete and accurate report" means that:

(i) The reported data accurately reflect information available to the Tribal TANF grantee in case records, financial records, and automated data systems;

(ii) The data are free from computational errors and are internally consistent (*e.g.*, items that should add to totals do so);

(iii) The Tribal TANF grantee reports data for all required elements (*i.e.*, no data are missing);

(iv) The Tribal TANF grantee provides data on all families; or

(v) If the Tribal TANF grantee opts to use sampling, the Tribal TANF grantee reports data on all families selected in a sample that meets the specification and procedures in the TANF Sampling Manual (except for families listed in error); and

(vi) Where estimates are necessary (*e.g.*, some types of assistance may require cost estimates), the Tribal TANF grantee uses reasonable methods to develop these estimates.

(2) For an aggregated data report, "a complete and accurate report" means that:

(i) The reported data accurately reflect information available to the Tribal TANF grantee in case records, financial records, and automated data systems;

(ii) The data are free from computational errors and are internally consistent (*e.g.*, items that should add to totals do so);

(iii) The Tribal TANF grantee reports data on all applicable elements; and

(iv) Monthly totals are unduplicated counts for all families (*e.g.*, the number of families and the number of out-of-wedlock births are unduplicated counts).

(3) For the Tribal TANF Financial Report, a "complete and accurate report" means that:

(i) The reported data accurately reflect information available to the Tribal TANF grantee in case records, financial records, and automated data systems;

(ii) The data are free from computational errors and are internally consistent (*e.g.*, items that should add to totals do so);

(iii) The Tribal TANF grantee reports data on all applicable elements; and

(iv) All expenditures have been made in accordance with 45 CFR part 75.

(4) We will review the data filed in the quarterly reports to determine if they meet these standards. In addition, we will use audits and reviews to verify the accuracy of the data filed by the Tribal TANF grantee.

(c) Tribal TANF grantees must maintain records to adequately support any report, in accordance with 45 CFR part 75.

(d) If we find reports so significantly incomplete or inaccurate that we seriously question whether the Tribe has met its participation rate, we may apply the penalty under § 286.195(a)(3).

[65 FR 8530, Feb. 18, 2000, as amended at 81 FR 3020, Jan. 20, 2016]

§ 286.210 What is the penalty for a Tribe's failure to repay a Federal loan?

(a) If a Tribe fails to repay the amount of principal and interest due at any point under a loan agreement:

(1) The entire outstanding loan balance, plus all accumulated interest, becomes due and payable immediately; and

(2) We will reduce the TFAG payable for the immediately succeeding fiscal year quarter by the outstanding loan amount plus interest.

(b) Neither the reasonable cause provisions at § 286.225 nor the corrective compliance plan provisions at § 286.230 apply when a Tribe fails to repay a Federal loan.

§ 286.215 When are the TANF penalty provisions applicable?

(a) A Tribe may be subject to penalties, as described in § 286.195(a)(1), § 286.195(a)(2) and § 286.195(a)(4), for conduct occurring on and after the first day of implementation of the Tribe's TANF program.

(b) A Tribe may be subject to penalties, as described in § 286.195(a)(3), for conduct occurring on and after the date that is six months after the Tribe begins operating the TANF program.

(c) We will not apply the regulations retroactively. We will judge Tribal actions that occurred prior to the effective date of these rules and expenditures of funds received prior to the effective date only against a reasonable interpretation of the statutory provisions in title IV-A of the Act.

(1) To the extent that a Tribe's failure to meet the requirements of the penalty provisions is attributable to the absence of Federal rules or guidance, Tribes may qualify for reasonable cause, as discussed in § 286.225.

(2) [Reserved]

§ 286.220 What happens if a Tribe fails to meet TANF requirements?

(a) If we determine that a Tribe is subject to a penalty, we will notify the Tribe in writing. This notice will:

(1) Specify what penalty provision(s) are in issue;

(2) Specify the amount of the penalty;

(3) Specify the reason for our determination;

(4) Explain how and when the Tribe may submit a reasonable cause justification under § 286.225 and/or a corrective compliance plan under § 286.230(d) for those penalties for which reasonable cause and/or corrective compliance plan apply; and

(5) Invite the Tribe to present its arguments if it believes that the data or method we used were in error or were insufficient, or that the Tribe's actions, in the absence of Federal regulations, were based on a reasonable interpretation of the statute.

(b) Within 60 days of receipt of our written notification, the Tribe may submit a written response to us that:

(1) Demonstrates that our determination is incorrect because our data or

the method we used in determining the penalty was in error or was insufficient, or that the Tribe acted prior to June 19, 2000, on a reasonable interpretation of the statute;

(2) Demonstrates that the Tribe had reasonable cause for failing to meet the requirement(s); and/or

(3) Provides a corrective compliance plan as discussed in § 286.230.

(c) If we find that the Tribe was correct and that a penalty was improperly determined, or find that a Tribe had reasonable cause for failing to meet a requirement, we will not impose the related penalty and so notify the Tribe in writing within two weeks of such a determination.

(d) If we determine that the Tribe has not demonstrated that our original determination was incorrect or that it had reasonable cause, we will notify the Tribe of our decision in writing.

(e) If we request additional information from a Tribe, it must provide the information within thirty days of the date of our request.

§ 286.225 How may a Tribe establish reasonable cause for failing to meet a requirement that is subject to application of a penalty?

(a) We will not impose a penalty against a Tribe if it is determined that the Tribe had reasonable cause for failure to meet the requirements listed at § 286.195(a)(1), § 286.195(a)(2), or § 286.195(a)(3). The general factors a Tribe may use to claim reasonable cause include, but are not limited to, the following:

(1) Natural disasters, extreme weather conditions, and other calamities (*e.g.*, hurricanes, earthquakes, fire, and economic disasters) whose disruptive impact was so significant that the Tribe failed to meet a requirement.

(2) Formally issued Federal guidance which provided incorrect information resulting in the Tribe's failure or prior to the effective date of these regulations, guidance that was issued after a Tribe implemented the requirements of the Act based on a different, but reasonable, interpretation of the Act.

(3) Isolated, non-recurring problems of minimal impact that are not indicative of a systemic problem.

(4) Significant increases in the unemployment rate in the TFAG service area and changes in the TFAG caseload size during the fiscal year being reported.

(b) We will grant reasonable cause to a Tribe that:

(1) Clearly demonstrates that its failure to submit complete, accurate, and timely data, as required at § 286.245, for one or both of the first two quarters of FY 2000, is attributable, in significant part, to its need to divert critical system resources to Year 2000 compliance activities; and

(2) Submits complete and accurate data for the first two quarters of FY 2000 by November 15, 2000.

(c) In addition to the reasonable cause criteria specified above, a Tribe may also submit a request for a reasonable cause exemption from the requirement to meet its work participation requirements in the following situation:

(1) We will consider that a Tribe has reasonable cause if it demonstrates that its failure to meet its work participation rate(s) is attributable to its provisions with regard to domestic violence as follows:

(i) To demonstrate reasonable cause, a Tribe must provide evidence that it achieved the applicable work rates, except with respect to any individuals receiving good cause waivers of work requirements (*i.e.*, when cases with good cause waivers are removed from the calculation in § 286.85); and

(ii) A Tribe must grant good cause waivers in domestic violence cases appropriately, in accordance with the policies in the Tribe's approved Tribal Family Assistance Plan.

(2) [Reserved]

(d) In determining reasonable cause, we will consider the efforts the Tribe made to meet the requirements, as well as the duration and severity of the circumstances that led to the Tribe's failure to achieve the requirement.

(e) The burden of proof rests with the Tribe to fully explain the circumstances and events that constitute reasonable cause for its failure to meet a requirement.

(1) The Tribe must provide us with sufficient relevant information and documentation to substantiate its claim of reasonable cause.

(2) [Reserved]

§ 286.230 What if a Tribe does not have reasonable cause for failing to meet a requirement?

(a) To avoid the imposition of a penalty under § 286.195(a)(1), § 286.195(a)(2), or § 286.195(a)(3), under the following circumstances a Tribe must enter into a corrective compliance plan to correct the violation:

(1) If a Tribe does not claim reasonable cause for failing to meet a requirement; or

(2) If we found that a Tribe did not have reasonable cause.

(b) A Tribe that does not claim reasonable cause will have 60 days from receipt of the notice described in § 286.220(a) to submit its corrective compliance plan to us.

(c) A Tribe that does not demonstrate reasonable cause will have 60 days from receipt of the second notice described in § 286.220(d) to submit its corrective compliance plan to us.

(d) In its corrective compliance plan the Tribe must outline:

(1) Why it failed to meet the requirements;

(2) How it will correct the violation in a timely manner; and

(3) What actions, outcomes and time line it will use to ensure future compliance.

(e) During the 60-day period beginning with the date we receive the corrective compliance plan, we may, if necessary, consult with the Tribe on modifications to the plan.

(f) A corrective compliance plan is deemed to be accepted if we take no action to accept or reject the plan during the 60-day period that begins when the plan is received.

(g) Once a corrective compliance plan is accepted or deemed accepted, we may request reports from the Tribe or take other actions to confirm that the Tribe is carrying out the corrective actions specified in the plan.

(1) We will not impose a penalty against a Tribe with respect to any violation covered by that plan if the Tribe corrects the violation within the time frame agreed to in the plan.

(2) We must assess some or all of the penalty if the Tribe fails to correct the violation pursuant to its corrective compliance plan.

§ 286.235 What penalties cannot be excused?

(a) The penalties that cannot be excused are:

(1) The penalty for failure to repay a Federal loan issued under section 406.

(2) The penalty for failure to replace any reduction in the TFAG resulting from other penalties that have been imposed.

(b) [Reserved]

§ 286.240 How can a Tribe appeal our decision to take a penalty?

(a) We will formally notify the Tribe of a potential reduction to the Tribe's TFAG within five days after we determine that a Tribe is subject to a penalty and inform the Tribe of its right to appeal to the Departmental Appeals Board (the Board) established in the Department of Health and Human Services. Such notification will include the factual and legal basis for taking the penalty in sufficient detail for the Tribe to be able to respond in an appeal.

(b) Within 60 days of the date it receives notice of the penalty, the Tribe may file an appeal of the action, in whole or in part, to the Board.

(c) The Tribe must include all briefs and supporting documentation when it files its appeal. A copy of the appeal and any supplemental filings must be sent to the Office of General Counsel, Children, Families and Aging Division, Room 411–D, 200 Independence Avenue, SW, Washington, DC 20201.

(d) ACF must file its reply brief and supporting documentation within 45 days after receipt of the Tribe's submission under paragraph (c) of this section.

(e) The Tribe's appeal to the Board must follow the provisions of this section and those at §§ 16.2, 16.9, 16.10, and 16.13 through 16.22 of this title to the extent they are consistent with this section.

(f) The Board will consider an appeal filed by a Tribe on the basis of the documentation and briefs submitted, along with any additional information the Board may require to support a final decision. Such information may include a hearing if the Board determines that it is necessary. In deciding whether to uphold an adverse action or any portion of such action, the Board will conduct a thorough review of the issues.

(g) The filing date shall be the date materials are received by the Board in a form acceptable to it.

(h) A Tribe may obtain judicial review of a final decision by the Board by filing an action within 90 days after the date of such decision with the district court of the United States in the judicial district where the Tribe or TFAG service area is located.

(1) The district court will review the final decision of the Board on the record established in the administrative proceeding, in accordance with the standards of review prescribed by 5 U.S.C. 706(2). The court's review will be based on the documents and supporting data submitted to the Board.

(2) [Reserved]

(i) No reduction to the Tribe's TFAG will occur until a final disposition of the matter has been made.

Subpart E—Data Collection and Reporting Requirements

§ 286.245 What data collection and reporting requirements apply to Tribal TANF programs?

(a) Section 412(h) of the Act makes section 411 regarding data collection and reporting applicable to Tribal TANF programs. This section of the regulations explains how we will collect the information required by section 411 of the Act and information to implement section 412(c) (work participation requirements).

(b) Each Tribe must collect monthly and file quarterly data on individuals and families as follows:

(1) Disaggregated data collection and reporting requirements in this part apply to families receiving assistance and families no longer receiving assistance under the Tribal TANF program; and

(2) Aggregated data collection and reporting requirements in this part apply to families receiving, families applying for, and families no longer receiving assistance under the Tribal TANF program.

(c) Each Tribe must file in its quarterly TANF Data Report and in the quarterly TANF Financial Report the specified data elements.

(d) Each Tribe must also submit an annual report that contains specified information.

(e) Each Tribe must submit the necessary reports by the specified due dates.

§ 286.250 What definitions apply to this subpart?

(a) Except as provided in paragraph (b) of this section, the general TANF definitions at §§ 286.5 and 286.10 apply to this subpart.

(b) For data collection and reporting purposes only, "TANF family" means:

(1) All individuals receiving assistance as part of a family under the Tribe's TANF program; and

(2) The following additional persons living in the household, if not included under paragraph (b)(1) of this section:

(i) Parent(s) or caretaker relative(s) of any minor child receiving assistance;

(ii) Minor siblings of any child receiving assistance; and

(iii) Any person whose income or resources would be counted in determining the family's eligibility for or amount of assistance.

§ 286.255 What quarterly reports must the Tribe submit to us?

(a) *Quarterly reports.* Each Tribe must collect on a monthly basis, and file on a quarterly basis, the data specified in the Tribal TANF Data Report and the Tribal TANF Financial Report.

(b) *Tribal TANF Data Report.* The Tribal TANF Data Report consists of three sections. Two sections contain disaggregated data elements and one section contains aggregated data elements.

(1) *TANF Data Report: Disaggregated Data—Sections one and two.* Each Tribe must file disaggregated information on families receiving TANF assistance (section one) and families no longer receiving TANF assistance (section two). These two sections specify identifying and demographic data such as the individual's Social Security Number; and

information such as the type and amount of assistance received, educational level, employment status, work participation activities, citizenship status, and earned and unearned income. These reports also specify items pertaining to child care and child support. The data requested cover adults (including non-custodial parents who are participating in work activities) and children.

(2) *TANF Data Report: Aggregated Data—Section three.* Each Tribe must file aggregated information on families receiving, applying for, and no longer receiving TANF assistance. This section of the Report asks for aggregate figures in the following areas: the total number of applications and their disposition; the total number of recipient families, adult recipients, and child recipients; the total number of births, out-of-wedlock births, and minor child heads-of-households; the total number of non-custodial parents participating in work activities; and the total amount of TANF assistance provided.

(c) *The Tribal TANF Financial Report.* Each Tribe must file quarterly expenditure data on the Tribe's use of Tribal Family Assistance Grant funds, any Tribal fund expenditures which are being substituted for TFAG funds withheld due to a penalty, and any State contributions. The report must be submitted on a form prescribed by ACF.

§ 286.260 May Tribes use sampling and electronic filing?

(a) Each Tribe may report disaggregated data on all recipient families (universal reporting) or on a sample of families selected through the use of a scientifically acceptable sampling method. The sampling method must be approved by ACF in advance of submitting reports.

(1) Tribes may not use a sample to generate the aggregated data.

(2) [Reserved]

(b) "Scientifically acceptable sampling method" means a probability sampling method in which every sampling unit has a known, non-zero chance to be included in the sample, and the sample size requirements are met.

(c) Each Tribe may file quarterly reports electronically, based on format specifications that we will provide. Tribes who do not have the capacity to submit reports electronically may submit quarterly reports on a disk or in hard copy.

§ 286.265 When are quarterly reports due?

(a) Upon a Tribe's initial implementation of TANF, the Tribe shall begin collecting data for the TANF Data Report as of the date that is six months after the initial effective date of its TANF program. The Tribe shall begin collecting financial data for the TANF Financial Report as of the initial effective date of its TANF program.

(b) Each Tribe must submit its TANF Data Report and TANF Financial Report within 45 days following the end of each quarter. If the 45th day falls on a weekend or on a national, State or Tribal holiday, the reports are due no later than the next business day.

§ 286.270 What happens if the Tribe does not satisfy the quarterly reporting requirements?

(a) If we determine that a Tribe has not submitted to us a complete and accurate Tribal TANF Data Report within the time limit, the Tribe risks the imposition of a penalty at § 286.205 related to the work participation rate targets since the data from the Tribal TANF Data Report is required to calculate participation rates.

(b) Non-reporting of the Tribal TANF Financial Report may give rise to a penalty under § 286.200 since this Report is used to demonstrate compliance with provisions of the Act, the provisions of 45 CFR part 75, or any Federal statutes and regulations applicable to the TANF program.

[65 FR 8530, Feb. 18, 2000, as amended at 81 FR 3020, Jan. 20, 2016]

§ 286.275 What information must Tribes file annually?

(a) Each Tribal TANF grantee must file an annual report containing information on its TANF program for that year. The report may be filed as:

(1) An addendum to the fourth quarter TANF Data Report; or

(2) A separate annual report.

(b) Each Tribal TANF grantee must provide the following information on its TANF program:

(1) The Tribal TANF grantee's definition of each work activity;

(2) A description of the transitional services provided to families no longer receiving assistance due to employment; and

(3) A description of how a Tribe will reduce the amount of assistance payable to a family when an individual refuses to engage in work without good cause pursuant to §286.145.

(4) The average monthly number of payments for child care services made by the Tribal TANF grantee through the use of disregards, by the following types of child care providers:

(i) Licensed/regulated in-home child care;

(ii) Licensed/regulated family child care;

(iii) Licensed/regulated group home child care;

(iv) Licensed/regulated center-based child care;

(v) Legally operating (*i.e.*, no license category available in Tribal TANF grantee's locality) in-home child care provided by a nonrelative;

(vi) Legally operating (*i.e.*, no license category available in Tribal TANF grantee's locality) in-home child care provided by a relative;

(vii) Legally operating (*i.e.*, no license category available in Tribal TANF grantee's locality) family child care provided by a nonrelative;

(viii) Legally operating (*i.e.*, no license category available in Tribal TANF grantee's locality) family child care provided by a relative;

(ix) Legally operating (*i.e.*, no license category available in Tribal TANF grantee's locality) group child care provided by a nonrelative;

(x) Legally operating (*i.e.*, no license category available in Tribal TANF grantee's locality) group child care provided by a relative; and

(xi) Legally operating (*i.e.*, no license category available in Tribal TANF grantee's locality) center-based child care.

(5) A description of any nonrecurring, short-term benefits provided, including:

(i) The eligibility criteria associated with such benefits, including any restrictions on the amount, duration, or frequency of payments;

(ii) Any policies that limit such payments to families that are eligible for TANF assistance or that have the effect of delaying or suspending a family's eligibility for assistance; and

(iii) Any procedures or activities developed under the TANF program to ensure that individuals diverted from assistance receive information about, referrals to, or access to other program benefits (such as Medicaid and food stamps) that might help them make the transition from Welfare-to-Work; and

(6) A description of the procedures the Tribal TANF grantee has established and is maintaining to resolve displacement complaints, pursuant to §286.110. This description must include the name of the Tribal TANF grantee agency with the lead responsibility for administering this provision and explanations of how the Tribal TANF grantee has notified the public about these procedures and how an individual can register a complaint.

(7) Tribes electing the FVO must submit a description of the strategies and procedures in place to ensure that victims of domestic violence receive appropriate alternative services, as well as an aggregate figure for the total number of good cause domestic waivers granted.

(c) If the Tribal TANF grantee has submitted the information required in paragraph (b) of this section in the TFAP, it may meet the annual reporting requirements by reference in lieu of re-submission. Also, if the information in the annual report has not changed since the previous annual report, the Tribal TANF grantee may reference this information in lieu of re-submission.

(d) If a Tribal TANF grantee makes a substantive change in certain data elements in paragraph (b) of this section, it must file a copy of the change either with the next quarterly data report or as an amendment to its TFAP. The Tribal TANF grantee must also indicate the effective date of the change.

This requirement is applicable to paragraphs (b)(1), (b)(2), and (b)(3) of this section.

§ 286.280 When are annual reports due?

(a) The annual report required by § 286.275 is due 90 days after the end of the Fiscal Year which it covers.

(b) The first annual report for a Tribe must include all months of operation since the plan was approved.

§ 286.285 How do the data collection and reporting requirements affect Public Law 102–477 Tribes?

(a) A Tribe that consolidates its Tribal TANF program into a Public-Law 102–477 plan is required to comply with the TANF data collection and reporting requirements of this section.

(b) A Tribe that consolidates its Tribal TANF program into a Public-Law 102–477 plan may submit the Tribal TANF Data Reports and the Tribal TANF Financial Report to the BIA, with a copy to us.

PART 287—THE NATIVE EMPLOYMENT WORKS (NEW) PROGRAM

Subpart A—General NEW Provisions

Subpart B—Eligible Tribes

Subpart C—NEW Program Funding

Subpart D—Plan Requirements

Subpart E—Program Design and Operations

Subpart F—Data Collection and Reporting Requirements

AUTHORITY: 42 U.S.C. 612.

SOURCE: 65 FR 8554, Feb. 18, 2000, unless otherwise noted.

Subpart A—General NEW Provisions

§ 287.1 What does this part cover?

(a) The regulations in this part prescribe the rules for implementing section 412(a)(2) of the Social Security Act (the Act), as amended by the Personal Responsibility and Work Opportunity Reconciliation Act of 1996 (PRWORA) (Pub. L. 104–193) and the Balanced Budget Act of 1997 (Pub. L. 105–33).

(b) Section 412(a)(2) of the Act, as amended, authorizes the Secretary to issue grants to eligible Indian tribes to operate a program that makes work activities available to "such population and such service area or areas as the tribe specifies."

(c) We call this Tribal work activities program the Native Employment Works (NEW) program.

(d) These regulations specify the Tribes who are eligible to receive NEW Program funding. They also prescribe requirements for: funding; program plan development and approval; program design and operation; and data collection and reporting.

§ 287.5 What is the purpose and scope of the NEW Program?

The purpose of the NEW Program is to provide eligible Indian tribes, including Alaska Native organizations, the opportunity to provide work activities and services to their needy clients.

§ 287.10 What definitions apply to this part?

The following definitions apply to this part:

ACF means the Administration for Children and Families;

Act means the Social Security Act, unless we specify otherwise;

Alaska Native organization means an Alaska Native village, or regional or village corporation, as defined in or established pursuant to the Alaska Native Claims Settlement Act (43 U.S.C. 1601 *et seq.*), that is eligible to operate a Federal program under the Indian Self-Determination and Education Assistance Act (25 U.S.C. 450);

Consortium means a group of Tribes working together for the same identified purpose and receiving combined NEW funding for that purpose.

Department means the Department of Health and Human Services;

Division of Tribal Services (DTS) means the unit in the Office of Community Services within the Department's Administration for Children and Families that has as its primary responsibility the administration of the Tribal family assistance program, called the Tribal Temporary Assistance for Needy Families (TANF) program, and the Tribal work program, called the Native Employment Works (NEW) program, as authorized by section 412(a);

Eligible Indian tribe means an Indian tribe, a consortium of Indian tribes, or an Alaska Native organization that operated a Tribal Job Opportunities and Basic Skills Training (JOBS) program in fiscal year 1995 under section 482(i) of the Act, as in effect during that fiscal year;

Fiscal year means the 12-month period beginning on October 1 of the preceding calendar year and ending on September 30;

FY means fiscal year;

Indian, Indian tribe, and Tribal organization—The terms Indian, Indian tribe, and Tribal organization have the meaning given such terms by section 4 of the Indian Self-Determination and Education Assistance Act (25 U.S.C. 450b);

Native Employment Works Program means the Tribal work program under section 412(a)(2) of the Act;

NEW means the Native Employment Works Program;

Program Year means, for the NEW Program, the 12-month period beginning on July 1 of the calendar year and ending on June 30;

PRWORA means the Personal Responsibility and Work Opportunity Reconciliation Act of 1996, Public Law 104–193;

Public Law 102–477 refers to the Indian Employment, Training and Related Services Demonstration Act of

1992, whose purpose is to provide for the integration of employment, training and related services to improve the effectiveness of those services;

Secretary means the Secretary of the Department of Health and Human Services;

State means, except as otherwise specifically provided, the 50 States of the United States, the District of Columbia, the Commonwealth of Puerto Rico, the United States Virgin Islands, Guam, and American Samoa;

TANF means the Temporary Assistance for Needy Families Program;

Temporary Assistance for Needy Families Program means a family assistance grant program operated either by a Tribe under section 412(a)(1) of the Act or by a State under section 403 of the Act;

Tribal TANF program means a Tribal program subject to the requirements of section 412 of the Act which is funded by TANF funds on behalf of eligible families;

We (and any other first person plural pronouns) refers to The Secretary of Health and Human Services, or any of the following individuals or organizations acting in an official capacity on the Secretary's behalf: The Assistant Secretary for Children and Families, the Regional Administrators for Children and Families, the Department of Health and Human Services, and the Administration for Children and Families.

Subpart B—Eligible Tribes

§ 287.15 Which Tribes are eligible to apply for NEW Program grants?

To be considered for a NEW Program grant, a Tribe must be an "eligible Indian tribe." An eligible Indian tribe is an Indian tribe or Alaska Native organization that operated a Job Opportunities and Basic Skills Training (JOBS) program in FY 1995.

§ 287.20 May a Public Law 102–477 Tribe operate a NEW Program?

Yes, if the Tribe is an "eligible Indian tribe."

§ 287.25 May Tribes form a consortium to operate a NEW Program?

(a) Yes, as long as each Tribe forming the consortium is an "eligible Indian tribe."

(b) To apply for and conduct a NEW Program, the consortium must submit a plan to ACF.

(c) The plan must include a copy of a resolution from each Tribe indicating its membership in the consortium and authorizing the consortium to act on its behalf in regard to administering a NEW Program. If an Alaska Native organization forms a consortium, submission of the required resolution from the governing board of the organization is sufficient to satisfy this requirement.

§ 287.30 If an eligible consortium breaks up, what happens to the NEW Program grant?

(a) If a consortium should break up or any Tribe withdraws from a consortium, it will be necessary to allocate unobligated funds and future grants among the Tribes that were members of the consortium, if each individual Tribe obtains ACF approval to continue to operate a NEW Program.

(b) Each withdrawing Tribe must submit to ACF a copy of the Tribal resolution that confirms the Tribe's decision to withdraw from the consortium and indicates whether the Tribe elects to continue its participation in the program.

(c) The allocation can be accomplished by any method that is recommended and agreed to by the leaders of those Tribes.

(d) If no recommendation is made by the Tribal leaders or no agreement is reached, the Secretary will determine the allocation of funds based on the best available data.

Subpart C—NEW Program Funding

§ 287.35 What grant amounts are available under the Personal Responsibility and Work Opportunity Reconciliation Act of 1996 (PRWORA) for the NEW Program?

Each Tribe shall receive a grant in an amount equal to the amount received by the Tribe in FY 1994 under section 482(i) of the Act (as in effect during FY 1994).

§ 287.40 Are there any matching funds requirements with the NEW Program?

No, Tribal grantees are not required to match NEW Federal funds.

§ 287.45 How can NEW Program funds be used?

(a) NEW grants are for making work activities available to such population as the Tribe specifies.

(b) NEW funds may be used for work activities as defined by the Tribal grantee.

(c) Work activities may include supportive services necessary for assisting NEW Program participants in preparing for, obtaining, and/or retaining employment.

§ 287.50 What are the funding periods for NEW Program grants?

NEW Program funds are for operation of the NEW Program for a 12-month period from July 1 through June 30.

§ 287.55 What time frames and guidelines apply regarding the obligation and liquidation periods for NEW Program funds?

(a) NEW Program funds provided for a FY are for use during the period July 1 through June 30 and must be obligated no later than June 30. Carry forward of an unobligated balance of NEW funds is not permitted. A NEW fund balance that is unobligated as of June 30 will be returned to the Federal government through the issuance of a negative grant award. Unobligated funds are to be reported on the SF–269A that Tribes must submit within 30 days after the funding period, *i.e.*, no later than July 30. This report is called the interim financial report.

(b) A Tribe must liquidate all obligations incurred under the NEW Program grant awards not later than one year after the end of the obligation period, *i.e.*, no later than June 30 of the following FY. An unliquidated balance at the close of the liquidation period will be returned to the Federal government through the issuance of a negative grant award. Unliquidated obligations are to be reported on the SF–269A that Tribes must submit within 90 days after the liquidation period, *i.e.*, by September 28. This report is called the final financial report.

§ 287.60 Are there additional financial reporting and auditing requirements?

(a) The reporting of expenditures are generally subject to the requirements of 45 CFR 75.341.

(b) NEW Program funds and activities are subject to the audit requirement of the Single Audit Act of 1984 (45 CFR part 75, subpart F).

(c) A NEW Program grantee must comply with all laws, regulations, and Departmental policies that govern submission of financial reports by recipients of Federal grants.

(d) Improper expenditure claims under this program are subject to disallowance.

(e) If a grantee disagrees with the Agency's decision to disallow funds, the grantee may follow the appeal procedures at 45 CFR part 16.

[65 FR 8554, Feb. 18, 2000, as amended at 81 FR 3021, Jan. 20, 2016]

§ 287.65 What OMB circulars apply to the NEW Program?

NEW Programs are subject to the following OMB circulars where applicable: A–87 "Cost Principles for State, Local, and Indian Tribal Governments," A–122 "Cost Principles for Non-Profit Organizations," and A–133 "Audits of States and Local Governments."

Subpart D—Plan Requirements

§ 287.70 What are the plan requirements for the NEW Program?

(a) To apply for and conduct a NEW Program, a Tribe must submit a plan to ACF.

(b) The plan must identify the agency responsible for administering the NEW Program and include a description of the following:

(1) Population to be served;

(2) Service area;

(3) Client services;

(4) Work activities to be provided;

(5) Supportive and job retention services to be provided;

(6) Anticipated program outcomes, and the measures the Tribe will use to determine them; and

(7) Coordination activities conducted and expected to be conducted with other programs and agencies.

(c) The plan must also describe how the Tribe will deliver work activities and services.

(d) The format is left to the discretion of each NEW grantee.

§ 287.75 When does the plan become effective?

NEW plans, which are three-year plans, become effective when approved by the Secretary. The plans are usually operative the beginning of a NEW Program year, July 1.

§ 287.80 What is the process for plan review and approval?

(a) A Tribe must submit its plan to the ACF Regional Office, with a copy sent to the Division of Tribal Services, Office of Community Services, Administration for Children and Families, Attention: Native Employment Works Team.

(b) To receive funding by the beginning of the NEW Program year (July 1), a Tribe must submit its plan by the established due date.

(c) ACF will complete its review of the plan within 45 days of receipt.

(d) After the plan review has occurred, if the plan is approvable, ACF will approve the plan, certifying that the plan meets all necessary requirements. If the plan is not approvable, the Regional Office will notify the Tribe regarding additional action needed for plan approval.

§ 287.85 How is a NEW plan amended?

(a) If a Tribe makes substantial changes in its NEW Program plan or operations, it must submit an amendment for the changed section(s) of the plan to the appropriate ACF Regional Office for review and approval, with a copy sent to the Division of Tribal Services, Office of Community Services, Administration of Children and Families, Attention: Native Employment Works Team. The review will verify consistency with section 412(a)(2) of the Act.

(b) A substantial change is a change in the agency administering the NEW Program, a change in the designated service area and/or population, a change in work activities provided or a change in performance standards.

(c) A substantial change in plan content or operations must be submitted to us no later than 45 days prior to the proposed implementation date.

(d) ACF will complete the review of the amended plan within 45 days of receipt.

(e) An amended plan becomes effective when it is approved by the Secretary.

§ 287.90 Are Tribes required to complete any certifications?

Yes. A Tribe must include in its NEW Program plan the following four certifications and any additional certifications that the Secretary prescribes in the planning guidance: Certification Regarding Debarment, Suspension, and Other Responsibility Matters—Primary Covered Transactions; Certification Regarding Drug Free Workplace Requirements for Grantees Other Than Individuals; Certification Regarding Tobacco Smoke, and Assurances—Non-Construction Programs.

§ 287.95 May a Tribe operate both a NEW Program and a Tribal TANF program?

Yes. However, the Tribe must adhere to statutory and regulatory requirements of the individual programs.

§ 287.100 Must a Tribe that operates both NEW and Tribal TANF programs submit two separate plans?

Yes. Separate plans are needed to reflect different program and plan requirements as specified in the statute and in plan guidance documents issued by the Secretary for each program.

Subpart E—Program Design and Operations

§ 287.105 What provisions of the Social Security Act govern the NEW Program?

NEW Programs are subject only to those requirements at section 412(a)(2) of the Act, as amended by PRWORA, titled "Grants for Indian Tribes that Received JOBS Funds."

§ 287.110 Who is eligible to receive assistance or services under a Tribe's NEW Program?

(a) A Tribe must specify in its NEW Program plan the population and service area to be served. In cases where a Tribe designates a service area for its NEW Program that is different from its Bureau of Indian Affairs (BIA) service area, an explanation must be provided.

(b) A Tribe must include eligibility criteria in its plan and establish internal operating procedures that clearly specify the criteria to be used to establish an individual's eligibility for NEW services. The eligibility criteria must be equitable.

§ 287.115 When a NEW grantee serves TANF recipients, what coordination should take place with the Tribal or State TANF agency?

The Tribe should coordinate with the Tribal or State TANF agency on:

(a) Eligibility criteria for TANF recipients to receive NEW Program services;

(b) Exchange of case file information;

(c) Changes in client status that result in a loss of cash assistance, food stamps, Medicaid or other medical coverage;

(d) Identification of work activities that may meet Tribal or State work participation requirements;

(e) Resources available from the Tribal or State TANF agency to ensure efficient delivery of benefits to the designated service population;

(f) Policy for exclusions from the TANF program (*e.g.*, criteria for exemptions and sanctions);

(g) Termination of TANF assistance when time limits become effective;

(h) Use of contracts in delivery of TANF services;

(i) Prevention of duplication of services to assure the maximum level of services is available to participants;

(j) Procedures to ensure that costs of other program services for which welfare recipients are eligible are not shifted to the NEW Program; and

(k) Reporting data for TANF quarterly and annual reports.

§ 287.120 What work activities may be provided under the NEW Program?

(a) The Tribe will determine what work activities are to be provided.

(b) Examples of allowable activities include, but are not limited to: Educational activities, alternative education, post secondary education, job readiness activity, job search, job skills training, training and employment activities, job development and placement, on-the-job training (OJT), employer work incentives related to OJT, community work experience, innovative approaches with the private sector, pre/post employment services, job retention services, unsubsidized employment, subsidized public or private sector employment, community service programs, entrepreneurial training, management training, job creation activities, economic development leading to job creation, and traditional subsistence activities.

§ 287.125 What supportive and job retention services may be provided under the NEW Program?

The NEW Program grantee may provide, pay for or reimburse expenses for supportive services, including but not limited to transportation, child care, traditional or cultural work related services, and other work or family sufficiency related expenses that the Tribe determines are necessary to enable a client to participate in the program.

§ 287.130 Can NEW Program activities include job market assessments, job creation and economic development activities?

(a) A Tribe may conduct job market assessments within its NEW Program. These might include the following:

(1) Consultation with the Tribe's economic development staff or leadership that oversees the economic and employment planning for the Tribe;

(2) Consultation with any local employment and training program, Workforce Development Boards, One-Stop Centers, or planning agencies that have undertaken economic and employment studies for the area in which the Tribe resides;

(3) Communication with any training, research, or educational agencies

that have produced economic development plans for the area that may or may not include the Tribe; and

(4) Coordination with any State or local governmental agency pursuing economic development options for the area.

(b) The Tribe's NEW Program may engage in activities and provide services to create jobs and economic opportunities for its participants. These services should be congruous with any available local job market assessments and may include the following:

(1) Tribal Employment Rights Office (TERO) services;

(2) Job creation projects and services;

(3) Self-employment;

(4) Self-initiated training that leads a client to improved job opportunities and employment;

(5) Economic development projects that lead to jobs, improved employment opportunities, or self-sufficiency of program participants;

(6) Surveys to collect information regarding client characteristics; and

(7) Any other development and job creation activities that enable Tribal members to increase their economic independence and reduce their need for benefit assistance and supportive services.

§ 287.135 Are bonuses, rewards and stipends allowed for participants in the NEW Program?

Bonuses, stipends, and performance awards are allowed. However, such allowances may be counted as income in determining eligibility for some TANF or other need-based programs.

§ 287.140 With whom should the Tribe coordinate in the operation of its work activities and services?

The administration of work activities and services provided under the NEW Program must ensure that appropriate coordination and cooperation is maintained with the following entities operating in the same service areas as the Tribe's NEW Program:

(a) State, local and Tribal TANF agencies, and agencies operating employment and training programs;

(b) Any other agency whose programs impact the service population of the NEW Program, including employment, training, placement, education, child care, and social programs.

§ 287.145 What measures will be used to determine NEW Program outcomes?

Each grantee must develop its own performance standards and measures to ensure accountability for its program results. A Tribe's program plan must identify planned program outcomes and the measures the Tribe will use to determine them. ACF will compare planned outcomes against outcomes reported in the Tribe's annual reports.

Subpart F—Data Collection and Reporting Requirements

§ 287.150 Are there data collection requirements for Tribes that operate a NEW Program?

(a) Yes, the Tribal agency or organization responsible for operation of a NEW Program must collect data and submit reports as specified by the Secretary.

(b) A NEW Program grantee must establish and maintain efficient and effective record-keeping systems to provide accurate and timely information regarding its service population.

(c) Required reports will provide Tribes, the Secretary, Congress, and other interested parties with information to assess the success of the NEW Program in meeting its goals. Also, the reports will provide the Secretary with information for monitoring program and financial operations.

§ 287.155 What reports must a grantee file with the Department about its NEW Program operations?

(a) Each eligible Tribe must submit an annual report that provides a summary of program operations.

(b) The Secretary has developed an annual operations report (OMB clearance number 0970–0174). The report specifies the data elements on which grantees must report, including elements that provide information regarding the number and characteristics of those served by the NEW Program. This report is in addition to any financial reports required by law, regulations, or Departmental policies.

(c) The report form and instructions are distributed through ACF's program instruction system.

(d) The program operations report will be due September 28th, 90 days after the close of the NEW Program year.

§ 287.160 What reports must a grantee file regarding financial operations?

(a) Grantees will use SF–269A to make an annual financial report of expenditures for program activities and services.

(b) Two annual financial reports will be due to the appropriate Regional Office. The interim SF–269A is due no later than July 30, *i.e.*, 30 days after the end of the obligation period. The final SF–269A is due 90 days after the end of the liquidation period.

§ 287.165 What are the data collection and reporting requirements for Public Law 102–477 Tribes that consolidate a NEW Program with other programs?

(a) Currently, there is a single reporting system for all programs operated by a Tribe under Public Law 102–477. This system includes a program report, consisting of a narrative report, a statistical form, and a financial report.

(1) The program report is required annually and submitted to BIA, as the lead Federal agency and shared with DHHS and DOL.

(2) The financial report is submitted on a SF–269A to BIA.

(b) Information regarding program and financial operations of a NEW Program administered by a Public Law 102–477 Tribe will be captured through the existing Public Law 102–477 reporting system.

§ 287.170 What are the data collection and reporting requirements for a Tribe that operates both the NEW Program and a Tribal TANF program?

Tribes operating both NEW and Tribal TANF programs must adhere to the separate reporting requirements for each program. NEW Program reporting requirements are specified in §§ 287.150–287.170.

PARTS 288–299 [RESERVED]

CHAPTER III—OFFICE OF CHILD SUPPORT ENFORCEMENT (CHILD SUPPORT ENFORCEMENT PROGRAM), ADMINISTRATION FOR CHILDREN AND FAMILIES, DEPARTMENT OF HEALTH AND HUMAN SERVICES

EDITORIAL NOTE: Nomenclature changes to chapter III appear at 66 FR 39452, July 31, 2001.

PART 300 [RESERVED]

PART 301—STATE PLAN APPROVAL AND GRANT PROCEDURES

AUTHORITY: 42 U.S.C. 651 through 658, 659a, 660, 664, 666, 667, 1301, and 1302.

SOURCE: 40 FR 27157, June 26, 1975, unless otherwise noted.

§ 301.0 Scope and applicability of this part.

This part deals with the administration of title IV-D of the Social Security Act by the Federal Government including actions on the State plan and amendments thereto and review of such actions; grants under the approved plan; review and audit of State and local expenditures; and reconsideration of disallowances of expenditures for Federal financial participation.

§ 301.1 General definitions.

When used in this chapter, unless the context otherwise indicates:

Act means the Social Security Act, and the title referred to is title IV-D of that Act.

Agent of a Child means a caretaker relative having custody of or responsibility for the child.

Applicable matching rate means the rate of Federal funding of State IV-D programs' administrative costs for the appropriate fiscal year. The applicable matching rate for FY 1990 and thereafter is 66 percent.

Assigned support obligation means, unless otherwise specified, any support obligation which has been assigned to the State under section 408(a)(3) of the Act or section 471(a)(17) of the Act, or any medical support obligation or payment for medical care from any third party which has been assigned to the State under 42 CFR 433.146.

Assignment means, unless otherwise specified, any assignment of rights to support under section 408(a)(3) of the Act or section 471(a)(17) of the Act, or any assignment of rights to medical support and to payment for medical care from any third party under 42 CFR 433.146.

Attorney of a Child means a licensed lawyer who has entered into an attorney-client relationship with either the child or the child's resident parent to provide legal representation to the child or resident parent related to establishment of paternity, or the establishment, modification, or enforcement of child support. An attorney-client relationship imposes an ethical and fiduciary duty upon the attorney to represent the client's best interests under applicable rules of professional responsibility.

Birthing hospital means a hospital that has an obstetric care unit or provides obstetric services, or a birthing center associated with a hospital. A birthing center is a facility outside a hospital that provides maternity services.

Central authority means the agency designated by a government to facilitate support enforcement with a foreign reciprocating country (FRC) pursuant to section 459A of the Act.

Central registry means a single unit or office within the State IV-D agency which receives, disseminates and has oversight responsibility for processing incoming interstate IV-D cases, including UIFSA petitions and requests for wage withholding in IV-D cases and, at the option of the State, intrastate IV-D cases.

Controlling order State means the State in which the only order was issued or, where multiple orders exist, the State in which the order determined by a tribunal to control prospective current support pursuant to the UIFSA was issued.

Country means a foreign country (or a political subdivision thereof) declared to be an FRC under section 459A of the Act and any foreign country (or political subdivision thereof) with which the State has entered into a reciprocal arrangement for the establishment and enforcement of support obligations to the extent consistent with Federal law pursuant to section 459A(d) of the Act.

Department means the Department of Health and Human Services.

Director means the Director, Office of Child Support Enforcement, who is the Secretary's designee to administer the Child Support Enforcement program under title IV-D.

Federal PLS means the Parent Locator Service operated by the Office of Child Support Enforcement pursuant to section 452(a)(9) of the Act.

Form means a federally-approved document used for the establishment and enforcement of support obligations whether compiled or transmitted in written or electronic format, including but not limited to the Income Withholding for Support form, and the National Medical Support Notice. In interstate IV–D cases, such forms include those used for child support enforcement proceedings under the UIFSA. *Form* also includes any federally-mandated IV–D reporting form, where appropriate.

Initiating agency means a State or Tribal IV–D agency or an agency in a country, as defined in this rule, in which an individual has applied for or is receiving services.

Intergovernmental IV–D case means a IV–D case in which the noncustodial parent lives and/or works in a different jurisdiction than the custodial parent and child(ren) that has been referred by an initiating agency to a responding agency for services. An intergovernmental IV–D case may include any combination of referrals between States, Tribes, and countries. An intergovernmental IV–D case also may include cases in which a State agency is seeking only to collect support arrearages, whether owed to the family or assigned to the State.

Interstate IV–D case means a IV–D case in which the noncustodial parent lives and/or works in a different State than the custodial parent and child(ren) that has been referred by an initiating State to a responding State for services. An interstate IV–D case also may include cases in which a State is seeking only to collect support arrearages, whether owed to the family or assigned to the State.

IV-D Agency means the single and separate organizational unit in the State that has the responsibility for administering or supervising the administration of the State plan under title IV-D of the Act.

Medicaid means medical assistance provided under a State plan approved under title XIX of the Act.

Medicaid agency means the single State agency that has the responsibility for the administration of, or supervising the administration of, the State plan under title XIX of the Act.

Non-IV-A Medicaid recipient means any individual who has been determined eligible for or is receiving Medicaid under title XIX of the Act but is not receiving, nor deemed to be receiving, title IV-A under title IV-A of the Act.

Office means the Office of Child Support Enforcement which is the separate organizational unit within the Department with the responsibility for the administration of the program under this title.

One-state remedies means the exercise of a State's jurisdiction over a non-resident parent or direct establishment, enforcement, or other action by a State against a non-resident parent in accordance with the long-arm provision of UIFSA or other State law.

Overdue support means a delinquency pursuant to an obligation determined under a court order, or an order of an administrative process established under State law, for support and maintenance of a minor child, which is owed to or on behalf of the child, or for the noncustodial parent's spouse (or former spouse) with whom the child is living, but only if a support obligation has been established with respect to the spouse and the support obligation established with respect to the child is being enforced under State's IV-D plan. At the option of the State, overdue support may include amounts which otherwise meet the definition in the previous sentence but which are owed to or on behalf of a child who is not a minor child. The option to include support owed to children who are not minors applies independently to the procedures required under §302.70 of this chapter.

Past-due support means the amount of support determined under a court order or an order of an administrative process established under State law for support and maintenance of a child, or of a child and the parent with whom the child is living, which has not been paid. Through September 30, 2007, for purposes of referral for Federal tax refund offset of support due an individual who is receiving services under §302.33 of this chapter, past-due support means support owed to or on behalf of a qualified child, or a qualified child and the parent with whom the child is living if the same support order includes support for the child and the parent.

Political subdivision means a legal entity of the State as defined by the State, including a legal entity of the political subdivision so defined, such as a Prosecuting or District Attorney or a Friend of the Court.

Procedures means a set of instructions in a record which describe in detail the step by step actions to be taken by child support enforcement personnel in the performance of a specific function under the State's IV–D plan. The IV-D agency may issue general instructions on one or more functions, and delegate responsibility for the detailed procedures to the office, agency, or political subdivision actually performing the function.

Qualified child, through September 30, 2007, means a child who is a minor or who, while a minor, was determined to be disabled under title II or XVI of the Act, and for whom a support order is in effect.

Record means information that is inscribed on a tangible medium or that is stored in an electronic or other medium and is retrievable in perceivable form.

Regional Office and *Central Office* refer to the Regional Offices and the Central Office of the Office of Child Support Enforcement, respectively.

Responding agency means the agency that is providing services in response to a referral from an initiating agency in an intergovernmental IV–D case.

Secretary means the Secretary of Health and Human Services.

Spousal support means a legally enforceable obligation assessed against an individual for the support of a spouse or former spouse who is living with a child or children for whom the individual also owes support.

State means the several States, the District of Columbia, the Commonwealth of Puerto Rico, the Virgin Islands, Guam and American Samoa.

The *State plan* means the State plan for child and spousal support under section 454 of the Act.

State PLS means the service established by the IV-D agency pursuant to section 454(8) of the Act to locate parents.

Tribunal means a court, administrative agency, or quasi-judicial entity authorized under State law to establish, enforce, or modify support orders or to determine parentage.

Uniform Interstate Family Support Act (UIFSA) means the model act promulgated by the National Conference of Commissioners on Uniform State Laws (NCCUSL) and mandated by section 466(f) of the Act to be in effect in all States.

[47 FR 57280, Dec. 23, 1982, as amended at 50 FR 19647, May 9, 1985; 50 FR 23958, June 7, 1985; 50 FR 31719, Aug. 6, 1985; 53 FR 5256, Feb. 22, 1988; 54 FR 32308, Aug. 4, 1989; 56 FR 8002, Feb. 26, 1991; 57 FR 30429, July 9, 1992; 58 FR 41437, Aug. 4, 1993; 59 FR 66249, Dec. 23, 1994; 61 FR 67240, Dec. 20, 1996; 64 FR 6247, Feb. 9, 1999; 68 FR 25303, May 12, 2003; 73 FR 74919, Dec. 9, 2008; 75 FR 38641, July 2, 2010; 75 FR 81906, Dec. 29, 2010; 81 FR 93560, Dec. 20, 2016]

§301.10 State plan.

The State plan is a comprehensive statement submitted by the IV-D agency describing the nature and scope of its program and giving assurance that it will be administered in conformity with the specific requirements stipulated in title IV-D, the regulations in Subtitle A and this chapter of this title, and other applicable official issuances of the Department. The State plan contains all information necessary for the Office to determine whether the plan can be approved, as a basis for Federal financial participation in the State program.

§ 301.11 State plan; format.

The State plan must be submitted to the Office in the format and containing the information prescribed by the Office, and within time limits set in implementing instructions issued by the Office. Such time limits will be adequate for proper preparation of plans and submittal in accordance with the requirements for State Governors' review (see § 301.12 of this chapter).

(Approved by the Office of Management and Budget under control number 0960–0253)

[40 FR 27147, June 26, 1975, as amended at 51 FR 37730, Oct. 24, 1986]

§ 301.12 Submittal of State plan for Governor's review.

The State plan must be submitted to the State Governor for his review and comments, and the State plan must provide that the Governor will be given opportunity to review State plan amendments and long-range program planning projections or other periodic reports thereon. This requirement does not apply to periodic statistical or budget and other fiscal reports. Under this requirement, the Office of the Governor will be afforded a specified period in which to review the material. Any comments made will be transmitted to the Office with the documents.

(Approved by the Office of Management and Budget under control number 0960–0253)

[40 FR 27147, June 26, 1975, as amended at 51 FR 37730, Oct. 24, 1986]

§ 301.13 Approval of State plans and amendments.

The State plan consists of records furnished by the State to cover its Child Support Enforcement program under title IV–D of the Act. After approval of the original plan by the Office, all relevant changes, required by new statutes, rules, regulations, interpretations, and court decisions, are required to be submitted currently so that the Office may determine whether the plan continues to meet Federal requirements and policies.

(a) *Submittal.* State plans and revisions of the plans are submitted first to the State governor or his designee for review in accordance with § 301.12, and then to the regional office. The States are encouraged to obtain consultation of the regional staff when a plan is in process of preparation or revision.

(b) *Review.* The Office of Child Support Enforcement in the regional offices is responsible for review of State plans and amendments. It also initiates discussion with the IV-D agency on clarification of significant aspects of the plan which come to its attention in the course of this review. State plan material on which the regional staff has questions concerning the application of Federal policy is referred with recommendations as required to the Office of Child Support Enforcement in the central office for technical assistance. Comments and suggestions, including those of consultants in specified areas, may be prepared by the central office for use by the regional staff in negotiations with the IV-D agency.

(c) *Action.* The Regional Office exercises delegated authority to take affirmative action on the State plan and amendments thereto on the basis of policy statements or precedents previously approved by the Director. The Director retains authority for determining that proposed plan material is not approvable, or that a previously approved plan no longer meets the requirements for approval, except that a final determination of disapproval may not be made without prior consultation and discussion by the Director with the Secretary. The Regional Office or the Director formally notifies the IV-D agency of the actions taken on the State plan or revisions thereto.

(d) *Basis for approval.* Determinations as to whether the State plan (including plan amendments and administrative practice under the plan) originally meets or continues to meet the requirements for approval are based on relevant Federal statutes and regulations. Guidelines are furnished to assist in the interpretation of the regulations.

(e) *Prompt approval of the State plan.* The determination as to whether the State plan submitted for approval conforms to the requirements for approval under the Act and regulations issued pursuant thereto shall be made promptly and not later than the 90th day following the date on which the plan submittal is received in OCSE Regional Program Office, unless the Regional Office has secured from the IV–D agency an agreement, which is reflected in a record, to extend that period.

(f) *Prompt approval of plan amendments.* Any amendment of an approved State plan may, at the option of the State, be considered as a submission of a new State plan. If the State requests that such amendments be so considered, the determination as to its conformity with the requirements for approval shall be made promptly and not later than the 90th day following the date on which such a request is received in the Regional Office with respect to an amendment that has been received in such office, unless the Regional Office has secured from the State agency an agreement, which is reflected in a record, to extend that period.

(g) *Effective date.* The effective date of a new plan may not be earlier than the first day of the calendar quarter in which an approvable plan is submitted.

(Approved by the Office of Management and Budget under control number 0960–0253)

[40 FR 27147, June 26, 1975, as amended at 51 FR 37730, Oct. 24, 1986; 81 FR 93560, Dec. 20, 2016]

§301.14 Administrative review of certain administrative decisions.

Any State dissatisfied with a determination of the Director pursuant to §301.13 (e) or (f) with respect to any plan or amendment may, within 60 days after the date of receipt of notification of such determination, file a petition with the Regional Office asking the Director for reconsideration of the issue of whether such plan or amendment conforms to the requirements for approval under the Act and pertinent Federal requirements. Within 30 days after receipt of such a petition, the Director shall notify the State of the time and place at which the hearing for the purpose of reconsidering such issue will be held. Such hearing shall be held not less than 30 days nor more than 60 days after the date notice of such hearing is furnished to the State, unless the Director and the State agree in writing on another time. The hearing procedures contained in 45 CFR part 213 applicable to §201.4 of this title shall apply to reconsiderations brought under this section. A determination affirming, modifying, or reversing the Director's original decision will be made within 60 days of the conclusion of the hearing. Action pursuant to an initial determination by the Director described in such §301.1 (e) or (f) that a plan or amendment is not approvable shall not be stayed pending the reconsideration, but in the event that the Director subsequently determines that his original decision was incorrect he shall certify restitution forthwith in a lump sum of any funds incorrectly withheld or otherwise denied.

§301.15 Grants.

To States with approved plans, a grant is made each quarter for expenditures under the plan for the administration of the Child Support Enforcement program. The determination as to the amount of a grant to be made to a State is based upon documents submitted by the IV-D agency containing information required under the Act and such other pertinent facts as may be found necessary.

(a) *Financial reporting forms*—(1) *Form OCSE–396: Child Support Enforcement Program Quarterly Financial Report.* States submit this form quarterly to report the actual amount of State and Federal share of title IV–D program expenditures and program income of the current quarter and to report the estimated amount of the State and Federal share of title IV–D program expenditures for the next quarter. This form is completed in accordance with published instructions. The digital signature of the authorized State program official on this document certifies that the reported expenditures and estimates are accurate and that the State has or will have the necessary State share of estimated program expenditures available when needed.

(2) *Form OCSE–34: Child Support Enforcement Program Quarterly Collection Report.* States submit this form quarterly to report the State and Federal share of child support collections received, distributed, disbursed, and remaining undistributed under the title IV–D program. This form is completed

in accordance with published instructions. The digital signature of the authorized State program official on this document certifies that the reported amounts are accurate. The Federal share of actual program expenditures and collections and the Federal share of estimated program expenditures reported on Form OCSE–396 and the Federal share of child support collections reported on Form OCSE–34 are used in the computation of quarterly grant awards issued to the State.

(b) *Submission, review, and approval*—(1) *Manner of submission.* The Administration for Children and Families (ACF) maintains an On-line Data Collection (OLDC) system available to every State. States must use OLDC to submit reporting information electronically. To use OLDC, a State must request access from the ACF Office of Grants Management and use an approved digital signature.

(2) *Schedule of submission.* Forms OCSE–396 and OCSE–34 must be electronically submitted no later than 45 days following the end of the each fiscal quarter. No submission, revisions, or adjustments of the financial reports submitted for any quarter of a fiscal year will be accepted by OCSE later than December 31, which is 3 months after the end of the fiscal year.

(3) *Review and approval.* The data submitted on Forms OCSE–396 and OCSE–34 are subject to analysis and review by the Regional Grants Officer in the appropriate ACF Regional Office and approval by the Director, Office of Grants Management, in the ACF central office. In the course of this analysis, review, and approval process, any reported program expenditures that cannot be determined to be allowable are subject to the deferral procedures found at 45 CFR 201.15 or the disallowance process found at 45 CFR 304.29 and 201.14 and 45 CFR part 16.

(c) *Grant award*—(1) *Award documents.* The grant award consists of a signed award letter and an accompanying "Computation of Grant Award" to detail the award calculation.

(2) *Award calculation.* The quarterly grant award is based on the information submitted by the State on the financial reporting forms and consists of:

(i) An advance of funds for the next quarter, based on the State's approved estimate; and

(ii) The reconciliation of the advance provided for the current quarter, based on the State's approved expenditures.

(3) *Access to funds.* A copy of the grant documents are provided to the HHS Program Support Center's Division of Payment Management, which maintains the Payment Management System (PMS). The State is able to request a drawdown of funds from PMS through a commercial bank and the Federal Reserve System against a continuing letter of credit. The letter of credit system for payment of advances of Federal funds was established pursuant to Treasury Department regulations. (Circular No. 1075).

(d) *General administrative requirements.* The provisions of part 95 of this title, establishing general administrative requirements for grant programs and part 75 of this title, establishing uniform administrative requirements and cost principles, shall apply to all grants made to the States under this part, with the following exceptions:

(1) 45 CFR 75.306, *Cost sharing or matching* and

(2) 45 CFR 75.341, *Financial reporting.*

(Approved by the Office of Management and Budget under control numbers 0960–0239 and 0960–0235)

[40 FR 27147, June 26, 1975, as amended at 51 FR 37731, Oct. 24, 1986; 61 FR 67240, Dec. 20, 1996; 81 FR 3021, Jan. 20, 2016; 81 FR 93560, Dec. 20, 2016]

§ 301.16 Withholding of advance funds for not reporting.

(a) No advance for any quarter will be made unless full and complete reports on expenditures and collections, as required by §§ 301.15 and 302.15 of this chapter, respectively, have been submitted to the Office by the IV-D agency for all quarters with the exception of the two quarters immediately preceding the quarter for which the advance is to be made.

(b) For purposes of this section, a report is full and complete if:

(1) All line items of information are reported in accordance with OCSE instructions; and

(2) The report contains all applicable information available to the State and

appropriate for inclusion in the report for the quarter being reported and prior quarters.

(Collection reporting form approved by the Office of Management and Budget under control number 0960–0238 and expenditure reporting form approved under control number 0960–0235)

[47 FR 8570, Mar. 1, 1982]

PART 302—STATE PLAN REQUIREMENTS

Sec.

AUTHORITY: 42 U.S.C. 651 through 658, 659a, 660, 664, 666, 667, 1302, 1396a(a)(25), 1396b(d)(2), 1396b(o), 1396b(p), and 1396(k).

SOURCE: 40 FR 27159, June 26, 1975, unless otherwise noted.

EDITORIAL NOTE: Nomenclature changes to part 302 appear at 64 FR 6247, Feb. 9, 1999.

§302.0 Scope of this part.

This part defines the State plan provisions required for an approved plan under title IV-D of the Act.

§302.1 Definitions.

The definitions found in §301.1 of this chapter also are applicable to this part.

§302.10 Statewide operations.

The State plan shall provide that:

(a) It will be in operation on a statewide basis in accordance with equitable standards for administration that are mandatory throughout the State;

(b) If administered by a political subdivision of the State, the plan will be mandatory on such political subdivision;

(c) The IV-D agency will assure that the plan is continuously in operation in all appropriate offices or agencies through:

(1) Methods for informing staff of State policies, standards, procedures and instructions; and

(2) Regular planned examination and evaluation of operations in local offices by regularly assigned State staff, including regular visits by such staff; and through reports, controls, or other necessary methods.

§302.11 State financial participation.

The State plan shall provide that the State will participate financially in the program.

§302.12 Single and separate organizational unit.

(a) The State plan shall provide for the establishment or designation of a single and separate organizational unit to administer the IV-D plan. Such unit is referred to as the IV-D agency. Under this requirement:

(1) The IV-D agency may be:

(i) Located in any other agency of the State; or,

(ii) Established as a new agency of the State.

(2) The IV-D agency shall be responsible and accountable for the operation of the IV-D program. Except as provided in § 303.20 of this part, the agency need not perform all the functions of the IV-D program so long as it insures that all these functions are being carried out properly, efficiently, and effectively;

(3) If the IV-D agency delegates any of the functions of the IV-D program to any other State or local agency or official, or any official with whom a cooperative agreement as described in § 302.34 has been entered into or purchases services from any person or private agency pursuant to § 304.22 of this part, the IV-D agency shall have responsibility for securing compliance with the requirements of the State plan by such agency or officials.

(b) The State plan shall describe the structure of the IV-D agency and the distribution of responsibilities among the major divisions within the unit, and if it is located within another agency, show its place in such agency. If any of the IV-D program functions are to be performed outside of the IV-D agency then these functions shall be listed with the name of the organization responsible for performing them.

(Approved by the Office of Management and Budget under control number 0960–0253)

[40 FR 27159, June 26, 1975, as amended at 51 FR 37731, Oct. 24, 1986; 64 FR 6247, Feb. 9, 1999]

§ 302.13 Plan amendments.

(a) The State plan shall provide that the plan will be amended whenever necessary to reflect new or revised Federal statutes or regulations, or material change in any phase of State law, organization, policy of IV-D agency operation.

(b) *Federal financial participation.* Except where otherwise provided, Federal financial participation is available in the additional expenditures resulting from an amended provision of the State plan as of the first day of the calendar quarter in which an approvable amendment is submitted or the date on which the amended provision becomes effective in the State, whichever is later.

(Approved by the Office of Management and Budget under control number 0960–0253)

[40 FR 27159, June 26, 1975, as amended at 51 FR 37731, Oct. 24, 1986]

§ 302.14 Fiscal policies and accountability.

The State plan shall provide that the IV–D agency, in discharging its fiscal accountability, will maintain an accounting system and supporting fiscal records adequate to assure that claims for Federal funds are in accord with applicable Federal requirements. The retention and custodial requirements for these records are prescribed in 45 CFR 75.361 through 75.370.

[81 FR 93561, Dec. 20, 2016]

§ 302.15 Reports and maintenance of records.

The State plan shall provide that:

(a) The IV-D agency will maintain records necessary for the proper and efficient operation of the plan, including records regarding:

(1) Applications pursuant to § 302.33 for support services available under the State plan;

(2) Location of noncustodial parents, actions to establish paternity and obtain and enforce support, and the costs incurred in such actions;

(3) Amount and sources of support collections and the distribution of these collections;

(4) Any fees charged or paid for support enforcement services;

(5) Any other administrative costs;

(6) Any other information required by the Office;

(7) Statistical, fiscal, and other records necessary for reporting and accountability required by the Secretary; and

(8) The retention and custodial requirements for the records in this section are prescribed in 45 CFR 75.361 through 75.370.

(b) The IV-D agency will make such reports in such form and containing such information, as the Secretary may from time to time require, and comply with such provisions as he may from time to time find necessary to assure the correctness and verification of such reports.

(Approved by the Office of Management and Budget under control numbers 0960–0154, 0960–0226 and 0960–0238)

[40 FR 27159, June 26, 1975, as amended at 47 FR 57281, Dec. 23, 1982; 48 FR 51917, Nov. 15, 1983; 51 FR 37731, Oct. 24, 1986; 61 FR 67240, Dec. 20, 1996; 81 FR 3021, Jan. 20, 2016; 81 FR 93561, Dec. 20, 2016]

§ 302.17 Inclusion of State statutes.

The State plan shall provide a copy of State statutes, or regulations promulgated pursuant to such statutes and having the force of law (including citations of such statutes and regulations), that provide procedures to determine the paternity of a child born out of wedlock, to establish the child support obligation of a responsible parent, and to enforce a support obligation, including spousal support if appropriate.

(Approved by the Office of Management and Budget under control numbers 0960–0253 and 0960–0385)

[50 FR 19647, May 9, 1985, as amended at 51 FR 37731, Oct. 24, 1986]

§ 302.19 Bonding of employees.

The State plan shall provide that the following requirements and criteria to bond employees are in effect:

(a) *IV-D responsibility*. The IV-D agency will insure that every person, who has access to or control over funds collected under the child support enforcement program, is covered by a bond against loss resulting from employee dishonesty.

(b) *Scope*. The requirement in paragraph (a) of this section applies to every person who, as a regular part of his or her employment, receives, disburses, handles or has access to support collections, which includes:

(1) IV-D agency employees and employees of any other State or local agency to which IV-D functions have been delegated.

(2) Employees of a court or law enforcement official performing under a cooperative agreement with the IV-D agency.

(3) Employees of any private or governmental entity from which the IV-D agency purchases services.

(c) *Bond*. The bond will be for an amount which the State IV-D agency deems adequate to indemnify the State IV-D program for loss resulting from employee dishonesty.

(d) *Self-bonding System*. A State or political subdivision may comply with the requirement in paragraph (a) of this section:

(1) By means of a self-bonding system established under State law or,

(2) In the case of a political subdivision, by means of a self-bonding system approved by the State IV-D agency.

(e) *IV-D liability*. The requirements of this section do not reduce or limit the ultimate liability of the IV-D agency for losses of support collections from the State's IV-D program.

[44 FR 28803, May 17, 1979; 44 FR 45137, Aug. 1, 1979, as amended at 47 FR 57281, Dec. 23, 1982]

§ 302.20 Separation of cash handling and accounting functions.

The State plan shall provide that the following requirements and criteria to separate the cash handling and accounting functions are in effect.

(a) *IV-D responsibility*. The IV-D agency will maintain methods of administration designed to assure that persons responsible for handling cash receipts of support do not participate in accounting or operating functions which would permit them to conceal in the accounting records the misuse of support receipts. Such methods of administration shall follow generally recognized accounting standards.

(b) *Scope*. The requirement in paragraph (a) of this section applies to persons who participate in the collection, accounting or operating functions which include:

(1) IV-D agency employees and employees of any other State or local agency to which IV-D functions have been delegated.

(2) Employees of a court or law enforcement official performing under a cooperative agreement with the IV-D agency.

(3) Employees of any private or governmental entity from which the IV-D agency purchases services.

(c) *Exception.* The Regional Office may grant a waiver to sparsely populated geographical areas, where the requirements in paragraph (a) of this section would necessitate the hiring of unreasonable numbers of additional staff. The IV-D agency must document such administrative infeasibility and provide an alternative system of controls that reasonably insures that support collections will not be misused.

[44 FR 28803, May 17, 1979, as amended at 47 FR 57281, Dec. 23, 1982]

§ 302.30 Publicizing the availability of support enforcement services.

Effective October 1, 1985, the State plan shall provide that the State will publicize regularly and frequently the availability of support enforcement services under the plan through public service announcements. Publicity must include information on any application fees which may be imposed for such services and a telephone number or postal address where further information may be obtained.

(Approved by the Office of Management and Budget under control number 0960–0385)

[50 FR 19647, May 9, 1985, as amended at 51 FR 37731, Oct. 24, 1986]

§ 302.31 Establishing paternity and securing support.

The State plan shall provide that:

(a) The IV-D agency will undertake:

(1) In the case of a child born out of wedlock with respect to whom an assignment as defined in § 301.1 of this chapter is effective, to establish the paternity of such child; and

(2) In the case of any individual with respect to whom an assignment as defined in § 301.1 of this chapter is effective, to secure support for a child or children from any person who is legally liable for such support, using State laws regarding intrastate and interstate establishment and enforcement of support obligations. Effective October 1, 1985, this includes securing support for a spouse or former spouse who is living with the child or children, but only if a support obligation has been established for that spouse and the child support obligation is being enforced under the title IV-D State plan.

(3) When assigned medical support payments are received and retained by a non-IV-A Medicaid recipient, the IV-D agency shall notify the Medicaid agency whenever it discovers that directly received medical support payments are being, or have been, retained.

(b) Upon receiving notice of a claim of good cause for failure to cooperate, the IV-D agency will suspend all activities to establish paternity or secure support until notified of a final determination by the appropriate agency.

(c) The IV-D agency will not undertake to establish paternity or secure support in any case for which it has received notice that there has been a finding of good cause unless there has been a determination that support enforcement may proceed without the participation of the caretaker or other relative. If there has been such a determination, the IV-D agency will undertake to establish paternity or secure support but may not involve the caretaker or other relative in such undertaking.

(Approved by the Office of Management and Budget under control numbers 0960–0385 and 0970–0107)

[50 FR 19647, May 9, 1985, as amended at 51 FR 25526, July 15, 1986; 51 FR 37731, Oct. 24, 1986; 56 FR 8003, Feb. 26, 1991; 64 FR 6247, Feb. 9, 1999; 68 FR 25303, May 12, 2003]

§ 302.32 Collection and disbursement of support payments by the IV–D agency.

The State plan shall provide that:

(a) The IV–D agency must establish and operate a State Disbursement Unit (SDU) for the collection and disbursement of payments under support orders—

(1) In all cases being enforced under the State IV–D plan; and

(2) In all cases not being enforced under the State IV–D plan in which the support order is initially issued in the State on or after January 1, 1994, and in which the income of the noncustodial parent is subject to withholding in accordance with section 466(a)(8)(B) of the Act.

(b) Timeframes for disbursement of support payments by SDUs under section 454B of the Act.

(1) In intergovernmental IV–D cases, amounts collected by the responding State on behalf of the initiating agency must be forwarded to the initiating agency within 2 business days of the date of receipt by the SDU in the responding State, in accordance with §303.7(d)(6)(v) of this chapter.

(2) Amounts collected by the IV-D agency on behalf of recipients of aid under the State's title IV-A or IV-E plan for whom an assignment under sections 408(a)(3) or 471(a)(17) of the Act is effective shall be disbursed by the SDU within the following timeframes:

(i) Except as specified under paragraph (b)(2)(iv) of this section, if the SDU sends payment to the family (other than payments sent to the family from the State share of assigned support collections), the SDU must send these payments within 2 business days of the end of the month in which the payment was received by the SDU. Any payment passed through to the family from the State share of assigned support collections must be sent to the family within 2 business days of the date of receipt by the SDU.

(ii) Except as specified under paragraph (b)(2)(iv) of this section, when the SDU sends collections to the family for the month after the month the family becomes ineligible for title IV-A, the SDU must send collections to the family within 2 business days of the date of receipt by the SDU.

(iii) Except as specified under paragraph (b)(2)(iv) of this section, when the SDU sends collections to the IV-E foster care agency under §302.52(b)(2) and (4) of this part, the SDU must send collections to the IV-E agency within 15 business days of the end of the month in which the support was received by the SUD.

(iv) Collections as a result of Federal tax refund offset paid to the family or distributed in title IV–E foster care cases under §302.52(b)(4) of this part, must be sent to the title IV–A family or title IV–E agency, as appropriate, within 30 calendar days of the date of initial receipt by the title IV–D agency, unless State law requires a post-offset appeal process and an appeal is filed timely, in which case the SDU must send any payment to the title IV–A family or title IV–E agency within 15 calendar days of the date the appeal is resolved.

(3)(i) Except as provided under paragraph (b)(3)(ii) of this section, amounts collected on behalf of individuals receiving services under §302.33 of this part shall be disbursed by the SDU pursuant to section 457 of the Act, within 2 business days of receipt by the SDU.

(ii) Collections due the family as a result of Federal tax refund offset must be sent to the family within 30 calendar days of the date of initial receipt in the title IV–D agency, except:

(A) If State law requires a post-offset appeal process and an appeal is timely filed, in which case the SDU must send any payment to the family within 15 calendar days of the date the appeal is resolved; or

(B) As provided in §303.72(h)(5) of this chapter.

[64 FR 6247, Feb. 9, 1999, as amended at 68 FR 25303, May 12, 2003; 73 FR 74919, Dec. 9, 2008; 81 FR 93561, Dec. 20, 2016]

§302.33 Services to individuals not receiving title IV–A assistance.

(a) *Availability of Services.* (1) The State plan must provide that the services established under the plan shall be made available to any individual who:

(i) Files an application for the services with the IV-D agency. In an interstate case, only the initiating State may require an application under this section; or

(ii) Is a non-IV-A Medicaid recipient; or

(iii) Has been receiving IV-D services and is no longer eligible for assistance under the title IV-A, IV-E foster care, and Medicaid program.

(2) The State may not require an application, other request for services or an application fee from any individual who is eligible to receive services under paragraphs (a)(1) (ii) and (iii) of this section. If an individual receiving services under paragraph (a)(1)(iii) of this section refuses services in response to a notice under paragraph (a)(4) of this section, and subsequently requests services, that individual must file an application and pay an application fee.

(3) The State may not charge fees or recover costs from any individual who is eligible to receive services under paragraph (a)(1)(ii) of this section.

(4) Whenever a family is no longer eligible for assistance under the State's title IV–A and Medicaid programs, the IV–D agency must notify the family, within 5 working days of the notification of ineligibility, that IV–D services will be continued unless the family notifies the IV–D agency that it no longer wants services but instead wants to close the case. This notice must inform the family of the benefits and consequences of continuing to receive IV–D services, including the available services and the State's fees, cost recovery, and distribution policies. This requirement to notify the family that services will be continued, unless the family notifies the IV–D agency to the contrary, also applies when a child is no longer eligible for IV–E foster care, but only in those cases that the IV–D agency determines that such services and notice would be appropriate.

(5) The State must provide all appropriate IV-D services, in addition to IV-D services related to securing medical support, to all individuals who are eligible to receive services under paragraph (a)(1)(ii) of this section unless the individual notifies the State that only IV-D services related to securing medical support are wanted.

(6) The State may elect in its State plan to allow an individual under paragraph (a)(1)(i) of this section who files an application to request paternity-only limited services in an intrastate case. If the State chooses this option, the State must define how this process will be implemented and must establish and use procedures, including domestic violence safeguards, which are reflected in a record, that specify when paternity-only limited services will be available. An application will be considered full-service unless the parent specifically applies for paternity-only limited services in accordance with the State's procedures. If one parent specifically requests paternity-only limited services and the other parent requests full services, the case will automatically receive full services. The State will be required to charge the application and service fees required under paragraphs (c) and (e) of this section for paternity-only limited services, and may recover costs in accordance with paragraph (d) of this section if the State has chosen this option in its State plan. The State must provide the applicant an application form with information on the availability of paternity-only limited services, consequences of selecting this limited service, and an explanation that the case will be closed when the limited service is completed.

(b) *Definitions.* For purposes of this section:

Applicant's income means the disposable income available for the applicant's use under State law.

(c) *Application fee.* (1) Beginning October 1, 1985, the State plan must provide that an application fee will be charged for each individual who applies for services under this section. Under this paragraph:

(i) The State shall collect the application fee from the individual applying for IV-D services or pay the application fee out of State funds.

(ii) The State may recover the application fee from the noncustodial parent who owes a support obligation to a non-IV-A family on whose behalf the IV-D agency is providing services and repay it to the applicant or itself.

(iii) State funds used to pay an application fee are not program expenditures under the State plan but are program income under § 304.50 of this chapter.

(iv) Any application fee charged must be uniformly applied on a statewide basis and must be:

(A) A flat dollar amount not to exceed $25 (or such higher or lower amount as the Secretary may determine to be appropriate for any fiscal year to reflect increases or decreases in administrative costs); or

(B) An amount based on a fee schedule not to exceed the flat dollar amount specified in paragraph (c)(2)(iv)(A) of this section. The fee schedule must be based on the applicant's income.

(v) The State may allow the jurisdiction that collects support for the State under this part to retain any application fee collected under this section.

(2) In an interstate case, the application fee is charged by the State where the individual applies for services under this section.

(d) *Recovery of costs.* (1) The State may elect in its State plan to recover any costs incurred in excess of any fees collected to cover administrative costs under the IV-D State plan. A State which elects to recover costs shall collect on a case by case basis either excess actual or standardized costs:

(i) From the individual who owes a support obligation to a non-IV-A family on whose behalf the IV-D agency is providing services under this section; or

(ii) From the individual who is receiving IV-D services under paragraph (a)(1) (i) or (iii) of this section, either directly or from the support collected on behalf of the individual, but only if the State has in effect a procedure for informing all individuals authorized within the State to establish an obligation for support that the State will recover costs from the individual receiving IV-D services under paragraphs (a)(1) (i) and (iii) of this section.

(2) A State that recovers standardized costs under paragraph (d)(1) of this section shall develop a methodology, which is reflected in a record, to determine standardized costs which are as close to actual costs as is possible. This methodology must be made available to any individual upon request.

(3) The IV-D agency shall not treat any amount collected from the individual as a recovery of costs under paragraph (d)(1)(i) of this section except amounts which exceed the current support owed by the individual under the obligation.

(4) If a State elects to recover costs under paragraph (d)(1)(ii) of this section, the IV-D agency may attempt to seek reimbursement from the individual who owes a support obligation for any costs paid by the individual who is receiving IV-D services and pay all amounts reimbursed to the individual who is receiving IV-D services.

(5) If a State elects to recover costs under this section, the IV-D agency must notify, consistent with the option selected, either the individual who is receiving IV-D services under paragraphs (a)(1) (i) or (iii) of this section, or the individual who owes a support obligation that such recovery will be made. In an interstate case, the IV-D agency where the case originated must notify the individual receiving IV-D services of the States that recover costs.

(6) The IV-D agency must notify the IV-D agencies in all other States if it recovers costs from the individual receiving IV-D services.

(e) *Annual $25 fee.* (1) A State must impose in, and report for, a Federal fiscal year an annual fee of $25 for each case if there is an individual in the case to whom IV–D services are provided and:

(i) For whom the State has collected and disbursed to the family at least $500 of support in that year; and

(ii) No individual in the case has received assistance under a former State AFDC program, assistance as defined in § 260.31 under a State TANF program, or assistance as defined in § 286.10 under a Tribal TANF program.

(2) The State must impose the annual $25 fee in international cases under section 454(32) of the Act in which the criteria for imposition of the annual $25 fee under paragraph (1) of this section are met.

(3) For each Federal fiscal year, after the first $500 of support is collected and disbursed to the family, the fee must be collected by one or more of the following methods:

(i) Retained by the State from support collected in cases subject to the fee in accordance with distribution requirements in § 302.51(a)(5) of this part, except that no cost will be assessed for such services against:

(A) A foreign obligee in an international case receiving IV–D services pursuant to section 454(32)(C) of the Act; and

(B) An individual who is required to cooperate with the IV–D program as a condition of Food Stamp eligibility as defined at § 273.11(o) and (p) of title 7;

(ii) Paid by the individual applying for services under section 454(4)(A)(ii) of the Act and implementing regulations in this section, provided that the individual is not required to cooperate with the IV–D program as a condition of Food Stamp eligibility as defined at § 273.11(o) and (p) of title 7;

(iii) Recovered from the noncustodial parent, provided that the noncustodial parent is not an individual required to cooperate with the IV–D program as a condition of Food Stamp eligibility as defined at § 273.11(o) and (p) of title 7; or

(iv) Paid by the State out of its own funds.

(4) The State must report, in accordance with § 302.15 of this part and instructions issued by the Secretary, the total amount of annual $25 fees imposed under this section for each Federal fiscal year as program income, regardless of which method or methods are used under paragraph (3) of this section.

(5) State funds used to pay the annual $25 fee shall not be considered administrative costs of the State for the operation of the title IV–D plan, and all annual $25 fees imposed during a Federal fiscal year must be considered income to the program, in accordance with § 304.50 of this chapter.

(Approved by the Office of Management and Budget under control numbers 0960–0253, 0960–0385, 0960–0402, and 0970–0107)

[49 FR 36772, Sept. 19, 1984, as amended at 50 FR 19648, May 9, 1985; 51 FR 37731, Oct. 24, 1986; 56 FR 8003, Feb. 26, 1991; 61 FR 67240, Dec. 20, 1996; 73 FR 74919, Dec. 9, 2008; 81 FR 93561, Dec. 20, 2016]

§ 302.34 Cooperative arrangements.

The State plan shall provide that the State will enter into agreements, which are reflected in a record, for cooperative arrangements under § 303.107 of this chapter with appropriate courts; law enforcement officials, such as district attorneys, attorneys general, and similar public attorneys and prosecutors; corrections officials; and Indian Tribes or Tribal organizations. Such arrangements may be entered into with a single official covering more than one court, official, or agency, if the single official has the legal authority to enter into arrangements on behalf of the courts, officials, or agencies. Such arrangements shall contain provisions for providing courts and law enforcement officials with pertinent information needed in locating noncustodial parents, establishing paternity and securing support, to the extent that such information is relevant to the duties to be performed pursuant to the arrangement. They shall also provide for assistance to the IV-D agency in carrying out the program, and may relate to any other matters of common concern. Under matters of common concern, such arrangements may include provisions for the investigation and prosecution of fraud directly related to paternity and child and spousal support, and provisions to reimburse courts and law enforcement officials for their assistance.

[54 FR 30222, July 19, 1989, as amended at 61 FR 67240, Dec. 20, 1996; 64 FR 6248, Feb. 9, 1999; 81 FR 93562, Dec. 20, 2016]

§ 302.35 State parent locator service.

The State plan shall provide as follows:

(a) *State PLS.* The IV–D agency shall maintain a State PLS to provide locate information to authorized persons for authorized purposes.

(1) *For IV–D cases and IV–D purposes by the IV–D agency.* The State PLS shall access the Federal PLS and all relevant sources of information and records available in the State, and in other States as appropriate, for locating custodial parents, noncustodial parents, and children for IV–D purposes.

(2) *For authorized non-IV–D individuals and purposes*—(i) The State PLS shall access and release information authorized to be disclosed under section 453(a)(2) and 453(j)(3) of the Act from the Federal PLS and, in accordance with State law, information from relevant in-State sources of information and records, as appropriate, for locating custodial parents, noncustodial parents, non-parent relatives, and children upon request of authorized individuals specified in paragraph (c) of this section, for authorized purposes specified in paragraph (d) of this section.

(ii) The State PLS shall not release information from the computerized support enforcement system required under part 307 of this chapter, IRS information, or financial institution data match information, nor shall the State PLS forward a non-IV–D request to another State IV–D agency.

(iii) The State PLS need not make subsequent location attempts if locate efforts fail to find the individual sought unless a new request is submitted.

(b) *Central State PLS requirement.* The IV–D program shall maintain a central State PLS to submit requests to the Federal PLS.

(c) *Authorized persons.* The State PLS shall accept requests for locate information only from the following authorized persons:

(1) Any State or local agency providing child and spousal support services under the State plan, and any Tribal IV–D agency providing child and spousal support services under a Tribal plan approved under 45 CFR part 309, provided the State and Tribe have in effect an intergovernmental agreement for the provision of Federal PLS services;

(2) A court that has authority to issue an order or to serve as the initiating court in an action to seek an order against a noncustodial parent for the support and maintenance of a child, or any agent of such court;

(3) The resident parent, legal guardian, attorney, or agent of a child who is not receiving assistance under title IV–A of the Act only if the individual:

(i) Attests that the request is being made to obtain information on, or to facilitate the discovery of, any individual in accordance with section 453(a)(2) of the Act for the purpose of establishing parentage, establishing, setting the amount of, modifying, or enforcing child support obligations;

(ii) Attests that any information obtained through the Federal or State PLS shall be used solely for these purposes and shall be otherwise treated as confidential;

(iii) Attests that the requestor is the resident parent, legal guardian, attorney, or agent of a child not receiving assistance under title IV–A; and

(iv) Pays the fee required for Federal PLS services under section 453(e)(2) of the Act and § 303.70(f)(2)(i) of this chapter, if the State does not pay the fee itself. The State may also charge a fee to cover its costs of processing the request, which must be as close to actual costs as possible, so as not to discourage requests to use the Federal PLS. If the State itself pays the fee for use of the Federal PLS or the State PLS in a non-IV–D case, Federal financial participation is not available in those expenditures.

(4) Authorized persons as defined in § 303.15 of this chapter in connection with parental kidnapping, child custody or visitation cases; or

(5) A State agency that is administering a program operated under a State plan under titles IV–B or IV–E of the Act.

(d) *Authorized purposes for requests and scope of information provided.* The State PLS shall obtain location information under this section only for the purpose specified in paragraphs (d)(1), (d)(2), (d)(3), and (d)(4) of this section.

(1) *To locate an individual with respect to a child in a IV–D, non-IV–D, IV–B, or IV–E case.* The State PLS shall locate individuals for the purpose of establishing parentage, or establishing, setting the amount of, modifying, or enforcing child support obligations or for determining who has or may have parental rights with respect to a child. For these purposes, only information in the Federal PLS or the State PLS may be provided. This information is limited to name, Social Security Number(s), most recent address, employer name and address, employer identification number, wages or other income from, and benefits of, employment, including rights to, or enrollment in, health care coverage, and asset or debt information.

(2) *To assist States in carrying out their responsibilities under title IV–D, IV–A, IV–B, and IV–E programs.* In addition to the information that may be released pursuant to paragraph (d)(1) of this section, State PLS information may be disclosed to State IV–D, IV–A, IV–B, and IV–E agencies for the purpose of assisting States to carry out their responsibilities to administer title IV–D, IV–A, IV–B, and IV–E programs, including information to locate an individual who is a child or a relative of a child in a IV–B or IV–E case. Information that may be disclosed about relatives of children involved in IV–B and IV–E cases is limited to name, Social Security Number(s), most recent address, employer name and address and employer identification number.

(3) *To locate an individual sought for the unlawful taking or restraint of a child or for child custody or visitation purposes.* The State PLS shall locate individuals for the purpose of enforcing a State law

with respect to the unlawful taking or restraint of a child or for making or enforcing a child custody or visitation determination as defined in section 463(d)(1) of the Act. This information is limited to most recent address and place of employment of a parent or child.

(e) *Locate information subject to disclosure.* Subject to the requirements of this section and the privacy safeguards required under section 454(26) of the Act and the family violence indicators under section 307.11(f)(1)(x) of this part, the State PLS shall disclose the following information to authorized persons for authorized purposes,

(1) Federal PLS information described in sections 453 and 463 of the Act; and

(2) Information from in-state locate sources.

[73 FR 56443, Sept. 26, 2008, as amended at 75 FR 81906, Dec. 29, 2010]

§ 302.36 Provision of services in intergovernmental IV–D cases.

(a) The State plan shall provide that, in accordance with § 303.7 of this chapter, the State will extend the full range of services available under its IV–D plan to:

(1) Any other State;

(2) Any Tribal IV–D program operating under § 309.65(a) of this chapter; and

(3) Any country as defined in § 301.1 of this chapter.

(b) The State plan shall provide that the State will establish a central registry for intergovernmental IV–D cases in accordance with the requirements set forth in § 303.7(b) of this chapter.

[75 FR 38641, July 2, 2010]

§ 302.37 [Reserved]

§ 302.38 Payments to the family.

The State plan shall provide that any payment required to be made under §§ 302.32 and 302.51 to a family will be made directly to the resident parent, legal guardian, caretaker relative having custody of or responsibility for the child or children, judicially-appointed conservator with a legal and fiduciary duty to the custodial parent and the child, or alternate caretaker designated in a record by the custodial parent. An alternate caretaker is a nonrelative caretaker who is designated in a record by the custodial parent to take care of the children for a temporary time period.

[81 FR 93562, Dec. 20, 2016]

§ 302.39 Standards for program operation.

The State plan shall provide that the IV–D agency will comply with the standards for program operation and the organizational and staffing requirements prescribed by part 303 of this chapter.

[41 FR 55348, Dec. 20, 1976]

§ 302.40 [Reserved]

§ 302.50 Assignment of rights to support.

The State plan shall provide as follows:

(a) An assignment of support rights, as defined in § 301.1 of this chapter, constitutes an obligation owed to the State by the individual responsible for providing such support. Such obligation shall be established by:

(1) Order of a court of competent jurisdiction or of an administrative process; or

(2) Except for obligations assigned under 42 CFR 433.146, other legal process as established by State laws, such as a legally enforceable and binding agreement.

(b) The amount of the obligation described in paragraph (a) of this section shall be:

(1) The amount specified in the order of a court of competent jurisdiction or administrative process which covers the assigned support rights.

(2) If there is no court or administrative order, an amount determined in a record by the IV–D agency as part of the legal process referred to in paragraph (a)(2) of this section in accordance with the requirements of § 302.56.

(c) The obligation described in paragraph (a) of this section shall be deemed for collection purposes to be collectible under all applicable State and local processes.

(d) Any amounts which represent support payments collected from an individual responsible for providing support under the State plan shall reduce, dollar for dollar, the amount of his obligation under this section.

(e) No portion of any amounts collected which represent an assigned support obligation defined under §301.1 of this chapter may be used to satisfy a medical support obligation unless the court or administrative order designates a specific dollar amount for medical purposes.

[64 FR 6248, Feb. 9, 1999, as amended at 68 FR 25303, May 12, 2003; 81 FR 93562, Dec. 20, 2016]

§302.51 Distribution of support collections.

The State plan shall provide as follows:

(a)(1) For purposes of distribution in a IV–D case, amounts collected, except as provided under paragraphs (a)(3) and (5) of this section, shall be treated first as payment on the required support obligation for the month in which the support was collected and if any amounts are collected which are in excess of such amount, these excess amounts shall be treated as amounts which represent payment on the required support obligation for previous months.

(2) In title IV-A and title IV-E foster care cases in which conversion to a monthly amount is necessary because support is ordered to be paid other than monthly, the IV-D agency may round off the converted amount to whole dollar amount for the purpose of distribution under this section and §302.52 of this part.

(3)(i) Except as provided in paragraph (a)(3)(ii), amounts collected through Federal tax refund offset must be distributed as arrearages in accordance with §303.72 of this chapter, and section 457 of the Act;

(ii) Effective October 1, 2009, or up to a year earlier at State option, amounts collected through Federal tax refund offset shall be distributed in accordance with §303.72 of this chapter and the option selected under section 454(34) of the Act.

(4)(i) Effective October 1, 1998 (or October 1, 1999 if applicable) except with respect to those collections addressed under paragraph (a)(3) of this section and except as specified under paragraph (a)(4)(ii) of this section, with respect to amounts collected and distributed under title IV-D of the Act, the date of collection for distribution purposes in all IV-D cases is the date of receipt in the State disbursement unit established under section 454B of the Act.

(ii) If current support is withheld by an employer in the month when due, and received by the State in a month other than the month when due, the date of withholding may be deemed to be the date of collection.

(iii) When the date of collection pursuant to this subparagraph is deemed to be the date the wage or other income was withheld, and the employer fails to report the date of withholding, the IV-D agency must reconstruct that date by contacting the employer or comparing actual amounts collected with the pay schedule specified in the court or administrative order.

(5)(i) Except as provided in paragraph (a)(5)(ii), a State must pay to a family that has never received assistance under a program funded or approved under title IV–A or foster care under title IV–E of the Act and to an individual who is not required to cooperate with the IV–D program as a condition of Food Stamp eligibility as defined at §273.11(o) and (p) of title 7 the portion of the amount collected that remains after withholding any annual $25 fee that the State imposes under §302.33(e) of this part.

(ii) If a State charges the noncustodial parent the annual $25 fee under §302.33(e) of this part, the State may retain the $25 fee from the support collected after current support and any payment on arrearages for the month under a court or administrative order have been disbursed to the family provided the noncustodial parent is not required to cooperate with the IV–D program as a condition of Food Stamp eligibility as defined at §273.11(o) and (p) of title 7.

(b) If an amount collected as support represents payment on the required support obligation for future months, the amount shall be applied to such future months. However, no such amounts shall be applied to future months unless amounts have been collected which fully satisfy the support obligation assigned under section

403(a)(8) of the Act for the current month and all past months.

(c)(1) The amounts collected by the IV-D agency which represent specific dollar amounts designated in the support order for medical purposes that have been assigned to the State under 42 CFR 433.146 shall be forwarded to the Medicaid agency for distribution under 42 CFR 433.154.

(2) When a family ceases receiving assistance under the State's title XIX plan, the assignment of medical support rights under section 1912 of the Act terminates, except for the amount of any unpaid medical support obligation that has accrued under such assignment. The IV-D agency shall attempt to collect any unpaid specific dollar amounts designated in the support order for medical purposes. Under this requirement, any medical support collection made by the IV-D agency under this paragraph shall be forwarded to the Medicaid agency for distribution under 42 CFR 433.154.

[64 FR 6248, Feb. 9, 1999, as amended at 68 FR 25303, May 12, 2003; 73 FR 74920, Dec. 9, 2008]

§ 302.52 Distribution of support collected in Title IV-E foster care maintenance cases.

Effective October 1, 1984, the State plan shall provide as follows:

(a) For purposes of distribution under this section, amounts collected in foster care maintenance cases shall be treated in accordance with the provisions of § 302.51(a) of this part.

(b) The amounts collected as support by the IV-D agency under the State plan on behalf of children for whom the State is making foster care maintenance payments under the title IV-E State plan and for whom an assignment under section 471(a)(17) of the Act is effective shall be distributed as follows:

(1) Any amount that is collected in a month which represents payment on the required support obligation for that month shall be retained by the State to reimburse itself for foster care maintenance payments. Of that amount retained by the State as reimbursement for that month's foster care maintenance payment, the State IV-D agency shall determine the Federal government's share so that the State may reimburse the Federal government to the extent of its participation in financing of the foster care maintenance payment.

(2) If the amount collected is in excess of the monthly amount of the foster care maintenance payment but not more than the monthly support obligation, the State must pay the excess to the State agency responsible for supervising the child's placement and care under section 472(a)(2) of the Act. The State agency must use the money in the manner it determines will serve the best interests of the child including:

(i) Setting aside amounts for the child's future needs; or

(ii) Making all or part of the amount available to the person responsible for meeting the child's daily needs to be used for the child's benefit.

(3) If the amount collected exceeds the amount required to be distributed under paragraphs (b) (1) and (2) of this section, but not the total unreimbursed foster care maintenance payments provided under title IV-E or unreimbursed assistance payments provided under title IV-A, the State shall retain the excess to reimburse itself for these payments. If past assistance or foster care maintenance payments are greater than the total support obligation owed, the maximum amount the State may retain as reimbursement for such payments is the amount of such obligation. If amounts are collected which represent the required support obligation for periods prior to the first month in which the family received assistance under the State's title IV-A plan or foster care maintenance payments under the State's title IV-E plan, such amounts may be retained by the State to reimburse the difference between such support obligation and such payments. Of the amounts retained by the State, the State IV-D agency shall determine the Federal government's share of the amount so that the State may reimburse the Federal government to the extent of its participation in financing the assistance payments and foster care maintenance payments.

(4) Any balance shall be paid to the State agency responsible for supervising the child's placement and care

and shall be used to serve the best interests of the child as specified in paragraph (b)(2) of this section.

(5) If an amount collected as support represents payment on the required support obligation for future months, the amount shall be applied to those future months. However, no amounts shall be applied to future months unless amounts have been collected which fully satisfy the support obligation assigned under sections 408(a)(3) and 471 (a)(17) of the Act for the current month and all past months.

(c) When a State ceases making foster care maintenance payments under the State's title IV-E State plan, the assignment of support rights under section 471(a)(17) of the Act terminates except for the amount of any unpaid support that has accrued under the assignment. The IV-D agency shall attempt to collect such unpaid support. Under this requirement, any collection made by the State under this paragraph must be distributed in accordance with paragraph (b)(3) of this section.

(Approved by the Office of Management and Budget under control number 0960–0385)

[50 FR 19648, May 9, 1985, as amended at 50 FR 31719, Aug. 6, 1985; 51 FR 37731, Oct. 24, 1986; 64 FR 6249, Feb. 9, 1999]

§ 302.54 Notice of collection of assigned support.

(a) Effective January 1, 1993, the State plan shall provide that the State has in effect procedures for issuing notices of collections as follows:

(1) The IV-D agency must provide a monthly notice of the amount of support payments collected for each month to individuals who have assigned rights to support under section 408(a)(3) of the Act, unless no collection is made in the month, the assignment is no longer in effect and there are no longer any assigned arrearages, or the conditions in paragraph (b) of this section are met.

(2) The monthly notice must list separately payments collected from each noncustodial parent when more than one noncustodial parent owes support to the family and must indicate the amount of current support collected, the amount of arrearages collected and the amount of support collected which was paid to the family.

(b)(1) The Office may grant a waiver to permit a State to provide quarterly, rather than monthly, notices, if the State:

(i) Until September 30, 1997, does not have an automated system that performs child support enforcement activities consistent with § 302.85 or has an automated system that is unable to generate monthly notices; or

(ii) Uses a toll-free automated voice response system which provides the information required under paragraph (a) of this section.

(2) A quarterly notice must be provided in accordance with conditions set forth in paragraph (a)(1) of this section and such notice must contain the information set forth in paragraph (a)(2) of this section.

[57 FR 30681, July 10, 1992, as amended at 61 FR 67241, Dec. 20, 1996; 64 FR 6249, Feb. 9, 1999; 68 FR 25303, May 12, 2003]

§ 302.55 Incentive payments to States and political subdivisions.

Effective October 1, 1985, in order for the State to be eligible to receive any incentive payments under § 304.12 and part 305 of this chapter, the State plan shall provide that, if one or more political subdivisions of the State participate in the costs of carrying out the activities under the State plan during any period, each such subdivision shall be entitled to receive an appropriate share of any incentive payments made to the State for such period, as determined by the State in accordance with § 303.52 of this chapter, taking into account the efficiency and effectiveness of the political subdivision in carrying out the activities under the State plan.

(Approved by the Office of Management and Budget under control number 0960–0385)

[50 FR 19649, May 9, 1985; 50 FR 23958, June 7, 1985, as amended at 51 FR 37731, Oct. 24, 1986; 54 FR 32309, Aug. 4, 1989; 65 FR 82208, Dec. 27, 2000]

§ 302.56 Guidelines for setting child support orders.

(a) Within 1 year after completion of the State's next quadrennial review of its child support guidelines, that commences more than 1 year after publication of the final rule, in accordance with § 302.56(e), as a condition of approval of its State plan, the State must establish one set of child support guidelines by law or by judicial or administrative action for setting and modifying child support order amounts within the State that meet the requirements in this section.

(b) The State must have procedures for making the guidelines available to all persons in the State.

(c) The child support guidelines established under paragraph (a) of this section must at a minimum:

(1) Provide that the child support order is based on the noncustodial parent's earnings, income, and other evidence of ability to pay that:

(i) Takes into consideration all earnings and income of the noncustodial parent (and at the State's discretion, the custodial parent);

(ii) Takes into consideration the basic subsistence needs of the noncustodial parent (and at the State's discretion, the custodial parent and children) who has a limited ability to pay by incorporating a low-income adjustment, such as a self-support reserve or some other method determined by the State; and

(iii) If imputation of income is authorized, takes into consideration the specific circumstances of the noncustodial parent (and at the State's discretion, the custodial parent) to the extent known, including such factors as the noncustodial parent's assets, residence, employment and earnings history, job skills, educational attainment, literacy, age, health, criminal record and other employment barriers, and record of seeking work, as well as the local job market, the availability of employers willing to hire the noncustodial parent, prevailing earnings level in the local community, and other relevant background factors in the case.

(2) Address how the parents will provide for the child's health care needs through private or public health care coverage and/or through cash medical support;

(3) Provide that incarceration may not be treated as voluntary unemployment in establishing or modifying support orders; and

(4) Be based on specific descriptive and numeric criteria and result in a computation of the child support obligation.

(d) The State must include a copy of the child support guidelines in its State plan.

(e) The State must review, and revise, if appropriate, the child support guidelines established under paragraph (a) of this section at least once every four years to ensure that their application results in the determination of appropriate child support order amounts. The State shall publish on the internet and make accessible to the public all reports of the guidelines reviewing body, the membership of the reviewing body, the effective date of the guidelines, and the date of the next quadrennial review.

(f) The State must provide that there will be a rebuttable presumption, in any judicial or administrative proceeding for the establishment and modification of a child support order, that the amount of the order which would result from the application of the child support guidelines established under paragraph (a) of this section is the correct amount of child support to be ordered.

(g) A written finding or specific finding on the record of a judicial or administrative proceeding for the establishment or modification of a child support order that the application of the child support guidelines established under paragraph (a) of this section would be unjust or inappropriate in a particular case will be sufficient to rebut the presumption in that case, as determined under criteria established by the State. Such criteria must take into consideration the best interests of the child. Findings that rebut the child support guidelines shall state the amount of support that would have been required under the guidelines and include a justification of why the order varies from the guidelines.

(h) As part of the review of a State's child support guidelines required under paragraph (e) of this section, a State must:

(1) Consider economic data on the cost of raising children, labor market data (such as unemployment rates, employment rates, hours worked, and earnings) by occupation and skill-level for the State and local job markets,

the impact of guidelines policies and amounts on custodial and noncustodial parents who have family incomes below 200 percent of the Federal poverty level, and factors that influence employment rates among noncustodial parents and compliance with child support orders;

(2) Analyze case data, gathered through sampling or other methods, on the application of and deviations from the child support guidelines, as well as the rates of default and imputed child support orders and orders determined using the low-income adjustment required under paragraph (c)(1)(ii) of this section. The analysis must also include a comparison of payments on child support orders by case characteristics, including whether the order was entered by default, based on imputed income, or determined using the low-income adjustment required under paragraph (c)(1)(ii). The analysis of the data must be used in the State's review of the child support guidelines to ensure that deviations from the guidelines are limited and guideline amounts are appropriate based on criteria established by the State under paragraph (g); and

(3) Provide a meaningful opportunity for public input, including input from low-income custodial and noncustodial parents and their representatives. The State must also obtain the views and advice of the State child support agency funded under title IV–D of the Act.

[81 FR 93562, Dec. 20, 2016]

§ 302.60 Collection of past-due support from Federal tax refunds.

The State plan shall provide that:

(a) The IV-D agency has in effect procedures necessary to obtain payment of past-due support from Federal tax refunds as set forth in section 464 of the Act, § 303.72 of this chapter, and regulations of the Internal Revenue Service at 26 CFR 304.6402–1; and

(b) The IV-D agency shall take the steps necessary to implement and use these procedures.

(Approved by the Office of Management and Budget under control number 0960–0253)

[47 FR 7428, Feb. 19, 1982]

§ 302.65 Withholding of unemployment compensation.

The State plan shall provide that the requirements of this section are met.

(a) *Definitions.* When used in this section:

Legal process means a writ, order, summons or other similar process in the nature of a garnishment, which is issued by a court of competent jurisdiction or by an authorized official pursuant to an order of such court or pursuant to State or local law.

State workforce agency or *SWA* means the State agency charged with the administration of the State unemployment compensation laws in accordance with title III of the Act.

Unemployment compensation means any compensation payable under State unemployment compensation law (including amounts payable in accordance with agreements under any Federal unemployment compensation law). It includes extended benefits, unemployment compensation for Federal employees, unemployment compensation for ex-servicemen, trade readjustment allowances, disaster unemployment assistance, and payments under the Redwood National Park Expansion Act.

(b) *Agreement.* The State IV–D agency shall enter into an agreement, which is reflected in a record, with the SWA in its State for the purpose of withholding unemployment compensation from individuals with unmet support obligations being enforced by the IV–D agency. The IV–D agency shall agree only to a withholding program that it expects to be cost effective and to reimbursement for the SWA's actual, incremental costs of providing services to the IV–D agency.

(c) *Functions to be performed by the IV-D agency.* The IV-D agency shall:

(1) Determine periodically from information provided by the SWA under section 508 of the Unemployment Compensation Amendments of 1976 whether individuals applying for or receiving unemployment compensation owe support obligations that are being enforced by the IV-D agency.

(2) Enforce unmet support obligations by arranging for the withholding of unemployment compensation based on a voluntary agreement with the individual who owes the support, or in

appropriate cases which meet the case selection criteria established under paragraph (c)(3), through legal process pursuant to State or local law. If a voluntary agreement is obtained, the IV-D agency must give the SWA a copy of the voluntary agreement.

(3) Establish and use criteria, which are reflected in a record, for selecting cases to pursue via the withholding of unemployment compensation for support purposes. These criteria must be designed to ensure maximum case selection and minimal discretion in the selection process.

(4) Provide a receipt at least annually to an individual who requests a receipt for the support paid via the withholding of unemployment compensation, if receipts are not provided through other means.

(5) Maintain direct contact with the SWA in its State:

(i) By processing cases through the SWA in its own State or through IV-D agencies in other States; and

(ii) By receiving all amounts withheld by the SWA in its own State and forwarding any amounts withheld on behalf of IV-D agencies in other States to those agencies.

(6) Reimburse the administrative costs incurred by the SWA that are actual, incremental costs attributable to the process of withholding unemployment compensation for support purposes insofar as these costs have been agreed upon by the SWA and the IV-D agency.

(7) Review and document, at least annually, program operations, including case selection criteria established under paragraph (c)(3), and costs of the withholding process versus the amounts collected and, as necessary, modify procedures and renegotiate the services provided by the SWA to improve program and cost effectiveness.

[49 FR 8927, Mar. 9, 1984, as amended at 68 FR 25303, May 12, 2003; 81 FR 93563, Dec. 20, 2016]

§ 302.70 Required State laws.

(a) *Required Laws.* The State plan shall provide that, in accordance with sections 454(20) and 466 of the Act and part 303 of this chapter, the State has in effect laws providing for, and has implemented procedures to improve, program effectiveness:

(1) Procedures for carrying out a program of withholding under which new or existing support orders are subject to the State law governing withholding so that a portion of the noncustodial parent's wages may be withheld, in accordance with the requirements set forth in § 303.100 of this chapter;

(2) Expedited processes to establish paternity and to establish and enforce child support orders having the same force and effect as those established through full judicial process, in accordance with the requirements set forth in § 303.101 of this chapter;

(3) Procedures for obtaining overdue support from State income tax refunds on behalf of individuals receiving IV-D services, in accordance with the requirements set forth in § 303.102 of this chapter;

(4) Procedures for the imposition of liens against the real and personal property of noncustodial parents who owe overdue support;

(5)(i) Procedures for the establishment of paternity for any child at least to the child's 18th birthday, including any child for whom paternity has not yet been established and any child for whom a paternity action was previously dismissed under a statute of limitations of less than 18 years; and

(ii) Effective November 1, 1989, procedures under which the State is required (except in cases where the individual involved has been found under section 454(29) of the Act to have good cause for refusing to cooperate or if, in accordance with § 303.5(b) of this chapter the IV-D agency has determined that it would not be in the best interest of the child to establish paternity in a case involving incest or forcible rape, or in any case in which legal proceedings for adoption are pending) to require the child and all other parties in a contested paternity case to submit to genetic tests upon the request of any such party, in accordance with § 303.5 (d) and (e) of this chapter.

(iii) Procedures for a simple civil process for voluntarily acknowledging paternity under which the State must provide that, before a mother and putative father can sign a voluntary acknowledgment of paternity, the mother and the putative father must be given notice, orally or through video or audio equipment, and in writing, of the alternatives to, the legal consequences of, and the rights (including any rights, if a parent is a minor, due to minority status) and responsibilities of acknowledging paternity, and ensure that due process safeguards are afforded. Such procedures must include:

(A) A hospital-based program in accordance with § 303.5(g) for the voluntary acknowledgment of paternity during the period immediately before or after the birth of a child to an unmarried mother, and a requirement that all public and private birthing hospitals participate in the hospital-based program defined in § 303.5(g)(2); and

(B) A process for voluntary acknowledgment of paternity in hospitals, State birth record agencies, and in other entities designated by the State and participating in the State's voluntary paternity establishment program; and

(C) A requirement that the procedures governing hospital-based programs and State birth record agencies must also apply to other entities designated by the State and participating in the State's voluntary paternity establishment program, including the use of the same notice provisions, the same materials, the same evaluation methods, and the same training for the personnel of these other entities providing voluntary paternity establishment services.

(iv) Procedures under which the voluntary acknowledgment of paternity creates a rebuttable or, at the option of the State, conclusive presumption of paternity, and under which such voluntary acknowledgment is admissible as evidence of paternity;

(v) Procedures which provide that any objection to genetic testing results must be made in writing within a specified number of days before any hearing at which such results may be introduced into evidence; and if no objection is made, a report of the test results, which is reflected in a record, is admissible as evidence of paternity without the need for foundation testimony or other proof of authenticity or accuracy;

(vi) Procedures which create a rebuttable or, at the option of the State, conclusive presumption of paternity upon genetic testing results indicating a threshold probability of the alleged father being the father of the child;

(vii) Procedures under which a voluntary acknowledgment must be recognized as a basis for seeking a support order without requiring any further proceedings to establish paternity; and

(viii) Procedures requiring a default order to be entered in a paternity case upon a showing that process was served on the defendant in accordance with State law, that the defendant failed to respond to service in accordance with State procedures, and any additional showing required by State law.

(6) Procedures which require that a noncustodial parent give security, post a bond, or give some other guarantee to secure payment of support, in accordance with the procedures set forth in § 303.104 of this chapter;

(7) Procedures for making information regarding the amount of overdue support owed by a noncustodial parent available to consumer reporting agencies;

(8) Procedures under which all child support orders which are issued or modified in the State will include provision for withholding from income, in order to assure that withholding as a means of collecting child support is available if arrearages occur without the necessity of filing an application for services under § 302.33, in accordance with § 303.100(g) of this chapter.

(9) Procedures which require that any payment or installment of support under any child support order, whether ordered through the State judicial system or through the expedited processes required by paragraph (a)(2) of this section, is (on and after the date it is due):

(i) A judgment by operation of law, with the full force, effect, and attributes of a judgment of the State, including the ability to be enforced;

(ii) Entitled as a judgment to full faith and credit in such State and in any other State; and

(iii) Not subject to retroactive modification by such State or by any other State, except as provided in § 303.106(b).

(10) Procedures for the review and adjustment of child support orders in accordance with § 303.8(b) of this chapter.

(11) Procedures under which the State must give full faith and credit to a determination of paternity made by any other State, whether established through voluntary acknowledgment or through administrative or judicial processes.

(b) A State need not apply a procedure required under paragraphs (a) (3), (4), (6) and (7) of this section in an individual case if the State determines that it is not appropriate using guidelines generally available to the public which take into account the payment record of the noncustodial parent, the availability of other remedies, and other relevant considerations. The guidelines may not determine a majority of cases in which no other remedy is being used to be inappropriate.

(c) State laws enacted under this section must give States sufficient authority to comply with the requirements of §§ 303.100 through 303.102 and § 303.104 of this chapter.

(d)(1) *Exemption.* A State may apply for an exemption from any of the requirements of section 466 of the Act by the submittal of a request for exemption to the appropriate Regional Office.

(2) *Basis for granting exemption.* The Secretary will grant a State, or political subdivision in the case of section 466(a)(2) of the Act, an exemption from any of the requirements of paragraph (a) of this section for a period not to exceed 5 years if the State demonstrates that compliance would not increase the effectiveness and efficiency of its Child Support Enforcement program. Demonstration of the program's efficiency and effectiveness must be shown by actual, or, if actual is not available, estimated data pertaining to caseloads, processing times, administrative costs, and average support collections or such other actual or estimated data as the Office may request. The State must demonstrate to the satisfaction of the Secretary that the program's effectiveness would not improve by using these procedures. Disapproval of a request for exemption is not subject to appeal.

(3) *Review of exemption.* The exemption is subject to continuing review by the Secretary and may be terminated upon a change in circumstances or reduced effectiveness in the State or political subdivision, if the State cannot demonstrate that the changed circumstances continue to warrant an exemption in accordance with this section.

(4) *Request for extension.* The State must request an extension of the exemption by submitting current data in accordance with paragraph (d)(2) of this section 90 days prior to the end of the exemption period granted under paragraph (d)(2) of this section.

(5) *When an exemption is revoked or an extension is denied.* If the Secretary revokes an exemption or does not grant an extension of an exemption, the State must enact the appropriate laws and procedures to implement the mandatory practice by the beginning of the fourth month after the end of the first regular, special, budget or other session of the State's legislature which ends after the date the exemption is revoked or the extension is denied. If no State law is necessary, the State must establish and be using the procedure by the beginning of the fourth month after the date the exemption is revoked.

(Approved by the Office of Management and Budget under control number 0960–0385)

[50 FR 19649, May 9, 1985, as amended at 51 FR 37731, Oct. 24, 1986; 54 FR 15764, Apr. 19, 1989; 56 FR 8004, Feb. 26, 1991; 56 FR 22354, May 15, 1991; 57 FR 30681, July 10, 1992; 57 FR 61581, Dec. 28, 1992; 59 FR 66249, Dec. 23, 1994; 64 FR 6249, Feb. 9, 1999; 64 FR 11809, Mar. 10, 1999; 68 FR 25303, May 12, 2003; 68 FR 53052, Sept. 9, 2003; 73 FR 74920, Dec. 9, 2008; 81 FR 93563, Dec. 20, 2016]

§ 302.75 Procedures for the imposition of late payment fees on noncustodial parents who owe overdue support.

(a) Effective September 1, 1984, the State plan may provide for imposition of late payment fees on noncustodial parents who owe overdue support.

(b) If a State opts to impose late payment fees—

(1) The late payment fee must be uniformly applied in an amount not less than 3 percent nor more than 6 percent of overdue support.

(2) The fee shall accrue as arrearages accumulate and shall not be reduced upon partial payment of arrears. The fee may be collected only after the full amount of overdue support is paid and

any requirements under State law for notice to the noncustodial parent have been met.

(3) The collection of the fee must not directly or indirectly reduce the amount of current or overdue support paid to the individual to whom it is owed.

(4) The late payment fee must be imposed in cases where there has been an assignment under section 408(a)(3) of the Act or section 471(a)(17) of the Act or the IV-D agency is providing services under §302.33 of this chapter.

(5) The State may allow fees collected to be retained by the jurisdiction making the collection.

(6) The State must reduce its expenditures claimed under the Child Support Enforcement program by any fees collected under this section in accordance with §304.50 of this chapter.

(Approved by the Office of Management and Budget under control number 0960–0385)

[50 FR 19650, May 9, 1985, as amended at 51 FR 37731, Oct. 24, 1986; 56 FR 8004, Feb. 26, 1991; 64 FR 6249, Feb. 9, 1999; 68 FR 25303, May 12, 2003]

§302.80 Medical support enforcement.

(a) The State plan may provide that the IV-D agency will secure and enforce medical support obligations under a cooperative agreement between the IV-D agency and the State Medicaid agency.

(b) The State plan must provide that the IV-D agency shall secure medical support information and establish and enforce medical support obligations in accordance with the requirements contained in §§303.30 and 303.31 of this chapter.

(Approved by the Office of Management and Budget under control number 0960–0420)

[50 FR 41894, Oct. 16, 1985, as amended at 51 FR 37731, Oct. 24, 1986; 54 FR 32309, Aug. 4, 1989; 61 FR 67241, Dec. 20, 1996; 64 FR 6249, Feb. 9, 1999]

§302.85 Mandatory computerized support enforcement system.

(a) *General.* The State plan shall provide that the State will have in effect a computerized support enforcement system:

(1) This guide is available on the OCSE Web site; and

(2) By October 1, 2000, which meets all the requirements of title IV-D of the Act enacted on or before the date of enactment of the Personal Responsibility and Work Opportunity Reconciliation Act of 1996, Pub. L. 104–193, in accordance with §§307.5 and 307.11 of this chapter and the OCSE guideline referenced in paragraph (a)(1) of this section.

(b) *Waiver*—(1) *Request for waiver.* The State may apply for a waiver of any condition for initial approval of an APD in §307.15(b) of this chapter, or any system functional requirement in §307.10 of this chapter, by the submission of a request for waiver under §307.5 of this chapter.

(2) *Basis for granting waiver.* The Secretary will grant a State a waiver if a State demonstrates that it has an alternative approach to APD requirements or an alternative system configuration, as defined in §307.1 of this chapter, that enables the State, in accordance with part 305 of this chapter, to be in substantial compliance with all other requirements of this chapter; and either:

(i) The waiver request meets the criteria set forth in section 1115(c)(1), (2) and (3) of the Act; or

(ii) The State provides assurances, which are reflected in a record, that steps will be taken to otherwise improve the State's Child Support Enforcement program.

[57 FR 47002, Oct. 14, 1992, as amended at 61 FR 67241, Dec. 20, 1996; 63 FR 44814, Aug. 21, 1998; 81 FR 93563, Dec. 20, 2016]

PART 303—STANDARDS FOR PROGRAM OPERATIONS

Sec.

AUTHORITY: 42 U.S.C. 651 through 658, 659a, 660, 663, 664, 666, 667, 1302, 1396a(a)(25), 1396b(d)(2), 1396b(o), 1396b(p), 1396(k), and 25 U.S.C. 1603(12) and 1621e.

SOURCE: 40 FR 27164, June 26, 1975, unless otherwise noted.

EDITORIAL NOTE: Nomenclature changes to part 303 appear at 64 FR 6249, Feb. 9, 1999.

§ 303.0 Scope and applicability of this part.

This part prescribes:

(a) The minimum organizational and staffing requirements the State IV-D agency must meet in carrying out the IV-D program, and

(b) The standards for program operation which the IV-D agency must meet.

[41 FR 55348, Dec. 20, 1976, as amended at 54 FR 32309, Aug. 4, 1989]

§ 303.1 Definitions.

The definitions found in § 301.1 of this chapter also are applicable to this part.

§ 303.2 Establishment of cases and maintenance of case records.

(a) The IV-D agency must:

(1) Make applications for child support services readily accessible to the public;

(2) When an individual requests an application for IV–D services, provide an application to the individual on the day the individual makes a request in person, or send an application to the individual within no more than 5 working days of a request received by telephone or in a record. Information describing available services, the individual's rights and responsibilities, and the State's fees, cost recovery and distribution policies must accompany all applications for services and must be provided to title IV-A, Medicaid and title IV-E foster care applicants or recipients within no more than 5 working days of referral to the IV-D agency; and

(3) Accept an application as filed on the day it and the application fee are received. An application is a record that is provided or used by the State which indicates that the individual is applying for child support enforcement services under the State's title IV–D program and is signed, electronically or otherwise, by the individual applying for IV–D services.

(b) For all cases referred to the IV-D agency or applying for services under § 302.33 of this chapter, the IV-D agency must, within no more than 20 calendar days of receipt of referral of a case or filing of an application for services under § 302.33, open a case by establishing a case record and, based on an assessment of the case to determine necessary action:

(1) Solicit necessary and relevant information from the custodial parent and other relevant sources and initiate verification of information, if appropriate; and

(2) If there is inadequate location information to proceed with the case, request additional information or refer the case for further location attempts, as specified in § 303.3.

(c) The case record must be supplemented with all information and documents pertaining to the case, as well as all relevant facts, dates, actions taken, contacts made and results in a case.

[54 FR 32309, Aug. 4, 1989, as amended at 81 FR 93563, Dec. 20, 2016]

§ 303.3 Location of noncustodial parents in IV–D cases.

(a) *Definition.* For purposes of this section, *location* means obtaining information concerning the physical whereabouts of the noncustodial parent, or the noncustodial parent's employer(s), other sources of income or assets, as appropriate, which is sufficient and necessary to take the next appropriate action in a IV–D case.

(b) For all cases referred to the IV–D program for IV–D services because of an assignment of support rights or cases opened upon application for IV–D services under § 302.33 of this chapter, the IV–D program must attempt to locate all noncustodial parents or their sources of income and/or assets when location is needed to take a necessary action. Under this standard, the IV–D program must:

(1) Use appropriate location sources such as the Federal PLS; interstate location networks; local officials and employees administering public assistance, general assistance, medical assistance, Supplemental Nutrition Assistance Program (SNAP) and social services (whether such individuals are employed by the State or a political subdivision); relatives and friends of the noncustodial parent; current or past employers; electronic communications and internet service providers; utility companies; the U.S. Postal Service; financial institutions; unions; corrections institutions; fraternal organizations; police, parole, and probation records if appropriate; and State agencies and departments, as authorized by State law, including those departments which maintain records of public assistance, wages and employment, unemployment insurance, income taxation, driver's licenses, vehicle registration, and criminal records and other sources;

(2) Establish working relationships with all appropriate agencies in order to use locate resources effectively;

(3) Within no more than 75 calendar days of determining that location is necessary, access all appropriate location sources and ensure that location information is sufficient to take the next appropriate action in a case;

(4) Refer appropriate IV–D cases to the IV–D program of any other State, in accordance with the requirements of § 303.7 of this part. The IV–D program of such other State shall follow the procedures in paragraphs (b)(1) through (b)(3) of this section for such cases, as necessary, except that the responding State is not required to access the Federal PLS;

(5) Repeat location attempts in cases in which previous attempts to locate noncustodial parents or sources of income and/or assets have failed, but adequate identifying and other information exists to meet requirements for submittal for location, either quarterly or immediately upon receipt of new information which may aid in location, whichever occurs sooner. Quarterly attempts may be limited to automated sources, but must include accessing State workforce files. Repeated attempts because of new information which may aid in location must meet the requirements of paragraph (b)(3) of this section; and

(6) Have in effect safeguards, applicable to all confidential information handled by the IV–D program, that are designed to protect the privacy rights of the parties and that comply with the requirements of sections 454(26) and 454A(d) and (f) of the Act and §§ 303.21 and 307.13.

(c) The State must establish guidelines defining diligent efforts to serve process. These guidelines must include periodically repeating service of process attempts in cases in which previous attempts to serve process have failed, but adequate identifying and other information exists to attempt service of process.

[73 FR 56443, Sept. 26, 2008, as amended at 81 FR 93563, Dec. 20, 2016]

§ 303.4 Establishment of support obligations.

For all cases referred to the IV-D agency or applying under § 302.33 of this chapter, the IV-D Agency must:

(a) When necessary, establish paternity pursuant to the standards of § 303.5;

(b) Use appropriate State statutes, procedures, and legal processes in establishing and modifying support obligations in accordance with § 302.56 of this chapter, which must include, at a minimum:

(1) Taking reasonable steps to develop a sufficient factual basis for the support obligation, through such means as investigations, case conferencing, interviews with both parties, appear and disclose procedures, parent questionnaires, testimony, and electronic data sources;

(2) Gathering information regarding the earnings and income of the noncustodial parent and, when earnings and income information is unavailable or insufficient in a case gathering available information about the specific circumstances of the noncustodial parent, including such factors as those listed under § 302.56(c)(1)(iii) of this chapter;

(3) Basing the support obligation or recommended support obligation amount on the earnings and income of the noncustodial parent whenever available. If evidence of earnings and income is unavailable or insufficient to use as the measure of the noncustodial parent's ability to pay, then the support obligation or recommended support obligation amount should be based on available information about the specific circumstances of the noncustodial parent, including such factors as those listed in § 302.56(c)(1)(iii) of this chapter.

(4) Documenting the factual basis for the support obligation or the recommended support obligation in the case record.

(c) Periodically review and adjust child support orders, as appropriate, in accordance with § 303.8.

(d) Within 90 calendar days of locating the alleged father or noncustodial parent, regardless of whether paternity has been established, establish an order for support or complete service of process necessary to commence proceedings to establish a support order and, if necessary, paternity (or document unsuccessful attempts to serve process, in accordance with the State's guidelines defining diligent efforts under § 303.3(c)).

(e) If the court or administrative authority dismisses a petition for a support order without prejudice, the IV-D agency must, at the time of dismissal, examine the reasons for dismissal and determine when it would be appropriate to seek an order in the future, and seek a support order at that time.

(f) Seek a support order based on a voluntary acknowledgment in accordance with § 302.70(a)(5)(vii).

[40 FR 27164, June 26, 1975, as amended at 50 FR 19650, May 9, 1985; 54 FR 32310, Aug. 4, 1989; 57 FR 30681, July 10, 1992; 59 FR 66250, Dec. 23, 1994; 81 FR 93563, Dec. 20, 2016]

§ 303.5 Establishment of paternity.

(a) For all cases referred to the IV-D agency or applying for services under § 302.33 of this chapter in which paternity has not been established, the IV-D agency must, as appropriate:

(1) Provide an alleged father the opportunity to voluntarily acknowledge paternity in accordance with § 302.70(a)(5)(iii); and

(2) Attempt to establish paternity by legal process established under State law.

(b) The IV-D agency need not attempt to establish paternity in any case involving incest or forcible rape, or in any case in which legal proceedings for adoption are pending, if, in the opinion of the IV-D agency, it would not be in the best interests of the child to establish paternity.

(c) The IV-D agency must identify and use through competitive procurement laboratories which perform, at reasonable cost, legally and medically acceptable genetic tests which tend to identify the father or exclude the alleged father. The IV-D agency must make available a list of such laboratories to appropriate courts and law enforcement officials, and to the public upon request.

(d)(1) Upon request of any party in a contested paternity case in accordance with section 466(a)(5)(B) of the Act, and subject to the provisions of paragraph

(b) of this section, the IV-D agency shall require all parties to submit to genetic tests unless, in the case of an individual receiving aid under the State's title IV-A, IV-E or XIX plan, or those recipients of the food stamp program, as defined under section 3(h) of the Food Stamp Act of 1977 who are required to cooperate with the child support program, there has been a determination of good cause for refusal to cooperate under section 454(29) of the Act.

(2) A contested paternity case is any action in which the issue of paternity may be raised under State law and one party denies paternity.

(e)(1) Except as provided in paragraph (e)(3) of this section, the IV-D agency may charge any individual who is not a recipient of aid under the State's title IV-A or XIX plan a reasonable fee for performing genetic tests.

(2) Any fee charged must be reasonable so as not to discourage those in need of paternity establishment services from seeking them and may not exceed the actual costs of the genetic tests.

(3) If paternity is established and genetic tests were ordered by the IV-D agency, the IV-D agency must pay the costs of such tests, subject to recoupment (if the agency elects) from the alleged father who denied paternity. If a party contests the results of an original test, the IV-D agency shall obtain additional tests but shall require the contestant to pay for the costs of any such additional testing in advance.

(4) The IV-D agency must use any amount collected under paragraphs (e) (1) and (3) of this section that exceeds the costs of performing genetic tests to reimburse any fee paid under paragraph (e)(1) of this chapter.

(f) The IV-D agency must seek entry of a default order by the court or administrative authority in a paternity case by showing that process has been served on the defendant in accordance with State law, that the defendant has failed to respond to service in accordance with State procedures, and any additional showing required by State law, in accordance with § 302.70(a)(5)(viii).

(g) *Voluntary paternity establishment programs.* (1) The State must establish, in cooperation with hospitals, State birth record agencies, and other entities designated by the State and participating in the State's voluntary paternity establishment program, a program for voluntary paternity establishment services.

(i) The hospital-based portion of the voluntary paternity establishment services program must be operational in all private and public birthing hospitals statewide and must provide voluntary paternity establishment services focusing on the period immediately before and after the birth of a child born out-of-wedlock.

(ii) The voluntary paternity establishment services program must also be available at the State birth record agencies, and at other entities designated by the State and participating in the State's voluntary paternity establishment program. These entities may include the following types of entities:

(A) Public health clinics (including Supplementary Feeding Program for Women, Infants, and Children (WIC) and Maternal and Child Health (MCH) clinics), and private health care providers (including obstetricians, gynecologists, pediatricians, and midwives);

(B) Agencies providing assistance or services under Title IV-A of the Act, agencies providing food stamp eligibility service, and agencies providing child support enforcement (IV-D) services;

(C) Head Start and child care agencies (including child care information and referral providers), and individual child care providers;

(D) Community Action Agencies and Community Action Programs;

(E) Secondary education schools (particularly those that have parenthood education curricula);

(F) Legal Aid agencies, and private attorneys; and

(G) Any similar public or private health, welfare or social services organization.

(2) The hospitals, State birth record agencies, and other entities designated by the State and participating in the State's voluntary paternity establishment program must, at a minimum:

(i) Provide to both the mother and alleged father:

(A) Written materials about paternity establishment,

(B) The forms necessary to voluntarily acknowledge paternity,

(C) Notice, orally or through video or audio equipment, and in writing, of the alternatives to, the legal consequences of, and the rights (including any rights, if a parent is a minor, due to minority status) and responsibilities or acknowledging paternity, and

(D) The opportunity to speak with staff, either by telephone or in person, who are trained to clarify information and answer questions about paternity establishment;

(ii) Provide the mother and alleged father the opportunity to voluntarily acknowledge paternity;

(iii) Afford due process safeguards; and

(iv) File signed original of voluntary acknowledgments or adjudications of paternity with the State registry of birth records (or a copy if the signed original is filed with another designated entity) for comparison with information in the State case registry.

(3) The hospitals, State birth record agencies, and other entities designated by the State and participating in the State's voluntary paternity establishment program need not provide services specified in paragraph (g)(2) of this section in cases where the mother or alleged father is a minor or a legal action is already pending, if the provision of such services is precluded by State law.

(4) The State must require that a voluntary acknowledgment be signed by both parents, and that the parents' signatures be authenticated by a notary or witness(es).

(5) The State must provide to all hospitals, State birth record agencies, and other entities designated by the State and participating in the State's voluntary paternity establishment program:

(i) Written materials about paternity establishment,

(ii) Form necessary to voluntarily acknowledge paternity, and

(iii) Copies of a written description of the alternatives to, the legal consequences of, and the rights (including any rights, if a parent is a minor, due to minority status) and responsibilities of acknowledging paternity.

(6) The State must provide training, guidance, and instructions, which are reflected in a record, regarding voluntary acknowledgment of paternity, as necessary to operate the voluntary paternity establishment services in the hospitals, State birth record agencies, and other entities designated by the State and participating in the State's voluntary paternity establishment program.

(7) The State must assess each hospital, State birth record agency, local birth record agency designated by the State, and other entity participating in the State's voluntary paternity establishment program that are providing voluntary paternity establishment services on at least an annual basis.

(8) Hospitals, State birth record agencies, and other entities designated by the State and participating in the State's voluntary paternity establishment program must forward completed voluntary acknowledgments or copies to the entity designated by the State. If any entity other than the State registry of birth records is designated by the State, a copy must be filed with the State registry of birth records, in accordance with § 303.5(g)(2)(iv). Under State procedures, the designated entity must be responsible for promptly recording identifying information about the acknowledgments with a statewide database, and the IV-D agency must have timely access to whatever identifying information and documentation it needs to determine in accordance with § 303.5(h) if an acknowledgment has been recorded and to seek a support order on the basis of a recorded acknowledgment in accordance with § 303.4(f).

(h) In IV-D cases needing paternity establishment, the IV-D agency must determine if identifying information about a voluntary acknowledgment has been recorded in the statewide database in accordance with § 303.5(g)(8).

[40 FR 27164, June 26, 1975, as amended at 50 FR 19650, May 9, 1985; 54 FR 32310, Aug. 4, 1989; 56 FR 22354, May 15, 1991; 59 FR 66250, Dec. 23, 1994; 64 FR 6249, Feb. 9, 1999; 64 FR 11809, Mar. 10, 1999; 81 FR 93564, Dec. 20, 2016]

§303.6 Enforcement of support obligations.

For all cases referred to the IV-D agency or applying for services under §302.33 in which the obligation to support and the amount of the obligation have been established, the IV-D agency must maintain and use an effective system for:

(a) Monitoring compliance with the support obligation;

(b) Identifying on the date the parent fails to make payments in an amount equal to the support payable for one month, or on an earlier date in accordance with State law, those cases in which there is a failure to comply with the support obligation; and

(c) Enforcing the obligation by:

(1) Initiating income withholding, in accordance with §303.100;

(2) Taking any appropriate enforcement action (except income withholding and Federal and State income tax refund offset) unless service of process is necessary, within no more than 30 calendar days of identifying a delinquency or other support-related non-compliance with the order or the location of the noncustodial parent, whichever occurs later. If service of process is necessary prior to taking an enforcement action, service must be completed (or unsuccessful attempts to serve process must be documented in accordance with the State's guidelines defining diligent efforts under §303.3(c)), and enforcement action taken if process is served, within no later than 60 calendar days of identifying a delinquency or other support-related non-compliance with the order, or the location of the noncustodial parent, whichever occurs later;

(3) Submitting once a year all cases which meet the certification requirements under §303.102 of this part and State guidelines developed under §302.70(b) of this title for State income tax refund offset, and which meet the certification requirements under §303.72 of this part for Federal income tax refund offset;

(4) Establishing guidelines for the use of civil contempt citations in IV–D cases. The guidelines must include requirements that the IV–D agency:

(i) Screen the case for information regarding the noncustodial parent's ability to pay or otherwise comply with the order;

(ii) Provide the court with such information regarding the noncustodial parent's ability to pay, or otherwise comply with the order, which may assist the court in making a factual determination regarding the noncustodial parent's ability to pay the purge amount or comply with the purge conditions; and

(iii) Provide clear notice to the noncustodial parent that his or her ability to pay constitutes the critical question in the civil contempt action; and

(5) In cases in which enforcement attempts have been unsuccessful, at the time an attempt to enforce fails, examining the reason the enforcement attempt failed and determining when it would be appropriate to take an enforcement action in the future, and taking an enforcement action in accordance with the requirements of this section at that time.

[54 FR 32310, Aug. 4, 1989, as amended at 55 FR 25840, June 25, 1990; 81 FR 93564, Dec. 20, 2016]

§303.7 Provision of services in intergovernmental IV–D cases.

(a) *General responsibilities.* A State IV–D agency must:

(1) Establish and use procedures for managing its intergovernmental IV–D caseload that ensure provision of necessary services as required by this section and include maintenance of necessary records in accordance with §303.2 of this part;

(2) Periodically review program performance on intergovernmental IV–D cases to evaluate the effectiveness of the procedures established under this section;

(3) Ensure that the organizational structure and staff of the IV–D agency are adequate to provide for the administration or supervision of the following functions specified in §303.20(c) of this part for its intergovernmental IV–D caseload: Intake; establishment of paternity and the legal obligation to support; location; financial assessment; establishment of the amount of child support; collection; monitoring; enforcement; review and adjustment; and investigation;

(4) Use federally-approved forms in intergovernmental IV–D cases, unless a country has provided alternative forms as part of its chapter in *A Caseworker's Guide to Processing Cases with Foreign Reciprocating Countries*. When using a paper version, this requirement is met by providing the number of complete sets of required documents needed by the responding agency, if one is not sufficient under the responding agency's law;

(5) Transmit requests for information and provide requested information electronically to the greatest extent possible;

(6) Within 30 working days of receiving a request, provide any order and payment record information requested by a State IV–D agency for a controlling order determination and reconciliation of arrearages, or notify the State IV–D agency when the information will be provided;

(7) Notify the other agency within 10 working days of receipt of new information on an intergovernmental case; and

(8) Cooperate with requests for the following limited services: Quick locate, service of process, assistance with discovery, assistance with genetic testing, teleconferenced hearings, administrative reviews, high-volume automated administrative enforcement in interstate cases under section 466(a)(14) of the Act, and copies of court orders and payment records. Requests for other limited services may be honored at the State's option.

(b) *Central registry*. (1) The State IV–D agency must establish a central registry responsible for receiving, transmitting, and responding to inquiries on all incoming intergovernmental IV–D cases.

(2) Within 10 working days of receipt of an intergovernmental IV–D case, the central registry must:

(i) Ensure that the documentation submitted with the case has been reviewed to determine completeness;

(ii) Forward the case for necessary action either to the central State Parent Locator Service for location services or to the appropriate agency for processing;

(iii) Acknowledge receipt of the case and request any missing documentation; and

(iv) Inform the initiating agency where the case was sent for action.

(3) If the documentation received with a case is incomplete and cannot be remedied by the central registry without the assistance of the initiating agency, the central registry must forward the case for any action that can be taken pending necessary action by the initiating agency.

(4) The central registry must respond to inquiries from initiating agencies within 5 working days of receipt of the request for a case status review.

(c) *Initiating State IV–D agency responsibilities*. The initiating State IV–D agency must:

(1) Determine whether or not there is a support order or orders in effect in a case using the Federal and State Case Registries, State records, information provided by the recipient of services, and other relevant information available to the State;

(2) Determine in which State a determination of the controlling order and reconciliation of arrearages may be made where multiple orders exist;

(3) Determine whether the noncustodial parent is in another jurisdiction and whether it is appropriate to use its one-state remedies to establish paternity and establish, modify, and enforce a support order, including medical support and income withholding;

(4) Within 20 calendar days of completing the actions required in paragraphs (1) through (3) and, if appropriate, receipt of any necessary information needed to process the case:

(i) Ask the appropriate intrastate tribunal, or refer the case to the appropriate responding State IV–D agency, for a determination of the controlling order and a reconciliation of arrearages if such a determination is necessary; and

(ii) Refer any intergovernmental IV–D case to the appropriate State Central Registry, Tribal IV–D program, or Central Authority of a country for action, if one-state remedies are not appropriate;

(5) Provide the responding agency sufficient, accurate information to act on the case by submitting with each

case any necessary documentation and intergovernmental forms required by the responding agency;

(6) Within 30 calendar days of receipt of the request for information, provide the responding agency with an updated intergovernmental form and any necessary additional documentation, or notify the responding agency when the information will be provided;

(7) Notify the responding agency at least annually, and upon request in an individual case, of interest charges, if any, owed on overdue support under an initiating State order being enforced in the responding jurisdiction;

(8) Submit all past-due support owed in IV–D cases that meet the certification requirements under § 303.72 of this part for Federal tax refund offset,

(9) Send a request for review of a child support order to another State within 20 calendar days of determining that a request for review of the order should be sent to the other State and of receipt of information from the requestor necessary to conduct the review in accordance with section 466(a)(10) of the Act and § 303.8 of this part;

(10) Distribute and disburse any support collections received in accordance with this section and §§ 302.32, 302.38, 302.51, and 302.52 of this chapter, sections 454(5), 454B, 457, and 1912 of the Act, and instructions issued by the Office;

(11) Notify the responding agency within 10 working days of case closure that the initiating State IV–D agency has closed its case pursuant to § 303.11 of this part, and the basis for case closure;

(12) Instruct the responding agency to close its interstate case and to stop any withholding order or notice the responding agency has sent to an employer before the initiating State transmits a withholding order or notice, with respect to the same case, to the same or another employer unless the two States reach an alternative agreement on how to proceed; and

(13) If the initiating agency has closed its case pursuant to § 303.11 and has not notified the responding agency to close its corresponding case, make a diligent effort to locate the obligee, including use of the Federal Parent Locator Service and the State Parent Locator Service, and accept, distribute and disburse any payment received from a responding agency.

(d) *Responding State IV–D agency responsibilities.* Upon receipt of a request for services from an initiating agency, the responding State IV–D agency must:

(1) Accept and process an intergovernmental request for services, regardless of whether the initiating agency elected not to use remedies that may be available under the law of that jurisdiction;

(2) Within 75 calendar days of receipt of an intergovernmental form and documentation from its central registry:

(i) Provide location services in accordance with § 303.3 of this part if the request is for location services or the form or documentation does not include adequate location information on the noncustodial parent;

(ii) If unable to proceed with the case because of inadequate documentation, notify the initiating agency of the necessary additions or corrections to the form or documentation;

(iii) If the documentation received with a case is incomplete and cannot be remedied without the assistance of the initiating agency, process the case to the extent possible pending necessary action by the initiating agency;

(3) Within 10 working days of locating the noncustodial parent in a different State, the responding agency must return the forms and documentation, including the new location, to the initiating agency, or, if directed by the initiating agency, forward/transmit the forms and documentation to the central registry in the State where the noncustodial parent has been located and notify the responding State's own central registry where the case has been sent.

(4) Within 10 working days of locating the noncustodial parent in a different political subdivision within the State, forward/transmit the forms and documentation to the appropriate political subdivision and notify the initiating agency and the responding State's own central registry of its action;

(5) If the request is for a determination of controlling order:

(i) File the controlling order determination request with the appropriate tribunal in its State within 30 calendar days of receipt of the request or location of the noncustodial parent, whichever occurs later; and

(ii) Notify the initiating State agency, the Controlling Order State and any State where a support order in the case was issued or registered, of the controlling order determination and any reconciled arrearages within 30 calendar days of receipt of the determination from the tribunal;

(6) Provide any necessary services as it would in an intrastate IV–D case including:

(i) Establishing paternity in accordance with § 303.5 of this part and, if the agency elects, attempting to obtain a judgment for costs should paternity be established;

(ii) Establishing a child support obligation in accordance with § 302.56 of this chapter and §§ 303.4, 303.31 and 303.101 of this part;

(iii) Reporting overdue support to Consumer Reporting Agencies, in accordance with section 466(a)(7) of the Act and § 302.70(a)(7) of this chapter;

(iv) Processing and enforcing orders referred by an initiating agency, whether pursuant to UIFSA or other legal processes, using appropriate remedies applied in its own cases in accordance with §§ 303.6, 303.31, 303.32, 303.100 through 303.102, and 303.104 of this part, and submit the case for such other Federal enforcement techniques as the State determines to be appropriate, such as administrative offset under 31 CFR 285.1 and passport denial under section 452(k) of the Act;

(v) Collecting and monitoring any support payments from the noncustodial parent and forwarding payments to the location specified by the initiating agency. The IV–D agency must include sufficient information to identify the case, indicate the date of collection as defined under § 302.51(a) of this chapter, and include the responding State's case identifier and locator code, as defined in accordance with instructions issued by this Office; and

(vi) Reviewing and adjusting child support orders upon request in accordance with § 303.8 of this part;

(7) Provide timely notice to the initiating agency in advance of any hearing before a tribunal that may result in establishment or adjustment of an order;

(8) Identify any fees or costs deducted from support payments when forwarding payments to the initiating agency in accordance with paragraph (d)(6)(v) of this section;

(9) Within 10 working days of receipt of instructions for case closure from an initiating State agency under paragraph (c)(12) of this section, stop the responding State's income withholding order or notice and close the intergovernmental IV–D case, unless the two States reach an alternative agreement on how to proceed; and

(10) Notify the initiating agency when a case is closed pursuant to §§ 303.11(b)(17) through (19) and 303.7(d)(9).

(e) *Payment and recovery of costs in intergovernmental IV–D cases.* (1) The responding IV–D agency must pay the costs it incurs in processing intergovernmental IV–D cases, including the costs of genetic testing. If paternity is established, the responding agency, at its election, may seek a judgment for the costs of testing from the alleged father who denied paternity.

(2) Each State IV–D agency may recover its costs of providing services in intergovernmental non-IV–A cases in accordance with § 302.33(d) of this chapter, except that a IV–D agency may not recover costs from an FRC or from a foreign obligee in that FRC, when providing services under sections 454(32) and 459A of the Act.

(f) *Imposition and reporting of annual $25 fee in interstate cases.* The title IV–D agency in the initiating State must impose and report the annual $25 fee in accordance with § 302.33(e) of this chapter.

[75 FR 38642, July 2, 2010, as amended at 81 FR 93564, Dec. 20, 2016]

§ 303.8 Review and adjustment of child support orders.

(a) Definition. For purposes of this section, *Parent* includes any custodial parent or noncustodial parent (or for purposes of requesting a review, any other person or entity who may have standing to request an adjustment to the child support order).

(b) *Required procedures.* Pursuant to section 466(a)(10) of the Act, when providing services under this chapter:

(1) The State must have procedures under which, within 36 months after establishment of the order or the most recent review of the order (or such shorter cycle as the State may determine), if there is an assignment under part A, or upon the request of either parent, the State shall, with respect to a support order being enforced under title IV–D of the Act, taking into account the best interests of the child involved:

(i) Review and, if appropriate, adjust the order in accordance with the State's guidelines established pursuant to section 467(a) of the Act if the amount of the child support award under the order differs from the amount that would be awarded in accordance with the guidelines;

(ii) Apply a cost-of-living adjustment to the order in accordance with a formula developed by the State; or

(iii) Use automated methods (including automated comparisons with wage or State income tax data) to identify orders eligible for review, conduct the review, identify orders eligible for adjustment, and apply the appropriate adjustment to the orders eligible for adjustment under any threshold that may be established by the State.

(2) The State may elect in its State plan to initiate review of an order, after learning that a noncustodial parent will be incarcerated for more than 180 calendar days, without the need for a specific request and, upon notice to both parents, review and, if appropriate, adjust the order, in accordance with paragraph (b)(1)(i) of this section.

(3) If the State elects to conduct the review under paragraph (b)(1)(ii) or (iii) of this section, the State must have procedures which permit either party to contest the adjustment, within 30 days after the date of the notice of the adjustment, by making a request for review and, if appropriate, adjustment of the order in accordance with the child support guidelines established pursuant to section 467(a) of the Act.

(4) If the State conducts a guideline review under paragraph (b)(1)(i) of this section:

(i) *Review* means an objective evaluation, conducted through a proceeding before a court, quasi-judicial process, or administrative body or agency, of information necessary for application of the State's guidelines for support to determine:

(A) The appropriate support award amount; and

(B) The need to provide for the child's health care needs in the order through health insurance coverage or other means.

(ii) *Adjustment* applies only to the child support provisions of the order, and means:

(A) An upward or downward change in the amount of child support based upon an application of State guidelines for setting and adjusting child support awards; and/or

(B) Provision for the child's health care needs, through health insurance coverage or other means.

(5) The State must have procedures which provide that any adjustment under paragraph (b)(1)(i) of this section shall be made without a requirement for proof or showing of a change in circumstances.

(6) The State must have procedures under which, in the case of a request for a review, and if appropriate, an adjustment outside the 3-year cycle (or such shorter cycle as the State may determine) under paragraph (b)(1) of this section, the State shall review and, if the requesting party demonstrates a substantial change in circumstances, adjust the order in accordance with the guidelines established pursuant to section 467(a) of the Act.

(7) The State must provide notice—

(i) Not less than once every 3 years to both parents subject to an order informing the parents of their right to request the State to review and, if appropriate, adjust the order consistent with this section. The notice must specify the place and manner in which the request should be made. The initial notice may be included in the order.

(ii) If the State has not elected paragraph (b)(2) of this section, within 15 business days of when the IV–D agency learns that a noncustodial parent will be incarcerated for more than 180 calendar days, to both parents informing them of the right to request the State to review and, if appropriate, adjust the order, consistent with this section. The notice must specify, at a minimum, the place and manner in which the request should be made. Neither the notice nor a review is required under this paragraph if the State has a comparable law or rule that modifies a child support obligation upon incarceration by operation of State law.

(c) Standard for adequate grounds. The State may establish a reasonable quantitative standard based upon either a fixed dollar amount or percentage, or both, as a basis for determining whether an inconsistency between the existent child support award amount and the amount of support determined as a result of a review is adequate grounds for petitioning for adjustment of the order. Such reasonable quantitative standard must not exclude incarceration as a basis for determining whether an inconsistency between the existing child support order amount and the amount of support determined as a result of a review is adequate grounds for petitioning for adjustment of the order.

(d) *Health care needs must be an adequate basis.* The need to provide for the child's health care needs in the order, through health insurance or other means, must be an adequate basis under State law to initiate an adjustment of an order, regardless of whether an adjustment in the amount of child support is necessary.

(e) Timeframes for review and adjustment. Within 180 calendar days of receiving a request for a review or locating the non-requesting parent, whichever occurs later, a State must: Conduct a review of the order and adjust the order or determine that the order should not be adjusted, in accordance with this section.

(f) Interstate review and adjustment. (1) In interstate cases, the State with legal authority to adjust the order must conduct the review and adjust the order pursuant to this section.

(2) The applicable laws and procedures for review and adjustment of child support orders, including the State guidelines for setting child support awards, established in accordance with § 302.56 of this chapter, are those of the State in which the review and adjustment, or determination that there be no adjustment, takes place.

[68 FR 25303, May 12, 2003, as amended at 69 FR 77661, Dec. 28, 2004; 73 FR 74920, Dec. 9, 2008; 81 FR 93564, Dec. 20, 2016]

§ 303.10 [Reserved]

§ 303.11 Case closure criteria.

(a) The IV–D agency shall establish a system for case closure.

(b) The IV–D agency may elect to close a case if the case meets at least one of the following criteria and supporting documentation for the case closure decision is maintained in the case record:

(1) There is no longer a current support order and arrearages are under $500 or unenforceable under State law;

(2) There is no longer a current support order and all arrearages in the case are assigned to the State;

(3) There is no longer a current support order, the children have reached the age of majority, the noncustodial parent is entering or has entered long-term care arrangements (such as a residential care facility or home health care), and the noncustodial parent has no income or assets available above the subsistence level that could be levied or attached for support;

(4) The noncustodial parent or alleged father is deceased and no further action, including a levy against the estate, can be taken;

(5) The noncustodial parent is living with the minor child (as the primary caregiver or in an intact two parent household), and the IV–D agency has determined that services are not appropriate or are no longer appropriate;

(6) Paternity cannot be established because:

(i) The child is at least 18 years old and an action to establish paternity is barred by a statute of limitations that meets the requirements of § 302.70(a)(5) of this chapter;

(ii) A genetic test or a court or an administrative process has excluded the alleged father and no other alleged father can be identified;

(iii) In accordance with § 303.5(b), the IV–D agency has determined that it would not be in the best interests of the child to establish paternity in a case involving incest or rape, or in any case where legal proceedings for adoption are pending; or

(iv) The identity of the biological father is unknown and cannot be identified after diligent efforts, including at least one interview by the IV–D agency with the recipient of services;

(7) The noncustodial parent's location is unknown, and the State has made diligent efforts using multiple sources, in accordance with § 303.3, all of which have been unsuccessful, to locate the noncustodial parent:

(i) Over a 2-year period when there is sufficient information to initiate an automated locate effort; or

(ii) Over a 6-month period when there is not sufficient information to initiate an automated locate effort; or

(iii) After a 1-year period when there is sufficient information to initiate an automated locate effort, but locate interfaces are unable to verify a Social Security Number;

(8) The IV–D agency has determined that throughout the duration of the child's minority (or after the child has reached the age of majority), the noncustodial parent cannot pay support and shows no evidence of support potential because the parent has been institutionalized in a psychiatric facility, is incarcerated, or has a medically-verified total and permanent disability. The State must also determine that the noncustodial parent has no income or assets available above the subsistence level that could be levied or attached for support;

(9) The noncustodial parent's sole income is from:

(i) Supplemental Security Income (SSI) payments made in accordance with sections 1601 *et seq.*, of title XVI of the Act, 42 U.S.C. 1381 *et seq.*; or

(ii) Both SSI payments and Social Security Disability Insurance (SSDI) benefits under title II of the Act.

(10) The noncustodial parent is a citizen of, and lives in, a foreign country, does not work for the Federal government or a company with headquarters or offices in the United States, and has no reachable domestic income or assets; and there is no Federal or State treaty or reciprocity with the country;

(11) The IV–D agency has provided location-only services as requested under § 302.35(c)(3) of this chapter;

(12) The non-IV–A recipient of services requests closure of a case and there is no assignment to the State of medical support under 42 CFR 433.146 or of arrearages which accrued under a support order;

(13) The IV–D agency has completed a limited service under § 302.33(a)(6) of this chapter;

(14) There has been a finding by the IV–D agency, or at the option of the State, by the responsible State agency of good cause or other exceptions to cooperation with the IV–D agency and the State or local assistance program, such as IV–A, IV–E, Supplemental Nutrition Assistance Program (SNAP), and Medicaid, has determined that support enforcement may not proceed without risk of harm to the child or caretaker relative;

(15) In a non-IV–A case receiving services under § 302.33(a)(1)(i) or (iii) of this chapter, or under § 302.33(a)(1)(ii) when cooperation with the IV–D agency is not required of the recipient of services, the IV–D agency is unable to contact the recipient of services despite a good faith effort to contact the recipient through at least two different methods;

(16) In a non-IV–A case receiving services under § 302.33(a)(1)(i) or (iii) of this chapter, or under § 302.33(a)(1)(ii) when cooperation with the IV–D agency is not required of the recipient of services, the IV–D agency documents the circumstances of the recipient's noncooperation and an action by the recipient of services is essential for the next step in providing IV–D services;

(17) The responding agency documents failure by the initiating agency to take an action that is essential for the next step in providing services;

(18) The initiating agency has notified the responding State that the initiating State has closed its case under § 303.7(c)(11);

(19) The initiating agency has notified the responding State that its intergovernmental services are no longer needed;

(20) Another assistance program, including IV–A, IV–E, SNAP, and Medicaid, has referred a case to the IV–D agency that is inappropriate to establish, enforce, or continue to enforce a child support order and the custodial

or noncustodial parent has not applied for services; or

(21) The IV–D case, including a case with arrears assigned to the State, has been transferred to a Tribal IV–D agency and the State IV–D agency has complied with the following procedures:

(i) Before transferring the State IV–D case to a Tribal IV–D agency and closing the IV–D case with the State:

(A) The recipient of services requested the State to transfer the case to the Tribal IV–D agency and close the case with the State; or

(B) The State IV–D agency notified the recipient of services of its intent to transfer the case to the Tribal IV–D agency and close the case with the State and the recipient did not respond to the notice to transfer the case within 60 calendar days from the date notice was provided;

(ii) The State IV–D agency completely and fully transferred and closed the case; and

(iii) The State IV–D agency notified the recipient of services that the case has been transferred to the Tribal IV–D agency and closed; or

(iv) The Tribal IV–D agency has a State-Tribal agreement approved by OCSE to transfer and close cases. The State-Tribal agreement must include a provision for obtaining the consent from the recipient of services to transfer and close the case.

(c) The IV–D agency must close a case and maintain supporting documentation for the case closure decision when the following criteria have been met:

(1) The child is eligible for health care services from the Indian Health Service (IHS); and

(2) The IV–D case was opened because of a Medicaid referral based solely upon health care services, including the Purchased/Referred Care program, provided through an Indian Health Program (as defined at 25 U.S.C. 1603(12)).

(d) The IV–D agency must have the following requirements for case closure notification and case reopening:

(1) In cases meeting the criteria in paragraphs (b)(1) through (10) and (b)(15) and (16) of this section, the State must notify the recipient of services in writing 60 calendar days prior to closure of the case of the State's intent to close the case.

(2) In an intergovernmental case meeting the criteria for closure under paragraph (b)(17) of this section, the responding State must notify the initiating agency, in a record, 60 calendar days prior to closure of the case of the State's intent to close the case.

(3) The case must be kept open if the recipient of services or the initiating agency supplies information in response to the notice provided under paragraph (d)(1) or (2) of this section that could lead to the establishment of paternity or a support order or enforcement of an order, or, in the instance of paragraph (b)(15) of this section, if contact is reestablished with the recipient of services.

(4) For cases to be closed in accordance with paragraph (b)(13) of this section, the State must notify the recipient of services, in writing, 60 calendar days prior to closure of the case of the State's intent to close the case. This notice must also provide information regarding reapplying for child support services and the consequences of receiving services, including any State fees, cost recovery, and distribution policies. If the recipient reapplies for child support services in a case that was closed in accordance with paragraph (b)(13) of this section, the recipient must complete a new application for IV–D services and pay any applicable fee.

(5) If the case is closed, the former recipient of services may request at a later date that the case be reopened if there is a change in circumstances that could lead to the establishment of paternity or a support order or enforcement of an order by completing a new application for IV–D services and paying any applicable fee.

(6) For notices under paragraphs (d)(1) and (4) of this section, if the recipient of services specifically authorizes consent for electronic notifications, the IV–D agency may elect to notify the recipient of services electronically of the State's intent to close the case. The IV–D agency must maintain documentation of the recipient's consent in the case record.

(e) The IV–D agency must retain all records for cases closed in accordance with this section for a minimum of 3 years, in accordance with 45 CFR 75.361.

[81 FR 93564, Dec. 20, 2016]

§ 303.15 Agreements to use the Federal Parent Locator Service (PLS) in parental kidnapping and child custody or visitation cases.

(a) *Definitions.* The following definitions apply to this section:

(1) *Authorized person* means the following:

(i) Any agent or attorney of any State having an agreement under this section, who has the duty or authority under the laws of the State to enforce a child custody or visitation determination;

(ii) Any court having jurisdiction to make or enforce a child custody or visitation determination, or any agent of the court; or

(iii) Any agent or attorney of the United States, or of a State having an agreement under this section, who has the duty or authority to investigate, enforce, or bring a prosecution with respect to the unlawful taking or restraint of a child.

(2) *Custody or visitation determination* means a judgment, decree, or other order of a court providing for custody or visitation of a child, and includes permanent and temporary orders, and initial orders and modifications.

(b) A State shall enter into an agreement with the Office that meets the requirements of section 463 of the Act and this section of the regulations so that the State IV-D agency may request information from the Federal PLS for the purpose of:

(1) Enforcing any State or Federal law with respect to the unlawful taking or restraint of a child; or

(2) Making or enforcing a child custody or visitation determination.

(c) An agreement under section 463 of the Act must contain the following provisions:

(1) The Director will provide the State IV-D agency with the most recent home address and place of employment of a parent or child if the information is requested for the purposes specified in paragraph (b) of this section.

(2) The State shall make requests for information under the agreement only for the purposes specified in paragraph (b) of this section.

(3) The State shall make requests to the Federal PLS through the State PLS established under § 302.35 of this chapter.

(4) The State shall submit requests in the standard format and exchange media normally available to or used by the State PLS.

(5) The State shall identify requests in a manner prescribed by the Office in instructions so that requests can be distinguished from other types of requests submitted to the Federal PLS.

(6) The State shall impose, collect and account for fees to offset the costs to the State and the Office incurred in processing requests.

(7) The State shall periodically transmit the fees collected to cover the costs to the Federal PLS of processing requests. Fees shall be transmitted in the amount and in the manner prescribed by the Office in instructions.

(8) The State shall adopt policies and procedures to ensure that information shall be used and disclosed solely for the purposes specified in paragraph (b) of this section. Under this requirement, the State shall:

(i) Restrict access to the information to authorized persons whose duties or responsibilities require access in connection with child custody and parental kidnapping cases;

(ii) Store the information during nonduty hours, or when not in use, in a locked container within a secure area that is safe from access by unauthorized persons;

(iii) Process the information under the immediate supervision and control of authorized personnel, in a manner which will protect the confidentiality of the information, and in such a way that unauthorized persons cannot retrieve the information by computer, remote terminal, or other means;

(iv) Brief all employees who will have access to the data on security procedures and instructions;

(v) Send the information directly to the requestor and make no other use of the information;

(vi) After the information is sent to the requestor, destroy any confidential records and information related to the request.

(d)(1) An agreement under section 463 of the Act must be signed by the Governor of the State or the Governor's designee.

(2) The agreement must also be signed by the Attorney General of the State who must certify that the signing State official has the authority under State law to commit the State to the agreement.

[46 FR 54557, Nov. 3, 1981, as amended at 64 FR 6250, Feb. 9, 1999; 68 FR 25304, May 12, 2003]

§ 303.20 Minimum organizational and staffing requirements.

(a) The organizational structure of the IV-D agency (see § 302.12) provides for administration or supervision of all the functions for which it is responsible under the State plan, is appropriate to the size and scope of the program in the State, and contains clearly established lines for administrative and supervisory authority.

(b) There is an organizational structure and sufficient staff to fulfill the following required State level functions:

(1) The establishment and administration of the State plan.

(2) Formal evaluation of the quality, efficiency, effectiveness, and scope of services provided under the plan.

(3) Coordination of activities pursuant to, and assurance of compliance with, the requirements of the State's Uniform Interstate Family Support Act for cases pursuant to a State plan.

(4) Requests to the DHHS Office of Child Support Enforcement for use of the Federal Parent Locator Service, the U.S. District Courts, and Secretary of the U.S. Treasury collection procedures.

(5) Preparation and submission of reports required by the Office.

(6) Financial control of the operation of the plan.

(7) Operation of the State PLS as required under §§ 302.35, 303.3, and 303.70 of this chapter.

(c) There is an organizational structure and sufficient resources at the State and local level to meet the performance and time standards contained in this part and to provide for the administration or supervision of the following support enforcement functions:

(1) *Intake.* Activities associated with initial support case opening.

(2) *Establishing the legal obligation to support.* Activities related to determining the noncustodial parent's legal obligation to support his or her dependent children, including paternity determination when necessary.

(3) *Locate.* Activities associated with locating a noncustodial parent.

(4) *Financial assessment.* Activities related to determining a noncustodial parent's ability to provide support.

(5) *Establishment of the amount of support.* Activities related to determining a noncustodial parent's child support obligation, including methods and terms of payment.

(6) *Collection.* Activities related to monitoring payment activities and processing cash flow.

(7) *Enforcement.* Activities to enforce collection of support, including income withholding and other available enforcement techniques.

(8) *Investigation.* Activities related to investigation necessary to accomplish the functions of this paragraph.

(d) The functions referred to in paragraphs (b) (1), (2) and (6) of this section may not be delegated by the IV-D agency. The functions referred to in paragraph (b)(5) of this section may be delegated to the extent necessary to report on activities delegated by the IV-D agency.

(e) No functions under the State plan may be delegated by the IV-D agency if such functions are to be performed by caseworkers who are also performing the assistance payments or social services functions under title IV-A or XX of the Act.

In the case of a sparsely populated geographic area, upon justification by the IV-D agency documenting a lack of administrative feasibility in not utilizing staff of the IV-A agency, the Office may approve alternate arrangements that include sufficient reporting and cost allocation methods that will assure compliance with Federal requirements and proper claims for Federal financial participation. Under this provision:

(1) *Caseworker* means any person who has decision-making authority over individual cases on a day-to-day basis and includes, but is not limited to such

designations as intake worker, eligibility technician, caseworker, and social worker.

(2) The *assistance payments function* means activities related to determination of eligibility for, and amount of financial assistance under the approved State plan under title I, IV-A, X, XIV, or XVI, State Supplemental income payments under title XVI of the Act, and State or local General Assistance programs. It includes the complete process of determining initial and continuing eligibility for financial and medical assistance and commodities distribution or food stamps.

(3) The *social services function* means those activities included in the approved State plan and carried out pursuant to title XX of the Act. It includes determination of eligibility for, and delivery of services to, families and individuals under the approved State plan or under title XX of the Act.

(f) There are the following types of staff in sufficient numbers to achieve the standards for an effective program prescribed in this part:

(1) Attorneys or prosecutors to represent the agency in court or administrative proceedings with respect to the establishment and enforcement of orders of paternity and support, and

(2) Other personnel such as legal, interviewer, investigative, accounting, clerical, and other supportive staff.

(g) If it is determined as a result of an audit conducted under part 305 of this chapter that a State is not in substantial compliance with the requirements of title IV-D of the Act, the Secretary will evaluate whether inadequate resources was a major contributing factor and, if necessary, may set resource standards for the State.

[40 FR 27164, June 26, 1975, as amended at 47 FR 57282, Dec. 23, 1982; 54 FR 32312, Aug. 4, 1989; 64 FR 6250, Feb. 9, 1999; 68 FR 25304, May 12, 2003; 73 FR 56443, Sept. 26, 2008; 75 FR 81907, Dec. 29, 2010]

§303.21 Safeguarding and disclosure of confidential information.

(a) *Definitions*—(1) *Confidential information* means any information relating to a specified individual or an individual who can be identified by reference to one or more factors specific to him or her, including but not limited to the individual's Social Security number, residential and mailing addresses, employment information, and financial information.

(2) *Independent verification* is the process of acquiring and confirming confidential information through the use of a second source. The information from the second source, which verifies the information about NDNH or FCR data, may be released to those authorized to inspect and use the information as authorized under the regulations or the Act.

(b) *Scope*. The requirements of this section apply to the IV–D agency, any other State or local agency or official to whom the IV–D agency delegates any of the functions of the IV–D program, any official with whom a cooperative agreement as described in §302.34 of this part has been entered into, and any person or private agency from whom the IV–D agency has purchased services pursuant to §304.22 of this chapter.

(c) *General rule*. Except as authorized by the Act and implementing regulations, an entity described in paragraph (b) of this section may not disclose any confidential information, obtained in connection with the performance of IV–D functions, outside the administration of the IV–D program.

(d) *Authorized disclosures*. (1) Upon request, the IV–D agency may, to the extent that it does not interfere with the IV–D agency meeting its own obligations and subject to such requirements as the Office may prescribe, disclose confidential information to State agencies as necessary to assist them to carry out their responsibilities under plans and programs funded under titles IV (including Tribal programs under title IV), XIX, or XXI of the Act, and the Supplemental Nutrition Assistance Program (SNAP), including:

(i) Any investigation, prosecution or criminal or civil proceeding conducted in connection with the administration of any such plan or program; and

(ii) Information on known or suspected instances of physical or mental injury, sexual abuse or exploitation, or negligent treatment or maltreatment of a child under circumstances which indicate that the child's health or welfare is threatened.

(2) Upon request, the IV–D agency may disclose information in the SDNH, pursuant to sections 453A and 1137 of the Act for purposes of income and eligibility verification.

(3) Authorized disclosures under paragraph (d)(1) and (2) of this section shall not include confidential information from the National Directory of New Hires or the Federal Case Registry, unless authorized under § 307.13 of this Chapter or unless it is independently verified information. No financial institution data match information may be disclosed outside the administration of the IV–D program and no IRS information may be disclosed, unless independently verified or otherwise authorized in Federal statute. States must have safeguards in place as specified in section 454A(d) and (f) of the Act.

(e) *Safeguards.* In addition to, and not in lieu of, the safeguards described in § 307.13 of this chapter, which governs computerized support enforcement systems, the IV–D agency shall establish appropriate safeguards to comply with the provisions of this section. These safeguards shall also include prohibitions against the release of information when the State has reasonable evidence of domestic violence or child abuse against a party or a child and that the disclosure of such information could be harmful to the party or the child, as required by section 454(26) of the Act, and shall include use of the family violence indicator required under § 307.11(f)(1)(x) of this chapter.

(f) Penalties for unauthorized disclosure. Any disclosure or use of confidential information in violation of 42 U.S.C. 653(l)(2) and implementing regulations shall be subject to:

(1) Any State and Federal statutes that impose legal sanctions for such disclosure; and

(2) The maximum civil monetary penalties associated with the statutory provisions authorizing civil monetary penalties under 42 U.S.C. 653(l)(2) as shown in the table at 45 CFR 102.3.

[73 FR 56444, Sept. 26, 2008, as amended at 75 FR 81907, Dec. 29, 2010; 81 FR 61582, Sept. 6, 2016]

§ 303.30 Securing medical support information.

(a) If the IV-A or IV-E agency does not provide the information specified in this paragraph to the Medicaid agency and if the information is available or can be obtained in a IV-D case for which an assignment as defined under § 301.1 of this chapter is in effect, the IV-D agency shall obtain the following information on the case:

(1) Title IV-A case number, title IV-E foster care case number, Medicaid number or the individual's social security number;

(2) Name of noncustodial parent;

(3) Social security number of noncustodial parent;

(4) Name and social security number of child(ren);

(5) Home address of noncustodial parent;

(6) Name and address of noncustodial parent's place of employment;

(7) Whether the noncustodial parent has a health insurance policy and, if so, the policy name(s) and number(s) and name(s) of person(s) covered.

(b) The IV-D agency shall provide the information obtained under paragraph (a) of this section to the Medicaid agency in a timely manner by the most efficient and cost-effective means available, using manual or automated systems.

(Approved by the Office of Management and Budget under control numbers 0960–0420 and 0970–0107)

[50 FR 41895, Oct. 15, 1985, as amended at 51 FR 37732, Oct. 24, 1986. Redesignated at 54 FR 32312, Aug. 4, 1989; 56 FR 8004, Feb. 26, 1991; 64 FR 6250, Feb. 9, 1999]

§ 303.31 Securing and enforcing medical support obligations.

(a) For purposes of this section:

(1) Cash medical support means an amount ordered to be paid toward the cost of health insurance provided by a public entity or by another parent through employment or otherwise, or for other medical costs not covered by insurance.

(2) Health care coverage includes fee for service, health maintenance organization, preferred provider organization, and other types of private health insurance and public health care coverage

under which medical services could be provided to the dependent child(ren).

(3) Cash medical support or the cost of health insurance is considered reasonable in cost if the cost to the parent responsible for providing medical support does not exceed five percent of his or her gross income or, at State option, a reasonable alternative income-based numeric standard defined in State law, regulations, or court rule having the force of law or State child support guidelines adopted in accordance with § 302.56(c) of this chapter.

(b) The State IV–D agency must:

(1) Petition the court or administrative authority to—

(i) Include health care coverage that is accessible to the child(ren), as defined by the State, and is available to the parent responsible for providing medical support and can be obtained for the child at reasonable cost, as defined under paragraph (a)(3) of this section, in new or modified court or administrative orders for support; and

(ii) Allocate the cost of coverage between the parents.

(2) If health care coverage described in paragraph (b)(1) of this section is not available at the time the order is entered or modified, petition to include cash medical support in new or modified orders until such time as health care coverage, that is accessible and reasonable in cost as defined under paragraph (a)(3) of this section, becomes available. In appropriate cases, as defined by the State, cash medical support may be sought in addition to health care coverage.

(3) Establish criteria, which are reflected in a record, to identify orders that do not address the health care needs of children based on—

(i) Evidence that health care coverage may be available to either parent at reasonable cost, as defined under paragraph (a)(3) of this section; and

(ii) Facts, as defined by State law, regulation, procedure, or other directive, and review and adjustment requirements under § 303.8(d) of this part, which are sufficient to warrant modification of the existing support order to address the health care needs of children in accordance with paragraph (b)(1) of this section.

(4) Petition the court or administrative authority to modify support orders, in accordance with State child support guidelines, for cases identified in paragraph (b)(3) of this section to include health care coverage and/or cash medical support in accordance with paragraphs (b)(1) and (2) of this section.

(5) Periodically communicate with the Medicaid agency to determine whether there have been lapses in health insurance coverage for Medicaid applicants and recipients.

(c) The IV–D agency shall inform an individual who is eligible for services under § 302.33 of this chapter that medical support services will be provided and shall provide the services specified in paragraph (b) of this section.

[73 FR 42441, July 21, 2008, as amended at 81 FR 93566, Dec. 20, 2016]

§ 303.32 National Medical Support Notice.

(a) *Mandatory State laws.* States must have laws, in accordance with section 466(a)(19) of the Act, requiring procedures specified under paragraph (c) of this section for the use, where appropriate, of the National Medical Support Notice (NMSN), to enforce the provision of health care coverage for children of noncustodial parents and, at State option, custodial parents who are required to provide health care coverage through an employment-related group health plan pursuant to a child support order and for whom the employer is known to the State agency.

(b) *Exception.* States are not required to use the NMSN in cases with court or administrative orders that stipulate alternative health care coverage to employer-based coverage.

(c) *Mandatory procedures.* The State must have in effect and use procedures under which:

(1) The State agency must use the NMSN to transfer notice of the provision for health care coverage of the child(ren) to employers.

(2) The State agency must transfer the NMSN to the employer within two business days after the date of entry of an employee who is an obligor in a IV-D case in the State Directory of New Hires.

(3) Employers must transfer the NMSN to the appropriate group health

plan providing any such health care coverage for which the child(ren) is eligible (excluding the severable Notice to Withhold for Health Care Coverage directing the employer to withhold any mandatory employee contributions to the plan) within twenty business days after the date of the NMSN.

(4) Employers must withhold any obligation of the employee for employee contributions necessary for coverage of the child(ren) and send any amount withheld directly to the plan.

(5) Employees may contest the withholding based on a mistake of fact. If the employee contests such withholding, the employer must initiate withholding until such time as the employer receives notice that the contest is resolved.

(6) Employers must notify the State agency promptly whenever the noncustodial parent's and, at State option, custodial parent's employment is terminated in the same manner as required for income withholding cases in accordance with § 303.100(e)(1)(x) of this part.

(7) The State agency must promptly notify the employer when there is no longer a current order for medical support in effect for which the IV-D agency is responsible.

(8) The State agency, in consultation with the custodial parent, must promptly select from available plan options when the plan administrator reports that there is more than one option available under the plan.

(d) *Effective date.* This section is effective October 1, 2001, or, if later, the effective date of State laws described in paragraph (a) of this section. Such State laws must be effective no later than the close of the first day of the first calendar quarter that begins after the close of the first regular session of the State legislature that begins after October 1, 2001. For States with 2-year legislative sessions, each year of such session would be regarded as a separate regular session.

[65 FR 82165, Dec. 27, 2000, as amended at 73 FR 42442, July 21, 2008]

§ 303.35 Administrative complaint procedure.

(a) Each State must have in place an administrative complaint procedure, defined by the State, in place to allow individuals the opportunity to request an administrative review, and take appropriate action when there is evidence that an error has occurred or an action should have been taken on their case. This includes both individuals in the State and individuals from other States.

(b) A State need not establish a formal hearing process but must have clear procedures in place. The State must notify individuals of the procedures, make them available for recipients of IV-D services to use when requesting such a review, and use them for notifying recipients of the results of the review and any actions taken.

[65 FR 82208, Dec. 27, 2000]

§ 303.52 Pass-through of incentives to political subdivisions.

The State must calculate and promptly pay incentives to political subdivisions as follows:

(a) The State IV-D agency must develop a standard methodology for passing through an appropriate share of its incentive payment to those political subdivisions of the State that participate in the costs of the program, taking into account the efficiency and effectiveness of the activities carried out under the State plan by those political subdivisions. In order to reward efficiency and effectiveness, the methodology also may provide for payment of incentives to other political subdivisions of the State that administer the program.

(b) To ensure that the standard methodology developed by the State reflects local participation, the State IV-D agency must submit a draft methodology to participating political subdivisions for review and comment or use the rulemaking process available under State law to receive local input.

[54 FR 32312, Aug. 4, 1989]

§ 303.69 Requests by agents or attorneys of the United States for information from the Federal Parent Locator Service (PLS).

(a) Agents or attorneys of the United States may request information directly from the Federal PLS in connection with a parental kidnapping or child custody case. (See § 303.15(a) of this part for a definition of persons authorized to request the information.)

(b) All requests under this section shall be made in the manner and form prescribed by the Office.

(c) All requests under this section shall contain the information specified in § 303.70(d) of this part.

(d) All requests under this section shall be accompanied by a statement, signed by the agent or attorney of the United States, attesting to the following:

(1) The request is being made solely to locate an individual in connection with a parental kidnapping or child custody case.

(2) Any information obtained through the Federal PLS shall be treated as confidential, shall be used solely for the purpose for which it was obtained and shall be safeguarded.

(e) A fee may be charged to cover the costs of processing requests for information. A separate fee may be charged to cover costs of searching for a social security number before processing a request for location information.

(Approved by the Office of Management and Budget under control number 0960–0258)

[48 FR 38645, Aug. 25, 1983, as amended at 51 FR 37731, Oct. 24, 1986; 75 FR 81907, Dec. 29, 2010]

§ 303.70 Procedures for submissions to the State Parent Locator Service (State PLS) or the Federal Parent Locator Service (Federal PLS).

(a) The State agency will have procedures for submissions to the State PLS or the Federal PLS for the purpose of locating parents, putative fathers, or children for the purpose of establishing parentage or establishing, setting the amount of, modifying, or enforcing child support obligations; for the purpose of enforcing any Federal or State law with respect to the unlawful taking or restraint of a child or making or enforcing a child custody or visitation determination as defined in section 463(d)(1) of the Act, or for the purpose of assisting State agencies to carry out their responsibilities under title IV–D, IV–A, IV–B, and IV–E programs.

(b) Only the central State PLS may make submittals to the Federal PLS for the purposes specified in paragraph (a) of this section.

(c) All submittals shall be made in the manner and form prescribed by the Office.

(d) All submittals shall contain the following information:

(1) The parent's, putative father's or non-parent relative's name;

(2) The parent's or putative father's Social Security Number (SSN). If the SSN is unknown, the IV–D program must make reasonable efforts to ascertain the individual's SSN before making a submittal to the Federal PLS; and

(3) The non-parent relative's SSN, if known.

(4) Any other information prescribed by the Office.

(e) The director of the IV–D agency or his or her designee shall attest annually to the following:

(1)(i) The IV–D agency will only obtain information to facilitate the location of any individual in accordance with section 453(a)(2) of the Act for the purpose of establishing parentage, establishing, setting the amount of, modifying, or enforcing child support obligations, or for determining who has or may have parental rights with respect to a child, or in accordance with section 453(a)(3) of the Act for enforcing a State law with respect to the unlawful taking or restraint of a child, or for making or enforcing a child custody or visitation determination as defined in section 463(d)(1) of the Act, or in accordance with section 453(j)(3) of the Act for the purpose of assisting State agencies to carry out their responsibilities under title IV–D, IV–A, IV–B, and IV–E programs.

(ii) The IV–D agency will only provide information to the authorized persons specified in sections 453(c) or 463(d) of the Act and § 302.35 of this chapter.

(2) In the case of a submittal made on behalf of a resident parent, legal guardian, attorney or agent of a child not receiving assistance under title IV–A, the IV–D agency must verify that the requesting individual has complied with the provisions of § 302.35 of this chapter.

(3) The IV–D agency will treat any information obtained through the Federal PLS and SPLS as confidential and shall safeguard the information under

the requirements of sections 453(b), 453(l), 454(8), 454(26), and 463(c) of the Act, § 303.21 of this part and instructions issued by the Office.

(f)(1) The IV–D agency shall reimburse the Secretary for the fees required under:

(i) Section 453(e)(2) of the Act whenever Federal PLS services are furnished to a resident parent, legal guardian, attorney or agent of a child not receiving assistance under title IV–A of the Act;

(ii) Section 454(17) of the Act whenever Federal PLS services are furnished in parental kidnapping and child custody or visitation determination;

(iii) Section 453(k)(3) of the Act whenever a State agency receives information from the Federal PLS pursuant to section 453 of the Act.

(2)(i) The IV–D agency may charge an individual requesting information, or pay without charging the individual, the fees required under sections 453(e)(2), 453(k)(3) or 454(17) of the Act except that the IV–D agency shall charge an individual specified in section 453(c)(3) of the Act the fee required under section 453(e)(2) of the Act

(ii) The IV–D agency may recover the fee required under section 453(e)(2) of the Act from the noncustodial parent who owes a support obligation to a family on whose behalf the IV–D agency is providing services and repay it to the individual requesting information or itself.

(iii) State funds used to pay the fee under section 453(e)(2) of the Act are not program expenditures under the State plan but are program income under § 304.50 of this chapter.

(3) The fees referenced in paragraph (f)(1) of this section shall be in an amount determined to be reasonable payment for the information exchange.

(4)(i) If a State fails to transmit the fees charged by the Office under this section, the services provided by the Federal PLS in cases subject to the fees may be suspended until payment is received.

(ii) Fees shall be transmitted in the amount and manner prescribed by the Office in instructions.

[73 FR 56445, Sept. 26, 2008, as amended at 75 FR 81907, Dec. 29, 2010]

§ 303.71 Requests for full collection services by the Secretary of the Treasury.

(a) *Definition. State collection mechanisms* means a comprehensive set of written procedures developed and used to maximize effective collection action within the State.

(b) *Families eligible.* Subject to the criteria and procedures in this section, the IV-D agency may request the Secretary to certify the amount of a child support obligation to the Secretary of the Treasury for collection under section 6305 of the Internal Revenue Code of 1986. Requests may be made on behalf of families who make assignments as defined in § 301.1 of this chapter and on behalf of families receiving services under § 302.33.

(c) *Cases eligible.* For a case to be eligible for certification to the Secretary of the Treasury:

(1) There shall be a court or administrative order for support;

(2) The amount to be collected under the support order shall be at least $750 in arrears;

(3) At least six months shall have elapsed since the last request for referral of the case to the Secretary of the Treasury;

(4) The IV-D agency, the client, or the client's representative shall have made reasonable efforts to collect the support through the State's own collection mechanisms. The agency need not repeat actions taken by the client or client's representative that the agency determines to be comparable to the State's collection mechanisms.

(5) Only the State that has taken an assignment as defined in § 301.1 of this chapter or an application or referral under § 302.33 of this chapter may request Secretary of the U.S. Treasury collection services on behalf of a given case.

(d) *Procedures for submitting requests.* (1) The IV-D agency shall submit requests for certification to the regional office in the manner and form prescribed by the Office.

(2) The Director of the State IV-D agency (or designee) shall sign requests for collection by the Secretary of the Treasury.

(e) *Criteria for acceptable requests.* The IV-D agency shall ensure that each request contains:

(1) Sufficient information to identify the debtor, including:

(i) The individual's name;

(ii) The individual's social security number;

(iii) The individual's address and place of employment, including the source of this information and the date it was last verified.

(2) A copy of all court or administrative orders for support;

(3)(i) The amount owed under the support orders;

(ii) A statement of whether the amount is in lieu of, or in addition to, amounts previously referred to Secretary of the U.S. Treasury for collection;

(4)(i) A statement that the agency, the client, or the client's representative has made reasonable efforts to collect the amount owed using the State's own collection mechanisms or mechanisms that are comparable;

(ii) A description of the actions taken, why they failed, and why further State action would be unproductive;

(5) The dates of any previous requests for referral of the case to the Secretary of the Treasury;

(6) A statement that the agency agrees to reimburse the Secretary of the Treasury for the costs of collection; and

(7)(i) A statement that the agency has reason to believe that the debtor has assets that the Secretary of the Treasury might levy to collect the support; and

(ii) A statement of the nature and location of the assets, if known.

(f) *Review of requests by the Office.* (1) The Regional Office will review each request to determine whether it meets the requirements of this section.

(2) If a request meets all requirements, the Regional Office will promptly certify and transmit the request with a copy of all supporting documentation to the Secretary of the Treasury. At the same time, the Regional Office will notify the IV-D agency in writing of the transmittal.

(3)(i) If a request does not meet all requirements, the Regional Office will attempt to correct the request in consultation with the IV-D agency.

(ii) If the request cannot be corrected through consultation, the Regional Office will return it to the agency with an explanation of why the request was not certified.

(g) *Notification of changes in case status.* (1) The IV-D agency shall immediately notify the Regional Office of the following changes in case status:

(i) A change in the amount due;

(ii) A change in the nature or location of assets;

(iii) A change in the address of the debtor.

(2) The Regional Office will transmit the revised information to the Secretary of the Treasury.

(Approved by the Office of Management and Budget under control number 0960–0281)

[47 FR 16030, Apr. 14, 1982; 48 FR 7179, Feb. 18, 1983, as amended at 51 FR 37731, Oct. 24, 1986; 56 FR 8004, Feb. 26, 1991; 64 FR 6251, Feb. 9, 1999]

§ 303.72 Requests for collection of past-due support by Federal tax refund offset.

(a) *Past-due support qualifying for offset.* Past-due support as defined in § 301.1 of this chapter qualifies for offset if:

(1) There has been an assignment of the support rights under section 408(a)(3) of the Act or section 471(a)(17) of the Act to the State making the request for offset or the IV-D agency is providing services under § 302.33 of this chapter.

(2) For support that has been assigned to the State under section 408(a)(3) of the Act or section 471(a)(17) of the Act, the amount of the support is not less than $150. The State may combine assigned support amounts from the same obligor in multiple cases to reach $150. Amounts under this paragraph may not be combined with amounts under paragraph (a)(3) of this section to reach the minimum amounts required under this paragraph or under paragraph (a)(3) of this section.

(3) For support owed in cases where the title IV–D agency is providing title IV–D services under § 302.33 of this chapter:

(i) The support is owed to or on behalf of a child, or a child and the parent with whom the child is living if the same support order includes support for the child and the parent.

(ii) The amount of support is not less than $500. The State may combine support amounts from the same obligor in multiple cases where the IV-D agency is providing IV-D services under § 302.33 of this chapter to reach $500. Amounts under this paragraph may not be combined with amounts under paragraph (a)(2) of this section to reach the minimum amounts required under this paragraph or under paragraph (a)(2) of this section.

(iii) At State option, the amount has accrued since the State IV-D agency began to enforce the support order; and

(iv) The State has checked its records to determine if a title IV-A or foster care maintenance assigned arrearage exists with respect to the non-IV-A individual or family.

(4) The IV-D agency has in its records:

(i) A copy of the order and any modifications upon which the amount referred is based which specify the date of issuance and amount of support;

(ii) A copy of the payment record, or, if there is no payment record, an affidavit signed by the custodial parent attesting to the amount of support owed; and

(iii) In non-IV-A cases, the custodial parent's current address.

(5) Before submittal, the State IV-D agency has verified the accuracy of the name and social security number of the noncustodial parent and the accuracy of the past-due support amount. If the State IV-D agency has verified this information previously, it need not reverify it.

(6) A notification of liability for past-due support has been received by the Secretary of the U.S. Treasury as prescribed by paragraph (c)(2) of this section.

(b) *Notification to OCSE of liability for past-due support.* (1) A State IV-D agency shall submit a notification (or notifications) of liability for past-due support to the Office according to the timeframes and in the manner specified by the Office in instructions.

(2) To the extent specified by the Office in instructions, the notification of liability for past-due support shall contain with respect to each delinquency:

(i) The name of the taxpayer who owes the past-due support;

(ii) The social security number of that taxpayer;

(iii) The amount of past-due support owed;

(iv) The State codes as contained in the Federal Information Processing Standards (FIPS) publication of the National Bureau of Standards and also promulgated by the General Services Administration in Worldwide Geographical Location Codes; and

(v) Whether the past-due support is due an individual who applied for services under § 302.33 of this chapter.

(3) The notification of liability for past-due support may contain with respect to each delinquency the taxpayer's IV-D identifier.

(c) *Review of requests by the Office.* (1) The Deputy Director will review each request to determine whether it meets the requirements of this section.

(2) If a request meets all requirements, the Deputy Director will transmit the request to the Secretary of the U.S. Treasury and will notify the State IV-D agency of the transmittal.

(3) If a request does not meet all requirements, the Deputy Director will attempt to correct the request in consultation with the State IV-D agency.

(4) If a request cannot be corrected through consultation, the Deputy Director will return it to the State IV-D agency with an explanation of why the request could not be transmitted to the Secretary of the U.S. Treasury.

(d) *Notification of changes in case status.* (1) The State referring past-due support for offset must, in interstate situations, notify any other State involved in enforcing the support order when it receives the offset amount from the Secretary of the U.S. Treasury.

(2) The State IV-D agency shall, within timeframes established by the Office in instructions, notify the Deputy Director of any deletion of, or any change in, the arrears balance, if the change is significant according to the guidelines developed by the State. The

notification shall contain the information specified in paragraph (b) of this section.

(e) *Notices of offset*—(1) *Advance.* The State IV-D agency, or the Office, if the State requests and the Office agrees, shall send a written advance notice to inform a noncustodial parent that the amount of his or her past-due support will be referred to the Secretary of the U.S. Treasury for collection by Federal tax refund offset. The notice must inform noncustodial parents:

(i) Of their right to contest the State's determination that past-due support is owed or the amount of past-due support;

(ii) Of their right to an administrative review by the submitting State or at the noncustodial parent's request the State with the order upon which the referral for offset is based;

(iii) Of the procedures and timeframe for contacting the IV-D agency in the submitting State to request administrative review; and

(iv) That, in the case of a joint return, the Secretary of the U.S. Treasury will notify the noncustodial parent's spouse at the time of offset regarding the steps to take to protect the share of the refund which may be payable to that spouse. If the IV-D agency sends the notice, it must meet the conditions specified by the Office in instructions.

(2) *At offset.* The Secretary of the U.S. Treasury will notify the noncustodial parent that the offset has been made. The Secretary of the U.S. Treasury will also notify any individual who filed a joint return with the noncustodial parent of the steps to take in order to secure a proper share of the refund.

(f) *Procedures for contesting in intrastate cases.* (1) Upon receipt of a complaint from a noncustodial parent in response to the advance notice required in paragraph (e)(1) of this section or concerning a tax refund which has already been offset, the IV-D agency must send a notice to the noncustodial parent and, in non-IV-A cases the custodial parent, of the time and place of the administrative review of the complaint and conduct the review to determine the validity of the complaint.

(2) If the complaint concerns a joint tax refund that has not yet been offset, the IV-D agency must inform the noncustodial parent that the Secretary of the U.S. Treasury will notify the noncustodial parent's spouse at the time of offset regarding the steps to take to secure his or her proper share of the refund. If the complaint concerns a joint tax refund which has already been offset, the IV-D agency must refer the noncustodial parent to the Secretary of the U.S. Treasury.

(3) If the administrative review results in a deletion of, or change in, the arrears balance, the IV-D agency must notify OCSE within timeframes established by the Office and include the information specified in paragraph (b) of this section.

(4) If, as a result of the administrative review, an amount which has already been offset is found to have exceeded the amount of past-due support owed, the IV-D agency must take steps to refund the excess amount to the noncustodial parent promptly.

(g) *Procedures for contesting in interstate cases.* (1) If the noncustodial parent requests an administrative review in the submitting State, the IV-D agency must meet the requirements in paragraph (f) of this section.

(2) If the complaint cannot be resolved by the submitting State and the noncustodial parent requests an administrative review in the State with the order upon which the referral for offset is based, the submitting State must notify the State with the order of the request for an administrative review and provide that State with all necessary information, including the information listed under paragraph (a)(4) of this section, within 10 days of the noncustodial parent's request for an administrative review.

(3) The State with the order must send a notice to the noncustodial parent and, in non-IV-A cases the custodial parent, of the time and place of the administrative review, conduct the review and make a decision within 45 days of receipt of the notice and information from the submitting State.

(4) If the administrative review results in a deletion of, or change in, the arrears balance, the State with the order upon which the referral for offset is based must notify the submitting State within timeframes established by

the Office and include the information specified in paragraph (b) of this section. The submitting State must then notify the Office within timeframes established by the Office and include the information specified in paragraph (b) of this section.

(5) Upon resolution of a complaint after an offset has been made, the State with the order must notify the submitting State of its decision promptly.

(6) When an administrative review is conducted in the State with the order, the submitting State is bound by the decision made by the State with the order.

(7) Based on the decision of the State with the order, the IV-D agency in the submitting State must take steps to refund any excess amount to the noncustodial parent promptly.

(8) In computing the arrearage collection performance level under § 305.2(a)(4) of this chapter, if the case is referred to the State with the order for an administrative review, the collections made as a result of Federal tax refund offset will be treated as having been collected in full by both the submitting State and the State with the order.

(h) *Distribution of collections.* (1) Collections received by the IV–D agency as a result of Federal tax refund offset to satisfy title IV–A or non-IV–A past-due support shall be distributed as required in accordance with section 457 and, effective October 1, 2009, or up to a year earlier at State option, in accordance with the option selected under section 454(34) of the Act.

(2) Collections received by the IV-D agency in foster care maintenance cases shall be distributed as past-due support under § 302.52(b) (3) and (4) of this chapter.

(3)(i) Except as provided in paragraph (h)(3)(ii), the IV–D agency must inform individuals receiving services under § 302.33 of this chapter in advance that amounts offset will be applied to satisfy any past-due support which has been assigned to the State and submitted for Federal tax refund offset.

(ii) Effective October 1, 2009, or up to a year earlier at State option, the IV–D agency need no longer meet the requirement for notice under paragraph (h)(3)(i) if the State has opted, under section 454(34) of the Act, to apply amounts submitted to Federal tax refund offset first to satisfy any current support due and past-due support owed to the family.

(4) If the amount collected is in excess of the amounts required to be distributed under section 457 of the Act, the IV-D agency must repay the excess to the noncustodial parent whose refund was offset or to the parties filing a joint return within a reasonable period in accordance with State law.

(5) In cases where the Secretary of the U.S. Treasury, through OCSE, notifies the State that an offset is being made to satisfy non-IV-A past-due support from a refund based on a joint return, the State may delay distribution until notified that the unobligated spouse's proper share of the refund has been paid or for a period not to exceed six months from notification of offset, whichever is earlier.

(6) Collections from offset may be applied only to cases that were being enforced by the IV-D agency at the time the advance notice described in paragraph (e)(1) of this section was sent.

(i) *Payment of fee.* (1) A refund offset fee, in such amount as the Secretary of the U.S. Treasury and the Secretary of Health and Human Services have agreed to be sufficient to reimburse the U.S. Department of Treasury for the full cost of the offset procedure, shall be deducted from the offset amount and credited to the U.S. Department of Treasury appropriations which bore all or part of the costs involved in making the collection. The full amount of the offset must be credited against the obligor's payment record. The fee which the Secretary of the U.S. Treasury may impose with respect to non-IV-A submittals shall not exceed $25 per submittal.

(2) The State IV-D agency may charge an individual who is receiving services under § 302.33(a)(1) (i) or (iii) of this chapter a fee not to exceed $25 for submitting past-due support for Federal tax refund offset. The State must inform the individual in advance of the amount of any fee charged.

(3) Any State which requests the Office to send the advance written notice under paragraph (e)(1) of this section

will be charged a fee, in an amount established by the Office in instructions, for printing and mailing of pre-offset notices. This fee shall be credited to the Health and Human Services appropriations which bore all or part of the costs involved in making the collection.

(j) Each State involved in a referral of past-due support for offset must comply with instructions issued by the Office.

(Approved by the Office of Management and Budget under control number 0960–0385)

[50 FR 19651, May 9, 1985; 50 FR 31719, Aug. 6, 1985, as amended at 51 FR 37731, Oct. 24, 1986; 53 FR 47710, Nov. 25, 1988; 54 FR 32312, Aug. 4, 1989; 56 FR 8005, Feb. 26, 1991; 58 FR 41437, Aug. 4, 1993; 64 FR 6251, Feb. 9, 1999; 68 FR 25304, May 12, 2003; 68 FR 37980, June 26, 2003; 68 FR 53052, Sept. 9, 2003; 69 FR 62415, Oct. 26, 2004; 73 FR 74920, Dec. 9, 2008; 81 FR 93566, Dec. 20, 2016]

§ 303.73 Applications to use the courts of the United States to enforce court orders.

The IV-D agency may apply to the Secretary for permission to use a United States district court to enforce a support order of a court of competent jurisdiction against a noncustodial parent who is present in another State if the IV-D agency can furnish evidence in accordance with instructions issued by the office.

[61 FR 67241, Dec. 20, 1996, as amended at 68 FR 25304, May 12, 2003]

§ 303.100 Procedures for income withholding.

(a) *General withholding requirements.* (1) The State must ensure that in the case of each noncustodial parent against whom a support order is or has been issued or modified in the State, and is being enforced under the State plan, so much of his or her income as defined in sections 466(b)(1) and (8) of the Act must be withheld, in accordance with this section, as is necessary to comply with the order.

(2) In addition to the amount to be withheld to pay the current month's obligation, the amount to be withheld must include an amount to be applied toward liquidation of overdue support.

(3) The total amount to be withheld under paragraphs (a)(1), (a)(2) and, if applicable, (f)(1)(iii) of this section may not exceed the maximum amount permitted under section 303(b) of the Consumer Credit Protection Act (15 U.S.C. 1673(b)).

(4) In the case of a support order being enforced under the State plan, the withholding must occur without the need for any amendment to the support order involved or any other action by the court or entity that issued it other than that required or permitted under this section.

(5) If there is more than one notice for withholding against a single noncustodial parent, the State must allocate amounts available for withholding giving priority to current support up to the limits imposed under section 303(b) of the Consumer Credit Protection Act (15 U.S.C. 1673(b)). The State must establish procedures for allocation of support among families, but in no case shall the allocation result in a withholding for one of the support obligations not being implemented.

(6) The withholding must be carried out in full compliance with all procedural due process requirements of the State.

(7) The State must have procedures for promptly terminating withholding:

(i) In all cases, when there is no longer a current order for support and all arrearages have been satisfied; or,

(ii) At State option, when the noncustodial parent requests termination and withholding has not been terminated previously and subsequently initiated, and the noncustodial parent meets the conditions for an alternative arrangement set forth under paragraph (b)(3) of this section.

(8) The State must have procedures for promptly refunding to noncustodial parents amounts which have been improperly withheld.

(9) Support orders issued or modified in IV-D cases must include a provision requiring the noncustodial parent to keep the IV-D agency informed of the name and address of his or her current employer, whether the noncustodial parent has access to health insurance coverage at reasonable cost and, if so, the health insurance policy information.

(b) *Immediate withholding on IV-D cases.* (1) In the case of a support order being enforced under this part that is issued or modified on or after November 1, 1990, the income of a noncustodial parent shall be subject to withholding, regardless of whether support payments by such parent are in arrears, on the effective date of the order, except that such income shall not be subject to withholding under this paragraph in any case where:

(i) Either the noncustodial or custodial parent demonstrates, and the court or administrative authority finds, that there is good cause not to require immediate withholding; or

(ii) A written agreement is reached between the absent and custodial parent, and, at State option, the State in IV-D cases in which there is an assignment of support rights to the State, which provides for an alternative arrangement.

(2) For the purposes of this paragraph, any finding that there is good cause not to require immediate withholding must be based on at least:

(i) A written determination that, and explanation by the court or administrative authority of why, implementing immediate income withholding would not be in the best interests of the child; and

(ii) Proof of timely payment of previously ordered support in cases involving the modification of support orders.

(3) For purposes of this paragraph, "written agreement" means a written alternative arrangement signed by both the custodial and noncustodial parent, and, at State option, by the State in IV-D cases in which there is an assignment of support rights to the State, and reviewed and entered in the record by the court or administrative authority.

(c) *Initiated withholding in IV-D cases.* In the case of income not subject to immediate withholding under paragraph (b) of this section, including cases subject to a finding of good cause or to a written agreement:

(1) The income of the noncustodial parent shall become subject to the withholding on the date on which the payments which the noncustodial parent has failed to make under a support order are at least equal to the support payable for one month or, if earlier, and without regard to whether there is an arrearage, the earliest of:

(i) The date on which the noncustodial parent requests that withholding begin;

(ii) The date on which the custodial parent requests that withholding begin, if the State determines, in accordance with such procedures and standards as it may establish, that the request should be approved; or

(iii) Such earlier date as State law or procedure may provide.

(2) The only basis for contesting a withholding under this paragraph is a mistake of fact, which for purposes of this paragraph means an error in the amount of current or overdue support or in the identity of the alleged noncustodial parent.

(d) *Notice to the noncustodial parent in cases of initiated withholding.* The State must send a notice to the noncustodial parent regarding the initiated withholding. The notice must inform the noncustodial parent:

(1) That the withholding has commenced;

(2) Of the amount of overdue support that is owed, if any, and the amount of wages that will be withheld;

(3) That the provision for withholding applies to any current or subsequent employer or period of employment;

(4) Of the procedures available for contesting the withholding and that the only basis for contesting the withholding is a mistake of fact;

(5) Of the information provided to the employer, pursuant to paragraph (e) of this section.

(e) *Notice to the employer for immediate and initiated withholding.* (1) To initiate withholding, the State must send the noncustodial parent's employer a notice using the required OMB-approved *Income Withholding for Support* form that includes the following:

(i) The amount to be withheld from the noncustodial parent's income, and a statement that the amount actually withheld for support and other purposes, including the fee specified under paragraph (e)(1)(iii) of this section, may not be in excess of the maximum amounts permitted under section 303(b) of the Consumer Credit Protection Act (15 U.S.C. 1673(b));

(ii) That the employer must send the amount to the SDU within 7 business days of the date the noncustodial parent is paid, and must report to the SDU the date on which the amount was withheld from the noncustodial parent's income;

(iii) That, in addition to the amount withheld for support, the employer may deduct a fee established by the State for administrative costs incurred for each withholding, if the State permits a fee to be deducted;

(iv) That the withholding is binding upon the employer until further notice by the State;

(v) That the employer is subject to a fine to be determined under State law for discharging a noncustodial parent from employment, refusing to employ, or taking disciplinary action against any noncustodial parent because of the withholding;

(vi) That, if the employer fails to withhold income in accordance with the provisions of the notice, the employer is liable for the accumulated amount the employer should have withheld from the noncustodial parent's income;

(vii) That the withholding under this section shall have priority over any other legal process under State law against the same income;

(viii) That the employer may combine withheld amounts from noncustodial parents' income in a single payment to each appropriate agency requesting withholding and separately identify the portion of the single payment which is attributable to each individual noncustodial parent;

(ix) That the employer must withhold from the noncustodial parent's income the amount specified in the notice and pay such amount to the State disbursement unit within 7 business days after the date the income would have been paid to the noncustodial parent.

(x) That the employer must notify the State promptly when the noncustodial parent terminates employment and provide the noncustodial parent's last known address and the name and address of the noncustodial parent's new employer, if known.

(2) In the case of an immediate withholding under paragraph (b) of this section, the State must issue the notice to the employer specified in paragraph (e)(1) of this section within 2 business days of the date the State's computerized support enforcement system receives notice of income and income source from a court, another State, an employer, the Federal Parent Locator Service, or another source recognized by the State, or the date information regarding a newly hired employee is entered into the State Directory of New Hires, or if information is not received by the State's computerized support enforcement system or its State Directory of New Hires, within 15 calendar days of the date the support order is received if the employer's address is known on that date, or, if the address is unknown on that date, within 2 business days of the date the State's computerized support enforcement system receives notice of income and income source from a court, another State, an employer, the Federal Parent Locator Service, or another source recognized by the State, or the date information regarding a newly hired employee is entered into the State Directory of New Hires, or if information is not received by the State's computerized support enforcement system or its State Directory of New Hires, within 15 calendar days of locating the employer's address.

(3) In the case of initiated withholding, the State must send the notice to the employer required under paragraph (e)(1) of this section within 2 business days of the date the State's computerized support enforcement system receives notice of income and income source from a court, another State, an employer, the Federal Parent Locator Service, or another source recognized by the State, or the date information regarding a newly hired employee is entered into the State Directory of New Hires, or if information is not received by the State's computerized support enforcement system or its State Directory of New Hires, within 15 calendar days of the date specified in paragraph (c)(1) of this section if the employer's address is known on that date, or, within 2 business days of the date the State's computerized support enforcement system receives notice of income and income source from a

court, another State, an employer, the Federal Parent Locator Service, or another source recognized by the State, or the date information regarding a newly hired employee is entered into the State Directory of New Hires, or if information is not received by the State's computerized support enforcement system or its State Directory of New Hires, within 15 calendar days of locating the employer's address.

(4) If the noncustodial parent changes employment within the State when a withholding is in effect, the State must notify the noncustodial parent's new employer, in accordance with the requirements of paragraph (e)(1) of this section, that the withholding is binding on the new employer.

(f) *Interstate withholding.* (1) The State law must require employers to comply with a withholding notice issued by any State.

(2) When an out-of-State IV-D agency requests direct withholding, the employer must be required to withhold funds as directed in the notice but to apply the income withholding laws of the noncustodial parent's principal place of employment to determine:

(i) The employer's fee for processing the withholding notice;

(ii) The maximum amount that may be withheld from the noncustodial parent's income;

(iii) The time periods to implement the withholding notice and to remit the withheld income;

(iv) The priorities for withholding and allocating income withheld for multiple child support obligees; and

(v) Any withholding term or conditions not specified in the withholding order.

(3) In other than direct withholding actions:

(i) A State may require registration for orders from other States for purposes of enforcement through withholding only if registration is for the sole purpose of obtaining jurisdiction for enforcement of the order; does not confer jurisdiction on the court or agency for any other purpose (such as modification of the underlying or original support order or resolution of custody or visitation disputes); and does not delay implementation of withholding beyond the timeframes established in paragraphs (e)(2) and (e)(3) of this section.

(ii) Within 20 calendar days of a determination that withholding is required in a particular case, and, if appropriate, receipt of any information necessary to carry out withholding, the initiating State must notify the IV-D agency of the State in which the noncustodial parent is employed to implement interstate withholding. The notice must contain all information necessary to carry out the withholding, including the amount requested to be withheld, a copy of the support order and a statement of arrearages, if appropriate. If necessary, the State where the support order is entered must provide the information necessary to carry out the withholding within 30 calendar days of receipt of a request for information by the initiating State.

(iii) The State in which the noncustodial parent is employed must implement withholding in accordance with this section upon receipt of the notice from the initiating State required in paragraph (f)(3)(ii) of this section.

(iv) The State in which the noncustodial parent is employed must notify the State in which the custodial parent is receiving services when the noncustodial parent is no longer employed in the State and provide the name and address of the noncustodial parent and new employer, if known.

(4) The withholding must be carried out in full compliance with all procedural due process requirements of the State in which the noncustodial parent is employed.

(5) Except with respect to when withholding must be implemented which is controlled by the State where the support order was entered, the law and procedures of the State in which the noncustodial parent is employed shall apply.

(g) *Provision for withholding in all child support orders.* Child support orders issued or modified in the State whether or not being enforced under the State IV-D plan must have a provision for withholding of income. This requirement does not alter the requirement governing all IV-D cases in paragraph (a)(4) of this section that enforcement under the State plan must proceed without the need for a withholding provision in the order.

(h) *Notice to employer in all child support orders.* The notice to employers in all child support orders must be on an OMB-approved *Income Withholding for Support* form.

(i) *Payments sent to the SDU in child support order not enforced under the State IV–D plan.* Income withholding payments made under child support orders initially issued in the State on or after January 1, 1994 that are not being enforced under the State IV–D plan must be sent to the State Disbursement Unit for disbursement to the family in accordance with sections 454B and 466(a)(8) and (b)(5) of the Act and § 302.32(a) of this chapter.

[57 FR 30682, July 10, 1992, as amended at 64 FR 6251, 6252, Feb. 9, 1999; 68 FR 25304, May 12, 2003; 81 FR 93566, Dec. 20, 2016]

§ 303.101 Expedited processes.

(a) *Definition. Expedited processes* means administrative and judicial procedures (including IV-D agency procedures) required under section 466(a)(2) and (c) of the Act;

(b) *Basic requirement.* (1) The State must have in effect and use, in interstate and intrastate cases, expedited processes as specified under this section to establish paternity and to establish, modify, and enforce support orders.

(2) Under expedited processes:

(i) In IV-D cases needing support order establishment, regardless of whether paternity has been established, action to establish support orders must be completed from the date of service of process to the time of disposition within the following timeframes: (A) 75 percent in 6 months; and (B) 90 percent in 12 months.

(ii) In IV-D cases where a support order has been established, actions to enforce the support order must be taken within the timeframes specified in §§ 303.6(c)(2) and 303.100;

(iii) For purposes of the timeframe at § 303.101(b)(2)(i), in cases where the IV-D agency uses long-arm jurisdiction and disposition occurs within 12 months of service of process on the alleged father or noncustodial parent, the case may be counted as a success within the 6 month tier of the timeframe, regardless of when disposition occurs in the 12 month period following service of process.

(iv) Disposition, as used in paragraphs (b)(2)(i) and (iii) of this section, means the date on which a support order is officially established and/or recorded or the action is dismissed.

(c) *Safeguards.* Under expedited processes:

(1) Paternities and orders established by means other than full judicial process must have the same force and effect under State law as paternities and orders established by full judicial process within the State;

(2) The due process rights of the parties involved must be protected;

(3) The parties must be provided a copy of the voluntary acknowledgment of paternity, paternity determination, and/or support order;

(4) Action taken may be reviewed under the State's generally applicable administrative or judicial procedures.

(d) *Functions.* The functions performed by presiding officers under expedited processes must include at minimum:

(1) Taking testimony and establishing a record;

(2) Evaluating evidence and making recommendations or decisions to establish paternity and to establish and enforce orders;

(3) Accepting voluntary acknowledgment of paternity or support liability and stipulated agreements setting the amount of support to be paid;

(4) Entering default orders upon a showing that process has been served on the defendant in accordance with State law, that the defendant failed to respond to service in accordance with State procedures, and any additional showing required by State law; and

(5) Ordering genetic tests in contested paternity cases in accordance with § 303.5(d)(1).

(e) *Exemption for political subdivisions.* A State may request an exemption from any of the requirements of this section for a political subdivision on the basis of the effectiveness and timeliness of paternity establishment, support order issuance or enforcement within the political subdivision in accordance with the provisions of § 302.70(d) of this chapter.

(Approved by the Office of Management and Budget under control number 0960–0385)

[50 FR 19655, May 9, 1985, as amended at 50 FR 23958, June 7, 1985; 59 FR 66251, Dec. 23, 1994; 64 FR 6252, Feb. 9, 1999; 68 FR 25305, May 12, 2003]

§ 303.102 Collection of overdue support by State income tax refund offset.

(a) *Overdue support qualifying for offset.* Overdue support qualifies for State income tax refund offset if:

(1) There has been an assignment of the support obligation under section 408(a)(3) of the Act or section 471(a)(17) of the Act or the IV-D agency is providing services under § 302.33 of this chapter, and

(2) The State does not determine, using guidelines it must develop which are generally available to the public, that the case is inappropriate for application of this procedure.

(b) *Accuracy of amounts referred for offset.* The IV-D agency must establish procedures to ensure that:

(1) Amounts referred for offset have been verified and are accurate; and

(2) The appropriate State office or agency is notified of any significant reductions in (including an elimination of) an amount referred for collection by State income tax refund offset.

(c) *Procedures for contesting offset and for reimbursing excess amounts offset.* (1) The State must establish procedures, which are in full compliance with the State's procedural due process requirements, for a noncustodial parent to use to contest the referral of overdue support for State income tax refund offset.

(2) If the offset amount is found to be in error or to exceed the amount of overdue support, the State IV-D agency must take steps to refund the excess amount in accordance with procedures that include a mechanism for promptly reimbursing the noncustodial parent.

(3) The State must establish procedures for ensuring that in the event of a joint return, the noncustodial parent's spouse can apply for a share of the refund, if appropriate, in accordance with State law.

(d) *Notice to custodial parent.* The IV-D agency must inform individuals receiving services under § 302.33 of this chapter, in advance that, for cases in which medical support rights have been assigned under 42 CFR 433.146, and amounts are collected which represent specific dollar amounts designated in the support order for medical purposes, amounts offset will be distributed under § 302.51(c) of this chapter.

(e) *Advance notice to noncustodial parent.* The State must send a written advance notice to inform the noncustodial parent of the referral for State income tax refund offset and of the opportunity to contest the referral.

(f) *Fee for certain cases.* The State IV-D agency may charge an individual who is receiving services under § 302.33(a)(1) (i) or (iii) of this chapter a reasonable fee to cover the cost of collecting past-due support using State tax refund offset. The State must inform the individual in advance of the amount of any fee charged.

(g) Distribution of collections. (1) The State must distribute collections received as a result of State income tax refund offset:

(i) In accordance with section 457 of the Act and §§ 302.51 and 302.52 of this chapter; and

(ii) For cases in which medical support rights have been assigned under 42 CFR 433.146, and amounts are collected which represent specific dollar amounts designated in the support order for medical purposes, under § 302.51(c) of this chapter.

(2) If the amount collected is in excess of the amounts required to be distributed under paragraph (g)(1) of this section, the IV-D agency must repay the excess to the noncustodial parent whose State income tax refund was offset within a reasonable period in accordance with State law.

(3) The State must credit amounts offset on individual payment records.

(h) *Information to the IV-D agency.* The State agency responsible for processing the State tax refund offset must notify the State IV-D agency of the noncustodial parent's home address and social security number or numbers. The State IV-D agency must provide this information to any other State involved in enforcing the support order.

(Approved by the Office of Management and Budget under control number 0960–0385)

[50 FR 19655, May 9, 1985; 50 FR 31720, Aug. 6, 1985, as amended at 51 FR 37731, Oct. 24, 1986; 54 FR 32312, Aug. 4, 1989; 56 FR 8005, Feb. 26, 1991; 64 FR 6252, Feb. 9, 1999; 68 FR 25305, May 12, 2003]

§ 303.104 Procedures for posting security, bond or guarantee to secure payment of overdue support.

(a) The State shall have in effect and use procedures which require that noncustodial parents post security, bond or give some other guarantee to secure payment of overdue support.

(b) The State must provide advance notice to the noncustodial parent regarding the delinquency of the support payment and the requirement of posting security, bond or guarantee, and inform the noncustodial parent of his or her rights and the methods available for contesting the impending action, in full compliance with the State's procedural due process requirements.

(c) The State must develop guidelines which are generally available to the public to determine whether the case is inappropriate for application of this procedure.

(Approved by the Office of Management and Budget under control number 0960–0385)

[50 FR 19656, May 9, 1985, as amended at 51 FR 37731, Oct. 24, 1986]

§ 303.106 Procedures to prohibit retroactive modification of child support arrearages.

(a) The State shall have in effect and use procedures which require that any payment or installment of support under any child support order is, on and after the date it is due:

(1) A judgment by operation of law, with the full force, effect, and attributes of a judgment of the State, including the ability to be enforced;

(2) Entitled as a judgment to full faith and credit in such State and in any other State; and

(3) Not subject to retroactive modification by such State or by any other State except as provided in paragraph (b) of this section.

(b) The procedures referred to in paragraph (a)(3) of this section may permit modification with respect to any period during which there is pending a petition for modification, but only from the date that notice of such petition has been given, either directly or through the appropriate agent, to the obligee or (where the obligee is the petitioner) to the obligor.

[54 FR 15764, Apr. 19, 1989]

§ 303.107 Requirements for cooperative arrangements.

The State must ensure that all cooperative arrangements:

(a) Contain a clear description of the specific duties, functions and responsibilities of each party;

(b) Specify clear and definite standards of performance which meet Federal requirements;

(c) Specify that the parties will comply with title IV-D of the Act, implementing Federal regulations and any other applicable Federal regulations and requirements;

(d) Specify the financial arrangements including budget estimates, covered expenditures, methods of determining costs, procedures for billing the IV-D agency, and any relevant Federal and State reimbursement requirements and limitations;

(e) Specify the kind of records that must be maintained and the appropriate Federal, State and local reporting and safeguarding requirements; and

(f) Specify the dates on which the arrangement begins and ends, any conditions for revision or renewal, and the circumstances under which the arrangement may be terminated.

[54 FR 30223, July 19, 1989]

§ 303.108 Quarterly wage and unemployment compensation claims reporting to the National Directory of New Hires.

(a) *What definitions apply to quarterly wage and unemployment compensation claims reporting?* When used in this section:

(1) *Reporting period* means time elapsed during a calendar quarter, e.g. January-March, April-June, July-September, October-December.

(2) *Wage information* means:

(i) The name of the employee;

(ii) The social security number of the employee;

(iii) The aggregate wages of the employee during the reporting period; and

(iv) The name, address (and optionally, any second address for wage withholding purposes), and Federal employer identification number of an employer reporting wages.

(3) *Unemployment compensation or claim information* means:

(i) Whether an individual is receiving, has received or has applied for unemployment compensation;

(ii) The individual's name and current (or most recent) home address;

(iii) The individual's social security number; and

(iv) The aggregate gross amount of compensation the claimant received during the reporting quarter.

(b) *What data must be transmitted to the National Directory of New Hires?* The State shall disclose quarterly, to the National Directory of New Hires, wage and claim information as defined in paragraph (a) of this section that is collected pursuant to a State's unemployment compensation program referenced in Title III of the Act or pursuant to section 1137 of the Act.

(c) *What time frames apply for reporting quarterly wage and unemployment compensation claims data?* The State shall report wage information for the reporting period no later than the end of the fourth month following the reporting period. The State shall report claim information for the reporting period no later than the end of the first month following the reporting period.

(d) *What reporting formats will be used for reporting data?* The State must use standardized formats established by the Secretary of Health and Human Services for reporting wage and claim information.

[63 FR 36190, July 2, 1998; 68 FR 62161, Oct. 31, 2003]

§ 303.109 Procedures for State monitoring, evaluation and reporting on programs funded by Grants to States for Access and Visitation Programs.

(a) *Monitoring.* The State must monitor all programs funded under Grants to States for Access and Visitation Programs to ensure that the programs are providing services authorized in section 469B(a) of the Act, are being conducted in an effective and efficient manner, are complying with Federal evaluation and reporting requirements, and contain safeguards to insure the safety of parents and children.

(b) *Evaluation.* The State:

(1) May evaluate all programs funded under Grants to States for Access and Visitation Programs;

(2) Must assist in the evaluation of significant or promising projects as determined by the Secretary;

(c) *Reporting.* The State must:

(1) Report a detailed description of each program funded, providing the following information, as appropriate: service providers and administrators, service area (rural/urban), population served (income, race, marital status), program goals, application or referral process (including referral sources), voluntary or mandatory nature of the programs, types of activities, and length and features of a completed program;

(2) Report data including: the number of applicants/referrals for each program, the total number of participating individuals, and the number of persons who have completed program requirements by authorized activities (mediation—voluntary and mandatory, counseling, education, development of parenting plans, visitation enforcement—including monitoring, supervision and neutral drop-off and pickup) and development of guidelines for visitation and alternative custody arrangements; and

(3) Report the information required in paragraphs (c)(1) and (c)(2) of this section annually, at such time, and in such form, as the Secretary may require.

[64 FR 15136, Mar. 30, 1999]

PART 304—FEDERAL FINANCIAL PARTICIPATION

Sec.

AUTHORITY: 42 U.S.C. 651 through 655, 657, 1302, 1396a(a)(25), 1396b(d)(2), 1396b(o), 1396b(p), and 1396(k).

SOURCE: 40 FR 27166, June 26, 1975, unless otherwise noted.

EDITORIAL NOTE: Nomenclature changes to part 304 appear at 64 FR 6252, Feb. 9, 1999.

§304.10 General administrative requirements.

As a condition for Federal financial participation, the provisions of 45 CFR part 75 (with the exception of 45 CFR 75.306, *Cost sharing or matching* and 45 CFR 75.341, *Financial reporting*) establishing uniform administrative requirements and cost principles shall apply to all grants made to States under this part.

[81 FR 93566, Dec. 20, 2016]

§304.11 Effect of State rules.

Subject to the provisions and limitations of title IV-D of the Act and chapter III, Federal financial participation will be available in expenditures made under the State plan (including the administration thereof) in accordance with applicable State laws, rules, regulations, and standards governing expenditures by State and local child support enforcement agencies.

§304.12 Incentive payments.

(a) *Definitions.* For the purposes of this section:

Non-title IV-A collections means support collections, on behalf of individuals receiving services under this title, satisfying a support obligation which has not been assigned under section 408(a)(3) of the Act or section 471(a)(17) of the Act, including collections treated in accordance with paragraph (b)(4)(ii) of this section .

Title IV-A collections means support collections satisfying an assigned support obligation under section 408(a)(3) of the Act or section 471(a)(17) of the Act, including collections treated in accordance with paragraph (b)(4)(ii) of this section.

Total IV-D administrative costs means total IV-D administrative expenditures claimed by a State in a specified fiscal year adjusted in accordance with paragraphs (b)(4)(iii), (b)(4)(iv) and (b)(4)(v) of this section.

(b) *Incentive payments to States.* Effective October 1, 1985, the Office shall compute incentive payments for States for a fiscal year in recognition of title IV-A collections and of non-title IV-A collections.

(1) A portion of a State's incentive payment shall be computed as a percentage of the State's title IV-A collections, and a portion of the incentive payment shall be computed as a percentage of its non-title IV-A collections. The percentages are determined separately for title IV-A and non-title IV-A portions of the incentive. The percentages are based on the ratio of the State's title IV-A collections to the State's total administrative costs and the State's non-title IV-A collections to the State's total administrative costs in accordance with the following schedule:

Ratio of collections to total IV-D administrative costs	Percent of collection paid as an incentive
Less than 1.4	6.0
At least 1.4	6.5
At least 1.6	7.0
At least 1.8	7.5
At least 2.0	8.0
At least 2.2	8.5
At least 2.4	9.0
At least 2.6	9.5
At least 2.8	10.0

(2) The ratios of the State's title IV-A and non-title IV-A collections to total IV-D administrative costs will be truncated at one decimal place.

(3) The portion of the incentive payment paid to a State for a fiscal year in recognition of its non-title IV-A collections is limited to the percentage of the portion of the incentive payment

paid for that fiscal year in recognition of its title IV-A collections, as follows:

(i) 100 percent in fiscal years 1986 and 1987;

(ii) 105 percent in fiscal year 1988;

(iii) 110 percent in fiscal year 1989; and

(iv) 115 percent in fiscal year 1990 and thereafter.

(4) In calculating the amount of incentive payments, the following conditions apply:

(i) Only those title IV-A and non-title IV-A collections distributed and expenditures claimed by the State in the fiscal year shall be used to determine the incentive payment payable for that fiscal year;

(ii) Support collected by one State on behalf of individuals receiving IV-D services in another State shall be treated as having been collected in full by each State;

(iii) Fees paid by individuals, recovered costs, and program income such as interest earned on collections shall be deducted from total IV-D administrative costs;

(iv) At the option of the State, laboratory costs incurred in determining paternity may be excluded from total IV-D administrative costs; and

(v) Effective January 1, 1990, amounts expended by the State in carrying out a special project under section 455(e) of the Act shall not be included in the State's total IV-D administrative costs.

(vi) Costs of demonstration projects for evaluating model procedures for reviewing child support awards under section 103(e) of Public Law 100–485 shall not be included in the State's total IV-D administrative costs.

(c) *Payment of incentives.* (1) The Office will estimate the total incentive payment that each State will receive for the upcoming fiscal year.

(2) Each State will include one-quarter of the estimated total payment in its quarterly collection report which will reduce the amount that would otherwise be paid to the Federal government to reimburse its share of assistance payments under §§ 302.51 and 302.52 of this chapter.

(3) Following the end of a fiscal year, the Office will calculate the actual incentive payment the State should have received based on the reports submitted for that fiscal year. If adjustments to the estimate made under paragraph (c)(1) of this section are necessary, the State's IV-A grant award will be reduced or increased because of over- or under-estimates for prior quarters and for other adjustments.

[54 FR 32312, Aug. 4, 1989, as amended at 56 FR 8005, Feb. 26, 1991; 64 FR 6252, Feb. 9, 1999; 81 FR 93567, Dec. 20, 2016]

§ 304.15 Cost allocation.

A State agency in support of its claims under title IV-D of the Social Security Act must have an approved cost allocation plan on file with the Department in accordance with the requirements contained in Subpart E of 45 CFR part 95. Subpart E also sets forth the effect on FFP if the requirements contained in that subpart are not met.

[47 FR 17509, Apr. 23, 1982]

§ 304.20 Availability and rate of Federal financial participation.

(a) Federal financial participation at the applicable matching rate is available for:

(1) Necessary and reasonable expenditures for child support services and activities to carry out the State title IV–D plan;

(2) Parent locator services for individuals eligible pursuant to § 302.33 of this title;

(3) Paternity and support services under the State plan for individuals eligible pursuant to § 302.33 of this chapter.

(b) Services and activities for which Federal financial participation will be available will be those made to carry out the State title IV–D plan, including obtaining child support, locating noncustodial parents, and establishing paternity, that are determined by the Secretary to be necessary and reasonable expenditures properly attributed to the Child Support Enforcement program including, but not limited to the following:

(1) The administration of the State Child Support Enforcement program, including but not limited to the following:

(i) The establishment and administration of the State plan;

(ii) Monitoring the progress of program development and operations and evaluating the quality, efficiency, effectiveness and scope of support enforcement services available in each political subdivision;

(iii) The establishment of all necessary agreements with other Federal, State, and local agencies or private providers to carry out Child Support Enforcement program activities in accordance with Procurement Standards, 45 CFR 75.326 through 75.340. These agreements may include:

(A) Necessary administrative agreements for support services;

(B) Utilization of State and local information resources;

(C) Cooperation with courts and law enforcement officials, and Indian Tribes or Tribal organizations pursuant to § 302.34 of this chapter;

(iv) Securing compliance with the requirements of the State plan in operations under any agreements;

(v) The development and maintenance of systems for fiscal and program records and reports required to be made to the Office based on these records;

(vi) The development of a cost allocation system pursuant to § 304.15 of this chapter;

(vii) The financial control of the State plan including the administration of Federal grants pursuant to § 301.15 of this chapter;

(viii) The establishment of agreements with agencies administering the State's title IV–A and IV–E plans including criteria for:

(A) Referring cases to and from the IV–D agency;

(B) Reporting on a timely basis information necessary to the determination and redetermination of eligibility and amount of assistance payments;

(C) The procedures to be used to transfer collections from the IV-D agency to the IV-A or IV-E agency before or after the distribution described in § 302.51 or § 302.52, respectively, of this chapter;

(D) The procedures to be used to coordinate services; and

(E) Agreements to exchange data as authorized by law.

(ix) The establishment of agreements with State agencies administering Medicaid or CHIP, including appropriate criteria for:

(A) Referring cases to and from the IV–D agency;

(B) The procedures to be used to coordinate services;

(C) Agreements to exchange data as authorized by law; and

(D) Transferring collections from the IV–D agency to the Medicaid agency in accordance with § 302.51(c) of this chapter.

(2) The establishment of paternity including, but not limited to:

(i) Reasonable attempts to determine the identity of the child's father such as:

(A) Investigation;

(B) The development of evidence including the use of the polygraph and genetic tests;

(C) Pre-trial discovery;

(ii) Court or other actions to establish paternity pursuant to procedures established under State statutes or regulations having the effect of law;

(iii) Identifying competent laboratories that perform genetic tests as described in § 303.5(c) of this chapter and making a list of those laboratories available;

(iv) Referral of cases to the IV-D agency of another State to establish paternity when appropriate;

(v) Cooperation with other States in determining paternity;

(vi) Payments up to $20 to hospitals, State birth record agencies, and other entities designated by the State and participating in the State's voluntary paternity establishment program, under § 303.5(g) of this chapter, for each voluntary acknowledgment obtained pursuant to an agreement with the IV-D agency;

(vii) Developing and providing to parents and family members, hospitals, State birth records agencies, and other entities designated by the State and participating in the State's voluntary paternity establishment program, under § 303.5(g) of this chapter, educational and outreach activities, written and audiovisual materials about paternity establishment and forms necessary to voluntarily acknowledge paternity; and

(viii) Reasonable and essential short-term training associated with the State's program of voluntary paternity establishment services under § 303.5(g).

(3) The establishment and enforcement of support obligations including, but not limited to:

(i) Investigation, the development of evidence and when appropriate, bringing court actions;

(ii) Determination of the amount of the child support obligation including developing the information needed for a financial assessment;

(iii) Referral of cases to the IV-D agency of another State to establish a child support obligation when appropriate;

(iv) Enforcement of a support obligation including those activities associated with collections and the enforcement of court orders, such as contempt citations, issuance of warrants, investigation, income withholding and processing, and the obtaining and enforcing of court-ordered support through civil or criminal proceedings either in the State that granted the order or in another State;

(v) Bus fare or other minor transportation expenses to enable custodial or noncustodial parties to participate in child support proceedings and related activities;

(vi) Services to increase *pro se* access to adjudicative and alternative dispute resolution processes in IV–D cases related to providing child support services; and

(vii) Investigation and prosecution of fraud related to child and spousal support.

(4) The collection and distribution of support payments including:

(i) An effective system for making collections of established support obligations and identifying delinquent cases and attempting to collect support from these cases;

(ii) Referral of cases to the IV-D agency of another State for collection when appropriate;

(iii) Making collections for another State;

(iv) The distribution of funds as required by this chapter;

(v) Making the IV-A agency aware of the amounts collected and distributed to the family for the purposes of determining eligibility for, and amount of, assistance under the State title IV-A plan;

(vi) Making the Medicaid agency aware of amounts collected and distributed to the family for the purposes of determining eligibility for assistance under the State XIX plan.

(5) The establishment and operation of the State parent locator service including:

(i) Utilization of appropriate State and local locate sources to locate noncustodial parents;

(ii) Utilization of the Federal Parent Locator Service;

(iii) Collection of the fee pursuant to § 303.70(e) of this chapter;

(iv) Referral of requests for location of a noncustodial parent to the IV-D agency of another State;

(v) Cooperation with another State in locating a noncustodial parent.

(6) Activities related to requests for certification of collection of support delinquencies by the Secretary of the Treasury pursuant to § 303.71 of this chapter.

(7) Activities related to requests for utilization of the United States district courts pursuant to § 303.73 of this chapter.

(8) Establishing and maintaining case records as required by § 303.2 of this chapter.

(9) The operation of systems that meet the conditions of § 307.35(a) of this chapter.

(10) Systems approved in accordance with 45 CFR part 95, subpart F. (See § 307.35(b) of this chapter.)

(11) Medical support activities as specified in §§ 303.30, 303.31, and 303.32 of this chapter.

(12) Educational and outreach activities intended to inform the public, parents and family members, and young people who are not yet parents about the Child Support Enforcement program, responsible parenting and co-parenting, family budgeting, and other financial consequences of raising children when the parents are not married to each other.

[40 FR 27166, June 26, 1975]

EDITORIAL NOTE: For FEDERAL REGISTER citations affecting § 304.20, see the List of CFR Sections Affected, which appears in the

Finding Aids section of the printed volume and at *www.fdsys.gov*.

§ 304.21 Federal financial participation in the costs of cooperative arrangements with courts and law enforcement officials.

(a) *General.* Subject to the conditions and limitations specified in this part, Federal financial participation (FFP) at the applicable matching rate is available in the costs of cooperative agreements with appropriate courts and law enforcement officials in accordance with the requirements of § 302.34 of this chapter. *Law enforcement officials* mean district attorneys, attorneys general, similar public attorneys and prosecutors and their staff, and corrections officials. When performed under agreement, which is reflected in a record, costs of the following activities are subject to reimbursement:

(1) The activities, including administration of such activities, specified in § 304.20(b)(2) through (8), (11), and (12);

(2) Reasonable and essential short term training of court and law enforcement staff assigned on a full or part time basis to support enforcement functions under the cooperative agreement.

(b) *Limitations.* Federal financial participation is not available in:

(1) Service of process and court filing fees unless the court or law enforcement agency would normally be required to pay the cost of such fees;

(2) Costs of compensation (salary and fringe benefits) of judges;

(3) Costs of travel and training related to the judicial determination process incurred by judges;

(4) Office-related costs, such as space, equipment, furnishings and supplies, incurred by judges;

(5) Compensation (salary and fringe benefits), travel and training, and office-related costs incurred by administrative and support staffs of judges;

(6) Costs of cooperative arrangements that do not meet the requirements of § 303.107 of this chapter.

(c) *Methods of determining costs.* The State IV-D agency has discretion with respect to the method of calculating eligible expenditures by courts and law enforcement officials under cooperative agreements. However, any method used must account for specific costs incurred on behalf of cases receiving services under the IV-D State plan.

(d) *When agreements take effect.* FFP is available in IV-D costs incurred as of the first day of the calendar quarter in which a cooperative agreement or amendment is signed by parties sufficient to create a contractual arrangement under State law.

[47 FR 53017, Nov. 24, 1982, as amended at 47 FR 57284, Dec. 23, 1982; 50 FR 19656, May 9, 1985; 54 FR 30223, July 19, 1989; 64 FR 6252, Feb. 9, 1999; 81 FR 93567, Dec. 20, 2016]

§ 304.22 Federal financial participation in purchased support enforcement services.

Federal financial participation is available at the applicable matching rate for the purchase of support enforcement services as provided for in the State plan to the extent that payment for such purchased services is in accordance with rates of payment established by the State which do not exceed the amounts reasonable and necessary to assure quality of such service and in the case of such services purchased from other public agencies, the cost reasonably assignable to such services. The determination that the amounts are reasonable and necessary and that the costs are reasonably assignable must be fully documented in the IV-D agency records. Support enforcement services which may be purchased with Federal financial participation are those for which Federal financial participation is otherwise available under § 304.20 and which are included under the approved State plan.

[40 FR 27166, June 26, 1975, as amended at 47 FR 57282, Dec. 23, 1982; 50 FR 19656, May 9, 1985]

§ 304.23 Expenditures for which Federal financial participation is not available.

Federal financial participation at the applicable matching rate is not available for:

(a) Activities related to administering titles I, IV–A, IV–B, IV–E, X, XIV, XVI, XIX, XX, or XXI of the Act or 7 U.S.C. Chapter 51.

(b) Purchased support enforcement services which are not secured in accordance with § 304.22.

(c) Construction and major renovations.

(d) Education and training programs and educational services for State and county employees and court personnel except direct cost of short-term training provided to IV–D agency staff in accordance with §§ 304.20(b)(2)(viii) and 304.21.

(e) Any expenditures which have been reimbursed by fees collected as required by this chapter.

(f) Any costs of those caseworkers described in § 303.20(e) of this chapter.

(g) Any expenditures made to carry out an agreement under § 303.15 of this chapter.

(h) The costs of counsel for indigent defendants in IV–D actions.

(i) Any expenditures for jailing of parents in child support enforcement cases.

(j) The costs of *guardians ad litem* in IV–D actions.

[81 FR 93567, Dec. 20, 2016]

§ 304.24 Equipment—Federal financial participation.

Claims for Federal financial participation in the cost of equipment under the Child Support Enforcement Program are to be determined in accordance with subpart G of 45 CFR part 95. Requirements concerning the management and disposition of equipment under the Child Support Enforcement Program are also prescribed in subpart G of 45 CFR part 95.

[47 FR 41576, Sept. 21, 1982]

§ 304.25 Treatment of expenditures; due date.

(a) *Treatment of expenditures.* Expenditures are considered to be made on the date on which the cash disbursements occur or the date to which allocated in accordance with part 75 of this title. In the case of local administration, the date of disbursements by the local agency governs. In the case of purchase of services from another public agency, the date of disbursements by such other public agency governs. Different rules may be applied with respect to a State, either generally or for particular classes of expenditures only upon justification by the State to the Office of Child Support Enforcement and approval by the Office.

(b) *Due date for expenditure statements.* The due date for the submission of the quarterly statement of expenditures under § 301.15 of this chapter is 45 days after the end of the quarter.

[42 FR 26427, May 24, 1977, as amended at 81 FR 3021, Jan. 20, 2016; 81 FR 93568, Dec. 20, 2016]

§ 304.26 Determination of Federal share of collections.

(a) From the amounts of support collected by the State and retained as reimbursement for title IV-A payments and foster care maintenance payments under title IV-E, the State shall reimburse the Federal government the Federal share of the support collections. In computing the Federal share of support collections for assistance payments made under titles IV-A and IV-E, the State shall use the Federal medical assistance percentage in effect for the fiscal year in which the amount is distributed. The Federal medical assistance percentage is:

(1) 75 percent for Puerto Rico, the Virgin Islands, Guam, and American Samoa for the distribution of retained IV–A collections; 55 percent for Puerto Rico, the Virgin Islands, Guam, the Northern Mariana Islands, and American Samoa for the distribution of retained IV–E collections; 70 percent for the District of Columbia for the distribution of retained IV–E collections; and

(2) As defined in section 1905(b) of the Act as in effect on September 30, 1995, for any other State.

(b) [Reserved]

[64 FR 6252, Feb. 9, 1999, as amended at 68 FR 25305, May 12, 2003; 81 FR 93568, Dec. 20, 2016]

§ 304.27 [Reserved]

§ 304.29 Applicability of other regulations.

Sections 201.14 and 201.15 of chapter II of title 45 of the Code of Federal Regulations, which establish procedures for disallowance, deferral and reconsideration of claims for expenditures submitted by the States, shall apply to all expenditures claimed for FFP under title IV-D of the Act. For purposes of applying those provisions under title

IV-D, *Service* shall read *Office* which refers to the Office of Child Support Enforcement; *Administrator* shall read *Director* which refers to the Director, Office of Child Support Enforcement; *Deputy Administrator* shall read *Deputy Director* which refers to the Deputy Director, Office of Child Support Enforcement; *Regional Commissioner* shall read *Regional Administrator* which refers to the Regional Administrator of the Administration for Children and Families; and *State* shall refer to the State IV-D agency.

[42 FR 3843, Jan. 21, 1977, as amended at 64 FR 6253, Feb. 9, 1999]

§ 304.30 Public sources of State's share.

(a) Public funds, other than those derived from private resources, used by the IV-D agency for its child support enforcement program may be considered as the State's share in claiming Federal reimbursement where such funds are:

(1) Appropriated directly to the IV-D agency; or

(2) Funds of another public agency which are:

(i) Transferred to the IV-D agency and are under its administrative control; or

(ii) Certified by the contributing public agency as representing expenditures under the State's IV-D plan, subject to the limitations of this part.

(b) Public funds used by the IV-D agency for its child support enforcement program may not be considered as the State's share in claiming Federal reimbursement where such funds are:

(1) Federal funds, unless authorized by Federal law to be used to match other Federal funds;

(2) Used to match other Federal funds.

[41 FR 7105, Feb. 17, 1976]

§ 304.40 Repayment of Federal funds by installments.

(a) *Basic conditions.* When a State has been reimbursed Federal funds for expenditures claimed under title IV-D, which is later determined to be unallowable for Federal financial participation, the State may make repayment of such Federal funds in installments provided:

(1) The amount of the repayment exceeds 2½ percent of the estimated annual State share of expenditures for the IV-D program as set forth in paragraph (b) of this section; and

(2) The State has notified the OCSE Regional Office in a record of its intent to make installment repayments. Such notice must be given prior to the time repayment of the total was otherwise due.

(b) *Criteria governing installment repayments.* (1) The number of quarters over which the repayment of the total unallowable expenditures will be made will be determined by the percentage the total of such repayment is of the estimated State share of the annual expenditures for the IV-D program as follows:

Total repayment amount as percentage of State share of annual expenditures for the IV-D program	Number of quarters to make repayment
2.5 percent or less	1
Greater than 2.5, but not greater than 5	2
Greater than 5, but not greater than 7.5	3
Greater than 7.5, but not greater than 10	4
Greater than 10, but not greater than 15	5
Greater than 15, but not greater than 20	6
Greater than 20, but not greater than 25	7
Greater than 25, but not greater than 30	8
Greater than 30, but not greater than 47.5	9
Greater than 47.5, but not greater than 65	10
Greater than 65, but not greater than 82.5	11
Greater than 82.5, but not greater than 100	12

The quarterly repayment amounts for each of the quarters in the repayment schedule shall not be less than the following percentages of estimated State share of the annual expenditures for the program against which the recovery is made.

For each of the following quarters	Repayment installment may not be less than these percentages
1 to 4	2.5
5 to 8	5.0
9 to 12	17.5

If the State chooses to repay amounts representing higher percentages during the early quarters, any corresponding reduction in required minimum percentages would be applied first to the last scheduled payment, then to the next to the last payment, and so forth as necessary.

(2) The latest required financial reports submitted by the State shall be used to estimatethe State's share of annual expenditures for the IV-D program. That estimated share shall be the sum of the State's share of the estimates for four quarters, beginning with the quarter in which the first installment is to be paid.

(3) In case of termination of the program, the actual State share—rather than the estimate—shall be used for determining whether the amount of the repayment exceeds 2½ percent of the annual State share for the IV-D program. The annual State share in these cases will be determined using payments computable for Federal funding as reported for the program by the State on its Quarterly Report of Expenditures and Estimates submitted for the last four quarters preceding the date on which the program was terminated.

(4) Repayment shall be accomplished through adjustment in the quarterly grants over the period covered by the repayment schedule.

(5) The amount of the repayment for purpose of paragraphs (a) and (b) of this section may not include any amount previously approved for installment repayment.

(6) The repayment schedule may be extended beyond 12 quarterly installments if the total repayment amount exceeds 100% of the estimated State share of annual expenditures.

In these circumstances, the criteria in paragraphs (b) (1) and (2) or (3) of this section, as appropriate, shall be followed for repayment of the amount equal to 100% of the annual State share. The remaining amount of the repayment shall be in quarterly amounts not less than those for the 9th through 12th quarters.

(7) The amount of a retroactive claim to be paid a State will be offset against any amounts to be, or already being, repaid by the State in installments, under the same title of the Social Security Act. Under this provision the State may choose to:

(i) Suspend payments until the retroactive claim due the State has, in fact, been offset; or

(ii) Continue payments until the reduced amount of its debt (remaining after the offset), has been paid in full. This second option would result in a shorter payment period.

A retroactive claim for the purpose of this regulation is a claim applicable to any period ending 12 months or more prior to the beginning of the quarter in which the payment is to be made by the Service.

[42 FR 28885, June 6, 1977, as amended at 52 FR 273, Jan. 5, 1987; 64 FR 6253, Feb. 9, 1999; 68 FR 25305, May 12, 2003; 81 FR 93568, Dec. 20, 2016]

§ 304.50 Treatment of program income.

The IV-D agency must exclude from its quarterly expenditure claims an amount equal to:

(a) All fees which are collected during the quarter under the title IV-D State plan; and

(b) All interest and other income earned during the quarter resulting from services provided under the IV-D State plan.

[49 FR 36772, Sept. 19, 1984]

§ 304.95 [Reserved]

PART 305—PROGRAM PERFORMANCE MEASURES, STANDARDS, FINANCIAL INCENTIVES, AND PENALTIES

Sec.

AUTHORITY: 42 U.S.C. 609(a)(8), 652(a)(4) and (g), 658a, and 1302.

SOURCE: 65 FR 82208, Dec. 27, 2000, unless otherwise noted.

§305.0 Scope.

This part implements the incentive system requirements as described in section 458A (to be redesignated as section 458 effective October 1, 2001) of the Act and the penalty provisions as required in sections 409(a)(8) and 452(g) of the Act. This part also implements Federal audit requirements under sections 409(a)(8) and 452(a)(4) of the Act. Sections 305.0 through 305.2 contain general provisions applicable to this part. Sections 305.31 through 305.36 of this part describe the incentive system. Sections 305.40 through 305.42 and §§305.60 through 305.66 describe the penalty and audit processes.

§305.1 Definitions.

The definitions found in §301.1 of this chapter are also applicable to this part. In addition, for purposes of this part:

(a) The term *IV-D case* means a parent (mother, father, or putative father) who is now or eventually may be obligated under law for the support of a child or children receiving services under the title IV-D program. A parent is a separate IV-D case for each family with a dependent child or children that the parent may be obligated to support. If both parents are absent and liable or potentially liable for support of a child or children receiving services under the IV-D program, each parent is considered a separate IV-D case. In counting cases for the purposes of this part, States may exclude cases closed under §303.11 and cases over which the State has no jurisdiction. Lack of jurisdiction cases are those in which a non-custodial parent resides in the civil jurisdictional boundaries of another country or federally recognized Indian Tribe and no income or assets of this individual are located or derived from outside that jurisdiction and the State has no other means through which to enforce the order.

(b) The term *Current Assistance collections* means collections received and distributed on behalf of individuals whose rights to support are required to be assigned to the State under title IV-A of the Act, under title IV-E of the Act, or under title XIX of the Act. In addition, a referral to the State's IV-D agency must have been made.

(c) The term *Former Assistance collections* means collections received and distributed on behalf of individuals whose rights to support were formerly required to be assigned to the State under title IV-A (TANF or Aid to Families with Dependent Children, AFDC), title IV-E (Foster Care), or title XIX (Medicaid) of the Act.

(d) The term *Never Assistance/Other collections* means all other collections received and distributed on behalf of individuals who are receiving child support enforcement services under title IV-D of the Act.

(e) The term *total IV-D dollars expended* means total IV-D administrative expenditures claimed by a State in a specified fiscal year adjusted in accordance with §305.32 of this part.

(f) The term *Consumer Price Index or CPI* means the last Consumer Price Index for all-urban consumers published by the Department of Labor. The CPI for a fiscal year is the average of the Consumer Price Index for the 12-month period ending on September 30 of the fiscal year.

(g) The term *State incentive payment share for a fiscal year* means the incentive base amount for the State for the fiscal year divided by the sum of the incentive base amounts for all of the States for the fiscal year.

(h) The term *incentive base amount for a fiscal year* means the sum of the State's performance level percentages (determined in accordance with §305.33) multiplied by the State's corresponding maximum incentive base on each of the following measures:

(1) The paternity establishment performance level;

(2) The support order performance level;

(3) The current collections performance level;

(4) The arrears collections performance level; and

(5) the cost-effectiveness performance level.

(i) The term *reliable data*, means the most recent data available which are found by the Secretary to be reliable and is a state that exists when data are sufficiently complete and error free to be convincing for their purpose and context. State data must meet a 95 percent standard of reliability effective beginning in fiscal year 2001. This is with the recognition that data may contain errors as long as they are not of a magnitude that would cause a reasonable person, aware of the errors, to doubt a finding or conclusion based on the data.

(j) The term *complete data* means all reporting elements from OCSE reporting forms, necessary to compute a State's performance levels, incentive base amount, and maximum incentive base amount, have been provided within timeframes established in instructions to these forms and § 305.32(f) of this part.

§ 305.2 Performance measures.

(a) The child support incentive system measures State performance levels in five program areas:

Paternity establishment; support order establishment; current collections; arrearage collections; and cost-effectiveness. The penalty system measures State performance in three of these areas: Paternity establishment; establishment of support orders; and current collections.

(1) *Paternity Establishment Performance Level.* States have the choice of being evaluated on one of the following two measures for their paternity establishment percentage (commonly known as the PEP). The count of children shall not include any child who is a dependent by reason of the death of a parent (unless paternity is established for that child). It shall also not include any child whose parent is found to have good cause for refusing to cooperate with the State agency in establishing paternity, or for whom the State agency determines it is against the best interest of the child to pursue paternity issues.

(i) *IV-D Paternity Establishment Percentage* means the ratio that the total number of children in the IV-D caseload in the fiscal year (or, at the option of the State, as of the end of the fiscal year) who have been born out-of-wedlock and for whom paternity has been established or acknowledged, bears to the total number of children in the IV-D caseload as of the end of the preceding fiscal year who were born out-of-wedlock. The equation to compute the measure is as follows (expressed as a percent):

$$\frac{\begin{array}{c}\text{Total \# of Children in IV - D Caseload in the Fiscal Year or,}\\ \text{at the option of the State, as of the end of the Fiscal Year who were}\\ \text{Born Out - of - Wedlock with Paternity Established or Acknowledged}\end{array}}{\begin{array}{c}\text{Total \# of Children in IV - D Caseload as of the end of the preceding}\\ \text{Fiscal Year who were Born Out - of - Wedlock}\end{array}}$$

(ii) *Statewide Paternity Establishment Percentage* means the ratio that the total number of minor children who have been born out-of-wedlock and for whom paternity has been established or acknowledged during the fiscal year, bears to the total number of children born out-of-wedlock during the preceding fiscal year. The equation to compute the measure is as follows (expressed as a percent):

$$\frac{\begin{array}{c}\text{Total \# of Minor Children who have been Born Out - of - Wedlock and for}\\ \text{Whom Paternity has been Established or Acknowledged During the Fiscal Year}\end{array}}{\text{Total \# of Children Born Out of Wedlock During the Preceding Fiscal Year}}$$

(2) *Support Order Establishment Performance Level.* This measure requires a determination of whether or not there is a support order for each case. These support orders include all types of legally enforceable orders, such as court, default, and administrative. Since the measure is a case count at a point-in-time, modifications to an order do not affect the count. The equation to compute the measure is as follows (expressed as a percent):

$$\frac{\text{Number of IV - D Cases with Support Orders During the Fiscal Year}}{\text{Total Number of IV - D Cases During the Fiscal Year}}$$

(3) *Current Collections Performance Level.* Current support is money applied to current support obligations and does not include payment plans for payment towards arrears. If included, voluntary collections must be included in both the numerator and the denominator. This measure is computed monthly and the total of all months is reported at the end of the year. The equation to compute the measure is as follows (expressed as a percent):

$$\frac{\text{Number Dollars Collected for Current Support in IV - D Cases}}{\text{Total Dollars Owed for Current Support in IV - D Cases}}$$

(4) *Arrearage Collection Performance Level.* This measure includes those cases where all of the past-due support was disbursed to the family, or retained by the State because all the support was assigned to the State. If some of the past-due support was assigned to the State and some was to be disbursed to the family, only those cases where some of the support actually went to the family can be included. The equation to compute the measure is as follows (expressed as a percent):

$$\frac{\text{Total number of eligible IV - D cases paying toward arrears}}{\text{Total number of IV - D cases with arrears due}}$$

(5) *Cost-Effectiveness Performance Level.* Interstate incoming and outgoing distributed collections will be included for both the initiating and the responding State in this measure. The equation to compute this measure is as follows (expressed as a ratio):

$$\frac{\text{Total IV - D Dollars Collected}}{\text{Total IV - D Dollars Expended}}$$

(b) For incentive purposes, the measures will be weighted in the following manner. Each State will earn five scores based on performance on each of the five measures. Each of the first three measures (paternity establishment, order establishment, and current collections) earn 100 percent of the collections base as defined in § 305.31(e) of this part. The last two measures (collections on arrears and cost-effectiveness) earn a maximum of 75 percent of the collections base as defined in § 305.31(e) of this part.

§ 305.31 Amount of incentive payment.

(a) The incentive payment for a State for a fiscal year is equal to the incentive payment pool for the fiscal year, multiplied by the State incentive payment share for the fiscal year.

(b) The incentive payment pool is:

(1) $422,000,000 for fiscal year 2000;

(2) $429,000,000 for fiscal year 2001;

(3) $450,000,000 for fiscal year 2002;

(4) $461,000,000 for fiscal year 2003;

(5) $454,000,000 for fiscal year 2004;

(6) $446,000,000 for fiscal year 2005;

(7) $458,000,000 for fiscal year 2006;

(8) $471,000,000 for fiscal year 2007;

(9) $483,000,000 for fiscal year 2008; and

(10) For any succeeding fiscal year, the amount of the incentive payment pool for the fiscal year that precedes such succeeding fiscal year multiplied by the percentage (if any) by which the CPI for such preceding fiscal year exceeds the CPI for the second preceding fiscal year. In other words, for each fiscal year following fiscal year 2008, the incentive payment pool will be multiplied by the percentage increase in the CPI between the two preceding years. For example, if the CPI increases by 1 percent between fiscal years 2007 and 2008, then the incentive pool for fiscal year 2009 would be a 1 percent increase over the $483,000,000 incentive payment pool for fiscal year 2008, or $487,830,000.

(c) The State incentive payment share for a fiscal year is the incentive base amount for the State for the fiscal year divided by the sum of the incentive base amounts for all of the States for the fiscal year.

(d) A State's maximum incentive base amount for a fiscal year is the State's collections base for the fiscal year for the paternity establishment, support order, and current collections performance measures and 75 percent of the State's collections base for the fiscal year for the arrearage collections and cost-effectiveness performance measures.

(e) A State's maximum incentive base amount for a State for a fiscal year is zero, unless a Federal audit performed under § 305.60 of this part determines that the data submitted by the State for the fiscal year and used to determine the performance level involved are complete and reliable.

(f) A State's collections base for a fiscal year is equal to: two times the sum of the total amount of support collected for Current Assistance cases plus two times the total amount of support collected in Former Assistance cases, plus the total amount of support collected in Never Assistance/other cases during the fiscal year, that is: 2(Current Assistance collections + Former Assistance collections) + all other collections.

§ 305.32 Requirements applicable to calculations.

In calculating the amount of incentive payments or penalties, the following conditions apply:

(a) Each measure is based on data submitted for the Federal fiscal year. The Federal fiscal year runs from October 1st of one year through September 30th of the following year.

(b) Only those Current Assistance, Former Assistance and Never Assistance/other collections disbursed and those expenditures claimed by the State in the fiscal year will be used to determine the incentive payment payable for that fiscal year;

(c) Support collected by one State at the request of another State will be treated as having been collected in full by each State;

(d) Amounts expended by the State in carrying out a special project under section 455(e) of the Act will be excluded from the State's total IV-D dollars expended in computing incentive payments;

(e) Fees paid by individuals, recovered costs, and program income such as interest earned on collections will be deducted from total IV-D dollars expended; and

(f) States must submit data used to determine incentives and penalties following instructions and formats as required by HHS on Office of Management and Budget (OMB) approved reporting instruments. Data necessary to calculate performance for incentives and penalties for a fiscal year must be submitted to the Office of Child Support Enforcement by December 31st, the end of the first quarter after the end of the fiscal year. Only data submitted as of December 31st will be used to determine the State's performance for the prior fiscal year and the amount of incentive payments due the States.

§ 305.33 Determination of applicable percentages based on performance levels.

(a) A State's paternity establishment performance level for a fiscal year is, at the option of the State, the IV-D paternity establishment percentage or the Statewide paternity establishment percentage determined under § 305.2 of this part. The applicable percentage for each level of a State's paternity establishment performance can be found in table 1 of this part, except as provided in paragraph (b) of this section.

(b) If the State's paternity establishment performance level for a fiscal year is less than 50 percent, but exceeds its paternity establishment performance level for the immediately preceding fiscal year by at least 10 percentage points, then the State's applicable percentage for the paternity establishment performance level is 50 percent.

(c) A State's support order establishment performance level for a fiscal year is the percentage of the total number of cases where there is a support order determined under §§ 305.2 and 305.32 of this part. The applicable percentage for each level of a State's support order establishment performance can be found on table 1 of this part, except as provided in paragraph (d) of this section.

(d) If the State's support order establishment performance level for a fiscal year is less than 50 percent, but exceeds the State's support order establishment performance level for the immediately preceding fiscal year by at least 5 percentage points, then the State's applicable percentage is 50 percent.

TABLE 1—IF THE PATERNITY ESTABLISHMENT OR SUPPORT ORDER ESTABLISHMENT PERFORMANCE LEVEL IS:

(Use this table to determine the applicable percentage levels for the paternity establishment and support order establishment performance measures.)

At least: (percent)	But less than: (percent)	The applicable percentage is:
80	....	100
79	80	98
78	79	96
77	78	94
76	77	92
75	76	90
74	75	88
73	74	86
72	73	84
71	72	82
70	71	80
69	70	79
68	69	78
67	68	77
66	67	76
65	66	75
64	65	74
63	64	73
62	63	72
61	62	71
60	61	70
59	60	69
58	59	68
57	58	67
56	57	66
55	56	65
54	55	64
53	54	63
52	53	62
51	52	61
50	51	60
0	50	0

(e) A State's current collections performance level for a fiscal year is equal to the total amount of current support collected during the fiscal year divided by the total amount of current support owed during the fiscal year in all IV-D cases, determined under §§ 305.2 and 305.32 of this part. The applicable percentage with respect to a State's current collections performance level can be found on table 2, except as provided in paragraph (f) of this section.

(f) If the State's current collections performance level for a fiscal year is less than 40 percent but exceeds the current collections performance level of the State for the immediately preceding fiscal year by at least 5 percentage points, then the State's applicable percentage is 50 percent.

(g) A State's arrearage collections performance level for a fiscal year is equal to the total number of IV-D cases in which payments of past-due child support were received and distributed during the fiscal year, divided by the total number of IV-D cases in which there was past-due child support owed, as determined under §§ 305.2 and 305.32 of this part. The applicable percentage with respect to a State's arrearage collections performance level can be found on table 2 except as provided in paragraph (h) of this section.

(h) If the State's arrearage collections performance level for a fiscal year is less than 40 percent but exceeds the arrearage collections performance level for the immediately preceding fiscal year by at least 5 percentage points, then the State's applicable percentage is 50 percent.

TABLE 2—IF THE CURRENT COLLECTIONS OR ARREARAGE COLLECTIONS PERFORMANCE LEVEL IS:

(Use this table to determine the percentage levels for the current collections and arrearage collections performance measures.)

At least (percent	But less than: (percent)	The applicable percentage is: (percent)
80		100
79	80	98
78	79	96
77	78	94
76	77	92
75	76	90
74	75	88
73	74	86
72	73	84
71	72	82
70	71	80
69	70	79
68	69	78
67	68	77
66	67	76
65	66	75
64	65	74
63	64	73
62	63	72
61	62	71
60	61	70
59	60	69
58	59	68
57	58	67
56	57	66
55	56	65
54	55	64
53	54	63
52	53	62
51	52	61
50	51	60
49	50	59
48	49	58
47	48	57
46	47	56
45	46	55
44	45	54
43	55	53
42	43	52
41	42	51
40	41	50
0	40	0

(i) A State's cost-effectiveness performance level for a fiscal year is equal to the total amount of IV-D support collected and disbursed or retained, as applicable during the fiscal year, divided by the total amount expended during the fiscal year, as determined under §§ 305.2 and 305.32 of this part. The applicable percentage with respect to a State's cost-effectiveness performance level can be found on table 3.

TABLE 3—IF THE COST-EFFECTIVENESS PERFORMANCE LEVEL IS:

(Use this table to determine the percentage level for the cost-effectiveness performance measure.)

At least:	But less than:	The app. % is
5.00		100
4.50	4.99	90
4.00	4.50	80
3.50	4.00	70
3.00	3.50	60
2.50	3.00	50
2.00	2.50	40
0.00	2.00	0

§ 305.34 Payment of incentives.

(a) Each State must report one-fourth of its estimated annual incentive payment on each of its four quarterly collections' reports for a fiscal year. When combined with the amounts claimed on each of the State's four quarterly expenditure reports, the portion of the annual estimated incentive payment as reported each quarter will be included in the calculation of the next quarterly grant awarded to the State under title IV-D of the Act.

(b) Following the end of each fiscal year, HHS will calculate the State's annual incentive payment, using the actual collection and expenditure data and the performance data submitted by December 31st by the State and other States for that fiscal year. A positive or negative grant will then be awarded to the State under title IV-D of the Act to reconcile an actual annual incentive payment that has been calculated to be greater or lesser, respectively, than the annual incentive payment estimated prior to the beginning of the fiscal year.

(c) Payment of incentives is contingent on a State's data being determined complete and reliable by Federal auditors.

§ 305.35 Reinvestment.

(a) A State must expend the full amount of incentive payments received under this part to supplement, and not supplant, other funds used by the State to carry out IV-D program activities or funds for other activities approved by the Secretary which may contribute to improving the effectiveness or efficiency of the State's IV-D program, including cost-effective contracts with local agencies, whether or not the expenditures for the activity are eligible for reimbursement under this part.

(b) In those States in which incentive payments are passed through to political subdivisions or localities, such payments must be used in accordance with this section.

(c) State IV-D expenditures may not be reduced as a result of the receipt and reinvestment of incentive payments.

(d) A base amount will be determined by subtracting the amount of incentive funds received and reinvested in the State IV-D program for fiscal year 1998 from the total amount expended by the State in the IV-D program during the same period. Alternatively, States have an option of using the average amount of the previous three fiscal years (1996, 1997, and 1998) as a base amount. This base amount of State spending must be maintained in future years. Incentive payments under this part must be used in addition to, and not in lieu of, the base amount. Noncompliance will result in disallowances of incentive amounts equal to the amount of funds supplanted.

(e) Using the Form OCSE–396, "Child Support Enforcement Program Quarterly Financial Report," the State Current Spending Level will be calculated by determining the State Share of Total Expenditures Claimed for all four quarters of the fiscal year minus State Share of IV–D Administrative Expenditures Made Using Funds Received as Incentive Payments for all four quarters of the fiscal year, plus the Federal Parent Locator Service (FPLS) fees for all four quarters of the fiscal year.

(1) The State Share of Expenditures Claimed is: Total Expenditures Claimed for the Current Quarter and the Prior Quarter Adjustments minus the Federal Share of Total Expenditures Claimed for the Current Quarter and Prior Quarter Adjustments claimed on the Form OCSE–396 for all four quarters of the fiscal year.

(2) The State Share of IV–D Administrative Expenditures Made Using Funds Received as Incentive Payments is: IV–D Administrative Expenditures Made Using Funds Received as Incentive Payments for the Current Quarter and the Prior Quarter Adjustments minus the Federal Share of IV–D Administrative Expenditures Made Using Funds Received as Incentive Payments for the Current Quarter and Prior Quarter Adjustments claimed on the Form OCSE–396 for all four quarters of the fiscal year.

(3) The Fees for the Use of the Federal Parent Locator Service (FPLS) can be computed by adding the FPLS fees claimed on the Form OCSE–396 for all four quarters of the fiscal year.

(f) Requests for approval of expending incentives on activities not currently eligible for funding under the IV-D program, but which would benefit the IV-D program, must be submitted in accordance with instructions issued by the Commissioner of the Office of Child Support Enforcement.

[65 FR 82208, Dec. 27, 2000, as amended at 81 FR 93568, Dec. 20, 2016]

§ 305.40 Penalty performance measures and levels.

(a) There are three performance measures for which States must achieve certain levels of performance in order to avoid being penalized for poor performance. These measures are the paternity establishment, support order establishment, and current collections measures set forth in § 305.2 of this part. The levels the State must meet are:

(1) *The paternity establishment percentage* which is required under section 452(g) of the Act for penalty purposes. States have the option of using either the IV-D paternity establishment percentage or the statewide paternity establishment percentage defined in § 305.2 of this part. Table 4 shows the level of performance at which a State will be subject to a penalty under the paternity establishment measure.

TABLE 4—STATUTORY PENALTY PERFORMANCE STANDARDS FOR PATERNITY ESTABLISHMENT

(Use this table to determine the level of performance for the paternity establishment measure that will incur a penalty.)

PEP	Increase required over previous year's PEP	Penalty FOR FIRST FAILURE if increase not met
90% or more	None	No Penalty.
75% to 89%	2%	1–2% TANF Funds.
50% to 74%	3%	1–2% TANF Funds.
45% to 49%	4%	1–2% TANF Funds.
40% to 44%	5%	1–2% TANF Funds.
39% or less	6%	1–2% TANF Funds.

(2) The support order establishment performance measure is set forth in § 305.2 of this part. For purposes of the penalty with respect to this measure, there is a threshold of 40 percent, below which a State will be penalized unless an increase of 5 percent over the previous year is achieved—which will qualify it for an incentive. Performance in the 40 percent to 49 percent range with no significant increase will not be penalized but neither will it qualify for an incentive payment. Table 5 shows at which level of performance a State will incur a penalty under the child support order establishment measure.

TABLE 5—PERFORMANCE STANDARDS FOR ORDER ESTABLISHMENT

(Use this table to determine the level of performance for the order establishment measure that will incur a penalty.)

Performance level	Increase over previous year	Incentive/Penalty
50% or more	no increase over previous year required	Incentive.
40% to 49%	w/5% increase over previous year	Incentive.
	w/out 5% increase	No Incentive/No Penalty.
Less than 40%	w/5% increase over previous year	Incentive.
	w/out 5% increase	Penalty equal to 1–2% of TANF funds for the first failure, 2–3% for second failure, and so forth, up to a maximum of 5% of TANF funds.

(3) The *current collections* performance measure is set forth in § 305.2 of this part. There is a threshold of 35 percent below which a State will be penalized unless an increase of 5 percent over the previous year is achieved (that qualifies it for an incentive). Performance in the 35 percent to 40 percent range with no significant increase will not be penalized but neither will it qualify for an incentive payment. Table 6 shows at which level of performance the State will incur a penalty under the current collections measure.

TABLE 6—PERFORMANCE STANDARDS FOR CURRENT COLLECTIONS

(Use this table to determine the level of performance for the current collections measure that will incur a penalty.)

Performance level	Increase over previous year	Incentive/Penalty
40% or more	no increase over previous year required	Incentive.
35% to 39%	w/5% increase over previous year	Incentive.
	w/out 5% increase	No Incentive/No Penalty.
less than 35%	w/5% increase over previous year	Incentive.

TABLE 6—PERFORMANCE STANDARDS FOR CURRENT COLLECTIONS—Continued

(Use this table to determine the level of performance for the current collections measure that will incur a penalty.)

Performance level	Increase over previous year	Incentive/Penalty
	w/out 5% increase	Penalty equal to 1–2% of TANF funds for the first failure, 2–3% for second failure, and so forth, up to a maximum of 5% of TANF funds.

(b) The provisions listed under § 305.32 of this part also apply to the penalty performance measures.

§ 305.42 Penalty phase-in.

States are subject to the performance penalties described in § 305.40 based on data reported for FY 2001. Data reported for FY 2000 will be used as a base year to determine improvements in performance during FY 2001. There will be an automatic one-year corrective action period before any penalty is assessed. The penalties will be assessed and then suspended during the corrective action period.

§ 305.60 Types and scope of Federal audits.

(a) OCSE will conduct audits, at least once every three years (or more frequently if the State fails to meet performance standards and reliability of data requirements) to assess the completeness, authenticity, reliability, accuracy and security of data and the systems used to process the data in calculating performance indicators under this part;

(b) Also, OCSE will conduct audits to determine the adequacy of financial management of the State IV-D program, including assessments of:

(1) Whether funds to carry out the State program are being appropriately expended, and are properly and fully accounted for; and

(2) Whether collections and disbursements of support payments are carried out correctly and are fully accounted for; and

(c) OCSE will conduct audits for such other purposes as the Secretary may find necessary.

(1) These audits include audits to determine if the State is substantially complying with one or more of the requirements of the IV-D program (with the exception of the requirements of section 454(24) of the Act relating to statewide-automated systems and section 454(27)(A) and (B)(i) relating to the State Disbursement Unit) as defined in § 305.63 of this part. Other audits will be conducted at the discretion of OCSE.

(2) Audits to determine substantial compliance will be initiated based on substantiated evidence of a failure by the State to meet IV-D program requirements. Evidence, which could warrant an audit to determine substantial compliance, includes:

(i) The results of two or more State self-reviews conducted under section 454(15)(A) of the Act which: Show evidence of sustained poor performance; or indicate that the State has not corrected deficiencies identified in previous self-assessments, or that those deficiencies are determined to seriously impact the performance of the State's program; or

(ii) Evidence of a State program's systemic failure to provide adequate services under the program through a pattern of non-compliance over time.

(d) OCSE will conduct audits of the State's IV-D program through inspection, inquiries, observation, and confirmation and in accordance with standards promulgated by the Comptroller General of the United States in "Government Auditing Standards."

§ 305.61 Penalty for failure to meet IV-D requirements.

(a) A State will be subject to a financial penalty and the amounts otherwise payable to the State under title IV-A of the Act will be reduced in accordance with § 305.66:

(1) If on the basis of:

(i) Data submitted by the State or the results of an audit conducted under § 305.60 of this part, the State's program failed to achieve the paternity establishment percentages, as defined in section 452(g)(2) of the Act and § 305.40 of this part, or to meet the support order establishment and current collections performance measures as set forth in § 305.40 of this part; or

(ii) The results of an audit under § 305.60 of this part, the State did not submit complete and reliable data, as defined in § 305.1 of the part; or

(iii) The results of an audit under § 305.60 of this part, the State failed to substantially comply with one or more of the requirements of the IV-D program, as defined in § 305.63; and

(2) With respect to the immediately succeeding fiscal year, the State failed to take sufficient corrective action to achieve the appropriate performance levels or compliance or the data submitted by the State are still incomplete and unreliable.

(b) The reductions under paragraph (c) of this section will be made for quarters following the end of the corrective action year and will continue until the end of the first quarter throughout which the State, as appropriate:

(1) Has achieved the paternity establishment percentages, the order establishment or the current collections performance measures set forth in § 305.40 of this part;

(2) Is in substantial compliance with IV-D requirements as defined in § 305.63 of this part; or

(3) Has submitted data that are determined to be complete and reliable.

(c) The payments for a fiscal year under title IV-A of the Act will be reduced by the following percentages:

(1) One to two percent for the first finding under paragraph (a) of this section;

(2) Two to three percent for the second consecutive finding; and

(3) Not less than three percent and not more than 5 percent for the third or a subsequent consecutive finding.

(d) The reduction will be made in accordance with the provisions of 45 CFR 262.1(b)–(e) and 262.7.

§ 305.62 Disregard of a failure which is of a technical nature.

A State subject to a penalty under § 305.61(a)(1)(ii) or (iii) of this part may be determined, as appropriate, to have submitted adequate data or to have achieved substantial compliance with one or more IV-D requirements, as defined in § 305.63 of this part, if the Secretary determines that the incompleteness or unreliability of the data, or the noncompliance with one or more of the IV-D requirements, is of a technical nature which does not adversely affect the performance of the State's IV-D program or does not adversely affect the determination of the level of the State's paternity establishment or other performance measures percentages.

§ 305.63 Standards for determining substantial compliance with IV-D requirements.

For the purposes of a determination under § 305.61(a)(1)(iii) of this part, in order to be found to be in substantial compliance with one or more of the IV-D requirements as a result of an audit conducted under § 305.60 of this part, a State must meet the standards set forth below for each specific IV-D State plan requirement or requirements being audited and contained in parts 302 and 303 of this chapter, measured as follows:

(a) The State must meet the requirements under the following areas:

(1) Statewide operations, § 302.10 of this chapter;

(2) Reports and maintenance of records, § 302.15(a) of this chapter;

(3) Separation of cash handling and accounting functions, § 302.20 of this chapter; and

(4) Notice of collection of assigned support, § 302.54 of this chapter.

(b) The State must provide services required under the following areas in at least 90 percent of the cases reviewed:

(1) Establishment of cases, § 303.2(a) of this chapter; and

(2) Case closure criteria, § 303.11 of this chapter.

(c) The State must provide services required under the following areas in at least 75 percent of the cases reviewed:

(1) Collection and distribution of support payments, including: collection and distribution of support payments by the IV-D agency under § 302.32(b) of this chapter; distribution of support

collections under § 302.51 of this chapter; and distribution of support collected in title IV-E foster care maintenance cases under § 302.52 of this chapter;

(2) Establishment of paternity and support orders, including: Establishment of a case under § 303.2(b) of this chapter; services to individuals not receiving TANF or title IV-E foster care assistance, under § 302.33(a)(1) through (4) of this chapter; provision of services in intergovernmental IV-D cases under § 303.7(a), (b), (c), (d)(1) through (5) and (7) through (10), and (e) of this chapter; location of non-custodial parents under § 303.3 of this chapter; establishment of paternity under § 303.5(a) and (f) of this chapter; guidelines for setting child support awards under § 302.56 of this chapter; and establishment of support obligations under § 303.4(d), (e) and (f) of this chapter;

(3) Enforcement of support obligations, including, in all appropriate cases: establishment of a case under § 303.2(b) of this chapter; services to individuals not receiving TANF or title IV-E foster care assistance, under § 302.33(a)(1) through (4) of this chapter; provision of services in intergovernmental IV-D cases under § 303.7(a), (b), (c), (d)(1) through (5) and (7) through (10), and (e) of this chapter; location of non-custodial parents under § 303.3 of this chapter; enforcement of support obligations under § 303.6 of this chapter and State laws enacted under section 466 of the Act, including submitting once a year all appropriate cases in accordance with § 303.6(c)(3) of this chapter to State and Federal income tax refund offset; and wage withholding under § 303.100 of this chapter. In cases in which wage withholding cannot be implemented or is not available and the non-custodial parent has been located, States must use or attempt to use at least one enforcement technique available under State law in addition to Federal and State tax refund offset, in accordance with State laws and procedures and applicable State guidelines developed under § 302.70(b) of this chapter;

(4) Review and adjustment of child support orders, including: Establishment of a case under § 303.2(b) of this chapter; services to individuals not receiving TANF or title IV-E foster care assistance, under § 302.33(a)(1) through (4) of this chapter; provision of services in intergovernmental IV-D cases under § 303.7(a), (b), (c), (d)(1) through (5) and (7) through (10), and (e) of this chapter; location of non-custodial parents under § 303.3 of this chapter; guidelines for setting child support awards under § 302.56 of this chapter; and review and adjustment of support obligations under § 303.8 of this chapter; and

(5) Medical support, including: establishment of a case under § 303.2(b) of this chapter; services to individuals not receiving TANF or title IV-E foster care assistance, under § 302.33(a)(1) through (4) of this chapter; provision of services in intergovernmental IV-D cases under § 303.7(a), (b), (c), (d)(1) through (5) and (7) through (10), and (e) of this chapter; location of non-custodial parents under § 303.3 of this chapter; securing medical support information under § 303.30 of this chapter; and securing and enforcing medical support obligations under § 303.31 and § 302.32 of this chapter; and

(6) Disbursement of support payments in accordance with the timeframes in section 454B of the Act and § 302.32 of this chapter.

(d) With respect to the 75 percent standard in paragraph (c) of this section:

(1) Notwithstanding timeframes for establishment of cases in § 303.2(b) of this chapter; provision of services in interstate IV-D cases under § 303.7(a)(4) through (8), (b), (c), (d)(2) through (5) and (7) and (10) of this chapter; location and support order establishment under § 303.3(b)(3) and (5), and § 303.4(d) of this chapter, if a support order needs to be established in a case and an order is established during the audit period in accordance with the State's guidelines for setting child support awards, the State will be considered to have taken appropriate action in that case for audit purposes.

(2) Notwithstanding timeframes for establishment of cases in § 303.2(b) of this chapter; provision of services in interstate IV-D cases under § 303.7(a)(4) through (8), (b), (c), (d)(2) through (5) and (7) and (10) of this chapter; and location and review and adjustment of support orders contained in § 303.3(b)(3)

and (5), and § 303.8 of this chapter, if a particular case has been reviewed and meets the conditions for adjustment under State laws and procedures and § 303.8 of this chapter, and the order is adjusted, or a determination is made, as a result of a review, during the audit period, that an adjustment is not needed, in accordance with the State's guidelines for setting child support awards, the State will be considered to have taken appropriate action in that case for audit purposes.

(3) Notwithstanding timeframes for establishment of cases in § 303.2(b) of this chapter; provision of services in interstate IV-D cases under § 303.7(a)(4) through (8), (b), (c), (d)(2) through (5) and (7) and (10) of this chapter; and location and wage withholding in § 303.3(b) (3) and (5), and § 303.100 of this chapter, if wage withholding is appropriate in a particular case and wage withholding is implemented and wages are withheld during the audit period, the State will be considered to have taken appropriate action in that case for audit purposes.

(4) Notwithstanding timeframes for establishment of cases in § 303.2(b) of this chapter; provision of services in interstate IV-D cases under § 303.7(a)(4) through (8), (b), (c), (d)(2) through (5) and (7) and (10) of this chapter; and location and enforcement of support obligations in § 303.3(b) (3) and (5), and § 303.6 of this chapter, if wage withholding is not appropriate in a particular case, and the State uses at least one enforcement technique available under State law, in addition to Federal and State income tax refund offset, which results in a collection received during the audit period, the State will be considered to have taken appropriate action in the case for audit purposes.

(e) The State must meet the requirements for expedited processes under § 303.101(b)(2)(i) and (iii), and (e) of this chapter.

[65 FR 82208, Dec. 27, 2000, as amended at 73 FR 42442, July 21, 2008; 75 FR 38644, July 2, 2010; 81 FR 93568, Dec. 20, 2016]

§ 305.64 Audit procedures and State comments.

(a) Prior to the start of the actual audit, Federal auditors will hold an audit entrance conference with the IV-D agency. At that conference, the auditors will explain how the audit will be performed and make any necessary arrangements.

(b) At the conclusion of audit fieldwork, Federal auditors will afford the State IV-D agency an opportunity for an audit exit conference at which time preliminary audit findings will be discussed and the IV-D agency may present any additional matter it believes should be considered in the audit findings.

(c) After the exit conference, Federal auditors will prepare and send to the IV-D agency a copy of their interim report on the results of the audit. Within a specified timeframe from the date the report was sent, the IV–D agency may submit comments, which are reflected in a record, on any part of the report which the IV–D agency believes is in error. The auditors will note such comments and incorporate any response into the final audit report.

[65 FR 82208, Dec. 27, 2000, as amended at 81 FR 93568, Dec. 20, 2016]

§ 305.65 State cooperation in audit.

(a) Each State shall make available to the Federal auditors such records or other supporting documentation (electronic and manual) as the audit staff may request, including records to support the data as submitted on the Federal statistical and financial reports that will be used to calculate the State's performance. The State shall also make available personnel associated with the State's IV-D program to provide information that the audit staff may find necessary in order to conduct or complete the audit.

(b) States must provide evidence to Office that their data are complete and reliable as defined in § 305.2 of this part.

(c) Failure to comply with the requirements of this section with respect to audits conducted to determine compliance with IV-D requirements under § 305.60 of this part, may necessitate a finding that the State has failed to comply with the particular criteria being audited.

§ 305.66 Notice, corrective action year, and imposition of penalty.

(a) If a State is found by the Secretary to be subject to a penalty as described in § 305.61, the OCSE will notify the State, in a record, of such finding.

(b) The notice will:

(1) Explain the deficiency or deficiencies which result in the State being subject to a penalty, indicate the amount of the potential penalty, and give reasons for the finding; and

(2) Specify that the penalty will be assessed in accordance with the provisions of 45 CFR 262.1(b) through (e) and 262.7 if the State is found to have failed to correct the deficiency or deficiencies cited in the notice during the automatic corrective action year (i.e., the succeeding fiscal year following the year with respect to which the deficiency occurred.)

(c) The penalty under § 305.61 of this part will be assessed if the Secretary determines that the State has not corrected the deficiency or deficiencies cited in the notice by the end of the corrective action year.

(d) Only one corrective action period is provided to a State with respect to a given deficiency where consecutive findings of noncompliance are made with respect to that deficiency. In the case of a State against which the penalty is assessed and which failed to correct the deficiency or deficiencies cited in the notice by the end of the corrective action year, the penalty will be effective for any quarter after the end of the corrective action year and ends for the first full quarter throughout which the State IV-D program is determined to have corrected the deficiency or deficiencies cited in the notice.

(e) A consecutive finding occurs only when the State does not meet the same criterion or criteria cited in the notice in paragraph (a) of this section.

[65 FR 82208, Dec. 27, 2000, as amended at 81 FR 93568, Dec. 20, 2016]

PART 306 [RESERVED]

PART 307—COMPUTERIZED SUPPORT ENFORCEMENT SYSTEMS

Sec.

AUTHORITY: 42 U.S.C. 652 through 658, 664, 666 through 669A, and 1302.

SOURCE: 49 FR 33260, Aug. 22, 1984, unless otherwise noted.

§ 307.0 Scope of this part.

This part implements sections 452(d) and (e), 454(16) and (24), 454A, and 455(a)(1)(A) and (B), and (a)(3)(A) of the Act which prescribe:

(a) The requirement for computerized support enforcement systems;

(b) The functional requirements that a statewide computerized support enforcement system must meet;

(c) Security and confidentiality requirements for computerized support enforcement systems;

(d) The criteria the Office must determine exist prior to approving an advance planning document (APD);

(e) The requirements and procedures for the submittal of an APD;

(f) The requirement for continuous review of each approved statewide computerized support enforcement system;

(g) The availability of FFP at the 90 percent rate;

(h) The availability of FFP at the applicable matching rate; and

(i) The conditions under which the Office will suspend approval of an APD.

[57 FR 47002, Oct. 14, 1992, as amended at 63 FR 44814, Aug. 21, 1998]

§ 307.1 Definitions.

(a) *Alternative approach to APD requirements* means that the State has developed an APD that does not meet all conditions for APD approval in § 307.15(b) resulting in the need for a waiver under § 307.5.

(b) *Business day* means a day on which State offices are open for business.

(c) *Alternative system* means the separate manual and/or automated processes that perform one or more of the required functions separately from the base system and that interfaces with the base system to ensure that the State can meet all requirements for purposes of the audit prescribed in section 403(h) of the Act. These separate processes may involve geographic areas, such as counties; administrative jurisdictions, such as courts; or separate means by which the State meets particular program requirements, e.g., collection of support for non-IV-A cases.

(d) *Alternative system configuration* means an alternative to a comprehensive computerized support enforcement system. It includes a base system with electronic linkages to an alternative system(s), which is not part of the State's computerized support enforcement project (i.e., not the State's sole system effort), but which is necessary to meet the functional requirements of the statewide, comprehensive computerized support enforcement system under § 307.10, or § 307.11.

(e) *Base system* means the hardware, operational software, applications software and electronic linkages in an alternative system configuration which allow the State to monitor, account for and control all support enforcement services and activities under the State plan.

(f) *Certification* means approval of an operational computerized support enforcement system based on a determination that the system has an efficient and effective design and is comprehensive, except where a waiver applies.

(g) *Comprehensive* means that a computerized support enforcement system meets the requirements prescribed in § 307.10, or § 307.11 of this part, as further defined in the OCSE guideline entitled "Automated Systems for Child Support Enforcement: A Guide for States."

(h) *Computerized support enforcement system* means a comprehensive, statewide system or an alternative system configuration which encompasses all political subdivisions within the State and which effectively and efficiently;

(1) Introduces, processes, accounts for and monitors data used by the Child Support Enforcement program in carrying out activities under the State plan; and

(2) Produces utilization and management information about support enforcement services as required by the State IV-D agency and Federal government for program administration and audit purposes.

(i) *Planning* means: (1) The preliminary project activity to determine the requirements necessitating the project, the activities to be undertaken, and the resources required to complete the project;

(2) The preparation of an APD;

(3) The preparation of a detailed project plan describing when and how the computer system will be designed or transferred and adapted; and

(4) The preparation of a detailed implementation plan describing specific training, testing, and conversion plans to install the computer system.

(j) The following terms are defined at 45 CFR part 95, subpart F, in § 95.605:

"Advance Planning Document";

"Annually Updated APD";

"Design" or "System Design";

"Development";

"Enhancement";

"Implementation Advance Planning Document";

"Initial APD";

"Installation";

"Operation";

"Planning Advance Planning Document";

"Requirements Analysis"; and

"Software".

(k) The definitions found in § 301.1 of this chapter are also applicable to this part.

[57 FR 47002, Oct. 14, 1992, as amended at 63 FR 44814, Aug. 21, 1998; 68 FR 25305, May 12, 2003]

§ 307.5 Mandatory computerized support enforcement systems.

(a) *Basic requirement.* (1) By October 1, 1997, each State must have in effect an operational computerized support enforcement system, which meets Federal requirements under § 302.85(a)(1) of this chapter, OCSE will review each system to certify that these requirements are met; and

(2) By October 1, 2000, each State must have in effect an operational computerized support enforcement system, which meets Federal requirements under § 302.85(a)(2) of this chapter. OCSE will review each system to certify that these requirements are met.

(b) *Waiver option.* A State may apply for a waiver of any functional requirement in § 307.10, or § 307.11 by presenting a plan for an alternative system configuration, or a waiver of any conditions for APD approval in § 307.15(b) by presenting an alternative approach. Waiver requests must be submitted and approved as part of the State's APD or APD update.

(c) *Conditions for waiver.* The Secretary may grant a State a waiver if:

(1) The State demonstrates that it has an alternative approach to the APD requirements or an alternative system configuration that enables the State, in accordance with part 305 of this chapter, to be in substantial compliance with the other requirements of this chapter; and either:

(2) The waiver request meets the criteria set forth in section 1115(c) (1), (2) and (3) of the Act; or

(3) The State provides assurance, which is reflected in a record, that steps will be taken to otherwise improve the State's Child Support Enforcement program.

(d) *APD submittal requirements for alternative system configuration.* APDs submitted by States which include requests for waiver for an alternative system configuration must, in addition to meeting conditions of § 307.15(b):

(1) Describe the State's base system;

(2) Include a detailed description of the separate automated or manual processes the State plans to use and how they will interface with the base system;

(3) Provide documentation that the alternative system configuration will enable the State to be in substantial compliance with title IV-D of the Act in accordance with section 403(h) of the Act and implementing regulations. In addition, if the State is subject to a Notice under § 305.99 of this part that it did not substantially comply with one or more of the requirements of title IV-D of the Act, at the time a waiver request is submitted, the State must:

(i) Demonstrate that the deficiency is not related to or caused by the performance of the system; or

(ii) Specify the corrective action taken to modify the system if the system contributed to the deficiency.

(e) *APD submittal requirements for alternative approach.* APDs submitted by States which include requests for waiver of conditions for APD approval in § 307.15(b) must demonstrate why meeting the conditions is unnecessary or inappropriate.

(f) *Review of waiver requests.* (1) The Office will review waiver requests to assure that all necessary information is provided, that all processes provide for effective and efficient program operation, and that the conditions for waiver in paragraph (d) of this section are met.

(2) When a waiver is approved, it becomes part of the State's approved APD. A waiver is subject to the APD suspension provisions in § 307.40.

(3) When a waiver is disapproved, the APD will be disapproved. The APD disapproval is a final administrative decision and is not subject to administrative appeal.

(g) *FFP limitations.* (1) The provisions of §§ 307.30 and 307.35 apply to requests for FFP for costs of computerized support enforcement systems.

(2) FFP for alternative system configurations is further limited as follows:

(i) FFP is available at the enhanced matching rate for development of the base system and for hardware, operational system software, and electronic linkages with the separate components of an alternative system configuration.

(ii) FFP is available at the applicable matching rate for minor alterations to the separate automated or manual processes that are part of an alternative system configuration and for operating costs including hardware, operational software and applications software of a computerized support enforcement system.

(iii) FFP is not available for developing new systems or making major changes and enhancements to separate automated or manual processes so that alternative system configurations meet conditions for waiver.

[57 FR 47003, Oct. 14, 1992, as amended at 61 FR 67241, Dec. 20, 1996; 63 FR 44814, Aug. 21, 1998; 81 FR 93568, Dec. 20, 2016]

§ 307.10 Functional requirements for computerized support enforcement systems in operation by October 1, 1997.

At a minimum, each State's computerized support enforcement system established under the title IV-D State plan at § 302.85(a)(1) of this chapter must:

(a) Be planned, designed, developed, installed or enhanced in accordance with an initial and annually updated APD approved under § 307.15; and

(b) Control, account for, and monitor all the factors in the support collection and paternity determination processes under the State plan. At a minimum this must include:

(1) Maintaining identifying information such as social security numbers, names, dates of birth, home addresses and mailing addresses (including postal zip codes) on individuals against whom support obligations are sought to be established or enforced and on individuals to whom support obligations are owed, and other data as required by the Office;

(2) Periodically verifying the information on individuals referred to in paragraph (b)(1) of this section with Federal, State and local agencies, both intrastate and interstate;

(3) Maintaining data necessary to meet Federal Reporting Requirements on a timely basis as prescribed by the Office;

(4) Maintaining information pertaining to:

(i) Delinquency and enforcement activities;

(ii) Intrastate, interstate and Federal location of absent parents;

(iii) The establishment of paternity; and

(iv) The establishment of support obligations;

(5) Collecting and distributing both intrastate and interstate support payments;

(6) Computing and distributing incentive payments to political subdivisions which share in the cost of funding the program and to other political subdivisions based on efficiency and effectiveness if the State has chosen to pay such incentives;

(7) Maintaining accounts receivable on all amounts owed, collected, and distributed;

(8) Maintaining costs of all services rendered, either directly or by interfacing with State financial management and expenditure information;

(9) Accepting electronic case referrals and update information from the State's title IV-A program and using that information to identify and manage support enforcement cases;

(10) Transmitting information electronically to provide data to the State's TANF system so that the IV-A agency can determine (and report back to the IV-D system) whether a collection of support causes a change in eligibility for, or the amount of aid under, the IV-A program;

(11) Providing security to prevent unauthorized access to, or use of, the data in the system;

(12) Providing management information on all IV-D cases under the State plan from initial referral or application through collection and enforcement;

(13) Providing electronic data exchange with the State Medicaid system to provide for case referral and the transfer of the medical support information specified in 45 CFR 303.30 and 303.31;

(14) Using automated processes to assist the State in meeting State plan requirements under part 302 of this chapter and Standards for program operations under part 303 of this chapter, including but not limited to:

(i) The automated maintenance and monitoring of accurate records of support payments;

(ii) Providing automated maintenance of case records for purposes of the management and tracking requirements in §303.2 of this chapter;

(iii) Providing title IV-D case workers with on-line access to automated sources of absent parent employer and wage information maintained by the State when available, by establishing an electronic link or by obtaining an extract of the data base and placing it on-line for access throughout the State;

(iv) Providing locate capability by automatically referring cases electronically to locate sources within the State (such as State motor vehicle department, State department of revenue, and other State agencies), and to the Federal Parent Locator Service and utilizing electronic linkages to receive return locate information and place the information on-line to title IV-D case workers throughout the State;

(v) Providing capability for electronic funds transfer for purposes of income withholding and interstate collections;

(vi) Integrating all processing of interstate cases with the computerized support enforcement system, including the central registry; and

(15) Providing automated processes to enable the Office to monitor State operations and assess program performance through the audit conducted under section 452(a) of the Act.

[57 FR 47003, Oct. 14, 1992, as amended at 63 FR 44815, Aug. 21, 1998; 68 FR 25305, May 12, 2003]

§307.11 Functional requirements for computerized support enforcement systems in operation by October 1, 2000.

At a minimum, each State's computerized support enforcement system established and operated under the title IV-D State plan at §302.85(a)(2) of this chapter must:

(a) Be planned, designed, developed, installed or enhanced, and operated in accordance with an initial and annually updated APD approved under §307.15 of this part;

(b) Control, account for, and monitor all the factors in the support collection and paternity determination processes under the State plan. At a minimum, this includes the following:

(1) The activities described in §307.10, except paragraphs (b)(3), (8) and (11); and

(2) The capability to perform the following tasks with the frequency and in the manner required under, or by this chapter:

(i) Program requirements. Performing such functions as the Secretary may specify related to management of the State IV-D program under this chapter including:

(A) Controlling and accounting for the use of Federal, State and local funds in carrying out the program either directly, through an auxiliary system or through an interface with State financial management and expenditure information; and

(B) Maintaining the data necessary to meet Federal reporting requirements under this chapter in a timely basis as prescribed by the Office;

(ii) Calculation of Performance Indicators. Enabling the Secretary to determine the incentive payments and penalty adjustments required by sections 452(g) and 458 of the Act by:

(A) Using automated processes to:

(*1*) Maintain the requisite data on State performance for paternity establishment and child support enforcement activities in the State; and

(*2*) Calculate the paternity establishment percentage for the State for each fiscal year;

(B) Having in place system controls to ensure the completeness, and reliability of, and ready access to, the data described in paragraph (b)(2)(i)(A)(1) of this section, and the accuracy of the calculation described in paragraph (b)(2)(i)(A)(2) of this section; and

(iii) System Controls: Having systems controls (e.g., passwords or blocking of fields) to ensure strict adherence to the policies described in Sec. 307.13(a); and

(3) Activities described in the Act that were added by the Personal Responsibility and Work Opportunity Reconciliation Act of 1996, Pub. L. 104–193, not otherwise addressed in this part.

(c) Collection and Disbursement of Support Payments. To the maximum extent feasible, assist and facilitate the collection and disbursement of support payments through the State disbursement unit operated under section 454B of the Act through the performance of functions which, at a minimum, include the following:

(1) Transmission of orders and notices to employers and other debtors for the withholding of income:

(i) Within 2 business days after receipt of notice of income, and the income source subject to withholding from a court, another State, an employer, the Federal Parent Locator Service, or another source recognized by the State; and

(ii) Using uniform formats prescribed by the Secretary;

(2) Ongoing monitoring to promptly identify failures to make timely payment of support; and

(3) Automatic use of enforcement procedures, including those under section 466(c) of the Act if payments are not timely, and the following procedures:

(i) Identify cases which have been previously identified as involving a noncustodial parent who is a recipient of SSI payments or concurrent SSI payments and Social Security Disability Insurance (SSDI) benefits under title II of the Act, to prevent garnishment of these funds from the noncustodial parent's financial account; and

(ii) Return funds to a noncustodial parent, within 5 business days after the agency determines that SSI payments or concurrent SSI payments and SSDI benefits under title II of the Act, in the noncustodial parent's financial account have been incorrectly garnished.

(d) Expedited Administrative Procedures. To the maximum extent feasible, be used to implement the expedited administrative procedures required by section 466(c) of the Act.

(e) State case registry. Have a State case registry that meets the requirements of this paragraph.

(1) Definitions. When used in this paragraph and paragraph (f) of this section, the following definitions shall apply.

(i) Participant means an individual who owes or is owed a duty of support, imposed or imposable by law, or with respect to or on behalf of whom a duty of support is sought to be established, or who is an individual connected to an order of support or a child support case being enforced.

(ii) Participant type means the custodial party, non-custodial parent, putative father, or child, associated with a case or support order contained in the State or Federal case registry.

(iii) locate request type refers to the purpose of the request for additional matching services on information sent to the Federal case registry, for example, a IV-D locate (paternity or support establishment or support enforcement), parental kidnapping or custody and visitation.

(iv) locate source type refers to the external sources a locate submitter desires the information sent to the Federal case registry to also be matched against.

(2) The State case registry shall contain a record of:

(i) Every IV-D case receiving child support enforcement services under an approved State plan; and

(ii) Every support order established or modified in the State on or after October 1, 1998.

(3) Standardized data elements shall be included for each participant. These data elements shall include:

(i) Names;

(ii) Social security numbers;

(iii) Dates of birth;

(iv) Case identification numbers;

(v) Other uniform identification numbers;

(vi) Data elements required under paragraph (f)(1) of this section necessary for the operation of the Federal case registry;

(vii) Issuing State of an order; and

(viii) Any other information that the Secretary may require.

(4) The record required under paragraph (e)(2) of this section shall include information for every case in the State case registry receiving services under an approved State plan that has a support order in effect. The information must include:

(i) The amount of monthly (or other frequency) support owed under the order;

(ii) Other amounts due or overdue under the order including arrearages, interest or late payment penalties and fees;

(iii) Any amounts described in paragraph (e)(4) (i) and (ii) of this section that have been collected;

(iv) The distribution of such collected amounts;

(v) The birth date and, beginning no later than October 1, 1999, the name and social security number of any child for whom the order requires the provision of support; and

(vi) The amount of any lien imposed in accordance with section 466(a)(4) of the Act to enforce the order.

(5) Establish and update, maintain, and regularly monitor case records in the State case registry for cases receiving services under the State plan. To ensure information on an established IV-D case is up to date, the State should regularly update the system to make changes to the status of a case, the participants of a case, and the data contained in the case record. This includes the following:

(i) Information on administrative and judicial orders related to paternity and support;

(ii) Information obtained from comparisons with Federal, State or local sources of information;

(iii) Information on support collections and distributions; and

(iv) Any other relevant information.

(6) States may link local case registries of support orders through an automated information network in meeting paragraph (e)(2)(ii) of this section provided that all other requirements of this paragraph are met.

(f) Information Comparisons and other Disclosures of Information. Extract information, at such times and in such standardized format or formats, as may be required by the Secretary, for purposes of sharing and comparing with, and receiving information from, other data bases and information comparison services, to obtain or provide information necessary to enable the State, other States, the Office or other Federal agencies to carry out this chapter. As applicable, these comparisons and disclosures must comply with the requirements of section 6103 of the Internal Revenue Code of 1986 and the requirements of section 453 of the Act. The comparisons and sharing of information include:

(1) Effective October 1, 1998, (or for the child data, not later than October 1, 1999) furnishing the following information to the Federal case registry on participants in cases receiving services under the State plan and in support orders established or modified on or after October 1, 1998, and providing updates of such information within five (5) business days of receipt by the IV-D agency of new or changed, information, including information which would necessitate adding or removing a Family Violence indicator and notices of the expiration of support orders:

(i) State Federal Information Processing Standard (FIPS) code and optionally, county code;

(ii) State case identification number;

(iii) State member identification number;

(iv) Case type (IV-D, non-IV-D);

(v) Social security number and any necessary alternative social security numbers;

(vi) Name, including first, middle, last name and any necessary alternative names;

(vii) Sex (optional);

(viii) Date of birth;

(ix) Participant type (custodial party, non-custodial parent, putative father, child);

(x) Family violence indicator (domestic violence or child abuse);

(xi) Indication of an order;

(xii) Locate request type (optional);

(xiii) Locate source (optional); and

(xiv) Any other information of the Secretary may require.

(2) Requesting or exchanging information with the Federal parent locator service for the purposes specified in section 453 of the Act;

(3) Exchanging information with State agencies, both within and outside of the State, administering programs under titles IV-A and XIX of the Act, as necessary to perform State agency responsibilities under this chapter and under such programs; and

(4) Exchanging information with other agencies of the State, and agencies of other States, and interstate information networks, as necessary and appropriate, to assist the State and

other States in carrying out the purposes of this chapter.

[63 FR 44815, Aug. 21, 1998, as amended at 81 FR 93568, Dec. 20, 2016]

§ 307.13 Security and confidentiality for computerized support enforcement systems in operation after October 1, 1997.

The State IV-D agency shall:

(a) *Information integrity and security.* Have safeguards protecting the integrity, accuracy, completeness of, access to, and use of data in the computerized support enforcement system. These safeguards shall include written policies concerning access to data by IV–D agency personnel, and the sharing of data with other persons to:

(1) Permit access to and use of data to the extent necessary to carry out the State IV–D program under this chapter;

(2) Specify the data which may be used for particular IV–D program purposes, and the personnel permitted access to such data;

(3) Permit disclosure of information to State agencies administering programs under titles IV (including Tribal programs under title IV), XIX, and XXI of the Act, and SNAP, to the extent necessary to assist them to carry out their responsibilities under such programs in accordance with section 454A(f)(3) of the Act, to the extent that it does not interfere with the IV–D program meeting its own obligations and subject to such requirements as prescribed by the Office.

(4) Prohibit the disclosure of NDNH, FCR, financial institution, and IRS information outside the IV–D program except that:

(i) IRS information is restricted as specified in the Internal Revenue Code;

(ii) Independently verified information other than financial institution information may be released to authorized persons;

(iii) NDNH and FCR information may be disclosed without independent verification to IV–B and IV–E agencies to locate parents and putative fathers for the purpose of establishing parentage or establishing parental rights with respect to a child; and

(iv) NDNH and FCR information may be disclosed without independent verification to title IV–D, IV–A, IV–B and IV–E agencies for the purpose of assisting States to carry out their responsibilities to administer title IV–D, IV–A, IV–B and IV–E programs.

(b) *Monitoring of access.* Monitor routine access to and use of the computerized support enforcement system through methods such as audit trails and feedback mechanisms to guard against, and promptly identify unauthorized access or use;

(c) *Training and information.* Have procedures to ensure that all personnel, including State and local staff and contractors, who may have access to or be required to use confidential program data in the computerized support enforcement system are:

(1) Informed of applicable requirements and penalties, including those in section 6103 of the Internal Revenue Service Code and section 453 of the Act; and

(2) Adequately trained in security procedures; and

(d) *Penalties.* Have administrative penalties, including dismissal from employment, for unauthorized access to, disclosure or use of confidential information.

[63 FR 44816, Aug. 21, 1998, as amended at 73 FR 56445, Sept. 26, 2008; 75 FR 81908, Dec. 29, 2010]

§ 307.15 Approval of advance planning documents for computerized support enforcement systems.

(a) *Approval of an APD.* The Office shall not approve the APD and annually updated APD unless the document, when implemented, will carry out the requirements of § 307.10, or § 307.11 of this part. Conditions for APD approval are specified in this section.

(b) *Conditions for initial approval.* In order to be approvable, an APD for a statewide computerized support enforcement system described under § 307.10, or § 307.11 must meet the following requirements:

(1) The APD must represent the sole systems effort being undertaken by the State in accordance with § 307.10, or § 307.11. If the State is requesting a waiver under § 302.85 of this chapter, the APD must specify the conditions for which waiver is requested;

(2) The APD must specify how the objectives of the computerized support enforcement system in §307.10, or §307.11 will be carried out throughout the State; this includes a projection of how the proposed system will meet the functional requirements of §307.10, or §307.11 and how the single State system will encompass all political subdivisions in the State by October 1, 1997, or October 1, 2000 respectively.

(3) The APD must assure the feasibility of the proposed effort and provide for the conduct of a requirements analysis study which address all system components within the State and includes consideration of the program mission, functions, organization, services and constraints related to the computerized support enforcement system;

(4) The APD must indicate how the results of the requirements analysis study will be incorporated into the proposed system design, development, installation or enhancement;

(5) The APD must contain a description of each component within the proposed computerized support enforcement system as required by §307.10, or §307.11 and must describe information flows, input data, and output reports and uses;

(6) The APD must describe the security requirements to be employed in the proposed computerized support enforcement system;

(7) The APD must describe the intrastate and interstate interfaces set forth in §307.10, or §307.11 to be employed in the proposed computerized support enforcement system;

(8) The APD must describe the projected resource requirements for staff, hardware, and other needs and the resources available or expected to be available to meet the requirements;

(9) The APD must contain a proposed budget and schedule of life-cycle milestones relative to the size, complexity and cost of the project which at a minimum address requirements analysis, program design, procurement and project management; and, a description of estimated expenditures by category and amount for:

(i) Items that are eligible for funding at the enhanced matching rate, and

(ii) Items related to developing and operating the system that are eligible for Federal funding at the applicable matching rate;

(10) The APD must contain an implementation plan and backup procedures to handle possible failures in system planning, design, development, installation or enhancement.

(i) These backup procedures must include provision for independent validation and verification (IV&V) analysis of a State's system development effort in the case of States:

(A) That do not have in place a statewide automated child support enforcement system that meets the requirements of the FSA of 1988;

(B) States which fail to meet a critical milestone, as identified in their APDs;

(C) States which fail to timely and completely submit APD updates;

(D) States whose APD indicates the need for a total system redesign;

(E) States developing systems under waivers pursuant to section 452(d)(3) of the Social Security Act; or,

(F) States whose system development efforts we determine are at risk of failure, significant delay, or significant cost overrun.

(ii) Independent validation and verification efforts must be conducted by an entity that is independent from the State (unless the State receives an exception from OCSE) and the entity selected must:

(A) Develop a project workplan. The plan must be provided directly to OCSE at the same time it is given to the State.

(B) Review and make recommendations on both the management of the project, both State and vendor, and the technical aspects of the project. The IV&V provider must provide the results of its analysis directly to OCSE at the same time it reports to the State.

(C) Consult with all stakeholders and assess the user involvement and buy-in regarding system functionality and the system's ability to meet program needs.

(D) Conduct an analysis of past project performance sufficient to identify and make recommendations for improvement.

(E) Provide risk management assessment and capacity planning services.

(F) Develop performance metrics which allow tracking project completion against milestones set by the State.

(iii) The RFP and contract for selecting the IV&V provider (or similar documents if IV&V services are provided by other State agencies) must include the experience and skills of the key personnel proposed for the IV&V analysis and specify by name the key personnel who actually will work on the project and must be submitted to OCSE for prior approval.

(11) The APD must describe each system considered during planning including the advantages of selecting the proposed solution. If a transfer system is not selected as the proposed solution, a transfer system must be among those systems considered. If a system that is already in place in the State could be enhanced to meet the requirements for a computerized support enforcement system, that system must be among the solutions considered;

(12) The APD must contain a cost benefit analysis of the proposed computerized support enforcement system and all alternatives considered that describes the proposed improvements to the IV-D program in both qualitative and quantitative terms;

(13) The APD must specify the basis for determining direct and indirect costs of the computerized support enforcement system during development and operation, including the methodology for determining costs of planning, design, development, installation or enhancement that are eligible for 90 percent Federal funding versus costs of development and operations that are eligible for Federal funding at the applicable matching rate;

(14) The APD must contain a statement indicating the period of time the State expects to use the proposed computerized support enforcement system; and

(15) The APD must include any waiver requested in accordance with § 307.5 of this chapter.

(c) *Conditions for approval of annual update.* The APD for a computerized support enforcement system described under § 307.10, or § 307.11 must be updated annually. In order to be approvable, the annual update of an APD for a computerized support enforcement system described under § 307.10 must meet only those requirements of paragraph (b) of this section that are prescribed by instructions issued by the Office.

(Approved by the Office of Management and Budget under control number 0960–0343)

[49 FR 33260, Aug. 22, 1984, as amended at 51 FR 37732, Oct. 24, 1986; 55 FR 4379, Feb. 7, 1990; 57 FR 47004, Oct. 14, 1992; 61 FR 67241, Dec. 20, 1996; 63 FR 44816, Aug. 21, 1998]

§ 307.20 Submittal of advance planning documents for computerized support enforcement systems.

The State IV-D agency must submit an APD for a computerized support enforcement system, approved and signed by the State IV-D Director and the appropriate State official, in accordance with the submission process prescribed in 45 CFR part 95, subpart F.

[55 FR 4379, Feb. 7, 1990, as amended at 57 FR 47005, Oct. 14, 1992]

§ 307.25 Review and certification of computerized support enforcement systems.

The Office will review, assess and inspect the planning, design, development, installation, enhancement and operation of computerized support enforcement systems developed under § 307.10, or § 307.11 to determine the extent to which such systems:

(a) Meet the requirements found in § 307.15; and

(b) Can be certified as meeting the requirements described in § 307.10 and in the OCSE guideline entitled "Automated Systems for Child Support Enforcement: A Guide for States".

[57 FR 47005, Oct. 14, 1992, as amended at 63 FR 44817, Aug. 21, 1998]

§ 307.30 Federal financial participation at the 90 percent rate for statewide computerized support enforcement systems.

(a) *Conditions that must be met for FFP.* During the Federal fiscal years 1996, and 1997, Federal financial participation is available at the 90 percent rate in expenditures for the planning, design, development, installation or enhancement of a computerized support enforcement system as described in §§307.5 and 307.10 limited to the amount in an advance planning document, or APDU submitted on or before September 30, 1995, and approved by OCSE if:

(1) The Office has approved an APD in accordance with §307.15 of this part;

(2) The system meets the requirements specified in §307.10;

(3) The Office determines that the expenditures incurred are consistent with the approved APD;

(4) The Office determines that the computerized support enforcement system or alternative system configuration is designed effectively and efficiently and will improve the management and administration of the State IV-D plan;

(5) The State IV-D agency agrees in writing to use the system for a period of time which is consistent with the APD approved by the Office; and

(6) The State or local government has ownership rights in software, software modifications and associated documentation that is designed, developed, installed, or enhanced with 90 percent FFP under this section subject to the Department of Health and Human Services license specified in paragraph (c) of this section.

(b) *Federal financial participation in the costs of hardware and proprietary software.* (1) Until September 30, 1997, FFP at the 90 percent rate is available in expenditures for the rental or purchase of hardware for the planning, design, development, installation or enhancement of a computerized support enforcement system as described in §307.10 in accordance with the limitation in paragraph (a) of this section.

(2) Until September 30, 1997, FFP at the 90 percent rate is available for expenditures for the rental or purchase of proprietary operating/vendor software necessary for the operation of hardware during the planning, design, development, installation or enhancement of a computerized support enforcement system in accordance with the limitation in paragraph (a) of this section, and the OCSE guideline entitled "Automated Systems for Child Support Enforcement: A Guide for States." FFP at the 90 percent rate is not available for proprietary application software developed specifically for a computerized support enforcement system. §307.35 of this part regarding reimbursement at the applicable matching rate.)

(c) *HHS rights to software.* The Department of Health and Human Services reserves a royalty-free, non-exclusive and irrevocable license to reproduce, publish or otherwise use, and to authorize others to use for Federal government purposes, software, software modifications, and documentation developed under §307.10. This license would permit the Department to authorize the use of software, software modifications and documentation developed under §307.10 in another project or activity funded by the Federal government.

(d) *Consequences of suspension of the APD.* If the Office suspends approval of an APD in accordance with §307.40 of this part during the planning design, development, installation, enhancement or operation of the system:

(1) The Office shall disallow FFP as of the date the State failed to comply substantially with the approved APD; and

(2) FFP at the 90 and applicable matching rates is not available in any expenditures incurred under the APD after the date of the suspension until the date the Office determines that the State has taken the actions specified in the notice of suspension described in §307.40(a)(2) of this part. The Office will notify the State in writing upon making such a determination. (See §307.35(b) regarding reimbursement for disallowed expenditures under part 95, subpart F of this title.)

[49 FR 33260, Aug. 22, 1984, as amended at 50 FR 19657, May 9, 1985; 55 FR 4379, Feb. 7, 1990; 57 FR 47005, Oct. 14, 1992; 63 FR 44817, Aug. 21, 1998]

§307.31 Federal financial participation at the 80 percent rate for computerized support enforcement systems.

(a) *Conditions that must be met for 80 percent FFP.* Until September 30, 2001, Federal financial participation is available at the 80 percent rate to States, Territories and systems defined in 42 U.S.C. 655(a)(3)(B)(iii) [455(a)(3)(B)(iii) of the Act] (hereafter referred to as "States") for expenditures for the planning, design, development, installation, or enhancement of a computerized support enforcement system meeting the requirements as described in §§ 307.5 and 307.10 or 42 U.S.C. § 654(16) [454(16) of the Act], if:

(1) The Office has approved an APD in accordance with § 307.15;

(2) The Office determines that the system meets the requirements specified in § 307.10, or 42 U.S.C. 654(16) [454(16) of the Act];

(3) The Office determines that the expenditures incurred are consistent with the approved APD;

(4) The Office determines that the computerized support enforcement system is designed effectively and efficiently and will improve the management and administration of the State IV-D plan;

(5) The State IV-D agency agrees in writing to use the system for a period of time which is consistent with the APD approved by the Office; and

(6) The State or local government has ownership rights in software, software modifications and associated documentation that is designed, developed, installed or enhanced under this section subject to the Department of Health and Human Services license specified in paragraph (c) of this section.

(b) *Federal financial participation in the costs of hardware and proprietary software.* (1) Until September 30, 2001, FFP at the 80 percent rate is available for expenditures for the rental or purchase of hardware for the planning, design, development, installation, or enhancement of a computerized support enforcement system as described in § 307.10 or 42 U.S.C. 654(16) [454(16) of the Act].

(2) Until September 30, 2001, FFP at the 80 percent rate is available for the rental or purchase of proprietary operating/vendor software necessary for the operation of hardware during the planning, design, development, installation, enhancement or operation of a computerized support enforcement system in accordance with the OCSE guideline entitled "Automated Systems for Child Support Enforcement: A Guide for States." FFP at the 80 percent rate is not available for proprietary application software developed specifically for a computerized support enforcement system. (See § 307.35 regarding reimbursement at the applicable matching rate.)

(c) *HHS rights to software.* The Department of Health and Human Services reserves a royalty-free, non-exclusive and irrevocable license to reproduce, publish or otherwise use, and to authorize others to use for Federal government purposes, software, software modifications, and documentation developed under § 307.10 or 42 U.S.C. 654(16) [454(16) of the Act]. This license would permit the Department to authorize the use of software, software modifications and documentation developed under § 307.10 or 42 U.S.C. 654(16) [454(16) of the Act] in another project or activity funded by the Federal government.

(d) *Consequences of suspension of the APD.* If the Office suspends approval of an APD in accordance with § 307.40 during the planning, design, development, installation, enhancement or operation of the system:

(1) The Office shall disallow FFP as of the date the State failed to comply substantially with the approved APD; and

(2) FFP at the 80 percent and applicable matching rates is not available in any expenditure incurred under the APD after the date of the suspension until the date the Office determines that the State has taken the actions specified in the notice of suspension described in § 307.40(a). The Office will notify the State in writing upon making such a determination.

(e) *Limitation on 80 percent funding.* Federal financial participation at the 80 percent rate may not exceed $400,000,000 in the aggregate for fiscal years 1996 through 2001.

(f) *Allocation formula.* Payments at the 80 percent rate to individual States, Territories and systems defined in 42 U.S.C. 655(a)(3)(B)(iii) [455(a)(3)(B)(iii) of the Act] (hereafter referred to as "States") will be equal to the sum of:

(1) A base amount of $2,000,000; and

(2) An additional amount defined as the Allocation Factor computed as follows:

(i) Allocation Factor—an average of the Caseload and Census Factors which yields the percentage that is used to calculate a State's allocation of the funds available, less amounts set aside pursuant to paragraph (f)(1) of this section.

(ii) Caseload Factor—a ratio of the six-year average IV-D caseload as reported by a State for fiscal years 1990 through 1995 to the total six-year average IV-D caseload in all States for the same period;

(iii) Census Factor—a ratio of the number of children in a State with one parent living elsewhere as reported in the 1992 Current Population Survey—Child Support Supplement to the total number of such children in all States.

[63 FR 44405, Aug. 19, 1998]

§307.35 Federal financial participation at the applicable matching rate for computerized support enforcement systems.

Federal financial participation at the applicable matching rate is available only in computerized support enforcement systems expenditures for:

(a) The operation of a system that meets the requirements specified in §307.10, or §307.11 if the conditions for APD approval in §§307.5 and 307.15 are met; or

(b) Systems approved in accordance with part 95, subpart F of this title. This may include expenditures for a system which were disallowed by the Office because the system failed to comply substantially with an APD approved under §307.15.

[49 FR 33260, Aug. 22, 1984, as amended at 50 FR 19658, May 9, 1985; 57 FR 47005, Oct. 14, 1992; 63 FR 44817, Aug. 21, 1998]

§307.40 Suspension of approval of advance planning documents for computerized support enforcement systems.

(a) *Suspension of approval.* The Office will suspend approval of the APD for a computerized support enforcement system approved and developed under §307.10, or §307.11 as of the date that the system ceases to comply substantially with the criteria, requirements, and other provisions in the APD, including conditions in §307.15(b) and the requirements in §307.10 or §307.11 of this part covered under a waiver granted in accordance with §307.5. Federal funding will be disallowed as described in §307.30(d) and §307.31(d).

(b) *Duration of suspension.* The suspension of approval of an APD under paragraph (a) shall remain in effect until the Office determines that actions required for Federal funding in the future, as specified in the notice of suspension, have been taken and the Office so notifies the State.

[49 FR 33260, Aug. 22, 1984, as amended at 57 FR 47005, Oct. 14, 1992; 63 FR 44405, Aug. 19, 1998; 63 FR 44817, Aug. 21, 1998]

PART 308—ANNUAL STATE SELF-ASSESSMENT REVIEW AND REPORT

AUTHORITY: 42 U.S.C. 654(15)(A) and 1302.

SOURCE: 65 FR 77750, Dec. 12, 2000, unless otherwise noted.

§308.0 Scope.

This part establishes standards and criteria for the State self-assessment review and report process required under section 454(15)(A) of the Act.

§308.1 Self-assessment implementation methodology.

(a) The IV-D agency must ensure the review meets Federal requirements and must maintain responsibility for and control of the results produced and contents of the annual report.

(b) *Sampling.* A State must either review all of its cases or conduct sampling which meets the following conditions:

(1) The sampling methodology maintains a minimum confidence level of 90 percent for each criterion;

(2) The State selects statistically valid samples of cases from the IV-D program universe of cases; and

(3) The State establishes a procedure for the design of samples and assures that no portions of the IV-D case universe are omitted from the sample selection process.

(c) *Scope of review.* A State must conduct an annual review covering all of the required criteria in Sec. 308.2.

(d) *Review period.* Each review period must cover a 12-month period. The first review period shall begin no later than 12 months after the effective date of the final rule and subsequent reviews shall each cover the same 12-month period thereafter.

(e) *Reporting.* (1) The State must provide a report of the results of the self-assessment review to the appropriate OCSE Regional Office, with a copy to the Commissioner of OCSE, no later than 6 months after the end of the review period.

(2) The report must include, but is not limited to:

(i) An executive summary, including a summary of the mandatory program criteria findings;

(ii) A description of optional program areas covered by the review;

(iii) A description of sampling methodology used, if applicable;

(iv) The results of the self-assessment reviews; and

(v) A description of the corrective actions proposed and/or taken.

§ 308.2 Required program compliance criteria.

(a) *Case closure.* (1) The State must have and use procedures for case closure pursuant to Sec. 303.11 of this chapter in at least 90 percent of the closed cases reviewed.

(2) If a IV-D case was closed during the review period, the State must determine whether the case met requirements pursuant to § 303.11 of this chapter.

(b) *Establishment of paternity and support order.* The State must have and use procedures required in this paragraph in at least 75 percent of the cases reviewed.

(1) If an order for support is required and established during the review period, the case meets the requirements, notwithstanding the timeframes for: establishment of cases as specified in Sec. 303.2(b) of this chapter; provision of services in intergovernmental IV-D cases per § 303.7(a)(4) through (8), (b), (c), (d)(2) through (5) and (7) and (10) of this chapter; and location and support order establishment under §§ 303.3(b)(3) and (5), and 303.4(d) of this chapter.

(2) If an order was required, but not established during the review period, the State must determine the last required action and determine whether the action was taken within the appropriate timeframe. The following is a list of possible last actions:

(i) Opening a case within 20 days pursuant to § 303.2(b) of this chapter;

(ii) If location activities are necessary, using all appropriate sources within 75 days according to § 303.3(b)(3) of this chapter. This includes all the following locate sources as appropriate: custodial parent, Federal and State Parent Locator Services, U.S. Postal Service, State workforce agency, employment data, Department of Motor Vehicles, and credit bureaus;

(iii) Repeating location attempts quarterly and when new information is received in accordance with § 303.3(b)(5) of this chapter;

(iv) Establishing an order or completing service of process necessary to commence proceedings to establish a support order, or if applicable, paternity, within 90 days of locating the non-custodial parent, or documenting unsuccessful attempts to serve process in accordance with the State's guidelines defining diligent efforts pursuant to §§ 303.3(c) and 303.4(d) of this chapter.

(c) *Enforcement of orders.* A State must have and use procedures required under this paragraph in at least 75 percent of the cases reviewed. Enforcement cases include cases in which ongoing income withholding is in place as well as cases in which new or repeated enforcement actions were required during the review period.

(1) If income withholding was appropriate and a withholding collection was received during the last quarter of the review period and the case was submitted for Federal and State income tax refund offset, if appropriate, the case meets the requirements of § 303.6(c)(3) of this chapter, notwithstanding the timeframes for: establishment of cases in § 303.2(b) of this chapter; provision of services in intergovernmental IV-D cases under § 303.7(a)(4) through (8), (b), (c), (d)(2) through (5) and (7) and (10) of this chapter; and location and income withholding in

§§ 303.3(b)(3) and (5), and 303.100 of this chapter.

(2) If income withholding was not appropriate, and a collection was received during the review period, and the case was submitted for Federal and State income tax refund offset, if appropriate, then the case meets the requirements of § 303.6(c)(3) of this chapter, notwithstanding the timeframes for: establishment of cases in § 303.2(b) of this chapter; provision of services in intergovernmental IV-D cases under § 303.7(a)(4) through (8), (b), (c), (d)(2) through (5) and (7) and (10) of this chapter; and location and enforcement of support obligations in §§ 303.3(b)(3) and (5), and 303.6 of this chapter.

(3) If an order needed enforcement during the review period, but income was not withheld or other collections were not received (when income withholding could not be implemented), the State must determine the last required action and determine whether the action was taken within the appropriate timeframes. The following is a list of possible last required actions:

(i) If location activities are necessary, using all appropriate location sources within 75 days according to § 303.3(b)(3) of this chapter. Location sources include: custodial parent, Federal and State Parent Locator Services, U.S. Postal Service, State workforce agency, Department of Motor Vehicles, and credit bureaus;

(ii) Repeating attempts to locate quarterly and when new information is received pursuant to § 303.3(b)(5) of this chapter;

(iii) If there is no immediate income withholding order, initiating income withholding upon identifying a delinquency equal to one month's arrears, in accordance with Sec. 303.100(c) of this chapter;

(iv) If immediate income withholding is ordered, sending a notice to the employer directing the employer to withhold from the income of the employee an amount equal to the monthly (or other periodic) support obligation (including any past due support obligation) of the employee, within:

(A) Two business days after the date information regarding a newly hired employee is entered into the State Directory of New Hires and in which an information comparison conducted under section 453A(f) of the Act reveals a match;

(B) Two business days after receipt of notice of, and the income source subject to withholding from a court, another State, an employer, the FPLS or another source recognized by the State.

(v) If income withholding is not appropriate or cannot be implemented, taking an appropriate enforcement action (other than Federal and State income tax refund offset), unless service of process is necessary, within no more than 30 days of identifying a delinquency or identifying the location of the non-custodial parent, whichever occurs later in accordance with § 303.6(c)(2) of this chapter;

(vi) If income withholding is not appropriate or cannot be implemented and service of process is needed, taking an appropriate enforcement action (other than Federal and State income tax refund offset), within no more than 60 days of identifying a delinquency or locating the non-custodial parent, whichever occurs later, or documenting unsuccessful attempts to serve process in accordance with the State's guidelines for defining diligent efforts and § 303.6(c)(2) of this chapter;

(vii) If the case has arrearages, submitting the case for Federal and State income tax refund offset during the review period, if appropriate, in accordance with §§ 303.72, 303.102 and 303.6(c)(3) of this chapter.

(d) *Disbursement of collections.* A State must have and use procedures required in this paragraph in at least 75 percent of the cases reviewed. With respect to the last payment received for each case:

(1) States must determine whether disbursement of collection was made within two business days after receipt by the State Disbursement Unit from the employer or other source of periodic income in accordance with section 457(a) of the Act, if sufficient information identifying the payee is provided pursuant to section 454B(c) of the Act.

(2) States may delay the distribution of collections toward arrearages until resolution of any timely appeals with respect to such arrearages pursuant to section 454B(c)(2) of the Act.

(e) Securing and enforcing medical support orders. A State must have and use procedures required under this paragraph in at least 75 percent of the cases reviewed. A State must:

(1) Determine whether support orders established or modified during the review period include medical support in accordance with § 303.31(b) of this chapter.

(2) If reasonable in cost and accessible private health insurance was available and required in the order, but not obtained, determine whether the National Medical Support Notice was used to enforce the order in accordance with requirements in § 303.32 of this chapter.

(3) Determine whether the State transferred notice of the health care provision, using the National Medical Support Notice required under § 303.32 of this chapter, to a new employer when a noncustodial parent, or at State option a custodial parent, was ordered to provide health insurance coverage and changed employment.

(f) *Review and adjustment of orders.* A State must have and use procedures required under this paragraph in at least 75 percent of the cases reviewed.

(1) If a case has been reviewed and meets the conditions for adjustment under State laws and procedures and § 303.8 of this chapter and the order is adjusted or a determination is made as a result of a review during the self-assessment period that an adjustment is not needed in accordance with the State's guidelines for setting child support awards, the State will be considered to have taken appropriate action in that case, notwithstanding the timeframes for: establishment of cases in § 303.2(b) of this chapter; provision of services in intergovernmental IV-D cases under § 303.7(a)(4) through (8), (b), (c), (d)(2) through (5) and (7) and (10) of this chapter; and location and review and adjustment of support orders contained in §§ 303.3(b)(3) and (5), and 303.8 of this chapter.

(2) If a case has not been reviewed, the State must determine the last required action and determine whether the action was taken within the appropriate timeframe. The following is a list of possible last required actions:

(i) If location is necessary to conduct a review, using all appropriate location sources within 75 days of opening the case pursuant to § 303.3(b)(3) of this chapter. Location sources include: custodial parent, Federal and State Parent Locator Services, U.S. Postal Service, State workforce agency, unemployment data, Department of Motor Vehicles, and credit bureaus;

(ii) Repeating location attempts quarterly and when new information is received pursuant to § 303.3(b)(5) of this chapter;

(iii) Within 180 calendar days of receiving a request for a review or locating the non-requesting parent, whichever occurs later, conducting a review of the order and adjusting the order or determining that the order should not be adjusted pursuant to sec. 303.8(e) of this chapter;

(iv) If an adjustment was made during the review period using cost of living or automated methods, giving both parties 30 days to contest any adjustment to that support order pursuant to sec. 466(a)(10)(A)(ii) of the Act.

(3) The State must provide the custodial and non-custodial parents notices, not less often than once every three years, informing them of their right to request the State to review and, if appropriate, adjust the order. The first notice may be included in the order pursuant to sec. 466(a)(10)(C) of the Act.

(g) Intergovernmental services. A State must have and use procedures required under this paragraph in at least 75 percent of the cases reviewed. For all intergovernmental cases requiring services during the review period, determine the last required action and determine whether the action was taken during the appropriate time frame:

(1) Initiating intergovernmental cases:

(i) Except when a State has determined that use of one-state remedies is appropriate in accordance with § 303.7(c)(3) of this Chapter, within 20 calendar days of completing the actions required in § 303.7(c)(1) through (3) of the Chapter, and, if appropriate, receipt of any necessary information needed to process the case, ask the appropriate intrastate tribunal or refer the case to the responding State agency, for a determination of the controlling order and a reconciliation of arrearages if such a determination is necessary, and refer any intergovernmental IV–D case to the appropriate State Central Registry, Tribal IV–D program, or Central Authority of a country for action, if one-state remedies are not appropriate;

(ii) If additional information is requested, providing the responding agency with an updated form and any necessary additional documentation, or notify the responding agency when the information will be provided, within 30 calendar days of the request pursuant to § 303.7(c)(6) of this chapter;

(iii) Within 20 calendar days after determining that a request for review of the order should be sent to another State IV–D agency and of receipt of information necessary to conduct the review, sending a request for review and adjustment pursuant to § 303.7(c)(9) of this chapter;

(iv) Within 10 working days of closing its case pursuant to § 303.11 of this chapter, notifying the responding agency pursuant to § 303.7(c)(11) of this chapter;

(v) Within 10 working days of receipt of new information on a case, notifying the responding State pursuant to § 303.7(a)(7) of this chapter;

(vi) Within 30 working days of receiving a request, providing any order and payment record information requested by a responding agency for a controlling order determination and reconciliation of arrearages, or notify the State IV–D agency when the information will be provided pursuant to § 303.7(a)(6) of this chapter.

(2) Responding intergovernmental cases:

(i) Within 10 working days of receipt of an intergovernmental IV–D case, the central registry reviewing submitted documentation for completeness, forwarding the case to the State Parent Locator Service (SPLS) for location services or to the appropriate agency for processing, acknowledging receipt of the case, and requesting any missing documentation from the initiating agency, and informing the initiating agency where the case was sent for action, pursuant to § 303.7(b)(2) of this chapter;

(ii) The central registry responding to inquiries from initiating agencies within 5 working days of a receipt of request for case status review pursuant to § 303.7(b)(4) of this chapter;

(iii) Within 10 working days of locating the noncustodial parent in a different jurisdiction within the State or in a different State, forwarding/transmitting the forms and documentation in accordance with Federal requirements pursuant to § 303.7(d)(3) and (4) of this chapter;

(iv) Within two business days of receipt of collections, forwarding any support payments to the initiating jurisdiction pursuant to section 454B(c)(1) of the Act;

(v) Within 10 working days of receipt of new information notifying the initiating jurisdiction of that new information pursuant to § 303.7(a)(7) of this chapter;

(vi) Within 30 working days of receiving a request, providing any order and payment record information requested by an initiating agency for a controlling order determination and reconciliation of arrearages, or notify the State IV–D agency when the information will be provided pursuant to § 303.7(a)(6) of this chapter;

(vii) Within 10 working days of receipt of instructions for case closure from an initiating agency under § 303.7(c)(12) of this chapter, stopping the responding State's income withholding order or notice and closing the responding State's case, pursuant to § 303.7(d)(9) of this chapter, unless the two States reach an alternative agreement on how to proceed.

(h) *Expedited processes.* The State must have and use procedures required under this paragraph in the amounts specified in this paragraph in the cases reviewed for the expedited processes criterion.

(1) In IV-D cases needing support orders established, regardless of whether paternity has been established, action to establish support orders must be completed from the date of service of process to the time of disposition within the following timeframes pursuant to Sec. 303.101(b)(2)(i) of this chapter:

(i) 75 percent in 6 months; and

(ii) 90 percent in 12 months.

(2) States may count as a success for the 6-month standard cases where the IV-D agency uses long-arm jurisdiction and disposition occurs within 12 months of service of process on the alleged father or non-custodial parent.

[65 FR 77750, Dec. 12, 2000, as amended at 73 FR 42442, July 21, 2008; 75 FR 38644, July 2, 2010; 81 FR 93568, Dec. 20, 2016]

§ 308.3 Optional program areas of review.

(a) *Program direction.* A State may include a program direction review in its self-assessment for the purpose of analyzing the relationships between case results relating to program compliance areas, and performance and program outcome indicators. This review is an opportunity for States to demonstrate how they are trying to manage their resources to achieve the best performance possible. A program direction analysis could describe the following:

(1) Initiatives that resulted in improved and achievable performance accompanied with supporting data;

(2) Barriers impeding progress; and

(3) Efforts to improve performance.

(b) *Program service enhancement.* A State may include a program service enhancement report in its self-assessment that describes initiatives put into practice that improved program performance and customer service. This is an opportunity for States to promote their programs and innovative practices. Some examples of innovative activities that States may elect to discuss in the report include:

(1) Steps taken to make the program more efficient and effective;

(2) Efforts to improve client services;

(3) Demonstration projects testing creative new ways of doing business;

(4) Collaborative efforts being taken with partners and customers;

(5) Innovative practices which have resulted in improved program performance;

(6) Actions taken to improve public image;

(7) Access/visitation projects initiated to improve non-custodial parents' involvement with the children and;

(8) Efforts to engage non-custodial parents who owe overdue child support to pay that support or engage in work activities, such as subsidized employment, work experience, or job search.

(c) A State may provide any of the optional information in paragraphs (a) and (b) of this section in narrative form.

PART 309—TRIBAL CHILD SUPPORT ENFORCEMENT (IV-D) PROGRAM

Subpart A—Tribal IV-D Program: General Provisions

Subpart B—Tribal IV-D Program Application Procedures

Subpart C—Tribal IV-D Plan Requirements

AUTHORITY: 42 U.S.C. 655(f) and 1302.

SOURCE: 69 FR 16672, Mar. 30, 2004, unless otherwise noted.

Subpart A—Tribal IV-D Program: General Provisions

§ 309.01 What does this part cover?

(a) The regulations in this part prescribe the rules for implementing section 455(f) of the Social Security Act. Section 455(f) of the Act authorizes direct grants to Indian Tribes and Tribal organizations to operate child support enforcement programs.

(b) These regulations establish the requirements that must be met by Indian Tribes and Tribal organizations to be eligible for grants under section 455(f) of the Act. They establish requirements for: Tribal IV-D plan and application content, submission, approval, and amendment; program funding; program operation; uses of funds; accountability; reporting; and other program requirements and procedures.

§ 309.05 What definitions apply to this part?

The following definitions apply to this part:

IV-D services are the services that are authorized or required for the establishment of paternity, establishment, modification, and enforcement of support orders, and location of noncustodial parents under title IV-D of the Act, this rule, the Tribal IV-D plan and program instructions issued by the Department.

ACF means the Administration for Children and Families, U.S. Department of Health and Human Services.

Act means the Social Security Act, unless otherwise specified.

Assistant Secretary means the Assistant Secretary for Children and Families, Department of Health and Human Services.

Central office means the Office of Child Support Enforcement.

Child support order and *child support obligation* mean a judgment, decree, or order, whether temporary, final or subject to modification, issued by a court of competent jurisdiction, tribunal or an administrative agency for the support and maintenance of a child, including a child who has attained the age of majority under the law of the issuing jurisdiction, or of the parent with whom the child is living, which provides for monetary support, health care, arrearages, or reimbursement, and which may include related costs and fees, interest and penalties, income withholding, attorneys' fees, and other relief.

The *Department* means the U.S. Department of Health and Human Services.

Income means any periodic form of payment due to an individual regardless of source, except that a Tribe may expressly decide to exclude per capita, trust, or Individual Indian Money (IIM) payments.

Indian means a person who is a member of an Indian Tribe.

Indian Tribe and *Tribe* mean any Indian or Alaska Native Tribe, band, nation, pueblo, village, or community that the Secretary of the Interior acknowledges to exist as an Indian Tribe and includes in the list of Federally-recognized Indian Tribal governments as published in the FEDERAL REGISTER pursuant to 25 U.S.C. 479a–1.

Location means information concerning the physical whereabouts of the noncustodial parent, or the noncustodial parent's employer(s), and other sources of income or assets, as appropriate, which is sufficient and necessary to take the next appropriate action in a case.

Non-cash support is support provided to a family in the nature of goods and/or services, rather than in cash, but which, nonetheless, has a certain and specific dollar value.

Notice of Disapproval refers to the written notification from the Department that the Tribal IV-D application, IV-D plan, or plan amendment fails to meet the requirements for approval under applicable Federal statutes and regulations.

OCSE refers to the Federal Office of Child Support Enforcement.

Program development plan means a document detailing the specific steps a Tribe or Tribal organization will take to come into compliance with the requirements of § 309.65(a), and the timeframe associated with each step.

Regional office refers to one of the regional offices of the Administration for Children and Families.

Secretary means the Secretary of the Department of Health and Human Services or designee.

TANF means the Temporary Assistance for Needy Families program as found at section 401 *et seq.* of the Social Security Act (42 U.S.C. 601 *et seq.*).

Title IV-D refers to the title of the Social Security Act that authorizes the Child Support Enforcement Program, including the Tribal Child Support Enforcement Program.

Tribal IV-D agency means the organizational unit in the Tribe or Tribal organization that has the authority for administering or supervising the Tribal IV-D program under section 455(f) of the Act.

Tribal custom means unwritten law having the force and effect of law within a particular Tribe.

Tribal organization means any legally established organization of Indian Tribes which is sanctioned or chartered as a single governing body representing two or more Indian Tribes.

§ 309.10 Who is eligible to apply for and receive Federal funding to operate a Tribal IV-D program?

The following Tribes or Tribal organizations are eligible to apply to receive Federal funding to operate a Tribal IV-D program meeting the requirements of this part:

(a) An Indian Tribe with at least 100 children under the age of majority as defined by Tribal law or code, in the population subject to the jurisdiction of the Tribal court or administrative agency.

(b) A Tribal organization that has been designated by two or more Indian Tribes to operate a Tribal IV-D program on their behalf, with a total of at least 100 children under the age of majority as defined by Tribal laws or codes, in the population of the Tribes subject to the jurisdiction of the Tribal court (or courts) or administrative agency (or agencies).

(c) A Tribe or Tribal organization that can demonstrate to the satisfaction of the Secretary the capacity to operate a child support enforcement program and provide justification for operating a program with less than the minimum number of children may be granted a waiver of paragraph (a) or (b) of this section as appropriate.

(1) A Tribe or Tribal organization's request for waiver of paragraph (a) or

(b) of this section must include documentation sufficient to demonstrate that meeting the requirement is not necessary. Such documentation must state:

(i) That the Tribe or Tribal organization otherwise complies with the requirements established in subpart C of these regulations;

(ii) That the Tribe or Tribal organization has the administrative capacity to support operation of a child support program under the requirements of this part;

(iii) That the Tribal IV-D program will be cost effective; and

(iv) The number of children under the jurisdiction of the Tribe or Tribal organization.

(2) A Tribe or Tribal organization's request for a waiver may be approved if the Tribe or Tribal organization demonstrates to the satisfaction of the Secretary that it can provide the services required under 45 CFR part 309 in a cost effective manner even though the population subject to Tribal jurisdiction includes fewer than 100 children.

Subpart B—Tribal IV-D Program Application Procedures

§ 309.15 What is a Tribal IV-D program application?

(a) *Initial application.* The initial application for funding under § 309.65(a) may be submitted at any time. The initial application must include:

(1) Standard Form (SF) 424, "Application for Federal Assistance;"

(2) SF 424A, "Budget Information—Non-Construction Programs," including the following information:

(i) A quarter-by-quarter estimate of expenditures for the funding period; and

(ii) Notification of whether the Tribe or Tribal organization is requesting funds for indirect costs and if so, an election of a method under paragraph (a)(3) of this section to calculate estimated indirect costs; and

(iii) A narrative justification for each cost category on the form; and either:

(iv) A statement that the Tribe or Tribal organization has or will have the non-Federal share of program expenditures available, as required; or

(v) A request for a waiver of the non-Federal share in accordance with § 309.130(e), if appropriate.

(3) If the Tribe or Tribal organization requests funding for indirect costs, estimated indirect costs may be submitted either by:

(i) Including documentation of the dollar amount of indirect costs allocable to the IV-D program; or

(ii) Submission of its current indirect cost rate negotiated with the Department of Interior and the estimated amount of indirect costs calculated using the negotiated cost rate.

(4) The Tribal IV-D plan. The initial application must include a comprehensive statement identifying how the Tribe or Tribal organization is meeting the requirements of subpart C of this part and that describes the capacity of the Tribe or Tribal organization to operate a IV-D program which meets the objectives of title IV-D of the Act, including establishment of paternity, establishment, modification, and enforcement of support orders, and location of noncustodial parents.

(b) *Additional application requirement for Tribal organizations.* The initial and subsequent annual budget submissions of a Tribal organization must document that each participating Tribe authorizes the Tribal organization to operate a Tribal IV-D program on its behalf.

(c) *Annual budget submission.* Following the initial funding period, the Tribe or Tribal organization operating a IV-D program must submit annually Form SF 424A, including all the necessary accompanying information and documentation described in paragraphs (a)(2) and (a)(3) of this section.

(d) *Plan Amendments.* Plan amendments must be submitted in accordance with the requirements of § 309.35(e).

§ 309.16 What rules apply to start-up funding?

(a) The application for start-up funding under § 309.65(b) must include:

(1) Standard Form (SF) 424, "Application for Federal Assistance';

(2) SF 424A, "Budget Information—Non-Construction Programs," including the following information:

(i) A quarter-by-quarter estimate of expenditures for the start-up period;

(ii) Notification of whether the Tribe or Tribal organization is requesting funds for indirect costs and, if so, an election of a method to calculate estimated indirect costs under paragraph (a)(3) of this section; and

(iii) A narrative justification for each cost category on the form;

(3) If the Tribe or Tribal organization requests funding for indirect costs as part of its application for Federal start-up funds, estimated indirect costs may be submitted either by:

(i) Including documentation of the dollar amount of indirect costs allocable to the IV-D program including the methodology used to arrive at these amounts; or

(ii) Submission of its current indirect cost rate negotiated with the Department of Interior and the amount of estimated indirect costs using that rate.

(iii) The amount of indirect costs must be included within the limit of $500,000 specified in paragraph (c) of this section.

(4) With respect to each requirement in § 309.65(a) that the Tribe or Tribal organization currently meets, a description of how the Tribe or Tribal organization satisfies the requirement; and

(5) With respect to each requirement in § 309.65(a) that the Tribe or Tribal organization does not currently meet, a program development plan which demonstrates to the satisfaction of the Secretary that the Tribe or Tribal organization has the capacity and will have in place a Tribal IV-D program that will meet the requirements outlined in § 309.65(a), within a reasonable, specific period of time, not to exceed two years. The Secretary must approve the program development plan. Disapproval of a program development plan is not subject to administrative appeal.

(b) The process for approval and disapproval of applications for start-up funding under this section is found in §§ 309.35, 309.40, 309.45, and 309.50. A disapproval of an application for start-up funding is not subject to administrative appeal.

(c) Federal funding for start-up costs is limited to $500,000, which must be obligated and liquidated within two years after the first day of the quarter after the start-up application was approved. In extraordinary circumstances, the Secretary will consider a request to extend the period of time during which start-up funding will be available and/or to increase the amount of start-up funding provided. Denial of a request to extend the time during which start-up funding will be available or for an increase in the amount of start-up funding is not subject to administrative appeal.

(1) The Secretary may grant a no-cost extension of time if the Tribe or Tribal organization demonstrates to the satisfaction of the Secretary that the extension will result in satisfaction of each requirement established in § 309.65(a) by the grantee and completion of the program development plan required under § 309.65(b)(2).

(2) The Secretary may grant an increase in the amount of Federal start-up funding provided beyond the limit specified at paragraph (c) of this section and § 309.150 if—

(i) The Tribe or Tribal organization demonstrates to the satisfaction of the Secretary that a specific amount of additional funds for a specific purpose or purposes will result in satisfaction of the requirements specified in § 309.65(a) which the Tribe or Tribal organization otherwise will be unable to meet; and

(ii) The Tribe or Tribal organization demonstrates to the satisfaction of the Secretary that it has satisfied every applicable reporting requirement.

(d) If a Tribe or Tribal organization receives start-up funding based on submission and approval of a Tribal IV-D application which includes a program development plan under § 309.65(b), a progress report that describes accomplishments to date in carrying out the plan must be submitted with the next annual refunding request.

§ 309.20 Who submits a Tribal IV-D program application and where?

(a) The authorized representative of the Tribe or Tribal organization must sign and submit the Tribal IV-D program application.

(b) Applications must be submitted to the Office of Child Support Enforcement, Attention: Tribal Child Support

Enforcement Program, 370 L'Enfant Promenade, SW., Washington, DC 20447, with a copy to the appropriate regional office.

§ 309.35 What are the procedures for review of a Tribal IV-D program application, plan or plan amendment?

(a) The Secretary will promptly review a Tribal IV-D program application, plan or plan amendment to determine whether it conforms to the requirements of the Act and these regulations. Not later than the 90th day following the date on which the Tribal IV-D application, plan or plan amendment is received by the Secretary, action will be taken unless additional information is needed. If additional information is needed from the Tribe or Tribal organization, the Secretary will promptly notify the Tribe or Tribal organization.

(b) The Secretary will take action on the application, plan or plan amendment within 45 days of receipt of any additional information requested from the Tribe or Tribal organization.

(c) Determinations as to whether the Tribal IV-D plan, including plan amendments, originally meets or continues to meet the requirements for approval are based on applicable Federal statutes, regulations and instructions applicable to Tribal IV-D programs. Guidance may be furnished to assist in the interpretation of the regulations.

(d) After approval of the original Tribal IV-D program application, all relevant changes required by new Federal statutes, rules, regulations, and Department interpretations are required to be submitted so that the Secretary may determine whether the plan continues to meet Federal requirements and policies.

(e) If a Tribe or Tribal organization intends to make any substantial or material change in any aspect of the Tribal IV-D program, a Tribal IV-D plan amendment must be submitted at the earliest reasonable time for approval under this section. The plan amendment must describe and, as appropriate, document the changes the Tribe or Tribal organization proposes to make to its IV-D plan, consistent with the requirements of applicable statutes and regulations.

(f) The effective date of a plan or plan amendment may not be earlier than the first day of the fiscal quarter in which an approvable plan or plan amendment is submitted.

§ 309.40 What is the basis for disapproval of a Tribal IV-D program application, plan or plan amendment?

(a) A IV-D application, plan, or plan amendment will be disapproved if:

(1) The Secretary determines that the application, plan, or plan amendment fails to meet or no longer meets one or more of the requirements set forth in this part or any other applicable Federal regulations, statutes and implementing instructions;

(2) The Secretary determines that required Tribal laws, code, regulations, and procedures are not in effect; and/or

(3) The Secretary determines that the application, plan, or plan amendment is not complete, after the Tribe or Tribal organization has had the opportunity to submit the necessary information.

(b)(1) Except as provided in paragraph (b)(2) of this section and § 309.45(h) of this part, a written Notice of Disapproval of the Tribal IV-D program application, plan, or plan amendment, as applicable, will be sent to the Tribe or Tribal organization upon the determination that any of the conditions of paragraph (a) of this section apply. The Notice of Disapproval will include the specific reason(s) for disapproval.

(2) Where the Secretary believes an approved Tribal IV-D plan should be disapproved, he will notify the Tribe of his intent to disapprove the plan.

(c) If the application, plan or plan amendment is incomplete and fails to provide enough information to make a determination to approve or disapprove, the Secretary will request the necessary information.

§ 309.45 When and how may a Tribe or Tribal organization request reconsideration of a disapproval action?

(a) Except as specified under paragraphs (g) and (h) of this section, a Tribe or Tribal organization may request reconsideration of the disapproval of a Tribal IV-D application, plan or plan amendment by filing a written Request for Reconsideration to the Secretary within 60 days of the date of the Notice of Disapproval.

(b) The Request for Reconsideration must include:

(1) All documentation that the Tribe or Tribal organization believes is relevant and supportive of its application, plan or plan amendment; and

(2) A written response to each ground for disapproval identified in the Notice of Disapproval, indicating why the Tribe or Tribal organization believes its application, plan or plan amendment conforms to the requirements for approval specified in applicable Federal statutes, regulations and office issuances; and

(3) Whether or not the Tribe or Tribal organization requests a meeting or conference call with the Secretary.

(c) After receiving a Request for Reconsideration that includes a request for a conference call or meeting, OCSE will determine whether to hold a conference call or a meeting with the Tribe or Tribal organization to discuss the reasons for disapproval of the application, plan, or plan amendment as well as the Tribe or Tribal organization's response. The Secretary will notify the Tribe or Tribal organization of the date and time of the conference call or meeting.

(d) A conference call or meeting under § 309.45(c) shall be held not less than 30 days nor more than 60 days after the date the notice of such call or meeting is furnished to the Tribe or Tribal organization, unless both parties agree in writing to another time.

(e) The Secretary will make a written determination affirming, modifying, or reversing disapproval of a Tribal IV-D program application, plan, or plan amendment within 60 days after the conference call or meeting is held, or within 60 days after the request for reconsideration that does not include a request for a meeting. This determination shall be the final decision of the Secretary.

(f) The Secretary's determination that a Tribal IV-D application, new plan or plan amendment is not approvable remains in effect pending the reconsideration under this part.

(g) Disapproval of start-up funding, a request for waiver of the 100-child rule, and a request for waiver of the non-Federal Tribal share is not subject to administrative appeal.

(h) Where the Secretary believes an approved Tribal IV-D plan should be disapproved, he will notify the Tribe of his intent to disapprove the plan. If the Tribe waives its right to reconsideration under this section, the Tribe may request a pre-decision hearing with 60 days of the date of the Notice of Intent to Disapprove the plan. The hearing will utilize the procedures at 45 CFR part 213.

§ 309.50 What are the consequences of disapproval of a Tribal IV-D program application, plan or plan amendment?

(a) If an application or plan submitted pursuant to § 309.15 is disapproved, the Tribe or Tribal organization will receive no funding under § 309.65(a) or this part until a new application or plan is submitted and approved.

(b) If a IV-D plan amendment is disapproved, there is no funding for the activity proposed in the plan amendment.

(c) A Tribe or Tribal organization whose application, plan or plan amendment has been disapproved may reapply at any time.

Subpart C—Tribal IV-D Plan Requirements

§ 309.55 What does this subpart cover?

This subpart defines the Tribal IV-D plan provisions that are required to demonstrate that a Tribe or Tribal organization has the capacity to operate a child support enforcement program meeting the objectives of title IV-D of the Act and these regulations, including establishment of paternity, establishment, modification, and enforcement of support orders, and location of noncustodial parents.

§ 309.60 Who is responsible for administration of the Tribal IV-D program under the Tribal IV-D plan?

(a) Under the Tribal IV-D plan, the Tribe or Tribal organization shall establish or designate an agency to administer the Tribal IV-D plan. That agency shall be referred to as the Tribal IV-D agency.

(b) The Tribe or Tribal organization is responsible and accountable for the operation of the Tribal IV-D program. Except where otherwise provided in this part, the Tribal IV-D agency need not perform all the functions of the Tribal IV-D program, so long as the Tribe or Tribal organization ensures that all approved functions are carried out properly, efficiently and effectively.

(c) If the Tribe or Tribal organization delegates any of the functions of the Tribal IV-D program to another Tribe, a State, and/or another agency or entity pursuant to a cooperative arrangement, contract, or Tribal resolution, the Tribe or Tribal organization is responsible for securing compliance with the requirements of the Tribal IV-D plan by such Tribe, State, agency or entity. The Tribe or Tribal organization is responsible for submitting copies and appending to the Tribal IV-D plan any agreements, contracts, or Tribal resolutions between the Tribal IV-D agency and a Tribe, State, other agency or entity.

§ 309.65 What must a Tribe or Tribal organization include in a Tribal IV-D plan in order to demonstrate capacity to operate a Tribal IV-D program?

(a) A Tribe or Tribal organization demonstrates capacity to operate a Tribal IV-D program meeting the objectives of title IV-D of the Act and these regulations by submission of a Tribal IV-D plan which contains the required elements listed in paragraphs (a)(1) through (14) of this section:

(1) A description of the population subject to the jurisdiction of the Tribal court or administrative agency for child support purposes as specified under § 309.70;

(2) Evidence that the Tribe or Tribal organization has in place procedures for accepting all applications for IV-D services and promptly providing IV-D services required by law and regulation;

(3) Assurance that the due process rights of the individuals involved will be protected in all activities of the Tribal IV-D program, including establishment of paternity, and establishment, modification, and enforcement of support orders;

(4) Administrative and management procedures as specified under § 309.75;

(5) Safeguarding procedures as specified under § 309.80;

(6) Assurance that the Tribe or Tribal organization will maintain records as specified under § 309.85;

(7) Copies of all applicable Tribal laws and regulations as specified under § 309.90;

(8) Procedures for the location of noncustodial parents as specified under § 309.95;

(9) Procedures for the establishment of paternity as specified under § 309.100;

(10) Guidelines for the establishment and modification of child support obligations as specified under § 309.105;

(11) Procedures for income withholding as specified under § 309.110;

(12) Procedures for the distribution of child support collections as specified under § 309.115;

(13) Procedures for intergovernmental case processing as specified under § 309.120; and

(14) Tribally-determined performance targets for paternity establishment, support order establishment, amount of current support to be collected, amount of past due support to be collected, and any other performance measures a Tribe or Tribal organization may want to submit.

(b) If a Tribe or Tribal organization currently is unable to satisfy any or all of the requirements specified in paragraph (a) of this section:

(1) It may demonstrate capacity to operate a Tribal IV-D program meeting the objectives of title IV-D of the Act and these regulations by submission of an application for start-up funding as required by § 309.16(a) of this part.

(2) The Secretary may cease start-up funding to a Tribe or Tribal organization if that Tribe or Tribal organization fails to satisfy one or more provisions or milestones described in its program development plan within the timeframe specified in such plan.

§ 309.70 What provisions governing jurisdiction must a Tribe or Tribal organization include in a Tribal IV-D plan?

A Tribe or Tribal organization must include in its Tribal IV-D plan a description of the population subject to the jurisdiction of the Tribal court or administrative agency for child support enforcement purposes and certify that there are at least 100 children under the age of majority in the population subject to the jurisdiction of the Tribe in accordance with § 309.10 of this part and subject to § 309.10(c).

§ 309.75 What administrative and management procedures must a Tribe or Tribal organization include in a Tribal IV-D plan?

A Tribe or Tribal organization must include in its Tribal IV-D plan the administrative and management provisions contained in this section:

(a) A description of the structure of the IV-D agency and the distribution of responsibilities within the agency.

(b) Evidence that all Federal funds and amounts collected by the Tribal IV-D agency are protected against loss. Tribes and Tribal organizations may comply with this paragraph by submitting documentation that establishes that every person who receives, disburses, handles, or has access to or control over funds collected under the Tribal IV-D program is covered by a bond or insurance sufficient to cover all losses.

(c) Procedures under which notices of support collected, itemized by month of collection, are provided to families receiving services under the Tribal IV-D program at least once a year. In addition, a notice must be provided at any time to either the custodial or noncustodial parent upon request.

(d) A certification that for each year during which the Tribe or Tribal organization receives or expends funds pursuant to section 455(f) of the Act and this part, it shall comply with the provisions of chapter 75 of Title 31 of the United States Code (the Single Audit Act of 1984, Pub. L. 98–502, as amended) and OMB Circular A–133.

(e) If the Tribe or Tribal organization intends to charge an application fee or recover costs in excess of the fee, the Tribal IV-D plan must provide that:

(1) The application fee must be uniformly applied by the Tribe or Tribal organization and must be:

(i) A flat amount not to exceed $25.00; or

(ii) An amount based on a fee schedule not to exceed $25.00.

(2) The Tribal IV-D agency may not charge an application fee in an intergovernmental case referred to the Tribal IV-D agency for services under § 309.120.

(3) No application fee may be charged to an individual receiving services under titles IV-A, IV-E foster care maintenance assistance, or XIX (Medicaid) of the Act.

(4) The Tribal IV-D agency must exclude from its quarterly expenditure claims an amount equal to all fees which are collected and costs recovered during the quarter.

§ 309.80 What safeguarding procedures must a Tribe or Tribal organization include in a Tribal IV-D plan?

A Tribe or Tribal organization must include in its Tribal IV-D plan safeguarding provisions in accordance with this section:

(a) Procedures under which the use or disclosure of personal information received by or maintained by the Tribal IV-D agency is limited to purposes directly connected with the administration of the Tribal IV-D program, or titles IV-A and XIX with the administration of other programs or purposes prescribed by the Secretary in regulations.

(b) Procedures for safeguards that are applicable to all confidential information handled by the Tribal IV-D agency and that are designed to protect the privacy rights of the parties, including:

(1) Safeguards against unauthorized use or disclosure of information relating to proceedings or actions to establish paternity, or to establish, modify or enforce support;

(2) Prohibitions against the release of information on the whereabouts of one party or the child to another party against whom a protective order with respect to the former party or the child has been entered;

(3) Prohibitions against the release of information on the whereabouts of one party or the child to another person if the Tribe has reason to believe that the release of the information to that person may result in physical or emotional harm to the party or child; and

(4) Procedures in accordance with any specific safeguarding regulations applicable to Tribal IV-D programs promulgated by the Secretary.

(c) Procedures under which sanctions must be imposed for the unauthorized use or disclosure of information covered by paragraphs (a) and (b) of this section.

§ 309.85 What records must a Tribe or Tribal organization agree to maintain in a Tribal IV-D plan?

A Tribal IV-D plan must provide that:

(a) The Tribal IV-D agency will maintain records necessary for the proper and efficient operation of the program, including records regarding:

(1) Applications for child support services;

(2) Efforts to locate noncustodial parents;

(3) Actions taken to establish paternity and obtain and enforce support;

(4) Amounts owed, arrearages, amounts and sources of support collections, and the distribution of such collections;

(5) IV-D program expenditures;

(6) Any fees charged and collected, if applicable; and

(7) Statistical, fiscal, and other records necessary for reporting and accountability required by the Secretary.

(b) The Tribal IV-D agency will comply with the retention and access requirements at 45 CFR 75.361 through 75.370, including the requirement that records be retained for at least three years.

[69 FR 16672, Mar. 30, 2004, as amended at 81 FR 3021, Jan. 20, 2016]

§ 309.90 What governing Tribal law or regulations must a Tribe or Tribal organization include in a Tribal IV-D plan?

(a) A Tribe or Tribal organization must include in its Tribal IV-D plan Tribal law, code, regulations, and/or other evidence that provides for:

(1) Establishment of paternity for any child up to and including at least 18 years of age;

(2) Establishment and modification of child support obligations;

(3) Enforcement of child support obligations, including requirements that Tribal employers comply with income withholding as required under § 309.110; and

(4) Location of custodial and noncustodial parents.

(b) In the absence of written laws and regulations, a Tribe or Tribal organization may provide in its plan detailed descriptions of any Tribal custom or common law with the force and effect of law which enables the Tribe or Tribal organization to satisfy the requirements in paragraph (a) of this section.

§ 309.95 What procedures governing the location of custodial and noncustodial parents must a Tribe or Tribal organization include in a Tribal IV-D plan?

A Tribe or Tribal organization must include in its Tribal IV-D plan the provisions governing the location of custodial and noncustodial parents and their assets set forth in this section.

(a) The Tribal IV-D agency must attempt to locate custodial or noncustodial parents or sources of income and/or assets when location is required to take necessary action in a case; and

(b) The Tribal IV-D agency must use all sources of information and records reasonably available to the Tribe or Tribal organization to locate custodial or noncustodial parents and their sources of income and assets.

§ 309.100 What procedures for the establishment of paternity must a Tribe or Tribal organization include in a Tribal IV-D plan?

(a) A Tribe or Tribal organization must include in its Tribal IV-D plan the procedures for the establishment of paternity included in this section. The Tribe must include in its Tribal IV-D plan procedures under which the Tribal IV-D agency will:

(1) Attempt to establish paternity by the process established under Tribal law, code, and/or custom in accordance with this section;

(2) Provide an alleged father the opportunity to voluntarily acknowledge paternity; and

(3) In a contested paternity case (unless otherwise barred by Tribal law) require the child and all other parties to submit to genetic tests upon the request of any such party, if the request is supported by a sworn statement by the party—

(i) Alleging paternity, and setting forth facts establishing a reasonable possibility of the requisite sexual contact between parties; or

(ii) Denying paternity, and setting forth facts establishing a reasonable possibility of the nonexistence of sexual contact between the parties.

(b) The Tribal IV-D agency need not attempt to establish paternity in any case involving incest or forcible rape, or in any case in which legal proceedings for adoption are pending, if, in the opinion of the Tribal IV-D agency, it would not be in the best interests of the child to establish paternity.

(c) When genetic testing is used to establish paternity, the Tribal IV-D agency must identify and use accredited laboratories which perform, at reasonable cost, legally and medically-acceptable genetic tests which intend to identify the father or exclude the alleged father.

(d) Establishment of paternity under this section has no effect on Tribal enrollment or membership.

§ 309.105 What procedures governing child support guidelines must a Tribe or Tribal organization include in a Tribal IV-D plan?

(a) A Tribal IV-D plan must: (1) Establish one set of child support guidelines by law or action of the tribunal for setting and modifying child support obligation amounts;

(2) Include a copy of child support guidelines governing the establishment and modification of child support obligations;

(3) Indicate whether non-cash payments will be permitted to satisfy support obligations, and if so;

(i) Require that Tribal support orders allowing non-cash payments also state the specific dollar amount of the support obligation; and

(ii) Describe the type(s) of non-cash support that will be permitted to satisfy the underlying specific dollar amount of the support order; and

(iii) Provide that non-cash payments will not be permitted to satisfy assigned support obligations;

(4) Indicate that child support guidelines will be reviewed and revised, if appropriate, at least once every four years;

(5) Provide that there shall be a rebuttable presumption, in any proceeding for the award of child support, that the amount of the award that would result from the application of the guidelines established consistent with this section is the correct amount of child support to be awarded; and

(6) Provide for the application of the guidelines unless there is a written finding or a specific finding on the record of the tribunal that the application of the guidelines would be unjust or inappropriate in a particular case in accordance with criteria established by the Tribe or Tribal organization. Such criteria must take into consideration the needs of the child. Findings that rebut the guidelines must state the amount of support that would have been required under the guidelines and include a justification of why the order varies from the guidelines.

(b) The guidelines established under paragraph (a) of this section must at a minimum:

(1) Take into account the needs of the child and the earnings and income of the noncustodial parent; and

(2) Be based on specific descriptive and numeric criteria and result in a computation of the support obligation.

§ 309.110 What procedures governing income withholding must a Tribe or Tribal organization include in a Tribal IV-D plan?

A Tribe or Tribal organization must include in its Tribal IV-D plan copies of Tribal laws providing for income withholding in accordance with this section.

(a) In the case of each noncustodial parent against whom a support order is or has been issued or modified under the Tribal IV-D plan, or is being enforced under such plan, so much of his or her income, as defined in § 309.05, must be withheld as is necessary to comply with the order.

(b) In addition to the amount to be withheld to pay the current month's obligation, the amount withheld must include an amount to be applied toward liquidation of any overdue support.

(c) The total amount to be withheld under paragraphs (a) and (b) of this section may not exceed the maximum amount permitted under section 303(b) of the Consumer Credit Protection Act (15 U.S.C. 1673(b)), but may be set at a lower amount.

(d) Income withholding must be carried out in compliance with the procedural due process requirements established by the Tribe or Tribal organization.

(e) The Tribal IV-D agency will promptly refund amounts which have been improperly withheld.

(f) The Tribal IV-D agency will promptly terminate income withholding in cases where there is no longer a current order for support and all arrearages have been satisfied.

(g) If the employer fails to withhold income in accordance with the provision of the income withholding order, the employer will be liable for the accumulated amount the employer should have withheld from the noncustodial parent's income.

(h) Income shall not be subject to withholding in any case where:

(1) Either the custodial or noncustodial parent demonstrates, and the tribunal enters a finding, that there is good cause not to require income withholding; or

(2) A signed written agreement is reached between the noncustodial and custodial parent, which provides for an alternative arrangement, and is reviewed and entered into the record by the tribunal.

(i) Where immediate income withholding is not in place, the income of the noncustodial parent shall become subject to withholding, at the earliest, on the date on which the payments which the noncustodial parent has failed to make under a Tribal support order are at least equal to the support payable for one month.

(j) The only basis for contesting a withholding is a mistake of fact, which for purposes of this paragraph, means an error in the amount of current or overdue support or in the identity of the alleged noncustodial parent.

(k) Tribal law must provide that the employer is subject to a fine to be determined under Tribal law for discharging a noncustodial parent from employment, refusing to employ, or taking disciplinary action against any noncustodial parent because of the withholding.

(l) To initiate income withholding, the Tribal IV-D agency must send the noncustodial parent's employer a notice using the standard Federal income withholding form.

(m) The Tribal IV-D agency must allocate withheld amounts across multiple withholding orders to ensure that in no case shall allocation result in a withholding for one of the support obligations not being implemented.

(n) The Tribal IV-D agency is responsible for receiving and processing income withholding orders from States, Tribes, and other entities, and ensuring orders are properly and promptly served on employers within the Tribe's jurisdiction.

§ 309.115 What procedures governing the distribution of child support must a Tribe or Tribal organization include in a Tribal IV-D plan?

A Tribe or Tribal organization must specify in its Tribal IV-D plan procedures for the distribution of child support collections in each Tribal IV-D case, in accordance with this section.

(a) *General Rule:* The Tribal IV-D agency must, in a timely manner:

(1) Apply collections first to satisfy current support obligations, except as provided in paragraph (e) of this section; and

(2) Pay all support collections to the family unless the family is currently receiving or formerly received assistance from the Tribal TANF program and there is an assignment of support rights to the Tribe's TANF agency, or the Tribal IV-D agency has received a request for assistance in collecting support on behalf of the family from a State or Tribal IV-D agency.

(b) *Current Receipt of Tribal TANF:* If the family is currently receiving assistance from the Tribal TANF program and has assigned support rights to the Tribe and:

(1) There is no request for assistance in collecting support on behalf of the family from a State or Tribal IV-D agency under § 309.120 of this part, the Tribal IV-D agency may retain collections on behalf of the family, not to exceed the total amount of Tribal TANF paid to the family. Any remaining collections must be paid to the family.

(2) There is a request for assistance in collecting support on behalf of the family from a State or Tribal IV-D agency under § 309.120, the Tribal IV-D agency may retain collections, not to exceed the total amount of Tribal TANF paid to the family. Except as provided in paragraph (f) of this section, the Tribal IV-D agency must send any remaining collections, as appropriate, to the requesting State IV-D agency for distribution under section 457 of the Act and 45 CFR 302.51 or 302.52, or to the requesting Tribal IV-D agency for distribution in accordance with this section.

(c) *Former Receipt of Tribal TANF:* If the family formerly received assistance from the Tribal TANF program and there is an assignment of support rights to the Tribe and:

(1) There is no request for assistance in collecting support from a State or Tribal IV-D agency under § 309.120 of this part, the Tribal IV-D agency must pay current support and any arrearages owed to the family to the family and may then retain any excess collections, not to exceed the total amount of Tribal TANF paid to the family. Any remaining collections must be paid to the family.

(2) There is a request for assistance in collecting support from a State or Tribal IV-D agency under § 309.120 of this part, the Tribal IV-D agency must send all support collected, as appropriate, to the requesting State IV-D agency for distribution under section 457 of the Act or 45 CFR 302.51 or 302.52, or to the requesting Tribal IV-D agency for distribution under this section, except as provided in paragraph (f) of this section.

(d) *Requests for Assistance from State or Tribal IV-D Agency:* If there is no assignment of support rights to the Tribe as a condition of receipt of Tribal TANF and the Tribal IV-D agency has received a request for assistance in collecting support on behalf of the family from a State or another Tribal IV-D agency under § 309.120 of this part, the Tribal IV-D agency must send all support collected to either the State IV-D agency for distribution in accordance with section 457 of the Act and 45 CFR 302.51 and 302.52, or to the Tribal IV-D agency for distribution under this section, as appropriate, except as provided in paragraph (f) of this section.

(e) *Federal Income Tax Refund Offset Collections:* Any collections received based on Federal income tax refund offset under section 464 of the Act and distributed by the Tribal IV-D agency must be applied to satisfy child support arrearages.

(f) *Option to Contact Requesting Agency for Appropriate Distribution:* Rather than send collections to a State or another Tribal IV-D agency for distribution as required under § 309.115 (b)(2), (c)(2) and (d), a Tribal IV-D agency may contact the requesting State IV-D agency to determine appropriate distribution under section 457 of the Act, or the other Tribal IV-D agency to determine appropriate distribution under this section, and distribute collections as directed by the other agency.

[69 FR 16672, Mar. 30, 2004, as amended at 81 FR 93569, Dec. 20, 2016]

§ 309.120 What intergovernmental procedures must a Tribe or Tribal organization include in a Tribal IV-D plan?

A Tribe or Tribal organization must specify in its Tribal IV-D plan:

(a) That the Tribal IV-D agency will extend the full range of services available under its IV-D plan to respond to all requests from, and cooperate with, State and other Tribal IV-D agencies; and

(b) That the Tribe or Tribal organization will recognize child support orders issued by other Tribes and Tribal organizations, and by States, in accordance with the requirements under the Full Faith and Credit for Child Support Orders Act, 28 U.S.C. 1738B.

Subpart D—Tribal IV-D Program Funding

§309.125 On what basis is Federal funding of Tribal IV-D programs determined?

Federal funding of Tribal IV-D programs is based on information contained in the Tribal IV-D application. The application must include a proposed budget and a description of the nature and scope of the Tribal IV-D program and must give assurance that the program will be administered in conformity with applicable requirements of title IV-D of the Act, regulations contained in this part, and other official issuances of the Department that specifically state applicability to Tribal IV-D programs.

§309.130 How will Tribal IV-D programs be funded and what forms are required?

(a) *General mechanism.* (1) Tribes and Tribal organizations with approved Tribal plans under title IV-D will receive Federal grant funds in an amount equal to the percentage specified in paragraph (c) of this section of the total amount of approved and allowable expenditures under the plan for the administration of the Tribal child support enforcement program.

(2) Tribes and Tribal organizations eligible for grants of less than $1 million per 12-month funding period will receive a single annual award. Tribes and Tribal organizations eligible for grants of $1 million or more per 12-month funding period will receive four equal quarterly awards.

(b) *Financial Form Submittal Requirements.* Tribes and Tribal organizations receiving Federal funding under this part are required to submit the following financial forms, and such other forms as the Secretary may designate, to OCSE:

(1) Standard Form (SF) 424, "Application for Federal Assistance," to be submitted with the initial grant application for funding under §309.65(a) and (b) (60 days prior to the start of the funding period);

(2) SF 424A, "Budget Information—Non-Construction Programs," to be submitted annually, no later than August 1 (60 days prior to the start of the funding period) in accordance with §309.15(a)(2) of this part. With each submission, the following information must be included:

(i) A quarter-by-quarter estimate of expenditures for the funding period; and

(ii) Notification of whether the Tribe or Tribal organization is requesting funds for indirect costs and an election of a method to calculate estimated indirect costs; and

(iii) A narrative justification for each cost category on the form; and for funding under §309.65(a) either:

(iv) A statement certifying that the Tribe or Tribal organization has or will have the non-Federal share of program expenditures available, as required, or

(v) A request for a waiver of the non-Federal share in accordance with paragraph (e) of this section;

(3) SF 425, "Federal Financial Report," to be submitted quarterly within 30 days after the end of each of the first three quarters of the funding period and within 30 days after the end of each of the first three quarters of the liquidation period. The final report for each period is due within 90 days after the end of the fourth quarter of both the funding and the liquidation period; and

(4) Form OCSE–34, "Child Support Enforcement Program Quarterly Collection Report" must be submitted no later than 45 days following the end of each fiscal quarter. No revisions or adjustments of the financial reports submitted for any quarter of the fiscal year will be accepted by OCSE later than December 31, which is 3 months after the end of the fiscal year.

(c) *Federal share of program expenditures.* (1) During the period of start-up funding specified in §309.16, a Tribe or Tribal organization will receive Federal grant funds equal to 100 percent of approved and allowable expenditures made during that period. Federal start-up funds are limited to a total of $500,000.

(2) During a 3-year period, beginning with the first day of the first quarter of the funding grant specified under §309.135(a)(2), a Tribe or Tribal organization will receive Federal grant funds equal to 90 percent of the total amount of approved and allowable expenditures

made during that period for the administration of the Tribal child support enforcement program.

(3)(i) Except as provided in paragraph (c)(3)(ii) of this section, for all periods following the three-year period specified in paragraph (c)(2) of this section, a Tribe or Tribal organization will receive Federal grant funds equal to 80 percent of the total amount of approved and allowable expenditures made for the administration of the Tribal child support enforcement program.

(ii) A Tribe or Tribal organization will receive Federal grant funds equal to 90 percent of pre-approved costs of installing the Model Tribal IV–D System.

(d) *Non-Federal share of program expenditures.* Each Tribe or Tribal organization that operates a child support enforcement program under title IV-D and § 309.65(a), unless the Secretary has granted a waiver pursuant to § 309.130(e), must provide the non-Federal share of funding, equal to:

(1) 10 percent of approved and allowable expenditures during the 3-year period specified in paragraph (c)(2) of this section or;

(2) 20 percent of approved and allowable expenditures during the subsequent periods specified in paragraph (c)(3) of this section.

(3) The non-Federal share of program expenditures must be provided either with cash or with in-kind contributions and must meet the requirements found in 45 CFR 75.306.

(e) *Waiver of non-Federal share of program expenditures.* (1) Under certain circumstances, the Secretary may grant a temporary waiver of part or all of the non-Federal share of expenditures.

(i) If a Tribe or Tribal organization anticipates that it will be temporarily unable to contribute part or all of the non-Federal share of funding under paragraph (d) of this section, it must submit a written request that this requirement be temporarily waived. A request for a waiver of part or all of the non-Federal share must be sent to ACF, included with the submission of SF 424A, no later than 60 days prior to the start of the funding period for which the waiver is being requested, except as provided in paragraph (e)(1)(ii) of this section. An untimely or incomplete request will not be considered.

(ii) If, after the start of the funding period, an emergency situation such as a hurricane or flood occurs such that the grantee would need to request a waiver of the non-Federal costs, it may do so. The request for a waiver must be submitted in accordance with the procedures specified in paragraphs (e)(2), (3) and (4) of this section. Any waiver request other than one submitted with the initial application must be submitted as soon as the adverse effect of the emergency situation giving rise to the request is known to the grantee.

(2) A request for a waiver of part or all of the non-Federal share must include the following:

(i) A statement of the amount of the non-Federal share that the Tribe is requesting be waived;

(ii) A narrative statement describing the circumstances and justification for the waiver request;

(iii) Portions of the Tribal budget for the funding period sufficient to demonstrate that any funding shortfall is not limited to the Tribal IV-D program and that any uncommitted Tribal reserve funds are insufficient to meet the non-Federal funding requirement;

(iv) Copies of any additional financial documents in support of the request;

(v) A detailed description of the attempts made to secure the necessary funds and in-kind contributions from other sources and the results of those attempts, including copies of all relevant correspondence; and

(vi) Any other documentation or other information that the Secretary may require to make this determination.

(3) The Tribe or Tribal organization must demonstrate to the satisfaction of the Secretary that it temporarily lacks resources to provide the non-Federal share. In its request for a temporary waiver, the Tribe or Tribal organization must be able to demonstrate that it:

(i) Lacks sufficient resources to provide the required non-Federal share of costs;

(ii) Has made reasonable, but unsuccessful, efforts to obtain non-Federal share contributions; and

(iii) Has provided all required information requested by the Secretary.

(4) All statements in support of a waiver request must be supported by evidence including, but not limited to, a description of how the Tribe or Tribal organization's circumstances relate to its capacity to provide child support enforcement services. The following statements will be considered insufficient to merit a waiver under this section without documentary evidence satisfactory to the Secretary:

(i) Funds have been committed to other budget items;

(ii) A high rate of unemployment;

(iii) A generally poor economic condition;

(iv) A lack of or a decline in revenue from gaming, fishing, timber, mineral rights and other similar revenue sources;

(v) A small or declining tax base; and

(vi) Little or no economic development.

(5)(i) If approved, a temporary waiver submitted under either paragraph (e)(1)(i) or (ii) of this section will expire on the last day of the funding period for which it was approved and is subject to review at any time during the funding period and may be revoked, if changing circumstances warrant.

(ii) Unless the Tribe receives a written approval of its waiver request, the funding requirements stated in paragraph (d) of this section remain in effect.

(iii) If the request for a waiver is denied, the denial is not subject to administrative appeal.

(f) *Increase in approved budget.* (1) A Tribe or Tribal organization may request an increase in the approved amount of its current budget by submitting a revised SF 424A to ACF and explaining why it needs the additional funds. The Tribe or Tribal organization should submit this request at least 60 days before additional funds are needed, to allow the Secretary adequate time to review the estimates and issue a revised grant award, if appropriate.

(2) If the change in Tribal IV-D budget estimate results from a change in the Tribal IV-D plan, the Tribe or Tribal organization must submit a plan amendment in accordance with § 309.35(e) of this part, a revised SF 424 and a revised SF 424A with its request for additional funding. The effective date of a plan amendment may not be earlier than the first day of the fiscal quarter in which an approvable plan is submitted in accordance with § 309.35(f) of this part. The Secretary must approve the plan amendment before approving any additional funding.

(3) Any approved increase in the Tribal IV-D budget will necessarily result in a proportional increase in the non-Federal share, unless a waiver of the non-Federal share has been granted.

(g) *Obtaining Federal funds.* Tribes and Tribal organizations will obtain Federal funds on a draw down basis from the Department's Payment Management System on a letter of credit system for payment of advances of Federal funds.

(h) *Grant administration requirements.* The provisions of part 75 of this title, establishing uniform administrative requirements and cost principles, shall apply to all grants made to Tribes and Tribal organizations under this part.

[69 FR 16672, Mar. 30, 2004, as amended at 75 FR 8520, Feb. 25, 2010; 81 FR 3021, Jan. 20, 2016; 81 FR 93569, Dec. 20, 2016]

§ 309.135 What requirements apply to funding, obligating and liquidating Federal title IV-D grant funds?

(a) *Funding period*—(1) *Ongoing funding.* Federal title IV-D grant funds will be awarded to Tribes and Tribal organizations for use during a 12-month period equivalent to the Federal fiscal year of October 1 through September 30.

(2) *Initial grant.* A Tribe or Tribal organization may request that its initial IV-D grant be awarded for a funding period of less than one year (but at least six months) or more than one year (but not to exceed 17 months) to enable its program funding cycle to coincide with the funding period specified in paragraph (a)(1) of this section.

(b) *Obligation period.* A Tribe or Tribal organization must obligate its Federal title IV-D grant funds no later than the last day of the funding period for which they were awarded. Any of these funds remaining unobligated after that date must be returned to the Department.

(c) *Liquidation period.* A Tribe or Tribal organization must liquidate the Federal title IV-D grant funds obligated during the obligation period specified in paragraph (b) of this section no later than the last day of the 12-month period immediately following the obligation period. Any of these funds remaining unliquidated after that date must be returned to the Department.

(d) *Funding reductions.* As required under § 309.130(b)(3), a Tribe or Tribal organization will report quarterly on Form SF 269A the amount of Federal title IV-D grant funds that have been obligated and liquidated and the amounts that remain unobligated and unliquidated at the end of each fiscal quarter during the obligation and liquidation periods. The Department will reduce the amount of the Tribe or Tribal organization's Federal title IV-D grant funds for the funding period by any amount reported as remaining unobligated on the report following the last day of the obligation period. The Department will further reduce the amount of the Tribe or Tribal organization's Federal title IV-D grant funds for the funding period by any amount reported as remaining unliquidated on the report following the last day of the liquidation period.

(e) *Extension requests.* A Tribe or Tribal organization may submit a written request for an extension of the deadline for liquidating Federal title IV-D grant funds. Such a request must be sent to ACF, to the attention of the Federal grants officer named on the most recent grant award. The request must be submitted as soon as it is clear that such an extension will be needed; any request received after the end of the liquidation period will not be considered. The request must include a detailed explanation of the extenuating circumstances or other reasons for the request and must state the date by which the Tribe anticipates all obligated funds will be liquidated. Unless the Tribe receives a written approval of its request, the deadline stated in paragraph (c) of this section remains in effect.

§ 309.145 What costs are allowable for Tribal IV-D programs carried out under § 309.65(a) of this part?

Federal funds are available for costs of operating a Tribal IV-D program under an approved Tribal IV-D application carried out under § 309.65(a) of this part, provided that such costs are determined by the Secretary to be reasonable, necessary, and allocable to the program. Allowable activities and costs include:

(a) Administration of the Tribal IV-D program, including but not limited to the following:

(1) Establishment and administration of the Tribal IV-D plan;

(2) Monitoring the progress of program development and operations, and evaluating the quality, efficiency, effectiveness, and scope of available support enforcement services;

(3) Establishment of all necessary agreements with other Tribal, State, and local agencies or private providers for the provision of child support enforcement services in accordance with Procurement Standards found in 45 CFR 75.326 through 75.340. These agreements may include:

(i) Necessary administrative agreements for support services;

(ii) Use of Tribal, Federal, State, and local information resources;

(iii) Cooperation with courts and law enforcement officials;

(iv) Securing compliance with the requirements of the Tribal IV-D program plan in operations under any agreements;

(v) Development and maintenance of systems for fiscal and program records and reports required to be made to OCSE based on these records; and

(vi) Development of cost allocation systems.

(b) Establishment of paternity, including:

(1) Establishment of paternity in accordance with Tribal law codes, and/or custom in accordance with § 309.100 of this part, as outlined in the approved Tribal IV-D plan;

(2) Reasonable attempts to determine the identity of a child's father, such as:

(i) Investigation;

(ii) Development of evidence, including the use of genetic testing performed by accredited laboratories; and

(iii) Pre-trial discovery;

(3) Actions taken by a tribunal to establish paternity pursuant to procedures established by Tribal law, and/or codes or custom in accordance with § 309.100 of this part;

(4) Identifying accredited laboratories that perform genetic tests (as appropriate); and

(5) Referrals of cases to another Tribal IV-D agency or to a State to establish paternity when appropriate.

(c) Establishment, modification, and enforcement of support obligations, including:

(1) Investigation, development of evidence and, when appropriate, court or administrative actions;

(2) Determination of the amount of the support obligation (including determination of income and allowable non-cash support under Tribal IV-D guidelines, if appropriate);

(3) Enforcement of a support obligation, including those activities associated with collections and the enforcement of court orders, administrative orders, warrants, income withholding, criminal proceedings, and prosecution of fraud related to child support; and

(4) Investigation and prosecution of fraud related to child and spousal support cases receiving services under the IV-D plan.

(d) Collection and disbursement of support payments, including:

(1) Establishment and operation of an effective system for making collections and identifying delinquent cases and collecting from them;

(2) Referral or transfer of cases to another Tribal IV-D agency or to a State IV-D program when appropriate; and

(3) Services provided for another Tribal IV-D program or for a State IV-D program.

(e) Establishment and operation of a Tribal Parent Locator Service (TPLS) or agreements for referral of cases to a State PLS, another Tribal PLS, or the Federal PLS for location purposes.

(f) Activities related to requests to State IV-D programs for enforcement services for the Federal Income Tax Refund Offset.

(g) Establishing and maintaining case records.

(h) Automated data processing computer systems, including:

(1) Planning efforts in the identification, evaluation, and selection of an automated data processing computer system solution meeting the program requirements defined in a Tribal IV–D plan and the automated systems requirements in part 310 of this chapter;

(2) Installation, operation, maintenance, and enhancement of a Model Tribal IV–D System as defined in and meeting the requirements of part 310 of this title;

(3) Procurement, installation, operation and maintenance of essential Office Automation capability;

(4) Establishment of Intergovernmental Service Agreements with a State and another comprehensive Tribal IV–D agency for access to the State or other Tribe's existing automated data processing computer system to support Tribal IV–D program operations, and Reasonable Costs associated with use of such a system;

(5) Operation and maintenance of a Tribal automated data processing system funded entirely with Tribal funds if the software ownership rights and license requirements in § 310.25(c)(1) are met; and

(6) Other automation and automated data processing computer system costs in accordance with instructions and guidance issued by the Secretary.

(i) Staffing and equipment that are directly related to operating a Tribal IV-D program.

(j) The portion of salaries and expenses of a Tribe's chief executive and staff that is directly attributable to managing and operating a Tribal IV-D program.

(k) The portion of salaries and expenses of tribunals and staff that is directly related to required Tribal IV-D program activities.

(l) Service of process.

(m) Training on a short-term basis that is directly related to operating a Tribal IV-D program.

(n) Costs associated with obtaining technical assistance that are directly related to operating a IV-D program, from non-Federal third-party sources, including other Tribes, Tribal organizations, State agencies, and private organizations, and costs associated with providing such technical assistance to public entities.

(o) Any other costs that are determined to be reasonable, necessary, and allocable to the Tribal IV-D program in accordance with the cost principles in 45 CFR part 75, subpart E. The total amount that may be claimed under the Tribal IV-D grant are allowable direct costs, plus the allocable portion of allowable indirect costs, minus any applicable credits.

(1) All claimed costs must be adequately documented; and

(2) A cost is allocable if the goods or services involved are assignable to the grant according to the relative benefit received. Any cost that is allocable to one Federal award may not be charged to other Federal awards to overcome funding deficiencies, or for any other reason.

[69 FR 16672, Mar. 30, 2004, as amended at 75 FR 8520, Feb. 25, 2010; 81 FR 3021, Jan. 20, 2016; 81 FR 93569, Dec. 20, 2016]

§ 309.150 What start-up costs are allowable for Tribal IV-D programs carried out under § 309.65(b) of this part?

Federal funds are available for costs of developing a Tribal IV-D program, provided that such costs are reasonable, necessary, and allocable to the program. Federal funding for Tribal IV-D program development under § 309.65(b) may not exceed a total of $500,000, unless additional funding is provided pursuant to § 309.16(c). Allowable start-up costs and activities include:

(a) Planning for the initial development and implementation of a Tribal IV-D program;

(b) Developing Tribal IV-D laws, codes, guidelines, systems, and procedures;

(c) Recruiting, hiring, and training Tribal IV-D program staff; and

(d) Any other reasonable, necessary, and allocable costs with a direct correlation to the initial development of a Tribal IV-D program, consistent with the cost principles in 45 CFR part 75, subpart E, and approved by the Secretary.

[69 FR 16672, Mar. 30, 2004, as amended at 81 FR 3021, Jan. 20, 2016]

§ 309.155 What uses of Tribal IV-D program funds are not allowable?

Federal IV-D funds may not be used for:

(a) Activities related to administering other programs, including those under the Social Security Act;

(b) Construction and major renovations;

(c) Any expenditures that have been reimbursed by fees or costs collected, including any fee collected from a State;

(d) Expenditures for jailing of parents in Tribal IV-D cases;

(e) The cost of legal counsel for indigent defendants in Tribal IV-D program actions;

(f) The cost of guardians ad litem in Tribal IV-D cases; and

(g) All other costs that are not reasonable, necessary, and allocable to Tribal IV-D programs, under the costs principles in OMB Circular A–87.

Subpart E—Accountability and Monitoring

§ 309.160 How will OCSE determine if Tribal IV-D program funds are appropriately expended?

OCSE will rely on audits conducted under 45 CFR part 75, *Subpart F—Audit Requirements*. The Department has determined that this program is to be audited as a major program in accordance with section 215(c) of the circular. The Department may supplement the required audits through reviews or audits conducted by its own staff.

[69 FR 16672, Mar. 30, 2004, as amended at 81 FR 3021, Jan. 20, 2016; 81 FR 93569, Dec. 20, 2016]

§ 309.165 What recourse does a Tribe or Tribal organization have to dispute a determination to disallow Tribal IV-D program expenditures?

If a Tribe or Tribal organization disputes a decision to disallow Tribal IV-D program expenditures, the grant appeals procedures outlined in 45 CFR part 16 are applicable.

Subpart F—Statistical and Narrative Reporting Requirements

§309.170 What statistical and narrative reporting requirements apply to Tribal IV-D programs?

(a) Tribes and Tribal organizations operating a Tribal IV-D program must submit to OCSE the *Child Support Enforcement Program: Quarterly Report of Collections* (Form OCSE–34A). The reports for each of the first three quarters of the funding period are due 30 days after the end of each quarterly reporting period. The report for the fourth quarter is due 90 days after the end of the fourth quarter of each funding period.

(b) Tribes and Tribal organizations must submit the following information and statistics for Tribal IV-D program activity and caseload for each annual funding period:

(1) Total number of cases and, of the total number of cases, the number that are State or Tribal TANF cases and the number that are non-TANF cases;

(2) Total number of out-of-wedlock births in the previous year and total number of paternities established or acknowledged;

(3) Total number of cases and the total number of cases with a support order;

(4) Total amount of current support due and collected;

(5) Total amount of past-due support owed and total collected;

(6) A narrative report on activities, accomplishments, and progress of the program, including success in reaching the performance targets established by the Tribe or Tribal organization;

(7) Total costs claimed;

(8) Total amount of fees and costs recovered; and

(9) Total amount of laboratory paternity establishment costs.

(c) A Tribe or Tribal organization must submit Tribal IV-D program statistical and narrative reports required by paragraph (b) of this section no later than 90 days after the end of each funding period.

PART 310—COMPUTERIZED TRIBAL IV-D SYSTEMS AND OFFICE AUTOMATION

Subpart A—General Provisions

Subpart B—Requirements for Computerized Tribal IV–D Systems and Office Automation

Subpart C—Funding for Computerized Tribal IV–D Systems and Office Automation

Subpart D—Accountability and Monitoring Procedures for Computerized Tribal IV–D Systems

AUTHORITY: 42 U.S.C. 655(f) and 1302.

SOURCE: 75 FR 8520, Feb. 25, 2010, unless otherwise noted.

Subpart A—General Provisions

§310.0 What does this part cover?

This part addresses conditions for funding and requirements governing Computerized Tribal IV-D Systems and Office Automation including:

(a) The automated systems options for comprehensive Tribal IV–D programs in § 310.5 of this part;

(b) The functional requirements for the Model Tribal IV–D Systems in § 310.10 of this part;

(c) The security and privacy requirements for Computerized Tribal IV–D Systems and Office Automation in § 310.15 of this part;

(d) The conditions for funding the installation, operation, maintenance, and enhancement of Computerized Tribal IV–D Systems and Office Automation in § 310.20 of this part;

(e) The conditions that apply to acquisitions of Computerized Tribal IV–D Systems in § 310.25 of this part; and

(f) The accountability and monitoring of Computerized Tribal IV–D Systems in § 310.40 of this part.

§ 310.1 What definitions apply to this part?

(a) The following definitions apply to this part and part 309:

(1) *Automated Data Processing Services (ADP Services)* means services for installation, maintenance, operation, and enhancement of ADP equipment and software performed by a comprehensive Tribal IV–D agency or for that agency through a services agreement or other contractual relationship with a State, another Tribe or private sector entity.

(2) *Comprehensive Tribal IV–D agency* means the organizational unit in the Tribe or Tribal organization that has the authority for administering or supervising a comprehensive Tribal IV–D program under section 455(f) of the Act and implementing regulations in part 309 of this chapter. This is an agency meeting all requirements of § 309.65(a) of this chapter which is not in the start-up phase under § 309.65(b) of this chapter.

(3) *Computerized Tribal IV–D System* means a comprehensive Tribal IV–D program's system of data processing that is performed by electronic or electrical machines so interconnected and interacting as to minimize the need for human assistance or intervention. A Computerized Tribal IV–D System is:

(i) The Model Tribal IV–D System; or

(ii) Access to a State or comprehensive Tribal IV–D agency's existing automated data processing computer system through an Intergovernmental Service Agreement;

(4) *Installation* means the act of installing ADP equipment and software, performing data conversion, and turnover to operation status.

(5) *Maintenance* is the totality of activities required to provide cost-effective support to an operational ADP system. Maintenance is generally routine in nature and can include activities such as: Upgrading ADP hardware, and revising/creating new reports, making limited data element/data base changes, minor data presentation changes, and other software corrections.

(6) *Model Tribal IV–D System* means an ADP system designed and developed by OCSE for comprehensive Tribal IV–D programs to include system specifications and requirements as specified in this part. The Model Tribal IV–D System effectively and efficiently allows a comprehensive Tribal IV–D agency to monitor, account for, and control all child support enforcement services and activities pursuant to part 309 of this chapter.

(7) *Office Automation* means a generic adjunct component of a computer system that supports the routine administrative functions in an organization (e.g., electronic mail, word processing, internet access), as well as similar functions performed as part of an automated data processing system. Office Automation is not specifically designed to meet the programmatic and business-centric needs of an organization.

(8) *Reasonable Cost* means a cost that is determined to be reasonable if, in its nature and amount, it does not exceed that which would be incurred by a prudent person under the circumstances prevailing at the time the decision was made to incur the cost. In determining reasonableness with regard to ADP systems cost, consideration shall be given to:

(i) Whether the cost is of a type generally recognized as ordinary and necessary for the operation of a comprehensive Tribal IV–D agency;

(ii) The restraints or requirements imposed by such factors as: Sound business practices; arms-length bargaining; Federal, Tribal laws and regulations;

and terms and conditions of any direct Federal funding;

(iii) Whether the individual concerned acted with prudence in the circumstances considering his or her responsibilities to the comprehensive Tribal IV–D agency, its employees, the public at large, and the Federal Government;

(iv) Market prices for comparable goods or services;

(v) Significant deviations from the established practices of the comprehensive Tribal IV–D agency which may unjustifiably increase the cost; and

(vi) Whether a project's Total Acquisition Cost is in excess of the comprehensive Tribal IV–D agency's total Tribal IV–D program grant award for the year in which the request is made.

(9) *Service Agreement* means a document signed by the Tribe or Tribal organization operating a comprehensive Tribal IV–D program under § 309.65(a) and the State or other comprehensive Tribal IV–D program whenever the latter provides data processing services to the former and identifies those ADP services that the State or other comprehensive Tribal IV–D program will provide to the Tribe or Tribal organization. Additionally, a Service Agreement would include the following details:

(i) Schedule of charges for each identified ADP service and a certification that these charges apply equally to all users;

(ii) Description of the method(s) of accounting for the services rendered under the agreement and computing service charges;

(iii) Assurances that services provided will be timely and satisfactory;

(iv) Assurances that information in the computer system as well as access, use and disposal of ADP data will be safeguarded in accordance with proposed § 310.15;

(v) Beginning and ending dates of the period of time covered by the Service Agreement; and

(vi) Schedule of expected total charges for the period of the Service Agreement.

(10) *Simplified Acquisition Threshold* for ADP systems, equipment, and service acquisitions means a Tribe or Tribal organization's monetary threshold for determining whether competitive acquisition rules are required for a given procurement or $100,000, whichever is less.

(b) The following terms apply to this part and are defined in § 95.605 of this title: "Acquisition"; "Advance Planning Document (APD)"; "Design or System Design"; "Development"; "Enhancement"; "Federal Financial Participation (FFP)"; "Operation"; "Project"; "Software"; and "Total Acquisition Cost".

(c) All of the terms defined in § 309.05 of this chapter apply to this part.

Subpart B—Requirements for Computerized Tribal IV–D Systems and Office Automation

§ 310.5 What options are available for Computerized Tribal IV–D Systems and office automation?

(a) *Allowable computerized support enforcement systems for a Comprehensive Tribal IV–D agency.* A comprehensive Tribal IV–D agency may have in effect an operational computerized support enforcement system that meets Federal requirements under this part.

(b) *Computerized Tribal IV–D Systems.* A Computerized Tribal IV–D System must be one of the design options listed below. A comprehensive Tribal IV–D program may automate its case processing and recordkeeping processes through:

(1) Installation, operation, maintenance, or enhancement of the Model Tribal IV–D System designed by OCSE to address the program requirements defined in a Tribal IV–D plan in accordance with § 309.65(a) of this chapter and the functional requirements in § 310.10 of this part;

(2) Establishment of Intergovernmental Service Agreements with a State or another comprehensive Tribal IV–D agency for access to that agency's existing automated data processing computer system to support comprehensive Tribal IV–D program operations.

(c) *Office Automation.* A comprehensive Tribal IV–D agency may opt to conduct automated data processing and recordkeeping activities through Office Automation. Allowable activities under this paragraph include procurement, installation, operation and maintenance of essential Office Automation capability as defined in § 310.1 of this part.

(d) *Alternative to Computerized Tribal IV–D Systems and Office Automation.* A comprehensive Tribal IV–D agency may design, develop, procure, or enhance an automated data processing system funded entirely with Tribal funds.

§ 310.10 What are the functional requirements for the Model Tribal IV–D System?

A Model Tribal IV–D System must:

(a) Accept, maintain and process the actions in the support collection and paternity determination processes under the Tribal IV–D plan, including:

(1) Identifying information such as Social Security numbers, names, dates of birth, home addresses and mailing addresses (including postal zip codes) on individuals against whom paternity and support obligations are sought to be established or enforced and on individuals to whom support obligations are owed, and other data as may be requested by OCSE;

(2) Verifying information on individuals referred to in paragraph (a)(1) of this section with Tribal, Federal, State and local agencies, both intra-tribal and intergovernmental;

(3) Maintaining information pertaining to:

(i) Applications and referrals for Tribal IV–D services, including:

(A) Case record;

(B) Referral to the appropriate processing unit (i.e., locate or paternity establishment);

(C) Caseworker notification;

(D) Case Identification Number; and

(E) Participant Identification Number;

(ii) Delinquency and enforcement activities;

(iii) Intra-tribal, intergovernmental, and Federal location of the putative father and noncustodial parents;

(iv) The establishment of paternity;

(v) The establishment of support obligations;

(vi) The payment and status of current support obligations;

(vii) The payment and status of arrearage accounts;

(4) Maintaining data on case actions administered by both the initiating and responding jurisdictions in intergovernmental cases;

(b) Update, maintain and manage all IV–D cases under the Tribal IV–D plan from initial application or referral through collection and enforcement, including any events, transactions, or actions taken therein;

(c) Record and report any fees collected, either directly or by interfacing with State or Tribal financial management and expenditure information;

(d) Distribute current support and arrearage collections in accordance with Federal regulations at § 309.115 of this chapter and Tribal laws;

(e) Maintain, process and monitor accounts receivable on all amounts owed, collected, and distributed with regard to:

(1) Detailed payment histories that include the following:

(i) Amount of each payment;

(ii) Date of each collection;

(iii) Method of payment;

(iv) Distribution of payments; and

(v) Date of each disbursement;

(2) Automated income withholding activities such as:

(i) Recording and maintaining any date the noncustodial parent defaults on payment of the support obligation in an amount equal to the support payable for one month;

(ii) Generating the Standard Federal Income Withholding Form; and

(iii) Allocating amounts received by income withholding according to §§ 309.110 and 309.115 of this chapter.

(f) Maintain and automatically generate data necessary to meet Federal reporting requirements on a timely basis as prescribed by OCSE. At a minimum this must include:

(1) Yearly notices on support collected, which are itemized by month of collection and provided to families receiving services under the comprehensive Tribal IV–D program as required in § 309.75(c) of this chapter, to all case participants regarding support collections; and

(2) Reports submitted to OCSE for program monitoring and program performance as required in § 309.170 of this chapter;

(g) Provide automated processes to enable OCSE to monitor Tribal IV–D program operations and to assess program performance through the audit of financial and statistical data maintained by the system; and

(h) Provide security to prevent unauthorized access to, or use of, the data in the system as detailed in § 310.15 of this part.

§ 310.15 What are the safeguards and processes that comprehensive Tribal IV–D agencies must have in place to ensure the security and privacy of Computerized Tribal IV–D Systems and Office Automation?

(a) *Information integrity and security.* The comprehensive Tribal IV–D agency must have safeguards on the integrity, accuracy, completeness, access to, and use of data in the Computerized Tribal IV–D System and Office Automation. Computerized Tribal IV–D Systems and Office Automation should be compliant with the Federal Information Security Management Act, and the Privacy Act. The required safeguards must include written policies and procedures concerning the following:

(1) Periodic evaluations of the system for risk of security and privacy breaches;

(2) Procedures to allow Tribal IV–D personnel controlled access and use of IV–D data, including:

(i) Specifying the data which may be used for particular IV–D program purposes, and the personnel permitted access to such data;

(ii) Permitting access to and use of data for the purpose of exchanging information with State and Tribal agencies administering programs under titles IV–A, IV–E and XIX of the Act to the extent necessary to carry out the comprehensive Tribal IV–D agency's responsibilities with respect to such programs;

(3) Maintenance and control of application software program data;

(4) Mechanisms to back-up and otherwise protect hardware, software, documents, and other communications; and,

(5) Mechanisms to report breaches or suspected breaches of personally identifiable information to the Department of Homeland Security, and to respond to those breaches.

(b) *Monitoring of access.* The comprehensive Tribal IV–D agency must monitor routine access to and use of the Computerized Tribal IV–D System and Office Automation through methods such as audit trails and feedback mechanisms to guard against, and promptly identify, unauthorized access or use;

(c) *Training and information.* The comprehensive Tribal IV–D agency must have procedures to ensure that all personnel, including Tribal IV–D staff and contractors, who may have access to or be required to use confidential program data in the Computerized Tribal IV–D System and Office Automation are adequately trained in security procedures.

(d) *Penalties.* The comprehensive Tribal IV–D agency must have administrative penalties, including dismissal from employment, for unauthorized access to, disclosure or use of confidential information.

Subpart C—Funding for Computerized Tribal IV–D Systems and Office Automation

§ 310.20 What are the conditions for funding the installation, operation, maintenance and enhancement of Computerized Tribal IV–D Systems and Office Automation?

(a) *Conditions that must be met for FFP at the applicable matching rate in § 309.130(c) of this chapter for Computerized Tribal IV–D Systems.* The following conditions must be met to obtain 90 percent FFP in the costs of installation of the Model Tribal IV–D System and FFP at the applicable matching rate under § 309.130(c) of this chapter in the costs of operation, maintenance, and enhancement of a Computerized Tribal IV–D System:

(1) A comprehensive Tribal IV–D agency must have submitted, and OCSE must have approved, an Advance Planning Document (APD) for the installation and enhancement of a Computerized Tribal IV–D System;

(2) An APD for installation of a Computerized Tribal IV–D System must:

(i) Represent the sole systems effort being undertaken by the comprehensive Tribal IV–D agency under this part;

(ii) Describe the projected resource requirements for staff, hardware, software, network connections and other needs and the resources available or expected to be available to meet the requirements;

(iii) Contain a proposed schedule of project milestones with detail sufficient to describe the tasks, activities, and complexity of the initial implementation project;

(iv) Contain a proposed budget including a description of expenditures by category and amount for items related to installing, operating, maintaining, and enhancing the Computerized Tribal IV–D System; and

(v) Contain a statement that the comprehensive Tribal IV–D agency agrees in writing to use the Computerized Tribal IV–D System for a minimum period of time;

(3) The following conditions, in addition to those in paragraphs (a)(1) and (2) of this section, must be met to obtain FFP in the installation costs of access to a State or another comprehensive Tribal IV–D program's ADP system established under an Intergovernmental Service Agreement. The comprehensive Tribal IV–D agency must:

(i) Maintain a copy of each intergovernmental cooperative agreement and Service Agreement in its files for Federal review; and

(ii) Ensure that the:

(A) Service Agreement for which FFP is being sought, meets the definition of a Service Agreement as defined in §310.1 of this title;

(B) Claims for FFP conform to the timely claim provisions of part 95 subpart A of this title; and

(C) Service Agreement was not previously disapproved by the Department.

(4) The following conditions, in addition to those in paragraphs (a)(1) through (3) of this section, must be met in order for a comprehensive Tribal IV–D agency to obtain FFP in the costs of enhancements to its Computerized Tribal IV–D System:

(i) The project's Total Acquisition Cost cannot exceed the comprehensive Tribal IV–D agency's total Tribal IV–D program grant award for the year in which the acquisition request is made; and

(ii) The APD budget, schedule and commitment to use the Computerized Tribal IV–D System for a specified minimum period of time must be updated to reflect the enhancement project.

(5) To receive FFP in the costs of the operation and maintenance of a Computerized Tribal IV–D System installed under §310.20 or developed under §309.145(h)(5), which refers to a Tribal automated data processing system that is funded entirely with Tribal funds, the comprehensive Tribal IV–D agency must include operation and maintenance costs in its annual Title IV–D program budget submission in accordance with §309.15(c) of this chapter;

(6) To receive FFP in the costs of the installation, operation, and maintenance of essential Office Automation capabilities, the comprehensive Tribal IV–D agency must include such costs in its annual Title IV–D program budget submission in accordance with §309.15(c) of this chapter;

(b) *Procedure for APD Submittal.* The comprehensive Tribal IV–D agency must submit an APD for a Computerized Tribal IV–D System to the Commissioner of OCSE, Attention: Division of State and Tribal Systems. The APD submitted by the comprehensive Tribal IV–D agency must be approved and signed by the comprehensive Tribal IV–D agency Director and the appropriate Tribal officials prior to submission to OCSE for approval.

§310.25 What conditions apply to acquisitions of Computerized Tribal IV–D Systems?

(a) *APD Approval.* A comprehensive Tribal IV–D agency must have an approved APD in accordance with the applicable requirements of §310.20 of this part prior to initiating acquisition of a Computerized Tribal IV–D System.

(b) *Procurements.* Requests for Proposals (RFP) and similar procurement documents, contracts, and contract amendments involving costs eligible for FFP, must be submitted to OCSE for approval prior to release of the procurement document, and prior to the execution of the resultant contract when a procurement is anticipated to or will exceed the Simplified Acquisition Threshold;

(c) *Software and ownership rights.* (1) All procurement and contract instruments must include a clause that provides that the comprehensive Tribal IV–D agency will have all ownership rights to Computerized Tribal IV–D System software or enhancements thereof and all associated documentation designed, developed or installed with FFP. Intergovernmental Service Agreements are not subject to this paragraph.

(2) OCSE reserves a royalty-free, nonexclusive, and irrevocable license to reproduce, publish, or otherwise use and to authorize others to use for Federal Government purposes, such software, modifications and documentation.

(3) FFP is not available for the costs of rental or purchase of proprietary application software developed specifically for a Computerized Tribal IV–D System. Commercial-off-the-shelf (COTS) software packages that are sold or leased to the general public at established catalog or market prices are not subject to the ownership and license provisions of this requirement.

(d) *Requirements for acquisitions under the threshold amount.* A comprehensive Tribal IV–D agency is not required to submit procurement documents, contracts, and contract amendments for acquisitions under the Simplified Acquisition Threshold unless specifically requested to do so in writing by OCSE.

§ 310.30 Under what circumstances would FFP be suspended or disallowed in the costs of Computerized Tribal IV–D Systems?

(a) *Suspension of APD approval.* OCSE will suspend approval of the APD for a Computerized Tribal IV–D System approved under this part as of the date that the system ceases to comply substantially with the criteria, requirements, and other provisions of the APD. OCSE will notify a Tribal IV–D agency in writing in a notice of suspension, with such suspension effective as of the date on which there is no longer substantial compliance.

(b) *Suspension of FFP.* If OCSE suspends approval of an APD in accordance with this part during the installation, operation, or enhancement of a Computerized Tribal IV–D System, FFP will not be available in any expenditure incurred under the APD after the date of the suspension until the date OCSE determines that the comprehensive Tribal IV–D agency has taken the actions specified in the notice of suspension described in paragraph (a) of this section. OCSE will notify the comprehensive Tribal IV–D agency in writing upon making such a determination.

§ 310.35 Under what circumstances would emergency FFP be available for Computerized Tribal IV–D Systems?

(a) *Conditions that must be met for emergency FFP.* OCSE will consider waiving the approval requirements for acquisitions in emergency situations, such as natural or man-made disasters, upon receipt of a written request from the comprehensive Tribal IV–D agency. In order for OCSE to consider waiving the approval requirements in § 310.25 of this part, the following conditions must be met:

(1) The comprehensive Tribal IV–D agency must submit a written request to OCSE prior to the acquisition of any ADP equipment or services. The written request must be sent by registered mail and include:

(i) A brief description of the ADP equipment and/or services to be acquired and an estimate of their costs;

(ii) A brief description of the circumstances which resulted in the comprehensive Tribal IV–D agency's need to proceed prior to obtaining approval from OCSE; and

(iii) A description of the harm that will be caused if the comprehensive Tribal IV–D agency does not acquire immediately the ADP equipment and services.

(2) Upon receipt of the information, OCSE will, within 14 working days of receipt, take one of the following actions:

(i) Inform the comprehensive Tribal IV–D agency in writing that the request has been disapproved and the reason for disapproval; or

(ii) Inform the comprehensive Tribal IV–D agency in writing that OCSE recognizes that an emergency exists and that within 90 calendar days from the date of the initial written request under paragraph (a)(1) of this section the comprehensive Tribal IV–D agency must submit a formal request for approval which includes the information specified at § 310.25 of this title in order for the ADP equipment or services acquisition to be considered for OCSE's approval.

(b) *Effective date of emergency FFP*. If OCSE approves the request submitted under paragraph (a)(2) of this section, FFP will be available from the date the comprehensive Tribal IV–D agency acquires the ADP equipment and services.

Subpart D—Accountability and Monitoring Procedures for Computerized Tribal IV–D Systems

§ 310.40 What requirements apply for accessing systems and records for monitoring Computerized Tribal IV–D Systems and Office Automation?

In accordance with part 95 of this title, a comprehensive Tribal IV–D agency must allow OCSE access to the system in all of its aspects, including installation, operation, and cost records of contractors and subcontractors, and of Service Agreements at such intervals as are deemed necessary by OCSE to determine whether the conditions for FFP approval are being met and to determine the efficiency, effectiveness, reasonableness of the system and its cost.

PARTS 311–399 [RESERVED]

CHAPTER IV—OFFICE OF REFUGEE RESETTLEMENT, ADMINISTRATION FOR CHILDREN AND FAMILIES, DEPARTMENT OF HEALTH AND HUMAN SERVICES

PART 400—REFUGEE RESETTLEMENT PROGRAM

Subpart A—Introduction

Subpart B—Grants to States for Refugee Resettlement

THE STATE PLAN

AWARD OF GRANTS TO STATES

Subpart C—General Administration

Subpart D—Immigration Status and Identification of Refugees

DOCUMENTATION OF REFUGEE STATUS

Subpart E—Refugee Cash Assistance

PUBLIC/PRIVATE RCA PROGRAM

PUBLICLY-ADMINISTERED RCA PROGRAMS

APPLICATIONS, DETERMINATIONS OF ELIGIBILITY, AND FURNISHING ASSISTANCE

CONDITIONS OF ELIGIBILITY FOR REFUGEE CASH ASSISTANCE

Subpart F—Requirements for Employability Services and Employment

GENERAL REQUIREMENTS

Subpart G—Refugee Medical Assistance

Subpart H—Child Welfare Services

Subpart I—Refugee Social Services

Subpart J—Federal Funding

Subpart K—Waivers and Withdrawals

AUTHORITY: Section 412(a)(9), Immigration and Nationality Act (8 U.S.C. 1522(a)(9)).

SOURCE: 45 FR 59323, Sept. 9, 1980, unless otherwise noted.

Subpart A—Introduction

§ 400.1 Basis and purpose of the program.

(a) This part prescribes requirements concerning grants to States and other public and private non-profit agencies, wherever applicable under title IV of the Immigration and Nationality Act.

(b) It is the purpose of this program to provide for the effective resettlement of refugees and to assist them to achieve economic self-sufficiency as quickly as possible.

(c) Under the authority in section 412(a)(6)(B) of the Immigration and Nationality Act, the Director has established the provision of employment services and English language training as a priority in accomplishing the purpose of this program.

[51 FR 3912, Jan. 30, 1986, as amended at 60 FR 33601, June 28, 1995]

§ 400.2 Definitions.

The following definitions are applicable for purposes of this part:

AABD means aid to the aged, blind, and disabled under title XVI of the Social Security Act.

AB means aid to the blind under title X of the Social Security Act.

Act means the Immigration and Nationality Act.

APTD means aid to the permanently and totally disabled under title XIV of the Social Security Act.

Case management services means the determination of which service(s) to refer a refugee to, referral to such service(s), and tracking of the refugee's participation in such service(s).

Cash assistance means financial assistance to refugees, including TANF, SSI, refugee cash assistance, and general assistance, as defined herein, under title IV of the Act.

Designee, when referring to the State agency's designee, means an agency designated by the State agency for the purpose of carrying out the requirements of this part.

Director means the Director, Office of Refugee Resettlement.

Economic self-sufficiency means earning a total family income at a level that enables a family unit to support itself without receipt of a cash assistance grant.

Family unit means an individual adult, married individuals without children, or parents, or custodial relatives, with minor children who are not eligible for TANF, who live in the same household.

Federal Funding or 'FF' means Federal funding for a State's expenditures under the refugee resettlement program.

General assistance program means a financial and/or medical assistance program existing in a State or local jurisdiction which: (a) Is funded entirely by State and/or local funds; (b) is generally available to needy persons residing in the State or locality who meet specified income and resource requirements; and (c) consists of one-time emergency, or ongoing assistance intended to meet basic needs of recipients, such as food, clothing, shelter, medical care, or other essentials of living.

HHS means the Department of Health and Human Services.

Local resettlement agency means a local affiliate or subcontractor of a national voluntary agency that has entered into a grant, contract, or cooperative agreement with the United States Department of State or other appropriate Federal agency to provide for the reception and initial placement of refugees in the United States.

Medical assistance means medical services to refugees, including Medicaid, refugee medical assistance, and general assistance, as defined herein, under title IV of the Act.

National voluntary agency means one of the national resettlement agencies or a State or local government that has entered into a grant, contract, or cooperative agreement with the United States Department of State or other appropriate Federal agency to provide for the reception and initial placement of refugees in the United States.

OAA means old age assistance under title I of the Social Security Act.

ORR means the Office of Refugee Resettlement.

Plan means a written description of the State's refugee resettlement program and a commitment by the State to administer or supervise the administration of the program in accordance with Federal requirements in this part.

RCA Plan means a written description of the public/private RCA program administered by local resettlement agencies under contract or grant with a State.

Refugee means an individual who meets the definitions of a refugee under section 101(a)(42) of the Act.

Refugee cash assistance (*RCA*) means cash assistance provided under section 412(e) of the Act to refugees who are ineligible for TANF, OAA, AB, APTD, AABD, or SSI.

Refugee medical assistance (*RMA*) means: (a) Medical assistance provided under section 412(e) of the Act to refugees who are ineligible for the Medicaid program; and (b) services provided in accordance with §§ 400.106 and 400.107 of this part.

Secretary means the Secretary of HHS.

Sponsor means an individual, church, civic organization, State or local government, or other group or organization which has agreed to help in the reception and initial placement of refugees in the United States and other public and private non-profit agencies, wherever.

SSI means supplemental security income under title XVI of the Social Security Act.

State means the 50 States, the District of Columbia, Guam, Puerto Rico, the Virgin Islands, the Commonwealth of the Northern Mariana Islands, American Samoa, and the Trust Territories of the Pacific.

State agency means the agency (or agencies) designated by the Governor or the appropriate legislative authority of the State to develop and administer, or supervise the administration of, the plan and includes any local agencies administering the plan under supervision of the State agency.

State Coordinator means the individual designated by the Governor or the appropriate legislative authority of the State to be responsible for, and who is authorized to, ensure coordination of public and private resources in refugee resettlement.

Support services means services provided or contracted for by a State, which are designed to meet resettlement needs of refugees, for which funding is available under title IV of the Act.

TANF means temporary assistance for needy families under Title IV-A of the Social Security Act.

Time-eligibility means the period for which FF (Federal funding) is provided under §§ 400.203 and 400.204 of this part, after applying the limitation "[s]ubject to the availability of funds" in accordance with § 400.202.

Title IV of the Act means title IV, Chapter 2, of the Immigration and Nationality Act.

[51 FR 3912, Jan. 30, 1986, as amended at 54 FR 5475, Feb. 3, 1989; 58 FR 46090, Sept. 1, 1993; 58 FR 64507, Dec. 8, 1993; 65 FR 15442, Mar. 22, 2000]

§ 400.3 [Reserved]

Subpart B—Grants to States for Refugee Resettlement

THE STATE PLAN

§ 400.4 Purpose of the plan.

(a) In order for a State to receive refugee resettlement assistance from funds appropriated under section 414 of the Act, it must submit to ORR a plan that meets the requirements of title IV of the Act and of this part and that is approved under § 400.8 of this part.

(b) A State must certify no later than 30 days after the beginning of each Federal fiscal year that the approved State plan is current and continues in effect. If a State wishes to change its plan, a State must submit a proposed amendment to the plan. The proposed amendment will be reviewed and approved or disapproved in accordance with § 400.8.

[51 FR 3912, Jan. 30, 1986, as amended at 60 FR 33602, June 28, 1995]

§ 400.5 Content of the plan.

The plan must:

(a) Provide for the designation of, and describe the organization and functions of, a State agency (or agencies) responsible for developing the plan and administering, or supervising the administration of, the plan;

(b) Describe how the State will coordinate cash and medical assistance with support services to ensure their successful use to encourage effective refugee resettlement and to promote employment and economic self-sufficiency as quickly as possible.

(c) Describe how the State will ensure that language training and employment services are made available to refugees receiving cash assistance, and to other refugees, including State efforts to actively encourage refugee registration for employment services;

(d) Identify an individual designated by the Governor or the appropriate legislative authority of the State, with the title of State Coordinator, who is employed by the State and will have the responsibility and authority to ensure coordination of public and private resources in refugee resettlement in the State;

(e) Provide for, and describe the procedures established for, the care and supervision of, and legal responsibility (including legal custody and/or guardianship under State law, as appropriate) for, unaccompanied refugee children in the State;

(f) Provide for and describe (1) the procedures established to identify refugees who, at the time of resettlement in the State, are determined to have medical conditions requiring, or medical histories indicating a need for, treatment or observation, and (2) the procedures established to monitor any necessary treatment or observation;

(g) Provide that assistance and services funded under the plan will be provided to refugees without regard to race, religion, nationality, sex, or political opinion; and

(h) Provide that the State will, unless exempted from this requirement by the Director, assure that meetings are convened, not less often than quarterly, whereby representatives of local resettlement agencies, local community service agencies, and other agencies that serve refugees meet with representatives of State and local governments to plan and coordinate the appropriate placement of refugees in advance of the refugees' arrival. All existing exemptions to this requirement will expire 90 days after the effective date of this rule. Any State that wishes to be exempted from the provisions regarding the holding and frequency of meetings may apply by submitting a written request to the Director. The request must set forth the reasons why the State considers these meetings unnecessary because of the absence of problems associated with the planning and coordination of refugee placement. An approved exemption will remain in effect for three years, at which time a State may reapply.

(i) Provide that the State will:

(1) Comply with the provisions of title IV, Chapter 2, of the Act and official issuances of the Director;

(2) Meet the requirements in this part;

(3) Comply with all other applicable Federal statutes and regulations in effect during the time that it is receiving grant funding; and

(4) Amend the plan as needed to comply with standards, goals, and priorities established by the Director.

(Approved by the Office of Management and Budget under control number 0960–0418)

[51 FR 3912, Jan. 30, 1986, as amended at 60 FR 33602, June 28, 1995; 65 FR 15443, Mar. 22, 2000]

§ 400.6 [Reserved]

§ 400.7 Submittal of the State plan and plan amendments for Governor's review.

A plan or plan amendment under title IV of the Act must be submitted to the State Governor or his or her designee, for review, comment, and signature before the plan is submitted to ORR.

[51 FR 3913, Jan. 30, 1986]

§ 400.8 Approval of State plans and plan amendments.

(a) The State agency must submit the State plan and plan amendments which have been signed by the Governor, or his or her designee, together with one copy of such plan or amendment, to the Director of ORR, or his or her designee, for approval. States are encouraged to consult with the Director, or his or her designee, when a plan or amendment is in preparation.

(b) The Director, or his or her designee, may initiate any necessary discussions with the State agency to clarify aspects of the plan.

(c) No later than 45 days after the State plan or plan amendment is submitted, the Director, or his or her designee, will—(1) Determine whether a State plan or plan amendment meets or continues to meet requirements for approval based on relevant Federal statutes and regulations, and (2) approve or disapprove the plan or plan amendment.

(d) The Director, or designee, will notify the State agency promptly of all actions taken on State plans and amendments.

(e) The effective date of an approved State plan or plan amendment may not be earlier than the first day of the calendar quarter in which the State agency submits the plan or plan amendment, except as otherwise approved by the Director.

[51 FR 3913, Jan. 30, 1986]

§ 400.9 Administrative review of decisions on approval of State plans and plan amendments.

(a) Any State dissatisfied with a determination by the Director, or his or her designee, under § 400.8 with respect to any plan or plan amendment may, within 60 days after the date of notification of such determination, file a petition with the Director, or designee, for reconsideration of the determination.

(b) A State may request that a hearing be held, but it is not required to do so.

(c) If a State requests a hearing, the Director, or designee, will notify the State within 30 days after receipt of such a petition, of the time and location of the hearing to reconsider the issue.

(d) The hearing must be held not less than 30 days nor more than 60 days after the date the notice of the hearing is furnished to the State, unless the Director, or designee, and the State agree in writing on another time.

(e) The hearing procedures in part 213 of this title will be used except that:

(1) "The Director" is substituted where there is a reference to "the Administrator," and

(2) "ORR Hearing Clerk" is substituted where there is reference to the "SRS Hearing Clerk."

(f) The Director will affirm, modify, or reverse the original decisions within 60 days of the receipt of the State's petition or, if a hearing is held, within 60 days after the hearing.

(g) The initial determination by the Director, or designee, that a plan or amendment is not approvable shall remain in effect pending the reconsideration.

(h) If the Director reverses the original decision, ORR will reimburse any funds incorrectly withheld or otherwise denied.

[51 FR 3913, Jan. 30, 1986]

§ 400.10 [Reserved]

AWARD OF GRANTS TO STATES

§ 400.11 Award of Grants to States.

(a) *Quarterly grants.* Subject to the availability of funds (and in accordance with the limitations of subpart J of this part), ORR will make two types of quarterly grants to eligible States:

(1) *Grants for cash assistance, medical assistance, and related administrative costs ("CMA grants"),* for the following purposes: Cash assistance provided by a State or local public agency under the program of temporary assistance for needy families (TANF) under part A of title IV of the Social Security Act, under the adult assistance programs (AABD, AB, APTD, or OAA) in the territories, or under section 412(e) of the Immigration and Nationality Act; foster care maintenance provided under part E of title IV of the Social Security Act; State supplementary payments under section 1616(a) of the Social Security Act or section 212 of the Pub. L.

93–66; medical assistance under title XIX of the Social Security Act or under section 412(e) of the Immigration and Nationality Act; assistance and services to unaccompanied minors under section 412(d)(2)(B) of the Immigration and Nationality Act; and cash or medical assistance provided under a public assistance program established under authority other than Federal law and under which such assistance is generally available to needy individuals or families in similar circumstances within the State; and

(2) *Grants for social services, as set forth in this part.* ORR will compute the amount of the quarterly awards based on documents submitted by the State agency in accordance with this section and such other pertinent facts as the Director may find necessary.

(b) *Form and manner of State application for grant award*—(1) *CMA grants.* For quarterly grants for cash assistance, medical assistance, and related administrative costs, including assistance and services to unaccompanied minors ("CMA grants"), a State must submit to the Director, or designee, yearly estimates for reimbursable costs for the fiscal year, identified by type of expense, and a justification statement in support of the estimates no later than 45 days prior to the beginning of the fiscal year in accordance with guidelines prescribed by the Director.

(2) *Grants for refugee social services.* For quarterly grants for refugee social services, a State must submit to the Director, or designee, an annual plan developed on the basis of local consultative process on a form and at a time prescribed by the Director.

(3) *Quarterly adjustments.* If a State revises its estimates required in paragraph (b)(1), it must submit to the Director, or designee, the revisions, accompanied by a justification statement, no later than 30 days prior to the beginning of the quarter in which the revision or adjustment applies.

(c) *Financial status report.* A State must submit to the Director, or designee, a financial status report described in §75.341 of this title, no later than 30 days after the end of each quarter. Final financial reports must be submitted in accordance with the requirements described in §400.210.

(d) *Review.* ORR will determine whether the State's description of services, estimates, other relevant information, and any adjustments to be made for prior periods meet the requirements under this part, and will compute the quarterly award.

(e) *Grant award.* (1) ORR will transmit to the State the grant award form showing, by type of assistance, the amount of the award.

(2) The State may draw funds, under the Department's Payment Management System (PMS), as needed, to meet the Federal share of disbursements.

(Approved by the Office of Management and Budget under control number 0960–0418)

[51 FR 3913, Jan. 30, 1986, as amended at 54 FR 5475, Feb. 3, 1989; 60 FR 33602, June 28, 1995; 65 FR 15443, Mar. 22, 2000; 81 FR 3021, Jan. 20, 2016]

§400.12 Adverse determinations concerning State grants.

(a) *Policy.* The Secretary has established a Departmental Grant Appeals Board for the purpose of reviewing and providing hearings on post-award disputes which may arise in the administration of certain grant programs by constituent agencies of HHS. Section 16.3(c) of this title mandates an appellant to exhaust any preliminary appeal process required by regulation before a formal appeal to the Board will be allowed. Paragraph (d) of this section provides an informal preliminary appeal process for resolution of such disputes within ORR prior to appeal to the Board.

(b) *Scope.* Adverse determinations to which this procedure is applicable are as follows:

(1) Termination, in whole or in part, of a grant for failure of the grantee to carry out its approved project or program in accordance with applicable law and the terms and conditions of such assistance or for failure of the grantee otherwise to comply with any law, regulation, assurance, term, or condition applicable to the grant.

(2) A determination that an expenditure not allowable under the grant has been charged to the grant or that the grantee has otherwise failed to discharge its obligation to account for grant funds.

(3) The disapproval of a grantee's written request for permission to incur an expenditure during the term of a grant.

(4) A determination that a grant is void because the award was obtained fraudulently, or was otherwise illegal or invalid from inception.

(c) *Notice of adverse determination.* If the Director, or his or her designee, makes an adverse determination with respect to a grant, he or she shall promptly issue a notice of adverse determination to the State which contains the reasons for the determination in sufficient detail to enable the State agency to respond and informing the State agency of the opportunity for review under paragraph (d) of this section.

(d) *Request for review of an adverse determination.* (1) If the State agency wants a review of the determination, it must submit a request for such review to the Director no later than 30 days after the postmark on the notice, unless an extension of time is granted for good cause.

(2) The request for review must contain a full statement of the State's position with respect to the determination being appealed and the pertinent facts and reasons in support of such position. The State agency must attach to the submission a copy of the notice.

(3) The Director may, at his or her discretion, invite the State to discuss pertinent issues and to submit such additional information as he or she deems appropriate.

(4) Based on his or her review, the Director will send a written response to the State. If the response is adverse to the State's position, the correspondence shall state the State's right to appeal to the Departmental Grant Appeals Board, pursuant to part 16 of this title.

(e) *Request for appeal of an adverse determination.* (1) To appeal an adverse determination, a State agency must file an appeal with the Departmental Grant Appeals Board, in accordance with requirements contained in part 16 of this title.

(2) The State's application for review must be postmarked no later than 30 days after the postmark on the Director's response to the State's request for review in paragraph (d)(4) of this section.

[51 FR 3914, Jan. 30, 1986]

§400.13 Cost allocation.

(a) A State must allocate costs, both direct and indirect, appropriately between the Refugee Resettlement Program (RRP) and other programs which it administers.

(b) Within the RRP, a State must allocate costs appropriately among its CMA grant, social services grant, and any other Refugee Resettlement Program (RRP) grants which it may receive, as prescribed by the Director.

(c) Certain administrative costs incurred for the overall management of the State's refugee program (e.g., development of the State plan, overall program coordination, and salary and travel costs of the State Refugee Coordinator), as identified by the Director, may be charged to the CMA grant. All other costs must be allocated among the CMA grant, social services grant, and any other Refugee Resettlement Program (RRP) grants.

(d) Costs of case management services, as defined in §400.2, may not be charged to the CMA grant.

(e) Administrative costs incurred by local resettlement agencies in the administration of the public/private RCA program (i.e., administrative costs of providing cash assistance) may be charged to the CMA grant. Administrative costs of managing the services component of the RCA program must be charged to the social services grant.

[54 FR 5476, Feb. 3, 1989, as amended at 60 FR 33602, June 28, 1995; 65 FR 15443, Mar. 22, 2000]

Subpart C—General Administration

SOURCE: 51 FR 3914, Jan. 30, 1986, unless otherwise noted.

§§400.20–400.21 [Reserved]

§400.22 Responsibility of the State agency.

(a) The State agency may not delegate, to other than its own officials, responsibility for administering or supervising the administration of the plan.

(b) The State agency must have—

(1) Methods for informing staff of State policies, standards, procedures, and instructions; and

(2) Systematic planned examination and evaluation of operations in local offices.

§ 400.23 Hearings.

(a) A State must provide applicants for, and recipients of, assistance and services under the Act with an opportunity for a hearing to contest adverse determinations using hearing procedures set forth in § 205.10(a) of this title for public assistance programs unless otherwise specified in this part.

(b) If the issue is the date of entry into the United States of an applicant for or recipient of assistance or services, the State or its designee must provide for prompt resolution of the issue by inspection of the individual's documentation issued by the Immigration and Naturalization Service (INS) or by information obtained from INS, rather than by hearing.

[51 FR 3914, Jan. 30, 1986, as amended at 65 FR 15443, Mar. 22, 2000]

§ 400.24 [Reserved]

§ 400.25 Residency requirements.

A State may not impose requirements as to duration of residence as a condition of participation in the State's program for the provision of assistance or services.

§ 400.26 [Reserved]

§ 400.27 Safeguarding and sharing of information.

(a) Except for purposes directly connected with, and necessary to, the administration of the program, a State must ensure that no information about, or obtained from, an individual and in possession of any agency providing assistance or services to such individual under the plan, will be disclosed in a form identifiable with the individual without the individual's consent, or if the individual is a minor, the consent of his or her parent or guardian.

(b) The provision by a State to a local resettlement agency or by a local resettlement agency to a State, of information as to whether an individual has applied for or is receiving cash assistance and the individual's address and telephone number is to be considered undertaken for a purpose directly connected with, and necessary to, the administration of the program during the first 36 months after such individual's entry into the United States.

[51 FR 3914, Jan. 30, 1986, as amended at 54 FR 5476, Feb. 3, 1989; 65 FR 15443, Mar. 22, 2000]

§ 400.28 Maintenance of records and reports.

(a) A State must provide for the maintenance of such operational records as are necessary for Federal monitoring of the State's refugee resettlement program in accordance with 45 CFR 75.361 through 75.370. This recordkeeping must include:

(1) Documentation of services and assistance provided, including identification of individuals receiving those services;

(2) Records on the location, progress, and status of unaccompanied minor refugee children, including the last known address of parents; and

(3) Documentation that necessary medical followup services and monitoring have been provided.

(b) A State must submit statistical or programmatic information that the Director determines to be required to fulfill his or her responsibility under the Act on refugees who receive assistance and services which are provided, or the costs of which are reimbursed, under the Act.

(Approved by the Office of Management and Budget under control number 0960–0418)

[51 FR 3914, Jan. 30, 1986, as amended at 81 FR 3021, Jan. 20, 2016]

Subpart D—Immigration Status and Identification of Refugees

SOURCE: 51 FR 3915, Jan. 30, 1986, unless otherwise noted.

§ 400.40 Scope.

This subpart sets forth requirements concerning the immigration status and identification of eligible applicants for assistance under title IV of the Act.

§ 400.41 Definitions

For purposes of this subpart—

Applicant for asylum means an individual who has applied for, but has not been granted, asylum under section 208 of the Act.

Asylee means an individual who has been granted asylum under section 208 of the Act.

DOCUMENTATION OF REFUGEE STATUS

§ 400.43 Requirements for documentation of refugee status.

(a) An applicant for assistance under title IV of the Act must provide proof, in the form of documentation issued by the Immigration and Naturalization Service (INS), of one of the following statuses under the Act as a condition of eligibility:

(1) Paroled as a refugee or asylee under section 212(d)(5) of the Act;

(2) Admitted as a refugee under section 207 of the Act;

(3) Granted asylum under section 208 of the Act;

(4) Cuban and Haitian entrants, in accordance with requirements in 45 CFR part 401;

(5) Certain Amerasians from Vietnam who are admitted to the U.S. as immigrants pursuant to section 584 of the Foreign Operations, Export Financing, and Related Programs Appropriations Act, 1988 (as contained in section 101(e) of Public Law 100–202 and amended by the 9th proviso under Migration and Refugee Assistance in title II of the Foreign Operations, Export Financing, and Related Programs Appropriations Acts, 1989 (Public Law 100–461 as amended)); or

(6) Admitted for permanent residence, provided the individual previously held one of the statuses identified above.

(b) The Director will issue instructions specifying the documentation that applicants for assistance must submit.

[51 FR 3915, Jan. 30, 1986, as amended at 65 FR 15443, Mar. 22, 2000]

§ 400.44 Restriction.

An applicant for asylum is not eligible for assistance under title IV of the Act unless otherwise provided by Federal law.

[51 FR 3915, Jan. 30, 1986, as amended at 65 FR 15443, Mar. 22, 2000]

Subpart E—Refugee Cash Assistance

SOURCE: 65 FR 15443, Mar. 22, 2000, unless otherwise noted.

§ 400.45 Requirements for the operation of an AFDC-type RCA program.

This section applies to a State's RCA program that follows the State's rules under the Aid to Families with Dependent Children (AFDC) program under title IV-A of the Social Security Act, prior to amendment by Public Law 104–33. A State must continue to apply these rules to its RCA program until it implements a new RCA program under § 400.56 or § 400.65. A State that receives an approved waiver under § 400.300 to continue an AFDC-type RCA program must follow the rules in this section.

(a) *Recovery of overpayments and correction of underpayments.* The State agency must comply with regulations at § 233.20(a)(13) of this title governing recovery of overpayments and correction of underpayments in the AFDC program.

(b) *Opportunity to apply for cash assistance.* (1) A State must provide any individual wishing to do so, an opportunity to apply for cash assistance and must determine the eligibility of each applicant.

(2) In determining eligibility for cash assistance, the State must—

(i) Comply with the regulations at part 206 of this title governing applications, determinations of eligibility, and furnishing assistance under public assistance programs, as applicable to the AFDC program;

(ii) Determine eligibility for other cash assistance programs in accordance with § 400.51; and

(iii) Comply with regulations at §§ 400.54(a)(3) and 400.68.

(c) *Emergency cash assistance to refugees*—A State must comply with the regulations at § 400.52.

(d) *General eligibility requirements*—A State must comply with the regulations at § 400.53.

(e) *Consideration of income and resources.* In considering the income and resources of applicants for and recipients of refugee cash assistance, the State agency must:

(1) Apply the regulations at § 233.20(a)(3) through (2) of this title for considering income and resources of AFDC applicants; and

(2) Apply the regulations at § 400.66(b) through (d).

(f) *Need standards and payment levels.* (1) In determining need for refugee cash assistance, a State agency must use the State's AFDC need standards established under § 233.20(a)(1) and (2) of this title.

(2) In determining the amount of the refugee cash assistance payment to an eligible refugee who meets the standards in paragraph (f)(1) of this section and applying the consideration of income and resources in paragraph (e) of this section and in § 400.66(b) through (d), a State must pay 100 percent of the payment level which would be appropriate for an eligible filing unit of the same size under the AFDC program.

(3) The State agency may use the date of application as the date refugee cash assistance begins in order to provide payments quickly to newly arrived refugees.

(g) *Proration of shelter, utilities, and similar needs*—If a State prorated allowances for shelter, utilities, and similar needs in its AFDC program under § 233.20(a)(5) of this title, it must prorate such allowances in the same manner in its refugee assistance programs.

(h) *Other AFDC requirements applicable to refugee cash assistance*—In administering the program of refugee cash assistance, the State agency must also apply the following AFDC regulations in this title:

233.31 Budgeting methods for AFDC.

233.32 Payment and budget months (AFDC).

233.33 Determining eligibility prospectively for all payment months (AFDC).

233.34 Computing the assistance payment in the initial one or two months (AFDC).

233.35 Computing the assistance payment under retrospective budgeting after the initial one or two months (AFDC).

233.36 Monthly reporting (AFDC)—which shall apply to recipients of refugee cash assistance who have been in the United States more than 6 months.

233.37 How monthly reports are treated and what notices are required (AFDC).

235.110 Fraud.

GENERAL

§ 400.48 Basis and scope.

This subpart sets forth requirements concerning grants to States under section 412(e) of the Act for refugee cash assistance (RCA). Sections 400.48 through 400.55 apply to both public/private RCA programs and publicly-administered RCA programs.

§ 400.49 Recovery of overpayments and correction of underpayments.

The State agency or its designee agency(s) must maintain a procedure to ensure recovery of overpayments and correction of underpayments in the RCA program.

§ 400.50 Opportunity to apply for cash assistance.

(a) A State or its designee agency(s) must provide any individual wishing to do so, an opportunity to apply for cash assistance and must determine the eligibility of each applicant as promptly as possible within no more than 30 days from the date of application.

(b) A State or its designee agency(s) must inform applicants about the eligibility requirements and the rights and responsibilities of applicants and recipients under the program.

(c) In determining eligibility for cash assistance, the State or its designee agency(s) must promptly refer elderly or disabled refugees and refugees with dependent children to other cash assistance programs to apply for assistance in accordance with § 400.51.

§ 400.51 Determination of eligibility under other programs.

(a) *TANF.* For refugees determined ineligible for cash assistance under the TANF program, the State or its designee must determine eligibility for refugee cash assistance in accordance with §§ 400.53 and 400.59 in the case of the public/private RCA program or

§§ 400.53 and 400.66 in the case of a publicly-administered RCA program.

(b) *Cash assistance to the aged, blind, and disabled*—(1) *SSI.* (i) The State agency or its designee must refer refugees who are 65 years of age or older, or who are blind or disabled, promptly to the Social Security Administration to apply for cash assistance under the SSI program.

(ii) If the State agency or its designee determines that a refugee who is 65 years of age or older, or blind or disabled, is eligible for refugee cash assistance, it must furnish such assistance until eligibility for cash assistance under the SSI program is determined, provided the conditions of eligibility for refugee cash assistance continue to be met.

(2) OAA, AB, APTD, or AABD. In Guam, Puerto Rico, and the Virgin Islands—

(i) Eligibility for cash assistance under the OAA, AB, APTD, or AABD program must be determined for refugees who are 65 years or older, or who are blind or disabled; and

(ii) If a refugee who is 65 years of age or older, or blind or disabled, is determined to be eligible for refugee cash assistance, such assistance must be furnished until eligibility for cash assistance under the OAA, AB, APTD, or AABD program is determined, provided the conditions of eligibility for refugee cash assistance continue to be met.

§ 400.52 Emergency cash assistance to refugees.

If the State agency or its designee determines that a refugee has an urgent need for cash assistance, it should process the application for cash assistance as quickly as possible and issue the initial payment to the refugee on an emergency basis.

§ 400.53 General eligibility requirements.

(a) Eligibility for refugee cash assistance is limited to those who—

(1) Are new arrivals who have resided in the U.S. less than the RCA eligibility period determined by the ORR Director in accordance with § 400.211;

(2) Are ineligible for TANF, SSI, OAA, AB, APTD, and AABD programs;

(3) Meet immigration status and identification requirements in subpart D of this part or are the dependent children of, and part of the same family unit as, individuals who meet the requirements in subpart D, subject to the limitation in § 400.208 with respect to nonrefugee children; and

(4) Are not full-time students in institutions of higher education, as defined by the Director.

(b) A refugee may be eligible for refugee cash assistance under this subpart during a period to be determined by the Director in accordance with § 400.211.

§ 400.54 Notice and hearings.

(a) *Timely and adequate notice.* (1) A written notice must be sent or provided to a recipient at least 10 days before the date upon which refugee cash assistance will be reduced, suspended, or terminated.

(2) In providing notice to an applicant or recipient to indicate that assistance has been authorized, denied, reduced, suspended, or terminated, the written notice must clearly state the action that will be taken, the reasons for the action, and the right to request a hearing.

(3) In providing notice to an applicant or recipient to indicate that assistance has been authorized, denied, reduced, suspended, or terminated, the State or its designee agency(s) must specify the program(s) to which the notice applies, clearly distinguishing between RCA and other assistance programs. For example, in the case of a publicly-administered program, if a refugee applies for assistance and is determined ineligible for TANF but eligible for refugee cash assistance, the notice to the applicant must specify clearly the determinations with respect both to TANF and to refugee cash assistance. When a recipient of refugee cash assistance is notified of termination because of reaching the time limit on such assistance, the State or its designee must review the case file to determine possible eligibility for TANF or GA due to changed circumstances and the notice to the recipient must indicate the result of that determination as well as the termination of RCA.

(b) *Hearings.* All applicants for and recipients of refugee cash assistance must be provided an opportunity for a hearing to contest adverse determinations. States must ensure that hearings meet the due process standards in *Goldberg* v. *Kelly*, 397 U.S. 254 (1970).

(1) *Public/private RCA programs.* The State must specify in the public/private RCA plan the hearing procedures to be used in the RCA program. The plan may specify that the local resettlement agency(s) will refer all hearing requests to a State-administered hearing process. If the plan does not specify the use of a State-administered hearing process, then the procedures to be followed must include:

(i) The State or local resettlement agency(s) responsible for the provision of RCA must provide an applicant for or recipient of refugee cash assistance an opportunity for an oral hearing to contest adverse determinations. Hearings must be conducted by an impartial official or designee of the State or local resettlement agency who has not been involved directly in the initial determination of the action in question.

(ii) The State must ensure that procedures are established to provide refugees a right of final appeal for an in-person hearing provided by an impartial, independent entity outside of the local resettlement agency.

(iii) Final administrative action must be taken within 60 days from the date of a request for a hearing.

(2) *Publicly-administered RCA programs.* The State must specify in the State Plan referenced in § 400.4 the public agency hearing procedures it intends to use in the RCA program.

(3) In both a public/private RCA program and a publicly-administered RCA program, the written notice of any hearing determination must adequately explain the basis for the decision and the refugee's right to request any further administrative or judicial review.

(4) In both a public/private RCA program and a publicly-administered RCA program, a refugee's benefits may not be terminated prior to completion of final administrative action, but are subject to recovery by the agency if the action is sustained.

(5) In both a public/private RCA program and a publicly-administered RCA program, a hearing need not be granted when Federal law requires automatic grant adjustments for classes of recipients unless the reason for an individual appeal is an incorrect grant computation.

(6) In both a public/private RCA program and a publicly-administered RCA program, a hearing need not be granted when assistance is terminated because the eligibility time period imposed by law has been reached, unless there is a disputed issue of fact that is unresolved by the process in § 400.23.

§ 400.55 Availability of agency policies.

A State, or the agency(s) responsible for the provision of RCA, must make available to refugees the written policies of the RCA program, including agency policies regarding eligibility standards, the duration and amount of cash assistance payments, the requirements for participation in services, the penalties for non-cooperation, and client rights and responsibilities to ensure that refugees understand what they are eligible for, what is expected of them, and what protections are available to them. The State, or the agency(s) responsible for the provision of RCA, must ensure that agency policy materials and all notices required in §§ 400.54, 400.82, and 400.83, are made available in written form in English and in appropriate languages where a significant number or proportion of the recipient population needs information in a particular language. In regard to refugee language groups that constitute a small number or proportion of the recipient population, the State, or the agency(s) responsible for the provision of RCA, at a minimum, must use an alternative method, such as verbal translation in the refugee's native language, to ensure that the content of the agency's policies is effectively communicated to each refugee.

PUBLIC/PRIVATE RCA PROGRAM

§ 400.56 Structure.

(a) States may choose to enter into a partnership agreement with local resettlement agencies for the operation of a public/private RCA program. Sections 400.56 through 400.63 apply to the public/private RCA program.

(b) The public/private RCA program must be administered by the State through contracts or grants with local resettlement agencies or a lead resettlement agency that provides initial resettlement services under the terms of the Department of State Cooperative Agreement for Reception and Placement.

(c) The public/private RCA program must be statewide, unless the State determines that it is not in the best interests of refugees to provide a public/private RCA program in a particular area of the State.

(d) Local resettlement agencies may be responsible for determining eligibility, and authorizing and providing payments to eligible refugees.

(e) States and local resettlement agencies may not propose to operate a public/private RCA program and a publicly-administered RCA program in the same geographic location.

(f) States must ensure the provision of RCA assistance to eligible refugees in the State who are sponsored by local resettlement agencies in bordering states, where applicable.

§400.57 Planning and consultation process.

A State that wishes to establish a public/private RCA program must engage in a planning and consultation process with the local agencies that resettle refugees in the State to develop a public/private RCA plan in accordance with the requirements under §400.58.

(a) Primary participants in the planning process must include representatives of the State and each local agency that resettles refugees in the State. During the planning process, the State must fully consult with representatives of counties, refugee mutual assistance associations (MAAs), local community services agencies, national voluntary agencies that resettle refugees in the State, representatives of each refugee ethnic group, and other agencies that serve refugees.

(b) Each local resettlement agency that resettles refugees in the State must inform its national resettlement agency of the proposed public/private RCA program and must obtain a letter of agreement from the national agency that indicates that the national agency supports the public/private RCA plan and will continue to place refugees in the State under the public/private RCA program.

§400.58 Content and submission of public/private RCA plan.

(a) States and local resettlement agencies must develop a public/private RCA plan which describes how the State and local resettlement agencies will administer and provide refugee cash assistance to eligible refugees. The plan must describe the agreed-upon public/private RCA program including:

(1) The proposed income standard to be used to determine RCA eligibility;

(2) The proposed payment levels to be used to provide cash assistance to eligible refugees;

(3) Assurance that the payment levels established are not lower than the comparable State TANF amounts;

(4) A detailed description of how benefit payments will be structured, including a description of employment incentives and/or income disregards to be used, if any, as well as methods of payment to be used, such as direct cash or vendor payments;

(5) A description of how all RCA eligible refugees residing in the State will have reasonable access to cash assistance and services;

(6) A description of the procedures to be used to ensure appropriate protections and due process for refugees, such as the correction of underpayments, notice of adverse action and the right to mediation, a pre-dermination hearing, and an appeal to an independent entity;

(7) A description of proposed exemptions from participation in employability services;

(8) A description of the employment and self-sufficiency services to be provided to RCA recipients by—

(i) Local resettlement agencies under contract or grant, and/or

(ii) Other refugee services providers;

(9) Procedures for providing RCA to eligible secondary migrants who move

to the State, including secondary migrants who were sponsored by a local resettlement agency that does not have a presence in the receiving State;

(10) If applicable, provisions for providing assistance to refugees resettling in the State who are sponsored by a local resettlement agency in a bordering State which does not have an office in the State of resettlement;

(11) A description of the procedures to be used to safeguard the disclosure of information regarding refugee clients;

(12) Letters of agreement from the national voluntary resettlement agencies that indicate support for the proposed public/private RCA program and indicate that refugee placements in the State will continue under the public/private RCA program;

(13) A breakdown of the proposed program and administrative costs of both the cash assistance and service components of the public/private RCA program, including any per capita caps on administrative costs only if a State proposes to use such caps; and

(14) The proposed implementation date for the State's public/private RCA program;

(b) In cases where the State, after consultation with the local resettlement agencies in the State, determines that a public/private RCA program is not feasible statewide and proposes to implement a public/private RCA program in only a portion of the State and to operate a publicly-administered RCA program in the balance of the State, the State's RCA plan must include the information required in §400.65(b).

(c) The plan must be signed by the Governor or his or her designee.

(d) The Director of ORR will follow the procedures in §400.8 for the approval of public/private RCA plans. An approved public/private RCA plan will be incorporated into the refugee program State Plan.

(e) Any amendments to the public/private RCA plan must be developed in consultation with the local resettlement agencies and must be submitted to ORR in accordance with §400.8. The Director of ORR will follow the procedures in §400.8 for approval of amendments to public/private RCA plans.

§400.59 Eligibility for the public/private RCA program.

(a) Eligibility for refugee cash assistance under the public/private program is limited to those who meet the income eligibility standard established by the State after consultation with local resettlement agencies in the State.

(b) Any resources remaining in the applicant's country of origin may not be considered in determining income eligibility.

(c) A sponsor's income and resources may not be considered to be accessible to a refugee solely because the person is serving as a sponsor.

(d) Any cash grant received by a refugee under the Department of State or Department of Justice Reception and Placement programs may not be considered in determining income eligibility.

§400.60 Payment levels.

(a) Under the public/private RCA program, States and the local resettlement agencies contracted or awarded grants to administer the RCA program must make monthly cash assistance payments to eligible refugees that do not exceed the following payment ceilings, according to the number of persons in the family unit, except as noted in paragraphs (b) and (c) of this section. For family units greater than 4 persons, the payment ceiling may be increased by $70 for each additional person.

Size of family unit	Monthly payment ceiling
1 person	$335
2 persons	450
3 persons	570
4 persons	685

(b) States and local resettlement agencies may not make payments to refugees that are lower than the State's TANF payment for the same sized family unit. In States that have TANF payment levels that are higher than the ceilings established in this section, States and local resettlement agencies must provide payment levels under the public/private RCA program that are comparable to the State's TANF payment levels.

(c) Income disregards and other incentives. (1) States and local resettlement agencies may design an assistance program that combines RCA payments with income disregards or other incentives such as employment bonuses, or graduated payments in order to encourage early employment and self-sufficiency, as long as the total combined payments to a refugee do not exceed the ORR monthly ceilings established in this section multiplied by the allowable number of months of RCA eligibility.

(2) States that elect to exceed monthly payment ceilings in order to provide employment incentives must budget their resources to ensure that sufficient RCA funds are available to cover a refugee's cash assistance needs in the latter months of a refugee's eligibility period, if needed.

(d) If the Director determines that the payment ceilings need to be adjusted for inflation, the Director will publish a document in the FEDERAL REGISTER announcing the new payment ceilings.

§ 400.61 Services to public/private RCA recipients.

(a) Services provided to recipients of refugee cash assistance in the public/private RCA program may be provided by the local resettlement agencies that administer the public/private RCA program or by other refugee service agencies.

(b) Allowable services under the public/private program are limited to those services described in §§ 400.154 and 400.155 and are to be funded in accordance with § 400.206.

(c) In public/private programs in which local resettlement agencies are responsible for administering both cash assistance and services, States and local resettlement agencies must coordinate on a regular basis with refugee mutual assistance associations and other ethnic representatives that represent or serve the ethnic populations that are being resettled in the U.S. to ensure that the services provided under the public/private RCA program:

(1) Are appropriate to the linguistic and cultural needs of the incoming populations; and

(2) Are coordinated with the longer-term resettlement services frequently provided by ethnic community organizations after the end of the time-limited RCA eligibility period.

(d) In public/private programs in which the agencies responsible for providing services to RCA recipients are not the same agencies that administer the cash assistance program, the State must:

(1) Establish procedures to ensure close coordination between the local resettlement agencies that provide cash assistance and the agencies that provide services to RCA recipients; and

(2) Set up a system of accountability that identifies the responsibilities of each participating agency and holds these agencies accountable for the results of the program components for which they are responsible.

§ 400.62 Treatment of eligible secondary migrants, asylees, and Cuban/Haitian entrants.

The State and local resettlement agencies must establish procedures to ensure that eligible secondary migrant refugees, asylees, and Cuban/Haitian entrants have access to public/private RCA assistance if they wish to apply. In developing these procedures, consideration must be given to ensuring coverage of eligible secondary migrants and other eligible applicants who were sponsored by a resettlement agency which does not have a presence in the State or who were not sponsored by any agency.

§ 400.63 Preparation of local resettlement agencies.

The State and the national voluntary agencies whose affiliate agencies will be responsible for implementing the public/private RCA program:

(a) Must determine the training needed to enable local resettlement agencies to achieve a smooth implementation of the RCA program; and

(b) Must provide the training in a uniform way to ensure that all local resettlement agencies in the State will implement the public/private RCA program in a consistent manner.

PUBLICLY-ADMINISTERED RCA PROGRAMS

§400.65 Continuation of a publicly-administered RCA program.

Sections 400.65 through 400.69 apply to publicly-administered RCA programs. If a State chooses to operate a publicly-administered RCA program:

(a) The State may operate its refugee cash assistance program consistent with its TANF program.

(b) The State must submit an amendment to its State Plan, describing the elements of its TANF program that will be used in its refugee cash assistance program.

§400.66 Eligibility and payment levels in a publicly-administered RCA program.

(a) In administering a publicly-administered refugee cash assistance program, the State agency must operate its refugee cash assistance program consistent with the provisions of its TANF program in regard to:

(1) The determination of initial and on-going eligibility (treatment of income and resources, budgeting methods, need standard);

(2) The determination of benefit amounts (payment levels based on size of the assistance unit, income disregards);

(3) Proration of shelter, utilities, and similar needs; and

(4) Any other State TANF rules relating to financial eligibility and payments.

(b) The State agency may not consider any resources remaining in the applicant's country of origin in determining income eligibility.

(c) The State agency may not consider a sponsor's income and resources to be accessible to a refugee solely because the person is serving as a sponsor.

(d) The State agency may not consider any cash grant received by the applicant under the Department of State or Department of Justice Reception and Placement programs.

(e) The State agency may use the date of application as the date refugee cash assistance begins in order to provide payments quickly to newly arrived refugees.

§400.67 Non-applicable TANF requirements.

States that choose to operate an RCA program modeled after TANF may not apply certain TANF requirements to refugee cash assistance applicants or recipients as follows: TANF work requirements may not apply to RCA applicants or recipients, and States must meet the requirements in subpart I of this part with respect to the provision of services for RCA recipients.

§400.68 Notification to local resettlement agency.

(a) The State must notify promptly the local resettlement agency which provided for the initial resettlement of a refugee whenever the refugee applies for refugee cash assistance under a publicly-administered RCA program.

(b) The State must contact the applicant's sponsor or the local resettlement agency concerning offers of employment and inquire whether the applicant has voluntarily quit employment or has refused to accept an offer of employment within 30 consecutive days immediately prior to the date of application, in accordance with §400.77(a).

§400.69 Alternative RCA programs.

A State that determines that a public/private RCA program or a publicly-administered program modeled after its TANF program is not the best approach for the State may choose instead to establish an alternative approach under the Wilson/Fish program, authorized by section 412(e)(7) of the INA.

Subpart F—Requirements for Employability Services and Employment

SOURCE: 54 FR 5477, Feb. 3, 1989, unless otherwise noted.

§400.70 Basis and scope.

This subpart sets forth requirements for applicants for and recipients of refugee cash assistance under both the public/private RCA program and the publicly-administered RCA program concerning registration for employment services, participation in social services or targeted assistance, and acceptance of appropriate employment under section 412(e)(2)(A) of the Act. A refugee who is an applicant for or recipient of refugee cash assistance must comply with the requirements in this subpart.

[60 FR 33602, June 28, 1995, as amended at 65 FR 15448, Mar. 22, 2000]

§ 400.71 Definitions.

For purposes of this subpart and Subpart I—

Appropriate agency providing employment services means an agency providing services specified under § 400.154(a) of this part which are specifically designed to assist refugees in becoming employed, which must include an established program of job referral to, and job placement with, private employers, and which must be determined acceptable by the State.

Employability plan means an individualized written plan for a refugee registered for employment services that sets forth a program of services intended to result in the earliest possible employment of the refugee.

Employability services means services, as specified in § 400.154 of this part, designed to enable an individual to obtain employment and to improve the employability or work skills of the individual.

Employable means not exempt from registration for employment services under § 400.76 of this part.

Employment services means the services specified in § 400.154(a) of this part.

Family self-sufficiency plan means a plan that addresses the employment-related service needs of the employable members in a family for the purpose of enabling the family to become self-supporting through the employment of one or more family members.

Registrant means an individual who has registered for employment services under § 400.75 of this part.

[54 FR 5477, Feb. 3, 1989, as amended at 60 FR 33602, June 28, 1995; 65 FR 15448, Mar. 22, 2000]

§ 400.72 Arrangements for employability services.

Paragraphs (a) and (b) of this section apply equally to States that operate a public/private RCA program and to States that operate a publicly-administered RCA program. Paragraph (c) applies only to publicly-administered RCA programs.

(a) The State agency must make such arrangements as are necessary to enable refugees to meet the requirements of, and receive the employability services specified in, this subpart.

(b) If a State agency makes such arrangements with another agency or agencies, it must retain responsibility for meeting the requirements in this subpart.

(c) In order for an agency to qualify to receive referrals from the State agency of refugees required to register for employability services, such agency must agree to advise the State agency whenever such a refugee fails or refuses to participate in the required services or to accept an offer of employment.

[54 FR 5477, Feb. 3, 1989, as amended at 65 FR 15448, Mar. 22, 2000]

GENERAL REQUIREMENTS

§ 400.75 Registration for employment services, participation in employability service programs and targeted assistance programs, going to job interviews, and acceptance of appropriate offers of employment.

(a) As a condition for receipt of refugee cash assistance, a refugee who is not exempt under § 400.76 of this subpart must, except for good cause shown—

(1) Register with an "appropriate agency providing employment services," as defined in § 400.71, and within 30 days of receipt of aid participate in the employment services provided by such agency, as defined in § 400.154(a) of this part.

(2) Go to a job interview which is arranged by the State agency or its designee.

(3) Accept at any time, from any source, an offer of employment, as determined to be appropriate by the State agency or its designee.

(4) Participate in any employability service program which provides job or language training in the area in which the refugee resides, which is funded under section 412(c) of the Act, and which is determined to be available and appropriate for that refugee; or if such a program funded under section

412(c) is not available or appropriate in the area in which the refugee resides, any other available and appropriate program in such area.

(5) Participate in any targeted assistance program in the area in which the refugee resides, which is funded under section 412(c) of the Act, and which is determined to be available and appropriate for that refugee.

(6)(i) Accept an offer of employment which is determined to be appropriate by the local resettlement agency which was responsible for the initial resettlement of the refugee or by the appropriate State or local employment service;

(ii) Go to a job interview which is arranged through such agency or service; and

(iii) Participate in a social service or targeted assistance program which such agency or service determines to be available or appropriate.

(b) The State agency or its designee must permit, but may not require, the voluntary registration for employment services of an applicant or recipient who is exempt under §400.76 of this part.

[54 FR 5477, Feb. 3, 1989, as amended at 60 FR 33602, June 28, 1995; 65 FR 15448, Mar. 22, 2000]

§400.76 Criteria for exemption from registration for employment services, participation in employability service programs, and acceptance of appropriate offers of employment.

States and local resettlement agencies operating a public/private RCA program, as well as States operating a publicly-administered RCA program, may determine what specific exemptions, if any, are appropriate for recipients of a time-limited RCA program in their State.

[65 FR 15448, Mar. 22, 2000]

§400.77 Effect of quitting employment or failing or refusing to participate in required services.

(a) As a condition of eligibility for refugee cash assistance, an employable applicant may not, without good cause, within 30 consecutive calendar days immediately prior to the application for assistance (or such longer period required by §400.82(c)(2), if applicable), have voluntarily quit employment or have refused to accept an offer of employment determined to be appropriate by the State agency or its designee, using criteria set forth in §400.81.

(b) As a condition of continued receipt of refugee cash assistance, an employable recipient may not, without good cause, voluntarily quit employment or fail or refuse to meet the requirements of §400.75(a).

[54 FR 5477, Feb. 3, 1989, as amended at 65 FR 15448, Mar. 22, 2000]

§400.79 Development of an employability plan.

(a) An individual employability plan must be developed as part of a family self-sufficiency plan where applicable for each recipient of refugee cash assistance in a family unit who is not exempt under §400.76 of this part.

(b) If such a plan has been developed by the local resettlement agency which sponsored the refugee, or its designee, the State agency, or its designee, may accept this plan if it determines that the plan is appropriate for the refugee and meets the requirements of this subpart.

(c) The employability plan must—

(1) Be designed to lead to the earliest possible employment and not be structured in such a way as to discourage or delay employment or job-seeking; and

(2) Contain a definite employment goal, attainable in the shortest time period consistent with the employability of the refugee in relation to job openings in the area.

[54 FR 5477, Feb. 3, 1989, as amended at 60 FR 33602, June 28, 1995; 65 FR 15448, Mar. 22, 2000]

Criteria for Appropriate Employability Services and Employment

§400.81 Criteria for appropriate employability services and employment.

The State agency or its designee must determine if employability services and employment are appropriate in accordance with the following criteria:

(a) The services or employment must meet the following criteria, or, if approved by the Director, the comparable criteria applied by the State in an alternative program for TANF recipients:

(1) All assignments must be within the scope of the individual's employability plan. The plan may be modified to reflect changed services or employment conditions.

(2) The services or employment must be related to the capability of the individual to perform the task on a regular basis. Any claim of adverse effect on physical or mental health must be based on adequate medical testimony from a physician or licensed or certified psychologist indicating that participation would impair the individual's physical or mental health.

(3) The total daily commuting time to and from home to the service or employment site must not normally exceed 2 hours, not including the transporting of a child to and from a child care facility, unless a longer commuting distance or time is generally accepted in the community, in which case the round trip commuting time must not exceed the generally accepted community standards.

(4) When child care is required, the care must meet the standards normally required by the State in its work and training programs for TANF recipients.

(5) The service or work site to which the individual is assigned must not be in violation of applicable Federal, State, or local health and safety standards.

(6) Assignments must not be made which are discriminatory in terms of age, sex, race, creed, color, or national origin.

(7) Appropriate work may be temporary, permanent, full-time, part-time, or seasonal work if such work meets the other standards of this section.

(8) The wage shall meet or exceed the Federal or State minimum wage law, whichever is applicable, or if such laws are not applicable, the wage shall not be substantially less favorable than the wage normally paid for similar work in that labor market.

(9) The daily hours of work and the weekly hours of work shall not exceed those customary to the occupation. And

(10) No individual may be required to accept employment if:

(i) The position offered is vacant due to a strike, lockout, or other bona fide labor dispute; or

(ii) The individual would be required to work for an employer contrary to the conditions of his existing membership in the union governing that occupation. However, employment not governed by the rules of a union in which he or she has membership may be deemed appropriate.

(11) In addition to meeting the other criteria of this paragraph, the quality of training must meet local employers' requirements so that the individual will be in a competitive position within the local labor market. The training must also be likely to lead to employment which will meet the appropriate work criteria.

(b) If an individual is a professional in need of professional refresher training and other recertification services in order to qualify to practice his or her profession in the United States, the training may consist of full-time attendance in a college or professional training program, provided that such training: Is approved as part of the individual's employability plan by the State agency, or its designee; does not exceed one year's duration (including any time enrolled in such program in the United States prior to the refugee's application for assistance); is specifically intended to assist the professional in becoming relicensed in his or her profession; and, if completed, can realistically be expected to result in such relicensing. This training may only be made available to individuals who are employed.

(c) A job offered, if determined appropriate under the requirements of this subpart, is required to be accepted by the refugee without regard to whether such job would interrupt a program of services planned or in progress unless the refugee is currently participating in a program *in progress* of on-the-job training (as described in § 400.154(c)) or vocational training (as described in § 400.154(e)) which meets the requirements of this part and which is being carried out as part of an approved employability plan.

[54 FR 5477, Feb. 3, 1989, as amended at 65 FR 15448, Mar. 22, 2000]

FAILURE OR REFUSAL TO ACCEPT EMPLOYABILITY SERVICES OR EMPLOYMENT

§ 400.82 Failure or refusal to accept employability services or employment.

(a) *Termination of assistance.* When, without good cause, an employable non-exempt recipient of refugee cash assistance under the public/private RCA program or under a publicly-administered RCA program has failed or refused to meet the requirements of § 400.75(a) or has voluntarily quit a job, the State, or the agency(s) responsible for the provision of RCA, must terminate assistance in accordance with paragraphs (b) and (c) of this section.

(b) *Notice of intended termination*—(1) In cases of proposed action to reduce, suspend, or terminate assistance, the State or the agency(s) responsible for the provision of RCA, must give timely and adequate notice, in accordance with adverse action procedures required at § 400.54.

(2) The State, or the agency(s) responsible for the provision of RCA, must provide written procedures in English and in appropriate languages, in accordance with requirements in § 400.55, for the determination of good cause, the sanctioning of refugees who do not comply with the requirements of the program, and for the filing of appeals by refugees.

(3) In addition to the requirements in § 400.54, the written notice must include—

(i) An explanation of the reason for the action and the proposed adverse consequences; and

(ii) Notice of the recipient's right to mediation and a hearing under § 400.83.

(4) A written notice in English and a written translated notice, or a verbal translation of the notice, in accordance with the requirements in § 400.55, must be sent or provided to a refugee at least 10 days before the date upon which the action is to become effective.

(c) *Sanctions.* (1) If the sanctioned individual is the only member of the filing unit, the assitance shall be terminated. If the filing unit includes other members, the State shall not take into account the sanctioned individual's needs in determining the filing unit's need for assistance.

(2) The sanction applied in paragraph (b)(3)(i) of this section shall remain in effect for 3 payment months for the first such failure and 6 payment months for any subsequent such failure.

[54 FR 5477, Feb. 3, 1989, as amended at 60 FR 33602, June 28, 1995; 65 FR 15448, Mar. 22, 2000]

§ 400.83 Mediation and fair hearings.

(a) *Mediation*—(1) *Public/private RCA program.* The State must ensure that a mediation period prior to imposition of sanctions is provided to refugees by local resettlement agencies under the public/private RCA program. Mediation shall begin as soon as possible, but no later than 10 days following the date of failure or refusal to participate, and may continue for a period not to exceed 30 days. Either the State (or local resettlement agency(s) responsible for the provision of RCA) or the recipient may terminate this period sooner when either believes that the dispute cannot be resolved by mediation.

(2) *Publicly-administered RCA programs.* Under a publicly-administered RCA program, the State must use the same procedures for mediation/conciliation as those used in its TANF program, if available.

(b) *Hearings.* The State or local resettlement agency(s) responsible for the provision of RCA must provide an applicant for, or recipient of, refugee cash assistance an opportunity for a hearing, using the same procedures and standards set forth in § 400.54, to contest a determination concerning employability, or failure or refusal to carry out job search or to accept an appropriate offer of employability services or employment, resulting in denial or termination of assistance.

[65 FR 15448, Mar. 22, 2000]

Subpart G—Refugee Medical Assistance

SOURCE: 54 FR 5480, Feb. 3, 1989, unless otherwise noted.

§ 400.90 Basis and scope.

This subpart sets forth requirements concerning grants to States under section 412(e) of the Act for refugee medical assistance (RMA), as defined at § 400.2 of this part.

§ 400.91 Definitions.

For purposes of this subpart—

Medically needy means individuals who are eligible for medical assistance under a State's approved Medicaid State plan in accordance with section 1902(a)(10)(C) of the Social Security Act.

Spend down means to deduct from countable income incurred medical expenses, thereby lowering the amount of countable income to a level that meets financial eligibility requirements in accordance with 42 CFR 435.831 (or, as applicable to Guam, the Virgin Islands, and Puerto Rico, 42 CFR 436.831).

APPLICATIONS, DETERMINATIONS OF ELIGIBILITY, AND FURNISHING ASSISTANCE

§ 400.93 Opportunity to apply for medical assistance.

(a) A State must provide any individual wishing to do so an opportunity to apply for medical assistance and must determine the eligibility of each applicant.

(b) In determining eligibility for medical assistance, the State agency must comply with regulations governing applications, determinations of eligibility, and furnishing Medicaid (including the opportunity for fair hearings) in the States and the District of Columbia under 42 CFR part 435, subpart J, and in Guam, Puerto Rico, and the Virgin Islands under 42 CFR part 436, subpart J, and 42 CFR part 431, subpart E.

(c) Notwithstanding any other provision of law, the State must notify promptly the agency (or local affiliate) which provided for the initial resettlement of a refugee whenever the refugee applies for medical assistance.

(d) In providing notice to an applicant or recipient to indicate that assistance has been authorized or that it has been denied or terminated, the State must specify the program(s) to which the notice applies, clearly distinguishing between refugee medical assistance and Medicaid or the State Children's Health Insurance Program (SCHIP). For example, if a refugee applies for assistance, is determined ineligible for Medicaid or the State Children's Health Insurance Program (SCHIP) but eligible for refugee medical assistance, the notice must specify clearly the determinations with respect both to Medicaid or the State Children's Health Insurance Program (SCHIP) and to refugee medical assistance.

[54 FR 5480, Feb. 3, 1989, as amended at 65 FR 15449, Mar. 22, 2000]

§ 400.94 Determination of eligibility for Medicaid.

(a) The State must determine Medicaid and SCHIP eligibility under its Medicaid and SCHIP State plans for each individual member of a family unit that applies for medical assistance.

(b) A State that provides Medicaid to medically needy individuals in the State under its State plan must determine a refugee applicant's eligibility for Medicaid as medically needy.

(c) A State must provide medical assistance under the Medicaid and SCHIP programs to all refugees eligible under its State plans.

(d) If the appropriate State agency determines that the refugee applicant is not eligible for Medicaid or SCHIP under its State plans, the State must determine the applicant's eligibility for refugee medical assistance.

[54 FR 5480, Feb. 3, 1989, as amended at 60 FR 33603, June 28, 1995; 65 FR 15449, Mar. 22, 2000]

CONDITIONS OF ELIGIBILITY FOR REFUGEE MEDICAL ASSISTANCE

§ 400.100 General eligibility requirements.

(a) Eligibility for refugee medical assistance is limited to those refugees who—

(1) Are ineligible for Medicaid or SCHIP but meet the financial eligibility standards under § 400.101;

(2) Meet immigration status and identification requirements in subpart D of this part or are the dependent children of, and part of the same assistance unit as, individuals who meet the

requirements in subpart D, subject to the limitation in § 400.208 of this part with respect to nonrefugee children;

(3) Meet eligibility requirements and conditions in this subpart;

(4) Provide the name of the resettlement agency which resettled them; and

(5) Are not full-time students in institutions of higher education, as defined by the Director, except where such enrollment is approved by the State, or its designee, as part of an individual employability plan for a refugee under § 400.79 of this part or a plan for an unaccompanied minor in accordance with § 400.112.

(b) A refugee may be eligible for refugee medical assistance under this subpart during a period of time to be determined by the Director in accordance with § 400.211.

(c) The State agency may not require that a refugee actually receive or apply for refugee cash assistance as a condition of eligibility for refugee medical assistance.

(d) All recipients of refugee cash assistance who are not eligible for Medicaid or SCHIP are eligible for refugee medical assistance.

[45 FR 59323, Sept. 9, 1980, as amended at 58 FR 46090, Sept. 1, 1993; 58 FR 64507, Dec. 8, 1993; 60 FR 33603, June 28, 1995; 65 FR 15449, Mar. 22, 2000]

§ 400.101 Financial eligibility standards.

In determining eligibility for refugee medical assistance, the State agency must use—

(a) In States with medically needy programs under 42 CFR part 435, subpart D:

(1) The State's medically needy financial eligibility standards established under 42 CFR part 435, subpart I, and as reflected in the State's approved title XIX State Medicaid plan; or

(2) A financial eligibility standard established at up to 200% of the national poverty level; and

(b) In States without a medically needy program:

(1) The State's AFDC payment standards and methodologies in effect as of July 16, 1996, including any modifications elected by the State under section 1931(b)(2) of the Social Security Act; or

(2) A financial eligibility standard established at up to 200% of the national poverty level.

[54 FR 5480, Feb. 3, 1989, as amended at 65 FR 15449, Mar. 22, 2000]

§ 400.102 Consideration of income and resources.

(a) Except as specified in paragraphs (b), (c), and (d) of this section, in considering financial eligibility of applicants for refugee medical assistance, the State agency must—

(1) In States with medically needy programs, use the standards governing determination of income eligibility in 42 CFR 435.831, and as reflected in the State's approved title XIX State Medicaid plan.

(2) In States without medically needy programs, use the standards and methodologies governing consideration of income and resources of AFDC applicants in effect as of July 16, 1996, including any modifications elected by the State under section 1931(b)(2) of the Social Security Act.

(b) The State may not consider in-kind services and shelter provided to an applicant by a sponsor or local resettlement agency in determining eligibility for and receipt of refugee medical assistance.

(c) The State may not consider any cash assistance payments provided to an applicant in determining eligibility for and receipt of refugee medical assistance.

(d) The State must base eligibility for refugee medical assistance on the applicant's income and resources on the date of application. The State agency may not use the practice of averaging income prospectively over the application processing period in determining income eligibility for refugee medical assistance.

[65 FR 15449, Mar. 22, 2000]

§ 400.103 Coverage of refugees who spend down to State financial eligibility standards.

States must allow applicants for RMA who do not meet the financial eligibility standards elected in § 400.101 to spend down to such standard using an appropriate method for deducting incurred medical expenses.

[65 FR 15449, Mar. 22, 2000]

§ 400.104 Continued coverage of recipients who receive increased earnings from employment.

(a) If a refugee who is receiving refugee medical assistance receives earnings from employment, the earnings shall not affect the refugee's continued medical assistance eligibility.

(b) If a refugee, who is receiving Medicaid and has been residing in the U.S. less than the time-eligibility period for refugee medical assistance, becomes ineligible for Medicaid because of earnings from employment, the refugee must be transferred to refugee medical assistance without an RMA eligibility determination.

(c) Under paragraphs (a) and (b) of this section, a refugee shall continue to receive refugee medical assistance until he/she reaches the end of his or her time-eligibility period for refugee medical assistance, in accordance with § 400.100(b).

(d) In cases where a refugee is covered by employer-provided health insurance, any payment of RMA for that individual must be reduced by the amount of the third party payment.

[65 FR 15449, Mar. 22, 2000]

SCOPE OF MEDICAL SERVICES

§ 400.105 Mandatory services.

In providing refugee medical assistance to refugees, a State must provide at least the same services in the same manner and to the same extent as under the State's Medicaid program, as delineated in 42 CFR part 440.

§ 400.106 Additional services.

If a State or local jurisdiction provides additional medical services beyond the scope of the State's Medicaid program to destitute residents of the State or locality through public facilities, such as county hospitals, the State may provide to refugees who are determined eligible under § 400.94, only to the extent that sufficient funds are appropriated, or § 400.100 of this part the same services through public facilities.

[54 FR 5480, Feb. 3, 1989, as amended at 60 FR 33603, June 28, 1995]

§ 400.107 Medical screening.

(a) As part of its refugee medical assistance program, a State may provide a medical screening to a refugee provided—

(1) The screening is in accordance with requirements prescribed by the Director, or his or her designee; and

(2) Written approval for the screening program or project has been provided to the State by the Director, or designee.

(b) If such screening is done during the first 90 days after a refugee's initial date of entry into the United States, it may be provided without prior determination of the refugee's eligibility under § 400.94 or § 400.100 of this part.

[54 FR 5480, Feb. 3, 1989, as amended at 60 FR 33603, June 28, 1995; 65 FR 15449, Mar. 22, 2000]

Subpart H—Child Welfare Services

SOURCE: 51 FR 3915, Jan. 30, 1986, unless otherwise noted.

§ 400.110 Basis and scope.

This subpart prescribes requirements concerning grants to States under section 412(d)(2)(B) of the Act for child welfare services to refugee unaccompanied minors.

§ 400.111 Definitions.

For purposes of this subpart—

Child welfare agency means an agency licensed or approved under State law to provide child welfare services to children in the State.

Unaccompanied minor means a person who has not yet attained 18 years of age (or a higher age established by the State of resettlement in its child welfare plan under title IV-B of the Social Security Act for the availability of child welfare services to any other child in the State); who entered the United States unaccompanied by and not destined to (a) a parent or (b) a close nonparental adult relative who is willing and able to care for the child or (c) an adult with a clear and court-verifiable claim to custody of the minor; and who has no parent(s) in the United States. *Limitation:* No child may be considered by a State to be *unaccompanied* for the purpose of this part unless such child was identified by INS at the time of entry as *unaccompanied*, except that a child who was correctly classified as *unaccompanied* by a State in accordance with Action Transmittal SSA-AT-79-04 (and official interpretations thereof by the Director) prior to the effective date of this definition may continue to be so classified until such status is terminated in accordance with §400.113(b) of this subpart; and the Director may approve the classification of a child as *unaccompanied* on the basis of information provided by a State showing that such child should have been classified as *unaccompanied* at the time of entry.

Title IV-B plan means a State's plan for providing child welfare services to children in the State under part B of title IV of the Social Security Act.

§400.112 Child welfare services for refugee children.

(a) In providing child welfare services to refugee children in the State, a State must provide the same child welfare services and benefits to the same extent as are provided to other children of the same age in the State under a State's title IV-B plan.

(b) A State must provide child welfare services to refugee children according to the State's child welfare standards, practices, and procedures.

(c) Foster care maintenance payments must be provided under a State's program under title IV-E of the Social Security Act if a child is eligible under that program.

§400.113 Duration of eligibility.

(a) Except as specified in paragraph (b), a refugee child may be eligible for services under §400.112 of this part during the 36-month period beginning with the first month the child entered the United States.

(b) An unaccompanied minor continues to meet the definition of "unaccompanied minor" and is eligible for benefits and services under §§400.115 through 400.120 of this part until the minor—

(1) Is reunited with a parent; or

(2) Is united with a nonparental adult (relative or nonrelative) willing and able to care for the child to whom legal custody and/or guardianship is granted under State law; or

(3) Attains 18 years of age or such higher age as the State's title IV-B plan prescribes for the availability of child welfare services to any other child in the State.

§400.114 [Reserved]

§400.115 Establishing legal responsibility.

(a) A State must ensure that legal responsibility is established, including legal custody and/or guardianship, as appropriate, in accordance with applicable State law, for each unaccompanied minor who resettles in the State. The State must initiate procedures for establishing legal responsibility for the minor, with an appropriate court (if action by a court is required by State law), within 30 days after the minor arrives at the location of resettlement.

(b) In establishing legal responsibility, including legal custody and/or guardianship under State law, as appropriate, the minor's natural parents should not be contacted in their native country since contact could be dangerous to the parents.

(c) Unaccompanied minors are not generally eligible for adoption since family reunification is the objective of the program. In certain rare cases, adoption may be permitted pursuant to adoption laws in the State of resettlement, provided a court finds that: (1) Adoption would be in the best interest of the child; and (2) there is termination of parental rights (for example, in situations where the parents are dead or are missing and presumed dead) as determined by the appropriate State court. When adoption occurs, the child's status as an unaccompanied minor terminates.

§400.116 Service for unaccompanied minors.

(a) A State must provide unaccompanied minors with the same range of child welfare benefits and services available in foster care cases to other children in the State. Allowable benefits and services may include foster care maintenance (room, board, and clothing) payments; medical assistance; support services; services identified in the State's plans under titles IV-B and IV-E of the Social Security Act; services permissible under title XX of the Social Security Act; and expenditures incurred in establishing legal responsibility.

(b) A State may provide additional services if the Director, or his or her designee, determines such services to be reasonable and necessary for a particular child or children and provides written notification of such determination to the State.

§ 400.117 Provision of care and services.

(a) A State may provide care and services to an unaccompanied minor directly or through arrangements with a public or private child welfare agency approved or licensed under State law.

(b) If a State arranges for the care and services through a public or private nonprofit child welfare agency, it must retain oversight responsibility for the appropriateness of the unaccompanied minor's care.

§ 400.118 Case planning.

(a) A State, or its designee under § 400.117, must develop and implement an appropriate plan for the care and supervision of, and services provided to, each unaccompanied minor, to ensure that the child is placed in a foster home or other setting approved by the legally responsible agency and in accordance with the child's need for care and for social, health, and educational services.

(b) Case planning for unaccompanied minors must, at a minimum, address the following elements:

(1) Family reunification;

(2) Appropriate placement of the unaccompanied child in a foster home, group foster care, residential facility, supervised independent living, or other setting, as deemed appropriate in meeting the best interest and special needs if the child.

(3) Health screening and treatment, including provision for medical and dental examinations and for all necessary medical and dental treatment.

(4) Orientation, testing, and counseling to facilitate the adjustment of the child to American culture.

(5) Preparation for participation in American society with special emphasis upon English language instruction and occupational as well as cultural training as necessary to facilitate the child's social integration and to prepare the child for independent living and economic self-sufficiency.

(6) Preservation of the child's ethnic and religious heritage.

(c) A State, or its designee under section 400.117 of this part, must review the continuing appropriateness of each unaccompanied minor's living arrangement and services no less frequently than every 6 months.

(Approved by the Office of Management and Budget under control number 0960–0418)

§ 400.119 Interstate movement.

After the initial placement of an unaccompanied minor, the same procedures that govern the movement of nonrefugee foster cases to other States apply to the movement of unaccompanied minors to other States.

§ 400.120 Reporting requirements.

A State must submit to ORR, on forms prescribed by the Director, the following reports on each unaccompanied minor:

(a) An initial report within 30 days of the date of the minor's placement in the State;

(b) A progress report every 12 months beginning with 12 months from the date of the initial report in paragraph (a);

(c) A change of status report within 60 days of the date that—

(1) The minor's placement is changed;

(2) Legal responsibility of any kind for the minor is established or transferred; or

(d) A final report within 60 days of the date of that the minor—

(1) Is reunited with a parent; or

(2) Is united with an adult, other than a parent, in accordance with § 400.113(b) or § 400.115(c) of this part.

(3) Is emancipated.

(Approved by the Office of Management and Budget under control number 0960–0418)

Subpart I—Refugee Social Services

§400.140 Basis and scope.

This subpart sets forth requirements concerning formula allocation grants to States under section 412(c) of the Act for refugee social services.

[54 FR 5481, Feb. 3, 1989, as amended at 60 FR 33603, June 28, 1995]

§400.141 Definitions.

For purposes of this subpart—

Refugee social services means any service set forth in §400.154 or §400.155 of this subpart.

[54 FR 5481, Feb. 3, 1989, as amended at 60 FR 33603, June 28, 1995]

APPLICATIONS, DETERMINATIONS OF ELIGIBILITY, AND PROVISION OF SERVICES

§400.145 Opportunity to apply for services.

(a) A State must provide any individual wishing to do so an opportunity to apply for services and determine the eligibility of each applicant.

(b) Except as otherwise specified in this subpart, a State must determine eligibility for and provide refugee social services specified in §§400.154 and 400.155 in accordance with the same procedures which it follows in its social service program under title XX of the Social Security Act with respect to determining eligibility, acting on applications and requests for services, and providing notification of right to a hearing.

(c) A State must insure that women have the same opportunities as men to participate in all services funded under this part, including job placement services.

[54 FR 5481, Feb. 3, 1989, as amended at 60 FR 33603, June 28, 1995]

FUNDING AND SERVICE PRIORITIES

§400.146 Use of funds.

The State must use its social service grants primarily for employability services designed to enable refugees to obtain jobs within one year of becoming enrolled in services in order to achieve economic self-sufficiency as soon as possible. Social services may continue to be provided after a refugee has entered a job to help the refugee retain employment or move to a better job. Social service funds may not be used for long-term training programs such as vocational training that last for more than a year or educational programs that are not intended to lead to employment within a year.

[60 FR 33603, June 28, 1995]

§400.147 Priority in provision of services.

A State must plan its social service program and allocate its social service funds in such a manner that services are provided to refugees in the following order of priority, except in certain individual extreme circumstances:

(a) All newly arriving refugees during their first year in the U.S., who apply for services;

(b) Refugees who are receiving cash assistance;

(c) Unemployed refugees who are not receiving cash assistance; and

(d) Employed refugees in need of services to retain employment or to attain economic independence.

[54 FR 5481, Feb. 3, 1989, as amended at 60 FR 33603, June 28, 1995]

PURCHASE OF SERVICES

§400.148 Purchase of services.

A state may provide services directly or it may purchase services from public or private service providers.

[54 FR 5481, Feb. 3, 1989]

CONDITIONS OF ELIGIBILITY FOR REFUGEE SOCIAL SERVICES

§400.150 General eligibility requirements.

Eligibility for refugee social services is limited to those refugees who—

(a) Meet immigration status and identification requirements in Subpart D of this part;

(b) Meet the other eligibility requirements and conditions in this subpart.

[54 FR 5481, Feb. 3, 1989]

§ 400.152 Limitations on eligibility for services.

(a) A State may provide the social services defined in § 400.154 to refugees who are 16 years of age or older and who are not full-time students in elementary or secondary school, except that such a student may be provided services under § 400.154 (a) and (b) in order to obtain part-time or temporary (e.g., summer) employment while a student or full-time permanent employment upon completion of schooling.

(b) A State may not provide services under this subpart, except for citizenship and naturalization preparation services and referral and interpreter services, to refugees who have been in the United States for more than 60 months.

[54 FR 5481, Feb. 3, 1989, as amended at 60 FR 33603, June 28, 1995; 65 FR 15449, Mar. 22, 2000]

SCOPE OF REFUGEE SOCIAL SERVICES

§ 400.154 Employability services.

A State may provide the following employability services—

(a) *Employment services*, including development of a family self-sufficiency plan and an individual employability plan, world-of-work and job orientation, job clubs, job workshops, job development, referral to job opportunities, job search, and job placement and followup.

(b) *Employability assessment services*, including aptitude and skills testing.

(c) *On-the job training*, when such training is provided at the employment site and is expected to result in full-time, permanent, unsubsidized employment with the employer who is providing the training.

(d) *English language instruction*, with an emphasis on English as it relates to obtaining and retaining a job.

(e) *Vocational training*, including driver education and training when provided as part of an individual employability plan.

(f) *Skills recertification*, when such training meets the criteria for appropriate training in § 400.81(b) of this part.

(g) *Day care for children*, when necessary for participation in an employability service or for the acceptance or retention of employment.

(h) *Transportation*, when necessary for participation in an employability service or for the acceptance or retention of employment.

(i) *Translation and interpreter services*, when necessary in connection with employment or participation in an employability service.

(j) *Case management services*, as defined in § 400.2 of this part, for refugees who are considered employable under § 400.76 and for recipients of TANF and GA who are considered employable, provided that such services are directed toward a refugee's attainment of employment as soon as possible after arrival in the United States.

(k) Assistance in obtaining Employment Authorization Documents (EADs).

[54 FR 5481, Feb. 3, 1989, as amended at 60 FR 33603, June 28, 1995; 65 FR 15449, Mar. 22, 2000]

§ 400.155 Other services.

A State may provide the following other services—

(a) *Information and referral services*.

(b) *Outreach services*, including activities designed to familiarize refugees with available services, to explain the purpose of these services, and facilitate access to these services.

(c) *Social adjustment services*, including:

(1) *Emergency services*, as follows: Assessment and short-term counseling to persons or families in a perceived crisis; referral to appropriate resources; and the making of arrangements for necessary services.

(2) *Health-related services*, as follows: Information; referral to appropriate resources; assistance in scheduling appointments and obtaining services; and counseling to individuals or families to help them understand and identify their physical and mental health needs and maintain or improve their physical and mental health.

(3) *Home management services*, as follows: Formal or informal instruction to individuals or families in management of household budgets, home maintenance, nutrition, housing standards, tenants' rights, and other consumer education services.

(d) *Day care for children*, when necessary for participation in a service other than an employability service.

(e) *Transportation*, when necessary for participation in a service other than an employability service.

(f) *Translation and interpreter services*, when necessary for a purpose other than in connection with employment or participation in an employability service.

(g) *Case management services*, when necessary for a purpose other than in connection with employment or participation in employability services.

(h) *Any additional service*, upon submission to and approval by the Director of ORR, aimed at strengthening and supporting the ability of a refugee individual, family, or refugee community to achieve and maintain economic self-sufficiency, family stability, or community integration which has been demonstrated as effective and is not available from any other funding source.

(i) Citizenship and naturalization preparation services, including English language training and civics instruction to prepare refugees for citizenship, application assistance for adjustment to legal permanent resident status and citizenship status, assistance to disabled refugees in obtaining disability waivers from English and civics requirements for naturalization, and the provision of interpreter services for the citizenship interview.

[54 FR 5481, Feb. 3, 1989, as amended at 60 FR 33603, June 28, 1995; 65 FR 15449, Mar. 22, 2000]

§ 400.156 Service requirements.

(a) In order to avoid interference with refugee employment, English language instruction and vocational training funded under this part must be provided to the fullest extent feasible outside normal working hours.

(b) In planning and providing services under §§ 400.154 and 400.155, a State must take into account those services which a resettlement agency is required to provide for a refugee whom it sponsors in order to ensure the provision of seamless, coordinated services to refugees that are not duplicative.

(c) English language instruction funded under this part must be provided in a concurrent, rather than sequential, time period with employment or with other employment-related services.

(d) Services funded under this part must be refugee-specific services which are designed specifically to meet refugee needs and are in keeping with the rules and objectives of the refugee program, except that vocational or job skills training, on-the-job training, or English language training need not be refugee-specific.

(e) Services funded under this part must be provided to the maximum extent feasible in a manner that is culturally and linguistically compatible with a refugee's language and cultural background.

(f) Services funded under this part must be provided to the maximum extent feasible in a manner that includes the use of bilingual/bicultural women on service agency staffs to ensure adequate service access by refugee women.

(g) A family self-sufficiency plan must be developed for anyone who receives employment-related services funded under this part.

[54 FR 5481, Feb. 3, 1989, as amended at 60 FR 33604, June 28, 1995]

Subpart J—Federal Funding

SOURCE: 51 FR 3916, Jan. 30, 1986, unless otherwise noted.

§ 400.200 Scope.

This subpart specifies when, and the extent to which, Federal funding (FF) is available under this regulation in expenditures for determining eligibility and for providing assistance and services to refugees determined eligible under this part, and prescribes limitations and conditions on FF for those expenditures.

FEDERAL FUNDING FOR EXPENDITURES FOR DETERMINING ELIGIBILITY AND PROVIDING ASSISTANCE AND SERVICES

§ 400.202 Extent of Federal funding.

Subject to the availability of funds and under the terms and conditions approved by the Director, FF will be provided for 100 percent of authorized allowable costs of determining eligibility and providing assistance and services in accordance with this part.

§ 400.203 Federal funding for cash assistance.

(a) To the extent that sufficient funds are appropriated, Federal funding is available for cash assistance provided to eligible refugees during the 36-month period beginning with the first month the refugee entered the United States, as follows—

(1) If a refugee is eligible for TANF, adult assistance programs, or foster care maintenance payments under title IV-E of the Social Security Act, FF is available only for the non-Federal share of such assistance.

(2) If a refugee is eligible for SSI, FF is available for any supplementary payment a State may provide under that program.

(b) Federal funding is available for refugees cash assistance (RCA) provided to eligible refugees during a period of time to be determined by the Director in accordance with § 400.211.

(c) To the extent that sufficient funds are appropriated, Federal funding is available for general assistance (GA) provided to eligible refugees during the 24-month period beginning with the 13th month after the refugee entered the United States.

[51 FR 3916, Jan. 30, 1986, as amended at 53 FR 32224, Aug. 24, 1988; 58 FR 46090, Sept. 1, 1993; 58 FR 64507, Dec. 8, 1993; 60 FR 33604, June 28, 1995; 65 FR 15450, Mar. 22, 2000]

§ 400.204 Federal funding for medical assistance.

(a) To the extent that sufficient funds are appropriated, Federal funding is available for the non-Federal share of medical assistance provided to refugees who are eligible for Medicaid or adult assistance programs during the 36-month period beginning with the first month the refugee entered the United States.

(b) Federal funding is available for refugee medical assistance (RMA) provided to eligible refugees during a period of time to be determined by the Director in accordance with § 400.211.

(c) To the extent that sufficient funds are appropriated, Federal funding is available for a State's expenditures for medical assistance under a general assistance (GA) program during the 24-month period beginning with the 13th month after the refugee entered the United States.

[51 FR 3916, Jan. 30, 1986, as amended at 53 FR 32225, Aug. 24, 1988; 58 FR 46090, Sept. 1, 1993; 58 FR 64507, Dec. 8, 1993; 60 FR 33604, June 28, 1995]

§ 400.205 Federal funding for assistance and services for unaccompanied minors.

Federal funding is available for a State's expenditures for service to unaccompanied minors under §§ 400.115 through 400.120 of this part until the minor's status as an unaccompanied minor is terminated as specified by § 400.113.

§ 400.206 Federal funding for social services and targeted assistance services.

(a) Federal funding is available for refugee social services as set forth in Subpart I of this part, including the reasonable and necessary identifiable administrative costs of providing such services, in accordance with allocations by the Director.

(b) Federal funding is available for targeted assistance services as set forth in subpart L of this part, including reasonable and necessary identifiable State administrative costs of providing such services, not to exceed 5 percent of the total targeted assistance award to the State.

[54 FR 5483, Feb. 3, 1989, as amended at 60 FR 33604, June 28, 1995]

§ 400.207 Federal funding for administrative costs.

Federal funding is available for reasonable and necessary identifiable administrative costs of providing assistance and services under this part only for those assistance and service programs set forth in §§ 400.203 through 400.205 for which Federal funding is currently made available under the refugee program. A State may claim only those costs that are determined to be reasonable and allowable as defined by the Administration for Children and Families. Such costs may include reasonable and necessary administrative costs incurred by local resettlement agencies in providing assistance and services under a public/private RCA program. Administrative costs may be included in a State's claims against its quarterly grants for the purposes set forth in §§400.203 through 400.205 of this part.

[60 FR 33604, June 28, 1995, as amended at 65 FR 15450, Mar. 22, 2000]

§400.208 Claims involving family units which include both refugees and nonrefugees.

(a) Federal funding is available for a State's expenditures for assistance and services to a family unit which includes a refugee parent or two refugee parents and one or more of their children who are nonrefugees, including children who are United States citizens.

(b) Federal funding is not available for a State's expenditures for assistance and services provided to a nonrefugee adult member of a family unit or to a nonrefugee child or children in a family unit if one parent in the family unit is a nonrefugee.

[51 FR 3916, Jan. 30, 1986, as amended at 65 FR 15450, Mar. 22, 2000]

§400.209 Claims involving family units which include refugees who have been in the United States more than 36 months.

Federal funding is not available for State expenditures for cash and medical assistance and child welfare services (except services for unaccompanied minors) provided to any refugee within a family unit who has been in the United States

(a) More than 36 months if the family unit is eligible for TANF, SSI, Medicaid, GA, or child welfare services (except services for unaccompanied minors), or

(b) More than a period of time to be determined by the Director in accordance with §400.211 if the family unit is eligible for RCA or RMA. A State agency must exclude expenditures made on behalf of such refugees from its claim.

[51 FR 3916, Jan. 30, 1986, as amended at 53 FR 32225, Aug. 24, 1988; 57 FR 1115, Jan. 10, 1992; 58 FR 46090, Sept. 1, 1993; 58 FR 64507, Dec. 8, 1993; 65 FR 15450, Mar. 22, 2000]

§400.210 Time limits for obligating and expending funds and for filing State claims.

Federal funding is available for a State's expenditures for assistance and services to eligible refugees for which the following time limits are met:

(a) *CMA grants*, as described at §400.11(a)(1) of this part:

(1) Except for services for unaccompanied minors, a State must use its CMA grants for costs attributable to the Federal fiscal year (FFY) in which the Department awards the grants. With respect to CMA funds used for services for unaccompanied minors, the State may use its CMA funds for services provided during the Federal fiscal year following the FFY in which the Department awards the funds.

(2) A State's final financial report on expenditures of CMA grants, including CMA expenditures for services for unaccompanied minors, must be received no later than one year after the end of the FFY in which the Department awarded the grant. At that time, the Department will deobligate any unexpended funds, including any unliquidated obligations.

(b) *Social service grants and targeted assistance grants*, as described, respectively, at §§400.11(a)(2) and 400.311 of this part:

(1) A State must obligate its social service and targeted assistance grants no later than one year after the end of the FFY in which the Department awards the grant.

(2) A State must expend its social service and targeted assistance grants no later than two years after the end of the FFY in which the Department awards the grant. A State's final financial report on expenditures of social services and targeted assistance grants must be received no later than 90 days after the end of the two-year expenditure period. At that time, if a State's final financial expenditure report has not been received, the Department will deobligate any unexpended funds, including any unliquidated obligations, based on a State's last submitted financial report.

[60 FR 33604, June 28, 1995, as amended at 65 FR 15450, Mar. 22, 2000]

§400.211 Methodology to be used to determine time-eligibility of refugees.

(a) The time-eligibility period for refugee cash assistance and refugee medical assistance will be determined by the Director each year, based on appropriated funds available for the fiscal year. The Director will make a determination of the eligibility period each year as soon as possible after funds are appropriated for the refugee program, and also at subsequent points during the fiscal year, only if a reduction in the eligibility period is indicated, based on updated information on refugee flows and State reports on receipt of assistance and expenditures. The method to be used to determine the RCA/RMA eligibility period will include the following steps and will be applied to various RCA/RMA time-eligibility periods in order to determine the time-eligibility period which will provide the most number of months without incurring a shortfall in funds for the fiscal year.

(1) The time-eligibility population for the projected fiscal year will be estimated on the basis of the refugee admissions ceiling established by the President for that fiscal year and the anticipated arrival of other persons eligible for refugee assistance, to the extent that data on these persons are available. The anticipated pattern of refugee flow for the projected fiscal year will be estimated based on the best available historical and current refugee flow information that will most accurately forecast the refugee flow for the projected fiscal year. These arrival figures will then be used to determine the time-eligible population for a given duration of RCA/RMA benefits.

(2) The average annual number of RCA and RMA recipients will be determined by multiplying the estimated time-eligible population established in paragraph (a)(1) of this section by the estimated RCA and RMA participation rates. The RMA participation rate will take into account both RCA recipients, who are also eligible for RMA, and RMA-only recipients. Recipient data from quarterly performance reports submitted by States for the most recent 4 quarters for which reports are available will be used to determine the appropriate participation rates for various RCA/RMA time-eligibility periods.

(3) The average annual per recipient cost for RCA and RMA will be estimated separately, based on estimated per recipient costs for the most recent fiscal year, using available data, and inflated for the projected fiscal year using projected increases in per capita cash assistance costs for RCA and per capita Medicaid costs for RMA.

(4) The expected average number of RCA recipients will be multiplied by the expected RCA per recipient cost to derive estimated RCA costs. The expected average annual number of RMA recipients will be multiplied by the expected RMA per recipient cost to derive estimated RMA costs.

(5) State administrative costs for the projected fiscal year for all States in the aggregate will be estimated based on total actual allowable expenditures for State administration for the most recent fiscal year. The variable portion of administrative costs will be adjusted for changes in program participation and inflated by the Consumer Price Index (CPI) for all items as estimated by the Office of Management and Budget (OMB). The fixed portion of administrative costs will be adjusted by the CPI inflator only.

(6) The total estimated costs for the projected fiscal year will equal the combined estimated costs for RCA, RMA, and State administration as calculated in paragraphs (a)(1) through (5) of this section.

(b) If, as the Director determines, the period of eligibility needs to be changed from the eligibility period in effect at the time, the Director will publish a final notice in the FEDERAL REGISTER, announcing the new period of eligibility for refugee cash assistance and refugee medical assistance and the effective date for implementing the new eligibility period. States will be given as much notice as available funds will allow without resulting in a further reduction in the eligibility period. At a minimum, States will be given 30 days' notice.

[58 FR 64507, Dec. 8, 1993, as amended at 65 FR 15450, Mar. 22, 2000]

§ 400.212 Restrictions in the use of funds.

Federal funding under this part is not available for travel outside the United States without the written approval of the Director.

[60 FR 33604, June 28, 1995]

§ 400.220 Counting time-eligibility of refugees.

A State may calculate the time-eligibility of a refugee under this part in either of the following ways:

(a) On the basis of calendar months, in which case the month of arrival in the United States must count as the first month; or

(b) On the basis of the actual date of arrival, in which case each month will be counted from that specific date.

[54 FR 5483, Feb. 3, 1989]

Subpart K—Waivers and Withdrawals

§ 400.300 Waivers.

If a State wishes to apply for a waiver of a requirement of this part, the Director may waive such requirement with respect to such State, unless required by statute, if the Director determines that such waiver will advance the purposes of this part and is appropriate and consistent with Federal refugee policy objectives. To the fullest extent practicable, the Director will approve or disapprove an application for a waiver within 130 days of receipt of such application. The Director shall provide timely written notice of the reasons for denial to States whose applications are disapproved.

[60 FR 33604, June 28, 1995]

§ 400.301 Withdrawal from the refugee program.

(a) In the event that a State decides to cease participation in the refugee program, the State must provide 120 days advance notice to the Director before withdrawing from the program.

(b) To participate in the refugee program, a State is expected to operate all components of the refugee program, including refugee cash and medical assistance, social services, preventive health, and an unaccompanied minors program if appropriate. A State is also expected to play a coordinating role in the provision of assistance and services in accordance with § 400.5(b). In the event that a State wishes to retain responsibility for only part of the refugee program, it must obtain prior approval from the Director of ORR. Such approval will be granted if it is in the best interest of the Government.

(c) When a State withdraws from all or part of the refugee program, the Director may authorize a replacement designee or designees to administer the provision of assistance and services, as appropriate, to refugees in that State. A replacement designee must adhere to the same regulations under this part that apply to a State-administered program, with the exception of the following provisions: 45 CFR 400.5(d), 400.7, 400.51(b)(2)(i), 400.58(c), 400.94(a), 400.94(b), 400.94(c), and subpart L. Replacement designees must also adhere to the Subpart L regulations regarding formula allocation grants for targeted assistance, if the State authorized the replacement designee appointed by the Director to act as its agent in applying for and receiving targeted assistance funds. Certain provisions are excepted because they apply only to States and become moot when a State withdraws from participation in the refugee program and is replaced by another entity. States would continue to be responsible for administering the other excepted provisions because these provisions refer to the administration of other State-run public assistance programs.

[60 FR 33604, June 28, 1995, as amended at 65 FR 15450, Mar. 22, 2000]

Subpart L—Targeted Assistance

SOURCE: 60 FR 33604, June 28, 1995, unless otherwise noted.

§ 400.310 Basis and scope.

This subpart sets forth requirements concerning formula allocation grants to States under section 412(c)(2) of the Act for targeted assistance.

§ 400.311 Definitions.

For purposes of this subpart—

"Targeted assistance grants" means formula allocation funding to States for assistance to counties and similar areas in the States where, because of factors such as unusually large refugee populations (including secondary migration), high refugee concentrations, and high use of public assistance by refugees, there exists and can be demonstrated a specific need for supplementation of available resources for services to refugees.

§ 400.312 Opportunity to apply for services.

A State must provide any individual wishing to do so an opportunity to apply for targeted assistance services and determine the eligibility of each applicant.

FUNDING AND SERVICE PRIORITIES

§ 400.313 Use of funds.

A State must use its targeted assistance funds primarily for employability services designed to enable refugees to obtain jobs with less than one year's participation in the targeted assistance program in order to achieve economic self-sufficiency as soon as possible. Targeted assistance services may continue to be provided after a refugee has entered a job to help the refugee retain employment or move to a better job. Targeted assistance funds may not be used for long-term training programs such as vocational training that last for more than a year or educational programs that are not intended to lead to employment within a year.

§ 400.314 Priority in provision of services.

A State must plan its targeted assistance program and allocate its targeted assistance funds in such a manner that services are provided to refugees in the following order of priority, except in certain individual extreme circumstances:

(a) Cash assistance recipients, particularly long-term recipients;

(b) Unemployed refugees who are not receiving cash assistance; and

(c) Employed refugees in need of services to retain employment or to attain economic independence.

§ 400.315 General eligibility requirements.

(a) For purposes of determining eligibility of refugees for services under this subpart, the same standards and criteria shall be applied as are applied in the determination of eligibility for refugee social services under §§ 400.150 and 400.152(a).

(b) A State may not provide services under this subpart, except for referral and interpreter services, to refugees who have been in the United States for more than 60 months, except that refugees who are receiving employability services, as defined in § 400.316, as of September 30, 1995, as part of an employability plan, may continue to receive those services through September 30, 1996, or until the services are completed, whichever occurs first, regardless of their length of residence in the U.S.

§ 400.316 Scope of targeted assistance services.

A State may provide the same scope of services under this subpart as may be provided to refugees under §§ 400.154 and 400.155, with the exception of § 400.155(h).

§ 400.317 Service requirements.

In providing targeted assistance services to refugees, a State must adhere to the same requirements as are applied to the provision of refugee social services under § 400.156.

§ 400.318 Eligible grantees.

Eligible grantees are those agencies of State governments which are responsible for the refugee program under 45 CFR 400.5 in States containing counties which qualify for targeted assistance awards. The use of targeted assistance funds for services to Cuban and Haitian entrants is limited to States which have an approved State plan under the Cuban/Haitian Entrant Program (CHEP).

§ 400.319 Allocation of funds.

(a) A State with more than one qualifying targeted assistance county may allocate its targeted assistance funds differently from the formula allocations for counties presented in the ORR targeted assistance notice in a fiscal year only on the basis of its population of refugees who arrived in the U.S. during the most recent 5-year period. A State may use welfare data as an additional factor in the allocation of targeted assistance funds if it so chooses; however, a State may not assign a greater weight to welfare data than it has assigned to population data in its allocation formula.

(b) A State must assure that not less than 95 percent of the total award to the State is made available to the qualified county or counties, except in those cases where the qualified county or counties have agreed to let the State administer the targeted assistance program in the county's stead.

PART 401—CUBAN/HAITIAN ENTRANT PROGRAM

AUTHORITY: Sec. 501(a), Pub. L. 96–422, 94 Stat. 1810 (8 U.S.C. 1522 note); Executive Order 12341 (January 21, 1982).

SOURCE: 47 FR 10850, Mar. 12, 1982, unless otherwise noted.

§401.1 [Reserved]

§401.2 Definitions.

For purposes of this part a *Cuban and Haitian entrant* or *entrant* is defined as:

(a) Any individual granted parole status as a Cuban/Haitian Entrant (Status Pending) or granted any other special status subsequently established under the immigration laws for nationals of Cuba or Haiti, regardless of the status of the individual at the time assistance or services are provided; and

(b) Any other national of Cuba or Haiti

(1) Who:

(i) Was paroled into the United States and has not acquired any other status under the Immigration and Nationality Act;

(ii) Is the subject of exclusion or deportation proceedings under the Immigration and Nationality Act; or

(iii) Has an application for asylum pending with the Immigration and Naturalization Service; and

(2) With respect to whom a final, nonappealable, and legally enforceable order of deportation or exclusion has not been entered.

§§401.3–401.11 [Reserved]

§401.12 Cuban and Haitian entrant cash and medical assistance.

Except as may be otherwise provided in this section, cash and medical assistance shall be provided to Cuban and Haitian entrants by the same agencies, under the same conditions, and to the same extent as such assistance is provided to refugees under part 400 of this title.

(a) For purposes of determining the eligibility of Cuban and Haitian entrants for cash and medical assistance under this section and the amount of assistance for which they are eligible under this section, the same standards and criteria shall be applied as are applied in the determination of eligibility for an amount of cash and medical assistance for refugees under subparts E and G of part 400 of this title.

(b) Federal reimbursement will be provided to States for the costs of providing cash and medical assistance (and related administrative costs) to Cuban and Haitian entrants according to procedures and requirements, including procedures and requirements relating to the submission and approval of a State plan, identical to those applicable to the Refugee Program and set forth in part 400 of this title.

(c) The number of months during which an entrant may be eligible for cash and medical assistance for which Federal reimbursement is available under this section shall be counted starting with the first month in which an individual meeting the definition of a Cuban and Haitian entrant in §401.2 was first issued documentation by the Immigration and Naturalization Service indicating:

(1) That the entrant has been granted parole by the Attorney General under the Immigration and Nationality Act,

(2) That the entrant is in a voluntary departure status, or

(3) That the entrant's residence in a United States community is known to the Immigration and Naturalization Service.

The amendments are to be issued under the authority contained in section 412(a)(9), Immigration and Nationality Act (8 U.S.C. 1522(a)(9)).

[47 FR 10850, Mar. 12, 1982, as amended at 65 FR 15450, Mar. 22, 2000]

PART 402—STATE LEGALIZATION IMPACT ASSISTANCE GRANTS

AUTHORITY: 8 U.S.C. 1255a note, as amended.

SOURCE: 53 FR 7858, Mar. 10, 1988, unless otherwise noted.

Subpart A—Introduction

§ 402.1 General.

(a) These regulations implement section 204 of Pub. L. 99–603, the Immigration Reform and Control Act of 1986 (IRCA), as amended. This act establishes a temporary program of State Legalization Impact Assistance Grants (SLIAG) for States. The purpose of SLIAG is to lessen the financial impact on State and local governments resulting from the adjustment of immigration status under the Act of certain groups of aliens residing in the States, the District of Columbia, Puerto Rico, the Virgin Islands, and Guam.

(b) Funds appropriated by section 204 may be applied by States with approved applications to certain State and local government costs incurred:

(1) In providing public assistance and public health assistance to eligible legalized aliens,

(2) For making payments to State educational agencies for the purpose of assisting local educational agencies in providing certain educational services to eligible legalized aliens,

(3) To provide public education and outreach to lawful temporary resident aliens concerning the adjustment to lawful permanent resident status and other matters,

(4) To make payments for education and outreach efforts by State agencies regarding unfair discrimination in employment practices based on national origin or citizenship status, and

(5) To administer the funds provided under this part.

[56 FR 21246, May 7, 1991]

§ 402.2 Definitions.

As used in this part—

The Act means the Immigration Reform and Control Act of 1986, Public Law 99–603, as amended.

Allocation means an amount designated for a State, as determined under § 402.31, § 402.33, or § 402.34.

Allotment means the total amount awarded to a State, as determined under § 402.31, § 402.33, or § 402.34.

Department means the U.S. Department of Health and Human Services.

Educational Services means:

(1) For eligible legalized aliens regardless of age enrolled in elementary or secondary school, services allowable under section 607 of the Emergency Immigrant Education Act, 20 U.S.C. 4101, *et seq.* (Pub. L. 98–511), as in effect on November 6, 1986.

(2) For adult eligible legalized aliens:

(i) Services authorized under the Adult Education Act, 20 U.S.C. 1201 *et seq.* (Pub. L. 89–750, as amended), as in effect November 6, 1986, and

(ii) English language and other programs designed to enable eligible legalized aliens to attain the citizenship skills required by section 245A(b)(1)(D)(i) of the INA.

Eligible legalized alien means an alien whose status has been adjusted to lawful temporary resident under section 245A, 210, or 210A of the Immigration and Nationality Act, beginning on the effective date of such adjustment as established by the Immigration and Naturalization Service, and continuing until the end of the five-year period beginning on the effective date of such adjustment, provided that during that time the alien remains in lawful temporary or permanent resident status granted under the Act.

Employment discrimination education and outreach means education and outreach efforts by State agencies regarding unfair discrimination in employment practices based on national origin or citizenship status.

INA means the Immigration and Nationality Act, 8 U.S.C. 1101, *et seq.*

Local educational agency means—

(a) A public board of education or other public authority legally constituted within a State for either administrative control of or direction of, or to perform service functions for, public elementary or secondary schools in—

(1) A city, county, township, school district, or other political subdivision of a State; or

(2) Such combination of school districts or counties a State recognizes as an administrative agency for its public elementary or secondary schools; or

(b) Any other public institution or agency that has administrative control and direction of a public elementary or secondary school.

Local government has the same meaning as in 45 CFR part 92.

Nonpublic, as applied to an agency, organization, or institution, means that the agency, organization, or institution is nonprofit and is not under Federal or public supervision or control.

Phase II outreach means public education and outreach (including the provision of information to individuals) to inform temporary resident aliens under section 210, 210A, 245A of the INA and aliens whose applications for such status are pending with the Immigration and Naturalization Service regarding:

(1) The requirements of sections 210, 210A, and 245A of the INA regarding the adjustment of resident status;

(2) Sources of assistance for such aliens obtaining the adjustment of status described in paragraph (1) of this definition, including educational, informational, and referral services, and the rights and responsibilities of such aliens and aliens lawfully admitted for permanent residence;

(3) The identification of health, employment, and social services; and,

(4) The importance of identifying oneself as a temporary resident alien to service providers.

Program administrative costs means those costs associated with administering public assistance, public health assistance, educational services, Phase II outreach, and employment discrimination education and outreach activities.

Public, as applied to an agency, organization, or institution, means that the agency, organization, or institution is under the administrative supervision or control of a government other than the Federal Government.

Public assistance means cash, medical, or other assistance provided to meet the basic subsistence needs or health needs of individuals.

(1) That is generally available to needy individuals residing in a State and

(2) That is provided with funds from units of State or local government.

As used in this definition, basic subsistence needs are minimal living requirements, including food, shelter and clothing. For purposes of this definition, assistance is considered to have been provided to needy individuals if specified income or resource requirements are used to determine eligibility or the amount of a fee or other charges to be paid for services. *Other assistance* means assistance and services, other than cash or medical assistance, that are directed at meeting basic subsistence needs, and that meet all of the criteria in this definition. *Other assistance* also means assistance and services in which participation is required as a condition of receipt of cash or medical assistance.

Public health assistance means health services (1) that are generally available to needy individuals residing in a State; (2) that receive funding from units of State or local government; and, (3) that are provided for the primary purpose of protecting the health of the general public, including, but not limited to, immunizations for immunizable diseases, testing and treatment for tuberculosis and sexually-transmitted diseases, and family planning services.

Recipient means grantee or subgrantee.

Secretary means the Secretary of the Department of Health and Human Services.

SLIAG administrative costs means the direct and indirect costs related to administration of funds provided under this part, including: planning and conferring with local officials, preparing the application, audits, allocation of funds, tracking and recordkeeping, monitoring use of funds, and reporting.

SLIAG-reimbursable activity means programs of public assistance, programs of public health assistance, educational services, employment discrimination education and outreach, Phase II outreach, program administrative costs, and SLIAG administrative costs, as those terms are defined in this part, that are included in a State's application approved pursuant to subpart E of this part.

SLIAG-related costs means expenditures made: To provide public assistance, public health assistance, or educational services, as defined in this part, to eligible legalized aliens; to provide public health assistance to aliens applying on a timely basis to become lawful temporary residents under sections 210, 210A, or 245A of the INA during such time as that alien's application with INS is pending approval; to provide employment discrimination education and outreach, as defined in this part; to provide Phase II outreach, as defined in this part; and for SLIAG administrative costs, as defined in this part. SLIAG-related costs include all allowable expenditures, including program administrative costs determined in accordance with § 402.21(c), regardless of whether those expenditures actually are reimbursed or paid for with funds allotted to the State under this part. SLIAG-related costs for educational services, Phase II outreach, and employment discrimination education and outreach are limited to the amount of payment that can be made under the Act for those activities, as described in § 402.11 (e), (k) and (l), respectively. SLIAG-related costs exclude: (1) Expenditures by a State or local government for costs which are reimbursed or paid for by Federal programs other than SLIAG; and (2) program income (as defined in 45 CFR 74.42 or 45 CFR 92.25(b), as applicable) received from or on behalf of eligible legalized aliens receiving services or benefits for which payment or reimbursement may be made under this part.

State means the 50 States, the District of Columbia, Puerto Rico, Guam, and the Virgin Islands of the United States.

State educational agency means—

(1) The State board of education or other agency or officer primarily responsible for the supervision of public elementary and secondary schools in a State. In the absence of this officer or agency, it is an officer or agency designated by the Governor or State law; or

(2) The State board of education or other agency or officer primarily responsible for the State supervision of public elementary and secondary schools; or if there is a separate State agency or officer primarily responsible for supervision of adult education in public schools, then that agency or officer may be designated for the purpose of the Act by the Governor or by State law. If no agency or officer qualifies under the preceding sentence, the term means an appropriate agency or officer

designated for the purpose of the Act by the Governor.

Unexpended funds means the amount by which allotments awarded to a State, as determined under §402.31 and §402.33 of this part, exceed the State's SLIAG-related costs, as defined in this part, reported in annual reports pursuant to §402.51 and accepted by the Department as of March 15, 1995.

Unreimbursed SLIAG-related costs means the amount by which a State's total SLIAG-related costs, as defined in this part, reported in annual reports pursuant to §402.51 and accepted by the Department as of March 15, 1995, exceed the allotments awarded to a State, as determined under §402.31 and §402.33 of this part.

[53 FR 7858, Mar. 10, 1988, as amended at 56 FR 19808, Apr. 30, 1991; 56 FR 21246, May 7, 1991; 59 FR 65726, Dec. 21, 1994]

Subpart B—Use of Funds

§402.10 Allowable use of funds.

(a) Funds provided under §402.31 and 402.33 of this part for a fiscal year may be used only with respect to SLIAG-related costs incurred in that fiscal year or succeeding fiscal years, except that funds provided for FY 1993 and FY 1994 may be used for SLIAG-related costs incurred in FY 1990 or succeeding years. Funds provided under §402.34 of this part may be used with respect to SLIAG-related costs incurred in any fiscal year of the program. Funds may be used, subject to §§402.11 and 402.26, for the following activities, as defined in this part:

(1) Public assistance;

(2) Public health assistance;

(3) Educational services;

(4) Employment discrimination education and outreach;

(5) Phase II outreach;

(6) SLIAG administrative costs; and

(7) Program administrative costs.

(b) Unless specifically prohibited by a statute enacted subsequent to November 6, 1986, a State may use SLIAG funds to pay the non-Federal share of costs allowable under (a) of this section incurred in providing assistance or services to eligible legalized aliens under Federal programs that have a matching or cost-sharing requirement, subject to the provisions of §402.11(f) of this part.

(c) [Reserved]

(d) Except as provided for in §402.11(n), funds awarded under this part may be used to reimburse or pay SLIAG-related costs incurred prior to the approval of a State's application or amendment to its application, pursuant to subpart E of this part, provided that such reimbursement or payment is consistent with the Act and this part.

[53 FR 7858, Mar. 10, 1988, as amended at 56 FR 19808, Apr. 30, 1991; 56 FR 21246, May 7, 1991; 59 FR 65726, Dec. 21, 1994]

§402.11 Limitations on Use of SLIAG Funds.

(a) Funds provided under this part may be used only for SLIAG-reimbursable activities that—

(1) Meet the definitions of §402.2 of this part; and

(2) Are otherwise consistent with the rules and procedures governing such activities.

(b) Funds provided under this part may not be used for costs to the extent that those costs are otherwise reimbursed or paid for under other Federal programs.

(c) The amount of reimbursement or payment may not exceed 100% of SLIAG-related costs, as defined in this part, associated with SLIAG-reimbursable activites.

(d) A State must use a minimum of 10 percent of its allotment under this part in any fiscal year for costs associated with each of the following program categories: public assistance, public health assistance, and educational services. In the event that a State does not require use of a full 10% in one of the above categories, it must allocate the unused portion equally among the remaining categories listed in this paragraph.

(e) Payments for educational services in any fiscal year may not exceed the amounts described in (e) (3), (4) and (5) of this section, and are subject to the limitations in (e) (1), (2), and (6) of this section.

(1) Payments may be made to a local educational agency in a fiscal year for the purpose of providing educational

services to eligible legalized aliens enrolled in elementary or secondary school only if 500 eligible legalized aliens meeting the conditions in (e)(2) of this section, are enrolled in elementary or secondary public or non-public schools in that local educational agency's jurisdiction in that fiscal year or if such eligible legalized aliens represent at least 3 percent of the total number of students enrolled in elementary or secondary public or non-public schools within that local educational agency's jurisdiction in that fiscal year.

(2) In computing payments to local education agencies or to providers of educational services described in section 204(c)(3)(C) of the Act, State educational agencies may take into account only eligible legalized aliens who have been enrolled in elementary or secondary school, public or non-public school or in educational activities for adults described in § 402.2 in the United States for fewer than three complete academic years.

(3) The amount that may be paid in any fiscal year to a local educational agency with respect to eligible legalized aliens enrolled in elementary and secondary public or non-public school may not exceed an amount equal to $500 (less, in States receiving Emergency Immigrant Education Act (EIEA) funds, the amount described in (e)(6) of this section) multiplied by the number of eligible legalized aliens meeting the criteria specified in (e)(2) of this section, who are enrolled in public or private non-profit elementary and secondary schools in the jurisdiction of that local educational agency in that fiscal year.

(4) The amount that may be paid in any fiscal year to a local educational agency or other provider of educational services for adults (who are not enrolled in elementary or secondary school), as described in section 204(c)(3)(C) of the Act, may not exceed an amount equal to $500 multiplied by the number of eligible legalized aliens meeting the criteria in paragraph (e)(2) of this section who receive educational services from that provider in that fiscal year.

(5) In no event may the amount paid to a local education agency or other provider of educational services exceed the actual costs of providing those services to eligible legalized aliens, as determined in accordance with 45 CFR part 74 (for grants awarded in FY 1988) or 45 CFR part 92 (for grants awarded in FY 1989 and succeeding fiscal years).

(6) The maximum amount of payment to a local educational agency with respect to eligible legalized aliens enrolled in elementary and secondary school will be reduced from the amount described in (e)(3) of this section, by an amount equal to the amount of funds received by the local educational agency with respect to such eligible legalized aliens pursuant to section 606 of the Emergency Immigrant Education Act.

(f) Funds provided under this part may not be used to provide assistance under the programs of financial assistance from which eligible legalized aliens are barred by section 245A(h)(1), 210(f), or 210A(d)(6) of the INA. However, such funds may be used for the State and local share of the costs of providing such assistance to eligible legalized aliens who are excepted from the bar by section 245A(h) (2) or (3), 210(f), or 210A(d)(6) of the INA, provided that such individuals are otherwise eligible for benefits under such programs, and that the costs of providing those benefits are otherwise allowable under the Act, this regulation, and the State's approved application.

(g) Funds provided under this part shall not be used to perform abortions except where the life of the mother would be endangered if the fetus were carrier to term.

(h) Funds provided under this part shall not be used to reimburse or pay costs inurred by any public or private entity or any individual, in the conduct of a medical examination as required for application for adjustment to lawful temporary resident status under 8 CFR 245a.2(i), 8 CFR 210.2(d), or 8 CFR 210a.6(f).

(i) Funds provided under this part shall not be used for client counselling or any other service which would assume responsibility for the adjustment of status of aliens to that of lawful temporary or permanent residence. This prohibition includes assisting an alien to appeal INS decisions or representation of an alien before any administrative or judicial body.

(j) Funds under this part shall not be used to investigate or prosecute discrimination complaints beyond initial intake and referral, to pay legal fees or other expenses incurred to provide legal counsel to a party alleging discrimination, or to represent such parties before any administrative or judicial body.

(k) A State may use funds to make payments for Phase II outreach activities, including related program administration, from allotments made to it under this part for FY 1989 and succeeding fiscal years. The maximum amount that a State may use for this purpose from a fiscal year's allotment is the greater of 1% of its allotment for that fiscal year or $100,000.

(l) A State may use funds to make payments for employment discrimination education and outreach activities, including related program administration, from allotments made to it under this part for FY 1989 and succeeding fiscal years. The maximum amount that a State may use from a fiscal year's allotment for this purpose is the greater of 1% of the State's allotment for that fiscal year or $100,000.

(m) [Reserved]

(n)(1) Except as provided for in paragraph (n)(2) of this section, a State may use SLIAG funds alloted to it for a fiscal year to reimburse or pay only those SLIAG-related costs for employment discrimination education and outreach activities which occurred after approval by the Department of an application or amendment describing those activities, as required by §402.41(d).

(2) Costs incurred in FY 1990 prior to approval by the Department of an application or amendment containing the information required by §402.41(d), but after December 18, 1989, for reproduction and dissemination of public information material certified by the Office of the Special Counsel for Immigration-Related Unfair Employment Practices, Department of Justice (hereafter, "Office of the Special Counsel"), pursuant to paragraph (o) of this section may be reimbursed with funds allotted under this part.

(o)(1) With respect to employment discrimination education and outreach, a State shall not use SLIAG funds to pay for the cost of producing or distributing materials prepared for public dissemination unless the Office of the Special Counsel has certified that those materials meet the criteria in paragraph (o)(2) of this section.

(2) Certification of materials described in paragraph (o)(1) of this section shall consist of a finding by the Office of the Special Counsel that information contained in such materials relating to the discrimination provision of the Act is legally accurate and that those materials include reference to the Office of the Special Counsel as a source of information and referral for complaints of discrimination based on citizenship status or national origin. Information regarding the Office of the Special Counsel shall include its address and telephone number, including the toll-free number and toll-free TDD number for the hearing impaired. The Office of the Special Counsel, in the exercise of discretion, may agree to the deletion of any portion of the information referenced in the previous sentence, in those instances where space limitations in printed materials, or time limitations in electronically recorded materials, make inclusion of all the required information impractical.

(p) Funds provided under this part may be used only for SLIAG-related costs submitted to the Department pursuant to §402.51 and accepted as allowable costs by March 15, 1995.

(q) Funds made available to a State pursuant to §402.34 shall be utilized by the State to reimburse all allowable costs within 90 days after such State has received a reallocation of funds from the Secretary, but in no event later than July 31, 1995.

[53 FR 7858, Mar. 10, 1991, as amended at 56 FR 19808, Apr. 30, 1991; 56 FR 21247, May 7, 1991; 59 FR 65726, Dec. 21, 1994]

§402.12 Use of SLIAG Funds for Costs Incurred Prior to October 1, 1987.

(a) Except as indicated in (b) and (c) of this section, States may not use funds provided under this part of costs incurred prior to October 1, 1987.

(b) A State may use funds provided under this part for administrative costs incurred prior to October 1, 1987, but after November 6, 1986, that are directly associated with implementation of this part. Such costs may include planning, preparing the application, establishing fund accounting and reporting systems, data development associated with the application, and other costs directly resulting from planning for implementation of this part.

(c) A State may use funds provided under this part for costs incurred prior to October 1, 1987, but after November 6, 1986, in providing public health assistance to eligible legalized aliens and to applicants for lawful temporary residence under sections 210, 210A and 245A of the INA, in conformity with the provisions of § 402.10(a).

[53 FR 7858, Mar. 10, 1988, as amended at 56 FR 21247, May 7, 1991]

Subpart C—Administration of Grants

§ 402.20 General provisions.

Except where otherwise required by Federal law, the Department rules codified at 45 CFR part 74 (for grants awarded in FY 1988) or 45 CFR part 92 (for grants awarded in FY 1989 and succeeding fiscal years), relating to the administration of grants, apply to funds awarded under this part. A State may, however, apply any or all provisions of part 92 to FY 1988 SLIAG funds.

[56 FR 19808, Apr. 30, 1991]

§ 402.21 Fiscal control.

(a) Fiscal control and accounting procedures must be sufficient to permit preparation of reports required by the Act, this regulation, and other applicable statutes and regulations.

(b) States must have accounting procedures in place which allow funds provided under this part to be traced from drawdown to allowable SLIAG-related costs. Allowability of the amount and purpose of expenditures must be established for each recipient of SLIAG funds. States must demonstrate that SLIAG-related costs, as defined in this part, incurred in SLIAG-reimbursable activities, equal or exceed the amount of SLIAG funds expended with respect to costs incurred in those activities. Documentation of the method of accounting and appropriate supporting information must be available for audit purposes and for Federal program reviews. To establish allowability of expenditures, States may use methods prescribed in (c) of this section. Alternatively, the State may use any other reliable method of cost calculation, subject to Federal review.

(c)(1) For public assistance, States may establish allowability by accounting for actual expenditures made to or on behalf of identifiable eligible legalized aliens who qualify for and receive assistance and/or services from the recipient, or by use of a statistically valid sampling of a recipient's public assistance caseload.

(2) For public health assistance, States may establish allowability by accounting for actual expenditures made to or on behalf of identifiable eligible legalized aliens, or applicants for lawful temporary resident status under sections 210, 210A, or 245A of the INA, who qualify for and receive such assistance and/or services, by use of a statistically valid sampling of clients in the public health system of the State or local government, or by using the ratio of eligible legalized aliens in a service population to all members of the relevant service population.

(3) For educational services, States must be able to demonstrate that:

(i) Funds provided under this part were used to provide educational services, as defined in this part, to eligible legalized aliens, as defined in this part; and,

(ii) Payments to local educational agencies or other providers of educational services, as described in section 204(c)(3)(C) of the Act, did not exceed the amounts described in § 402.11(e) of this part.

(4) With respect to Phase II outreach, as defined in this part, a State must demonstrate that the costs of activities that provide information directly to specific individuals are attributable only to lawful temporary residents under sections 210, 210A, or 245A of the INA, and applicants for such status whose applications were pending with the Immigration and Naturalization Service at the time information is provided. For Phase II outreach activities

that do not involve the provision of information directly to specific individuals, States must demonstrate that such activities are targeted predominantly to or intended primarily for lawful temporary residents under sections 210, 210A, or 245A of the INA or applicants for such status whose applications are pending with the Immigration and Naturalization Service at the time information is provided. The State must demonstrate that the amount of any fiscal year's allotment used for this purpose did not exceed the amount described in §402.11(k) and was consistent with the limitations of §402.11(i).

(5) With respect to employment discrimination education and outreach, as defined in this part, the State must demonstrate that funds were expended only for activities described in the State's approved application pursuant to §402.41(d) and the limitations of §402.11 (i), (n), and (o) and that the amount of any fiscal year's allotment used for this purpose did not exceed the amount described in §402.11(1).

(6)(i) For program administrative costs, as defined in this part, a State may establish allowability by use of the proportion of eligible legalized aliens provided assistance and/or services allowable under this part by a recipient, as defined in this part, relative to all persons provided such assistance and/or services; by use of the proportion of program or service costs actually incurred in providing assistance and/or services allowable under this part by a recipient, relative to all costs of providing the same assistance and/or services allowable under this part by the recipient; or by use of such other basis as will document that administrative costs incurred in providing such assistance and/or services and reimbursed under this part are allowable, allocable to SLIAG, and reasonable.

(ii) Consistent with section 604 of the Emergency Immigrant Education Act, of the amount paid to a State educational agency for educational services, only 1.5 percent may be used for administrative costs incurred by the State educational agency in carrying out its function under this part.

[53 FR 7858, Mar. 10, 1988, as amended at 56 FR 21247, May 7, 1991]

§402.22 [Reserved]

§402.23 Repayment.

The Department will order a State to repay amounts found not to have been expended in accordance with Federal law, regulations, the State's approved application, or terms of the State's grant. If a State refuses to repay such amounts, the Department may offset the amount against any other amount to which the State is or may become entitled under this part.

§402.24 Withholding.

After notice and opportunity for a hearing, the Secretary may withhold payment of funds to any State which is not using its allotment in accordance with the Act, these regulations, 45 CFR part 74 (for grants awarded in FY 1988) or 45 CFR part 92 (for grants awarded in FY 1989 and succeeding fiscal years), and terms of the grant award.

[56 FR 19808, Apr. 30, 1991]

§402.25 Appeals.

Appeals under this Subpart will be subject to 45 CFR part 16, Procedures of the Departmental Grant Appeals Board.

§402.26 Time period for obligation and expenditure of grant funds.

(a) Any amount awarded to a State for a fiscal year and remaining unobligated at the end of such year shall remain available to the State for obligation in subsequent fiscal years, but not after September 30, 1994. The funding period of a SLIAG grant begins on October 1 of the Federal fiscal year for which the allotment is made and ends on September 30, 1994.

(b) Obligations by the State of funds awarded under §402.31 and §402.33 must be liquidated within the time limit set by 45 CFR 92.23(b). This time limit will not be extended. The time limit established by 45 CFR 92.23(b) does not apply to funds awarded under §402.34.

[53 FR 7858, Mar. 10, 1988, as amended at 56 FR 19808, Apr. 30, 1991; 59 FR 65727, Dec. 21, 1994]

Subpart D—State Allocations

§ 402.30 Basis of awards.

The Secretary will award funds in a fiscal year under § 402.31 or § 402.33 to States with approved applications for that fiscal year in accordance with the apportionment of funds from the Office of Management and Budget. The Secretary will award funds under § 402.34 to States whose annual reports submitted pursuant to § 402.51 establish that their allowable SLIAG-related costs exceed the total of their allotments, as determined under § 402.31 and § 402.33. The grant award constitutes the authority to draw and expend funds for the purposes set forth in the Act and this regulation.

[53 FR 7858, Mar. 10, 1988, as amended at 59 FR 65727, Dec. 21, 1994]

§ 402.31 Determination of allocations.

(a) *Allocation formula.* Allocations will be computed according to a formula using the following factors and weights:

(1) 50 percent based on the State's eligible legalized alien population, with 49 percent based upon the number of eligible legalized aliens in a State relative to the number of such aliens in all States, and 1 percent to States which have higher-than-average ratios of eligible legalized aliens to total population relative to the average for all States, based on the proportional number of such aliens; and

(2) 50 percent based on the ratio of SLIAG-related costs in a State to the total of all such costs in all States.

(b) *Calculation of allocations.* (1) Each time the Department calculates State allocations, it will use the best data then available to the Secretary on the distribution of eligible legalized aliens by State.

(2) For all years except fiscal years 1993 and 1994, the Department will determine each State's SLIAG-related costs to be included in the computation of its allocation for a fiscal year by adding to the sum of SLIAG-related costs reported for all previous fiscal years by that State, pursuant to § 402.51(e) (1) and (2), the total amount of estimated SLIAG-related costs included in the State's approved application for that fiscal year, pursuant to § 402.41(c) (1) and (2). For fiscal years 1993 and 1994, the Department will add to the amount of estimated SLIAG-related costs included in the State's approved applications for fiscal years 1993 and 1994, respectively, the sum of SLIAG-related costs for all previous years ending with FY 1991 (for FY 1993 applications) or FY 1992 (for FY 1994 applications), and the first and second quarters of FY 1992 (for FY 1993 applications) or FY 1993 (for FY 1994 applications), pursuant to § 402.52(e)(4). In the event that a State has not submitted an approved report for a fiscal year, the Department will include no costs for that fiscal year in its calculation.

[53 FR 7858, Mar. 10, 1988, as amended at 56 FR 21248, May 7, 1991; 57 FR 19386, May 6, 1992; 58 FR 31913, June 7, 1993; 59 FR 65727, Dec. 21, 1994]

§ 402.32 Determination of state allotments.

Except as noted below, a State's allotment is the difference between the amount determined under § 402.31(b) of this regulation and the cumulative amount previously allotted to the State. In the event that the amount determined under § 402.31(b) is less than the cumulative amount previously allotted to a State, that State's allotment will be zero. The allotments of the remaining States would be calculated by multiplying the difference between the amount determined under § 402.31(b) of this regulation and the cumulative amount previously allotted to the State by the ratio of the amount of funds available for grants to States to the sum of the differences between the amounts determined under § 402.31(b) and the amounts previously awarded to those States.

[56 FR 21248, May 7, 1991]

§ 402.33 Allotment of excess funds.

If a State fails to qualify for an allotment in a particular fiscal year because it did not submit an approvable application by the deadline established in § 402.43 of this part, or is not allotted its designated allocation amount because it indicated in its application that it does not intend to use, in the fiscal year for which the application is made or in any succeeding fiscal year before FY 1995, the full amount of its allocation, funds which would otherwise have been allotted to the State in that fiscal year shall be allotted among the remaining States submitting timely approved applications in proportion to the amount that otherwise would have been allotted to such State in that fiscal year.

[56 FR 19808, Apr. 30, 1991]

§402.34 Allocation of unexpended funds.

(a) Any unexpended funds, as defined in this part, from allotments awarded to States under §402.31 and §402.33 of this part, will be allocated to States with unreimbursed SLIAG-related costs, as defined in this part.

(b) To determine the allocations, the ratio of each State's unreimbursed SLIAG-related costs to the total of all such costs in all States will be calculated. The ratio for each State with unreimbursed SLIAG-related costs will be multiplied by total unexpended funds to determine the allocation for each State. The amount allotted to a State will be the amount of the State's allocation under this section or the amount of the State's unreimbursed SLIAG-related costs, whichever is less.

[59 FR 65727, Dec. 21, 1994]

Subpart E—State Applications

§402.40 General.

In order to be eligible for funds available under §402.31 and §402.33 of this part in a fiscal year, a State must submit an annual application. A State's application must be approved by the Secretary prior to the award of funds to that State. In order to be eligible for funds under §402.34 of this part, a State must submit annual reports pursuant to §402.51 which establish that the State has incurred SLIAG-related costs in excess of the amount of the allotments it received under §402.31 and §402.33 of this part.

[53 FR 7858, Mar. 10, 1988, as amended at 59 FR 65727, Dec. 21, 1994]

§402.41 Application content.

A State application must:

(a) Contain certifications by the chief executive officer or an individual specifically designated to make such certifications on behalf of the chief executive officer that, notwithstanding other contents of the application, the State assures that:

(1) Funds allotted to the State will be used only to carry out the purposes described in the Act and this part.

(2) The State will provide a fair method for the allocation of funds among State and local agencies (as determined by the State) in accordance with the information in the application as required under (b) and (c) of this section and in accordance with the provisions of §402.11(d) of this part, which sets forth minimum funding levels for program categories.

(3) Fiscal control and accounting procedures used in the administration of SLIAG funds will be established that are adequate to meet the requirements established by the Act and this regulation.

(4) The State will comply with the prohibitions against discrimination on the basis of age under the Age Discrimination Act of 1975, on the basis of handicap under section 504 of the Rehabilitation Act of 1973, on the basis of sex under title IX of the Education Amendments of 1972, on the basis of race, color, or national origin under title VI of the Civil Rights Act of 1964, and on the basis of sex or religion under section 204(h)(1)(B) of the Immigration Reform and Control Act of 1986.

(b) Contain information on the number of eligible legalized aliens residing in the State. A State may either (1) adopt as its official State-level estimate the estimate of the State's number of eligible legalized aliens provided by the Department, or (2) provide its own estimate, including detailed information on the method and data used in deriving the estimate. If a State has previously provided this information to the Department, it need not be included in the application unless the information has changed.

(c) Contain an estimate of likely SLIAG-related costs for the fiscal year for which application is being made for each program or activity in which SLIAG-related costs will be incurred.

Programs and activities must be identified by the purposes listed in § 402.10(a). Such estimates for FY 1988 should include, as a discrete subset, costs incurred in FY 1987, pursuant to § 402.12.

(d) Contain the following information pertaining to the estimates required by paragraph (c) of this section (the application must include sufficient detail to permit assessment by the Department of the reasonableness of such estimates and the allowability of such costs under the Act and this part):

(1)(i) Descriptions of the programs and activities for which SLIAG-related costs will be incurred; and,

(ii) If a State elects to use its allotment for employment discrimination education and outreach, a description of the State's planned education and outreach activities, including: descriptions of the kinds of government or private agencies or other entities, if any, through which these activities will be conducted; brief descriptions of the targeted audience(s) for these activities; and, preproduction copies or the text of any material intended for distribution to the public to be produced or disseminated with SLIAG funds, if available at the time the application is submitted.

(2) Descriptions of the methodologies used to determine SLIAG-related cost. This description is to include (i) the methodology used in determining the proportion (or actual number) of eligible legalized aliens who are likely to participate in or benefit from the program or service, and (ii) a description of how a unit or other measure of the cost of providing services or benefits was calculated, or, if the estimate is based on actual cost data, a description of how the data were obtained. For SLIAG administrative costs, Phase II outreach, and employment discrimination education and outreach, the descriptions must instead include the basis for the estimate of SLIAG-related costs, as defined in this part.

(e) Contain information on the criteria for and administrative methods of disbursing funds received under this part.

(f) Designate a single point of contact (SPOC) in the State responsible for securing and submitting information required by the Act and this regulation and provide the name, title, mailing address, and telephone number of such official. If the grantee agency is different from the SPOC, also provide the name, title, mailing address, and telephone number of the official in that agency responsible for State administration of funds available under this part. In either case, provide the employer identification number of the grantee agency. If the State elects to use SLIAG funds for employment discrimination education and outreach, it must also designate in its application a contact person for this activity, if different from the single point of contact.

[53 FR 7858, May 7, 1991, as amended at 56 FR 21248, May 7, 1991; 56 FR 49707, Oct. 1, 1991]

§ 402.42 Application format.

A State may determine the format of its application as long as it contains all the information required by § 402.41.

§ 402.43 Application deadline.

(a) An application from a State for SLIAG funds for any Federal fiscal year except fiscal years 1993 and 1994 must be received by the Department by October 1 of that fiscal year. Applications for fiscal years 1993 and 1994 must be received by July 1, 1992, and July 1, 1993, respectively. If a State fails to submit an application by this date, funds which it may otherwise have been eligible to receive shall be distributed among States submitting timely approved applications in accordance with § 402.33 of this part.

(b) In order to receive funds under this part, a State's application for any fiscal year except fiscal years 1993 and 1994 must be approvable by the Secretary by December 15 of that fiscal year. Applications for fiscal years 1993 and 1994 must be approvable by the Secretary by September 15, 1992, and September 15, 1993, respectively. This may necessitate a State's providing clarification, revision, or additional material, as required, to render its application approvable by the Secretary. If a State fails to render its application approvable by the Secretary by these dates, funds which it may otherwise have been eligible to receive shall be distributed among States which have submitted approvable applications in accordance with § 402.32 of this part.

(Approved by the Office of Management and Budget under control number 0970–0079)

[53 FR 7858, Mar. 10, 1988, as amended at 54 FR 23984, June 5, 1989; 55 FR 26207, June 27, 1990; 56 FR 21248, May 7, 1991; 57 FR 19386, May 6, 1992; 58 FR 31913, June 7, 1993]

§ 402.44 Basis for approval.

(a) The Department will review each State's application to ensure that it contains all of the required assurances and information and otherwise is consistent with the Act and this part.

(b) The Department will assess the reasonableness of each State's estimates of SLIAG-related costs, as required by § 402.41(c) (1) and (2), based on the following:

(1) Are the activities for which estimates are included in the application allowable under the Act and this part?

(2) Are the rates of participation by eligible legalized aliens in the activities for which estimates of SLIAG-related costs are included in the application and other assumptions underlying the cost estimates based on reliable empirical data?

(3) To what extent are the estimates based on actual costs incurred? Are actual costs based on methodologies described in this part or other methodologies likely to result in valid measures of SLIAG-related costs?

(4) Do current estimates appear to be consistent with past estimates, known actual costs pursuant to § 402.41(c)(2), and current INS eligible legalized alien population data?

(5) Are revised estimates a result (all or in part) of changes in program activities?

(c) The Department will notify the State that (1) its application has been approved or (2) its application has been disapproved, together with the reasons for disapproval.

(d)(1) The Department will forward to the Office of Special Counsel information provided by a State pursuant to § 402.41(d).

(2) The Office of the Special Counsel will review information forwarded to it by the Department pursuant to paragraph (d) (1) of this section to determine whether the activities described therein conflict with or unnecessarily duplicate other employment discrimination education and outreach efforts. Certification to the Department by the Office of the Special Counsel that the State's submission meets this criterion is a prerequisite for approval by the Department.

[53 FR 7858, Mar. 10, 1988, as amended at 56 FR 21248, May 7, 1991]

§ 402.45 Amendments to applications.

(a)(1) If, during the course of a fiscal year, a State adds a program or activity for which it intends to claim reimbursement or make payment in that fiscal year, it must submit an amendment (containing appropriate information pursuant to § 402.41(c)) to its approved application for that fiscal year prior to the due date for reports required by § 402.51 of this part.

(2) If a State plans to initiate employment discrimination education and outreach activities not described in its application pursuant to § 402.41(d), it must submit an application amendment, which shall be reviewed in accordance with procedures described in § 402.41(d) of this part. The Department's approval of such an amendment is a prerequisite for the initiation of such new activities, except as provided for in § 402.11(n) (2).

(b) Except as provided for in § 402.11(k) and (n), a State may use SLIAG funds received for a fiscal year to reimburse or pay SLIAG related costs for programs or activities described in paragraph (a) of this section retroactive to the date the activity began, but no earlier than the first day of the fiscal year and only to the extent described in § 402.10(d), except that funds received in FY 1992, if any, may be used for costs incurred on or after October 1, 1989. Costs incurred prior to October 1, 1987, are allowable only to the extent described in § 402.12.

[53 FR 7858, Mar. 10, 1988, as amended at 56 FR 21249, May 7, 1991]

Subpart F—Recordkeeping and Reporting

§ 402.50 Recordkeeping.

A State must provide for the maintenance of such records as are necessary:

(a) To meet the requirements of the Act and Department regulations relating to retention of and access to records.

(b) To allow the State to provide to the Department (1) an accurate description of its activities undertaken with SLIAG funds, and (2) a complete record of the purposes for which SLIAG funds were spent, and of the recipients of such funds; and

(c) To allow the Department and auditors of the State to determine the extent to which SLIAG funds were expended consistent with the Act and this regulation.

§ 402.51 Reporting.

(a)(1) After the end of each Federal fiscal year through FY 1994 for which it received or during which it obligated or expended SLIAG funds and by the due date indicated below, a State must submit annual reports containing the information identified in (c) and (e) of this section. The reports are due no later than 90 days after the end of a Federal fiscal year.

(2) A State which receives funds pursuant to § 402.31 and § 402.33 and which expends funds pursuant to § 402.26(b) must submit a report containing the information identified in paragraph (e) of this section. The report is due no later than December 29, 1994.

(b)(1) Failure to submit the annual report required in (a) of this section by the deadline, without prior written permission from the Secretary, constitutes a basis for withholding of SLIAG funds.

(2) Failure by a State to submit the required information prior to the calculation of allocations pursuant to Subpart D will result in the Secretary's including no SLIAG-related costs for the fiscal year for that State in the calculation of State allocations.

(c) A State's annual report must provide information on the status of each fiscal year's funds, as of September 30, for the fiscal year for funds received under § 402.31 and § 402.33, including:

(1) Identification of the amount obligated and the amount expended by the State grantee agency;

(2) Identification of any amount remaining unobligated at the end of the fiscal year which the State intends to carry over to succeeding fiscal years; and,

(3) Identification of any amount remaining unobligated at the end of the fiscal year which the State does not desire to carry over to the succeeding fiscal year.

(d) A State must use SF–269 in its reporting under paragraph (c) of this section, but it may determine the format of its annual report content under paragraph (e) of this section.

(e)(1) For all years except fiscal years 1992 and 1993, a State's annual report must also provide the actual SLIAG-related costs incurred during the fiscal year. The report must provide, for each program or activity identified in the State's application, the amount of SLIAG-related costs, as defined in this part, incurred in that program or activity, identified as public assistance, public health assistance, educational services, Phase II outreach, employment discrimination education and outreach, and SLIAG administrative costs, as defined in this part, the amount of SLIAG funds obligated for that program or activity, and the time period for which the funds were obligated.

(2) The report must contain a description of the methodology used to determine actual SLIAG-related costs, if different from the description provided in the State's application pursuant to § 402.41 (d) (2) of this part.

(3) Federal and State costs of providing assistance under a State plan approved under title XIX of the Social Security Act to aliens whose status has been adjusted under sections 245A and 210A of the INA by virtue of the exceptions to the bar to Medicaid eligibility (sections 245A (h) (2) and (3) of the INA) must be shown separately in States' reports.

(4) For fiscal years 1992 and 1993, a State must report actual SLIAG-related costs, pursuant to paragraphs (e) (1), (2) and (3) of this section, for the first and second quarters, along with its application for SLIAG funding for fiscal years 1993 and 1994, respectively, in accordance with § 402.43(a) of this

part, and for the third and fourth quarters in accordance with paragraph (a) of this section.

(Approved by the Office of Management and Budget under control number 0970–0079)

[53 FR 7858, Mar. 10, 1988, as amended at 56 FR 21249, May 7, 1991; 57 FR 19386, May 6, 1992; 58 FR 31913, June 7, 1993; 59 FR 65727, Dec. 21, 1994]

PARTS 403–410 [RESERVED]

PART 411—STANDARDS TO PREVENT, DETECT, AND RESPOND TO SEXUAL ABUSE AND SEXUAL HARASSMENT INVOLVING UNACCOMPANIED CHILDREN

Subpart L—Audits and Corrective Action

AUTHORITY: 42 U.S.C. 15607 (d).

SOURCE: 79 FR 77789, Dec. 24, 2014, unless otherwise noted.

§411.5 General definitions.

For the purposes of this part, the following definitions apply:

ACF means the Administration for Children and Families.

Care provider facility means any ORR funded program that is licensed, certified, or accredited by an appropriate State or local agency to provide residential or group services to UCs, including a program of group homes or facilities for children with special needs or staff-secure services for children. Emergency care provider facilities are included in this definition but may or may not be licensed, certified, or accredited by an appropriate State or local agency.

Contractor means a person who, or entity that, provides services on a recurring basis pursuant to a contractual agreement with ORR or with a care provider facility or has a sub-contractual agreement with the contractor.

DHS means the Department of Homeland Security.

Director means the Director of the Office of Refugee Resettlement.

DOJ means the Department of Justice.

Emergency means a sudden, urgent, usually unexpected occurrence or occasion requiring immediate action.

Emergency care provider facility is a type of care provider facility that is temporarily opened to provide temporary emergency shelter and services for UCs during an influx. Emergency care provider facilities may or may not be licensed by an appropriate State or local agency.

Exigent circumstances means any set of temporary and unforeseen circumstances that require immediate action in order to combat a threat to the security of a care provider facility or a threat to the safety and security of any person.

Gender refers to the attitudes, feelings, and behaviors that a given culture associates with a person's biological sex.

Gender identity refers to one's sense of oneself as male, female, or transgender.

Gender nonconforming means a person whose appearance or manner does not conform to traditional societal gender expectations.

HHS means the Department of Health and Human Services.

Intersex means a person whose sexual or reproductive anatomy or chromosomal pattern does not seem to fit typical definitions of male or female. Intersex medical conditions are sometimes referred to as disorders of sex development.

Law enforcement means any local, State, or Federal enforcement agency with the authority and jurisdiction to investigate whether any criminal laws were violated.

LGBTQI means lesbian, gay, bisexual, transgender, questioning, or intersex.

Limited English proficient (LEP) means individuals for whom English is not the primary language and who may have a limited ability to read, write, speak, or understand English.

Medical practitioner means a health professional who, by virtue of education, credentials, and experience, is permitted by law to evaluate and care for patients within the scope of his or her professional practice. A "qualified medical practitioner" refers to a professional who also has successfully completed specialized training for treating sexual abuse victims.

Mental health practitioner means a mental health professional who, by virtue of education, credentials, and experience, is permitted by law to evaluate and care for patients within the scope of his or her professional practice. A "qualified mental health practitioner" refers to a professional who also has successfully completed specialized training for treating sexual abuse victims.

ORR refers to the Office of Refugee Resettlement.

Pat-down search means a sliding or patting of the hands over the clothed body of an unaccompanied child by staff to determine whether the individual possesses contraband.

Secure care provider facility is a type of care provider facility with a physically secure structure and staff responsible for controlling violent behavior. ORR uses a secure care provider facility as the most restrictive placement option for a UC who poses a danger to him or herself or others or has been charged with having committed a criminal offense. A secure care provider facility is a juvenile detention center.

Sex refers to a person's biological status and is typically categorized as male, female, or intersex. There are a number of indicators of biological sex, including sex chromosomes, gonads, internal reproductive organs, and external genitalia.

Sexual Assault Forensic Examiner (SAFE) means a "medical practitioner" who has specialized forensic training in treating sexual assault victims and conducting forensic medical examinations.

Sexual Assault Nurse Examiner (SANE) means a registered nurse who has specialized forensic training in treating sexual assault victims and conducting forensic medical examinations.

Special needs means mental and/or physical conditions that require special services and treatment by staff. A UC may have special needs due to a disability as defined in section 3 of the Americans with Disabilities Act of 1990, 42 U.S.C. 12102(2).

Staff means employees or contractors of ORR or a care provider facility, including any entity that operates within a care provider facility.

Strip search means a search that requires a person to remove or arrange some or all clothing so as to permit a visual inspection of the person's breasts, buttocks, or genitalia.

Substantiated allegation means an allegation that was investigated and determined to have occurred.

Traditional foster care means a type of care provider facility where a UC is placed with a family in a community-based setting. The State or locally licensed foster family is responsible for providing basic needs in addition to responsibilities as outlined by the State or local licensed child placement agency, State and local licensing regulations, and any ORR policies related to foster care. The UC attends public school and receives on-going case management and counseling services. The care provider facility facilitates the provision of additional psychiatric, psychological, or counseling referrals as needed. Traditional foster care may include transitional or short-term foster care as well as long-term foster care providers.

Transgender means a person whose gender identity (*i.e.*, internal sense of feeling male or female) is different from the person's assigned sex at birth.

Unaccompanied child (UC) means a child:

(1) Who has no lawful immigration status in the United States;

(2) Who has not attained 18 years of age; and

(3) With respect to whom there is no parent or legal guardian in the United States or there is no parent or legal guardian in the United States available to provide care and physical custody.

Unfounded allegation means an allegation that was investigated and determined not to have occurred.

Unsubstantiated allegation means an allegation that was investigated and the investigation produced insufficient evidence to make a final determination as to whether or not the event occurred.

Volunteer means an individual who donates time and effort on a recurring basis to enhance the activities and programs of ORR or the care provider facility.

Youth care worker means employees primarily responsible for the supervision and monitoring of UCs in housing units, educational areas, recreational areas, dining areas, and other program areas of a care provider facility.

§411.6 Definitions related to sexual abuse and sexual harassment.

For the purposes of this part, the following definitions apply:

Sexual abuse means—

(1) Sexual abuse of a UC by another UC; and

(2) Sexual abuse of a UC by a staff member, grantee, contractor, or volunteer.

Sexual abuse of a UC by another UC includes any of the following acts, if the victim does not consent, is coerced into such act by overt or implied threats of violence, or is unable to consent or refuse:

(1) Contact between the penis and the vulva or the penis and the anus, including penetration, however slight;

(2) Contact between the mouth and the penis, vulva, or anus;

(3) Penetration of the anal or genital opening of another person, however slight, by a hand, finger, object, or other instrument; and

(4) Any other intentional touching, either directly or through the clothing, of the genitalia, anus, groin, breast, inner thigh, or the buttocks of another person, excluding contact incidental to a physical altercation.

Sexual abuse of a UC by a staff member, grantee, contractor, or volunteer includes any of the following acts, with or without the consent of the UC:

(1) Contact between the penis and the vulva or the penis and the anus, including penetration, however slight;

(2) Contact between the mouth and the penis, vulva, or anus;

(3) Contact between the mouth and any body part where the staff member, contractor, or volunteer has the intent to abuse, arouse, or gratify sexual desire;

(4) Penetration of the anal or genital opening, however slight, by a hand, finger, object, or other instrument, that is unrelated to official duties or where the staff member, grantee, contractor, or volunteer has the intent to abuse, arouse, or gratify sexual desire;

(5) Any other intentional contact, either directly or through the clothing, of or with the genitalia, anus, groin, breast, inner thigh, or the buttocks, that is unrelated to official duties or where the staff member, grantee, contractor, or volunteer has the intent to abuse, arouse, or gratify sexual desire;

(6) Any attempt, threat, or request by a staff member, grantee, contractor, or volunteer to engage in the activities described in paragraphs (1) through (5) of this definition;

(7) Any display by a staff member, grantee, contractor, or volunteer of his or her uncovered genitalia, buttocks, or breast in the presence of a UC; and

(8) Voyeurism by a staff member, grantee, contactor, or volunteer.

Sexual harassment includes—

(1) Repeated and unwelcome sexual advances, requests for sexual favors, or verbal comments, gestures, phone calls, emails, texts, social media messages, pictures sent or shown, other electronic communication, or actions of a derogatory or offensive sexual nature by one UC towards another; and

(2) Repeated verbal comments, gestures, phone calls, emails, texts, social media messages, pictures sent or shown, or other electronic communication of a sexual nature to a UC by a staff member, grantee, contractor, or volunteer, including demeaning references to gender, sexually suggestive or derogatory comments about body or clothing, or obscene language or gestures.

Voyeurism by a staff member, grantee, contractor, or volunteer means an invasion of privacy of a UC by a staff member, grantee, contractor, or volunteer for reasons unrelated to official duties, such as inappropriately viewing a UC perform bodily functions or bathing; requiring a UC to expose his or her buttocks, genitals, or breasts; or recording images of all or part of a UC's naked body or of a UC performing bodily functions.

Subpart A—Coverage

§ 411.10 Coverage of ORR care provider facilities.

(a) This part applies to all ORR care provider facilities except secure care provider facilities and traditional foster care homes. Secure care provider facilities must, instead, follow the Department of Justice's National Standards to Prevent, Detect, and Respond to Prison Rape, 28 CFR part 115. Traditional foster care homes are not subject to this part.

(b) Emergency care provider facilities are subject to every section in this part except:

(1) Section 411.22(c);

(2) Section 411.71(b)(4);

(3) Section 411.101(b);

(4) Section 411.102(c), (d), and (e); and

(5) Subpart L.

(c) Emergency care provider facilities must implement the standards in this rule, excluding the standards listed above, within fifteen (15) days of opening. The Director, however, may, using unreviewable discretion, waive or modify specific sections for a particular emergency care provider facility for good cause. Good cause would only be found in cases where the temporary nature of the emergency care provider facility makes compliance with the provision impracticable or impossible, and the Director determines that the emergency care provider facility could not, without substantial difficulty, meet the provision in the absence of the waiver or modification.

(d) For the purposes of this part, the terms related to sexual abuse and sexual harassment refer specifically to the sexual abuse or sexual harassment of a UC that occurs at an ORR care provider facility while in ORR care and custody. Incidents of past sexual abuse or sexual harassment or sexual abuse or sexual harassment that occurs in any other context other than in ORR care and custody are not within the scope of this regulation.

Subpart B—Prevention Planning

§411.11 Zero tolerance toward sexual abuse and sexual harassment; Prevention of Sexual Abuse Coordinator and Compliance Manager.

(a) ORR must have a written policy mandating zero tolerance toward all forms of sexual abuse and sexual harassment and outlining ORR's approach to preventing, detecting, and responding to such conduct. ORR must ensure that all policies and services related to this rule are implemented in a culturally-sensitive and knowledgeable manner that is tailored for a diverse population.

(b) ORR must employ or designate an upper-level, ORR-wide Prevention of Sexual Abuse Coordinator (PSA Coordinator) with sufficient time and authority to develop, implement, and oversee ORR efforts to comply with these standards in all of its care provider facilities.

(c) Care provider facilities must have a written policy mandating zero tolerance toward all forms of sexual abuse and sexual harassment and outlining the care provider facility's approach to preventing, detecting, and responding to such conduct. The care provider facility also must ensure that all policies and services related to this rule are implemented in a culturally-sensitive and knowledgeable manner that is tailored for a diverse population. ORR will review and approve each care provider facility's written policy.

(d) Care provider facilities must employ or designate a Prevention of Sexual Abuse Compliance Manager (PSA Compliance Manager) with sufficient time and authority to develop, implement, and oversee the care provider facility's efforts to comply with the provisions set forth in this part and serve as a point of contact for ORR's PSA Coordinator.

§411.12 Contracting with or having a grant from ORR for the care of UCs.

(a) When contracting with or providing a grant to a care provider facility, ORR must include in any new contracts, contract renewals, cooperative agreements, or cooperative agreement renewals the entity's obligation to adopt and comply with these standards.

(b) For organizations that contract, grant, or have a sub-grant with a care provider facility to provide residential services to UCs, the organization must, as part of the contract or cooperative agreement, adopt and comply with the provisions set forth in this part.

(c) All new contracts, contract renewals, and grants must include provisions for monitoring and evaluation to ensure that the contractor, grantee, or sub-grantee is complying with these provisions.

§411.13 UC supervision and monitoring.

(a) Care provider facilities must develop, document, and make their best effort to comply with a staffing plan that provides for adequate levels of staffing, and, where applicable under State and local licensing standards, video monitoring, to protect UCs from sexual abuse and sexual harassment.

(b) In determining adequate levels of UC supervision and determining the need for video monitoring, the care provider facility must take into consideration the physical layout of the facility, the composition of the UC population, the prevalence of substantiated and unsubstantiated incidents of sexual abuse and sexual harassment, and any other relevant factors. Video monitoring equipment may not be placed in any bathroom, shower or bathing area, or other area where UCs routinely undress.

(c) Care provider facilities must conduct frequent unannounced rounds to identify and deter sexual abuse and sexual harassment. Such rounds must be implemented during night as well as day shifts. Care provider facilities must prohibit staff from alerting others that rounds are occurring, unless such announcement is related to the legitimate operational functions of the care provider facility.

§411.14 Limits to cross-gender viewing and searches.

(a) Cross-gender pat-down searches of UCs must not be conducted except in exigent circumstances. For a UC that identifies as transgender or intersex, the ORR care provider facility must ask the UC to identify the gender of staff with whom he/she would feel most comfortable conducting the search.

(b) All pat-down searches must be conducted in the presence of one additional care provider facility staff member unless there are exigent circumstances and must be documented and reported to ORR.

(c) Strip searches and visual body cavity searches of UCs are prohibited.

(d) Care provider facilities must permit UCs to shower, perform bodily functions, and change clothing without being viewed by staff, except: In exigent circumstances; when such viewing is incidental to routine room checks; is otherwise appropriate in connection with a medical examination or monitored bowel movement; if a UC is under age 6 and needs assistance with such activities; a UC with special needs is in need of assistance with such activities; or the UC requests and requires assistance. If the UC has special needs and requires assistance with such activities, the care provider facility staff member must be of the same gender as the UC when assisting with such activities.

(e) Care provider facilities must not search or physically examine a UC for the sole purpose of determining the UC's sex. If the UC's sex is unknown, it may be determined during conversations with the UC, by reviewing medical records, or, if necessary, learning that information as part of a broader medical examination conducted in private by a medical practitioner.

(f) Care provider facilities must train youth care worker staff in proper procedures for conducting pat-down searches, including cross-gender pat-down searches and searches of transgender and intersex UCs. All pat-down searches must be conducted in a professional and respectful manner, and in the least intrusive manner possible, consistent with security needs and existing ORR policy, including consideration of youth care worker staff safety.

§411.15 Accommodating UCs with disabilities and UCs who are limited English proficient (LEP).

(a) Care provider facilities must take appropriate steps to ensure that UCs with disabilities (including, for example, UCs who are deaf or hard of hearing, those who are blind or have low vision, or those who have intellectual, psychiatric, or speech disabilities) have an equal opportunity to participate in or benefit from all aspects of the care provider facility's efforts to prevent, detect, and respond to sexual abuse and sexual harassment. Such steps must include, when necessary to ensure effective communication with UCs who are deaf or hard of hearing, providing access to in-person, telephonic, or video interpretive services that enable effective, accurate, and impartial interpretation, both receptively and expressively, using any necessary specialized vocabulary. In addition, the care provider facility must ensure that any written materials related to sexual abuse and sexual harassment are translated and provided in formats or through methods that ensure effective communication with UCs with disabilities, including UCs who have intellectual disabilities, limited reading skills, or who are blind or have low vision.

(b) Care provider facilities must take appropriate steps to ensure that UCs who are limited English proficient have an equal opportunity to participate in or benefit from all aspects of the care provider facility's efforts to prevent, detect, and respond to sexual abuse and sexual harassment, including steps to provide quality in-person or telephonic interpretive services and quality translation services that enable effective, accurate, and impartial interpretation and translation, both receptively and expressively, using any necessary specialized vocabulary.

(c) In matters relating to allegations of sexual abuse or sexual harassment, the care provider facility must provide quality in-person or telephonic interpretation services that enable effective, accurate, and impartial interpretation by someone other than another UC. Care provider facilities also must ensure that any written materials related to sexual abuse and sexual harassment, including notification, orientation, and instruction not provided by ORR, are translated either verbally or in written form into the preferred languages of UCs.

§411.16 Hiring and promotion decisions.

(a) Care provider facilities are prohibited from hiring or promoting any individual who may have contact with UCs and must not enlist the services of any contractor or volunteer who may have contact with UCs and who engaged in: Sexual abuse in a prison, jail, holding facility, community confinement facility, juvenile facility, other institution (as defined in 42 U.S.C. 1997), or care provider facility; who was convicted of engaging or attempting to engage in sexual activity facilitated by force, overt or implied threats of force, or coercion, or if the victim did not consent or was unable to consent or refuse; or who was civilly or administratively adjudicated to have engaged in such activity.

(b) Care provider facilities considering hiring or promoting staff must ask all applicants who may have direct contact with UCs about previous misconduct described in paragraph (a) of this section in written applications or interviews for hiring or promotions and in any interviews or written self-evaluations conducted as part of performance evaluations of current employees. Care provider facilities also must impose upon employees a continuing affirmative duty to disclose any such misconduct, whether the conduct occurs on or off duty. Care provider facilities, consistent with law, must make their best efforts to contact all prior institutional employers of an applicant for employment to obtain information on substantiated allegations of sexual abuse or sexual harassment or any resignation during a pending investigation of alleged sexual abuse or sexual harassment.

(c) Prior to hiring new staff who may have contact with UCs, the care provider facility must conduct a background investigation to determine whether the candidate for hire is suitable for employment with minors in a residential setting. Upon ORR request, the care provider facility must submit all background investigation documentation for each staff member and the care provider facility's conclusions.

(d) Care provider facilities also must perform a background investigation before enlisting the services of any contractor or volunteer who may have contact with UCs. Upon ORR request, the care provider facility must submit all background investigation documentation for each contractor or volunteer and the care provider facility's conclusions.

(e) Care provider facilities must either conduct a criminal background records check at least every five years for current employees, contractors, and volunteers who may have contact with UCs or have in place a system for capturing the information contained in a criminal background records check for current employees.

(f) Material omissions regarding such misconduct or the provision of materially false information by the applicant or staff will be grounds for termination or withdrawal of an offer of employment, as appropriate.

(g) Unless prohibited by law, the care provider facility must provide information on substantiated allegations of sexual abuse or sexual harassment involving a former employee upon receiving a request from another care provider facility or institutional employer for whom such employee has applied to work.

(h) In the event the care provider facility contracts with an organization to provide residential services and/or other services to UCs, the requirements of this section also apply to the organization and its staff.

§411.17 Upgrades to facilities and technologies.

(a) When designing or acquiring any new facility and in planning any substantial expansion or modification of existing facilities, the care provider facility, as appropriate, must consider the effect of the design, acquisition, expansion, or modification upon their ability to protect UCs from sexual abuse and sexual harassment.

(b) When installing or updating a video monitoring system, electronic surveillance system, or other monitoring technology in a care provider facility, the care provider facility, as appropriate, must consider how such technology may enhance its ability to protect UCs from sexual abuse and sexual harassment while maintaining UC privacy and dignity.

Subpart C—Responsive Planning

§411.21 Victim advocacy, access to counselors, and forensic medical examinations.

(a) Care provider facilities must develop procedures to best utilize available community resources and services to provide valuable expertise and support in the areas of crisis intervention and counseling to most appropriately address victims' needs. Each care provider facility must establish procedures to make available outside victim services following incidents of sexual abuse and sexual harassment; the care provider facility must attempt to make available to the victim a victim advocate from a rape crisis center. If a rape crisis center is not available or if the UC prefers, the care provider facility may provide a licensed clinician on staff to provide crisis intervention and trauma services for the UC. The outside or internal victim advocate must provide emotional support, crisis intervention, information, and referrals.

(b) Where evidentiarily or medically appropriate, and only with the UC's consent, the care provider facility must arrange for an alleged victim UC to undergo a forensic medical examination as soon as possible and that is performed by Sexual Assault Forensic Examiners (SAFEs) or Sexual Assault Nurse Examiners (SANEs) where possible. If SAFEs or SANEs cannot be made available, the examination may be performed by a qualified medical practitioner.

(c) As requested by a victim, the presence of his or her outside or internal victim advocate, including any available victim advocacy services offered at a hospital conducting a forensic examination, must be allowed to the extent possible for support during a forensic examination and investigatory interviews.

(d) To the extent possible, care provider facilities must request that the investigating agency follow the requirements of paragraphs (a) through (c) of this section.

§411.22 Policies to ensure investigation of allegations and appropriate agency oversight.

(a) ORR and care provider facilities must ensure that each allegation of sexual abuse and sexual harassment, including a third-party or anonymous allegation, is immediately referred to all appropriate investigating authorities, including Child Protective Services, the State or local licensing agency, and law enforcement. Care provider facilities also must immediately report each allegation of sexual abuse and sexual harassment to ORR according to ORR policies and procedures. The care provider facility has an affirmative duty to keep abreast of the investigation(s) and cooperate with outside investigators. ORR also must remain informed of ongoing investigations and fully cooperate as necessary.

(b) Care provider facilities must maintain or attempt to enter into a written memorandum of understanding or other agreement specific to investigations of sexual abuse and sexual harassment with the law enforcement agency, designated State or local Child Protective Services, and/or the State or local licensing agencies responsible for conducting sexual abuse and sexual harassment investigations, as appropriate. Care provider facilities must maintain a copy of the agreement or documentation showing attempts to enter into an agreement.

(c) Care provider facilities must maintain documentation for at least ten years of all reports and referrals of allegations of sexual abuse and sexual harassment.

(d) ORR will refer an allegation of sexual abuse to the Department of Justice or other investigating authority for further investigation where such reporting is in accordance with its policies and procedures and any memoranda of understanding.

(e) All allegations of sexual abuse that occur at emergency care provider facilities operating on fully Federal properties must be reported to the Department of Justice in accordance with ORR policies and procedures and any memoranda of understanding.

Subpart D—Training and Education

§411.31 Care provider facility staff training.

(a) Care provider facilities must train or require the training of all employees who may have contact with UCs to be able to fulfill their responsibilities under these standards, including training on:

(1) ORR and the care provider facility's zero tolerance policies for all forms of sexual abuse and sexual harassment;

(2) The right of UCs and staff to be free from sexual abuse and sexual harassment and from retaliation for reporting sexual abuse and sexual harassment;

(3) Definitions and examples of prohibited and illegal sexual behavior;

(4) Recognition of situations where sexual abuse or sexual harassment may occur;

(5) Recognition of physical, behavioral, and emotional signs of sexual abuse and methods of preventing and responding to such occurrences;

(6) How to avoid inappropriate relationships with UCs;

(7) How to communicate effectively and professionally with UCs, including UCs who are lesbian, gay, bisexual, transgender, questioning, or intersex;

(8) Procedures for reporting knowledge or suspicion of sexual abuse and sexual harassment as well as how to comply with relevant laws related to mandatory reporting;

(9) The requirement to limit reporting of sexual abuse and sexual harassment to personnel with a need-to-know in order to make decisions concerning the victim's welfare and for law enforcement, investigative, or prosecutorial purposes;

(10) Cultural sensitivity toward diverse understandings of acceptable and unacceptable sexual behavior and appropriate terms and concepts to use when discussing sex, sexual abuse, and sexual harassment with a culturally diverse population;

(11) Sensitivity and awareness regarding past trauma that may have been experienced by UCs;

(12) Knowledge of all existing resources for UCs both inside and outside the care provider facility that provide treatment and counseling for trauma and legal advocacy for victims; and

(13) General cultural competency and sensitivity to the culture and age of UC.

(b) All current care provider facility staff and employees who may have contact with UCs must be trained within six months of the effective date of these standards, and care provider facilities must provide refresher information, as appropriate.

(c) Care provider facilities must document that staff and employees who may have contact with UCs have completed the training.

§411.32 Volunteer and contractor training.

(a) Care provider facilities must ensure that all volunteers and contractors who may have contact with UCs are trained on their responsibilities under ORR and the care provider facility's sexual abuse and sexual harassment prevention, detection, and response policies and procedures as well as any relevant Federal, State, and local laws.

(b) The level and type of training provided to volunteers and contractors may be based on the services they provide and the level of contact they will have with UCs, but all volunteers and contractors who have contact with UCs must be trained on the care provider facility's zero tolerance policies and procedures regarding sexual abuse and sexual harassment and informed how to report such incidents.

(c) Each care provider facility must maintain written documentation that contractors and volunteers who may have contact with UCs have completed the required trainings.

§411.33 UC education.

(a) During the intake process and periodically thereafter, each care provider facility must ensure that during orientation or a periodic refresher session, UCs are notified and informed of the care provider facility's zero tolerance policies for all forms of sexual abuse and sexual harassment in an age and culturally appropriate fashion and in accordance with §411.15 that includes, at a minimum:

(1) An explanation of the UC's right to be free from sexual abuse and sexual harassment as well as the UC's right to be free from retaliation for reporting such incidents;

(2) Definitions and examples of UC-on-UC sexual abuse, staff-on-UC sexual abuse, coercive sexual activity, appropriate and inappropriate relationships, and sexual harassment;

(3) An explanation of the methods for reporting sexual abuse and sexual harassment, including to any staff member, outside entity, and to ORR;

(4) An explanation of a UC's right to receive treatment and counseling if the UC was subjected to sexual abuse or sexual harassment;

(b) Care provider facilities must provide the UC notification, orientation, and instruction in formats accessible to all UCs at a time and in a manner that is separate from information provided about their immigration cases.

(c) Care provider facilities must document all UC participation in orientation and periodic refresher sessions that address the care provider facility's zero tolerance policies.

(d) Care provider facilities must post on all housing unit bulletin boards who a UC can contact if he or she is a victim or is believed to be at imminent risk of sexual abuse or sexual harassment in accordance with §411.15.

(e) Care provider facilities must make available and distribute a pamphlet in accordance with §411.15 that contains, at a minimum, the following:

(1) Notice of the care provider facility's zero-tolerance policy toward sexual abuse and sexual harassment;

(2) The care provider facility's policies and procedures related to sexual abuse and sexual harassment;

(3) Information on how to report an incident of sexual abuse or sexual harassment;

(4) The UC's rights and responsibilities related to sexual abuse and sexual harassment;

(5) How to contact organizations in the community that provide sexual abuse counseling and legal advocacy for UC victims of sexual abuse and sexual harassment;

(6) How to contact diplomatic or consular personnel.

§411.34 Specialized training: Medical and mental health care staff.

(a) All medical and mental health care staff employed or contracted by care provider facilities must be specially trained, at a minimum, on the following:

(1) How to detect and assess signs of sexual abuse and sexual harassment;

(2) How to respond effectively and professionally to victims of sexual abuse and sexual harassment;

(3) How and to whom to report allegations or suspicions of sexual abuse and sexual harassment; and

(4) How to preserve physical evidence of sexual abuse. If medical staff conduct forensic examinations, such medical staff must receive training to conduct such examinations.

(b) Care provider facilities must document that medical and mental health practitioners employed or contracted by the care provider facility received the training referenced in this section.

(c) Medical and mental health practitioners employed or contracted by the care provider facility also must receive the training mandated for employees under §411.31 or for contractors and volunteers under §411.32, depending on the practitioner's status at the care provider facility.

Subpart E—Assessment for Risk of Sexual Victimization and Abusiveness

§411.41 Assessment for risk of sexual victimization and abusiveness.

(a) Within 72 hours of a UC's arrival at a care provider facility and periodically throughout a UC's stay, the care provider facility must obtain and use information about each UC's personal history and behavior using a standardized screening instrument to reduce the risk of sexual abuse or sexual harassment by or upon a UC.

(b) The care provider facility must consider, at a minimum and to the extent that the information is available, the following criteria to assess UCs for risk of sexual victimization:

(1) Prior sexual victimization or abusiveness;

(2) Any gender nonconforming appearance or manner or Self-identification as lesbian, gay, bisexual, transgender, questioning, or intersex and whether the resident may therefore be vulnerable to sexual abuse or sexual harassment;

(3) Any current charges and offense history;

(4) Age;

(5) Any mental, physical, or developmental disability or illness;

(6) Level of emotional and cognitive development;

(7) Physical size and stature;

(8) The UC's own perception of vulnerability; and

(9) Any other specific information about an individual UC that may indicate heightened needs for supervision, additional safety precautions, or separation from certain other UCs.

(c) This information must be ascertained through conversations with the UC during the intake process and medical and mental health screenings; during classification assessments; and by reviewing court records, case files, care provider facility behavioral records, and other relevant documentation from the UC's files. Only trained staff are permitted to talk with UCs to gather information about their sexual orientation or gender identity, prior sexual victimization, history of engaging in sexual abuse, mental health status, and mental disabilities for the purposes of the assessment required under paragraph (a) of this section. Care provider facilities must provide UCs an opportunity to discuss any safety concerns or sensitive issues privately.

(d) The care provider facility must implement appropriate controls on the dissemination within the care provider facility of responses to questions asked pursuant to this standard in order to ensure that sensitive information is not exploited to the UC's detriment by staff or other UCs.

§411.42 Use of assessment information.

(a) The care provider facility must use the information from the risk assessment under §411.41 to inform assignment of UCs to housing, education, recreation, and other activities and services. The care provider facility must make individualized determinations about how to ensure the safety and health of each UC.

(b) Care provider facilities may not place UCs on one-on-one supervision as a result of the assessment completed in §411.41 unless there are exigent circumstances that require one-on-one supervision to keep the UC, other UCs, or staff safe, and then, only until an alternative means of keeping all residents and staff safe can be arranged. During any period of one-on-one supervision, a UC may not be denied any required services, including but not limited to daily large-muscle exercise, required educational programming, and social services, as reasonable under the circumstances. UCs on one-on-one supervision must receive daily visits from a medical practitioner or mental health care clinician as necessary unless the medical practitioner or mental health care clinician determines daily visits are not required. The medical practitioner or mental health care clinician, however, must continue to meet with the UC on a regular basis while the UC is on one-on-one supervision.

(c) When making assessment and housing assignments for a transgender or intersex UCs, the care provider facility must consider the UC's gender self-identification and an assessment of the effects of a housing assignment on the UC's health and safety. The care provider facility must consult a medical or mental health professional as soon as practicable on this assessment. The care provider facility must not base housing assignment decisions of transgender or intersex UCs solely on the identity documents or physical anatomy of the UC; a UC's self-identification of his/her gender and self-assessment of safety needs must always be taken into consideration as well. An identity document may include but is not limited to official U.S. and foreign government documentation, birth certificates, and other official documentation stating the UC's sex. The care provider facility's housing assignment of a transgender or intersex UCs must be consistent with the safety and security considerations of the care provider facility, State and local licensing standards, and housing and programming assignments of each transgender or intersex UCs must be regularly reassessed to review any threats to safety experienced by the UC.

Subpart F—Reporting

§411.51 UC reporting.

(a) The care provider facility must develop policies and procedures in accordance with §411.15 to ensure that UCs have multiple ways to report to the care provider: Sexual abuse and sexual harassment, retaliation for reporting sexual abuse or sexual harassment, and staff neglect or violations of responsibilities that may have contributed to such incidents. The care provider facility also must provide access to and instructions on how UCs may contact their consular official, ORR's headquarters, and an outside entity to report these incidents. Care provider facilities must provide UCs access to telephones with free, preprogrammed numbers for ORR headquarters and the outside entity designated under §411.51(b).

(b) The care provider facility must provide and inform the UC of at least one way for UCs to report sexual abuse and sexual harassment to an entity or office that is not part of the care provider facility and is able to receive and immediately forward UC reports of sexual abuse and sexual harassment to ORR officials, allowing UCs to remain anonymous upon request. The care provider facility must maintain or attempt to enter into a memorandum of understanding or other agreement with the entity or office and maintain copies of agreements or documentation showing attempts to enter into agreements.

(c) The care provider facility's policies and procedures must include provisions for staff to accept reports made verbally, in writing, anonymously, and from third parties. Staff must promptly document any verbal reports.

(d) All allegations or knowledge of sexual abuse and sexual harassment by staff or UCs must be immediately reported to the State or local licensing agency, the State or local Child Protective Services agency, State or local law enforcement, and to ORR according to ORR's policies and procedures.

§411.52 Grievances.

(a) The care provider facility must implement written policies and procedures for identifying and handling time-sensitive grievances that involve an immediate threat to UC health, safety, or welfare related to sexual abuse and sexual harassment. All such grievances must be reported to ORR according to ORR policies and procedures.

(b) The care provider facility's staff must bring medical emergencies to the immediate attention of proper medical and/or emergency services personnel for further assessment.

(c) The care provider facility must issue a written decision on the grievance within five days of receipt.

(d) To prepare a grievance, a UC may obtain assistance from another UC, care provider facility staff, family members, or legal representatives. Care provider facility staff must take reasonable steps to expedite requests for assistance from these other parties.

§411.53 UC access to outside confidential support services.

(a) Care provider facilities must utilize available community resources and services to provide valuable expertise and support in the areas of crisis intervention, counseling, investigation, and the prosecution of sexual abuse perpetrators to most appropriately address a sexual abuse victim's needs. The care provider facility must maintain or attempt to enter into memoranda of understanding or other agreements with community service providers, or if local providers are not available, with national organizations that provide legal advocacy and confidential emotional support services for immigrant victims of crime. The care provider facility must maintain copies of its agreements or documentation showing attempts to enter into such agreements.

(b) Care provider facilities must have written policies and procedures to include outside agencies in the care provider facility's sexual abuse and sexual harassment prevention and intervention protocols, if such resources are available.

(c) Care provider facilities must make available to UC information about local organizations that can assist UCs who are victims of sexual abuse and sexual harassment, including mailing addresses and telephone numbers (including toll-free hotline numbers where available). If no such local organizations exist, the care provider facility must make available the same information about national organizations. The care provider facility must enable reasonable communication between UCs and these organizations and agencies in a confidential manner and inform UCs, prior to giving them access, of the extent to which such communications will be confidential.

§411.54 Third-party reporting.

ORR must establish a method to receive third-party reports of sexual abuse and sexual harassment and must make available to the public information on how to report sexual abuse and sexual harassment on behalf of a UC.

§411.55 UC access to attorneys or other legal representatives and families.

(a) Care provider facilities must provide UCs confidential access to their attorney or other legal representative in accordance with the care provider's attorney-client visitation rules. The care provider's visitation rules must include provisions for immediate access in the case of an emergency or exigent circumstance. The care provider's attorney-client visitation rules must be approved by ORR to ensure the rules are reasonable and appropriate and include provisions for emergencies and exigent circumstances.

(b) Care provider facilities must provide UCs access to their families, including legal guardians, unless ORR has documentation showing that certain family members or legal guardians should not be provided access because of safety concerns.

Subpart G—Official Response Following a UC Report

§411.61 Staff reporting duties.

(a) All care provider facility staff, volunteers, and contractors must immediately report to ORR according to ORR policies and procedures and to State or local agencies in accordance with mandatory reporting laws: any knowledge, suspicion, or information regarding an incident of sexual abuse or sexual harassment that occurred while a UC was in ORR care; retaliation against UCs or staff who reported such an incident; and any staff neglect or violation of responsibilities that may have contributed to an incident or retaliation. ORR must review and approve the care provider facility's policies and procedures and ensure that the care provider facility specifies appropriate reporting procedures.

(b) Care provider facility staff members who become aware of alleged sexual abuse or sexual harassment must immediately follow reporting requirements set forth by ORR's and the care provider facility's policies and procedures.

(c) Apart from such reporting, care provider facility staff must not reveal any information related to a sexual abuse or sexual harassment report to anyone within the care provider facility except to the extent necessary for medical or mental health treatment, investigations, notice to law enforcement, or other security and management decisions.

(d) Care provider facility staff must report any sexual abuse and sexual harassment allegations to the designated State or local services agency under applicable mandatory reporting laws in addition to law enforcement and the State and local licensing agency.

(e) Upon receiving an allegation of sexual abuse or sexual harassment that occurred while a UC was in ORR care, the care provider facility head or his or her designee must report the allegation to the alleged victim's parents or legal guardians, unless ORR has evidence showing the parents or legal guardians should not be notified or the victim does not consent to this disclosure of information and is 14 years of age or older and ORR has determined the victim is able to make an independent decision.

(f) Upon receiving an allegation of sexual abuse or sexual harassment that occurred while a UC was in ORR care, ORR will share this information with the UC's attorney of record within 48 hours of learning of the allegation unless the UC does not consent to this disclosure of information and is 14 years of age or older and ORR has determined the victim is able to make an independent decision.

§ 411.62 Protection duties.

If a care provider facility employee, volunteer, or contractor reasonably believes that a UC is subject to substantial risk of imminent sexual abuse or sexual harassment, he or she must take immediate action to protect the UC.

§ 411.63 Reporting to other care provider facilities and DHS.

(a) Upon receiving an allegation that a UC was sexually abused or sexually harassed while at another care provider facility, the care provider facility whose staff received the allegation must immediately notify ORR, but no later than 24 hours after receiving the allegation. ORR will then notify the care provider facility where the alleged abuse or harassment occurred.

(b) The care provider facility must document that it provided such notification to ORR.

(c) The care provider facility that receives such notification, to the extent that such care provider facility is covered by this part, must ensure that the allegation is referred for investigation in accordance with these standards.

(d) Upon receiving an allegation that a UC was sexually abused or sexually harassed while in DHS custody, the care provider facility whose staff received the allegation must immediately notify ORR, but no later than 24 hours after receiving an allegation. ORR will then report the allegation to DHS in accordance with DHS policies and procedures.

(e) The care provider facility must document that it provided such notification to ORR.

§ 411.64 Responder duties.

(a) Upon learning of an allegation that a UC was sexually abused while in an ORR care provider facility, the first care provider facility staff member to respond to the report must be required to:

(1) Separate the alleged victim, abuser, and any witnesses;

(2) Preserve and protect, to the greatest extent possible, any crime scene until the appropriate authorities can take steps to collect any evidence;

(3) If the abuse occurred within a time period that still allows for the collection of physical evidence, request that the alleged victim not take any actions that could destroy physical evidence, including, as appropriate, washing, brush teeth, changing clothes, urinating, defecating, smoking, drinking, or eating; and

(4) If the abuse occurred within a time period that still allows for the collection of physical evidence, request that the alleged abuser(s) and/or witnesses, as necessary, do not take any actions that could destroy physical evidence, including, as appropriate, washing, brushing teeth, changing clothes, urinating, defecating, smoking, drinking, or eating.

(b) [Reserved]

§ 411.65 Coordinated response.

(a) Care provider facilities must develop a written institutional plan to coordinate actions taken by staff first responders, medical and mental health practitioners, outside investigators, victim advocates, and care provider facility leadership in response to an incident of sexual abuse to ensure that victims receive all necessary immediate and ongoing medical, mental health, and support services and that investigators are able to obtain usable evidence. ORR must approve the written institutional plan.

(b) Care provider facilities must use a coordinated, multidisciplinary team approach to responding to sexual abuse.

(c) If a victim of sexual abuse is transferred between ORR care provider facilities, ORR must, as permitted by law, inform the receiving care provider facility of the incident and the victim's potential need for medical or social services.

(d) If a victim of sexual abuse is transferred from an ORR care provider facility to a non-ORR facility or sponsor, ORR must, as permitted by law, inform the receiving facility or sponsor of the incident and the victim's potential need for medical or social services, unless the victim requests otherwise.

§411.66 Protection of UCs from contact with alleged abusers.

ORR and care provider facility staff, contractors, and volunteers suspected of perpetrating sexual abuse or sexual harassment must be suspended from all duties that would involve or allow access to UCs pending the outcome of an investigation.

§411.67 Protection against retaliation.

Care provider facility staff, contractors, volunteers, and UCs must not retaliate against any person who reports, complains about, or participates in an investigation of alleged sexual abuse or sexual harassment. For the remainder of the UC's stay in ORR custody following a report of sexual abuse or sexual harassment, ORR and the care provider facility must monitor to see if there are facts that may suggest possible retaliation by UCs or care provider facility staff and must promptly remedy any such retaliation. ORR and the care provider facility must also monitor to see if there are facts that may suggest possible retaliation by UCs or care provider facility staff against any staff member, contractor, or volunteer and must promptly remedy any such retaliation. Items ORR and the care provider facility should monitor include but are not limited to any UC disciplinary reports, housing or program changes, negative performance reviews, or reassignments of staff. Care provider facilities must discuss any changes with the appropriate UC or staff member as part of their efforts to determine if retaliation is taking place and, when confirmed, immediately takes steps to protect the UC or staff member.

§411.68 Post-allegation protection.

(a) Care provider facilities must ensure that UC victims of sexual abuse and sexual harassment are assigned to a supportive environment that represents the least restrictive housing option possible to keep the UC safe and secure, subject to the requirements of §411.42.

(b) The care provider facility should employ multiple protection measures to ensure the safety and security of UC victims of sexual abuse and sexual harassment, including but not limited to: Housing changes or transfers for UC victims and/or abusers or harassers; removal of alleged UC abusers or harassers from contact with victims; and emotional support services for UCs or staff who fear retaliation for reporting sexual abuse or sexual harassment or cooperating with investigations.

(c) A UC victim may be placed on one-on-one supervision in order to protect the UC in exigent circumstances. Before taking the UC off of one-on-one supervision, the care provider facility must complete a re-assessment taking into consideration any increased vulnerability of the UC as a result of the sexual abuse or sexual harassment. The re-assessment must be completed as soon as possible and without delay so that the UC is not on one-on-one supervision longer than is absolutely necessary for safety and security reasons.

Subpart H—ORR Incident Monitoring and Evaluation

§411.71 ORR monitoring and evaluation of care provider facilities following an allegation of sexual abuse or sexual harassment.

(a) Upon receiving an allegation of sexual abuse or sexual harassment that occurs at an ORR care provider facility, ORR will monitor and evaluate the care provider facility to ensure that the care provider facility complied with the requirements of this section or ORR policies and procedures. Upon conclusion of an outside investigation, ORR must review any available completed investigation reports to determine whether additional monitoring and evaluation activities are required.

(b) ORR must develop written policies and procedures for incident monitoring and evaluation of sexual abuse and sexual harassment allegations, including provision requiring:

(1) Reviewing prior complaints and reports of sexual abuse and sexual harassment involving the suspected perpetrator;

(2) Determining whether actions or failures to act at the care provider facility contributed to the abuse or harassment;

(3) Determining if any ORR policies and procedures or relevant legal authorities were broken; and

(4) Retention of such reports for as long as the alleged abuser or harasser is in ORR custody or employed by ORR or the care provider facility, plus ten years.

(c) ORR must ensure that its incident monitoring and evaluation does not interfere with any ongoing investigation conducted by State or local Child Protective Services, the State or local licensing agency, or law enforcement.

(d) When outside agencies investigate an allegation of sexual abuse or sexual harassment, the care provider facility and ORR must cooperate with outside investigators.

§411.72 Reporting to UCs.

Following an investigation by the appropriate investigating authority into a UC's allegation of sexual abuse or sexual harassment, ORR must notify the UC in his/her preferred language of the result of the investigation if the UC is still in ORR care and custody and where feasible. If a UC has been released from ORR care when an investigation is completed, ORR should attempt to notify the UC. ORR may encourage the investigating agency to also notify other complainants or additional parties notified of the allegation of the result of the investigation.

Subpart I—Interventions and Discipline

§411.81 Disciplinary sanctions for staff.

(a) Care provider facilities must take disciplinary action up to and including termination against care provider facility staff with a substantiated allegation of sexual abuse or sexual harassment against them or for violating ORR or the care provider facility's sexual abuse and sexual harassment policies and procedures.

(b) Termination must be the presumptive disciplinary sanction for staff who engaged in sexual abuse or sexual harassment.

(c) All terminations for violations of ORR and/or care provider facility sexual abuse and sexual harassment policies and procedures or resignations by staff, who would have been terminated if not for their resignation, must be reported to law enforcement agencies and to any relevant State or local licensing bodies.

(d) Any staff member with a substantiated allegation of sexual abuse or sexual harassment against him/her at an ORR care provider facility is barred from employment at any ORR care provider facility.

§411.82 Corrective actions for contractors and volunteers.

(a) Any contractor or volunteer with a substantiated allegation of sexual abuse or sexual harassment against him/her must be prohibited from working or volunteering at the care provider facility and at any ORR care provider facility.

(b) The care provider facility must take appropriate remedial measures and must consider whether to prohibit further contact with UCs by contractors or volunteers who have not engaged in sexual abuse or sexual harassment but violated other provisions within these standards, ORR sexual abuse and sexual harassment policies and procedures, or the care provider's sexual abuse and sexual harassment policies and procedures.

§411.83 Interventions for UCs who engage in sexual abuse.

UCs must receive appropriate interventions if they engage in UC-on-UC sexual abuse. Decisions regarding which types of interventions to use in particular cases, including treatment, counseling, or educational programs, are made with the goal of promoting improved behavior by the UC and ensuring the safety of other UCs and staff. Intervention decisions should take into account the social, sexual, emotional, and cognitive development of the UC and the UC's mental health status. Incidents of UC-on-UC abuse are referred to all investigating authorities, including law enforcement entities.

Subpart J—Medical and Mental Health Care

§411.91 Medical and mental health assessments; history of sexual abuse.

(a) If the assessment pursuant to §411.41 indicates that a UC experienced prior sexual victimization or perpetrated sexual abuse, the care provider facility must ensure that the UC is immediately referred to a qualified medical or mental health practitioner for medical and/or mental health follow-up as appropriate. Care provider facility staff must also ensure that all UCs disclosures are reported in accordance with these standards.

(b) When a referral for medical follow-up is initiated, the care provider facility must ensure that the UC receives a health evaluation no later than seventy-two (72) hours after the referral.

(c) When a referral for mental health follow-up is initiated, the care provider facility must ensure that the UC receives a mental health evaluation no later than seventy-two (72) hours after the referral.

§411.92 Access to emergency medical and mental health services.

(a) Care provider facilities must provide UC victims of sexual abuse timely, unimpeded access to emergency medical treatment, crisis intervention services, emergency contraception, and sexually transmitted infections prophylaxis, in accordance with professionally accepted standards of care, where appropriate under medical or mental health professional standards.

(b) Care provider facilities must provide UC victims of sexual abuse access to all medical treatment and crisis intervention services regardless of whether the victim names the abuser or cooperates with any investigation arising out of the incident.

§411.93 Ongoing medical and mental health care for sexual abuse and sexual harassment victims and abusers.

(a) Care provider facilities must offer ongoing medical and mental health evaluations and treatment to all UCs who are victimized by sexual abuse or sexual harassment while in ORR care and custody.

(b) The evaluation and treatment of such victims must include, as appropriate, follow-up services, treatment plans, and, when necessary, referrals for continued care following their transfer to or placement in other care provider facilities or their release from ORR care and custody.

(c) The care provider facility must provide victims with medical and mental health services consistent with the community level of care.

(d) Care provider facilities must ensure that female UC victims of sexual abuse by a male abuser while in ORR care and custody are offered pregnancy tests, as necessary. If pregnancy results from an instance of sexual abuse, care provider facility must ensure that the victim receives timely and comprehensive information about all lawful pregnancy-related medical services and timely access to all lawful pregnancy-related medical services. In order for UCs to make informed decisions regarding medical services, including, as appropriate, medical services provided under §411.92, care provider facilities should engage the UC in discussions with family members or attorneys of record in accordance with § 411.55 to the extent practicable and follow appropriate State laws regarding the age of consent for medical procedures.

(e) Care provider facilities must ensure that UC victims of sexual abuse that occurred while in ORR care and custody are offered tests for sexually transmitted infections as medically appropriate.

(f) Care provider facilities must ensure that UC victims are provided access to treatment services regardless of whether the victim names the abuser or cooperates with any investigation arising out of the incident.

(g) The care provider facility must attempt to conduct a mental health evaluation of all known UC-on-UC abusers within seventy-two (72) hours of learning of such abuse and/or abuse history and offer treatment when deemed appropriate by mental health practitioners.

Subpart K—Data Collection and Review

§ 411.101 Sexual abuse and sexual harassment incident reviews.

(a) Care provider facilities must conduct sexual abuse or sexual harassment incident reviews at the conclusion of every investigation of sexual abuse or sexual harassment and, where the allegation was either substantiated or unable to be substantiated but not determined to be unfounded, prepare a written report recommending whether the incident review and/or investigation indicates that a change in policy or practice could better prevent, detect, or respond to sexual abuse and sexual harassment. The care provider facility must implement the recommendations for improvement or must document its reason for not doing so in a written response. Both the report and response must be forwarded to ORR's Prevention of Sexual Abuse Coordinator. Care provider facilities also must collect accurate, uniform data for every reported incident of sexual abuse and sexual harassment using a standardized instrument and set of definitions.

(b) Care provider facilities must conduct an annual review of all sexual abuse and sexual harassment investigations and resulting incident reviews to assess and improve sexual abuse and sexual harassment detection, prevention, and response efforts. The results and findings of the annual review must be provided to ORR's Prevention of Sexual Abuse Coordinator.

§ 411.102 Data collection.

(a) Care provider facilities must maintain all case records associated with claims of sexual abuse and sexual harassment, including incident reports, investigative reports, offender information, case disposition, medical and counseling evaluation findings, and recommendations for post-release treatment and/or counseling in accordance with these standards and applicable Federal and State laws and ORR policies and procedures.

(b) On an ongoing basis, the PSA Compliance Manager must work with care provider facility management and ORR to share data regarding effective care provider facility response methods to sexual abuse and sexual harassment.

(c) On a quarterly basis, the PSA Compliance Manager must prepare a report for ORR compiling information received about all incidents and allegations of sexual abuse and sexual harassment of UCs in the care provider facility during the period covered by the report as well as ongoing investigations and other pending cases.

(d) On an annual basis, the PSA Compliance Manager must aggregate incident-based sexual abuse and sexual harassment data, including the number of reported sexual abuse and sexual harassment allegations determined to be substantiated, unsubstantiated, unfounded, or for which an investigation is ongoing. For each incident, information concerning the following also must be included:

(1) The date, time, location, and nature of the incident;

(2) The demographic background of the victim and perpetrator (including citizenship, nationality, age, and sex) that excludes specific identifying information;

(3) The reporting timeline for the incident (including the name of the individual who reported the incident; the date and time the report was received

by the care provider facility; and the date and time the incident was reported to ORR);

(4) Any injuries sustained by the victim;

(5) Post-report follow-up responses and action taken by the care provider facility (*e.g.*, housing placement changes, medical examinations, mental health counseling);

(6) Any interventions imposed on the perpetrator.

(e) Care provider facilities must provide all data described in this section from the previous calendar year to ORR no later than August 31.

§411.103 Data review for corrective action.

(a) ORR must review data collected and aggregated pursuant to §§411.101 and 411.102 in order to assess and improve the effectiveness of its sexual abuse and sexual harassment prevention, detection, and response policies, procedures, practices, and training, including:

(1) Identifying problem areas;

(2) Taking corrective actions on an ongoing basis; and

(3) Preparing an annual report of its findings and corrective actions for each care provider facility as well as ORR as a whole.

(b) Such report must include a comparison of the current year's data and corrective actions with those from prior years and must provide an assessment of ORR's progress in preventing, detecting, and responding to sexual abuse and sexual harassment.

(c) The Director of ORR must approve ORR's annual report on ORR's UC Program as a whole and make the report available to the public through its Web site or otherwise make the report readily available to the public.

(d) ORR may redact specific material from the reports when necessary for safety and security reasons but must indicate the nature of the material redacted.

§411.104 Data storage, publication, and destruction.

(a) ORR must ensure that data collected pursuant to §§411.101 and 411.102 is securely retained in accordance with Federal and State laws and ORR record retention policies and procedures.

(b) ORR must make all aggregated sexual abuse and sexual harassment data from ORR care provider facilities with which it provides a grant to or contracts with, excluding secure care providers and traditional foster care providers, available to the public at least annually on its Web site consistent with existing ORR information disclosure policies and procedures.

(c) Before making any aggregated sexual abuse and sexual harassment data publicly available, ORR must remove all personally identifiable information.

(d) ORR must maintain sexual abuse and sexual harassment data for at least 10 years after the date of its initial collection unless Federal, State, or local law requires for the disposal of official information in less than 10 years.

Subpart L—Audits and Corrective Action

§411.111 Frequency and scope of audits.

(a) Within three years of February 22, 2016, each care provider facility that houses UCs will be audited at least once; and during each three-year period thereafter.

(b) ORR may expedite an audit if it believes that a particular care provider facility may be experiencing problems related to sexual abuse or sexual harassment.

(c) ORR must develop and issue an instrument that is coordinated with the HHS Office of the Inspector General that will provide guidance on the conduct and contents of the audit.

(d) The auditor must review all relevant ORR-wide policies, procedures, reports, internal and external audits, and licensing requirements for each care provider facility type.

(e) The audits must review, at a minimum, a sampling of relevant documents and other records and other information for the most recent one-year period.

(f) The auditor must have access to, and must observe, all areas of the audited care provider facilities.

(g) ORR and the care provider facility must provide the auditor with the relevant documentation to complete a thorough audit of the care provider facility.

(h) The auditor must retain and preserve all documentation (including, *e.g.*, videotapes and interview notes) relied upon in making audit determinations. Such documentation must be provided to ORR upon request.

(i) The auditor must interview a representative sample of UCs and staff, and the care provider facility must make space available suitable for such interviews.

(j) The auditor must review a sampling of any available video footage and other electronically available data that may be relevant to the provisions being audited.

(k) The auditor must be permitted to conduct private interviews with UCs.

(l) UCs must be permitted to send confidential information or correspondence to the auditor.

(m) Auditors must attempt to solicit input from community-based or victim advocates who may have insight into relevant conditions in the care provider facility.

(n) All sensitive and confidential information provided to auditors will include appropriate designations and limitations on further dissemination. Auditors must follow appropriate procedures for handling and safeguarding such information.

(o) Care provider facilities bear the affirmative burden on demonstrating compliance with the standards to the auditor.

§ 411.112 Auditor qualifications.

(a) An audit must be conducted by an entity or individual with relevant auditing or evaluation experience and is external to ORR.

(b) All auditors must be certified by ORR, and ORR must develop and issue procedures regarding the certification process within six months of December 24, 2014, which must include training requirements.

(c) No audit may be conducted by an auditor who received financial compensation from the care provider, the care provider's agency, or ORR (except for compensation received for conducting other audits) within the three years prior to ORR's retention of the auditor.

(d) ORR, the care provider, or the care provider's agency must not employ, contract with, or otherwise financially compensate the auditor for three years subsequent to ORR's retention of the auditor, with the exception of contracting for subsequent audits.

§ 411.113 Audit contents and findings.

(a) Each audit must include a certification by the auditor that no conflict of interest exists with respect to his or her ability to conduct an audit of the care provider facility under review.

(b) Audit reports must state whether care provider facility policies and procedures comply with all standards.

(c) For each of these standards, the auditor must determine whether the audited care provider facility reaches one of the following findings: Exceeds Standard (substantially exceeds requirement of standard); Meets Standard (substantial compliance; complies in all material ways with the standard for the relevant review period); Does Not Meet Standard (requires corrective action). The audit summary must indicate, among other things, the number of provisions the care provider facility achieved at each grade level.

(d) Audit reports must describe the methodology, sampling sizes, and basis for the auditor's conclusions with regard to each standard provision for each audited care provider facility and must include recommendations for any required correction action.

(e) Auditors must redact any personally identifiable information of UCs or staff information from their reports but must provide such information to ORR upon request.

(f) ORR must ensure that aggregated data on final audit reports is published on ORR's Web site, or is otherwise made readily available to the public. ORR must redact any sensitive or confidential information prior to providing such reports publicly.

§ 411.114 Audit corrective action plan.

(a) A finding of "Does Not Meet Standard" with one or more standards must trigger a 90-day corrective action period.

(b) The auditor and ORR must jointly develop a corrective action plan to achieve compliance.

(c) The auditor must take necessary and appropriate steps to verify implementation of the corrective action plan, such as reviewing updated policies and procedures or re-inspecting portions of a care provider facility.

(d) After the 180-day corrective action period ends, the auditor must issue a final determination as to whether the care provider facility achieved compliance with those standards requiring corrective action.

(e) If the care provider facility does not achieve compliance with each standard, it may (at its discretion and cost) request a subsequent audit once it believes that it achieved compliance.

§411.115 Audit appeals.

(a) A care provider facility may file an appeal with ORR regarding any specific audit finding that it believes to be incorrect. Such appeal must be filed within 90 days of the auditor's final determination.

(b) If ORR determines that the care provider facility stated good cause for re-evaluation, the care provider facility may commission a re-audit by an auditor mutually agreed upon by ORR and the care provider facility. The care provider facility must bear the costs of the re-audit.

(c) The findings of the re-audit are considered final.

PARTS 412–499 [RESERVED]

FINDING AIDS

A list of CFR titles, subtitles, chapters, subchapters and parts and an alphabetical list of agencies publishing in the CFR are included in the CFR Index and Finding Aids volume to the Code of Federal Regulations which is published separately and revised annually.

Table of CFR Titles and Chapters

(Revised as of October 1, 2017)

Title 1—General Provisions

Title 2—Grants and Agreements

Title 2—Grants and Agreements—Continued

Chap.	
XXVII	Small Business Administration (Parts 2700—2799)
XXVIII	Department of Justice (Parts 2800—2899)
XXIX	Department of Labor (Parts 2900—2999)
XXX	Department of Homeland Security (Parts 3000—3099)
XXXI	Institute of Museum and Library Services (Parts 3100—3199)
XXXII	National Endowment for the Arts (Parts 3200—3299)
XXXIII	National Endowment for the Humanities (Parts 3300—3399)
XXXIV	Department of Education (Parts 3400—3499)
XXXV	Export-Import Bank of the United States (Parts 3500—3599)
XXXVI	Office of National Drug Control Policy, Executive Office of the President (Parts 3600—3699)
XXXVII	Peace Corps (Parts 3700—3799)
LVIII	Election Assistance Commission (Parts 5800—5899)
LIX	Gulf Coast Ecosystem Restoration Council (Parts 5900—5999)

Title 3—The President

I	Executive Office of the President (Parts 100—199)

Title 4—Accounts

I	Government Accountability Office (Parts 1—199)

Title 5—Administrative Personnel

I	Office of Personnel Management (Parts 1—1199)
II	Merit Systems Protection Board (Parts 1200—1299)
III	Office of Management and Budget (Parts 1300—1399)
IV	Office of Personnel Management and Office of the Director of National Intelligence (Parts 1400—1499)
V	The International Organizations Employees Loyalty Board (Parts 1500—1599)
VI	Federal Retirement Thrift Investment Board (Parts 1600—1699)
VIII	Office of Special Counsel (Parts 1800—1899)
IX	Appalachian Regional Commission (Parts 1900—1999)
XI	Armed Forces Retirement Home (Parts 2100—2199)
XIV	Federal Labor Relations Authority, General Counsel of the Federal Labor Relations Authority and Federal Service Impasses Panel (Parts 2400—2499)
XVI	Office of Government Ethics (Parts 2600—2699)
XXI	Department of the Treasury (Parts 3100—3199)
XXII	Federal Deposit Insurance Corporation (Parts 3200—3299)
XXIII	Department of Energy (Parts 3300—3399)
XXIV	Federal Energy Regulatory Commission (Parts 3400—3499)
XXV	Department of the Interior (Parts 3500—3599)
XXVI	Department of Defense (Parts 3600—3699)

Chap.	
XXVIII	Department of Justice (Parts 3800—3899)
XXIX	Federal Communications Commission (Parts 3900—3999)
XXX	Farm Credit System Insurance Corporation (Parts 4000—4099)
XXXI	Farm Credit Administration (Parts 4100—4199)
XXXIII	Overseas Private Investment Corporation (Parts 4300—4399)
XXXIV	Securities and Exchange Commission (Parts 4400—4499)
XXXV	Office of Personnel Management (Parts 4500—4599)
XXXVI	Department of Homeland Security (Parts 4600—4699)
XXXVII	Federal Election Commission (Parts 4700—4799)
XL	Interstate Commerce Commission (Parts 5000—5099)
XLI	Commodity Futures Trading Commission (Parts 5100—5199)
XLII	Department of Labor (Parts 5200—5299)
XLIII	National Science Foundation (Parts 5300—5399)
XLV	Department of Health and Human Services (Parts 5500—5599)
XLVI	Postal Rate Commission (Parts 5600—5699)
XLVII	Federal Trade Commission (Parts 5700—5799)
XLVIII	Nuclear Regulatory Commission (Parts 5800—5899)
XLIX	Federal Labor Relations Authority (Parts 5900—5999)
L	Department of Transportation (Parts 6000—6099)
LII	Export-Import Bank of the United States (Parts 6200—6299)
LIII	Department of Education (Parts 6300—6399)
LIV	Environmental Protection Agency (Parts 6400—6499)
LV	National Endowment for the Arts (Parts 6500—6599)
LVI	National Endowment for the Humanities (Parts 6600—6699)
LVII	General Services Administration (Parts 6700—6799)
LVIII	Board of Governors of the Federal Reserve System (Parts 6800—6899)
LIX	National Aeronautics and Space Administration (Parts 6900—6999)
LX	United States Postal Service (Parts 7000—7099)
LXI	National Labor Relations Board (Parts 7100—7199)
LXII	Equal Employment Opportunity Commission (Parts 7200—7299)
LXIII	Inter-American Foundation (Parts 7300—7399)
LXIV	Merit Systems Protection Board (Parts 7400—7499)
LXV	Department of Housing and Urban Development (Parts 7500—7599)
LXVI	National Archives and Records Administration (Parts 7600—7699)
LXVII	Institute of Museum and Library Services (Parts 7700—7799)
LXVIII	Commission on Civil Rights (Parts 7800—7899)
LXIX	Tennessee Valley Authority (Parts 7900—7999)
LXX	Court Services and Offender Supervision Agency for the District of Columbia (Parts 8000—8099)
LXXI	Consumer Product Safety Commission (Parts 8100—8199)
LXXIII	Department of Agriculture (Parts 8300—8399)

Title 5—Administrative Personnel—Continued

Title 6—Domestic Security

Title 7—Agriculture

Title 8—Aliens and Nationality

Chap.	
I	Department of Homeland Security (Immigration and Naturalization) (Parts 1—499)
V	Executive Office for Immigration Review, Department of Justice (Parts 1000—1399)

Title 9—Animals and Animal Products

I	Animal and Plant Health Inspection Service, Department of Agriculture (Parts 1—199)
II	Grain Inspection, Packers and Stockyards Administration (Packers and Stockyards Programs), Department of Agriculture (Parts 200—299)
III	Food Safety and Inspection Service, Department of Agriculture (Parts 300—599)

Title 10—Energy

I	Nuclear Regulatory Commission (Parts 0—199)
II	Department of Energy (Parts 200—699)
III	Department of Energy (Parts 700—999)
X	Department of Energy (General Provisions) (Parts 1000—1099)
XIII	Nuclear Waste Technical Review Board (Parts 1300—1399)
XVII	Defense Nuclear Facilities Safety Board (Parts 1700—1799)
XVIII	Northeast Interstate Low-Level Radioactive Waste Commission (Parts 1800—1899)

Title 11—Federal Elections

I	Federal Election Commission (Parts 1—9099)
II	Election Assistance Commission (Parts 9400—9499)

Title 12—Banks and Banking

I	Comptroller of the Currency, Department of the Treasury (Parts 1—199)
II	Federal Reserve System (Parts 200—299)
III	Federal Deposit Insurance Corporation (Parts 300—399)
IV	Export-Import Bank of the United States (Parts 400—499)
V	Office of Thrift Supervision, Department of the Treasury (Parts 500—599)
VI	Farm Credit Administration (Parts 600—699)
VII	National Credit Union Administration (Parts 700—799)
VIII	Federal Financing Bank (Parts 800—899)
IX	Federal Housing Finance Board (Parts 900—999)
X	Bureau of Consumer Financial Protection (Parts 1000—1099)
XI	Federal Financial Institutions Examination Council (Parts 1100—1199)
XII	Federal Housing Finance Agency (Parts 1200—1299)

Title 12—Banks and Banking—Continued

Title 13—Business Credit and Assistance

Title 14—Aeronautics and Space

Title 15—Commerce and Foreign Trade

Title 15—Commerce and Foreign Trade—Continued

Chap.

XI National Technical Information Service, Department of Commerce (Parts 1100—1199)

XIII East-West Foreign Trade Board (Parts 1300—1399)

XIV Minority Business Development Agency (Parts 1400—1499)

SUBTITLE C—REGULATIONS RELATING TO FOREIGN TRADE AGREEMENTS

XX Office of the United States Trade Representative (Parts 2000—2099)

SUBTITLE D—REGULATIONS RELATING TO TELECOMMUNICATIONS AND INFORMATION

XXIII National Telecommunications and Information Administration, Department of Commerce (Parts 2300—2399) [Reserved]

Title 16—Commercial Practices

I Federal Trade Commission (Parts 0—999)

II Consumer Product Safety Commission (Parts 1000—1799)

Title 17—Commodity and Securities Exchanges

I Commodity Futures Trading Commission (Parts 1—199)

II Securities and Exchange Commission (Parts 200—399)

IV Department of the Treasury (Parts 400—499)

Title 18—Conservation of Power and Water Resources

I Federal Energy Regulatory Commission, Department of Energy (Parts 1—399)

III Delaware River Basin Commission (Parts 400—499)

VI Water Resources Council (Parts 700—799)

VIII Susquehanna River Basin Commission (Parts 800—899)

XIII Tennessee Valley Authority (Parts 1300—1399)

Title 19—Customs Duties

I U.S. Customs and Border Protection, Department of Homeland Security; Department of the Treasury (Parts 0—199)

II United States International Trade Commission (Parts 200—299)

III International Trade Administration, Department of Commerce (Parts 300—399)

IV U.S. Immigration and Customs Enforcement, Department of Homeland Security (Parts 400—599) [Reserved]

Title 20—Employees' Benefits

I Office of Workers' Compensation Programs, Department of Labor (Parts 1—199)

II Railroad Retirement Board (Parts 200—399)

Title 20—Employees' Benefits—Continued

Chap.

III Social Security Administration (Parts 400—499)

IV Employees' Compensation Appeals Board, Department of Labor (Parts 500—599)

V Employment and Training Administration, Department of Labor (Parts 600—699)

VI Office of Workers' Compensation Programs, Department of Labor (Parts 700—799)

VII Benefits Review Board, Department of Labor (Parts 800—899)

VIII Joint Board for the Enrollment of Actuaries (Parts 900—999)

IX Office of the Assistant Secretary for Veterans' Employment and Training Service, Department of Labor (Parts 1000—1099)

Title 21—Food and Drugs

I Food and Drug Administration, Department of Health and Human Services (Parts 1—1299)

II Drug Enforcement Administration, Department of Justice (Parts 1300—1399)

III Office of National Drug Control Policy (Parts 1400—1499)

Title 22—Foreign Relations

I Department of State (Parts 1—199)

II Agency for International Development (Parts 200—299)

III Peace Corps (Parts 300—399)

IV International Joint Commission, United States and Canada (Parts 400—499)

V Broadcasting Board of Governors (Parts 500—599)

VII Overseas Private Investment Corporation (Parts 700—799)

IX Foreign Service Grievance Board (Parts 900—999)

X Inter-American Foundation (Parts 1000—1099)

XI International Boundary and Water Commission, United States and Mexico, United States Section (Parts 1100—1199)

XII United States International Development Cooperation Agency (Parts 1200—1299)

XIII Millennium Challenge Corporation (Parts 1300—1399)

XIV Foreign Service Labor Relations Board; Federal Labor Relations Authority; General Counsel of the Federal Labor Relations Authority; and the Foreign Service Impasse Disputes Panel (Parts 1400—1499)

XV African Development Foundation (Parts 1500—1599)

XVI Japan-United States Friendship Commission (Parts 1600—1699)

XVII United States Institute of Peace (Parts 1700—1799)

Title 23—Highways

I Federal Highway Administration, Department of Transportation (Parts 1—999)

Title 24—Housing and Urban Development

Chap.

Chap.	
XXIV	Board of Directors of the HOPE for Homeowners Program (Parts 4000—4099) [Reserved]
XXV	Neighborhood Reinvestment Corporation (Parts 4100—4199)

Title 25—Indians

I	Bureau of Indian Affairs, Department of the Interior (Parts 1—299)
II	Indian Arts and Crafts Board, Department of the Interior (Parts 300—399)
III	National Indian Gaming Commission, Department of the Interior (Parts 500—599)
IV	Office of Navajo and Hopi Indian Relocation (Parts 700—899)
V	Bureau of Indian Affairs, Department of the Interior, and Indian Health Service, Department of Health and Human Services (Part 900)
VI	Office of the Assistant Secretary, Indian Affairs, Department of the Interior (Parts 1000—1199)
VII	Office of the Special Trustee for American Indians, Department of the Interior (Parts 1200—1299)

Title 26—Internal Revenue

I	Internal Revenue Service, Department of the Treasury (Parts 1—End)

Title 27—Alcohol, Tobacco Products and Firearms

I	Alcohol and Tobacco Tax and Trade Bureau, Department of the Treasury (Parts 1—399)
II	Bureau of Alcohol, Tobacco, Firearms, and Explosives, Department of Justice (Parts 400—699)

Title 28—Judicial Administration

I	Department of Justice (Parts 0—299)
III	Federal Prison Industries, Inc., Department of Justice (Parts 300—399)
V	Bureau of Prisons, Department of Justice (Parts 500—599)
VI	Offices of Independent Counsel, Department of Justice (Parts 600—699)
VII	Office of Independent Counsel (Parts 700—799)
VIII	Court Services and Offender Supervision Agency for the District of Columbia (Parts 800—899)
IX	National Crime Prevention and Privacy Compact Council (Parts 900—999)
XI	Department of Justice and Department of State (Parts 1100—1199)

Title 29—Labor

Title 30—Mineral Resources

Title 31—Money and Finance: Treasury

Title 31—Money and Finance: Treasury—Continued

Title 32—National Defense

Title 33—Navigation and Navigable Waters

Title 34—Education

Title 34—Education—Continued

Chap.	
II	Office of Elementary and Secondary Education, Department of Education (Parts 200—299)
III	Office of Special Education and Rehabilitative Services, Department of Education (Parts 300—399)
IV	Office of Career, Technical and Adult Education, Department of Education (Parts 400—499)
V	Office of Bilingual Education and Minority Languages Affairs, Department of Education (Parts 500—599) [Reserved]
VI	Office of Postsecondary Education, Department of Education (Parts 600—699)
VII	Office of Educational Research and Improvement, Department of Education (Parts 700—799) [Reserved]
	SUBTITLE C—REGULATIONS RELATING TO EDUCATION
XI	[Reserved]
XII	National Council on Disability (Parts 1200—1299)

Title 35 [Reserved]

Title 36—Parks, Forests, and Public Property

I	National Park Service, Department of the Interior (Parts 1—199)
II	Forest Service, Department of Agriculture (Parts 200—299)
III	Corps of Engineers, Department of the Army (Parts 300—399)
IV	American Battle Monuments Commission (Parts 400—499)
V	Smithsonian Institution (Parts 500—599)
VI	[Reserved]
VII	Library of Congress (Parts 700—799)
VIII	Advisory Council on Historic Preservation (Parts 800—899)
IX	Pennsylvania Avenue Development Corporation (Parts 900—999)
X	Presidio Trust (Parts 1000—1099)
XI	Architectural and Transportation Barriers Compliance Board (Parts 1100—1199)
XII	National Archives and Records Administration (Parts 1200—1299)
XV	Oklahoma City National Memorial Trust (Parts 1500—1599)
XVI	Morris K. Udall Scholarship and Excellence in National Environmental Policy Foundation (Parts 1600—1699)

Title 37—Patents, Trademarks, and Copyrights

I	United States Patent and Trademark Office, Department of Commerce (Parts 1—199)
II	U.S. Copyright Office, Library of Congress (Parts 200—299)
III	Copyright Royalty Board, Library of Congress (Parts 300—399)
IV	National Institute of Standards and Technology, Department of Commerce (Parts 400—599)

Title 38—Pensions, Bonuses, and Veterans' Relief

Title 39—Postal Service

Title 40—Protection of Environment

Title 41—Public Contracts and Property Management

Title 41—Public Contracts and Property Management—Continued

Chap.

SUBTITLE E—FEDERAL INFORMATION RESOURCES MANAGEMENT REGULATIONS SYSTEM [RESERVED]

SUBTITLE F—FEDERAL TRAVEL REGULATION SYSTEM

300 General (Parts 300–1—300–99)

301 Temporary Duty (TDY) Travel Allowances (Parts 301–1—301–99)

302 Relocation Allowances (Parts 302–1—302–99)

303 Payment of Expenses Connected with the Death of Certain Employees (Part 303–1—303–99)

304 Payment of Travel Expenses from a Non-Federal Source (Parts 304–1—304–99)

Title 42—Public Health

I Public Health Service, Department of Health and Human Services (Parts 1—199)

ii—III [Reserved]

IV Centers for Medicare & Medicaid Services, Department of Health and Human Services (Parts 400—699)

V Office of Inspector General-Health Care, Department of Health and Human Services (Parts 1000—1099)

Title 43—Public Lands: Interior

SUBTITLE A—OFFICE OF THE SECRETARY OF THE INTERIOR (PARTS 1—199)

SUBTITLE B—REGULATIONS RELATING TO PUBLIC LANDS

I Bureau of Reclamation, Department of the Interior (Parts 400—999)

II Bureau of Land Management, Department of the Interior (Parts 1000—9999)

III Utah Reclamation Mitigation and Conservation Commission (Parts 10000—10099)

Title 44—Emergency Management and Assistance

I Federal Emergency Management Agency, Department of Homeland Security (Parts 0—399)

IV Department of Commerce and Department of Transportation (Parts 400—499)

Title 45—Public Welfare

SUBTITLE A—DEPARTMENT OF HEALTH AND HUMAN SERVICES (PARTS 1—199)

SUBTITLE B—REGULATIONS RELATING TO PUBLIC WELFARE

II Office of Family Assistance (Assistance Programs), Administration for Children and Families, Department of Health and Human Services (Parts 200—299)

Title 45—Public Welfare—Continued

Title 46—Shipping

Title 47—Telecommunication

Chap.

IV National Telecommunications and Information Administration, Department of Commerce, and National Highway Traffic Safety Administration, Department of Transportation (Parts 400—499)

V The First Responder Network Authority (Parts 500—599)

Title 48—Federal Acquisition Regulations System

1 Federal Acquisition Regulation (Parts 1—99)

2 Defense Acquisition Regulations System, Department of Defense (Parts 200—299)

3 Health and Human Services (Parts 300—399)

4 Department of Agriculture (Parts 400—499)

5 General Services Administration (Parts 500—599)

6 Department of State (Parts 600—699)

7 Agency for International Development (Parts 700—799)

8 Department of Veterans Affairs (Parts 800—899)

9 Department of Energy (Parts 900—999)

10 Department of the Treasury (Parts 1000—1099)

12 Department of Transportation (Parts 1200—1299)

13 Department of Commerce (Parts 1300—1399)

14 Department of the Interior (Parts 1400—1499)

15 Environmental Protection Agency (Parts 1500—1599)

16 Office of Personnel Management, Federal Employees Health Benefits Acquisition Regulation (Parts 1600—1699)

17 Office of Personnel Management (Parts 1700—1799)

18 National Aeronautics and Space Administration (Parts 1800—1899)

19 Broadcasting Board of Governors (Parts 1900—1999)

20 Nuclear Regulatory Commission (Parts 2000—2099)

21 Office of Personnel Management, Federal Employees Group Life Insurance Federal Acquisition Regulation (Parts 2100—2199)

23 Social Security Administration (Parts 2300—2399)

24 Department of Housing and Urban Development (Parts 2400—2499)

25 National Science Foundation (Parts 2500—2599)

28 Department of Justice (Parts 2800—2899)

29 Department of Labor (Parts 2900—2999)

30 Department of Homeland Security, Homeland Security Acquisition Regulation (HSAR) (Parts 3000—3099)

34 Department of Education Acquisition Regulation (Parts 3400—3499)

51 Department of the Army Acquisition Regulations (Parts 5100—5199)

52 Department of the Navy Acquisition Regulations (Parts 5200—5299)

53 Department of the Air Force Federal Acquisition Regulation Supplement (Parts 5300—5399) [Reserved]

Title 49—Transportation

Title 50—Wildlife and Fisheries

Alphabetical List of Agencies Appearing in the CFR

(Revised as of October 1, 2017)

Agency	CFR Title, Subtitle or Chapter
Administrative Committee of the Federal Register	1, I
Administrative Conference of the United States	1, III
Advisory Council on Historic Preservation	36, VIII
Advocacy and Outreach, Office of	7, XXV
Afghanistan Reconstruction, Special Inspector General for	5, LXXXIII
African Development Foundation	22, XV
Federal Acquisition Regulation	48, 57
Agency for International Development	2, VII; 22, II
Federal Acquisition Regulation	48, 7
Agricultural Marketing Service	7, I, IX, X, XI
Agricultural Research Service	7, V
Agriculture Department	2, IV; 5, LXXIII
Advocacy and Outreach, Office of	7, XXV
Agricultural Marketing Service	7, I, IX, X, XI
Agricultural Research Service	7, V
Animal and Plant Health Inspection Service	7, III; 9, I
Chief Financial Officer, Office of	7, XXX
Commodity Credit Corporation	7, XIV
Economic Research Service	7, XXXVII
Energy Policy and New Uses, Office of	2, IX; 7, XXIX
Environmental Quality, Office of	7, XXXI
Farm Service Agency	7, VII, XVIII
Federal Acquisition Regulation	48, 4
Federal Crop Insurance Corporation	7, IV
Food and Nutrition Service	7, II
Food Safety and Inspection Service	9, III
Foreign Agricultural Service	7, XV
Forest Service	36, II
Grain Inspection, Packers and Stockyards Administration	7, VIII; 9, II
Information Resources Management, Office of	7, XXVII
Inspector General, Office of	7, XXVI
National Agricultural Library	7, XLI
National Agricultural Statistics Service	7, XXXVI
National Institute of Food and Agriculture	7, XXXIV
Natural Resources Conservation Service	7, VI
Operations, Office of	7, XXVIII
Procurement and Property Management, Office of	7, XXXII
Rural Business-Cooperative Service	7, XVIII, XLII
Rural Development Administration	7, XLII
Rural Housing Service	7, XVIII, XXXV
Rural Telephone Bank	7, XVI
Rural Utilities Service	7, XVII, XVIII, XLII
Secretary of Agriculture, Office of	7, Subtitle A
Transportation, Office of	7, XXXIII
World Agricultural Outlook Board	7, XXXVIII
Air Force Department	32, VII
Federal Acquisition Regulation Supplement	48, 53
Air Transportation Stabilization Board	14, VI
Alcohol and Tobacco Tax and Trade Bureau	27, I
Alcohol, Tobacco, Firearms, and Explosives, Bureau of	27, II
AMTRAK	49, VII
American Battle Monuments Commission	36, IV
American Indians, Office of the Special Trustee	25, VII

Agency	CFR Title, Subtitle or Chapter
Animal and Plant Health Inspection Service	7, III; 9, I
Appalachian Regional Commission	5, IX
Architectural and Transportation Barriers Compliance Board	36, XI
Arctic Research Commission	45, XXIII
Armed Forces Retirement Home	5, XI
Army Department	32, V
Engineers, Corps of	33, II; 36, III
Federal Acquisition Regulation	48, 51
Bilingual Education and Minority Languages Affairs, Office of	34, V
Blind or Severely Disabled, Committee for Purchase from People Who Are	41, 51
Broadcasting Board of Governors	22, V
Federal Acquisition Regulation	48, 19
Career, Technical and Adult Education, Office of	34, IV
Census Bureau	15, I
Centers for Medicare & Medicaid Services	42, IV
Central Intelligence Agency	32, XIX
Chemical Safety and Hazardous Investigation Board	40, VI
Chief Financial Officer, Office of	7, XXX
Child Support Enforcement, Office of	45, III
Children and Families, Administration for	45, II, III, IV, X, XIII
Civil Rights, Commission on	5, LXVIII; 45, VII
Civil Rights, Office for	34, I
Council of the Inspectors General on Integrity and Efficiency	5, XCVIII
Court Services and Offender Supervision Agency for the District of Columbia	5, LXX
Coast Guard	33, I; 46, I; 49, IV
Coast Guard (Great Lakes Pilotage)	46, III
Commerce Department	2, XIII; 44, IV; 50, VI
Census Bureau	15, I
Economic Analysis, Bureau of	15, VIII
Economic Development Administration	13, III
Emergency Management and Assistance	44, IV
Federal Acquisition Regulation	48, 13
Foreign-Trade Zones Board	15, IV
Industry and Security, Bureau of	15, VII
International Trade Administration	15, III; 19, III
National Institute of Standards and Technology	15, II; 37, IV
National Marine Fisheries Service	50, II, IV
National Oceanic and Atmospheric Administration	15, IX; 50, II, III, IV, VI
National Technical Information Service	15, XI
National Telecommunications and Information Administration	15, XXIII; 47, III, IV
National Weather Service	15, IX
Patent and Trademark Office, United States	37, I
Secretary of Commerce, Office of	15, Subtitle A
Commercial Space Transportation	14, III
Commodity Credit Corporation	7, XIV
Commodity Futures Trading Commission	5, XLI; 17, I
Community Planning and Development, Office of Assistant Secretary for	24, V, VI
Community Services, Office of	45, X
Comptroller of the Currency	12, I
Construction Industry Collective Bargaining Commission	29, IX
Consumer Financial Protection Bureau	5, LXXXIV; 12, X
Consumer Product Safety Commission	5, LXXI; 16, II
Copyright Royalty Board	37, III
Corporation for National and Community Service	2, XXII; 45, XII, XXV
Cost Accounting Standards Board	48, 99
Council on Environmental Quality	40, V
Court Services and Offender Supervision Agency for the District of Columbia	5, LXX; 28, VIII
Customs and Border Protection	19, I
Defense Contract Audit Agency	32, I
Defense Department	2, XI; 5, XXVI; 32, Subtitle A; 40, VII
Advanced Research Projects Agency	32, I

Agency	CFR Title, Subtitle or Chapter
Air Force Department	32, VII
Army Department	32, V; 33, II; 36, III; 48, 51
Defense Acquisition Regulations System	48, 2
Defense Intelligence Agency	32, I
Defense Logistics Agency	32, I, XII; 48, 54
Engineers, Corps of	33, II; 36, III
National Imagery and Mapping Agency	32, I
Navy Department	32, VI; 48, 52
Secretary of Defense, Office of	2, XI; 32, I
Defense Contract Audit Agency	32, I
Defense Intelligence Agency	32, I
Defense Logistics Agency	32, XII; 48, 54
Defense Nuclear Facilities Safety Board	10, XVII
Delaware River Basin Commission	18, III
Denali Commission	45, IX
District of Columbia, Court Services and Offender Supervision Agency for the	5, LXX; 28, VIII
Drug Enforcement Administration	21, II
East-West Foreign Trade Board	15, XIII
Economic Analysis, Bureau of	15, VIII
Economic Development Administration	13, III
Economic Research Service	7, XXXVII
Education, Department of	2, XXXIV; 5, LIII
Bilingual Education and Minority Languages Affairs, Office of	34, V
Career, Technical and Adult Education, Office of	34, IV
Civil Rights, Office for	34, I
Educational Research and Improvement, Office of	34, VII
Elementary and Secondary Education, Office of	34, II
Federal Acquisition Regulation	48, 34
Postsecondary Education, Office of	34, VI
Secretary of Education, Office of	34, Subtitle A
Special Education and Rehabilitative Services, Office of	34, III
Career, Technical, and Adult Education, Office of	34, IV
Educational Research and Improvement, Office of	34, VII
Election Assistance Commission	2, LVIII; 11, II
Elementary and Secondary Education, Office of	34, II
Emergency Oil and Gas Guaranteed Loan Board	13, V
Emergency Steel Guarantee Loan Board	13, IV
Employee Benefits Security Administration	29, XXV
Employees' Compensation Appeals Board	20, IV
Employees Loyalty Board	5, V
Employment and Training Administration	20, V
Employment Standards Administration	20, VI
Endangered Species Committee	50, IV
Energy, Department of	2, IX; 5, XXIII; 10, II, III, X
Federal Acquisition Regulation	48, 9
Federal Energy Regulatory Commission	5, XXIV; 18, I
Property Management Regulations	41, 109
Energy, Office of	7, XXIX
Engineers, Corps of	33, II; 36, III
Engraving and Printing, Bureau of	31, VI
Environmental Protection Agency	2, XV; 5, LIV; 40, I, IV, VII
Federal Acquisition Regulation	48, 15
Property Management Regulations	41, 115
Environmental Quality, Office of	7, XXXI
Equal Employment Opportunity Commission	5, LXII; 29, XIV
Equal Opportunity, Office of Assistant Secretary for	24, I
Executive Office of the President	3, I
Environmental Quality, Council on	40, V
Management and Budget, Office of	2, Subtitle A; 5, III, LXXVII; 14, VI; 48, 99
National Drug Control Policy, Office of	2, XXXVI; 21, III
National Security Council	32, XXI; 47, 2

Agency	CFR Title, Subtitle or Chapter
Indian Arts and Crafts Board	25, II
Indian Health Service	25, V
Industry and Security, Bureau of	15, VII
Information Resources Management, Office of	7, XXVII
Information Security Oversight Office, National Archives and Records Administration	32, XX
Inspector General	
Agriculture Department	7, XXVI
Health and Human Services Department	42, V
Housing and Urban Development Department	24, XII, XV
Institute of Peace, United States	22, XVII
Inter-American Foundation	5, LXIII; 22, X
Interior Department	2, XIV
American Indians, Office of the Special Trustee	25, VII
Endangered Species Committee	50, IV
Federal Acquisition Regulation	48, 14
Federal Property Management Regulations System	41, 114
Fish and Wildlife Service, United States	50, I, IV
Geological Survey	30, IV
Indian Affairs, Bureau of	25, I, V
Indian Affairs, Office of the Assistant Secretary	25, VI
Indian Arts and Crafts Board	25, II
Land Management, Bureau of	43, II
National Indian Gaming Commission	25, III
National Park Service	36, I
Natural Resource Revenue, Office of	30, XII
Ocean Energy Management, Bureau of	30, V
Reclamation, Bureau of	43, I
Safety and Enforcement Bureau, Bureau of	30, II
Secretary of the Interior, Office of	2, XIV; 43, Subtitle A
Surface Mining Reclamation and Enforcement, Office of	30, VII
Internal Revenue Service	26, I
International Boundary and Water Commission, United States and Mexico, United States Section	22, XI
International Development, United States Agency for	22, II
Federal Acquisition Regulation	48, 7
International Development Cooperation Agency, United States	22, XII
International Joint Commission, United States and Canada	22, IV
International Organizations Employees Loyalty Board	5, V
International Trade Administration	15, III; 19, III
International Trade Commission, United States	19, II
Interstate Commerce Commission	5, XL
Investment Security, Office of	31, VIII
James Madison Memorial Fellowship Foundation	45, XXIV
Japan–United States Friendship Commission	22, XVI
Joint Board for the Enrollment of Actuaries	20, VIII
Justice Department	2, XXVIII; 5, XXVIII; 28, I, XI; 40, IV
Alcohol, Tobacco, Firearms, and Explosives, Bureau of	27, II
Drug Enforcement Administration	21, II
Federal Acquisition Regulation	48, 28
Federal Claims Collection Standards	31, IX
Federal Prison Industries, Inc.	28, III
Foreign Claims Settlement Commission of the United States	45, V
Immigration Review, Executive Office for	8, V
Independent Counsel, Offices of	28, VI
Prisons, Bureau of	28, V
Property Management Regulations	41, 128
Labor Department	2, XXIX; 5, XLII
Employee Benefits Security Administration	29, XXV
Employees' Compensation Appeals Board	20, IV
Employment and Training Administration	20, V
Employment Standards Administration	20, VI
Federal Acquisition Regulation	48, 29
Federal Contract Compliance Programs, Office of	41, 60

Agency	CFR Title, Subtitle or Chapter
Federal Procurement Regulations System	41, 50
Labor-Management Standards, Office of	29, II, IV
Mine Safety and Health Administration	30, I
Occupational Safety and Health Administration	29, XVII
Public Contracts	41, 50
Secretary of Labor, Office of	29, Subtitle A
Veterans' Employment and Training Service, Office of the Assistant Secretary for	41, 61; 20, IX
Wage and Hour Division	29, V
Workers' Compensation Programs, Office of	20, I, VII
Labor-Management Standards, Office of	29, II, IV
Land Management, Bureau of	43, II
Legal Services Corporation	45, XVI
Library of Congress	36, VII
Copyright Royalty Board	37, III
U.S. Copyright Office	37, II
Local Television Loan Guarantee Board	7, XX
Management and Budget, Office of	5, III, LXXVII; 14, VI; 48, 99
Marine Mammal Commission	50, V
Maritime Administration	46, II
Merit Systems Protection Board	5, II, LXIV
Micronesian Status Negotiations, Office for	32, XXVII
Military Compensation and Retirement Modernization Commission	5, XCIX
Millennium Challenge Corporation	22, XIII
Mine Safety and Health Administration	30, I
Minority Business Development Agency	15, XIV
Miscellaneous Agencies	1, IV
Monetary Offices	31, I
Morris K. Udall Scholarship and Excellence in National Environmental Policy Foundation	36, XVI
Museum and Library Services, Institute of	2, XXXI
National Aeronautics and Space Administration	2, XVIII; 5, LIX; 14, V
Federal Acquisition Regulation	48, 18
National Agricultural Library	7, XLI
National Agricultural Statistics Service	7, XXXVI
National and Community Service, Corporation for	2, XXII; 45, XII, XXV
National Archives and Records Administration	2, XXVI; 5, LXVI; 36, XII
Information Security Oversight Office	32, XX
National Capital Planning Commission	1, IV, VI
National Commission for Employment Policy	1, IV
National Commission on Libraries and Information Science	45, XVII
National Council on Disability	5, C; 34, XII
National Counterintelligence Center	32, XVIII
National Credit Union Administration	5, LXXXVI; 12, VII
National Crime Prevention and Privacy Compact Council	28, IX
National Drug Control Policy, Office of	2, XXXVI; 21, III
National Endowment for the Arts	2, XXXII
National Endowment for the Humanities	2, XXXIII
National Foundation on the Arts and the Humanities	45, XI
National Geospatial-Intelligence Agency	32, I
National Highway Traffic Safety Administration	23, II, III; 47, VI; 49, V
National Imagery and Mapping Agency	32, I
National Indian Gaming Commission	25, III
National Institute of Food and Agriculture	7, XXXIV
National Institute of Standards and Technology	15, II; 37, IV
National Intelligence, Office of Director of	5, IV; 32, XVII
National Labor Relations Board	5, LXI; 29, I
National Marine Fisheries Service	50, II, IV
National Mediation Board	29, X
National Oceanic and Atmospheric Administration	15, IX; 50, II, III, IV, VI
National Park Service	36, I
National Railroad Adjustment Board	29, III
National Railroad Passenger Corporation (AMTRAK)	49, VII
National Science Foundation	2, XXV; 5, XLIII; 45, VI

Agency	CFR Title, Subtitle or Chapter
Federal Acquisition Regulation	48, 25
National Security Council	32, XXI
National Security Council and Office of Science and Technology Policy	47, II
National Telecommunications and Information Administration	15, XXIII; 47, III, IV, V
National Transportation Safety Board	49, VIII
Natural Resources Conservation Service	7, VI
Natural Resource Revenue, Office of	30, XII
Navajo and Hopi Indian Relocation, Office of	25, IV
Navy Department	32, VI
Federal Acquisition Regulation	48, 52
Neighborhood Reinvestment Corporation	24, XXV
Northeast Interstate Low-Level Radioactive Waste Commission	10, XVIII
Nuclear Regulatory Commission	2, XX; 5, XLVIII; 10, I
Federal Acquisition Regulation	48, 20
Occupational Safety and Health Administration	29, XVII
Occupational Safety and Health Review Commission	29, XX
Ocean Energy Management, Bureau of	30, V
Oklahoma City National Memorial Trust	36, XV
Operations Office	7, XXVIII
Overseas Private Investment Corporation	5, XXXIII; 22, VII
Patent and Trademark Office, United States	37, I
Payment From a Non-Federal Source for Travel Expenses	41, 304
Payment of Expenses Connected With the Death of Certain Employees	41, 303
Peace Corps	2, XXXVII; 22, III
Pennsylvania Avenue Development Corporation	36, IX
Pension Benefit Guaranty Corporation	29, XL
Personnel Management, Office of	5, I, XXXV; 5, IV; 45, VIII
Human Resources Management and Labor Relations Systems, Department of Homeland Security	5, XCVII
Federal Acquisition Regulation	48, 17
Federal Employees Group Life Insurance Federal Acquisition Regulation	48, 21
Federal Employees Health Benefits Acquisition Regulation	48, 16
Pipeline and Hazardous Materials Safety Administration	49, I
Postal Regulatory Commission	5, XLVI; 39, III
Postal Service, United States	5, LX; 39, I
Postsecondary Education, Office of	34, VI
President's Commission on White House Fellowships	1, IV
Presidential Documents	3
Presidio Trust	36, X
Prisons, Bureau of	28, V
Privacy and Civil Liberties Oversight Board	6, X
Procurement and Property Management, Office of	7, XXXII
Public Contracts, Department of Labor	41, 50
Public and Indian Housing, Office of Assistant Secretary for	24, IX
Public Health Service	42, I
Railroad Retirement Board	20, II
Reclamation, Bureau of	43, I
Refugee Resettlement, Office of	45, IV
Relocation Allowances	41, 302
Research and Innovative Technology Administration	49, XI
Rural Business-Cooperative Service	7, XVIII, XLII
Rural Development Administration	7, XLII
Rural Housing Service	7, XVIII, XXXV
Rural Telephone Bank	7, XVI
Rural Utilities Service	7, XVII, XVIII, XLII
Safety and Environmental Enforcement, Bureau of	30, II
Saint Lawrence Seaway Development Corporation	33, IV
Science and Technology Policy, Office of	32, XXIV
Science and Technology Policy, Office of, and National Security Council	47, II
Secret Service	31, IV

Agency	CFR Title, Subtitle or Chapter
Securities and Exchange Commission	5, XXXIV; 17, II
Selective Service System	32, XVI
Small Business Administration	2, XXVII; 13, I
Smithsonian Institution	36, V
Social Security Administration	2, XXIII; 20, III; 48, 23
Soldiers' and Airmen's Home, United States	5, XI
Special Counsel, Office of	5, VIII
Special Education and Rehabilitative Services, Office of	34, III
State Department	2, VI; 22, I; 28, XI
Federal Acquisition Regulation	48, 6
Surface Mining Reclamation and Enforcement, Office of	30, VII
Surface Transportation Board	49, X
Susquehanna River Basin Commission	18, VIII
Technology Administration	15, XI
Technology Policy, Assistant Secretary for	37, IV
Tennessee Valley Authority	5, LXIX; 18, XIII
Thrift Supervision Office, Department of the Treasury	12, V
Trade Representative, United States, Office of	15, XX
Transportation, Department of	2, XII; 5, L
Commercial Space Transportation	14, III
Emergency Management and Assistance	44, IV
Federal Acquisition Regulation	48, 12
Federal Aviation Administration	14, I
Federal Highway Administration	23, I, II
Federal Motor Carrier Safety Administration	49, III
Federal Railroad Administration	49, II
Federal Transit Administration	49, VI
Maritime Administration	46, II
National Highway Traffic Safety Administration	23, II, III; 47, IV; 49, V
Pipeline and Hazardous Materials Safety Administration	49, I
Saint Lawrence Seaway Development Corporation	33, IV
Secretary of Transportation, Office of	14, II; 49, Subtitle A
Transportation Statistics Bureau	49, XI
Transportation, Office of	7, XXXIII
Transportation Security Administration	49, XII
Transportation Statistics Bureau	49, XI
Travel Allowances, Temporary Duty (TDY)	41, 301
Treasury Department	2, X;5, XXI; 12, XV; 17, IV; 31, IX
Alcohol and Tobacco Tax and Trade Bureau	27, I
Community Development Financial Institutions Fund	12, XVIII
Comptroller of the Currency	12, I
Customs and Border Protection	19, I
Engraving and Printing, Bureau of	31, VI
Federal Acquisition Regulation	48, 10
Federal Claims Collection Standards	31, IX
Federal Law Enforcement Training Center	31, VII
Financial Crimes Enforcement Network	31, X
Fiscal Service	31, II
Foreign Assets Control, Office of	31, V
Internal Revenue Service	26, I
Investment Security, Office of	31, VIII
Monetary Offices	31, I
Secret Service	31, IV
Secretary of the Treasury, Office of	31, Subtitle A
Thrift Supervision, Office of	12, V
Truman, Harry S. Scholarship Foundation	45, XVIII
United States and Canada, International Joint Commission	22, IV
United States and Mexico, International Boundary and Water Commission, United States Section	22, XI
U.S. Copyright Office	37, II
Utah Reclamation Mitigation and Conservation Commission	43, III
Veterans Affairs Department	2, VIII; 38, I
Federal Acquisition Regulation	48, 8
Veterans' Employment and Training Service, Office of the Assistant Secretary for	41, 61; 20, IX
Vice President of the United States, Office of	32, XXVIII

Agency	CFR Title, Subtitle or Chapter
Wage and Hour Division	29, V
Water Resources Council	18, VI
Workers' Compensation Programs, Office of	20, I, VII
World Agricultural Outlook Board	7, XXXVIII

List of CFR Sections Affected

All changes in this volume of the Code of Federal Regulations (CFR) that were made by documents published in the FEDERAL REGISTER since January 1, 2012 are enumerated in the following list. Entries indicate the nature of the changes effected. Page numbers refer to FEDERAL REGISTER pages. The user should consult the entries for chapters, parts and subparts as well as sections for revisions.

For changes to this volume of the CFR prior to this listing, consult the annual edition of the monthly List of CFR Sections Affected (LSA). The LSA is available at *www.fdsys.gov*. For changes to this volume of the CFR prior to 2001, see the "List of CFR Sections Affected, 1949–1963, 1964–1972, 1973–1985, and 1986–2000" published in 11 separate volumes. The "List of CFR Sections Affected 1986–2000" is available at *www.fdsys.gov*.

2012

45 CFR

77 FR Page

301.1 Correctly amended; CFR correction 59339

2013

(No regulations published)

2014

45 CFR

79 FR Page

411 Added; interim 77789

2015

(No regulations published)

2016

45 CFR

81 FR Page

261.64 (c) amended; interim 3020
262 Authority citation revised 2104
262.1 (a)(16) added; (c)(2) revised 2104
262.2 (e) added 2105
262.3 (g) added 2105
(a) and (f) amended; interim 3020
263.2 (e)(1) amended; interim 3020
263.11 (b) amended; interim 3020
263.14 Amended; interim 3020
264 Authority citation revised 2105
264.0 (b) amended 2105
264.60 Added 2105

45 CFR—Continued

81 FR Page

264.61 Added 2105
265.7 (d)(4) and (f) amended; interim 3020
265.9 (b)(10) and (11) added 2105
286.30 (c) and (f)(2) amended; interim 3020
286.45 (c) and (d) amended; interim 3020
286.200 (b) amended; interim 3020
286.205 (b)(3)(iv) and (c) amended; interim 3020
286.270 (b) amended; interim 3020
287.60 (a) and (b) amended; interim 3021

Chapter III

301.1 Amended 93560
301.13 Introductory text amended; (e) and (f) revised 93560
301.15 (e) revised; interim 3021
(a) through (d) revised; (e) removed 93560
302.14 Amended; interim 3021
Revised 93561
302.15 (a)(7) amended; interim 3021
(a)(6) amended; (a)(7) revised; (a)(8) added 93561
302.32 Heading, introductory text, (a), (b) introductory text and (1) revised 93561
302.33 (a)(4) revised; (a)(6) added; (d)(2) amended 93561
302.34 Amended 93562
302.38 Revised 93562
302.50 (b)(2) revised 93562

45 CFR—Continued

81 FR Page

45 CFR—Continued

81 FR Page

2017

(No regulations published from January 1, 2017, through October 1, 2017)

○

CPSIA information can be obtained
at www.ICGtesting.com
Printed in the USA
LVHW080005081122
732619LV00024B/365

9 781640 241954